P9-DFZ-037

Fodor's

NINTH New EDITION

Philadelphia & the Pennsylvania Dutch Country

Fodor's Travel Publications, Inc.
New York • Toronto • London • Sydney • Auckland

Fodor's Philadelphia & the Pennsylvania Dutch Country

Editor: Robert I.C. Fisher

Area Editor: Rathe Miller

Editorial Contributors: Steven Amsterdam, Robert Andrews, Suzanne De Galan, Joyce Eisenberg, Rathe Miller, Tracy Patruno, Mary Ellen Schultz, Michael Schwager, M.T. Schwartzman (Gold Guide editor), Dinah Spritzer

Art Director: Fabrizio La Rocca

Cartographer: David Lindroth

Cover Photograph: H. Mark Weidman

Text Design: Between the Covers

Copyright

Special Sales

CONTENTS

ON THE ROAD WITH FODOR'S

A GOOD TRAVEL GUIDE is like a wonderful traveling companion. It's charming, it's brimming with sound recommendations and solid ideas, it gives the lowdown on lodging and dining establishments, and is loaded with fascinating facts that make you view what you've traveled to see in a rich new light. In the creation of *Philadelphia & the Pennsylvania Dutch Country,* we at Fodor's have gone to great lengths to make this guide the very best of all possible traveling companions—and to make your trip the best of all possible vacations.

About Our Writers

The information in these pages is a collaboration by several extraordinary writers.

As a writer who specializes in Philadelphia, **Rathe Miller** has watched his hometown undergo startling changes for the better in the past few years. While he celebrates the new Philadelphia, he almost wistfully recalls some of the town's former ways: "I miss the fistfights in the City Council, the political free-for-alls, the demonstrators camping outside the city's fanciest hotel." Actually, Rathe loves what's happening to the City of Brotherly Love, which he writes up for the *Philadelphia Inquirer, Philadelphia Magazine,* as well as other newspapers and publications. "New York City may be the Big Apple but Philadelphia is the Big Pretzel," says Rathe. "Yes, Philly is a food lover's cornucopia, but there's nothing like the soft pretzels served up at the Reading Terminal Market—hot, drizzled with butter, and slathered with mustard—to subdue a raging hunger."

A newspaper editor, travel writer, and tireless adventurer, **Joyce Eisenberg** has trekked through the poppy fields of Northern Thailand, eaten banana hotcakes on the beaches of Bali, and dined with ambassadors in Singapore. But like Dorothy in *The Wizard of Oz,* she says "there's no place like home." For her, that home is Philadelphia, which she loves for its unpretentious small-town feel and big-town cultural attractions. She makes her nest in the city with her husband and two young children, who delight in having heart-to-hearts with Big Bird at Sesame Place, the theme park in nearby Bucks County.

Michael Schwager writes articles and books ranging from Philadelphia history to personal finance. His work has appeared in many publications, including the *Philadelphia Inquirer Magazine* and the *Boston Globe.*

What's New

A New Design

If this is not the first Fodor's guide you've purchased, you'll immediately notice our new look. More readable and easier to use than ever? We think so—and we hope you do, too.

Let Us Do Your Booking

Our writers have scoured Philadelphia and the beautiful counties of Eastern Pennsylvania to come up with an extensive and well-balanced list of the best B&Bs, inns, and hotels, both small and large, new and old. But you don't have to beat the bushes to come up with a reservation. Now we've teamed up with an established hotel-booking service to make it easy for you to secure a room at the property of your choice. It's fast, it's free, and confirmation is guaranteed. If your first choice is booked, the operators can line up your second right away. Just call 1–800/FODORS–1 or 1–800/363–6771 (0800–89–1030 in Great Britain; 0014–800–12–8271 in Australia; 1–800/55–9101 in Ireland).

Travel Updates

In addition, just before your trip, you may want to order a Fodor's Worldview Travel Update. From local publications in and around Philadelphia, the lively, cosmopolitan editors at Worldview gather information on concerts, plays, opera, dance performances, gallery and museum shows, sports competitions, and other special events that coincide with your visit. See the order blank at the back of this book, call 800/799–9609, or fax 800/799–9619.

And in Philadelphia

Major plans were announced in 1995 for "America's most historic square mile,"

the **Independence National Historical Park.** A new visitors center to be built just north of Independence Hall will serve as a "gateway" to the park. A new National Constitution center will also be built, as will an educational center called the Independence Park Institute. Our guess is the new **Liberty Bell Pavilion** being built will keep visitors from walking up and touching the bell—so touch it while you can!

Stroll through the district around Independence Hall and you'll now encounter historical street theater: a fife-and-drum corps, town criers, and colonial-costumed hosts giving out information and directions. In Franklin Court, Ben Franklin sits under a Mulberry Tree dispensing Poor Richard's wisdom and wit to visitors.

Philadelphia's main north–south artery will still be named Broad Street, but if city planners succeed with their vision it will be better known as the **Avenue of the Arts.** Tagged at about $350 million, there are plans for new theaters, performance and rehearsal spaces, galleries, a jazz hall, and a creative-arts high school. The street itself will be lined with new diamond-patterned sidewalks, old-fashioned street lamps, and public artworks. Some of the smaller projects are already up and running, while others, including a new $90 million concert hall for the Philadelphia Orchestra—the centerpiece of the scheme—are still on the drawing board. The hope is that the new venues will join established ones such as the Academy of Music and the Merriam Theater, to create an artistic-critical mass that will see thousands of patrons strolling a grand boulevard of culture.

Philadelphia is hosting more out-of-town guests than ever before, thanks to the great success of the **Pennsylvania Convention Center.** The $522 million complex opened in 1993 with seven football fields' worth of exhibition space. The jewel of the center is the old **Reading Railroad train shed.** The magnificent Victorian-era terminal—the largest remaining single-span terminal in the world—was transformed into a grand hall complete with ballroom and a spectacular mixed-media sculpture by Judy Pfaff that has almost become as famous as Oldenburg's *Clothespin.* In 1996 the center is projected to host more

than 400,000 out of town guests bringing in $200 million to the city.

Penn's Landing has a new $15 million centerpiece: the **Independence Seaport Museum**—a bigger, better incarnation of the old Philadelphia Maritime Museum. Housed in the former Port of History Museum, many of the nautical artifacts and ship models are still on display, but now the emphasis is on kid-pleasing interactive displays.

From Penn's Landing at Walnut Street you can catch the "ferry to the fishies": the **Riverbus** crosses the Delaware River to Camden in about ten minutes and you arrive a few steps away from the $52 million **New Jersey State Aquarium.** It opened in 1992, was jazzed-up and expanded in 1995, and now 6,000 fish call it home. Interactive shows let you balance a ball on the nose of a seal and pet a shark.

After completing a major reorganization of the collection in 1995, the big news at the **Philadelphia Museum of Art** is the summer 1996 Cézanne exhibition, making its only North American stop here in Philly. The show—the art "event" of the year—will include 180 oils, water colors, and drawings from public and private collections, and is expected to outdraw the 1995 Barnes Collection exhibit, which had almost a half-million visitors.

After being closed for over two years of renovations and touring, the **Barnes Foundation,** one of the world's greatest collections of Impressionist art, is scheduled to reopen in November 1995. User-friendly innovations planned for the hitherto antisocial museum, include a giftshop, catalogue, CD-ROM, and audio tour system.

Hollywood came back to the streets of Philadelphia in 1995 to film *Up Close and Personal* with Robert Redford and Michelle Pfeiffer, and *12 Monkeys* with Bruce Willis and Brad Pitt. On the small screen, *Brotherly Love, Minor Adjustments,* and *Maybe This Time* are three sitcoms set in Philadelphia, scheduled to debut in the '95 fall season. Philly hasn't gotten this much tube-time since Gary of *Thirtysomething* died in a crash on the Schuylkill Expressway.

Yuppies and Boomers who have abandoned South Street—still the city's main entertainment strip—and the waterfront

to more youthful partygoers now head to **Main Street, Manayunk,** in the northwest part of the city. Shops and restaurants stay open late, and you can enjoy a peaceful stroll along the street or the Manayunk Canal.

The streets are definitely cleaner, colonies of homeless have been provided shelters, and with the 1995 opening of the new criminal justice center, the streets should be safer, too. Philadelphia has long been saying to the tourist, "Your visit is important to us," and under the new mayor Ed Rendell, they are starting to act like they really mean it.

How to Use This Book

Organization

Up front is the **Gold Guide,** comprising two sections on gold paper that are chockfull of information about traveling within your destination and traveling in general. Both are in alphabetical order by topic. **Important Contacts A to Z** gives addresses and telephone numbers of organizations and companies that offer destination-related services and detailed information or publications. Here's where you'll find information about how to get to Philadelphia from wherever you are. **Smart Travel Tips A to Z,** the Gold Guide's second section, gives specific tips on how to get the most out of your travels, as well as information on how to accomplish what you need to in Philly and its surrounding counties.

After our complete coverage of Philadelphia, you'll find separate chapters on Bucks and Lancaster Counties and some suggestions for excursions to the Brandywine Valley, Valley Forge, and Reading. Each of these chapters covers exploring, shopping, sports, dining, lodging, and arts and nightlife, and ends with a section called **Essentials,** which tells you how to get there and get around and gives you important local addresses and telephone numbers.

At the end of the book you'll find **Portraits,** wonderful essays about the city of Brotherly Love and the Amish culture, followed by suggestions for pretrip reading, both fiction and nonfiction.

Stars

Stars in the margin are used to denote highly recommended sights, attractions, hotels, and restaurants.

Dress Code in Restaurants

In general, we note a dress code only when men are required to wear a jacket or a jacket and tie.

Credit Cards

The following abbreviations are used: **AE,** American Express; **D,** Discover; **DC,** Diners Club; **MC,** MasterCard; and **V,** Visa.

Please Write to Us

Everyone who has contributed to *Philadelphia & the Pennsylvania Dutch Country* has worked hard to make the text accurate. All prices and opening times are based on information supplied to us at press time, and Fodor's cannot accept responsibility for any errors that may have occurred. The passage of time will bring changes, so it's always a good idea to call ahead and confirm information when it matters—particularly if you're making a detour to visit specific sights or attractions. When making reservations at a hotel or inn, be sure to speak up if you have a disability or are traveling with children, if you prefer a private bath or a certain type of bed, or if you have specific dietary needs or any other concerns.

Were the restaurants we recommended as described? Did our hotel picks exceed your expectations? Did you find a museum we recommended a waste of time? We would love your feedback, positive and negative. If you have complaints, we'll look into them and revise our entries when the facts warrant it. If you've happened upon a special place that we haven't included, we'll pass the information along to the writers so they can check it out. So please send us a letter or postcard (we're at 201 East 50th Street, New York, New York 10022). We'll look forward to hearing from you. And in the meantime, have a wonderful trip!

Karen Cure
Editorial Director

Philadelphia

Poplar St.

Parrish St.

Brown St.

Aspen St.

Fairmount Ave.

Mt. Vernon St.

George St.

Corinthian Ave.

Vineyard St.

Parrish St.

Ridge Ave.

North St.

Wallace St.

Rte. 611

28th St.

27th St.

26th St.

25th St.

24th St.

23rd St.

19th St.

Fairmount
Park

Green St.

Brandywine St.

Spring Garden St.

Hamilton St.

Philadelphia
Museum of Art

Rodin
Museum

Benjamin Franklin Parkway

Buttonwood St.

Button

Broad St.

Callowhill St.

18th St.

Tours 3 and 4

I-76

I-30

I-676 I-30

Schuylkill River

Logan
Circle

Franklin Institute

17th St.

Race St.

Broad St. Subway

Con
Readin

Cherry St.

Academy
of Natural
Sciences

Arch St.

19th St.

Parkway

Suburban
Station

23rd St.

John F. Kennedy Blvd.

**30th St.
Station**

Market-Frankford Subway

Subway-Surface

Market St.

City Hall

Ludlow St.

**University
City**

TO U.
OF
PENN.

TO
AIRPORT

Airport Train (R1)

30th St.

I-76

Schuylkill River

Chestnut St.

Sansom St.

Walnut St.

Rittenhouse
Square

Locust St.

21st St.

20th St.

16th St.

Broad St.

Juniper St.

Locust St.

15th St.

Broad St. Subway

Center City

Spruce St.

19th St.

Rte. 611

Pine St.

Lombard St.

25th St.

24th St.

South St.

Bainbridge St.

Pemberton St.

Fitzwater St.

22nd St.

Schuylkill Ave.

Grays Ferry Ave.

23rd St.

Webster St.

Christian St.

Catharine St.

Carpenter St.

N

0 ———— 440 yards

0 ———— 400 meters

KEY

- - - - Market-Frankford Subway
——— Broad St. Subway
- - - - Subway-Surface Subway
——— Airport Train

Poplar St.

9th St.
Franklin St.
Marshall St.
Lawrence St.
Orianna St.
Wildey St.
Germantown Ave.
Market St.
2nd St.
American St.
Penn St.

Brown St.

Fairmount Ave.

8th St.
7th St.
5th St.

Green St.

Spring Garden St.

Delaware Ave.

Clay St.

Ridge Ave.

wood St.

Broad St. Subway

Willow St.

Callowhill St.

6th St.

Front St.

Ben Franklin Br.

Vine St.

10th St.

30

Franklin Square

30 676

Philadelphia vention Center/ g Terminal Market

Chinatown

Race St.

Old City

Front St.

Delaware River

U.S. Mint

Arch St.

Market East Station

Filbert St.

7th St.

Independence National Historical Park

Market St.

Delaware Ave.

Front St.

13th St.

11th St.

Sansom St.

Independence Hall

Chestnut St.

2nd St.

Penn's Landing

Independence Square

Washington Square

Walnut St.

Locust St.

4th St.
3rd St.

Spruce St.

Society Hill

Quince St.

9th St.
8th St.

Tours 1 and 2

Pine St.

Lombard St.

South St.

5th St.

95

12th St.

Bridge St.

7th St.

Fitzwater St.

South Philadelphia and Southwark

Fitzwater St.

TO WALT WHITMAN BRIDGE

Christian St.

Catharine St.

Queen St.

World Time Zones

Numbers below vertical bands relate each zone to Greenwich Mean Time (0 hrs.).
Local times frequently differ from these general indications,
as indicated by light-face numbers on map.

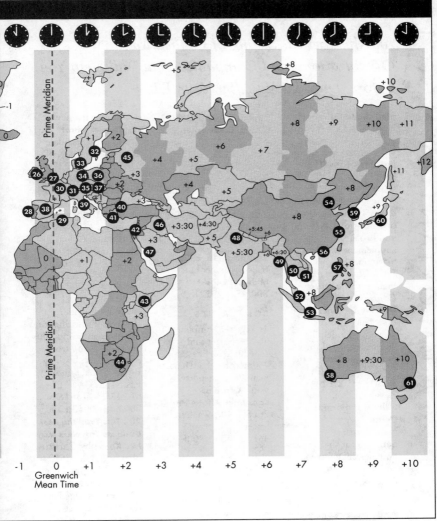

IMPORTANT CONTACTS A TO Z

An Alphabetical Listing of Publications, Organizations, and Companies That Will Help You Before, During, and After Your Trip

Half the fun of traveling is looking forward to your trip—but when you look forward, don't just daydream. There are plans to be made, things to learn about, serious work to be done. The following organizations, books, and brochures will supplement the information in *Fodor's Philadelphia & the Pennsylvania Dutch Country.* For related information, including both basic tips on visiting Philadelphia and background information on many of the topics below, study Smart Travel Tips A to Z, the section that follows Important Contacts A to Z. The main information numbers for the various Philadelphia convention and tourist bureaus are listed below under Visitor Information.

A

AIR TRAVEL

The major gateway to Philadelphia is **Philadelphia International Airport** (☎ 215/492–3181) in the southwest part of the city, 8 miles from downtown. Flying time is approximately 50 minutes from New York, two hours from Chicago, and five hours from Los Angeles.

CARRIERS

Carriers serving Philadelphia include **American** (☎ 800/433–7300), **Continental** (☎ 800/525–0280), **Delta** (☎ 800/221–1212), **TWA** (☎ 800/221–2000), **Midwest** (☎ 800/452–2022), **Northwest** (☎ 800/225–2525), **United** (☎ 800/241–6522), and **USAir** (☎ 800/231–3131).

For inexpensive, no-frills flights, contact **Midwest Express** (☎ 800/452–2022).

COMPLAINTS

To register complaints about charter and scheduled airlines, contact the U.S. Department of Transportation's **Office of Consumer Affairs** (400 7th St. NW, Washington, DC 20590, ☎ 202/366–2220 or 800/322–7873).

PUBLICATIONS

For general information about charter carriers, ask for the Office of Consumer Affairs' brochure **"Plane Talk: Public Charter Flights."** The Department of Transportation also publishes a 58-page booklet, **"Fly Rights"** ($1.75; Consumer Information Center, Dept. 133B, Pueblo, CO 81009).

For other tips and hints, consult the Consumers Union's monthly **"Consumer Reports Travel Letter"** ($39 a year; Box 53629, Boulder, CO 80322, ☎ 800/234–1970) and the newsletter **"Travel Smart"** ($37 a year; 40 Beechdale Rd., Dobbs Ferry, NY 10522, ☎ 800/327–3633); *The Official Frequent Flyer Guidebook,* by Randy Petersen ($14.99 plus $3 shipping; 4715-C Town Center Dr., Colorado Springs, CO 80916, ☎ 719/597–8899 or 800/487–8893); *Airfare Secrets Exposed,* by Sharon Tyler and Matthew Wonder (Universal Information Publishing; $16.95 plus $3.75 shipping from Sandcastle Publishing, Box 3070-A, South Pasadena, CA 91031, ☎ 213/255–3616 or 800/655–0053); and *202 Tips Even the Best Business Travelers May Not Know,* by Christopher McGinnis ($10 plus $3 shipping; Irwin Professional Publishing, 1333 Burr Ridge Parkway, Burr Ridge, IL 60521, ☎ 800/634–3966).

AIRPORT TRANSFERS

BY CAR OR TAXI

Allow at least a half hour, more during rush hour, for the 8-mile trip between the airport and Center City. By car, the airport is accessible via I–95 south or I–76 east.

Taxis at the airport are plentiful but expensive—about $20 plus tip. "Limos" (vans, not

stretch limousines) cost about $10 per person, but service is less frequent and most limos stop only at certain hotels and downtown points. Among them are **Deluxe Transportation** (☎ 215/463–8787) and **Limelight Limousine** (☎ 215/342–5557).

BY TRAIN

SEPTA's Airport Express leaves the airport every 30 minutes from 6:10 AM to 12:10 AM. The trip to downtown takes about 20 minutes and costs $5. For $1 more you can transfer to any train in the regional rail system. Trains serve the 30th Street, Suburban, Market East, and North Broad stations. For schedules and other information, call the **Airport Information Desk** (☎ 215/492–3181) or **SEPTA** (☎ 215/580–7800).

B

BETTER BUSINESS BUREAU

Contact the Better Business Bureau of Philadelphia (1930 Chestnut St., Box 2297, Philadelphia, PA 19103; ☎ 215/448–6100).

BUS TRAVEL

Greyhound Lines (☎ 215/931–4014 or 800/231–2222) operates long-haul service out of a new terminal at 10th and Filbert streets, just north of the Market East commuter rail station. **NJ Transit** (☎ 215/569–3752) stops at the Greyhound terminal and offers service between Philadelphia and Atlantic City and other New Jersey destinations.

WITHIN PHILADELPHIA

The Southeastern Pennsylvania Transportation Authority (SEPTA) operates an extensive network of buses, subways, and commuter trains. For route information, call 215/580–7800. Though SEPTA's new automated answering system has cut down on the wait somewhat, be prepared for a busy signal and, once you get through, a long time on hold. To have a schedule mailed to you, call **SEPTA** (☎ 215/580–7777).

C

CAR RENTAL

Major car-rental companies represented in Philadelphia include **Alamo** (☎ 800/327–9633, 0800/272–2000 in the U.K.), **Avis** (☎ 800/331–1212, 800/879–2847 in Canada), **Budget** (☎ 800/527–0700, 0800/181–181 in the U.K.), **Dollar** (known as Eurodollar outside North America, ☎ 800/800–4000, 0181/952–6565 in the U.K.), **Hertz** (☎ 800/654–3131, 800/263–0600 in Canada, 0181/679–1799 in the U.K.), and **National** (☎ 800/227–7368, 0181/950–5050 in the U.K., where it is known as Europcar). Lower-price companies include **Enterprise** (☎ 215/521–3700). Rates in Philadelphia begin at $21 a day and $147 a week for an economy car with unlimited mileage.

BABY-SITTING

Rocking Horse Child-Care Center (6th and Walnut Sts., Curtis Center, Suite 25 LL, Philadelphia 19106, ☎ 215/592–8257) offers part- and full-time care for children ages 6 weeks to 10 years.

FLYING

Look into **"Flying With Baby"** ($5.95 plus $1 shipping; Third Street Press, Box 261250, Littleton, CO 80126, ☎ 303/595–5959), cowritten by a flight attendant. **"Kids and Teens in Flight,"** free from the U.S. Department of Transportation's Office of Consumer Affairs, offers tips for children flying alone. Every two years the February issue of *Family Travel Times* (see Know-How, *below*) details children's services on three dozen airlines.

KNOW-HOW

Family Travel Times, published four times a year by Travel With Your Children (TWYCH, 45 W. 18th St., New York, NY 10011, ☎ 212/206–0688; annual subscription $40), covers destinations, types of vacations, and modes of travel.

The *Family Travel Guides* catalogue ($1 postage; ☎ 510/527–5849) lists about 200 books and articles on family travel. *Great Vacations with Your Kids,* by Dorothy Jordon and Marjorie Cohen ($13; Penguin

USA, 120 Woodbine St., Bergenfield, NJ 07621, ☎ 201/387–0600 or 800/253–6476), and *Traveling with Children—And Enjoying It,* by Arlene K. Butler ($11.95 plus $3 shipping; Globe Pequot Press, Box 833, 6 Business Park Rd., Old Saybrook, CT 06475, ☎ 203/395–0440 or 800/243–0495, 800/962–0973 in CT) help plan your trip with children, from toddlers to teens. Also check *Take Your Baby and Go! A Guide for Traveling with Babies, Toddlers and Young Children,* by Sheri Andrews, Judy Bordeaux, and Vivian Vasquez ($5.95 plus $1.50 shipping; Bear Creek Publications, 2507 Minor Ave., Seattle, WA 98102, ☎ 206/322–7604 or 800/326–6566).

LODGING

The Four Seasons Hotel Philadelphia (1 Logan Sq., Philadelphia 19103, ☎ 215/963–1500) allows children under 17 to stay free in their parents' room, runs holiday tea parties for kids, and provides a *Family Activities and Children's Services* brochure for guests. The **Doubletree Guest Suite Hotels** in the Philadelphia area (☎ 800/424–2900) offer the luxury of two-room suites with kitchen facilities plus children's menus in the restaurants; children under 18 stay free in their parents' suite. Most **Days Inn** hotels (☎ 800/325–2525) allow children under 18 to stay free in their par-

ents' room and allow kids 12 and under to eat free.

CUSTOMS

CANADIANS

Contact **Revenue Canada** (2265 St. Laurent Blvd. S, Ottawa, Ontario K1G 4K3, ☎ 613/993–0534) for a copy of the free brochure *"I Declare/Je Déclare"* and for details on duties that exceed the standard duty-free limit.

U.K. CITIZENS

HM Customs and Excise (Dorset House, Stamford St., London SE1 9NG, ☎ 0171/202–4227) can answer questions about U.K. customs regulations and publishes *"A Guide for Travellers,"* detailing standard procedures and import rules.

D

FOR TRAVELERS WITH DISABILITIES

COMPLAINTS

To register complaints under the provisions of the Americans With Disabilities Act, contact the U.S. Department of Justice's **Public Access Section** (Box 66738, Washington, DC 20035, ☎ 202/514–0301, TTY 202/514–0383, FAX 202/307–1198).

ORGANIZATIONS

FOR TRAVELERS WITH HEARING IMPAIRMENTS➤ Contact the **American Academy of Otolaryngology** (1 Prince St., Alexandria, VA 22314, ☎ 703/836–4444, FAX 703/683–5100, TTY 703/519–1585).

FOR TRAVELERS WITH MOBILITY PROBLEMS➤ Contact the **Information Center for Individuals with Disabilities** (Fort Point Pl., 27–43 Wormwood St., Boston, MA 02210, ☎ 617/727–5540, 800/462–5015 in MA, TTY 617/345–9743); **Mobility International USA** (Box 10767, Eugene, OR 97440, ☎ and TTY 503/343–1284, FAX 503/343–6812), the U.S. branch of an international organization based in Belgium (*see below*) that has affiliates in 30 countries; **MossRehab Hospital Travel Information Service** (1200 W. Tabor Rd., Philadelphia, PA 19141, ☎ 215/456–9603, TTY 215/456–9602); the **Society for the Advancement of Travel for the Handicapped** (347 5th Ave., Suite 610, New York, NY 10016, ☎ 212/447–7284, FAX 212/725–8253); the **Travel Industry and Disabled Exchange** (TIDE, 5435 Donna Ave., Tarzana, CA 91356, ☎ 818/344–3640, FAX 818/344–0078); and **Travelin' Talk** (Box 3534, Clarksville, TN 37043, ☎ 615/552–6670, FAX 615/552–1182).

FOR TRAVELERS WITH VISION IMPAIRMENTS➤ Contact the **American Council of the Blind** (1155 15th St. NW, Suite 720, Washington, DC 20005, ☎ 202/467–5081, FAX 202/467–5085) or the **American Foundation for the Blind** (15 W. 16th St., New York, NY 10011, ☎ 212/620–2000, TTY 212/620–2158).

IN THE U.K.

Contact the **Royal Association for Disability and Rehabilitation** (RADAR, 12 City Forum, 250 City Rd., London EC1V 8AF, ☎ 0171/250–3222) or **Mobility International** (Rue de Manchester 25, B–1070 Brussels, Belgium, ☎ 00–322–410–6297), an international clearinghouse of travel information for people with disabilities.

PUBLICATIONS

Several publications for travelers with disabilities are available from the Consumer Information Center (Box 100, Pueblo, CO 81009, ☎ 719/948–3334). Call or write for a free catalogue of current titles.

Fodor's **Great American Vacations for Travelers with Disabilities** ($18; available in bookstores, or call 800/533–6478) details accessible attractions, restaurants, and hotels in U.S. destinations. The 500-page **Travelin' Talk Directory** ($35; Box 3534, Clarksville, TN 37043, ☎ 615/552–6670) lists people and organizations who help travelers with disabilities. For specialist travel agents worldwide, consult the **Directory of Travel Agencies for the Disabled** ($19.95 plus $2 shipping; Twin Peaks Press, Box 129, Vancouver, WA 98666, ☎ 206/694–2462 or 800/637–2256).

TRAVEL AGENCIES, TOUR OPERATORS

The Americans with Disabilities Act requires that travel firms serve the needs of all travelers. However, some agencies and operators specialize in making group and individual arrangements for travelers with disabilities, among them **Access Adventures** (206 Chestnut Ridge Rd., Rochester, NY 14624, ☎ 716/889–9096), run by a former physical-rehab counselor; and **Sprout, Inc.** (893 Amsterdam Ave., New York, NY 10025, ☎ 212/222–9575), which specializes in custom-designed itineraries. In addition, many general-interest operators and agencies (*see* Tour Operators, *below*) can also arrange vacations for travelers with disabilities.

FOR TRAVELERS WITH MOBILITY PROBLEMS➤ Two operators are **Hinsdale Travel Service** (201 E. Ogden Ave., Suite 100, Hinsdale, IL 60521, ☎ 708/325–1335 or 800/303–5521), a travel agency that will give you access to the services of wheelchair traveler Janice Perkins, and **Wheelchair Journeys** (16979 Redmond Way, Redmond, WA 98052, ☎ 206/885–2210), which can handle arrangements worldwide.

FOR TRAVELERS WITH DEVELOPMENTAL DISABILITIES➤ Contact the nonprofit **New Directions** (5276 Hollister Ave., Suite 207, Santa Barbara, CA 93111, ☎ 805/967–2841), as well as the general-interest operators, *above*.

DISCOUNT CLUBS

Options include **Entertainment Travel Editions** (fee $28–$53, depending on destination; Box 1068, Trumbull, CT 06611, ☎ 800/445–4137), **Great American Traveler** ($49.95 annually; Box 27965, Salt Lake City, UT 84127, ☎ 800/548–2812), **Moment's Notice Discount Travel Club** ($25 annually, single or family; 163 Amsterdam Ave., Suite 137, New York, NY 10023, ☎ 212/486–0500), **Privilege Card** ($74.95 annually; 3391 Peachtree Rd. NE, Suite 110, Atlanta, GA 30326, ☎ 404/262–0222 or 800/236–9732), **Travelers Advantage** ($49 annually, single or family; CUC Travel Service, 49 Music Sq. W, Nashville, TN 37203, ☎ 800/548–1116 or 800/648–4037), and **Worldwide Discount Travel Club** ($50 annually for family, $40 single; 1674 Meridian Ave., Miami Beach, FL 33139, ☎ 305/534–2082).

DRIVING

AUTO CLUBS

For routing information, AAA members can call the **Keystone Automobile Club** (☎ 215/569–4321).

E

EMERGENCIES

Police, fire, and **ambulance,** ☎ 911.

HOSPITALS

Near the historic area: **Pennsylvania Hospital** (8th and Spruce Sts., ☎ 215/829–3358). Near City Hall: **Hahnemann University Hospital** (Broad and Vine Sts., ☎ 215/448–7963). Near Rittenhouse Square:

Graduate Hospital (1800 Lombard St., ☎ 215/893–2350).

LATE-NIGHT PHARMACIES

CVS Pharmacy (10th and Reed Sts., ☎ 215/465–2130) is the 24-hour pharmacy closest to downtown, located in South Philadelphia, 10 minutes by car. Downtown, **Corson's Pharmacy** (15th and Spruce Sts., ☎ 215/735–1386) is open 9 AM–9:45 PM Monday through Friday, until 5 PM Saturday, and until 2 PM Sunday. **Medical Tower Pharmacy** (255 S. 17th St., ☎ 215/545–3525) is open weekdays 8:30 AM–7:30 PM and Saturday until 5 PM.

G
GAY AND LESBIAN TRAVEL

ORGANIZATIONS

The **International Gay Travel Association** (Box 4974, Key West, FL 33041, ☎ 800/448–8550), a consortium of 800 businesses, can supply names of travel agents and tour operators.

PUBLICATIONS

The premier international travel magazine for gays and lesbians is **Our World** ($35 for 10 issues; 1104 N. Nova Rd., Suite 251, Daytona Beach, FL 32117, ☎ 904/441–5367). The 16-page monthly **"Out & About"** ($49 for 10 issues; ☎ 212/645–6922 or 800/929–2268) covers gay-friendly resorts, hotels, cruise lines, and airlines.

TOUR OPERATORS

Toto Tours (1326 W. Albion, Suite 3W, Chicago, IL 60626, ☎ 312/274–8686 or 800/565–1241) offers group tours worldwide.

TRAVEL AGENCIES

The largest agencies serving gay travelers are **Advance Travel** (10700 Northwest Freeway, Suite 160, Houston, TX 77092, ☎ 713/682–2002 or 800/695–0880), **Islanders/Kennedy Travel** (183 W. 10th St., New York, NY 10014, ☎ 212/242–3222 or 800/988–1181), **Now Voyager** (4406 18th St., San Francisco, CA 94114, ☎ 415/626–1169 or 800/255–6951), and **Yellowbrick Road** (1500 W. Balmoral Ave., Chicago, IL 60640, ☎ 312/561–1800 or 800/642–2488). **Skylink Women's Travel** (746 Ashland Ave., Santa Monica, CA 90405, ☎ 310/452–0506 or 800/225–5759) works with lesbians.

I
INSURANCE

Travel insurance covering baggage, health, and trip cancellation or interruptions is available from **Access America** (Box 90315, Richmond, VA 23286, ☎ 804/285–3300 or 800/284–8300), **Carefree Travel Insurance** (Box 9366, 100 Garden City Plaza, Garden City, NY 11530, ☎ 516/294–0220 or 800/323–3149), **Near Services** (Box 1339, Calumet City, IL 60409, ☎ 708/868–6700 or 800/654–6700), **Tele-Trip** (Mutual of Omaha

Plaza, Box 31716, Omaha, NE 68131, ☎ 800/228–9792), **Travel Insured International** (Box 280568, East Hartford, CT 06128–0568, ☎ 203/528–7663 or 800/243–3174), **Travel Guard International** (1145 Clark St., Stevens Point, WI 54481, ☎ 715/345–0505 or 800/826–1300), and **Wallach & Company** (107 W. Federal St., Box 480, Middleburg, VA 22117, ☎ 703/687–3166 or 800/237–6615).

IN THE U.K.

The **Association of British Insurers** (51 Gresham St., London EC2V 7HQ, ☎ 0171/600–3333; 30 Gordon St., Glasgow G1 3PU, ☎ 0141/226–3905; Scottish Provident Bldg., Donegall Sq. W, Belfast BT1 6JE, ☎ 01232/249176; and other locations) gives advice by phone and publishes the free **"Holiday Insurance,"** which sets out typical policy provisions and costs.

L
LODGING

HOME EXCHANGE

Principal clearinghouses include **Intervac International** ($65 annually; Box 590504, San Francisco, CA 94159, ☎ 415/435–3497), which has three annual directories; and **Loan-a-Home** ($35–$45 annually; 2 Park La., Apt. 6E, Mount Vernon, NY 10552-3443, ☎ 914/664–7640), which specializes in long-term exchanges.

M
MONEY MATTERS

ATMS

For specific **Cirrus** locations in the United States and Canada, call 800/424–7787. For U.S. **Plus** locations, call 800/843–7587 and enter the area code and first three digits of the number you're calling from (or of the calling area where you want an ATM).

WIRING FUNDS

Funds can be wired via **American Express MoneyGram℠** (☎ 800/926–9400 from the U.S. and Canada for locations and information) or **Western Union** (☎ 800/325–6000 for agent locations or to send using MasterCard or Visa, 800/321–2923 in Canada).

P
PASSPORTS
AND VISAS

U.K. CITIZENS

For fees, documentation requirements, and to get an emergency passport, call the **London Passport Office** (☎ 0171/271–3000). For visa information, call the **U.S. Embassy Visa Information Line** (☎ 0891/200–290; calls cost 49p per minute or 39p per minute cheap rate) or write the **U.S. Embassy Visa Branch** (5 Upper Grosvenor St., London W1A 4JB). If you live in Northern Ireland, write the **U.S. Consulate General** (Queen's House, Queen St., Belfast BTI 6EQ).

PHOTO HELP

The **Kodak Information Center** (☎ 800/242–2424) answers consumer questions about film and photography.

R
RAIL TRAVEL

For long-distance rail service to and from Philadelphia, contact **Amtrak** (☎ 215/824–1600 or 800/872–7245).

WITHIN PHILADELPHIA

PATCO (Port Authority Transit Corporation, ☎ 215/922–4600.) High Speed Line trains run underground from 16th and Locust streets to Lindenwold, New Jersey. Trains stop at 13th and Locust, 9th and Locust, and 8th and Market streets, then continue across the Benjamin Franklin Bridge to Camden. Fares run 75¢ to $1.60. Sit in the very front seat for a great view going across the bridge.

S
SENIOR CITIZENS

EDUCATIONAL TRAVEL

The nonprofit **Elderhostel** (75 Federal St., 3rd Floor, Boston, MA 02110, ☎ 617/426–7788), for people 60 and older, has offered inexpensive study programs since 1975. The nearly 2,000 courses cover everything from marine science to Greek myths and cowboy poetry. Fees for programs in the United States and Canada, which usually last one week, run

about $300, not including transportation.

ORGANIZATIONS

Contact the **American Association of Retired Persons** (AARP, 601 E St. NW, Washington, DC 20049, ☎ 202/434–2277; $8 per person or couple annually). Its Purchase Privilege Program gets members discounts on lodging, car rentals, and sightseeing, and the AARP Motoring Plan furnishes domestic trip-routing information and emergency road-service aid for an annual fee of $39.95 per person or couple ($59.95 for a premium version).

For other discounts on lodgings, car rentals, and other travel products, along with magazines and newsletters, contact the **National Council of Senior Citizens** (membership $12 annually; 1331 F St. NW, Washington, DC 20004, ☎ 202/347–8800) and **Mature Outlook** (subscription $9.95 annually; 6001 N. Clark St., Chicago, IL 60660, ☎ 312/465–6466 or 800/336–6330).

PUBLICATIONS

The 50¢ Traveler's Guidebook: Where to Go, Where to Stay, What to Do, by Anita Williams and Merrimac Dillon ($12.95; St. Martin's Press, 175 5th Ave., New York, NY 10010, ☎ 212/674–5151 or 800/288–2131), offers many useful tips. **"The Mature Traveler"** ($29.95; Box 50400, Reno, NV 89513, ☎ 702/786–

THE GOLD GUIDE / IMPORTANT CONTACTS

7419), a monthly newsletter, covers travel deals.

SIGHTSEEING

CARRIAGE RIDES

Numerous horse-drawn carriages wend their way through the narrow streets of the historic area. Tours last anywhere from 15 minutes to an hour and cost from $15 to $60. Carriages line up on Chestnut and 5th streets near Independence Hall and at Head House Square, 2nd Street between Pine and Lombard streets, from about 10 AM to 2 AM. You can reserve a carriage and be picked up anywhere downtown. Carriages operate year-round, except when the temperature is below 20°F or above 94°F. Carriage operators include **Ben Franklin Carriages** (☎ 215/923–8516), **Philadelphia Carriage Company** (☎ 215/922–6840), **76 Carriage Company** (☎ 215/923–8516), and **Society Hill Carriage Company** (☎ 215/627–6128).

MULTILINGUAL TOURS

Some tour companies provide interpreters and foreign-language guides. **Centipede Tours** (☎ 215/735–3123) can supply German-, French-, Spanish-, Russian-, Chinese-, Japanese-, Swedish-, Finnish-, Danish- or Italian-speaking guides for all parts of Philadelphia.

ORIENTATION TOURS

Two companies offer tours in buses designed to resemble Victorian–style trolleys, with driver/guides narrating. With both companies the fare is an all–day pass, allowing unlimited on/offs. Board at any stop including the Visitors Center, the Pennsylvania Convention Center, and the Liberty Bell.

The **Philadelphia Trolley Works** (☎ 215/923–8522) tour takes about 90 minutes and costs $10 for adults, $5 for children 6–12. The tour makes 15 stops on a route covering the historic area, the Benjamin Franklin Parkway, the Avenue of the Arts (South Broad St.), and Penn's Landing.

For an extra $5 for adults, we recommend the **Old Town Trolley** (☎ 215/928–8687) whose two-hour tour includes most of their competitor's route plus stops in Fairmount Park such as the Waterworks behind the Museum of Art, Memorial Hall, and the Zoo.

Gray Line Tours (☎ 215/569–3666) gives a three-hour tour of the city focusing on the historic and cultural areas, plus tours of Valley Forge, Bucks County, and Rittenhousetown. Most tours cost $16 and leave from 30th Street Station at 1:30 PM.

RIVER CRUISES

The *Spirit of Philadelphia* (☎ 215/923–1419) runs lunch and dinner cruises along the Delaware River. This three-deck ship leaves Pier 3 (Delaware Ave. and Market St.) for lunch, dinner, and "Moonlight Cruises." Dinner cruises include a band and singing waitstaff, while "moonlight" cruises feature a bar, band, and dancing.

The *Liberty Belle II* (☎ 215/629–1131), a 93-foot Great Lakes steamer, offers lunch, dinner, and Sunday brunch cruises with a banjo player, singalongs, and a buffet. Occasional private charters affect the daily schedule. Board at Penn's Landing (Columbus Blvd. at Spruce St.).

SPECIAL-INTEREST TOURS

If the sites of bizarre crimes, scandals, and infamous events beckons you, *noTOURious* (☎ 215/625–2680) gives a two-hour bus tour to some of Philly's legendary locales. The route also includes the original home of American Bandstand, Eastern State Penitentiary, and a medical oddities museum. The multimedia narration includes clips from movies filmed in Philadelphia (such as *Rocky* and *Blowup*), as you are at the very site. Tours leave Saturday at 10 AM and 1 PM from the Visitors Center, 16th St. and JFK Boulevard.

The **Foundation for Architecture** (☎ 215/569–3187) offers the "Hidden River Tour: A View of the Schuylkill," and several other Schuylkill River boat tours, on some Saturdays and Sundays.

WALKING TOURS

Several walking tours of historic Philadelphia are

available. **Audio Walk and Tour** (☎ 215/925–1234) from the Norman Rockwell Museum, 6th and Sansom streets, offers go-at-your-own-pace tours of historic Philadelphia with cassette players and an accompanying map. **Centipede Tours** (☎ 215/735–3123) offers a candlelight stroll through Society Hill led by guides in Colonial dress. Tours begin at the Thomas Bond House (129 S. 2nd St) Friday and Saturday at 6:30 PM, May–October. Theme and area tours given by the **Foundation for Architecture** (*see above*) focus on architecture but also touch on the history of each destination. Area tours include Chestnut Hill, Manayunk, and Spruce Hill. Theme tours include Art Deco, skyscrapers, the University of Pennsylvania campus, Washington Square, and Judaic architecture and influence. Most tours begin weekends at 2 PM, and occasionally on Wednesday at 6 PM.

GROUPS

Major tour operators include **Contiki Holidays** (300 Plaza Alicante, Suite 900, Garden Grove, CA 92640, ☎ 714/740–0808 or 800/466–0610).

HOSTELING

Contact **Hostelling International–American Youth Hostels** (733 15th St. NW, Suite 840, Washington, DC 20005, ☎ 202/783–6161) in the United States, **Hostelling Inter-** national–Canada (205 Catherine St., Suite 400, Ottawa, Ontario K2P 1C3, ☎ 613/237–7884) in Canada, and the **Youth Hostel Association of England and Wales** (Trevelyan House, 8 St. Stephen's Hill, St. Albans, Hertfordshire AL1 2DY, ☎ 01727/855215 or 01727/845047) in the United Kingdom. Membership ($25 in the U.S., C$26.75 in Canada, and £9 in the U.K.) gets you access to 5,000 hostels worldwide that charge $7–$20 nightly per person.

I.D. CARDS

To be eligible for discounts on transportation and admissions, get the **International Student Identity Card** (ISIC) if you're a bona fide student or the **International Youth Card** (IYC) if you're under 26. In the United States, the ISIC and IYC cards cost $16 each and include basic travel accident and illness coverage, plus a toll-free travel hot line. Apply through the Council on International Educational Exchange (*see Organizations, below*). Cards are available for $15 each in Canada from Travel Cuts (*see below*) and in the United Kingdom for £5 each at student unions and student travel companies.

ORGANIZATIONS

A major contact is the **Council on International Educational Exchange** (CIEE, 205 E. 42nd St., 16th Floor, New York, NY 10017, ☎ 212/661–1450) with locations in Boston (729 Boylston St., 02116, ☎ 617/266–1926), Miami (9100 S. Dadeland Blvd., 33156, ☎ 305/670–9261), Los Angeles (10904 Lindbrook Dr., 90024, ☎ 310/208–3551), 43 college towns nationwide, and the United Kingdom (28A Poland St., London W1V 3DB, ☎ 0171/437–7767). Twice a year, it publishes *Student Travels* magazine. The CIEE's Council Travel Service offers domestic air passes for bargain travel within the United States and is the exclusive U.S. agent for several student-discount cards.

Campus Connections (325 Chestnut St., Suite 1101, Philadelphia, PA 19106, ☎ 215/625–8585 or 800/428–3235) specializes in discounted accommodations and airfares for students. The **Educational Travel Centre** (438 N. Frances St., Madison, WI 53703, ☎ 608/256–5551) offers rail passes and low-cost airline tickets, mostly for flights departing from Chicago.

In Canada, also contact **Travel Cuts** (187 College St., Toronto, Ontario M5T 1P7, ☎ 416/979–2406 or 800/667–2887).

Contact **SEPTA** (☎ 215/580–7800); *see* Bus Travel, *above*.

T

The main cab companies are **Quaker City Cab** (☎ 215/728–8000), **United Cab** (☎ 215/238–9500), and

THE GOLD GUIDE / IMPORTANT CONTACTS

Yellow Cab (☎ 215/ 922–8400).

TOUR OPERATORS

Among the companies selling tours and packages to Philadelphia, the following have a proven reputation, are nationally known, and offer plenty of options.

GROUP TOURS

Escorted tours of Philadelphia typically include a tour of Amish country and the quaint sights of Buck's County. For a deluxe tour, contact **Maupintour** (Box 807, Lawrence KS 66044, ☎ 800/255– 4266 or 913/843– 1211) and **Tauck Tours** (11 Wilton Rd., Westport, CT 06880, ☎ 800/468–2825 or 203/226–6911). Another operator falling between deluxe and first-class is **Globus** (5301 South Federal Circle, Littleton, CO 80123, ☎ 800/221– 0090 or 303/797– 2800). For first-class and tourist programs, try **Mayflower Tours** (1225 Warren Ave., Downers Grove, IL 60515, ☎ 708/960– 3430 or 800/323– 7064) and **Collette Tours** (162 Middle Street, Pawtucket, RI 02860, ☎ 800/832–4656 or 401/728–3805). For budget and tourist class programs, try **Cosmos** (*see* Globus, *above*).

PACKAGES

Independent vacation packages are available from major airlines and tour operators. Contact **American Airlines Fly AAway Vacations** (☎ 800/321–2121), **Delta Dream Vacations** (800/ 872–7786), **SuperCities**

(☎ 800/333–1234), **United Airlines Vacation Planning Center** (☎ 800/328–6877).

THEME TRIPS

AMISH LIFE➤ For personal interaction with the Amish, such as sharing a meal with an Amish family or riding in a horse-drawn buggy while your host explains local Amish farming techniques, contact **Lang's Great Escapes** (Box 117386, Dept. STI, Burlingame, CA 94011, ☎ 415/ 343–9705, FAX 415/ 343–9044). Trips also include a visit to area attractions such as Longwood Gardens and Valley Forge.

SPORTS➤ For packages that include hotel accommodations, air transportation, and tickets to see the baseball Phillies, football Eagles, and other local Philadelphia teams, contact **Dan Chavez's Sports Empire** (Box 6169, Lakewood, CA 90714, ☎ 310/809– 6930 or 800/255– 5258).

FROM THE U.K.

Tour operators offering packages to Philadelphia include **British Airways Holidays** (Astral Towers, Betts Way, London Rd., Crawley, West Sussex RH10 2XA, ☎ 01293/ 518–022) **Cosmosair** (Ground Floor, Dale House, Tiviot Dale, Stockport, Cheshire SK1 1TB, ☎ 0161/ 480–5799), **Jetsave** (Sussex House, London Rd., East Grinstead, W. Sussex RH19 1LD, ☎ 01342/312–033), **Kuoni Travel** (Kuoni House,

Dorking, Surrey RH5 4AZ, ☎ 01306/742– 222), and **Premier Holidays** (Premier Travel Centre, Westbrook, Milton Rd., Cambridge CB4 1YG, ☎ 01223/516–688).

Travel agencies that offer cheap fares to Philadelphia include **Trailfinders** (42–50 Earl's Court Rd., London W8 6FT, ☎ 0171/ 937–5400), **Travel Cuts** (295a Regent St., London W1R 7YA, ☎ 0171/637–3161; *see* Students, *above*), and **Flightfile** (49 Tottenham Court Rd., London W1P 9RE, ☎ 0171/ 700–2722).

ORGANIZATIONS

The **National Tour Association** (546 E. Main St., Lexington, KY 40508, ☎ 606/ 226–4444 or 800/755– 8687) and **United States Tour Operators Association** (USTOA, 211 E. 51st St., Suite 12B, New York, NY 10022, ☎ 212/750–7371) can provide lists of member operators and information on booking tours.

PUBLICATIONS

Consult the brochure **On Tour** and ask for a current list of member operators from the National Tour Association (*see* Organizations, *above*). Also get a copy of the **"Worldwide Tour & Vacation Package Finder"** from the USTOA (*see* Organizations, *above*) and the Better Business Bureau's **"Tips on Travel Packages"** (publication No. 24-195, $2; 4200 Wilson Blvd., Arlington, VA 22203).

TRAVEL AGENCIES

For names of reputable agencies in your area, contact the **American Society of Travel Agents** (1101 King St., Suite 200, Alexandria, VA 22314, ☎ 703/739–2782).

VISITOR INFORMATION

Contact the **Philadelphia Convention and Visitors Bureau** (1515 Market St., Suite 2020, Philadelphia 19102, ☎ 215/636–3300), the **Philadelphia Visitors Center** (16th St. and John F. Kennedy Blvd., Philadelphia 19102, ☎ 215/636–1666 or 800/321–9563), and the

Pennsylvania Office of Travel Marketing (453 Forum Bldg., Harrisburg 17120, ☎ 717/787–5453 or 800/847–4872).

The **Philadelphia Visitors Center** (☎ 215/636–1666), located at 16th Street and John F. Kennedy Boulevard, one block from City Hall, is open 9–5 daily, until 6 in summer. The **National Park Service** (☎ 215/597–8974 or 215/627–1776 for recorded message) operates a Visitor Center at 3rd and Chestnut streets in the heart of the historic district; open daily 9–5.

In the U.K., also contact the **United States Travel and Tourism Administra-** tion (Box 1EN, London W1A 1EN, ☎ 0171/495–4466). For a free USA pack, write the USTTA at Box 170, Ashford, Kent TN24 0ZX. Enclose stamps worth £1.50.

W WEATHER

For current conditions and forecasts, plus the local time and helpful travel tips, call the **Weather Channel Connection** (☎ 900/932–8437; 95¢ per minute) from a touch-tone phone.

THE GOLD GUIDE / IMPORTANT CONTACTS

SMART TRAVEL TIPS A TO Z

Basic Information on Traveling in Philadelphia and Savvy Tips to Make Your Trip a Breeze

The more you travel, the more you know about how to make trips run like clockwork. To help make your travels hassle-free, Fodor's editors have rounded up dozens of tips from our contributors and travel experts all over the world, as well as basic information on visiting Philadelphia. For names of organizations to contact and publications that can give you more information, *see* Important Contacts A to Z, *above.*

A

AIR TRAVEL

If time is an issue, **always look for nonstop flights,** which require no change of plane. If possible, **avoid connecting flights,** which stop at least once and can involve a change of plane, although the flight number remains the same; if the first leg is late, the second waits.

CUTTING COSTS

The Sunday travel section of most newspapers is a good source of deals.

MAJOR AIRLINES➤ The least-expensive airfares from the major airlines are priced for round-trip travel and are subject to restrictions. You must usually **book in advance and buy the ticket within 24 hours** to get cheaper fares, and you may have to **stay over a Saturday night.** The lowest fare is subject to availability, and only a small percentage of the plane's total seats are sold at that price. It's good to **call a number of airlines, and when you are quoted a good price, book it on the spot**—the same fare on the same flight may not be available the next day. Airlines generally allow you to change your return date for a $25 to $50 fee, but most low-fare tickets are nonrefundable. However, if you don't use it, you can apply the cost toward the purchase price of a new ticket, again for a small charge.

CONSOLIDATORS➤ Consolidators, who buy tickets at reduced rates from scheduled airlines, sell them at prices below the lowest available from the airlines directly—usually without advance restrictions. Sometimes you can even get your money back if you need to return the ticket. Carefully read the fine print detailing penalties for changes and cancellations. If you doubt the reliability of a consolidator, **confirm your reservation with the airline.**

ALOFT

AIRLINE FOOD➤ If you hate airline food, **ask for special meals when booking.** These can be vegetarian, low-cholesterol, or kosher, for example; commonly prepared to order in smaller quantities than standard catered fare, they can be tastier.

SMOKING➤ Smoking is banned on all flights within the United States of less than six hours' duration and on all Canadian flights; the ban also applies to domestic segments of international flights aboard U.S. and foreign carriers. Delta has banned smoking system-wide.

B

BUS TRAVEL

Buses comprise the bulk of the SEPTA system, with 110 routes extending throughout the city and into the suburbs. Bus route 76, called the "Ben FrankLine," connects the zoo in west Fairmount Park with Penn's Landing at the Delaware River, stopping at major tourist sites along the way including the Pennsylvania Convention Center and the Museum of Art. Route 76 costs 50¢ and operates daily from around 9 AM to 6 PM, and later on Wednesday evenings when the Philadelphia Museum of Art is open.

The funny purple mini-buses you'll see around Center City are SEPTA's newest convenience line for visitors,

the PHILLY PHLASH. The line runs from Logan Circle on the Benjamin Franklin Parkway, through Center City to Penn's Landing. **Since a ride on the PHLASH costs $1.50 for a one-way ticket, consider the handy all-day, unlimited-ride pass available for $3.** These special buses run daily from 10 AM to midnight in the summer, 11 AM to 6 PM from Labor Day to Memorial Day.

The base fare for subways, trolleys, and buses is $1.60 in exact change or a token. Transfers cost 40¢. Senior citizens (with valid ID) ride free during off-peak hours and holidays. Tokens sell for $1.15 and can be purchased in packages of two, five or 10 from cashiers along the Broad Street Subway and Market–Frankford lines, and in many downtown stores (including some Rite Aid pharmacies).

If you plan to travel extensively within Center City, it's a good idea to **get a SEPTA pass.** A Day Pass costs $5 and is good for 24 hours of unlimited use on all SEPTA vehicles within the city, plus one trip on any regional rail line including the Airport Express train. A weekly transit pass costs $17.50. Tokens and transit passes are good on buses and subways but not on commuter rail lines.

You can purchase tokens and transit passes in the SEPTA Sales Offices located in the concourse below the

northwest corner of 15th and Market streets, in Market East Station at 8th and Market streets, and in 30th Street Station at 30th and Market streets.

C
CAMERAS, CAMCORDERS, AND COMPUTERS

LAPTOPS

Before you depart, **check your portable computer's battery,** because you may be asked at security to turn on the computer to prove that it is what it appears to be. At the airport, you may prefer to **request a manual inspection,** although security X-rays do not harm hard-disk or floppy-disk storage.

PHOTOGRAPHY

If your camera is new or if you haven't used it for a while, **shoot and develop a few rolls of film** before you leave. Always **store film in a cool, dry place**—never in the car's glove compartment or on the shelf under the rear window.

Every pass of film through an X-ray machine increases the chance of clouding. To protect it, carry it in a clear plastic bag and **ask for hand inspection at security.** Such requests are virtually always honored at U.S. airports. Don't depend on a lead-lined bag to protect film in checked luggage—the airline may increase the radiation to see what's inside.

VIDEO

Before your trip, **test your camcorder, invest in a skylight filter to protect the lens, and charge the batteries.** (Airport security personnel may ask you to turn on the camcorder to prove that it's what it appears to be.)

Videotape is not damaged by X-rays, but it may be harmed by the magnetic field of a walk-through metal detector, so **ask that videotapes be hand-checked.**

CHILDREN AND TRAVEL

BABY-SITTING

For recommended local sitters, **check with your hotel desk.** *See also* Children and Travel *in* Important Contacts A to Z, *above.*

DRIVING

If you are renting a car, **arrange for a car seat when you reserve.** Sometimes they're free.

FLYING

On domestic flights, children under 2 not occupying a seat travel free, and older children currently travel on the lowest applicable adult fare.

BAGGAGE➤ In general, the adult baggage allowance applies for children paying half or more of the adult fare.

SAFETY SEATS➤ According to the Federal Aviation Administration (FAA), it's a good idea to **use safety seats aloft.** Airline policy varies. U.S. carriers allow FAA-approved models, but airlines usually require

that you buy a ticket, even if your child would otherwise ride free, because the seats must be strapped into regular passenger seats.

FACILITIES➤ When making your reservation, **ask for children's meals or freestanding bassinets** if you need them; the latter are available only to those with seats at the bulkhead, where there's enough legroom. If you don't need a bassinet, **think twice before requesting bulkhead seats**—the only storage for in-flight necessities is in the inconveniently distant overhead bins.

LODGING

Most hotels allow children under a certain age to stay in their parents' room at no extra charge, while others charge them as extra adults; be sure to **ask about the cut-off age.**

CUSTOMS AND DUTIES

IN PHILADELPHIA

British visitors aged 21 or over may import the following into the United States: 200 cigarettes or 50 cigars or 2 kilograms of tobacco; one U.S. liter of alcohol; gifts to the value of $100. Restricted items include meat products, seeds, plants, and fruits. Never carry illegal drugs.

BACK HOME

IN CANADA➤ Once per calendar year, when you've been out of Canada for at least seven days, you may bring in C$300 worth

of goods duty-free. If you've been away less than seven days but more than 48 hours, the duty-free exemption drops to C$100 but can be claimed any number of times (as can a C$20 duty-free exemption for absences of 24 hours or more). You cannot combine the yearly and 48-hour exemptions, use the C$300 exemption only partially (to save the balance for a later trip), or pool exemptions with family members. Goods claimed under the C$300 exemption may follow you by mail; those claimed under the lesser exemptions must accompany you.

Alcohol and tobacco products may be included in the yearly and 48-hour exemptions but not in the 24-hour exemption. If you meet the age requirements of the province through which you reenter Canada, you may bring in, duty-free, 1.14 liters (40 imperial ounces) of wine or liquor *or* 24 12-ounce cans or bottles of beer or ale. If you are 16 or older, you may bring in, duty-free, 200 cigarettes, 50 cigars or cigarillos, and 400 tobacco sticks or 400 grams of manufactured tobacco. Alcohol and tobacco must accompany you on your return.

An unlimited number of gifts valued up to C$60 each may be mailed to Canada duty-free. These do not count as part of your exemption. Label the package "Unsolicited Gift— Value Under $60."

Alcohol and tobacco are excluded.

IN THE U.K.➤ From countries outside the EU, including the United States, you may import duty-free 200 cigarettes, 100 cigarillos, 50 cigars or 250 grams of tobacco; 1 liter of spirits or 2 liters of fortified or sparkling wine; 2 liters of still table wine; 60 milliliters of perfume; 250 milliliters of toilet water; plus £136 worth of other goods, including gifts and souvenirs.

D FOR TRAVELERS WITH DISABILITIES

When discussing accessibility with an operator or reservationist, **ask hard questions.** Are there any stairs, inside *or* out? Are there grab bars next to the toilet *and* in the shower/tub? How wide is the doorway to the room? To the bathroom? For the most extensive facilities, meeting the latest legal specifications, **opt for newer accommodations,** which more often have been designed with access in mind. Older properties or ships must usually be retrofitted and may offer more limited facilities as a result. Be sure to **discuss your needs before booking.**

DISCOUNT CLUBS

Travel clubs offer members unsold space on airplanes, cruise ships, and package tours at as much as 50% below regular prices. Membership may include a regular bulletin or access to a

toll-free hot line giving details of available trips departing from three or four days to several months in the future. Most also offer 50% discounts off hotel rack rates. Before booking with a club, **make sure the hotel or other supplier isn't offering a better deal.**

DRIVING

Getting to and around Philadelphia by car is often difficult and, at rush hour, can be a nightmare. The main east–west freeway through the city, the Schuylkill Expressway (I–76), is often tied up for miles.

The main north–south highway through Philadelphia is the Delaware Expressway (I–95). To reach Center City heading southbound on I–95, take the Vine Street exit.

From the west, the Pennsylvania Turnpike begins at the Ohio border and intersects the Schuylkill Expressway (I–76) at Valley Forge. The Schuylkill Expressway, with recently completed renovations, has several exits in Center City. The Northeast Extension of the turnpike runs from Scranton to Plymouth Meeting, north of Philadelphia. From the east, the New Jersey Turnpike and I–295 access U.S. 30, which enters the city via the Benjamin Franklin Bridge, or New Jersey Route 42 and the Walt Whitman Bridge into South Philadelphia.

Parking in Center City can be tough. A spot at a parking meter, if you're lucky enough to find one, costs 25¢ per 15 minutes. Parking garages charge up to $1.50 per 15 minutes.

I
INSURANCE

BAGGAGE

Airline liability for your baggage is limited to $1,250 per person on domestic flights. On international flights, the airlines' liability is $9.07 per pound or $20 per kilogram for checked baggage (roughly $640 per 70-pound bag) and $400 per passenger for unchecked baggage. Insurance for losses exceeding the terms of your airline ticket can be bought directly from the airline at check-in for about $10 per $1,000 of coverage; note that it excludes a rather extensive list of items, shown on your airline ticket.

FLIGHT

You should **think twice before buying flight insurance.** Often purchased as a last-minute impulse at the airport, it pays a lump sum when a plane crashes, either to a beneficiary if the insured dies or sometimes to a surviving passenger who loses eyesight or a limb. Supplementing the airlines' coverage described in the limits-of-liability paragraphs on your ticket, it's expensive and basically unnecessary. Charging an airline ticket to a major credit card often automatically entitles you to coverage and

may also embrace travel by bus, train, and ship.

U.K. TRAVELERS

According to the Association of British Insurers, a trade association representing 450 insurance companies, it's wise to **buy extra medical coverage when you visit the United States.** You can buy an annual travel-insurance policy valid for most vacations during the year in which it's purchased. If you go this route, make sure it covers you if you have a preexisting medical condition or are pregnant.

TRIP

Without insurance, you will lose all or most of your money if you must cancel your trip due to illness or any other reason. Especially if your airline ticket, cruise, or package tour is nonrefundable and cannot be changed, it's essential that you **buy trip-cancellation-and-interruption insurance.** When considering how much coverage you need, look for a policy that will cover the cost of your trip plus the nondiscounted price of a one-way airline ticket should you need to return home early. Read the fine print carefully, especially sections defining "family member" and "preexisting medical conditions." Also **consider default or bankruptcy insurance,** which protects you against a supplier's failure to deliver. However, such policies often do not cover default by a travel agency, tour operator, airline, or

cruise line if you bought your tour and the coverage directly from the firm in question.

L
LODGING

HOME EXCHANGE

If you would like to find a house, an apartment, or other vacation property to exchange for your own while on vacation, **become a member of a home-exchange organization,** which will send you its annual directories listing available exchanges and will include your own listing in at least one of them. Arrangements for the actual exchange are made by the two parties to it, not by the organization.

M
MONEY
AND EXPENSES

ATMS

Chances are that you can **use your bank card at ATMs** to withdraw money from an account and get cash advances on a credit-card account if your card has been programmed with a personal identification number, or PIN. Before leaving home, **check in on frequency limits** for withdrawals and cash advances.

On cash advances you are charged interest from the day you receive the money, whether from a teller or an ATM. Transaction fees for ATM withdrawals outside your home turf may be higher than for withdrawals at home.

TAXES

SALES➤ The main sales tax in Pennsylvania is 7%. Various other taxes—including a liquor tax—apply. Visitors are delighted to learn there is no sales tax on clothing.

HOTEL➤ In addition to the room rate, travelers pay a 13% hotel tax (7% state, 6% city).

TRAVELER'S CHECKS

Whether or not to buy traveler's checks depends on where you are headed; **take cash to rural areas and small towns, traveler's checks to cities.** The most widely recognized are American Express, Citicorp, Thomas Cook, and Visa, which are sold by major commercial banks for 1% to 3% of the checks' face value—it pays to **shop around.** Both American Express and Thomas Cook issue checks that can be countersigned and used by you or your traveling companion. Record the numbers of the checks, cross them off as you spend them, and keep this information separate from your checks.

WIRING MONEY

You don't have to be a cardholder to send or receive funds through MoneyGramSM from American Express. Just go to a MoneyGram agent, located in retail and convenience stores and in American Express Travel Offices. Pay up to $1,000 with cash or a credit card, anything over that in cash. The money can be picked up within 10 minutes in cash or check at the nearest MoneyGram agent. There's no limit, and the recipient need only present photo identification. The cost, which includes a free long-distance phone call, runs from 3% to 10%, depending on the amount sent, the destination, and how you pay.

You can also send money using Western Union. Money sent from the United States or Canada will be available for pickup at agent locations in 100 countries within 15 minutes. Once the money is in the system, it can be picked up at any one of 25,000 locations. Fees range from 4% to 10%, depending on the amount you send.

P
PACKAGES
AND TOURS

A package or tour to Philadelphia can make your vacation less expensive and more convenient. Firms that sell tours and packages purchase airline seats, hotel rooms, and rental cars in bulk and pass some of the savings on to you. In addition, the best operators have local representatives to help you out at your destination.

A GOOD DEAL?

The more your package or tour includes, the better you can predict the ultimate cost of your vacation. Make sure you know exactly what is included, and

beware of hidden costs. Are taxes, tips, and service charges included? Transfers and baggage handling? Entertainment and excursions? These can add up.

Most packages and tours are rated deluxe, first-class superior, first class, tourist, and budget. The key difference is usually accommodations. If the package or tour you are considering is priced lower than in your wildest dreams, **be skeptical.** Also, **make sure your travel agent knows the hotels** and other services. Ask about location, room size, beds, and whether it has a pool, room service, or programs for children, if you care about these. Has your agent been there or sent others you can contact?

BUYER BEWARE

Each year consumers are stranded or lose their money when operators go out of business—even very large ones with excellent reputations. If you can't afford a loss, take the time to **check out the operator**—find out how long the company has been in business, and ask several agents about its reputation. Next, **don't book unless the firm has a consumer-protection program.** Members of the United States Tour Operators Association and the National Tour Association are required to set aside funds exclusively to cover your payments and travel arrangements in case of default. Nonmember

operators may instead carry insurance; look for the details in the operator's brochure—and the name of an underwriter with a solid reputation. Note: When it comes to tour operators, **don't trust escrow accounts.** Although there are laws governing those of charter-flight operators, no governmental body prevents tour operators from raiding the till.

Next, **contact your local Better Business Bureau and the attorney general's office** in both your own state and the operator's; have any complaints been filed? Last, **pay with a major credit card.** Then you can cancel payment, provided that you can document your complaint. Always **consider trip-cancellation insurance** (*see* Insurance, *above*).

USING AN AGENT

Travel agents are an excellent resource. In fact, large operators accept bookings only through travel agents. But it's good to **collect brochures from several agencies,** because some agents' suggestions may be skewed by promotional relationships with tour and package firms that reward them for volume sales. If you have a special interest, **find an agent with expertise in that area;** the American Society of Travel Agents can give you leads in the United States. (Don't rely solely on your agent, though; agents may be unaware of small-niche operators, and some special-interest travel

companies only sell direct.)

SINGLE TRAVELERS

Prices are usually quoted per person, based on two sharing a room. If traveling solo, you may be required to pay the full double-occupancy rate. Some operators eliminate this surcharge if you agree to be matched up with a roommate of the same sex, even if one is not found by departure time.

PACKING FOR
PHILADELPHIA

Portage and luggage trolleys are hard to find, so **pack light.** Philadelphia is a fairly casual city, although men will need a jacket and tie in some of the better restaurants. Jeans and sneakers or other casual clothing are fine for sightseeing. You'll need a heavy coat for winter, which can be cold and snowy. Summers are hot and humid, but you'll need a shawl or jacket for air-conditioned restaurants. Many areas are best explored on foot, so **bring good walking shoes.**

Bring an extra pair of eyeglasses or contact lenses in your carry-on luggage, and if you have a health problem, **pack enough medication** to last the trip. **Don't put prescription drugs or valuables in luggage to be checked,** for it could go astray.

LUGGAGE

Free airline baggage allowances depend on the airline, the route, and the class of your

THE GOLD GUIDE / SMART TRAVEL TIPS

ticket; ask in advance. In general, on domestic flights you are entitled to check two bags—neither exceeding 62 inches, or 158 centimeters (length + width + height), or weighing more than 70 pounds (32 kilograms). A third piece may be brought aboard; its total dimensions are generally limited to less than 45 inches (114 centimeters), so it will fit easily under the seat in front of you or in the overhead compartment. In the United States, the FAA gives airlines broad latitude to limit carry-on allowances and tailor them to different aircraft and operational conditions. Charges for excess, oversize, or overweight pieces vary.

SAFEGUARDING YOUR LUGGAGE➤ Before leaving home, **itemize your bags' contents** and their worth, and label them with your name, address, and phone number. (If you use your home address, cover it so that potential thieves can't see it.) Inside your bag, **pack a copy of your itinerary.** At check-in, **make sure that your bag is correctly tagged** with the airport's three-letter destination code. If your bags arrive damaged or not at all, file a written report with the airline before leaving the airport.

PASSPORTS
AND VISAS

CANADIANS

No passport is necessary to enter the United States.

U.K. CITIZENS

British citizens need a valid passport. If you are staying fewer than 90 days and traveling on a vacation, with a return or onward ticket, you will probably not need a visa. However, you will need to fill out the Visa Waiver Form, 1-94W, supplied by the airline.

While traveling, **keep one photocopy of the data page** separate from your wallet and leave another copy with someone at home. If you lose your passport, promptly call the nearest embassy or consulate, and the local police; having the data page can speed replacement.

R
RAIL TRAVEL

ARRIVING BY TRAIN

Philadelphia's 30th Street Station (30th and Market Sts.) is a major stop on **Amtrak's Northeast Corridor line.** You can travel by train between Philadelphia and New York City on the cheap by taking the **SEPTA commuter line R7** to Trenton, New Jersey, and transferring to a NJ Transit commuter line to Manhattan. Ask for the excursion rate. The trip takes an extra 30 minutes, but costs about $14, versus Amtrak's $39. Amtrak also serves Philadelphia from points west, including Harrisburg, Pittsburgh, and Chicago.

At the 30th Street Station, you can connect with Southeastern Pennsylvania Trans-

portation Authority (SEPTA) commuter trains to two downtown stations—Suburban Station at 16th Street and John F. Kennedy Boulevard (near major hotels), and Market East Station at 10th and Market streets (near the historic district)—and to outlying areas. Travelers should **avoid North Philadelphia Station,** which is in a deteriorated neighborhood.

WITHIN PHILADELPHIA

Philadelphia's fine network of commuter trains, operated by SEPTA, serves both the city and the suburbs. The famous Main Line got its start—and its name—from the Pennsylvania Railroad route that ran westward from Center City.

All trains serve 30th Street Station (30th and Market Sts.), where they connect to Amtrak trains, Suburban Station (16th St. and John F. Kennedy Blvd., across from the Visitors Center), and the new Market East Station (10th and Market Sts.) beneath the Gallery at Market East shopping complex. Fares, which vary according to route and time of travel, range from $2.50 to $5 one way. These trains are your best bet for reaching Germantown, Chestnut Hill, Merion (site of the Barnes Foundation), and other suburbs.

RENTING A CAR

CUTTING COSTS

To get the best deal, **book through a travel**

agent and shop around. When pricing cars, **ask where the rental lot is located.** Some off-airport locations offer lower rates—even though their lots are only minutes away from the terminal via complimentary shuttle. You may also want to **price local car-rental companies,** whose rates may be lower still, although service and maintenance standards may not be up to those of a national firm. Also **ask your travel agent about a company's customer-service record.** How has it responded to late plane arrivals and vehicle mishaps? Are there often lines at the rental counter, and, if you're traveling during a holiday period, does a confirmed reservation guarantee you a car?

INSURANCE

When you drive a rented car, you are generally responsible for any damage or personal injury that you cause as well as damage to the vehicle. Before you rent, **see what coverage you already have** by means of your personal auto-insurance policy and credit cards. For about $14 a day, rental companies sell insurance, known as a collision damage waiver (CDW), that eliminates your liability for damage to the car; it's always optional and should never be automatically added to your bill.

FOR U.K. CITIZENS

In the United States you must be 21 to rent a car; rates may be higher for those under 25.

Extra costs cover child seats, compulsory for children under five (about $3 per day), and additional drivers (about $1.50 per day). To pick up your reserved car you will need the reservation voucher, a passport, a U.K. driver's license, and a travel policy covering each driver.

SURCHARGES

Before picking up the car in one city and leaving it in another, **ask about drop-off charges or one-way service fees,** which can be substantial. Note, too, that some rental agencies charge extra if you return the car before the time specified on your contract. To avoid a hefty refueling fee, **fill the tank just before you turn in the car.**

S

SENIOR-CITIZEN DISCOUNTS

To qualify for age-related discounts, **mention your senior-citizen status up front** when booking hotel reservations, not when checking out, and before you're seated in restaurants, not when paying your bill. Note that discounts may be limited to certain menus, days, or hours. When renting a car, **ask about promotional car-rental discounts**—they can net lower costs than your senior-citizen discount.

Seniors should avail themselves of an enormous array of discounts. From cut-rate Amtrak tickets to free rides on SEPTA buses,

from numerous hotel discount rates to free admissions at many cultural museums and attractions, from 10% senior discounts at various restaurants to flat-rate programs at leading car rental companies, Philly promises its senior-citizen visitors will leave the city richer in more ways than one. Benjamin Franklin—inventor of bifocals—would be proud of his hometown. For a complete list on all the discount options, ask for the "Seniors on the Go" booklet available from the Philadelphia Convention and Visitors Bureau.

STUDENTS
ON THE ROAD

To save money, **look into deals available through student-oriented travel agencies.** To qualify, you'll need to have a bona fide student I.D. card. Members of international student groups also are eligible. *See* Students *in* Important Contacts A to Z, *above.*

SUBWAY TRAVEL

The Broad Street Subway runs from Fern Rock Station in the northern part of the city to Pattison Avenue and the sports complex in South Philadelphia. The Market-Frankford Line runs across the city from the western suburb of Upper Darby to Frankford in the northeast. Both lines shut down from midnight to 5 AM, during which time "Night Owl" buses operate along the same routes.

SMART TRAVEL TIPS / THE GOLD GUIDE

Subway cars are crowded and safe during the day. Subway crime has diminished in recent years, but platforms and cars can be relatively empty in the late evening hours—**take a cab late at night.** The station at 13th and Market streets is once again usable now that the city has cleared out the large number of street people who had made it their home.

For information on subway fares and passes, *see* Bus Travel, *above*.

T

TAXIS

Cabs cost about $2 for the flag throw and then $1.80–$2.30 per mile. They are plentiful during the day downtown—especially along Broad Street and near hotels and train stations. At night and outside Center City,

taxis are scarce. You can call for a cab, but they frequently show up late and occasionally never arrive. Be persistent: Calling back if the cab is late will often yield results.

TELEPHONES

LONG-DISTANCE

The long-distance services of AT&T, MCI, and Sprint make calling home relatively convenient and let you avoid hotel surcharges; typically, you dial an 800 number in the United States.

TROLLEYS

Philadelphia once had an extensive trolley network, and nostalgia buffs can still ride on two SEPTA lines in some of the few remaining Presidential Conference Committee cars, popular in the 1940s. The new "Welcome Line" runs a short downtown loop, with some cars continuing

out to the zoo in West Fairmount Park. The "Chestnut Hill Trolley" operates on Saturday and Sunday along Germantown Avenue in the northwest section of the city.

W

WHEN TO GO

Like other northern American cities, Philadelphia can be uncomfortably hot and humid in the summer and freezing cold in winter (winter snowfall averages 21 inches). However, any time is right to enjoy the special pleasures offered throughout the year. *See* Festivals and Seasonal Events *in* Chapter 1 for the city's special-events calendar.

CLIMATE

The following are average daily maximum and minimum temperatures for Philadelphia.

Climate in Philadelphia

Jan.	40F	4C	May	72F	22C	Sept.	76F	24C
	27	- 3		54	12		61	16
Feb.	41F	5C	June	81F	27C	Oct.	67F	19C
	27	- 3		63	17		50	10
Mar.	49F	9C	July	85F	29C	Nov.	54F	12C
	34	- 1		68	20		40	- 4
Apr.	61F	16C	Aug.	83F	28C	Dec.	43F	6C
	43	6		67	19		31	- 1

1 Destination: Philadelphia and the Pennsylvania Dutch Country

YO, PHILADELPHIA!

YO, WORLD! Which is not a mere "hello," but a run-them-all-together salutation of "Hithere," "Howareya," and "Have-a-good-day."

Philadelphians claim credit for "Yo" as a greeting, although they concede it wasn't in vogue when Quaker William Penn founded Philadelphia or when the city's most distinguished citizen, Benjamin Franklin, prowled the streets in pensive solitude. Instead, a muscle-bound movie hero may be the source of its popularity.

In the movie *Rocky*, Philadelphians shout "Yo, Rocky!" as the underdog boxer jogs over some of the city's cobbled streets, through the open-air Italian market, up the Benjamin Franklin Parkway ("America's Champs Elysées"), and up the expansive steps of the Philadelphia Art Museum. Reaching the top, he raises his arms in a "V" in sweet anticipation of victory.

Today, many visitors try to imitate Rocky's dash up the 98 steps of this sandstone-color Greco-Roman building before entering to browse through its fabled art treasures. That irony is only one of the many examples of Philadelphia's audacious uniqueness.

Philadelphia is a fountainhead of superlatives cherished by both historians and tourists: the world's largest city-owned park, Fairmount Park; the oldest art school in America, the Pennsylvania Academy of Fine Arts; the first U.S. medical school to admit women, Women's Medical College of Pennsylvania; the oldest natural-science museum, the Academy of Natural Sciences; the oldest U.S. opera house still in use, the Academy of Music; the first library in America to circulate books, the Library Company founded by Benjamin Franklin; the world's largest sculpture atop a building, the statue of William Penn atop City Hall; the oldest black newspaper in America, the *Philadelphia Tribune;* the oldest African Methodist Episcopal church, Mother Bethel AME; and the nation's oldest street of continuous occupation, Elfreth's Alley, a narrow,

one-block street of 33 Colonial homes in Center City (downtown). All of these buildings still breathe architectural vitality. Or as that popular song cheerfully promises, "Everything old is new again."

But if love is a many-splendored thing, the name, Philadelphia, is a many-storied legend.

The "Philadelphia Lawyer," long a symbol of legal genius, was probably invented when a gout-ravaged, white-haired Philadelphian, Andrew Hamilton, successfully defended Peter Zenger in the nation's first libel case. The plaintiff was New York governor William Cosby (no relation, of course, to a famous and cherished Philadelphia son, Bill Cosby).

The Philadelphia Story amused theatergoers with its inside peek at upper-class eccentricities. *The Philadelphia Negro,* by W.E.B. duBois, set a standard for sociological research. Philadelphia Cream Cheese enhances hors d'oeuvres (although the name alone doesn't claim to titillate taste buds). And Philadelphians still yearn to make the world forget W.C. Fields's suggested impudence for his epitaph: "On the whole, I'd rather be in Philadelphia."

Classical-music lovers around the world pay homage to the Philadelphia Orchestra for its buoyant interpretations of Tchaikovsky. During the winter, the orchestra delights its fans in the Academy of Music's chandeliered splendor, a building modeled after La Scala Opera House. When summer comes, the orchestra moves to Fairmount Park's outdoor Frederic Mann Music Center, where music lovers can lie on blankets under the stars and soar with the classics.

Musical diversity is a Philadelphia tradition. Jazz still reflects the swinging sassiness of three Philadelphia jazz greats, Dizzy Gillespie, Stan Getz, and John Coltrane. Popular music went through a golden period when South Philadelphia's "Golden Boys"—Frankie Avalon, Fabian, Jimmy Darren, and Bobby Rydell—seduced a whole generation into swooning to their love songs. "Philly Sounds" still

transform contemporary music with Teddy Pendergrass, the Ojays, the Stylistics, and the irrepressible Patti LaBelle, who can blow a hole in your soul every time she belts out a tune. If Americans have "danced by the light of the moon," they owe that terpsichorean pleasure to a Philadelphian. South Philadelphian Chubby Checker popularized the "Twist"— and America's sacroiliacs have never been the same since.

The Philadelphia metropolitan area also has an amazing array of institutions of higher education, including a University for the Arts. *Parade Magazine* nominated Philadelphia's Central High School as one of the nation's 12 best high schools.

Given this explosive creativity, it's easy to understand why no city has nurtured the arts more lovingly. Visitors can share that affection when they visit the majestic Free Library with its Parthenon-like facade, the famed Rodin Museum, and the Pennsylvania Academy of the Fine Arts, a spectacular urban maharajah's palace.

But this "Athens of America" has also encouraged commerce to be an equally dominant force. Four of the city's most distinctive buildings are the ovalfront Philadelphia Merchants Exchange (1832) that majestically adjoins a cobblestones street, the huge glass-paned dome that capacious Memorial Hall wears like a Victorian dowager's tiara, Independence Blue Cross's blue-glass-tinted headquarters, and the stately City Hall, an exquisite example of Second French Empire style.

Visitors to the nation's capital may have noticed the City Hall's architectural twin, the Executive Office Building, across the street from the White House. Ironically, this City Hall also became as excuse for resisting progress. An unspoken rule decreed that no building could be constructed higher than City Hall with its statue of William Penn on top. Eventually, Philadelphia's plow-resisting mentality succumbed to American ingenuity. Today, Liberty Place, the Mellon Bank Center, and four new skyscrapers have virtually doubled the height of the city's skyline.

In the wintertime, Philadelphians follow convention. They lunch indoors. But when summer arrives, they lunch in their ubiquitous park. Fairmount Park winds through the city, an urban oasis from smoke-clogged, noisy traffic jams. Visitors can relax in its verdant serenity with noon-day picnics, softball tournaments, and family barbecues. A meandering Schuylkill River through the park also attracts a daily stream of neighborhood anglers and rowers from the city's 13 rowing clubs.

Because Quaker William Penn founded Philadelphia, Quakers quickly dominated the city's early political and commercial life. The Quaker City influence has diminished, but the memory lingers. Today, the nation's most enduring exercise in multiethnicity flavors the city's political and social life.

Although all of the city's founding fathers were WASPs, Philadelphia soon opened its arms to the world's "tired . . . huddled masses, yearning to be free." Successive waves of immigrants swarmed into Philadelphia as they did into New York City. Mention the name of a neighborhood and Philadelphians will candidly identify its ethnic abundance: Italian South Philadelphia, black North Philadelphia, Irish Olney, Jewish Northeast, Puerto Rican Hunting Park, Chestnut Hill WASPs, Center City Chinatown, Vietnamese West Philadelphia, Polish Port Richmond, and Ukrainian Nicetown. Each enclave's lifestyles and restaurants exalt is ethnic heritage.

AT THE SAME TIME, the city's peoplescape is changing. Recently arrived yuppies are gentrifying black and Puerto Rican low-income neighborhoods within walking distance of Center City office buildings and the art museum. The relentless survival of ethnic neighborhoods, however, unfrocks a won't-lie-down-and-die spirit behind the city's name.

William Penn chose the name "Philadelphia" (Greek for "brotherly love"). He hoped it would fill expectations for his "Holy Experiment"—"you shall be governed by laws of your own making, and live a free, and if you will, a sober and industrious people." Since 1682, Philadelphia has diligently met all of those goals, even if the great journalist Lincoln Steffens dubbed it in 1903 "the worst-governed city in the country."

But Philadelphians have been forced to cope with the reality that their "City of Brotherly Love" is no more brotherly—nor even sisterly—than any other American city. Philadelphia has endured its share of white-black confrontations, other interethnic battles (early Colonialists roaming the streets, beating up the Germans and Quakers), and electoral decisions decided solely on race.

When the controversial ex-cop and colorful mayor Frank L. Rizzo held office, the Italian-American community provided his staunchest electoral base. When the city's first black mayor, W. Wilson Goode, made a more perverse kind of history by approving the bombing of a neighborhood, black voters supported his reelection with 98% of their vote, even though an entire city block of black homes was incinerated and 11 blacks (including five children) were killed.

Every city should enjoy an interlude of greatness. Between 1949 and 1962 Richardson Dilworth and Joseph Clark dominated the city's politics, and "For one brief moment there was Camelot." Although the "Dilworth-Clark Renaissance" lasted only 13 years, it set a standard by which Philadelphia is still judged. These men dared to envision a people who would owe a higher loyalty to their city than their neighborhoods.

But Philadelphia's neighborhoods have triumphed because they are more than houses on a street. They are daily celebrations of life where families still sit on the marble steps of sentry-like rowhouses and gossip as the sun sets. They lounge in their bucolic backyards behind 12-room flagstone houses, attend religious services in Colonial-period churches, or just hang out on the street corner. "Yo, Angelo, your mother's lookin' for ya. Dinner's ready."

A *Washington Post* feature installed Philadelphia in the Culinary Hall of Fame with this observation of stunning authority: "There are four kinds of cuisine, Italian, French, Chinese and Philadelphia." Not only will the truth set you free, it will emancipate your taste buds. Succulent crabs are served in joyous heaps at world-famed Bookbinder's, Walt's, or DiNardo's. Cheesesteaks (as Philadelphian as the Liberty Bell), barbecue ribs (that will remind Southerners of home),

hoagies (subs or hero sandwiches), pepper pot soup, Jewish deli corned beef, and Philadelphia's ubiquitous mustard-smeared pretzels cover the city's foodscape like a midwinter blizzard.

For food shopping, either the Reading Terminal Market in a cavernous railroad shed with its Amish farmers and Asian proprietors, or the outdoor Italian Market with barrel-by-carton sidewalk displays of fruits, vegetables, and exotic foods offer great money-saving values.

And then there's South Street, a one-thoroughfare adventure that combines the fascinations of New York's Greenwich Village and San Francisco's Ghirardelli Square. As Philadelphia Daily News writer Kathy Sheehan summed it up: "South Street must be the only street in America where, in one trip, you can do your laundry, watch live Jello-O wrestling, and buy a bridal gown, used books, natural foods, crazy hats, a mattress and box spring, wind-up toys, toilet paper, a VCR, key chains with condoms, Central American art, a box of wood screws, fresh flowers, used clothing, a fountain pen, window shades, water ice, margaritas, mint juleps, rolling papers, healing crystals, and Halloween masks."

Along the east bank of the Schuylkill River, boathouses are contoured by strings of white lights that brighten the dark night. It's a year-round festival of lights.

As the seasons change, so do the sports teams. Philadelphia's Eagles, the Flyers, the Phillies and the 76ers are supported by fanatically loyal fans. How fanatic? "Philadelphia fans will boo Santa Claus," a national news magazine once groused.

O N NEW YEAR'S DAY, while Americans are recovering from night-before revelry and blearily watching football bowl games, energetic Philadelphians strut into the national limelight with the Mummers, gaudily plummeted string bands. After kicking up their frisky heels in an all-day parade of skits and dances, they dissolve into all-night neighborhood revelries.

But with all of Philadelphia's festive enticements, *caveat peregrinator* (let the tourist beware). As with any big city,

Philadelphia does have a crime problem, although the efficiency of the PAVies might lead you to believe that illegal parking is the city's most serious offense.

PAVies (Parking Authority Vultures) will ticket your car if you pause one minute on a street to buy a hotdog or pick up a package. If you're parked in a "No stopping" zone, your car stands a good chance of being towed. Unsuspecting tourists have filled the columns of letters-to-the-editor with tales of horror because they erroneously assumed that the Philadelphia Parking Authority fanatics would exercise a reciprocal civility respected in their hometowns. In Philadelphia, PAVies don't. Beware of these ticket-writing zealots.

Yo, America!

Check out your "Cradle of Liberty" with its Independence Hall, Liberty Bell, Art Museum, cheesesteaks, Reading Terminal Market, ethnic neighborhoods, cobbled streets, hoagies, Center City boutiques, theaters, buoyant classical music, jazz nightclubs, the South Street cornucopia, and the neighborhood streets teeming with life.

As the rock groups at two simultaneous Live Aid concerts in London and Philadelphia sang, "We are the world, We are the children." In Philadelphia, we are the neighborhoods, we are the people—just like all of America.

— *Chuck Stone*

A former editor of the Philadelphia Daily News, *Chuck Stone is currently a professor at the School of Journalism and Mass Communication of the University of North Carolina, Chapel Hill.*

WHAT'S WHERE

Back in the 18th century, William Penn laid out his new city of Philadelphia as though it were a huge chessboard. Charles Dickens lamented in 1842 that "it is a handsome city but distractingly regular: After walking about it for an hour or two, I felt that I would have given the world for a crooked street," but today's tourists readily give thanks to Billy. The center of the city is intersected by two main thoroughfares: Broad Street (the city's spinal column, runs north to south), and Market Street (which runs east to west). Where Broad and Market meet (neatly dividing the city center into four segments), you find City Hall, Philadelphia's center of gravity.

What makes Philadelphia different from other urban centers around the world? Simply stated, this sprawling cosmopolis has the feel of a friendly small town. Actually, several small towns—as Philly is a city of distinct neighborhoods, each with its own personality, rhythm, and lore. Here's a quick overview of the city's main districts, plus some of the other destinations covered in this guide.

The Historic District

No matter how you first approach Philadelphia, all things start at Independence National Historical Park. As the birthplace of the country, "America's most historic square mile" was the arena across which the nation strode to its national identity and independence. One can't list the historical highlights because *everything* is a highlight. Independence Hall—where the Declaration of Independence was approved and the U.S. Constitution adopted—Congress Hall, Old City Hall, Carpenter's Hall, Franklin Court, Declaration House, and, of course, the Liberty Bell Pavilion, are just some of the attractions. If seeing these sights doesn't bring out the gee-whiz patriotism in your 9-year-old, nothing will.

Society Hill

Society Hill is Philadelphia as it has been for 200 years. A gem of a preserved district, it is easily the city's most photogenic neighborhood. Old chimney pots, hidden courtyards, ornate door knockers, and cobblestone streets: Untouched by neons, Society Hill basks in its own patina. While many houses are "trinity" abodes—one room to a floor—other are numbered among America's Federal-style showplaces, including the Hill-Physick-Keith House and the Howell House. Sit a while outside them and watch the people go by—and not just those of the 20th century: Guides in Colonial dress sometimes lead candlelight strolls through the district.

Center City

As a cultural palimpsest, Philadelphia has many pasts, but if you're interested in its present and future head for Center City. This is Philly's business district, anchored by Oz-like skyscrapers and City Hall, crowned by the enormous statue of William Penn. Now that the observation tower atop City Hall has reopened, go up and see him sometime. From Chinatown to Rittenhouse, Center City is crammed with sights. A sample? How about the Academy of Music; that leviathan horn of plenty, the Reading Terminal Market; the spanking new Pennsylvania Convention Center; Thomas Jefferson University (its Gallery holds Philly's greatest painting, Thomas Eakins's *Gross Clinic*) and, for those with itchy credit cards, John Wanamaker and the Shops at Liberty Place.

Old City

Long considered one of Society Hill's poorer neighbors and known as a melting pot for immigrants, Old City is associated in tourists' minds and itineraries with three historic monuments: Christ Church, Elfreth's Alley, and the Betsy Ross House. Landmarked by its gleaming white spire, Christ Church is a gem of English Palladian architecture (its central window was the model for the one in Independence Hall). A few blocks north you'll find Elfreth's Alley, the most beautifully preserved street in the city—by some magical flick of a Wellsian time machine, you feel transported back to the 18th century here. To find the Betsy Ross House, look for the 13 stars and the 13 stripes flying from a second story window of 239 Arch Street, a splendid example of a Colonial Philadelphia house.

Penn's Landing

Ever since William Penn sailed up the Delaware into Dock Creek, Philadelphia's waterfront has been a vibrant part of the city's life. Once home to sailing ships and counting houses, and still one of the world's largest freshwater ports, Penn's Landing today has become a 37-acre-long riverside park, home to the Independence Seaport Museum, the Great Plaza—where an open-air stage hosts concerts all summer long—and a flotilla of ship museums: the USS *Becuna*, the USS *Olympia*, and the *Gazela of Philadelphia*. New hotels, restaurants, and condominiums sprout regularly.

Southwark

Chiseled in stone on the facade of an old Southwark building are the words: "On this site in 1897, nothing happened!" Today, a great deal is happening in this district, which stretches from Front to Sixth streets and from South to Washington avenues. The renovation generation has helped make the Queen Village area a winner in the revival-of-the-fittest contest among Philly's neighborhoods. As a result, rents here are catching up to nearby Society Hill. While Southwark has never been as renowned as its neighbor, it offers some of the most charming streets in the city, such as Hancock and Queen. For real Philly flash, check out the Mummers Museum on Washington Avenue.

South Philadelphia

Yes, this is the neighborhood that gave the world Rocky Balboa, as well as Bobby Rydell, Frankie Avalon, Fabian, and Geno's cheesesteaks. The city's "Little Italy" can sometimes be more Naples than Philly—just take in the five-block-long outdoor Italian Market, where piles of peppers and mountains of mozzarella make your taste buds sit up and beg. To satisfy them, head for the Victor Cafe, where opera-singing waiters serve up *That-sa-good!* meals—Mario Lanza once sang for his supper here. After lunch at the Victor, why not head over to the Mario Lanza Museum—recently included on the *Philadelphia Daily News'* bad-taste list, but a great supporter of up-and-coming musical talent.

Rittenhouse

Like a grande dame, Rittenhouse Square is never in a hurry. The prettiest of Philadelphia's public parks, it beckons frazzled city dwellers to slow down and find balm among its blades. Today, the park is the heart of upper-crust Philly. Christopher Morley, the humorist and author of *Kitty Foyle,* was alluding to a district like Rittenhouse when he described Philadelphia as being situated "at the confluence of the Drexel and Biddle families." Swank hotels and modern office buildings now intrude, but the trappings of one-time grandeur remain on view in its Victorian town houses. Many treasures are tucked away here, including the Curtis Institute of Music, the Church of the Holy Trinity, and the Rosenbach Museum and Li-

brary, home to 130,000 manuscripts, including James Joyce's *Ulysses.*

Benjamin Franklin Parkway

From City Hall, the Benjamin Franklin Parkway stretches northwest to a Greco-Roman temple on a hill—the Philadelphia Museum of Art. The parkway is the city's Champs-Elysées, a grand boulevard designed by French architects and alive with flowers, trees, and fountains. Along the way are many of the city's finest cultural institutions: the Academy of Natural Sciences, the Franklin Institute, the Rodin Museum, and, nearby, the Pennsylvania Academy of the Fine Arts. Don't forget to check out the great paintings of Thomas Eakins at the Museum of Art. If Philadelphia's soul could be said to have been captured in a single image, it would likely be Eakins's *Concert Singer,* a portrait of Weda Cook, a friend of Walt Whitman.

University City

Once known as the "Athens of America," Philadelphia boasts an astonishing concentration of colleges and universities, nearly unrivalled in the country. Two of the larger institutions, the University of Pennsylvania and Drexel University, are located in an area dubbed University City in West Philadelphia, near 34th and Walnut streets. City buses travel along Walnut Street from Society Hill to University City; 34th and Walnut is the stop for Penn. On the southwest corner is the Institute of Contemporary Art, with its innovative exhibitions. Take Locust Walk to explore this Ivy League campus; ivy really does cling to the stately stone buildings.

Fairmount Park

When in need of elbow room, Philadelphians head for Fairmount Park, whose 8,500 acres make it the largest landscaped city park in the world. Considered by many Philly dwellers to be their own backyard, Fairmount beckons with a wide range of pleasures. Along Kelly Drive are the Victorian houses of Boathouse Row, headquarters to the many rowing clubs that make up the "Schuylkill Navy." The Mann Music Center and Robin Hood Dell East hosts open-air concerts in the summer. Children flock to the Zoological Gardens, America's oldest zoo. Tourists, particularly, are drawn to the centuries-old

houses that dot the park, including Mount Pleasant, Strawberry Mansion, and Lemon Hill. Here, also, can be found the noted Greek Revival Fairmount Water Works.

Bucks County

Long a vacation spot for New Yorkers as well as for Philadelphians, Bucks County is a day-tripper's delight, filled with historic sites, artist's colonies, nature preserves, old fieldstone inns, and country-chic restaurants. Once hailed as "The Genius Belt" and home to such luminaries as Dorothy Parker, James Michener, and Oscar Hammerstein II, the region is packed with attractions: New Hope and Lahaska offer delightful antiquing; Doylestown has Fonthill, a millionaire's do-it-yourself castle right out of the Brothers Grimm; and the Delaware Canal Towpath runs through countryside that conjures up England's Cotswolds.

Lancaster County

An hour's drive from Philadelphia will take you to Pennsylvania Dutch Country, an area known for delicious foods and stunning farmlands. The folks responsible are the "Plain People," who still use horse-drawn buggies and dress as their families have dressed for centuries, unfussily. Around the hub of Lancaster, you can tour farmers' markets (top of the take-home goody list is shoofly pie) or replicas of Amish villages, or stop in at the oldest pretzel bakery in the country and twist your own pretzel. For dessert, head for Hershey, the only town in the world that has streetlights shaped like foil-wrapped Hershey Kisses. About 55 miles distant, you'll arrive at Gettysburg, where on July 3, 1863, the greatest artillery battle held on this continent was fought—immortalized through the words of Lincoln's *Gettysburg Address.*

From Brandywine to Valley Forge

Think of the Brandywine Valley and the beloved paintings of Andrew Wyeth come to mind: clapboard farmhouses, forests that could tell a story or two, meadows with getaway space and privacy. The valley's palette is quintessentially Wyeth, too—russet, fieldstone gray, shades of amber. A journey through this valley makes for a restful experience. From Chadds Ford, the heart of Wyeth Country, head south to discover the splendid homes and estates of the Du

Ponts: Winterthur, Nemours, and Longwood Gardens. Nearby, Valley Forge, the site of George Washington's heroic 1778–79 encampment awaits. For some retail shopping therapy, don't forget to check out Reading, the "outlet capital of the world."

PLEASURES & PASTIMES

The Spirit of 1776

Many Americans think they know something about the birthplace of the nation: Benjamin Franklin, Thomas Jefferson's drafting of the Declaration of Independence, the sayings of Poor Richard, the signing of the Constitution. Still, these grade-school facts and figures do little to prepare travelers for the actual Philadelphia experience. To walk through "America's most historic square mile"—Independence National Historical Park—is a tour that exercises not only the feet but the spirit. Who can fail to be moved by the words "Proclaim Liberty thro' all the Land" inscribed on America's best loved relic, the Liberty Bell? Or be moved by sitting where James Madison sat in Congress Hall?

The story begins in 1753, when the Provincial Assembly, meeting at Independence Hall, notified Parliament of its refusal to "make laws by direction." The meeting of the Second Continental Congress in 1775 then lit the fuse for the Revolution. The spirit of 1776 found its fullest expression as Congress acted on Richard Henry Lee's famous Resolution for Independence. Today, Independence National Historical Park continues to embody America's noblest ideals.

Oh! Dem Golden Slippers

Buttoned-up Philadelphia explodes in a tidal wave of sequins, feathers, riotous sound, and pageantry every New Year's Day: the Mummer's Parade. For this day of sudden liberation, the City of Brotherly Love dons "dem Golden Slippers" and cakewalks up Broad Street in a parade that outglitters Las Vegas. This little shindig, initially brought from England, had its American beginnings early in the 19th century when gaily costumed groups rang doorbells seeking donations after reciting rhymes intended to explain their strange garb. Add in Philly's heritage of minstrel shows and vaudeville, and you wind up with today's 12 non-stop hours of song, dance, and costumed splendor.

Philly Fare

Philadelphia has finally managed to beat those cordon bleus. For decades gourmet groupies wrote the city off as a lackluster dining center. How things have changed! In 1994, Philly was named the best restaurant city in the nation, according to the *Condé Nast Traveler*'s reader's poll. The soufflé continued to rise with the opening of the Striped Bass, recently hailed by Esquire as Restaurant of the Year. And the béarnaise never curdles at Le Bec-Fin, which some epicureans cite as the greatest temple of French gastronomy in America. Quintessential Philly dining spots include the City Tavern—called by John Adams "the most genteel tavern in America", Bookbinder's, Lee's Hoagie House, and Pat's King of Steaks. As Pat's aficionados will attest, nothing is more delicious than a cheesesteak—served with onions, spitting fat, and drizzled with real melt-in-your-mouth provolone.

The Emerald City

Envisioned by William Penn as a "green countrie town," Philadelphia is famous as a city with a green thumb. It counts its trees as avidly as a miser counts his gold, and now boasts more than 2 million—maples, elms, oaks, beeches, and poplars—scattered among city squares, parks, streets, and innumerable backyards. The city's main "garden" is Fairmount Park, the largest municipal park in the world. For Philly at its flower-spangled best, check out some of the great Society Hill house gardens. Continuing evidence that Philly is "the city with the country heart" is the annual Flower Show—the largest indoor horticultural event in the world—held every March at the Civic Center.

Artistically Speaking

Artistically, Philadelphia has always been fertile aesthetic territory. From the innovative, probing realism of such 19th-century masters as Thomas Eakins and Robert Henri to famous collectors like the Wintersteens, the McIlhennys, and the Arens-

bergs—among the first Americans to collect Monets, Matissses, and Duchamps—Philadelphia has always played off the contrast between its traditionally staid origins and a lively interest in the new. Nowhere is this better seen than in the Barnes Collection—175 Renoirs alone—which recently returned to its Merion mansion after a world tour. Thanks to the Philadelphia Art Alliance, the Painted Bride Art Center, the Tyler School of Art, the Institute of Contemporary Art, and the Pennsylvania Academy of the Fine Arts, the city's art scene remains as spirited as ever.

Sportsmania

Philadelphia is one of the only three cities on the East Coast with four professional sports teams—the Phillies (baseball), the Eagles (football), the 76ers (basketball), and the Flyers (hockey)—teams that often make it to payoffs and are as good as they come. But there's another sport that Philadelphians are expert at: spectating. Forget about just passing the popcorn; be prepared to throw snowballs at Santa Claus! Visiting teams say they've never seen anything like the behavior of Philly's sports fans, whose hijinks make events at the Spectrum and Veterans Stadium shake, rattle, and roll.

FODOR'S CHOICE

Picking the exceptional (from inexpensive to extravagant) is what our writers do best. We asked them which places and pleasures would help make a perfect trip, and here's what they said. For detailed information about each entry, refer to the appropriate chapters in this guidebook.

Quintessential Philadelphia

★ **The Philadelphia Museum of Art.** If you saw Sylvester Stallone do it in the *Rocky* movies, you *will* have the urge to run up the steps. Go ahead, indulge! Then, unlike Rocky, *go inside*—wander through the 200 galleries and discover one of the world's great collections of art.

★ **Independence National Historical Park.** Even if you're not a history-buff, we predict a few quivers. Start at the Visitor Center and follow the red-brick road past a dozen stirring sites, including Independence Hall and the Liberty Bell.

● **The Wissahickon.** A wilderness outing in the city! A 20-minute drive from downtown brings you to this 5-mile forested gorge with cliffs, trails and wildlife. Have lunch at Valley Green Inn, feed the ducks, then visit the nearby neighborhoods of Chestnut Hill and Manayunk.

★ **Rittenhouse Square.** With majestic elms, Victorian statues, and playing children, Philadelphia's toniest downtown park seems to have sprung from the brush of Mary Cassatt.

Philly Food

★ **Cheesesteaks.** While the hoagie (a.k.a. the submarine sandwich) is the town's "official" sandwich, for our money the cheesesteak—dripping with fried onions, hot cherry peppers, oil, fats and cholesterol—is the quintessential Philly sandwich. The best can be found at Pat's in South Philadelphia.

★ **Bassett's Ice Cream.** Just sweet enough, just rich enough. Favorite flavor: butterscotch-vanilla. Favorite place to get it: the counter at Reading Terminal Market.

★ **Tastykakes.** What's for dessert in the junkfood capital of the country? How about these locally produced snackcakes, especially the Coconut Juniors and Peanut Butter TandyKakes. Their theme song says it all: Clap, clap, clap, and yum, yummy-yummy; so much fun to put in your tummy.

Off the Beaten Track

★ **Bryn Athyn Cathedral.** You'll find this spectacular cathedral, built in 12th-century Romanesque and 14th-century Gothic styles, set on a hill overlooking a valley—one of the most beautiful sites in the Philadelphia region.

★ **The Benjamin Franklin Bridge.** From dawn to dusk you can jog or walk the 1.8-mile span, on a metal walkway 150 feet over the Delaware River, and take in a terrific view of the waterfront.

★ **The Insectarium.** A horrible, ugly, beautiful, diverse collection of 1,500 different creepy crawlers—dead and alive. Best bug gift shop in town!

After Hours

★ **South Street.** From fine restaurants to tattoo parlors, from art galleries to condom boutiques, South Street—from Front to Seventh—is the hippest place in town.

★ **Delaware River Waterfront.** You can club-hop by river taxi to more than a dozen nightspots along the water near the Ben Franklin Bridge.

★ **Boathouse Row.** From the art museum, walk a half mile out West River Drive for a view of these delightfully Tudoresque, neo-Victorian buildings, outlined with hundreds of tiny lights and shimmering on the river.

★ **Zanzibar Blue.** The hottest *and* the coolest jazz room in town, with the best local and national talent.

Hotels

★ **Four Seasons.** Philly's most luxurious hotel, with the best restaurants, service, and—if you get a room overlooking the fountains in Logan Circle—the most romantic views. $$$$

★ **Hotel Atop the Bellevue.** This is the beauty-contest winner: a first-rate hotel that is worth a visit just to see the magnificently restored interior of this sumptuous 19th-century building. $$$$

★ **The Barclay.** Built in 1929 and for decades one of Philadelphia's two best hotels. You can stay on Rittenhouse Square, Philadelphia's prestigious downtown park, for half of what you'd pay across the square at the newer Rittenhouse Hotel. $$$

★ **Shippen Way Inn.** Two 18th-century houses converted to a colonial inn, with exposed wooden beams, wide plank floors and antiques: If the Betsy Ross House were turned into a bed-and-breakfast, it would look like this. $$

Restaurants

★ **Le Bec-Fin.** *Formidable!* As the most prestigious and expensive restaurant in town, the Bec has become internationally renowned for its impeccable service, elegant decor, and the *soufflés tous parfums* of owner-chef Georges Perrier. $$$$

★ **Striped Bass.** At this chic-and-be-seen spot, the food is delicious and so is the stunning decor. *Esquire*'s 1994 Restaurant of

the Year has taken the laurel as Philly's leading scene-arena. $$$$

★ **Café Nola.** Shrimp Creole, Cajun popcorn, jambalaya, and all the Big Easy favorites—most with a distinctive twist—make this the closest you'll get to New Orleans in Philadelphia. $$$

★ **Susanna Foo.** Is this America's finest Chinese restaurant? Try Madame Foo's pheasant dumplings with shiitake mushroom sauce, and you'll probably say "yes." Don't forget the chocolate covered fortune cookies! $$$

★ **Victor Café.** If you love opera, don't miss dinner at Victor. Northern Italian cuisine is served by a waitstaff that bursts into song every few minutes. When Luciano Pavarotti dines there, however, he doesn't join in on "Nessun Dorma." $$

★ **Marrakesh.** No chairs? No utensils? You mean we sit on these cushions and eat a 7-course Moroccan meal with our hands? Yes! Enjoy! $$

★ **The Restaurant School.** Because it's run by students, you get haute cuisine and European service in a beautiful atrium setting—all for around $15. Talk about a deal! $$

★ **Joe's Peking Duck.** Small, crowded, noisy, and the best of the more than 50 restaurants in Philly's Chinatown. $

★ **Famous Deli.** Huge corned beef and pastrami sandwiches, herring, Nova lox, sour pickles, bickering counter men, and waitresses who call you "hon"—everything you want in a deli. $

Brandywine Valley

★ **Longwood Gardens.** The number one attraction in the Brandywine Valley, it has over 1,000 acres of flowers, trees, color and beauty, 365 days a year.

★ **Brandywine River Museum.** A converted 19th-century gristmill on the banks of the Brandywine is the showcase for the beloved art of Andrew Wyeth and the Wyeth family.

★ **Winterthur Museum and Gardens.** The most glamorous attic in the world, Henry Francis du Pont's nine-story mansion is filled with an unrivalled collection of American decorative arts from 1640–1860. Visi-

tors also enjoy 1,000 acres of gardens, lawns and forest.

Bucks County

★ **Fonthill.** The storybook castle-home of Henry Chapman Mercer in Doylestown takes on an air of magic and fantasy during its Christmas and candlelight tours. If you're out for a touch of mystery and murder, attend the on-site theatrical performances of "The Ghost of Grimsley Hall."

★ **Tubing on the Delaware.** For a summer delight, float down the Delaware River in an inner tube rented from Bucks County River Tubing.

★ **Exploring along River Road.** Drive north out of New Hope (Route 32) along the Delaware River Towpath, past old stone farmhouses, 18th-century mills, and lush rolling hills.

Lancaster County

★ **Visit a farmer's market.** For the best "sweets and sours" and chowchow, head for the Central Market in downtown Lancaster or the Green Dragon Farmers Market and Auction in Ephrata.

★ **Exploring Amish Country.** Drive along the back-country roads between Routes 23 and 340 to see the Amish farms and roadside stands.

★ **Eat "Family Style."** No menu, just sit down and they'll bring you all the Pennsylvania Dutch food you can eat.

FESTIVALS AND SEASONAL EVENTS

For exact dates and other information about the following events, contact the **Philadelphia Visitors Center** (*see* Visitor Information *in* The Gold Guide's Important Contacts A to Z).

WINTER

DEC. 31–JAN. 1➤ New Year's Eve fireworks are set to music over the Delaware River at Penn's Landing. *Columbus Blvd. and Chestnut St.,* ☎ *215/923–4992.*

JAN. 1➤ Mummer's Parade is an all-day event during which some 30,000 sequined and feathered paraders—members of string bands, "fancies," "brigades," and comics—march north on Broad Street to City Hall.

FEB.➤ Black History Month features exhibits, lectures, and music at the Afro-American Historical and Cultural Museum, plus related events around the city. *Afro-American Historical and Cultural Museum, 7th and Arch Sts., Philadelphia 19106,* ☎ *215/574–0380.*

FEB.➤ The **Philadelphia Boat Show** displays more than 500 yachts, sailboats, and powerboats. *Pennsylvania Convention Center, 12th and Arch Sts., Philadelphia 19107,* ☎ *610/449–9910.*

LATE FEB.➤ Comcast U.S. Indoor Tennis Championships attracts many of the world's top men tennis pros. *The Spectrum, Broad St. and Pattison Ave., Philadelphia 19148,* ☎ *215/336–3600.*

SPRING

FEB.–MAY➤ Chinese New Year celebrations include 10-course banquets Tuesday through Sunday nights beginning at 6:30. Chefs come from China to prepare the feast. *Chinese Cultural Center, 125 N. 10th St., Philadelphia 19107,* ☎ *215/636–1666.*

MAR.➤ The **St. Patrick's Day Parade** brings the wearing of the green to the Benjamin Franklin Parkway.

MAR.➤ The **Philadelphia Flower Show,** the nation's largest indoor flower show, features acres of exhibits. *Pennsylvania Convention Center, 12th and Arch Sts., Philadelphia 19107,* ☎ *215/625–8250.*

MAR.➤ The Book and the Cook teams the city's best chefs and the world's top cookbook authors in a four-day event. Meet the authors and sample their dishes. For information, contact the Visitors Center (☎ 215/636–1666).

MAR.–JUNE➤ The **American Music Theater Festival** presents opera, musical comedy, cabaret-style revues, children's programs, and experimental works at indoor and outdoor theaters around the city. ☎ *215/893–1579.*

APR.➤ The **Philadelphia Antiques Show** offers museum-quality antiques, lectures, and appraisals to benefit the Hospital of the University of Pennsylvania. *103rd Engineers Armory, 33rd St. above Market St., Philadelphia 19104,* ☎ *215/387–3500.*

APR.➤ The **Easter Promenade** features a parade down South Street with music, entertainment, celebrities, and a fashion contest. *8th and South Sts.,* ☎ *215/636–1666.*

LATE APR.➤ Penn Relays is one of the world's oldest and largest amateur track meets. *Franklin Field, 33rd and Spruce Sts., Philadelphia 19104,* ☎ *215/898–6154.*

LATE APR.➤ St. Walpurgis Night Festival, the traditional Swedish welcome to spring, offers food, song, dance, and bonfires. *American Swedish Historical Museum, 1900 Pattison Ave., Philadelphia 19145,* ☎ *215/389–1776.*

LATE APR.–MAY➤ Philadelphia Open House is a two-week period when selected private homes, gardens, and historic buildings in neighborhoods around the city—including Society Hill, Germantown, and the Main Line—open their doors to the public. ☎ *215/928–1188.*

MAY➤ Riverblues is a weekend waterfront festival featuring the top names in blues. *On the Great Plaza at Penn's Landing,* ☎ *215/636–1666.*

MAY➤ The **Dad Vail Regatta** is the largest collegiate rowing event in the country. Up to 500 shells from over 100 colleges race on a 2,000-meter course on the Schuylkill River along Kelly Drive in Fairmount Park. ☎ 215/248–2600.

3RD THURS. IN MAY➤ **Rittenhouse Square Flower Market** for 82 years has held this one-day sale of plants, flowers, and food, including the traditional candy lemon stick in a fresh lemon. *18th and Walnut Sts.,* ☎ 215/271–7149.

LATE MAY➤ **Jambalaya Jam** is a New Orleans–style festival featuring bands on five stages playing jazz, zydeco, funk, and Dixieland music; specialties such as pralines, gumbo, jambalaya, and other Creole and Cajun food favorites; and Louisiana crafts. *On the Great Plaza at Penn's Landing,* ☎ 215/923–4992.

LATE MAY–EARLY JUNE➤ The **Devon Horse Show and Country Fair,** first held in 1896, is a nine-day event in which top riders compete for more than $200,000 in prize money. *Devon Fairgrounds, U.S. 30, Devon 19333,* ☎ 610/964–0550.

SUMMER

JUNE➤ The **Rittenhouse Square Fine Arts Annual,** America's oldest (1931) and largest outdoor juried art show, exhibits paintings and sculpture by more than 100 Delaware

Valley artists. *Rittenhouse Sq., 18th and Walnut Sts.,* ☎ 215/636–1666.

1ST WEEKEND IN JUNE➤ **Elfreth's Alley Days** features open houses on America's oldest continuously occupied street, along with food, fife-and-drum music, and Colonial crafts. *Elfreth's Alley, between Front, 2nd, Arch, and Race Sts.,* ☎ 215/574–0560.

JUNE➤ The **Mellon PSFS Jazz Festival** presents music from local talent to the top names in jazz in a week-long series of concerts (many free) at locations around town. ☎ 610/667–3559.

JUNE➤ **CoreStates Pro Cycling Championship,** the country's premier bicycle race, attracts the world's top cyclists. ☎ 215/636–1666.

JUNE–AUG.➤ At the **Head House Crafts Fair,** more than 40 artisans exhibit jewelry, stained glass, leather, and quilts on summer weekends, noon–11 PM Saturday and noon–6 PM Sunday. *2nd and Pine Sts.,* ☎ 215/790–0782.

JUNE–AUG.➤ The **Philadelphia Orchestra's Summer Season** showcases noted guest conductors and soloists in outdoor concerts with free lawn seating. *Mann Music Center, 52nd St. and Parkside Ave., Philadelphia 19131,* ☎ 215/878–7707 or 215/567–0707.

JULY➤ The **Welcome America! Festival** celebrates the nation's birth with several days of parades (including the Mummers), hot-air-balloon races, a drum-and-bugle competition,

Independence Day ceremonies at Independence Hall, and the Old City Outdoor Restaurant Festival. It all culminates in a grand old-fashioned July 4 fireworks display. ☎ 215/636–1666.

LATE AUG.➤ The **Philadelphia Folk Festival,** America's oldest (1962) continuous folk festival, consists of three days of concerts and workshops. Performers featured range from the relatively new and unknown to folk superstars. There's also food, crafts, folk dancing, impromptu jam sessions, and sing-alongs. Many "folkies" camp out on the grounds. *Old Pool Farm, Schwenksville 19473,* ☎ 215/242–0150.

AUTUMN

SEPT.➤ **Penn's Landing In-Water Boat Show,** one of the largest in-water boat show on the East Coast, fills the 10-acre basin in Penn's Landing with yachts and other pleasure craft. *Penn's Landing,* ☎ 610/449–9910.

SEPT.➤ The **Philadelphia Distance Run** is the country's premier half-marathon with more than 7,000 runners completing a 13.1-mile course through the streets of downtown and along the Schuylkill River. ☎ 215/685–0052.

LATE SEPT.➤ The **Von Steuben Day Parade,** along Benjamin Franklin Parkway, honors the general who trained the Continental soldiers at

Valley Forge. ☎ *215/636–1666.*

OCT.➤ The **Pulaski Day Parade** marches up Broad Street; the Polish American Congress honors a hero of the Revolutionary War, the Polish general known as the "father of the American Cavalry." ☎ *215/636–1666.*

OCT.➤ **Super Sunday** is Philadelphia's largest block party with food, entertainment, rides, games, more than 400 exhibit booths, and as many as 250,000 guests. *Benjamin Franklin Parkway,* ☎ *215/299–1044.*

2ND MON. IN OCT.➤ The **Columbus Day Parade** includes both a parade on South Broad Street and a festival at Marconi Plaza. ☎ *215/636–1666.*

EARLY NOV.➤ The **Philadelphia Craft Show** is three days of exhibits by 100 craftspeople from

around the country. *103rd Engineers Armory, 33rd St. above Market St.,* ☎ *215/636–1666.*

NOV.➤ The **Philadelphia Marathon** draws several thousand runners for the 26.2-mile race along the Schuylkill River. ☎ *215/686–3645.*

NOV. OR DEC.➤ The **Dog Show,** sponsored by the Kennel Club of Philadelphia, draws more than 2,500 entries. *Pennsylvania Convention Center, 12th and Arch Sts., Philadelphia 19107,* ☎ *215/947–1677.*

LATE NOV.➤ The **Thanksgiving Day Parade** features thousands of marchers, floats, and local personalities. The finale is the arrival of Santa Claus, ushering in the Christmas shopping season. *Benjamin Franklin Pkwy.,* ☎ *215/636–1666.*

DEC.➤ **Christmas Tours of Historic Houses** take visitors around historic Fairmount Park and Germantown houses decorated with Christmas finery. ☎ *215/763–8100 or 215/848–1777.*

DEC.➤ **The Nutcracker,** the Pennsylvania Ballet's production of the Tchaikovsky classic, is a Philadelphia Yuletide tradition. *Academy of Music, Broad and Locust Sts.,* ☎ *215/893–1935.*

DEC. 25➤ **Washington Crossing the Delaware** is re-enacted by more than 200 participants with four 40-foot replicas of Durham boats. It was on Christmas Day 1776 when George Washington and his troops took the Hessian camp at Trenton by surprise. *Washington Crossing Historic Park, Washington Crossing 18977,* ☎ *215/493–4076.*

2 Exploring Philadelphia

By Rathe Miller
and Joyce
Eisenberg

Updated by
Rathe Miller

O**N THE WHOLE I'D RATHER BE IN PHILADELPHIA."** W. C. Fields may have been joking when he wrote his tombstone epitaph, but if he were here today he would eat his words. They no longer roll up the sidewalks at night in Philadelphia. An entertainment boom, a restaurant renaissance, and a cultural revival have helped transform the city. For the past decade, there has been a new optimistic mood, aggressive civic leadership, and national recognition of what the natives have long known: Philadelphia can be a very pleasant place to live—a city with an impressive past and an fascinating future. Indeed, the verdict's in: Not only was Philly ranked the safest of the nation's twelve largest metropolitan areas according to the latest FBI Crime Index, *Condé Nast Traveler* recently proclaimed it "the nation's friendliest city." For many observers, Philadelphia really *is* the only civilized big city in America.

FROM BENJAMIN FRANKLIN TO GRACE KELLY

As the city that gave us the Declaration of Independence *and* the Twist, the birthplace of the nation remains a place of charming contrasts: Grace Kelly and Rocky Balboa; Le Bec Fin—perhaps the nation's finest French haute cuisine restaurant—and the fast-food heaven of Pat's King of Steaks; Independence Hall and the Mario Lanza Museum; 18th-century landmarks that are national icons and 21st-century skyscrapers that soar above them. The world-renowned Philadelphia Orchestra performs at the Academy of Music, a dignified, opulent opera house on Broad Street. Along the same street, 25,000 Mummers dressed in outrageous sequins and feathers pluck their banjos and strut their stuff to the strains of "Oh, 'Dem Golden Slippers" on New Year's Day. City residents include descendants of the staid Quaker founding fathers, the self-possessed socialites of the Main Line (remember Katherine Hepburn and Cary Grant in *The Philadelphia Story*?), and the unrestrained sports fans who are as vocal as they are loyal. Some have been accused of booing the Easter Bunny when their teams have failed them. Together all these folks make for an wonderful mix.

Historically speaking, Philadelphia is a city of superlatives: the world's largest municipal park, the best public collection of art in the United States, the widest variety of urban architecture in America, and according to some experts, the greatest concentration of institutions of higher learning in the country.

A CITY OF NEIGHBORHOODS

In addition, Philadelphia is known as a city of neighborhoods (109 by one count). Shoppers haggle over the price of tomatoes in South Philly's Italian Market; families picnic in the parks of Germantown; street vendors hawk soft pretzels in Logan; and all over town, kids play street games such as stickball, stepball, wireball, and chink. It's a city of neighborhood loyalty: Ask a native where he's from and he'll tell you Fairmount, Fishtown, or Frankford, rather than Philadelphia. The city's population is less transient than in other large cities; people who are born here generally remain and many who leave home to study or work eventually return. Although the population is close to 2 million, residents are intricately connected; on any given day, a Philadelphian is likely to encounter someone with whom he grew up. The "it's-a-small-world" syndrome makes people feel like they belong.

THE PHILADELPHIA STORY

William Penn founded the city in 1682 and chose to name it Philadelphia—Greek for "brotherly love"—after an ancient Syrian city, site of

one of the most venerated and earliest Christian churches. Penn's Quakers settled on a tract of land he described as his "greene countrie towne." After the Quakers, the next wave of immigrants to arrive were Anglicans and Presbyterians (who had a running conflict with the "stiff Quakers" and their distaste for music and dancing). The new residents forged traditions that remain strong in parts of Philadelphia today: united families, comfortable houses, handsome furniture, and good education. From these early years came the attitude Mark Twain summed up as: "In Boston, they ask: 'What does he know?' In New York, 'How much does he make?' In Philadelphia, 'Who were his parents?'."

The city became the queen of the English-speaking New World from the late 1600s to the early 1800s. In the last half of the 1700s, Philadelphia was the largest city in the Colonies, a great and glorious city second only to London in the British Empire. So, when the delegates from the Colonies wanted to meet in a centrally located, thriving city, they chose Philadelphia. They convened the First Continental Congress in 1774 at Carpenters' Hall. The rest, as they say, is history. It is here that the Declaration of Independence was written and adopted, the Constitution was framed, the capital of the United States was established, the Liberty Bell was rung, the nation's flag was sewn by Betsy Ross (though scholars debate this), and George Washington served most of his presidency.

GETTING YOUR BEARINGS

Today, visitors will find Philadelphia's compact 2-square-mile downtown (William Penn's original city) nestled between the Delaware and the Schuylkill (pronounced *skoo*-kill) rivers. Thanks to Penn's grid system of streets—laid out in 1681—the downtown area is a breeze to navigate. The traditional heart of the city is Broad and Market streets (Penn's Center Square), where City Hall now stands. Market Street divides the city north and south; 130 S. 15th Street, for example, is in the second block south of Market. North–south streets are numbered, starting with Front (First) Street, at the Delaware River, and increasing to the west. Broad Street is equivalent to 14th Street.

The city extends north, south, and west from downtown for more than 130 square miles. The Benjamin Franklin Parkway breaks the rigid grid pattern by leading out of Center City into Fairmount Park, which straddles the Schuylkill River and the Wissahickon Creek for 10 miles. It's a distance of 30 miles from the northeast corner to the southwest tip.

Sections of Philadelphia range from posh old-money enclaves to inner-city slums. The downtown is comparatively safe during the day. After dark, exercise caution, especially in areas like Market Street east of Broad Street, 13th Street, and the neighborhoods ringing the downtown. Ask hotel personnel about the safety of places you're interested in visiting. At night, cabs are safer than walking.

Philadelphia has too many attractions to see in one day. Unless you severely limit your itinerary, figure on spending several days. This chapter divides downtown into four walking tours (Tour 3 can be done in a day—if you move fast; each of the other tours takes more than a day of sightseeing.) Although Philadelphia is the fifth largest city in the nation, it maintains a small-town feel. It's a cosmopolitan, exciting, but not overwhelming city, a town that's easy to explore on foot but big enough to keep surprising even those most familiar with it.

Tour 1 **Around Independence Hall:
The Most Historic Square Mile in America**

*Numbers in the margin correspond to points of interest on the Tours
1 and 2 map.*

Whether this is your first day or your only day in Philadelphia, it should
be savored in the city area that comprises Independence National His-
torical Park. Philadelphia was the birthplace of the United States, the
home of the country's first government, and nowhere is the spirit of
those miraculous early days—the boldness of conceiving a brand new
nation—more palpable than along the cobbled streets of the city's
most historic district. The park, which covers forty-two acres and
holds close to forty buildings, has been administered by the National
Park Service since 1951.

In the late 1940s, before civic-minded citizens banded together to save
the area and before the Park Service stepped in, Independence Hall was
crowded with sooty factories and rundown warehouses. Then the city,
state, and federal government took interest. Some buildings were re-
stored, others were reconstructed on their original sites, with several
attractions built for the 1976 Bicentennial celebration. The fine urban
renewal efforts at Independence Mall plaza and in Washington Square
East (Society Hill) ensure that Independence Hall will never again
keep unsightly company. Today, besides being the city's most historic
area, it is also one of the loveliest.

❶ The best place to orient yourself is at the **Visitor Center** (3rd and Chest-
nut Sts.), where you can get a map of the park's important sites and
see the Founding Fathers come to life in the 30-minute movie, *Inde-
pendence.* The center is staffed by park rangers who answer questions
and distribute maps and brochures on Independence National Historical
Park and other sites in the historic area. The bell atop the tower, cast
at the same foundry as the Liberty Bell, was a Bicentennial birthday
gift from Queen Elizabeth II. The main attraction is *Promise of Per-
manency,* a video-computer exhibit that gives visitors an opportunity
to deliberate on key constitutional cases; it was installed to mark the
Constitution's 200th birthday. A city information desk is inside the cen-
ter, plus an excellent bookstore where you can stock up on books, videos,
brochures, prints, and wall hangings about historic figures and events.
For $2.00 you can buy a reproduction of a 1787 map of Philadelphia;
copies of the Declaration and the Constitution on parchment-like
paper cost just one dollar. The most popular items are the tiny Liberty
Bell reproductions.

Here, you can pick up free tickets to some of the park's various at-
tractions. Except as noted, all are free and have the same telephone
number (☎ 215/597–8974) and hours (9–5, with extended evening
hours in summer). A 24-hour hot line (☎ 215/627–1776) will give you
the basic information. You'll need to reserve a spot for the tours of two
Colonial homes: the Bishop White House, where the wealthy first
Episcopal bishop of Pennsylvania lived in grand style, and the modest
home of Quaker John Todd, from whence Todd's widow, Dolley Payne,
emerged to become the first lady of President James Madison. No tick-
ets will be required to see the park's most famous site, Independence
Hall; admission is first come, first served (note that from early May
to Labor Day, you may wait from 15 minutes to an hour for the In-
dependence Hall Tour).

This walking tour covers many of the more important historic sights in the park. During the summer, the Visitor Center offers suggestions for half-day and full-day do-it-yourself tours: "Washington Walk" departs from the Visitor Center at 11 and 3; "Franklin Family Tour" departs from Franklin Court at 11, 1, 2, 3, 4, and 5; and the "Friends Walking Tour" departs from the front of Independence Hall at 6. "Ranger's Choice Walk" departs from the Visitor Center at 11 and 3 with individual rangers choosing their itinerary of interest.

② Directly across 3rd Street is the **First Bank of the United States,** the oldest bank building in the country and headquarters of the government's bank from 1797 to 1811. Head first to the right, to the north side of the structure, to find a beautiful wrought-iron gateway topped by an eagle. Pass through it and you magically step out of modern-day Philadelphia and into Colonial America. Before you do so, check out the bank's beautiful pediment: Executed in 1797 by Clodius F. Legrand and Sons, its cornucopia, oak branch, and American eagle are carved from mahogany—it's amazing to see that this late-18th century masterpiece has withstood acid rain better than the bank's marble pillars.

A redbrick path alongside manicured lawns and ancient oaks and maples leads to the first group of historic buildings, Carpenter's Court, **③** which includes **Carpenter's Hall.** Built in 1770, this was the headquarters of the Carpenters' Company, a guild founded to teach carpenters architecture and to aid their families. In September 1774 the First Continental Congress convened here and addressed a declaration of rights and grievances to King George III. Recreations of Colonial settings include original chairs and candle sconces and displays of 18th-century carpentry tools. The building is still owned and operated by the Carpenters' Company. *320 Chestnut St.,* ☎ *215/597–8974.* ☉ *Tues.–Sun. 10–4.*

Next door the former Army-Navy Museum and the Marine Crops National Memorial have been combined to create the new **New Hall Military Museum.** On display are uniforms, medals, and authentic weapons **④** including powder horns, swords, and a 1763 flintlock musket. Dioramas depict highlights of the Revolutionary War. New to New Hall is the Pemberton House, scheduled to become a book shop and gift store. *Chestnut St. east of 4th St.,* ☎ *215/597–8974.* ☉ *Daily 9–5.*

Leave Carpenter's Court and continue west on the redbrick path across **⑤** 4th Street to the Parthenon look-alike, the **Second Bank of the United States.** Built in 1824, the Second Bank is an excellent example of Greek Revival architecture. Housed in the building are portraits of prominent Colonial Americans by noted artists such as Charles Willson Peale, William Rush, and Gilbert Stuart. Don't miss Peale's portrait of Jefferson: It's the only one that shows him with red hair. The permanent exhibit, "Portraits of the Capital City," opened in 1988, has a life-size wooden statue of George Washington by William Rush; a mural of Philadelphia in the 1830s by John A. Woodside Jr.; and the only known likeness of William Floyd, a lesser-known signer of the Declaration of Independence. *420 Chestnut St.,* ☎ *215/597–8974.* ☉ *Daily 9–5.*

As you continue west on the redbrick path, which now runs along cobblestoned Library Street, you'll see on your right **Library Hall,** the library of the American Philosophical Society. This was the first public **⑥** library in the Colonies and a "library of congress" for members of the Continental and Federal congresses that met in Philadelphia. Although now basically a research library for scholars, its vaults contain such artifacts as a copy of the Declaration of Independence handwritten by

Tours 1 and 2

0 220 yards N
0 200 meters

KEY
---- Market-Frankford
Subway

Arch St.

Commerce St.

Market-Frankford Subway

Market St.

Ranstead St.

Chestnut St.

Sansom St.

*Independence
Square*

Walnut St.

*Washington
Square*

Locust St.

SOCIETY HILL

Marshalls Ct.

Spruce St.

Cypress St. Cypress St.

Panama St.

Pine St.

7th St. 6th St. 5th St. 4th St.

Willings

St. Joseph's Way

Lawrence Ct.

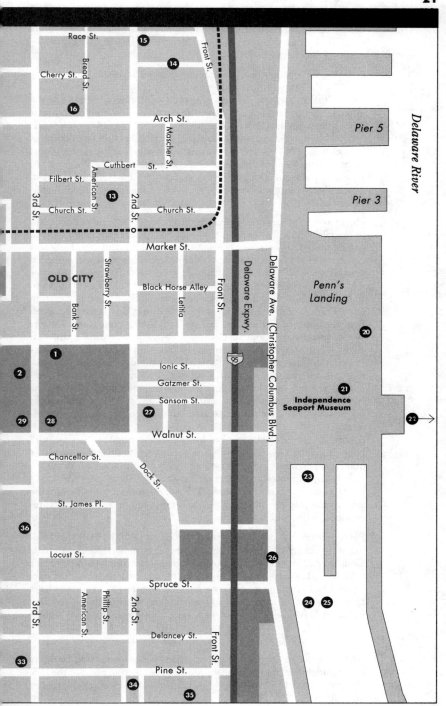

Thomas Jefferson, William Penn's 1701 Charter of Privileges, and Benjamin Franklin's will, and there are fascinating changing exhibits in the lobby that are open to the public. *105 S. 5th St., ☎ 215/440–3400. ⊙ Weekdays 9–4:45.*

Crossing 5th Street, you arrive at **Independence Square,** where, on July 8, 1776, the Declaration of Independence was first read in public. Although the square is not as imposing today, you can easily imagine the impact that this setting had on the colonists. The first building on your right is **Philosophical Hall** (104 S. 5th St., ☎ 215/440–3400), the headquarters of the American Philosophical Society. Founded by Benjamin Franklin in 1743 to promote "useful knowledge," it is the oldest learned society in America; its membership has included Washington, Jefferson, Lafayette, Emerson, Darwin, Edison, Churchill, and Einstein. The building (dating from 1785) is closed to the public except by appointment.

Hurry over to **Independence Hall** to get a place at the head of the classes of schoolchildren who've come to see the birthplace of the United States, one of our nation's greatest gems. America's most historic building was constructed in 1732 as the Pennsylvania State House. What happened here between 1775 and 1787 changed the course of American history— and the name of the building to Independence Hall. The delegates to the Second Continental Congress met in the hall's Assembly Room in May 1776, united in anger over the blood that had been shed when British troops fired on citizens in Concord. In this same room, George Washington was appointed Commander-in-Chief of the Continental Army, Thomas Jefferson's eloquent Declaration of Independence was signed, and later the Constitution of the United States was adopted. Here, the first foreign minister to visit the United States was welcomed, the news of Cornwallis's defeat was announced signaling the end of the Revolutionary War, and John Adams and Abraham Lincoln lay in state. The memories that this building holds linger in the collection of polished muskets, the silver inkstand that was used by delegates to sign the Declaration of Independence, and the "Rising Sun" chair in which George Washington sat. (After the Constitution was adopted, Benjamin Franklin said about the sun carving on the chair, "I have the happiness to know that it is a rising and not a setting sun.") Upstairs on the second floor you'll find the 100-foot Long Room, the site of many of the fledgling nation's most important banquets, receptions, balls, and suppers.

Part of the Independence Hall complex today is Old City Hall, the building at the corner of 5th and Chestnut streets, home of the U.S. Supreme Court from 1791 to 1800. In the East Wing—attached to Independence Hall by a short colonnade—you can embark on free tours that start every 15 to 20 minutes; The tour lasts 35 minutes, but you may have to wait in line up to an hour during the busy season from early May to Labor Day. The West Wing of Independence Hall contains a book shop and gift store. *Chestnut St. between 5th and 6th Sts., ☎ 215/597–8974. ⊙ Daily 9–5; early July–early Sept. 9–8.*

At the corner of 6th and Chestnut streets is **Congress Hall,** formerly the Philadelphia County Courthouse and the meeting place of the U.S. Congress from 1790 to 1800—one of the most important decades in our nation's history. Here, during that time, the Bill of Rights was added to the Constitution; Alexander Hamilton's proposals for a mint and a national bank were enacted; and Vermont, Kentucky, and Tennessee became the first new states. On the first floor is the House of Representatives, where President John Adams was inaugurated in 1797. On

the second floor is the Senate chamber, where George Washington was inaugurated for his second term in 1793. Both chambers have been authentically restored. *6th and Chestnut Sts.,* ☎ *215/597–8974.* ⊙ *Daily 9–5.*

In front of Independence Hall, next to the statue of George Washington, note the plaques marking the spot where Abraham Lincoln stood on February 22, 1861, and a few steps away where John F. Kennedy delivered an address on July 4th, 1962. On July 4th, 1993, President Bill Clinton joined in the presentation of the Philadelphia Liberty Medal to African National Congress President Nelson Mandela and South African President F. W. de Klerk. With Independence Hall in front of you and the Liberty Bell behind you, it's a place to stand for a moment and soak up a sense of history.

North of Independence Hall, one block up the mall, is Philadelphia's best-known symbol, the **Liberty Bell.** The bell fulfilled the biblical words of its inscription when it rang to "proclaim liberty throughout all the land unto all the inhabitants thereof," beckoning Philadelphians to the State House Yard to hear the first reading of the Declaration of Independence. Ordered in 1751 and originally cast in England, the bell cracked during testing and was recast in Philadelphia by Pass and Stow in 1753. To keep it from falling into British hands during the Revolution—they would have melted it down for ammunition—the bell was spirited away by horse and wagon to Allentown 60 miles north. The bell is the subject of much legend; one story says that it cracked when tolled at the funeral of Chief Justice John Marshall in 1835. Actually, the bell cracked slowly over a period of years. It was repaired but cracked again in 1846 and was then forever silenced. It was called the State House Bell until 1839, when a group of Abolitionists adopted it as a symbol of freedom and renamed it the Liberty Bell. After being housed in Independence Hall for more than 200 years, the bell was moved to a glass-enclosed pavilion for the 1976 Bicentennial. The new home is an incongruous setting for such a historic object, but it does display the bell 24 hours a day. While the building is open, rangers and volunteers tell the story. After hours you can press a button on the outside walls to hear a recorded account of the bell's history. *Market St. between 5th and 6th Sts.,* ☎ *215/597–8974.* ⊙ *Daily 9–5; early July–early Sept. 9–8.*

Head west on the walkway between Market and Chestnut streets under the Rohm and Haas Building. You'll pass the sculpture-fountain *Milkweed Pod.* Installed in 1959, it was one of the first examples of Philadelphia's law requiring public buildings to spend 1% of construction costs for art. The walkway will lead you to 7th Street and **Declaration House** (formerly the Graff House), where Thomas Jefferson wrote the rough draft of the Declaration of Independence in June 1776. Jefferson rented rooms from bricklayer Jacob Graff. The bedroom and parlor in which he lived that summer have been re-created with period furnishings. The first floor has a Jefferson exhibit and a seven-minute film, *The Extraordinary Citizen.* The display on the Declaration of Independence shows changes Jefferson made in the writing. You can see Jefferson's original version—which would have abolished slavery had the passage not been stricken by the committee that included Benjamin Franklin and John Adams. *7th and Market Sts.,* ☎ *215/597–8974.* ⊙ *Daily 9–5.*

TIME OUT Enter the **Bourse** (on 5th Street across from the Liberty Bell Pavilion) and you're in another century. The skylit Great Hall, with its Corinthian columns, marble, wrought-iron stairways, and Victorian gingerbread de-

tails, has been magnificently restored. Built in 1895 as a stock exchange, it's now a festive complex of shops, offices, and eateries.

If you have time to see just one site other than Independence Hall and the Liberty Bell, make it **Franklin Court,** eastward at 316 Market Street. This underground museum on the site of Benjamin Franklin's home is an imaginative tribute to the Renaissance man, and the imagination used in its construction is almost a match for that of its famous owner. In 1763, at the age of 57, Dr. Franklin built his first permanent home in Philadelphia, in a courtyard off Market Street. Within the museum, the accomplishments of the statesman, diplomat, scientist, inventor, printer, and author are brought to life. Dial-a-quote to hear his thoughts or pick up a telephone and call his contemporaries to find out what they really thought of him. There also an informative 20-minute film on Franklin's life. At the Market Street side are several houses, now exhibit halls, that Ben had rented. In one, visitors can see how Franklin fireproofed the building: His interest in fireproofing led him to experiment with kite flying and lightning (remember the delightful rendition of those experiments in Disney's animated cartoon *Ben and Me?*). Here, too, you'll find a restoration of a Colonial-era print shop and a post office (nice touch: manned by employees in Colonial dress). Don't forget to get a letter hand-stamped with a "B. Free Franklin" cancellation. *314– 322 Market St. (or enter from Chestnut St. walkway),* ☎ *215/597– 2760.* ☉ *Daily 9–5; summer Sept. 10–6.*

Walk one block east on Market Street and a half block north on 2nd Street to **Christ Church,** the oldest Episcopal Church in America and a gem of 18th-century architecture, where noted colonists, including 15 original signers of the Declaration of Independence, worshipped. The congregation was organized in 1695 on this site; the present church— a fine example of Georgian architecture—was completed in 1754. The bells and the steeple were financed by lotteries run by Benjamin Franklin. Brass plaques mark the pews of Washington, Robert Morris, Betsy Ross, and others. (The church burial ground, two blocks west, is No. 20 on this tour.) *2nd St. north of Market St.,* ☎ *215/922–1695.* ☉ *Mon.–Sat. 9–5, Sun. 1–5. Services Sun. at 9 and 11.*

Continuing north on 2nd Street for a block and passing Arch Street, you come to a small street on the right. **Elfreth's Alley** is the oldest continuously occupied residential street in America, dating back to 1702. Much of Colonial Philadelphia resembled this area, with its cobblestone streets and narrow two-story houses. The Elfreth's Alley Association has restored No. 126, a Colonial craftsman's home, with authentic furnishings and a Colonial kitchen. On the first weekend in June residents celebrate Elfreth's Alley Days by dressing in Colonial garb and opening their houses to the public. In December the houses are open for a one-night Christmas tour. The rest of the year, only No. 126 is open. *Off Front and 2nd Sts. between Arch and Race Sts.,* ☎ *215/574–0560.* ☉ *Daily 10–4, Mar.–Dec.; weekends 10–4, Jan. and Feb.*

Walk back to 2nd Street, turn right, and a few footsteps take you to the **Fireman's Hall Museum.** Housed in an authentic 1876 firehouse, the museum traces the history of firefighting, from the volunteer company founded in Philadelphia by Benjamin Franklin in 1736 to the professional departments of the 20th century. The collection includes early hand- and horse-drawn fire engines (such as an 1815 hand pumper and a 1907 three-horse Metropolitan steamer), fire marks, uni-

forms, and other memorabilia. *147 N. 2nd St., ☎ 215/923–1438.* ⊙ *Tues.–Sat. 9–5.*

If you walk south on 2nd Street and turn right to 239 Arch Street, you'll find the most popular residence in Philadelphia. It's easy to find: Just look for the 13-star flag displayed from its second-floor window. Whether Betsy Ross—who worked in her family's flag-making and upholstery business—actually lived in the **Betsy Ross House,** and whether or not she really made the first Stars and Stripes, is debatable. Nonetheless, the house is a splendid example of a Colonial Philadelphia home and is fun to visit. Owned and maintained by the City of Philadelphia, the eight-room house is crammed with artifacts such as a family Bible and Betsy Ross's wardrobe and yardstick. The small rooms are furnished with period pieces to reflect the life of this hardworking Quaker lady (who died at the age of 84, outliving three husbands). You may have to wait in line here, as this is one of the city's most popular tourist attractions. Alongside the house is brick-paved Atwater Kent Park, with a fountain, benches, and the graves of Betsy Ross and her third husband, John Claypoole. *239 Arch St., ☎ 215/627–5343.* ⊙ *Tues.–Sun. 10–5.*

Continuing west on Arch Street, you'll see an eight-foot-high bust of Benjamin Franklin made of 80,000 pennies donated by Philadelphia schoolchildren and the children of city firefighters.

⑰ Across 4th Street, the **United States Mint** stands just two blocks from the first U.S. mint, which opened in 1792. Built in 1969, this is the largest mint in the world. A self-guided tour shows how blank discs are turned into U.S. coins. The visitors' gallery has an exhibit of medals from the nation's wars, including the Medal of Honor, the Purple Heart, and the Bronze Star—once made at the mint. Seven beautiful Tiffany glass-tile mosaics depict coin making in ancient Rome. A shop in the lobby sells special coins and medals—in mint condition. Note that no cameras or video equipment is allowed. *5th and Arch Sts., ☎ 215/597–7350.* ⊙ *Daily 9–4:30; closed weekends Sept.–Apr., Sun. May–June. Coinage machinery operates weekdays only.*

A bit farther along, between 321 and 323 Arch Street is **Loxely Court.** The court's claim to fame, according to its residents, is as the spot where Benjamin Franklin flew his kite; the key tied to it was the key to carpenter Benjamin Loxley's front door.

⑱ Catercorner is the **Arch Street Meeting House,** built in 1804 for the Philadelphia Yearly Meeting of the Society of Friends. It is still used for that purpose—aside from bi-weekly services, 13,000 Quakers congregate here in the largest Friends meeting house in the world for five days each March. A small museum in the church presents a series of dioramas and a 14-minute slide show depicting the life and accomplishments of William Penn—who gave the land on which the meeting house sits to the Society of Friends—and from April 15 to October 30, Quaker guides give tours. *4th and Arch Sts., ☎ 215/627–2667.* ⊙ *Mon.–Sat. 10–4; services Thurs. at 10 and Sun. at 10:30.*

⑲ A block west on Arch Street is the **Christ Church Burial Ground,** resting place of five signers of the Declaration and other Colonial patriots. The best-known "resident" is Benjamin Franklin. According to local legend, throwing a penny on Franklin's grave will bring you good luck. Take a moment out to savor the peace of this cloistered spot in the center of the city. *5th and Arch Sts., ☎ 215/922–1695.* ⊙ *Hours vary,*

but generally late spring to early fall, Mon. and Wed.–Sat. 11:30–3, or by appointment.

Tour 2 Enduring Grace: Society Hill and Penn's Landing

Society Hill was—and still is—Philadelphia's showplace. A gem of a preserved district, it is easily the city's most charming and photogenic neighborhood, filled with hidden courtyards, delightful decorative touches like chimney pots and brass door knockers, wrought-iron footscrapers, and other remnants from the days of horse-drawn carriages and muddy, unpaved streets. Here, time has not quite stopped, but meanders down the cobblestone streets, whiling away the hours.

A trove of Federal-style, brick row houses and quaint streets, Society Hill stretches from the Delaware River to 6th Street. Here lived the "World's People," wealthier Anglicans who arrived after William Penn and loved music and dancing (pursuits the Quakers shunned when they set up their enclave in Old City, "the other side of the tracks," north of Market Street). The "Society" in the neighborhood's moniker refers, however, to the Free Society of Traders, a group of business investors who settled here on William Penn's advice.

Today, many homes in this area have been lovingly restored by modern pioneers who began moving in to the area thirty years ago and rescued Society Hill from becoming a slum. Inspired urban renewal efforts have since transformed vast empty factory spaces into airy lofts; Colonial houses have been rehabbed, and picturesque city corners rediscovered. As a result, Society Hill is not just a showcase for historic churches and mansions, but a living, breathing neighborhood.

Before setting out to explore Society Hill, however, many visitors will want to tour Philadelphia's nearby waterfront, with its many attractions, including a seaport museum, historic marine vessels, and an aquarium. Those who don't wish to enjoy this waterside detour should jump ahead in the following tour to Welcome Park.

②⓪ Our waterfront tour begins at **Penn's Landing,** the spot where William Penn stepped ashore in 1682. This is the hub of a 37-acre park that stretches from Market Street on the north to Lombard Street on the south. The development of this area—an ambitious effort to reclaim the Delaware River waterfront—began in 1967. Plans include condominiums, offices, more recreation areas, hotels, and restaurants. In warm weather, the Great Plaza at Penn's Landing—an outdoor amphitheater— is the scene of concerts, jamborees, festivals, and other special events; pick up a calendar at the Visitor Center (3rd and Chestnut Sts.) or call the Penn's Landing Info-Line (☎ 215/923–4992). Walk along the waterfront and you'll see scores of pleasure boats moored at the marina, and cargo ships chugging up and down the Delaware. Philadelphia's harbor, which includes docking facilities in New Jersey and Delaware, is one of the world's largest freshwater ports.

②① At the foot of Walnut Street, you'll see the new $15 million centerpiece of Penn's Landing, the **Independence Seaport Museum**—a bigger, better incarnation of the old Philadelphia Maritime Museum that was previously located on Chestnut Street. Housed in the former Port of History Museum, many of the nautical artifacts, figureheads, and ship models are still on display, but now the emphasis is on kid-pleasing interactive exhibits, ranging from fishing off an indoor pier to operating a miniature crane. Enter the museum by passing under the three-story replica of the Benjamin Franklin Bridge. *211 S. Columbus Blvd.*

at Walnut St, ☎ *215/925–5439.* ☉ *Daily 10–5.* ☛ *$7.50 adults, $3 children, $6 senior citizens; includes entry to the USS* Olympia *and USS* Becuna (see below).

From Penn's Landing at Walnut Street you can catch the "ferry to the fishies:" The **Riverbus** crosses the Delaware River to Camden in about 10 minutes, leaving you a few steps from the $52 million **New Jersey State Aquarium.** This new marvel opened in 1992, and 6,000 fish now call it home. A diver inside the 760,000-gallon tank (the second largest in the United States) can answer your questions via a "scubaphone." Interactive shows let you balance a ball on the nose of a seal or pet a shark. No kidding. *Riverbus: Penn's Landing near Walnut St.,* ☎ *609/365–1400.* ☛ *$4 round-trip, $3 children and senior citizens.* ☉ *Departs every 30 min on the ¼ hr, weekdays 8–5:45, weekends and summer 9–8:45. Aquarium: S. Riverside Dr., Camden, New Jersey,* ☎ *609/365–3300.* ☛ *$9.95 adults, $8.45 students and senior citizens, $6.95 children under 12.* ☉ *Daily 9:30–5:30, extended hrs Sun. in summer.*

Docked next to the Seaport Museum is the **Gazela of Philadelphia,** formerly *Gazela Primeiro.* Built in 1883, this 177-foot square-rigger is the last of a Portuguese fleet of cod-fishing ships. Still in use as late as 1969, it is the oldest and largest wooden square-rigger still sailing. As the Port of Philadelphia's ambassador of goodwill, the *Gazela* sails up and down the Atlantic Coast to participate in harbor festivals and celebrations. It is also a school ship and a museum. An all-volunteer crew of 35 work all winter on ship maintenance; in summer they set sail. *Penn's Landing at Market St.,* ☎ *215/923–9030.* ☛ *Suggested donation $2.50.* ☉ *Memorial Day–Labor Day, daily 10–6; rest of yr, weekends noon–5. Call ahead; open frequently when in port, but no regular hrs.*

A five-minute stroll along the river brings you to two historic ships well worth a visit. Descend the steep metal ladder into the **USS Becuna.** This 318-foot-long "guppy class" was commissioned in 1944 and conducted search-and-destroy missions in the South Pacific. Hear the guides—all WWII submarine vets—tell amazing stories of what life was like for a crew of 88 men, at sea for months at a time, in these claustrophobic quarters. Then step through the narrow walkways, climb the ladders, and glimpse the torpedoes in their firing chambers. Kids will love it, but it's fascinating for adults, too. *Penn's Landing at Spruce St.,* ☎ *215/922–1898.* ☛ *$3 adults, $2 children under 12 (includes USS* Olympia*).* ☉ *Daily 10–5, summer weekends 10–6.*

Arise from the depths of the USS *Becuna* and cross the gangplank for a decidedly different shipboard experience. The **USS Olympia** was Commodore George Dewey's flagship at the Battle of Manila in the Spanish-American War. Dewey entered Manila Harbor after midnight on May 1, 1898. At 5:40 AM, he told his captain, "You may fire when ready, Gridley," and the battle began. By 12:30 the Americans had destroyed the entire Spanish fleet. The *Olympia* was the last ship of the "New Navy" of the 1880s and 1890s, the beginning of the era of steel ships, and it is the only remaining ship from the Spanish-American War. You can tour the entire restored ship, including the officers' staterooms, engine room, galley, gun batteries, pilothouse, and conning tower. *Penn's Landing at Spruce St.,* ☎ *215/922–1898.* ☛ *$3 adults, $2 children under 12 (includes USS* Becuna*).* ☉ *Daily 10–5, summer weekends 10–6.*

In the middle of Delaware Avenue (also called Christopher Columbus Boulevard) are the tracks of the **Penn's Landing Trolley Company.** You can board an authentic turn-of-the-century trolley at Dock Street or Spruce Street for a 20-minute round-trip along the Delaware River waterfront. The conductor provides a guided tour as you ride. *Delaware Ave. at Spruce St., ☎ 215/627–0807.* ☛ *$1.50 adults, 75¢ children under 12, for an all-day pass.* ☯ *Runs 11–dusk weekends and holidays from mid-Apr. to late Nov.; also Thurs. and Fri. in July and Aug.*

Watch out for traffic as you leave the trolley, and head back to Front Street where it crosses Sansom Street. As you walk west on Sansom Street, you'll find **Welcome Park,** site of the slate-roof house where William Penn lived briefly and where he granted the Charter of Privileges in 1701. (The *Welcome* was the ship that transported Penn to America.) Here, on a 60-foot-long map of Penn's Philadelphia carved in the pavement sits a scale model of the Penn statue that sits atop City Hall. The wall surrounding the park displays a time line of his life, with information about his philosophy and quotations from his writings.

TIME OUT Walk north one block to the corner of 2nd and Chestnut streets for a wide selection of bars and restaurants, including Rib-It, Serrano, Los Amigos, the Middle East, and Philadelphia Fish and Company.

A half block west on Walnut Street, the **Philadelphia Merchant's Exchange** (3rd and Walnut Sts., ☎ 215/597–8974) stands behind Dock Street, a cobblestone thoroughfare that is closed to traffic. Designed by the well-known Philadelphia architect William Strickland and built in 1832, the Greek Revival structure served as the city's commercial center for 50 years. It was both the stock exchange and a place where merchants met to trade goods. In the tower, a watchman scanned the Delaware and notified merchants of arriving ships. Now it's the regional offices of the National Park Service and the interior is not open to the public.

On the corner of 3rd and Walnut streets a small, lovingly maintained garden leads to the **Bishop White House,** home of Bishop William White, rector of Christ Church, first Episcopal bishop of Pennsylvania, and spiritual leader of Philadelphia for 60 years. Built in 1786, this upper-class house has been restored to Colonial elegance. White, who was chaplain to the Continental Congress, entertained many members of the country's first families, including Washington and Franklin. The second-floor study contains much of the bishop's own library. Unlike most houses of the period, the bishop's house had an early form of flush toilet. The house tour is not recommended for small children (they get bored). *309 Walnut St., ☎ 215/597–8974.* ☯ *Daily 9:30–4:30; obtain tickets at the Visitor Center for a free 1-hr tour that includes the Bishop White House and the Todd House.*

On the same block, the simply furnished **Todd House** stands in direct contrast to the lavish Bishop White House. Built in 1775, it has been restored to its 1790s' appearance, when its best-known resident lived here. Dolley Payne Todd lost her husband, the lawyer John Todd, to the yellow-fever epidemic of 1793. She later married James Madison, who became the fourth president. Her time in the White House was quite a contrast to her years in this house. *4th and Walnut Sts., ☎ 215/597–8974.* ☯ *Daily 9:30–4:30; obtain tickets at the Visitor Center for a free 1-hr tour that includes the Todd House and the Bishop White House.*

A few steps south on 4th Street is the nation's oldest fire-insurance company, the **Philadelphia Contributionship for the Insurance of Houses from Loss by Fire.** The contributionship was founded by Benjamin Franklin in 1752; the present building dates from 1836 and boasts some magnificently elegant salons (particularly the board room, where a seating plan on the wall lists Benjamin Franklin as the first incumbent of seat Number One). This is still an active business, but a small museum is open to the public; supervised visits to the upstairs room and the beautiful garden are available by appointment. *212 S. 4th St.,* ☎ *215/627–1752.* ☉ *Weekdays 10–3.*

③② Two blocks south on 4th Street is the 22-room **Hill-Physick-Keith House,** built in 1786 and the only freestanding house in Society Hill. (You should have noticed the famous Philadelphia row houses by now). It is also one of the most beautiful homes in America, with elegantly restored interiors containing some of the finest Federal and Empire furniture in Philadelphia. Touches of Napoléon's France are everywhere: the golden bee motif woven into upholstery, the magenta-hued Aubusson rug (the emperor's favorite color), and stools in the Pompeian style. Upstairs in the parlor, note the inkstand that still retains Benjamin Franklin's fingerprints. The house's most famous owner was Philip Syng Physick, a leading physician in the days before anesthesia, and known as the "Father of American Surgery." His most celebrated patient was Chief Justice John Marshall. Enjoy the garden planted on three sides, filled with plants common in the 19th century: complete with an Etruscan sarcophagus, a natural grotto, and antique cannon, it is considered by some to be the city's loveliest garden. *321 S. 4th St.,* ☎ *215/925–7866.* ☛ *$3 adults, $2 children and senior citizens.* ☉ *Thurs.–Sat., guided tours at 11, noon, 1, and 2.*

③③ Take a pleasant walk east on Delancey Street and then turn right on 3rd Street to Pine Street. At the northwest corner is the **Thaddeus Kosciuszko National Memorial.** A Polish general who later became a national hero in his homeland, Kosciuszko came to the United States in 1776 to help fight the Revolution; he distinguished himself as one of the first foreign volunteers in the war. Visit the portrait gallery or view a six-minute film (in English and Polish) that portrays his activities during the Revolution. *301 Pine St.,* ☎ *215/597–8974.* ☉ *Daily 9–5, July and Aug. 10–5.*

③④ A block east is **Head House Square** (2nd and Pine Sts.), an open-air Colonial marketplace that extends from Pine Street to Lombard Street. It was established as New Market in 1745. George Washington shopped here. Built in 1804, the Head House was both the home of the market master and a firehouse. Today, on summer weekends, the square is used for craft fairs, food festivals, and other activities. A host of street performers, including jugglers, magicians, and mimes, draw crowds.

③⑤ East of Head House Square is **Newmarket,** a once-thriving but mostly vacant complex of boutiques and restaurants. It's still worth a walk-through, from the 18th-century homes on 2nd Street to the contemporary glass facades on Front Street. New life may be stirring here—a restaurant and small theater have recently opened.

TIME OUT You can find food and drink on both sides of 2nd Street between Pine and South streets, including the Dickens Inn, a British-style pub and restaurant.

Heading north on 2nd Street to Locust Street, note Society Hill Towers, three of the most elegant high-rise apartment buildings in Amer-

ica, and the Society Hill Townhouses at 3rd and Locust streets. Both were designed to great acclaim in the early '60s by I. M. Pei.

36 Cross Locust and turn right on 3rd to the **Powel House,** one of the most elegant homes in Philadelphia. Built in 1765, the brick Georgian house was purchased by Samuel Powel in 1769. Powel—the "Patriot Mayor"— was the last mayor of Philadelphia under the Crown and the first in the new republic. The lavish home is furnished with highly important pieces of 18th-century Philadelphia furniture; the front hall is embellished with a mahogany staircase from Santo Domingo, and there is a signed Gilbert Stuart portrait in the parlor. In the second floor ballroom, Mrs. Powel—the city's hostess-with-the-mostest—served floating islands and whipped sillibubs to distinguished guests (including Adams, Franklin, and Lafayette) on Nanking china that had been a gift from George and Martha Washington. Today, the ballroom can be rented for parties and special events. *244 S. 3rd St.,* ☎ *215/627- 0364.* ☛ *$3 adults; $2 students with ID and senior citizens; 50¢ children under 12.* ☉ *Tues.–Sat. 10–4. Call ahead; hrs can vary.*

The brownstones on this stretch of 3rd Street are often called Bouvier's Row, as three of the Victorian houses at 260 South 3rd Street were once owned by Jacqueline Kennedy Onassis's ancestors (Michel Bouvier, her great-great grandfather—the first of the family to come from France— and many of his descendants lie in the family vault at Old St. Mary's Church, a few blocks away on 4th Street)—a fitting high-society finale to our Society Hill tour.

Tour 3 Center City: City Hall and Environs

Numbers in the margin correspond to points of interest on the Tours 3 and 4 map.

For a grand introduction to the downtown area, climb the few steps to the plaza in front of the **Municipal Services Building** at 15th Street and John F. Kennedy Boulevard to get a great up-close overview of the city. You'll feel surrounded by Philadelphia—City Hall, the PSFS building, the art museum, the new skyscrapers at Liberty Place, Oldenburg's *Clothespin* statue, and other places covered here, spread out around you.

There's a story behind this glittering skyline. It begins with Philadelphia's historic City Hall, which reaches to 40 stories and was the tallest structure in the metropolis until 1987. No law prohibited taller buildings, but the tradition sprang from a gentleman's agreement not to build higher. In May 1984, when a developer proposed building two office towers that would break the 491-foot barrier, it became evident how much Philadelphians cared about their city—and how entrenched this tradition was. The proposal provoked a public outcry. The traditionalists contended that the height limitation had made Philadelphia a city of human scale, given its streets and public places intimacy, and showed respect for tradition. The opposing camp thought that a dramatic new skyline would shatter the city's conservative image and encourage economic growth. After painstaking debate, the go-ahead was granted. In short order, the midtown area became the hub of the city's commercial center, Market Street west of City Hall became a district of high-rise office buildings, and the area became a symbol of the city's transformation from a dying industrial town to a major center of service industries.

❶ One block west of the Municipal Services Building plaza is the **Philadelphia Visitors Center.** Here you can get maps, brochures about the city and surroundings, lists of restaurants and hotels, and information about current events. Volunteers and staff members are on hand to answer your questions. What are the most common questions they hear? Where's the Liberty Bell? Where's Independence Hall? Where's the nearest bathroom? In the gift shop—where the staff wear Colonial garb—you can buy a Philadelphia T-shirt, a Liberty Bell necktie, or a bumper sticker showing a tombstone inscribed, "I would rather be in Philadelphia." *16th St. and John F. Kennedy Blvd.,* ☎ *215/636–1666.* ☉ *Daily 9–5, until 6 in summer.*

❷ Walk east on Kennedy Boulevard to 15th Street for an incomparable, unobstructed view of **City Hall.** Topped by a 37-foot bronze statue of William Penn, the city's founder, City Hall was Philadelphia's tallest building until 1987. With 642 rooms, it is the largest city hall in the country and the tallest masonry-bearing building in the world: no steel structure supports it. It took 30 years to build (1871 to 1900) and cost taxpayers more than $23 million. Placed about the facade are hundreds of statues by Alexander Milne Calder, who also designed the statue of William Penn at the top.

Not only the geographic center of Penn's original city, City Hall is also the center of municipal and state government. Start at the northeast corner and ascend one flight to the mayor's ornate reception room (Room 202), and the recently restored Conversation Hall (Room 201). Many of the magnificent interiors—splendidly decorated with mahogany paneling, gold-leaf ceilings, and marble pillars—are patterned after the salons of the Second Empire–style New Louvre in Paris. Take a look, too, at the City Council Chambers (Room 400) and the Supreme Court of Pennsylvania (municipal court sessions are open to the public). To top off your visit, take the elevator to the observation deck at the foot of Billy Penn's statue for a 30-mile panoramic view of the city and surroundings. *Broad and Market Sts.,* ☎ *215/686–1776; Tour Office, East Portal, Room 121,* ☎ *215/686–2840.* ☉ *90-min tours including tower: weekdays at 12:30 PM; tower open weekdays 9:30–4:15.*

❸ Leave City Hall by the northern exit and cross Kennedy Boulevard to the **Masonic Temple.** Philadelphia is the mother city of American Masonry, and the temple is home to the Grand Lodge of Free and Accepted Masons of Pennsylvania. The trowel used here at the laying of the cornerstone in 1868 is the same one that Brother George Washington used to set the cornerstone of the U.S. Capitol. Designed by Brother James H. Windrim and built by Masons, the temple's ornate interior consists of seven Lodge Halls built to represent seven styles of architecture: Corinthian, Ionic, Italian Renaissance, Norman, Gothic, Oriental, and Egyptian. The collection of Masonic items includes handwritten letters from Washington to brothers of the Grand Lodge and Benjamin Franklin's printing of the first book on Freemasonry published in America. *1 N. Broad St.,* ☎ *215/988–1917. Free 45-min tours weekdays at 10, 11, 1, 2, and 3; Sat. 10 and 11. Closed Sat. July and Aug.*

❹ Walk to 15th and Market streets and you'll see Claes Oldenburg's 45-foot-high, 10-ton steel *Clothespin* in front of the Center Square Building. Lauded by some and scorned by others, this pop art piece contrasts with the traditional statuary so common in Philadelphia.

TIME OUT Grab a pita sandwich and a fresh fruit cup from one of the sidewalk vendors along 15th Street around Market Street, and munch and relax

32

Nectarine St.
Buttonwood St.

Broad St. Subway

Ridge Ave.

18th St.

19th St.

Callowhill St.
Carlton St.
Wood St.

Broad St.

Vine St.

19

Logan
Circle
17

17th St.

16th St.

15th St.

18

Race St.

20

19th St.

15

16

Philadelphia
Convention Center

13

14

Suburban
Station
1

3

Commerce St.

Commerce St.

Subway-Surface

5

4

2

11

12

Ludlow St.

Chestnut St.

18th St.

15th St.

Broad St.

Juniper St.

13th St.

12th St.

11th St.

Ranstead St.

Moravian St.

10

17th St.

6

Rittenhouse
Square

Locust St.

9

Quince St.

7

19th St.

Broad St. Subway

N

0 ————— 440 yards
0 ————— 400 meters

KEY
▪▪▪▪ Market-Frankford Subway
▬▬ Broad St. Subway
▬ ▬ Subway-Surface Subway
— Airport Train

in Dilworth Plaza (on the west apron of City Hall) or JFK Plaza (15th St. and JFK Blvd.).

⑤ Two blocks west is **Liberty Place. One Liberty Place** (1650 Market St.) is the 945-foot, 63-story office building that propelled Philadelphia into the "ultra-high" skyscraper era. Built in 1987 at a cost of $225 million, it became the tallest structure in Philadelphia. The Art Deco–style structure, vaguely reminiscent of New York's Chrysler Building, is visible from almost everywhere in the city. In 1990, the adjacent 58-story tower, **Two Liberty Place,** opened with a shopping complex, food court, and the Ritz-Carlton Hotel.

⑥ Walk to 18th Street, head south, and you soon come upon **Rittenhouse Square** (between 18th and 19th Sts. at Walnut St.). Once grazing ground for cows and sheep, this is now Philadelphia's most elegant square, one reminiscent of a Parisian park. Another of William Penn's original five city squares, the park was named in honor of David Rittenhouse, astronomer, clockmaker, and the first director of the United States Mint. Many of Philadelphia's movers, shakers, and celebrities have lived here. Extra paths were made for Dr. William White, a leader in beautifying the square, so that he could walk directly from his home to the exclusive Rittenhouse Club across the square and lunch with the likes of Henry James. Until 1950 town houses bordered the square, but they have now been replaced on three sides by swank apartment buildings and hotels. Some great town houses remain, including the celebrated residence of Henry P. McIlhenny (on the southwest corner), once home to one of the world's great art collections, now on view at the Philadelphia Museum of Art. Today, the good life continues in Rittenhouse Square: Annual events include the Rittenhouse Square Flower Market, the Clothesline Art Exhibit, and the Mozart on the Square Festival. If you want to join the office workers who have lunch-hour picnics in the park, you'll find scores of restaurants and sandwich shops along Walnut, Sansom, and Chestnut streets, east of the square.

East of the square are the Barclay Hotel, celebrated for decades as the most fashionable hotel in the city and home-away-from-home for visiting actors; the Philadelphia Art Alliance, housed in a Gay Nineties **⑦** mansion with galleries open to the public; and the **Curtis Institute of Music** (1726 Locust St., ☎ 215/893–5261), a tuition-free school for outstanding students. Graduates include Leonard Bernstein, Samuel Barber, Ned Rorem, and Anna Moffo. You may recognize the exterior of the Curtis Institute from the Eddie Murphy film *Trading Places.* Free student and faculty concerts are given from October through May at 8 PM on Monday, Wednesday, and Friday (as well as other occasional) evenings.

West of the square you'll find a branch of the Free Library of Philadelphia, the Rittenhouse Hotel, and the Church of the Holy Trinity, presided over in the mid-19th century by the Reverend Phillips Brooks, who achieved renown as the lyricist of "O Little Town of Bethlehem."

Leave the square on its southern side and continue south on 19th Street to Delancey Place, then turn right and take a look at this urban residential showcase with its grand houses, once the address of Pearl S. Buck (at 2019 Delancy) and Rudolf Serkin. At the corner (320 South Eighteenth) there is an interesting old sea captain's house. However, the 2000 block of Delancey Place wins the prize. At 2010 is the **⑧** **Rosenbach Museum and Library,** which has more than 130,000 manuscripts and 30,000 rare books. This 1863 three-floor town house is furnished with Persian rugs and 18th-century British, French, and

American antiques (plus an entire living room that once belonged to poet Marianne Moore). Amassed by Philadelphia collectors Philip H. and A.S.W. Rosenbach, the collection includes paintings by Canaletto, Sully, and Lawrence; drawings by Daumier, Fragonard, and Blake; book illustrations ranging from medieval illuminations to Maurice Sendak; the only known copy of the first edition of Benjamin Franklin's *Poor Richard's Almanack;* and the library's most famous treasure—the original manuscript of James Joyce's *Ulysses. 2010 Delancey Pl.,* ☎ *215/732–1600.* ☛ *$3.50 adults, $2.50 senior citizens and students.* ⊙ *Tues.–Sun. 11–4. Guided 1-hr tour (arrive no later than 2:45). Closed Aug. and national holidays.*

On your way back to Rittenhouse Square, you may want to wander through the neighborhood west of the square. Cypress Street just north of Delancey Place, and Panama Street (especially the 1900 block, one block south of Delancey), are two of the many intimate streets lined with trees and town houses characteristic of the area. Back at the square, an elegant teatime can be had in the Mary Cassatt Tearoom and adjoining cloistered garden at the Rittenhouse Hotel.

⑨ From Rittenhouse Square walk east on Locust Street four blocks to the **Academy of Music** (Broad and Locust Sts., ☎ 215/893–1900 or 215/893–1930 for the box office). Modeled after Milan's La Scala opera house, it opened with a lavish ball in 1857. Home of the Philadelphia Orchestra, the academy attracts not only music lovers and students but also many members of Philadelphia's elite. Friday afternoon concerts are legendary for their audience of "Main Line matrons." Tickets are available at the box office; if you're willing to wait in line and sit in the cramped amphitheater four levels above the stage, you can take advantage of one of the music world's great bargains—the $4 "nose-bleed" seats. The academy is also home to the Opera Company of Philadelphia and the Luciano Pavarotti International Voice Competition, and the site of the Pennsylvania Ballet's annual Christmas production of *The Nutcracker.* Tours are given on occasional Tuesdays at 2 PM by reservation (☎ 215/893–1935).

As you walk along the west side of Broad Street, between Spruce and Walnut streets, notice the more than 30 plaques in the sidewalk honoring some of those who contributed to Philadelphia's cultural history. Where else could Frankie Avalon and Dizzy Gillespie rub shoulders with Anna Moffo and Eugene Ormandy?

⑩ A block north of the academy is the second "Grande Dame of South Broad Street," the former **Bellevue Stratford Hotel** (Broad and Walnut Sts., ☎ 215/893–1776). The epitome of the thirst for opulence characteristic of the early 1900s, it was the city's leading hotel for decades. It closed in 1976 after the first outbreak of Legionnaire's disease (which spread through the building's air-conditioning system during an American Legion convention). Reopened as the Fairmont several years later, it failed to regain its luster and closed again in 1986. When renovations were completed in 1989, this magnificent building re-opened as home to a number of shops and offices, as well as the luxurious Hotel Atop the Bellevue (*see* Chapter 6, Lodging).

As you continue up Broad Street, you pass a French Renaissance–style building, the **Union League of Philadelphia** (140 S. Broad St.). A bastion of Philadelphia conservatism, the Union League is a social club founded during the Civil War to preserve the Union.

⑪ Just east of City Hall is the **John Wanamaker** store, almost as prominent a Philadelphia landmark as the Liberty Bell. Wanamaker began

with a clothing store in 1861 and became one of America's most innovative and prominent retailers. The building was designed by the Chicago firm of D. H. Burnham and Company. Its focal point is the nine-story grand court with its 30,000-pipe organ—the largest ever built—and a 2,500-pound statue of an eagle, both remnants of the 1904 Louisiana Purchase Exposition in St. Louis. "Meet me at the Eagle" is a popular way for Philadelphians to arrange a rendezvous. Organ performances are held at 11:15 and 5:15. The store is famous for its Christmas sound-and-light show. In 1995 Philadelphians were dismayed to hear that this city institution was up for sale, and its future uncertain. *13th and Market Sts.,* ☎ *215/422–2000.* ☽ *Mon.–Sat. 10–7, Wed. 10–8, Sun. noon–6.*

⑫ Leave Wanamaker's via the Market Street exit, turn right, and go one block to 12th Street. Here is the **Philadelphia Saving Fund Society (PSFS) Building,** one of the city's first skyscrapers. Built in 1930, this still modern-looking structure was influential in the design of other American skyscrapers. Pay special attention to the enormous escalators and the main banking floor, two striking contrasts to the utilitarian approach of architecture today. This floor is now part of the Mellon Bank; if you have any banking needs, here's a place to take care of them and see an interesting sight at the same time. *12th and Market Sts.,* ☎ *215/928– 2000.* ☽ *Weekdays 8–4.*

⑬ Across Market Street at 12th Street is the old Reading Railroad Headhouse, purchased by the city to become the grand entrance to the new **Pennsylvania Convention Center.** Opened in June 1993 with galas, parties, and Vice President Al Gore cutting the ribbon, the $522 million center is being counted on to help rejuvenate Philadelphia's struggling economy. After visitors enter the headhouse, escalators take them through the magnificently restored Reading Train Shed, then across another bridge over Arch Street to the main exhibition hall. (With 313,000 square feet, its area equals seven football fields.) Free 45-minute tours are given on Tuesdays and Thursdays by reservation (☎ 215/418– 4728); but you can sneak a peek at the best part—the train shed—any day by crossing over the skybridge from the third floor of the Philadelphia Marriott next door.

⑭ A half block north on 12th Street is the **Reading Terminal Market**— food heaven to Philadelphians and visitors alike. One floor beneath the former Reading Railroad's 1891 train shed, the sprawling market has 80 stores, food stalls, and other places of business. Some stalls change daily, offering items like hooked rugs and handmade jewelry to Mexican and African crafts. Here, amidst the local color, you can sample Bassett's ice cream, Philadelphia's best; down a cheesesteak or a bowl or chowder; or nibble Greek, Mexican, and Indian specialties. On certain days, the Amish from Lancaster County cart in their goodies, including Lebanon bologna, shoofly pie, and scrapple. Many stalls have their own counters with seating; there's also a central eating area, where at lunchtime on the second Friday of each month a group of amateur musicians (a politician, a doctor, and a lawyer) called the Reading Terminals play jazz. You can also buy a large variety of fresh food to cook from vegetable and fruit stands, butchers, fish stores, and Pennsylvania Dutch markets. The entire building is a National Historic Landmark and the train shed is a National Engineering Landmark. So, while the city's new convention center is being built above and behind the market, pledges and legal guarantees are in place to preserve this Philadelphia treasure. *12th and Filbert Sts.,* ☎ *215/922–2317.* ☽ *Mon.–Sat. 8–6 PM.*

Tour 4 **Museums and Marvels:**
Along the Benjamin Franklin Parkway

⑮ From City Hall, the **Benjamin Franklin Parkway** stretches northwest to the Greco-Roman temple on a hilltop—the Philadelphia Museum of Art. The parkway is the city's Champs-Elysées, a boulevard home to many great cultural institutions and alive with flowers, trees, and fountains. Lined with a distinguished assemblage of museums, institutions, hotels, and apartment buildings that compete with each other in grandeur, this 250-foot-wide boulevard was designed by French architect Jacques Greber and built in the 1920s. Here you'll find the Free Library of Philadelphia and the Family Court, both copies from the palaces on Paris's Place de la Concorde. The newest addition is the Four Seasons Hotel on the south side of Logan Circle, though its dignified design made it look like a local institution from the day it opened. A grand processional route, the parkway occasionally lets down its hair as the route for city parades and the site of many festivals and events, including the Thanksgiving parade, "Super Sunday," the Big Apple Circus, and the CoreStates Pro Cycling championship.

⑯ Before heading out the parkway, we'll take a short detour to the **Pennsylvania Academy of the Fine Arts.** Starting at the Visitors Center (16th St. and Kennedy Blvd.), walk east on Kennedy Boulevard and turn left on Broad Street; go two blocks to Cherry Street and you'll see a High Victorian Gothic structure that's a work of art in itself. Designed in 1876 by the noted, and sometimes eccentric, Philadelphia architects Frank Furness and George Hewitt, the multicolored stone-and-brick exterior is an extravagant blend of columns, friezes, Richardsonian Romanesque and Moorish flourishes. Inside, the oldest art institution in the United States (founded 1804) boasts a collection that ranges from Winslow Homer and Benjamin West to Andrew Wyeth and Red Grooms. The academy faculty has included Thomas Sully, Thomas Eakins, and Charles Willson Peale. The permanent collection is supplemented by constantly changing exhibits of sculpture, paintings, and mixed-media artwork. *Broad and Cherry Sts.,* ☎ *215/972–7600.* ☛ *$5.95 adults, $4.95 senior citizens and students with ID; free Sat. 10– 1.* ☺ *Tues.–Sat. 10–5, Sun. 11–5.*

Head west on Cherry Street past the American Friends Service Committee and the Race Street Friends Meeting House. At 17th Street, you'll find yourself on the Benjamin Franklin Parkway.

⑰ Walk northwest on the parkway one block to **Logan Circle.** Originally this was one of four squares Penn had built at the corners of a rectangle around Center Square, where City Hall now stands. (The others are Franklin Square to the northeast, Washington Square to the southeast, and Rittenhouse Square to the southwest.) The focal point of Logan Circle is the Swann Fountain of 1920, designed by Alexander Stirling Calder, son of Alexander Milne Calder who did the William Penn statue atop City Hall. (In the nearby Philadelphia Museum of Art, you'll find many works by a third generation of the family, noted modern sculptor Alexander Calder, the mobile- and stabile-maker.) The main figures in the fountain symbolize Philadelphia's three leading waterways: the Delaware and Schuylkill rivers and Wissahickon Creek. Around Logan Circle are some examples of Philadelphia's magnificent collection of outdoor art, including *General Galusha Pennypacker,* the *Shakespeare Memorial,* and *Jesus Breaking Bread.*

⑱ The **Cathedral of Saints Peter and Paul** at 18th Street and the parkway is the basilica of the Archdiocese of Philadelphia and the spiritual

center for the Philadelphia area's 1.4 million Roman Catholics. Topped by a huge copper dome, it was built between 1846 and 1864 in the Italian Renaissance style. Many of the interior decorations were done by Constantino Brumidi, who painted the dome of the United States Capitol. Six Philadelphia bishops and archbishops are buried beneath the altar. *18th and Race Sts.,* ☎ *215/561–1313.* ⊙ *7–3:30.*

Walking counterclockwise around Logan Circle, you'll see twin, marble, Greek Revival buildings off to your right. The nearer of the two

⑲ is the city's Family Court; the other is the **Free Library of Philadelphia.** Along with a collection of more than one million volumes (*see* Libraries and Museums, *below*), the central unit of the public library system presents concerts, movies, lectures, and historical displays. *19th St. and Benjamin Franklin Pkwy.,* ☎ *215/686–5322.* ⊙ *Mon.–Wed. 9–9, Thurs. and Fri. 9–6, Sat. 9–5, Sun. (Sept.–May) 1–5. Closed Sun. in summer.*

TIME OUT The rooftop cafeteria of the **Free Library** (19th St. and Benjamin Franklin Pkwy.) provides inexpensive meals at umbrellaed tables.

⑳ Cross Logan Circle to the **Academy of Natural Sciences,** America's first museum of natural history, founded in 1812. (The present building dates from 1868.) The collection is famous for its stuffed animals from around the world, displayed in 35 natural settings. The third-floor "Outside In" exhibit is a mini-museum where children can handle fossils, dinosaur teeth, and even live animals such as snakes and lizards. The most popular attraction is "Discovering Dinosaurs": movies, computer videos, reconstructed skeletons of a tyrannosaurus and others, and a Cretaceous landscape complete with animals and plants. *19th St. and Benjamin Franklin Pkwy.,* ☎ *215/299–1020.* ☛ *$6.50 adults, $5.50 children.* ⊙ *Weekdays 10–4:30, weekends and holidays 10–5.*

From the Academy, walk west on Race Street to 20th Street and the

㉑ **Franklin Institute Science Museum.** Founded to honor Benjamin Franklin, the institute is a science museum that is as clever as its namesake, thanks to an abundance of dazzling hands-on exhibits. You can sit in the cockpit of a T-33 jet trainer, trace the route of a corpuscle through the world's largest artificial heart (15,000 times life-size), and ride to nowhere on a 350-ton Baldwin steam locomotive. The many exhibits cover energy, motion, sound, physics, astronomy, aviation, ships, mechanics, electricity, time, and other scientific subjects. You'll also find a working weather station, computers to operate, and the world's largest pinball machine. The Fels Planetarium features shows about the stars, space exploration, comets, and other phenomena. The $72 million Mandell Center includes an Omniverse Theater, with a 79-foot domed screen and a 56-speaker high-tech sound system. *20th St. and Benjamin Franklin Pkwy.,* ☎ *215/448–1200.* ☛ *Ticket packages range from $7 to $12.50.* ⊙ *Daily 9:30–5; Omniverse Theater evening shows.*

Winter Street borders the Franklin Institute to the north. Take it west

㉒ one block to 21st Street; cross it and turn left to the **Please Touch Museum,** the first U.S. museum designed specifically for children seven and younger. All the exhibits are interactive. "Foodtastic Journey" lets kids simulate taking part in a food product's trip from farm to store, from milking the cow to stocking the shelves. An oversize exhibit on author Maurice Sendak lets kids really get into his *Where the Wild Things Are* and *In the Night Kitchen*. The museum shares an outdoor science park with its neighbor the Franklin Institute. There is also a theater program with high school students performing for the younger kids.

210 N. 21st St., ☎ *215/963–0667.* ☛ *$6.50.* ⊘ *Daily 9–4:30, in summer until 6.*

Cross to the north side of the parkway and walk northwest. On your right is the Youth Study Center (a detention center for juvenile offenders) with two striking tableaux depicting families.

㉓ At the next corner, guarded by the statue of *The Thinker,* is the **Rodin Museum.** Considered a jewel of a museum, this 20th-century building houses the best collection, outside of France, of Auguste Rodin's work. You'll pass through Rodin's *Gates of Hell*—a 21-foot-high sculpture with more than 100 human and animal figures—into an exhibition hall where the sculptor's masterworks are made even more striking by the use of light and shadow. Here are the French master's *The Kiss, The Burghers of Calais,* and *Eternal Springtime.* A small room is devoted to one of Rodin's most famous sitters, the French novelist Balzac. Photographs by Edward Steichen showing Rodin at work round out the collection. *22nd St. and Benjamin Franklin Pkwy.,* ☎ *215/586–6026.* ☛ *Donation requested.* ⊘ *Tues.–Sun. 10–5.*

㉔ Atop Faire Mount, the plateau at the end of Franklin Parkway, stands the **Philadelphia Museum of Art,** the city's premier cultural attraction and one of the country's leading museums. Actually, one of the greatest treasures of the museum is the building itself. Constructed in 1928 of Minnesota dolomite, it's modeled after ancient Greek temples but on a grander scale. Covering 10 acres, it has 200 galleries and a collection of over 300,000 works. You can enter the museum from the front or the rear; we recommend the front, where you can run up the 99 steps made famous in the movie *Rocky* (Rocky ran up only 72). From the expansive terrace, look up to the pediment on your right at a group of 13 glazed, multicolored statues of classical gods. After passing Jacques Lipchitz's statue *Prometheus Strangling the Vulture,* climb the last flight of steps, and, before entering the museum, turn around to savor the impressive view down the parkway.

Once inside, you'll see the grand staircase and Saint-Gaudens's statue of *Diana;* she formerly graced New York's old Madison Square Garden. The museum has several outstanding permanent collections: The John G. Johnson Collection covers Western art from the Renaissance to the 19th century; the Arensberg and A. E. Gallatin collections contain modern and contemporary works by artists such as Brancusi, Braque, Matisse, and Picasso. Famous paintings from among these collections include Van Eyck's *St. Francis Receiving the Stigmata,* Rubens's *Prometheus Bound,* Benjamin West's *Benjamin Franklin Drawing Electricity from the Sky,* Van Gogh's *Sunflowers,* Renoir's *The Bathers,* and Picasso's *Three Musicians.* The most recent collection to arrive was that of Henry P. McIlhenny: It contains world-famous paintings by Ingres and van Gogh, along with Toulouse-Lautrec's incomparable *Bal at the Moulin-Rouge.*

Marcel Duchamp is a specialty of the house; the museum has the world's most extensive collection of his works, including the world-famous *Woman Descending a Staircase.* The most spectacular "objects" in the museum are entire structures and great rooms moved lock, stock and barrel from around the world: a 12th-century French cloister, a 16th-century Indian temple hall, a 16th-century Japanese Buddhist temple, a 17th-century Chinese palace hall, and a Japanese ceremonial teahouse. Among the other collections: costumes, early American furniture, and Amish and Shaker crafts. An unusual touch—and one that children especially like—is the Kienbusch Collection of Arms and Armor.

Pick up a map of the museum at either of the two entrances and wander on your own; or choose from a variety of guided tours. Special exhibitions scheduled for 1996 include a Cézanne blockbuster and a retrospective devoted to Philadelphia realist, Sidney Goodman. *26th St. and Benjamin Franklin Pkwy.,* ☎ *215/763–8100, 215/787–5488 for 24-hr taped message.* ☛ *$7 adults, $4 senior citizens, students, and children; free Sun. 10–1.* ☉ *Tues.–Sun. 10–5; closed on legal holidays. Special programs on some Wed. evenings.*

The Emerald City:
A Tour of Fairmount Park

Numbers in the margin correspond to points of interest on the Fairmount Park map.

Stretching from the edge of downtown to the city's northwest corner, Fairmount Park is the largest landscaped city park in the world. With more than 8,500 acres and two million trees (someone claims to have counted), the park winds along the banks of the Schuylkill River and through parts of the city. Quite a few city dwellers consider the park to be their backyard. On weekends, the four-mile stretch along Kelly Drive is crowded with joggers, bicycling moms and dads with children strapped into kiddie seats atop the back wheel, hand-holding senior citizens out for some fresh air, collegiate crew teams sculling along the river, and budding artists trying to capture the sylvan magic as Thomas Eakins once did.

The park encompasses beautiful natural areas—woodlands, meadows, rolling hills, two scenic waterways, and a forested 5½-mile gorge. It also contains tennis courts, ball fields, playgrounds, trails, exercise courses, several celebrated cultural institutions, and some beautiful and historic Early American country houses open to visitors. Philadelphia has more works of outdoor art than any other city in North America. More than 200 of these works—including statues by Frederic Remington, Jacques Lipchitz, and Auguste Rodin—are scattered throughout Fairmount Park.

The park was established in 1812 when the city purchased five acres behind Faire Mount, the hill upon which the Philadelphia Museum of Art now stands, for waterworks and public gardens. Through private bequests and public purchases (which continue today), it grew to its present size and stature.

The following tour highlights many of the park's treasures. Take a narrated tour on the Fairmount Park Trolley Bus or do it by car, starting near the art museum. The trolley bus visits many of these sites, and you can get on and off all day (*see* Sightseeing *and* Trolleys *in* The Gold Guide). Although some of the directions may sound complicated, signs help point the way. An excellent map of the park is available at Memorial Hall and most park mansions and sites for 25¢.

❶ The park tour starts where the park began, at **Faire Mount,** now the site of the Philadelphia Museum of Art (*see* Tour 4, *above*). In 1812 a reservoir was built here to distribute water throughout the city. Park **❷** behind the art museum and walk down to the **Waterworks.** Designed by Frederick Graff, this National Historic Engineering Landmark was the first steam pumping station of its kind in the country. The notable assemblage of Greek Revival buildings—one of the city's most beautiful sights—is undergoing extensive renovation.

Fairmont Park

Belmont Plateau, **10**
Boathouse Row, **3**
Cedar Grove, **14**
Ellen Phillips Samuel
Memorial Sculpture
Garden, **4**
Faire Mount, **1**
Japanese House, **11**
Laurel Hill, **7**
Lemon Hill, **5**
Memorial Hall, **12**
Mt. Pleasant, **6**
Smith Civil War
Memorial, **13**
Strawberry
Mansion, **9**
Sweetbriar, **15**
Waterworks, **2**
Woodford, **8**

215 685-0722
Fairmount Water Works
Interp. Center

Tues → Sat. 10-5
Sun. 1-5
closed mon.

❸ A few steps north of the Waterworks, **Boathouse Row** begins. These 11 architecturally varied 19th-century buildings are home to the 13 rowing clubs that make up the "Schuylkill Navy." The view of the houses from the west side of the river is splendid—especially at night, when they're outlined with hundreds of small lights.

❹ Continuing north along Kelly Drive, you soon reach the **Ellen Phillips Samuel Memorial Sculpture Garden.** Bronze and granite statues by 16 artists stand in a series of tableaux and groupings on riverside terraces. Portraying American themes and traits, they include *The Quaker* by Harry Rosen, *Birth of a Nation* by Henry Kreis, and *Spirit of Enterprise* by Jacques Lipchitz.

Drive north on Kelly Drive for about 200 yards. Take the second right **❺** (at the end of Boathouse Row) and go up to **Lemon Hill.** Built in 1800 on a 350-acre farm, this is a beautiful example of a Federal-style country house. *Poplar Dr., East Fairmount Park, ☎ 215/232–4337. ☛ $1.50. ☉ Wed.–Sun. 10–4:30. Closed Jan.–Feb. Call ahead as hrs may vary.*

Head back to Kelly Drive, turn right, and then right again at the equestrian statue of Ulysses S. Grant. The first left takes you to **Mt. Pleas-**
❻ **ant.** Built in 1761 by Captain John Macpherson, a pirate, the house was later purchased by the Revolutionary War traitor Benedict Arnold. John Adams called the Georgian mansion "the most elegant seat in Pennsylvania." *Mt. Pleasant Dr., East Fairmount Park, ☎ 215/763–8100, ext. 333. ☛ $1.50. ☉ Tues.–Sun. 10–4:15.*

Double back to Reservoir Drive, pass Rockland and Ormiston (two **❼** other park mansions), and take the next left, Randolph Drive, to **Laurel Hill.** Built around 1767 on a laurel-covered hill overlooking the Schuylkill, the Georgian house was once owned by Dr. Philip Syng Physick (also proprietor of Society Hill's Hill-Physick-Keith house; *see* Tour 2, *above*). On some Sunday evenings during the summer, Women for Greater Philadelphia sponsors candlelight chamber-music concerts here. *E. Edgely Dr., East Fairmount Park, ☎ 215/235–1776. ☛ $1.50. ☉ Wed.–Sun. 10–4.*

Edgely Drive turns into Dauphin Street. Just before reaching 33rd **❽** Street, turn left on Strawberry Mansion Drive and you're at **Woodford,** a fine Georgian mansion built about 1756. Inside is the Naomi Wood collection of household goods, including furniture, unusual clocks, and English delftware. *Near 33rd and Dauphin Sts., East Fairmount Park, ☎ 215/229–6115. ☛ $1.50. ☉ Tues.–Sun. 10–4.*

A few steps northwest of Woodford stands the house that gave its name **❾** to the nearby section of Philadelphia, **Strawberry Mansion.** The largest mansion in Fairmount Park, it has furniture from the three main phases of its history: Federal, Regency, and Empire. In the parlor is a collection of rare Tucker porcelain; in the attic is a fine assortment of antique dolls. *Near 33rd and Dauphin Sts., East Fairmount Park, ☎ 215/228–8364. ☛ $1.50. ☉ Tues.–Sun. 10–4.*

Go back to Strawberry Mansion Drive, turn left, and cross the Strawberry Mansion Bridge to West Fairmount Park. Looping through the park, you'll reach Chamounix Drive, a long straightaway. Turn left on **❿** Belmont Mansion Drive to **Belmont Plateau.** Here are the Playhouse in the Park and the Belmont Mansion, but the main attraction is the view, from 243 feet above river level. In front of you lie the park, the Schuylkill River winding down to the Philadelphia Museum of Art, and— 4 miles away—the Philadelphia skyline.

Follow Belmont Mansion Drive down the hill. Where it forks, stay to the left, cross Montgomery Drive and turn left to reach the Horticulture Center (*see* Parks, Zoos, and Gardens, *below*). Loop all the way around the Horticulture Center to the **Japanese House,** a reconstructed 16th-century house and garden built in Japan. It was exhibited temporarily at the Museum of Modern Art in New York, then reassembled here in 1958. Enjoy the serenity of this architectural setting and the waterfall, gardens, Japanese trees, and pond. The house is called Shofu-So, which means "pine breeze villa." *Lansdowne Dr. east of Belmont Ave., West Fairmount Park,* ☎ *215/878–5097.* ☛ *$2.50.* ☉ *June–Aug., Tues.–Sun. 11–4; May, Sept., and Oct., weekends 11–4.*

Go back around the Horticulture Center and continue through the gates straight to Belmont Avenue. Turn left and then left again at the first light (North Concourse Drive). On your left is **Memorial Hall,** the only major building remaining from the Philadelphia Centennial Exposition of 1876. This grand stone building with a glass dome and Palladian windows served as the exposition's art museum. Sometimes open for viewing is a 20-by-40-foot model of the exposition. *N. Concourse Dr., West Fairmount Park,* ☎ *215/686–1776.* ☛ *Free.* ☉ *Daily 8:30–5.*

The two towers to your left as you leave Memorial Hall are part of the **Smith Civil War Memorial** (N. Concourse Dr., West Fairmount Park). Built from 1897 to 1912 with funds donated by wealthy foundry owner Richard Smith, the memorial honors Pennsylvania heroes of the Civil War. Among those immortalized in bronze are Generals Meade and Hancock—and Smith himself. At the base of each tower is a curved wall with a bench. If you sit at one end and listen to a person whispering at the other end, you'll understand why they're called the Whispering Benches. Unfortunately, the litter around the site reflects its location near a declining neighborhood.

To the east stands **Cedar Grove,** where five styles of furniture—Jacobean, William and Mary, Queen Anne, Chippendale, and Federal—reflect the accumulations of five generations of the Paschall-Morris family. The house stood in Frankford for 180 years before being moved to this location in 1927. *Lansdowne Dr. off N. Concourse Dr., West Fairmount Park,* ☎ *215/763–8100, ext. 4013.* ☛ *$1.50.* ☉ *Tues.–Sun. 10–4:15.*

Just south of Cedar Grove atop a hill sloping gently down to the Schuylkill is **Sweetbriar.** Built in 1797, it was the park's first year-round residence. *Lansdowne Dr. off N. Concourse Dr., West Fairmount Park,* ☎ *215/222–1333.* ☛ *$1.50.* ☉ *Wed.–Mon. 10–4. Call ahead.*

A trip farther down Lansdowne Drive takes you to the Philadelphia Zoological Gardens (*see* Parks, Zoos, and Gardens, *below*).

The northwest section of Fairmount Park is the **Wissahickon.** A gorge carved out by the Wissahickon Creek, it is 5½ miles of towering trees, cliffs, trails, and animals, and retains many traces of history.

Of the Philadelphia areas that William Penn encountered, the Wissahickon has changed the least. You can easily visualize the Lenni-Lenape Indians who lived here, beat its trails, and gave the creek its name. *Wissahickon* is an Anglicized version of the Lenni-Lenape words for yellow creek and catfish creek.

Forbidden Drive, a dirt-and-gravel pathway along the west side of the creek, is a haunt of joggers, bikers, horseback riders, fishermen, and nature lovers. For the more adventuresome there are foot trails along both sides of the creek.

Many inns once stood along the banks of the Wissahickon; only two remain. One is now a police station; the other is the **Valley Green Inn,** built in 1850 on the site of an earlier inn. Today it's a restaurant filled with restored antiques and a focal point of the Wissahickon. The inn is nestled in one of the loveliest parts of the Wissahickon gorge. Sit on a bench alongside the creek, feed bread crumbs to the ducks, look at the stone bridge reflected in the water, and savor the beauty and tranquillity of this spot. It's an experience you'll long remember.

Valley Green Inn is an excellent departure point for exploring the Wissahickon. You can saunter along one of the trails, enjoy the stream, lose yourself in the wilderness, and investigate some of the sights. To find the sights listed here, ask a mounted policeman or inquire at the inn; a map of the Wissahickon showing all the trails and sites is available ($4) at the inn's snack-booth window.

To reach Valley Green Inn, take the Schuylkill Expressway west to the Lincoln Drive–Wissahickon Park exit (Exit 32). Follow Lincoln Drive to Allen's Lane, then turn right. At Germantown Avenue turn left, go about a mile, turn left at Springfield Avenue, and follow it to the end.

South of Valley Green Inn

About a quarter mile south of Valley Green Inn on the east side of the creek, near where Cresheim Creek joins the Wissahickon, is a picturesque spot with an intriguing name—**Devil's Pool.** Neighborhood kids dive off the rocks into the pool, which local legend says is bottomless. (It's really about 10 feet deep.) Along the path near the pool, look for **Shakespeare Rock,** with a quotation, appropriate to the setting, carved on its face:

The current that with gentle murmur glides
. . . makes sweet music with th' enamell'd stones,
Giving a gentle kiss to every sedge . . .
And so by many winding nooks he strays
With willing sport, to the wild ocean.

Fingerspan, the newest addition to the Wissahickon, is a steel sculpture of a bridge spanning a ravine. It was done by local artist Jody Pinto.

Toleration, a granite statue of William Penn erected in 1883, stands on Mom Rinker's Rock. This dramatic spot affords a magnificent view of the Wissahickon Valley.

Rittenhousetown, near where Forbidden Drive runs into Lincoln Drive, is a cluster of six small historic whitewashed Colonial buildings. One house, built in 1707, is the birthplace of David Rittenhouse, the clockmaker, astronomer, and patriot after whom Rittenhouse Square is named (*see* Tour 3, *above*). Built around 1683, the mill is the sole survivor of the 60 mills that once lined the Wissahickon. It was the first paper mill in America.

Hermit's Cave was a favorite hangout of the Wissahickon's most famous inhabitant, the German mystic Johannes Kelpius. In 1694, Kelpius and his followers, the Society of the Woman in the Wilderness, moved to the Wissahickon to await the millennium. Kelpius is buried in an unmarked grave near his cave. Look up and you'll see the graceful arch of the Henry Avenue Bridge and, nearby, the broad rock outcropping called **Lover's Leap**—for obvious reasons.

North of Valley Green Inn

On the east side of the Rex Avenue Bridge (1 mile north of Valley Green Inn), a path through a stone arch leads up, up, up to **Indian Rock,** where

the Lenni-Lenape held council until their disappearance from the valley around 1750. Atop the rock is a stone statue of a kneeling warrior, called *Tedyuscung* after a local chief.

The red wooden **Covered Bridge** at the foot of Thomas Mill Road is 97 feet long and 14 feet wide. Built in 1855, it's the last covered bridge still standing within the boundaries of a major American city.

At the north end of Forbidden Drive (2½ miles north of Valley Green Inn) is the **Andorra Natural Area.** Its Tree House Visitors Center has exhibits, a reference library, self-guiding materials including trail maps, and a changing collection of local fauna—toads, rabbits, turtles, and snakes. Tree House hours vary, but the information center is always open (☎ 215/685–9285). The center's director, Sioux Baldwin, is probably the world's foremost authority on the Wissahickon.

To explore the Wissahickon in more detail, see *Rediscovering the Wissahickon,* by Sarah West. Published in 1993, the book gives mapped geology and history walks, plus information on the ecology, flora, and fauna of the valley.

Local Color:
Five Great Neighborhoods to Explore

Southwark

Directly south of Society Hill, Southwark is neither as glamorous nor as historically renowned as its neighbor. Chiseled in stone on one facade are these words: "On this site in 1879, nothing happened!" Yet, today, the district is buzzing with the sounds of restoration, and young professionals and teachers are busily gentrifying Southwark's Queen Village neighborhood, attracting chic restaurants and interesting shops.

Southwark, stretching from Front to Sixth Street and from South Street to Washington Avenue, was the center of the commercial and ship-building activity that made Philadelphia the biggest port in the Colonies and in the young United States. A leisurely stroll through Southwark, neighboring South Philadelphia, and along South Street is a fun day's outing. Begin your tour with breakfast at Famous Delicatessen, at Fourth and Banbridge, one block south of South Street), one of the city's most popular culinary institutions and a holdover from the era when this was a Jewish neighborhood and immigrants hawked their wares from pushcarts.

Walk east on Bainbridge and then proceed south on Second Street, which old-timers call "Two Street." The homes along these streets are the oldest in the city. Even when their construction dates are not chiseled on the facades, the ravages of years of settling lines of bricks above the overhangs, crooked windows, and shutters that don't hang straight attest to their vintage. Turn east on Catharine Street and then south on Hancock. This is one of the most charming streets in the city. The tiny clapboard houses at 813 and 815 were built by a shipwright and are the last of their type. Detour onto Queen Street to see the old firehouse with the gas lamps at 117. It has been converted to a single home, and you'll be awed by the beautiful restoration.

Continue down Hancock to Christian Street; go east about one block (under the I–95 overpass) to Swanson Street. Here is **Gloria Dei,** the oldest church in Pennsylvania. One of the few remnants of the Swedes who settled Pennsylvania before William Penn, Gloria Dei (Old Swedes') Church was organized in 1642. Built in 1698, the church has numerous religious artifacts, such as a 1608 Bible once owned by Sweden's

Queen Christina, and carvings on the lectern and balcony salvaged from the congregation's first church that was destroyed by fire. Models of two of the ships that transported the first Swedish settlers hang from the ceiling—right in the center of the church. Grouped around the church are the parish hall, caretaker's house, rectory, and guild house. The church sits in the center of its graveyard; it forms a picture pleasing in its toy-like simplicity and tranquillity. *916 Swanson St., near Christian and Delaware Aves.,* ☏ *215/389–1513.* ☉ *Usually daily 9–5, but call first.*

Back on Second Street walk south, past a neighborhood landmark, the Shot Tower, where lead shot was made during the War of 1812. At Washington Avenue is the **Mummers Museum.** Even if you aren't in Philadelphia on New Year's Day, here's a chance to see a unique local institution and phenomenon. Famous for extravagant sequin-and-feather costumes and string bands, the Mummers spend the entire year preparing for an all-day parade up Broad Street every January 1. The museum has costumes, photos of parades from as far back as the turn of the century, and audiovisual displays of Mummerabilia. You can push buttons to compose your own Mummers medley with banjos, saxophones, and xylophones, and dance the Mummers strut to the strains of "Oh, 'Dem Golden Slippers." A 45-inch screen shows filmed highlights of past parades. On most Tuesday evenings from May to September, the museum presents free outdoor concerts (weather permitting). *2nd St. and Washington Ave.,* ☏ *215/336–3050.* ☛ *$2.50 adults, $2 children under 12 and senior citizens.* ☉ *Tues.–Sat. 9:30–5, Sun. noon–5.*

South Philadelphia

The city's "Little Italy"—the neighborhood that gave the world Mario Lanza, Bobby Rydell, Frankie Avalon, Fabian, and Rocky Balboa—is a huge area of identical row houses with gleaming white marble steps. From Southwark's Mummers Museum (*see above*), walk west on Washington Avenue to Ninth Street and then proceed north. The heart of the neighborhood is the five-block-long, open-air Italian Market, more Naples than Philadelphia: vendors crowd the sidewalks and spill out onto the streets; live crabs and caged chickens wait for the kill; picture-perfect produce is piled up high. Although there are chic eateries in South Philadelphia, the majority of the neighborhood restaurants are not fancy (decor such as red-checked vinyl tablecloths and plastic grapes hanging from plastic vines is not uncommon), but occasionally the food can be terrific—and more importantly—authentic. You'll wonder if Mama is in kitchen preparing a Southern-Italian specialty for you. (Though the restaurants are always crowded, streets here can be quiet at night; so it's best to have a waiter call you a cab.)

Restaurants proudly display gold records earned by neighborhood celebrities, but to really enjoy a delightful stroll down South Philly's memory lane, head for its unique **Mario Lanza Museum,** devoted to the famous tenor and Hollywood star. Here you'll find thousands of photos, selected memorabilia, videocassette showings of Lanza's films, and souvenirs for sale. Lanza was supposedly moving a piano into the Academy of Music when he seized the opportunity to sing from its stage—and was first discovered. Lanza's birthplace at 634 Christian Street is a few blocks away. *Settlement Music School, 416 Queen Street,* ☏ *215/468–3623.* ☉ *Mon.–Sat. 10–3. Closed Sat. in July and Aug.*

Today, aspiring opera stars sing arias while you eat antipasto at the Victor Cafe (*see* Chapter 5, Dining), where the young Lanza sang for his supper, literally. However, many visitors like to head for South Philly's

culinary shrine, Pat's King of Steaks, at the corner of 9th and Passyunk. One of their cheesesteaks makes a perfect prelude to an evening spent at the city's sports complex—the Spectrum, Veterans Stadiums, and John F. Kennedy Stadium—at the southern end of South Philadelphia (*see* Chapter 4, Sports and the Outdoors).

University City

University City is the portion of West Philadelphia across the Schuylkill that includes the campuses of the University of Pennsylvania, Drexel University, and the Philadelphia College of Pharmacy and Science. It also has the University City Science Center (a leading think tank), a large and impressive collection of houses, and a variety of moderately priced restaurants, movie theaters, stores, and lively bars catering to more than 32,000 students and other residents.

Prominent on your itinerary here should be the **University of Pennsylvania.** For a good look at the Ivy League campus stop at the **Information Center** at 34th and Walnut streets (☎ 215/898–1000), then follow **Locust Walk** between 33rd Street and 40th Street. The campus is charming, and ivy really does cling to the stately stone buildings.

Starting at 33rd Street, you see **Franklin Field,** the university football stadium and home of the Penn Relays (*see* Festivals and Seasonal Events *in* Chapter 1 *and* Spectator Sports *in* Chapter 4). At 33rd and Spruce is the **University Museum** (*see* Libraries and Museums, *below*). And just north of Locust Walk along 33rd Street is the Moore School of Engineering, home of **ENIAC,** the world's first all-electronic general-purpose digital computer (*see* Off the Beaten Track, *below*).

At 34th Street and Locust Walk is the **Furness Building.** Formerly the university's main library and now the graduate-school fine arts library, it is an architectural gem by the innovative Frank Furness. A $16.5 million restoration by the architectural firm of Robert Venturi was completed in February 1991 to celebrate the building's centennial.

You're now at the edge of **College Green** (Blanche Levy Park), the crossroads of the campus. In the middle stands a statue of Benjamin Franklin, who founded the university in 1740. To your right, the huge **Van Pelt Library** stretches from 34th Street to 36th Street. In front is Claes Oldenburg's *Broken Button* statue. To your left is **College Hall,** an administration building said to be the inspiration for the scary Addams House in cartoonist Charles Addams' work.

Just west of 36th Street, the **Annenberg School of Communication** and the **Annenberg Center** (*see* Chapter 7, The Arts and Nightlife) are to the right; the famed **Wharton School of Economics** is to the left. As you pass the intersection of 37th Street, say hello to Ben Franklin sitting on a bench.

At 38th Street is the well-stocked **University Bookstore** (*see* Chapter 3, Shopping). A footbridge takes you over 38th Street (turn around for a good view of Center City) to **Superblock,** three high-rise student dormitories. Locust Walk ends at 40th Street with the Dental School, a row of stores, restaurants, and two movie theaters.

Two other notable university sights a short distance from Locust Walk are the **Quad,** near 37th and Spruce, and the **Richards Laboratories,** a modernist monument created by one of the 20th century's greatest architects. The university's first dorm buildings, the Quad was designed by Cope and Stewardson in 1895 and became the prototype of the Collegiate Gothic style prevalent in campuses coast to coast. These dormitory buildings—awash with gargoyles and gables—easily conjure up

the England of everyone's dreams. Not far away, on Hamilton Walk, you're smack back in the 20th century, thanks to Louis Kahn's Alfred Newton Richards Medical Research Laboratories building, an award-winning masterpiece of this important architect. Kahn, a brilliant teacher and architectural theorist did not leave many completed buildings.

Chinatown

Centered on 10th and Race streets just two blocks north of Market Street, Chinatown serves as the residential and commercial hub of the Chinese community. Along with more than 50 restaurants (*see* Chapter 5, Dining), Chinatown attractions include grocery stores, souvenir and gift shops, martial arts studios, a fortune cookie store, bilingual street signs, and red-and-green pagoda-style telephone booths.

One striking Chinatown site is the **Chinese Friendship Gate** straddling 10th Street at Arch Street. This intricate and colorful 40-foot-tall arch—the largest authentic Chinese gate outside China—was created by Chinese artisans, who brought their own tools and construction materials. The citizens of Tianjin, Philadelphia's sister city in the People's Republic of China, donated the building materials, including the ornamental tile.

From February to May, you can celebrate Chinese New Year with a 10-course banquet at the **Chinese Cultural Center** (125 N. 10th St., ☎ 215/923–6767). The center occupies an 1831 example of the Peking Mandarin-palace style.

Germantown and Chestnut Hill

About 6 miles northwest of Center City is Germantown, which has been an integrated, progressive community since thirteen German Quaker and Mennonite families settled here in 1683 and soon welcomed English, French, and other Europeans seeking religious freedom. Germantown has a tradition of free thinking—the first written protest against slavery came from its residents. For the visitor today, more importantly, it houses a wealth of still-occupied and exceptionally well-preserved architectural masterpieces.

The Germantown area is rich in history. It was the site of Philadelphia's first gristmill (1683) and America's first paper mill (1690). The American Colonies' first English-language Bible was printed here (1743). By the time of the Revolution, Germantown had become a bustling industrial town. In 1777, Colonial troops under George Washington attacked part of the British force here and fought the Battle of Germantown in various skirmishes. After the Revolutionary War, Germantown became a rural retreat for the city's wealthy residents who wanted to escape summer heat and disease. The Deshler-Morris House was the summer White House where President Washington and his family resided in 1793 and 1794, when the yellow-fever epidemic drove them from the city.

You can reach Germantown from Center City via Trolley 23, by the two Chestnut Hill SEPTA commuter trains, or by car. The best way to tour the area is by car. From City Hall, drive north on Broad Street for about 3½ miles to Pike Street (two blocks north of Erie Ave.). Turn left, go one block to Germantown Avenue, and turn right.

About a mile up Germantown Avenue on the left side is **Loudon,** an 1801 Greek Revival house filled with antique furniture, household goods, and paintings. A fire in 1993 destroyed some of the home's contents.

4650 Germantown Ave., ☎ 215/685–2067. ◷ Tues., Thurs., and Sat. 1–4.

Six blocks farther north is **Grumblethorpe.** Built by John Wister in 1744, this Georgian house is one of Germantown's leading examples of early 18th-century architecture. *5267 Germantown Ave., ☎ 215/843–4820. ◷ Tues. and Thurs. 10–4.*

Two blocks north is the **Deshler-Morris House,** where President Washington lived in 1793–94, making it the seat of government of the new Republic for a short time. Beautiful antiques accent the rooms, and—as one of the many Germantown houses built flush with the road—it features enchanting side and back gardens. *5442 Germantown Ave., ☎ 215/596–1748. ☛ $1 adults, 50¢ students. ◷ Tues.–Sun. 1–4. Closed Dec.–Mar.*

Across the street is the **Germantown Historical Society,** with a historical and genealogical library and collections of industrial and decorative arts. It also serves as an orientation point for visiting all the Germantown houses. *5501 Germantown Ave., ☎ 215/844–0514. ◷ Tues. and Thurs. 10–4, Sun. 1–5.*

For a look at one of the most charming of Quaker-style houses, visit **Wyck** and its idyllic gardens, complete with old pump, barn, and carriage house. The house remained the property of the same Quaker family from 1736 to 1973. *6026 Germantown Ave., ☎ 215/848–1690. ◷ Tues., Thurs., Sat. 1-4, and by appointment. Closed mid-Dec.–Mar.*

To see fabulous Germantown architecture, wander the area west of Wyck, between Walnut Lane and Tulpehocken Street. Included here is the **Ebenezer Maxwell House.** Built in 1859, this Victorian Gothic extravaganza of elongated windows, arches, and a three-story tower is the incarnation of an old haunted house and Philadelphia's only mid-19th-century house-museum. *200 W. Tulpehocken St., ☎ 215/438–1861. ☛ $4 adults, $3 senior citizens, $2 students. ◷ Thurs.–Sun. 1–4.*

If you have time for only one site in Germantown, make it **Cliveden.** Built in 1763 by Benjamin Chew, Germantown's most elaborate country house was occupied by the British during the Revolution. On October 4, 1777, Washington's unsuccessful attempt to dislodge the British resulted in his defeat at the Battle of Germantown. You can still see bullet marks on the outside walls. Today a museum, the house occupies a 6-acre plot with outbuildings and a barn converted into offices and a gift shop. It remained in the Chew family until 1972, when it was donated to the National Trust for Historic Preservation. *6401 Germantown Ave., ☎ 215/848–1777. ☛ $4 adults, $3 students. ◷ Tues.–Sat. 10–4, Sun. 1–4.*

Across the street from Cliveden is **Upsala,** built about 1755 and one of Germantown's best examples of Georgian-style architecture. Continental troops set up their cannons on Upsala's front lawn and shelled the British at Cliveden. *6430 Germantown Ave., ☎ 215/842–1798. ◷ Tues. and Thurs. 1–4. Closed Jan.–Mar.*

North of Germantown is the residential community of Mount Airy, and further north, at the "top" of Germantown Avenue, is **Chestnut Hill.** Though it's part of the city, Chestnut Hill is more like a classy, Main Line suburb. One of Philadelphia's poshest neighborhoods, it has numerous impressive mansions, more than 120 shops and restaurants, several art galleries, two train stations, and an arboretum. For tours

and guest information, contact the Chestnut Hill Development Group. *8434 Germantown Ave., ☎ 215/247–6696.*

Chestnut Hill sights include **Pastorius Park** at Lincoln Drive and Abington Avenue (one block west of the 8100 block of Germantown Ave.) and **Morris Arboretum** (*see* Parks, Zoos, and Gardens, *below*). The **Woodmere Art Museum** (9201 Germantown Ave., ☎ 215/247–0476) displays paintings, tapestries, sculpture, porcelains, ivories, Japanese rugs, and works by contemporary local artists.

Historical Buildings and Sites

Many of Philadelphia's historic sites have been described in the Exploring tours, *above.* Here is a selection of other historic attractions that many travelers will find of interest.

Andalusia. In the early 1800s, Philadelphia banker Nicholas Biddle toured Greece and returned determined to re-create its architecture in his backyard. He commissioned the prominent architect Thomas U. Walter to add a Doric colonnade and other alterations to his 18th-century farmhouse, Andalusia, transforming it into one of the nation's first examples of Greek Revival architecture. Wander throughout the 220-acre estate to see the boxwood and rose gardens, various outbuildings, and the grotto. The house remains in the Biddle family; it is administered by the National Trust for Historic Preservation. *State Rd., Andalusia, Bucks County, ☎ 215/848–1777. ☛ $9 per person, 7-person minimum. ☉ For guided tours Tues.–Sat. 10–2, by appointment only; 10 days' notice requested.*

Mikveh Israel Synagogue and Cemetery. Nathan Levy, a Colonial merchant whose ship, *The Myrtilla*, brought the Liberty Bell to America, helped found this synagogue in 1740. It is the oldest synagogue in Philadelphia and the second-oldest in the United States. Originally located at 3rd and Cherry streets, it now occupies the same building as the National Museum of American Jewish History (*see* Libraries and Museums, *below*). The cemetery was established in 1738. Levy acquired the land from William Penn as a family burial ground; it was later expanded to accommodate the Jewish community. Buried there are Haym Salomon, financier of the American Revolution, and Rebecca Gratz, the inspiration for Rebecca in Sir Walter Scott's novel *Ivanhoe*. *Synagogue: 44 N. 4th St., ☎ 215/922–5446. ☉ Mon.–Thurs. 10–5, Fri. 10–3, Sun. noon–5. Services Sat. 9 AM and Fri. evenings. Cemetery: Spruce St. between 8th and 9th Sts., ☎ 215/922–5446. A guide is present in summer, weekdays 10–4. From Sept. to June, visiting arrangements can be made through the Park Service or the synagogue.*

Fort Mifflin. Because of its Quaker origins, Philadelphia had no defenses until 1772, when the British began building Fort Mifflin. It was completed in 1776 by Revolutionary forces under General Washington. In a 40-day battle in 1777, 300 Continental defenders held off British forces long enough for Washington's troops to flee to Valley Forge. The fort was almost totally destroyed and was rebuilt in 1798 from plans by French architect Pierre Charles L'Enfant, who designed the plan for Washington, D.C. In use until 1962, the fort has served as a prisoner-of-war camp, an artillery battalion, and a munitions dump. Within this 49-acre National Historic Landmark, you can see cannons and carriages, officers' quarters, soldiers' barracks (which contain an exhibit called "Defense of the Delaware"), an artillery shed, a blacksmith shop, a bomb shelter, and a museum. *Island Rd. and Hog Island Rd. on the Delaware River near Philadelphia International Airport, ☎*

215/365–9781. ☛ *$2 adults, $1 children under 12.* ⊘ *Wed.–Sun. 10–4. Tours at 11, 1, and 3. Closed mid-Dec.–early Mar.*

Pennsylvania Hospital. Another in the long list of "firsts" and institutions founded by Benjamin Franklin is Pennsylvania Hospital, the oldest hospital in the United States. Inside the fine 18th-century original buildings are the nation's first medical library and first surgical amphitheater, an 1804 innovation with a skylight, and the only one still in existence. It also has a portrait gallery, early medical instruments, art objects, and a rare-book library with items that date from 1762. The artwork includes the Benjamin West painting *Christ Healing the Sick in the Temple.* Today Pennsylvania Hospital is a full-service, modern medical center. Pick up a copy of *Pennsylvania Hospital: A Walking Tour* in the marketing department on the second floor of the Pine Building. *8th and Spruce Sts.,* ☎ *215/829–3971.* ☛ *Free.* ⊘ *Weekdays 8:30–5. Call to arrange a guided group tour.*

Libraries and Museums

Libraries

When it comes to Philadelphia's libraries, the words *oldest, largest,* and *best* are commonly used to describe the city's holdings and collections. Many are, in truth, museums, filled with treasured paintings and furnishings. In addition to the Free Library—the vast public-library system—Philadelphia also has some of the oldest, largest, and most comprehensive private collections in the country. All five libraries described below are located within the boundaries of our downtown Exploring tours (*see above*), and all are open to the public.

Housed in a national landmark Italianate brownstone dating from the mid-1800s, the **Athenaeum** of Philadelphia is a research library specializing in 19th-century social and cultural history. Founded in 1814, the library contains significant materials on the French in America and early American travel, exploration, and transportation. Its American Architecture Collection has close to a million items. Besides books, the Athenaeum houses notable paintings and period furniture. *219 S. 6th St.,* ☎ *215/925–2688.* ☛ *Free; tours by appointment.* ⊘ *Weekdays 9–5.*

The Free Library of Philadelphia. Philadelphia calls its public-library system the "Fabulous Freebie." Founded in 1891, the central library has more than 1 million volumes. With its grand entrance hall, sweeping marble staircase, 30-foot ceilings, enormous reading rooms with long tables, and spiral staircases leading to balconies, this Greek Revival building looks the way libraries ought to look. With more than 12,000 musical scores, the Edwin S. Fleisher Collection is the largest of its kind in the world. Tormented by a tune whose name you can't recall? Hum it to one of the Music Room's librarians and he'll track it down. The Department of Social Science and History has nearly 100,000 charts, maps, and guidebooks. The Newspaper Room stocks papers (back issues are on microfilm) from all major U.S. and foreign cities , some going all the way back to Colonial times. The Rare Book Room is a beautiful suite housing first editions of Dickens, ancient Sumerian clay tablets, illuminated medieval manuscripts, and more modern manuscripts, including Poe's *Murders in the Rue Morgue* and "The Raven." *19th St. and Benjamin Franklin Pkwy.,* ☎ *215/686–5322.* ⊘ *Mon.–Wed. 9–9, Thurs. and Fri. 9–6, Sat. 9–5, Sun. 1–5. Closed Sun. June–Aug. Tours of Rare Book Room weekdays at 11.*

The **Historical Society of Pennsylvania** contains more than a half-million books and 14 million manuscripts—the largest privately owned manuscript collection in the United States. Founded in 1824 for the purpose of "elucidating the history of the state," the society has expanded its scope to cover the original 13 colonies. Notable items from the collection include the Penn family archives, President Buchanan's papers, a printer's proof of the Declaration of Independence, and the first draft of the Constitution. The staff in the genealogical library will help you trace your roots. The first floor has changing exhibits from the permanent collection of portraits and artifacts. Paintings include the earliest portrait of Washington (1772) and the last of Franklin (1789), both by Charles Willson Peale. *1300 Locust St., ☎ 215/732–6200. ☛ Use of library $5; museum and exhibits $2.50. ⊙ Tues.–Sat. 10–5, Wed. 1–9.*

The **Library of the American Philosophical Society** is one of the country's leading institutions for the study of science. Its collection includes first editions of Newton's *Principia Mathematica*, Franklin's *Experiments and Observations*, and Darwin's *On the Origin of Species*. The collection also covers American natural history, medical science, and American Indians. Here you'll find many of Franklin's original books and papers as well as journals from the Lewis and Clark expedition of 1803–06. Nonresearch visitors can view the lobby exhibit, recently "Thomas Jefferson Statesman of Science." *105 S. 5th St., ☎ 215/440–3400. ☛ Free. ⊙ Weekdays 9–4:45.*

Founded in 1731, the **Library Company of Philadelphia** is one of the oldest cultural institutions in the United States and the only major Colonial American library that has survived virtually intact. From 1774 to 1800 it functioned as the de facto Library of Congress, and until the late 19th century it was the city library. Its membership has included 10 signers of the Declaration of Independence, among them Robert Morris, Benjamin Rush, and Thomas McKean. The 400,000-volume collection includes 200,000 rare books. First editions—many of which were acquired when they were first published—include Melville's *Moby Dick* and Whitman's *Leaves of Grass*. The library is particularly rich in Americana up to 1880, black history to 1915, the history of science, and women's history. *1314 Locust St., ☎ 215/546–3181. ☛ Free. ⊙ Weekdays 9–4:45.*

Museums
While some of Philadelphia's most interesting museums fall outside the confines of the tours described in the Exploring section, many are certainly worth a visit.

Afro-American Historical and Cultural Museum. Opened in the Bicentennial year of 1976, this is the first museum of its kind funded and built by a city. Exhibits are dedicated to the history, arts, crafts, and culture of African-Americans in the United States—with a focus on Philadelphia and Pennsylvania. Recent exhibits included "The Great Migration" from the South to the North between the 1880s and World War I and "Black Photographers Bear Witness." Every year the museum presents a "Jazz and Music" series and a literary series with appearances by major black writers. Its bookshop offers the area's widest selection on black culture, history, fiction, poetry, and drama. The gift shop features carvings from Togo, Senegal, and Ghana, and hand-cut jewelry from Zaire. *7th and Arch Sts., ☎ 215/574–0380. ☛ $3.50 adults, $1.75 senior citizens and children. ⊙ Tues.–Sat. 10–5, Sun. noon–6.*

American-Swedish Historical Museum. The Swedes settled the Delaware Valley in the mid-1600s before William Penn, but few traces remain other than Old Swedes' Church (Gloria Dei) (*see* Southwark *in* Neighborhoods to Explore, *above*) and the American-Swedish Historical Museum. Modeled after a 17th-century Swedish manor house and located on land settled by the Swedes, the museum's 14 galleries trace the history of Swedes in the United States. The newest exhibit is "Before Penn," the nation's only permanent exhibit on the New Sweden colony. The John Ericsson room honors the designer of the Civil War ironclad ship, the *Monitor;* the Jenny Lind room contains memorabilia from the Swedish Nightingale's American tour of 1848 to 1851; other rooms display handmade, costumed Swedish peasant dolls; crafts; paintings; and drawings. *1900 Pattison Ave.,* ☎ *215/389–1776.* ☛ *$2 adults, $1 students and senior citizens, children under 12 free.* ☉ *Tues.–Fri. 10–4, weekends noon–4.*

Atwater Kent Museum. Founded in 1938 and housed in an elegant 1826 Greek Revival building, the museum portrays Philadelphia history from the beginning to the present day. It includes exhibits on municipal services such as police, fire, water, and gas; shipbuilding; model streets and railroads; and maps showing the city's development. One gallery, "The City Beneath Our Feet," has changing exhibits culled from the thousands of artifacts uncovered during 20th-century excavations. Recent temporary exhibits have included "Tune In—Philadelphia Radio, 1920–1950." *15 S. 7th St.,* ☎ *215/922–3031.* ☛ *Free.* ☉ *Tues.–Sat. 9:30–4:45.*

Balch Institute for Ethnic Studies. More a research center than a museum, the Balch Institute has a 60,000-volume library on immigration history and ethnicity. The institute's permanent exhibit, "Freedom's Doors— Immigrant Points of Entry to the U.S.," focuses on immigration in port cities such as Philadelphia, Boston, and Baltimore. Recent temporary exhibits have included "The Korean Community in the Delaware Valley" and "Ethnic Images in Toys and Games." *18 S. 7th St.,* ☎ *215/925– 8090.* ☛ *Suggested donation: $2 adults; $1 students, senior citizens, and children.* ☉ *Exhibits Mon.–Sat. 10–4, library 9–5.*

Barnes Foundation. It used to be pretty much of a secret that one of the world's greatest collections of Impressionist and Post-Impressionist art—175 Renoirs, 66 Cézannes (including his *Card Players*), 65 Matisses, plus masterpieces by Van Gogh, Degas, Picasso, and others, estimated by some experts to be worth $500 million, by others to be incalculable—was on view in the little town of Merion, PA, 8 miles west of Center City. That was the way Albert C. Barnes actually wanted it. The son of a Philadelphia butcher who made millions by inventing a miracle-drug, Barnes considered art an educational tool, and until a 1961 court order the collection was open only to students. Now that the enlightened trustees of Lincoln University have taken over, Barnes's public-be-dammed attitude is a thing of the past. Thanks to the recent spectacularly successful world-wide tour of the collection (which allowed the trustees to renovate Barnes's French Renaissance–style mansion), the secret is out and tickets—now that the museum reopened in November 1995—are a very hot commodity. The Gauguins, Tintorettos, and Degases are displayed as they have always been: wallpapered floor to ceiling and check-by-jowl with household tools, Amish chests, and New Mexican folk icons (Dr. Barnes felt that a Matisse and an antique door latch shared many of the same aesthetic qualities). Whether Dr. Barnes would appreciate all the glitzy publicity his museum has received is doubtful but, having always believed

art should be appreciated by the masses, he undoubtedly would have approved of the new Renoir T-shirts. *300 Latches La., Merion,* ☎ *610/667–0290. Hrs unavailable at press time. Call for new schedule and admission fees.*

Mutter Museum. Skulls, antique microscopes, and a cancerous tumor removed from President Grover Cleveland's mouth in 1893 form just part of the medical collection in the Mutter Museum. The museum has hundreds of anatomical and pathological specimens, medical instruments, and organs removed from patients, including John Marshall's bladder stones and a piece of John Wilkes Booth's neck tissue. The collection contains 139 skulls plus items belonging to Madame Curie, Louis Pasteur, and Joseph Lister. Also included is a 7-foot-6-inch skeleton, the tallest on public exhibition in the United States. The autopsy of Chang and Eng (the original Siamese twins) was done here, and the museum displays their joined livers and a plaster cast of their torsos. *19 S. 22nd St.,* ☎ *215/563–3737 ext. 241.* ☛ *Free (donations accepted).* ⊙ *Tues.–Fri. 10–4.*

National Museum of American Jewish History. This is the only museum in the country devoted to Jewish participation in the growth and development of America. It opened on July 4, 1976. Its permanent exhibit, the "American Jewish Experience," documents American Jewish history from 1654 to the present. It also has changing exhibits, lectures, workshops, films, and theater; and a collection of art, artifacts, and archival material. *55 N. 5th St.,* ☎ *215/923–3811.* ☛ *$2.50 adults, $1.75 senior citizens and students, $1.25 children under 12.* ⊙ *Mon.–Thurs. 10–5, Fri. 10–3, Sun. noon–5.*

Poe House. Edgar Allan Poe lived here, the only one of his Philadelphia residences still standing, from 1843 to 1844. During that time, some of his best-known short stories were published: "The Telltale Heart," "The Black Cat," and "The Gold Bug." You can tour the 19th-century three-story brick house; to evoke the spirit of Poe, the National Park Service deliberately keeps the house empty. The adjoining house has exhibits on Poe and his family, his work habits, and his literary contemporaries; there is also an eight-minute slide show and a small Poe library and reading room. At night, a statue in the garden casts the eerie shadow of a raven across the side of the house. *532 N. 7th St.,* ☎ *215/597–8780.* ☛ *Free.* ⊙ *Daily 9–5.*

Norman Rockwell Museum. The Curtis Publishing Company Building, where Rockwell delivered his paintings to the editors of the *Saturday Evening Post,* now has the world's largest collection of the artist's works. Displays include all 324 Rockwell *Post* cover illustrations; lithographs, prints, collotypes, and sketches; and a replica of his studio in Stockbridge, Massachusetts. A 10-minute video illustrates Rockwell's life. The lobby of the Curtis building, incidentally, has a great treasure: a 15-by-50 foot glass mosaic mural based on a Maxfield Parrish painting executed by the Louis C. Tiffany Studios in 1916. With 260 different colors of opalescent, hand-fired glass, it is perhaps the finest Tiffany mural in the world. *6th and Sansom Sts. (lower level),* ☎ *215/922–4345.* ☛ *$2 adults, $1.50 senior citizens.* ⊙ *Mon.–Sat. 10–4, Sun. 11–4.*

Shoe Collection. Housed on the sixth floor of the Pennsylvania College of Podiatric Medicine, this unusual museum displays 500 pairs of "Footwear Through the Ages." The collection includes burial sandals from ancient Egypt, Eskimo snowshoes, Moroccan two-heeled shoes, and shoes used in the foot binding of Chinese women. Celebrity items

include basketball player Julius Erving's huge sneakers, Joe Frazier's boxing shoes, Billie Jean King's tennis shoes, and Bernie Parent's hockey skates. *8th and Race Sts.,* ☎ *215/629–0300 ext. 185.* ⊙ *Weekdays 9–4. Call to arrange a tour.*

University Museum. Indiana Jones, look out! Rare treasures from the deepest jungles and most ancient tombs make this one of the finest archaeological/anthropological museums in the world. The collection of more than a million objects, gathered largely during worldwide expeditions by University of Pennsylvania scholars, includes a 12-ton sphinx from Egypt, a crystal ball once owned by China's Dowager Empress, the world's oldest writing—Sumerian cuneiform clay tablets—and the 4,500-year-old golden jewels from the royal tombs of the kingdom of Ur. Kids run to "The Egyptian Mummy: Secrets and Science" exhibit. *33rd and Spruce Sts.,* ☎ *215/898–4000.* ☛ *Suggested donation: $5 adults, $2.50 children and senior citizens.* ⊙ *Tues.–Sat. 10–4:30, Sun. 1–5. Closed Sun. from Memorial Day to Labor Day.*

The War Library and Museum. This is one of the premier collections of Civil War memorabilia in the Union. Artifacts include two life masks of Abraham Lincoln, dress uniforms and swords of Generals Grant and Meade, plus many other weapons, uniforms, and personal effects of Civil War officers and enlisted men. The library has more than 12,000 volumes on the war. *1805 Pine St.,* ☎ *215/735–8196.* ☛ *$3.* ⊙ *Mon.–Sat. 10–4, Sun. 11–4.*

Wagner Free Institute of Science. Well worth the trip to one of Philadelphia's poorest inner-city neighborhoods, this museum consists of an 1865 building with one huge exhibition hall. It's like a museum of a museum—hardly anything has changed in 125 years. The 21,000-specimen collection includes mollusks, minerals, birds, fish, and dinosaur bones. The building and museum are a National Historic Landmark. *17th St. and Montgomery Ave.,* ☎ *215/763–6529.* ☛ *Free.* ⊙ *Tues.–Fri. 9–4. Call ahead for groups.*

Parks, Zoos, and Gardens

In addition to Fairmount Park (*see* Tour of Fairmount Park, *above*), Philadelphia boasts recreational areas that range from peaceful landscaped grounds to wilderness preserves.

Bartram's Garden is a 44-acre oasis tucked into a heavily industrialized and depressed corner of southwest Philadelphia. Begun in 1728 by John Bartram, America's oldest surviving botanic garden has remained relatively unchanged while the surrounding areas have altered dramatically. With stone columns and carvings by Bartram himself, the 18th-century farmhouse on the grounds reflects his peculiar vision of classical and Colonial architecture. The self-trained Bartram became botanist to King George III, traveling throughout the Colonies and returning with many unusual species. The house is a National Historic Landmark, and the trails extending to the Schuylkill River are part of the National Recreation Trails System. *54th St. and Lindbergh Blvd.,* ☎ *215/729–5281.* ⊙ *Garden daily, House May–Oct. Wed.–Sun. noon–4; Nov.–Apr. Wed.–Fri.* ☛ *House and garden tour $4.50 adults, $3 children 6–18; house tour only $2 adults, $1 children; garden free. Trolley 36 from City Hall stops at the entrance.*

Horticulture Center. Standing on the site of the 1876 Centennial Exposition's Horticultural Hall, the Horticulture Center consists of 22 wooded acres, a display house, and a greenhouse where plants and flowers used on city property are grown. Don't miss the whimsical *Seaweed*

Girl fountain in the display house. *N. Horticultural Dr., West Fairmount Park,* ☎ *215/879–4062.* ☛ *$1 donation requested.* ⊙ *Daily 9–3. Fairmount Park Trolley Bus stops at door.*

Morris Arboretum. In the very northwest corner of the city, you'll find 166 acres of romantic landscaped seclusion. Morris Arboretum of the University of Pennsylvania is an eclectic retreat with a formal rose garden, English garden, Japanese garden, meadows, and woodlands. Begun in 1887 by siblings John and Lydia Morris and bequeathed to the University of Pennsylvania in 1932, the arboretum typifies Victorian-era garden design, with winding paths, a hidden grotto, tropical ferns, and natural woodland. It has 3,500 trees and shrubs from around the world, including one of the finest collections of Asian plants outside Asia. *Hillcrest Ave. between Germantown and Stenton Aves., Chestnut Hill,* ☎ *215/247–5777.* ☛ *$3 adults, $1.50 children and senior citizens.* ⊙ *Daily 10–5 Apr.–Oct.; 10–4 Nov.–Mar. Guided tours weekends at 2. Chestnut Hill East or West commuter trains stop ½ mi away; Bus L stops at corner of Hillcrest and Germantown Aves.*

Schuylkill Center for Environmental Education consists of more than 500 acres of wildflowers, ferns, and thickets; ponds, streams, and woodlands; 6 miles of winding trails; and the 8-acre Pine Plantation. You may spot deer, hawks, Canada geese, red fox, and other animals. Hands-on exhibits in the Discovery Museum explain the flora and fauna you see outside. Nature programs on weekends. The bookstore and gift shop follow the nature theme. *8480 Hagy's Mill Rd., Roxborough,* ☎ *215/482–7300.* ☛ *$5 adults, $3 children.* ⊙ *Mon.–Sat. 8:30–5, Sun. 1–5. Closed Sun. in Aug. Bus 27 stops at Ridge Pike and Port Royal Ave. 1 mi away.*

Tinicum National Environmental Center hosts more than 280 species of ducks, herons, egrets, geese, gallinules, and other birds. Resident earthbound animals include turtles, foxes, muskrats, deer, raccoons, weasels, and snakes. Facilities in this 900-acre wetland, the largest remaining in Pennsylvania (it used to be 6,000 acres), include 8 miles of foot trails, an observation blind, observation deck, boardwalks through the wet areas, and a canoe launch into the 4½-mile stretch of Darby Creek that runs through the preserve (the best way to see it). Bird-watchers can prepare for their visit by calling 215/567–BIRD for recent sightings. *86th St. and Lindbergh Blvd.,* ☎ *215/365–3118 or 215/521–0662.* ☛ *Free.* ⊙ *Daily 8 ᴀᴍ–sunset; visitor center daily 9–4. Buses "U" and 37 stop nearby.*

Philadelphia Zoological Gardens. Opened in 1874, America's first zoo displays 1,600 animals on 42 acres. Orangutans, gorillas, gibbons, mandrills, and lemurs romp in the World of Primates, a 1-acre outdoor jungle. The African Plain is the stomping ground of giraffes, zebras, and rhinoceroses. Bear Country offers up-close views of sloths, spectacled bears, and polar bears diving off 12-foot cliffs. The George D. Widener Memorial Treehouse provides an animal's-eye view of a four-story tropical tree. The Children's Zoo has pony rides, a petting area, and a sea lion show. In 1993, two rare white lions were added to the zoo. *34th St. and Girard Ave.,* ☎ *215/243–1100.* ☛ *$7 adults, $5.50 children 2–11 and senior citizens; additional charge for Treehouse.* ⊙ *Weekdays 9:30–5, weekends 9:30–6.*

What to See and Do with Children

W. C. Fields may have disliked children, but children love his hometown. In addition to places and events that appeal to children and adults

alike, Philadelphia has many special attractions just for kids. This section describes some of the best; others are covered in other chapters.

Annenberg Center Theater for Children (37th and Walnut Sts., ☎ 215/898–6791). Part of a distinguished full-scale theater program, the Annenberg Center Theater for Children schedules productions in October, February, and April. The annual Philadelphia International Theater Festival for Children, held for five days at the end of May, features professional theater companies from around the world specializing in music, magic, dance, and circus performances.

Free Library Children's Department. With 100,000 books for preschoolers to eighth-graders, the Children's Department houses the city's largest collection of children's books in a made-for-kids setting. Historical collections include copies of the Hardy Boys and Nancy Drew series, over which adults wax nostalgic. The foreign-language collection has children's books in more than 50 languages. The department also sponsors story hours and film festivals. *19th St. and Benjamin Franklin Pkwy.*, ☎ 215/686–5372. ⊗ *Weekdays 9–6, Sat. 9–5, Sun. 1–5.*

Philadelphia Marionette Theater schedules hour-long performances featuring puppets, music, and magic introduced by a lecture-demonstration. Scheduled shows include *Jack and the Beanstalk, Pinocchio,* and *Peter and the Wolf.* Reservations a must. *Playhouse in the Park, Belmont Mansion Dr., West Fairmount Park,* ☎ 215/879–1213. ☛ *$4.50.* ⊗ *Performances weekdays at 10:30, some Sun. at 2.*

Sesame Place. A one-hour drive from Center City, Sesame Place is an amusement park based on the popular public-television show. Children play and learn, just as they are encouraged to on the show. It has Muppet characters, animal shows, computer games, climbing tunnels, playgrounds, a water park (bring a bathing suit), and healthful food. It's geared to children ages 3 to 13. *100 Sesame Rd., Langhorne,* ☎ 215/757–1100. ☛ *$22.95; children under 3 free.* ⊗ *Mid May–mid-Sept., daily; early May and mid-Sept.–mid-Oct., weekends only. Peak season hrs (July–Aug.), 9–8; call for spring and fall hrs.*

Smith Playground. This mansion, built just for kids, was donated to the city in 1899 by Richard and Sarah Smith in memory of their son Stanfield. For kids five and under the mansion has playrooms, a nature den, and a minivillage with metal kiddie cars from the 1950s. The playground has picnic tables, grills, Jungle Gyms, swings, and an enclosed wooden slide wide enough for 10 children. It also has a wading pool, swimming pool, and equipment for disabled children. Although located at the edge of a disadvantaged inner-city neighborhood, it's a wonderful place to take the children. *33rd and Oxford Sts., East Fairmount Park,* ☎ 215/765–4325. ⊗ *House, Mon.–Sat. 10–3:30; playground, 9–4:45.*

The following children's activities are discussed in other sections, as noted.

Academy of Natural Sciences (*see* Tour 4, *above*).

Franklin Institute Science Museum and Fels Planetarium (*see* Tour 4, *above*).

Penn's Landing: sailing ships, battleships, submarine, pleasure boats (*see* Tour 2, *above*).

Philadelphia Zoological Gardens—especially the Children's Zoo, tree house, jungle bird walk, and wolf woods (*see* Parks, Zoos, and Gardens, *above*).

Please Touch Museum (*see* Tour 4, *above*).
University Museum of the University of Pennsylvania (*see* Libraries and Museums, *above*).

Off the Beaten Track

Benjamin Franklin Bridge. Cars, trucks, and trains zoom past, and brisk winds make your face tingle as you cross the Delaware River (150 feet below) and get the best view of riverfront Philadelphia. Walking across the Benjamin Franklin Bridge is an adventure few people undertake. When it opened in 1926, its 1,750-foot main span made it the longest suspension bridge in the world. It was designed by Paul Cret, architect of the Rodin Museum. After a new, blue paint job and a lighting system specially designed to show off its contours, the bridge is more beautiful than ever. Start the 1.8-mile walk from either the Philadelphia or the Camden side. Only the south walkway is open, but that's the best view anyway. *5th and Vine Sts.,* ☎ *215/925–8780.* ☛ *Free.* ☉ *Daily (except a few days in winter when it gets too icy)* 6 AM*–around* 7 PM *(closes earlier in winter).*

Bryn Athyn Cathedral. Located at one of the most beautiful spots in the Philadelphia area is a spectacular cathedral built in 12th-century Romanesque and 14th-century Gothic styles. Atop a hill overlooking the Pennypack Valley, the cathedral is the episcopal seat of the Church of the New Jerusalem, a sect based on the writings of the Swedish scientist and mystic Emanuel Swedenborg. The main patrons of the church are descendants of John Pitcairn, an industrialist who made his fortune in paint and plate glass. Construction of the cathedral began in 1914 and went on for decades. It was built according to the medieval guild system: All materials—wood, metal, glass, stone—were brought to craftsmen at the site, and everything was fashioned by hand. The stained glass includes two colors, striated ruby and cobalt blue, found nowhere else in the Americas. Also on the hill is the former home of Raymond and Mildred Pitcairn, Glencairn, a neo-Romanesque building that's now a museum. *Rte. 232 (Huntingdon Pike) and Paper Mill Rd., Bryn Athyn 19009, 15 mi north of Center City,* ☎ *215/947–0266.* ☛ *Free.* ☉ *Weekdays 10–5. Visitors are welcome at services Sun. 9:30 and 11* AM*. Tours weekends 1–4:30* PM*. Visiting hrs sometimes preempted by special church events. Directions: Go north on Broad St. to Rte. 611, right on County Line Rd., south on Rte. 232 to the 2nd traffic light. Cathedral will be on your right.*

Philadelphia City Council. For drama, comedy, and adventure, nothing rivals the Philadelphia city government. Some of the 17-member legislative branch of municipal government are capable and dedicated, but lawmaking often takes a back seat to righteous indignation, playing to the crowd, outrage, and profanity. Fistfights between council members occasionally break out. In the past 20 years, a half dozen council members (including one former council president) have been convicted of crimes. Under the leadership of John Street, who became Council President in 1992, the council is becoming less "theater of the absurd" and more "political process." Bad news for theatergoers, good news for Philadelphians. *City Hall, Broad and Market Sts., Council Chamber, Room 400,* ☎ *215/686–3432.* ☛ *Free.* ☉ *Meets Thurs. at 10* AM*.*

ENIAC. Here's a chance for computer aficionados to see the place where the computer age dawned. During World War II, engineers at the Moore School of Engineering at the University of Pennsylvania undertook a secret project to develop the world's first all-electronic, large-scale, general-purpose digital computer. They called it ENIAC,

an acronym for electronic numerical integrator and calculator. The largest electronic machine in the world, it weighed 30 tons and contained 18,000 vacuum tubes—one of which, in the beginning, burned out every few seconds. While most of ENIAC is now in the Smithsonian Institution, a small portion is still on view at the Moore School (the room containing ENIAC, at the top of the right-hand staircase, is usually locked, but you can always see the exhibit through the glass wall). In addition, photos and informative signs tell ENIAC's story. *Moore School of Electrical Engineering, University of Pennsylvania, 200 S. 33rd St., ☎ 215/898–8294. Enter on 33rd St. just below Walnut St. ☛ Free. ☉ Weekdays 9–5.*

Laurel Hill Cemetery is beautiful and a great place for a stroll. John Notman, architect of the Athenaeum (*see* Libraries and Museums, *above*) and many other noted local buildings, designed Laurel Hill in 1836. It is an important example of an early, rural burial ground and the first cemetery in America designed by an architect. Its rolling hills that overlook the Schuylkill River, its rare trees, and monuments and mausoleums sculpted by greats such as Notman, Alexander Milne Calder, Alexander Stirling Calder, William Strickland, and Thomas U. Walter made it a popular picnic spot in the 19th century. Those buried in this 99-acre necropolis include prominent Philadelphians and Declaration of Independence signers. Burials still take place. *3822 Ridge Ave., East Fairmount Park, ☎ 215/228–8200. ☉ Weekdays 8–4, Sat. 9–1, closed Sun. Friends of Laurel Hill Cemetery arranges tours (☎ 215/648–0824). Directions: Go north on East River Dr., turn right on Ferry Rd. (1st street after 1st traffic light), go 1 block to Ridge Ave., turn right. Cemetery entrance is about ½ mi on your right.*

The Insectarium. Here you'll find a horrible, ugly, beautiful, diverse collection of 1,500 different creepy crawlers—tarantulas, giant centipedes, scorpions, assassin bugs, butterflies, and metallic beetles that look like gold pieces of jewelry. Even if you hate bugs, you'll love this place. Don't forget to check out the amazing bug gift shop. *8046 Frankfurt Ave., Northeast Philadelphia, ☎ 215/338–3000. ☛ $3. ☉ Mon.–Sat. 10–4.*

3 Shopping

EVEN WHEN IT COMES TO SHOPPING, tradition runs strong in Philadelphia. The leading department stores are city institutions: John Wanamaker has been at its current Chestnut Street location since 1877; Strawbridge & Clothier has been a family-run business since 1868. But Philadelphia—like all vibrant, cosmopolitan centers—is also fashion-forward in outlook. While you can buy a Chippendale-style grandfather clock at Wanamaker, you can also find the latest chartreuse-hued jeans at Zipperhead.

Updated by
Rathe Miller

For consumers with consuming passions, Philadelphia offers a vast array of goodies. Diamond baubles, bangles, and beads from Bailey, Banks, and Biddle? A photojournalist vest from Banana Republic? High-style Italian shoes from Bottini (Sylvester Stallone bought 12 pairs on his last visit)? A $500 reproduction of the inkwell used in the signing of the Declaration of Independence? Or, for that matter, a $1 mini-Liberty Bell? From the homey to the haute, Philadelphia can be a great shopping town.

The city has an upscale shopping district centered on 17th and Walnut streets, a jewelers' row, an antiques row, the first downtown indoor shopping mall in the United States, an outdoor food market that covers five city blocks, and department stores, including one of the oldest and most elegant in the country. Bargains are available, too—from discount stores, street vendors, and factory outlets (for the lowdown on Philly thrift stores, check out the book *The Thrift Shop Maniac's Guided Tours,* by Nancy Berman).

Here's a quick run-down of the city's leading shopping attractions. Most shop-till-you-droppers first head for the main shopping area of **Walnut Street,** between Broad Street and Rittenhouse Square, and the intersecting streets just north and south. These blocks are filled with boutiques, art galleries, jewelers, fine clothing stores, and many other unusual shops. At Broad and Walnut, the **Shops at the Bellevue** include Polo/Ralph Lauren, Gucci, and Tiffany & Company. On 18th Street in the block north of Rittenhouse Square, you'll find entrepreneurs both indoors and out: the youthful and trendy department store Urban Outfitters, a sidewalk vendor selling handmade Peruvian shawls, street artist Joe Barker painting watercolors of Philadelphia cityscapes, and a shop—Scoop De Ville—that sells more than 40 flavors of frozen yogurt.

The **Chestnut Street Transitway,** though somewhat seedy after dark, buzzes with urban vitality during the day. It has rare-book sellers, custom tailors, sporting goods stores, pinball arcades, and discount drugstores. At 17th and Chestnut you'll find **The Shops at Liberty Place.** The city's newest shopping complex includes more than 70 stores and restaurants arranged in two circular levels within a striking 90-foot glass-roofed atrium.

A block north of Chestnut Street is Philadelphia's landmark effort at urban renewal cum shopping, the **Gallery at Market East** (☎ 215/925–7162), America's first enclosed downtown shopping mall. The four-level, glass-roofed structure on Market Street between 8th and 11th contains 160 retailers, including 50 food outlets and two department stores—Strawbridge and Clothier (☎ 215/629–6000) and JCPenney (☎ 215/238–9100).

Across from the Gallery, at Market between 7th and 8th streets is **Market Place East** (☎ 215/592–8905). Saved from the wrecker's ball at

the eleventh hour, the former Lit Brothers Department Store went through a $75 million renovation to emerge as an office building featuring a five-level atrium with stores and restaurants.

Jewelers' Row, centered on Sansom Street between 7th and 8th, is one of the world's oldest and largest markets of precious stones: More than 350 retailers, wholesalers, and craftsmen operate here. The 700 block of Sansom Street is a brick-paved enclave occupied almost exclusively by jewelers.

Pine Street from 9th Street to 12th Street is Philadelphia's **Antiques Row.** The three-block area has dozens of antiques stores and curio shops, many specializing in period furniture and Colonial heirlooms.

Across the street from the Liberty Bell is the **Bourse** (5th St. between Market and Chestnut Sts., ☎ 215/625–0300), an elegantly restored 1895 commodities exchange building. The Bourse failed as an upscale minimall, but while the designer boutiques are gone, the six-story skylit atrium still contains a few fun shops catering to tourists such as Destination Philadelphia (Philly-related T-shirts) and Best of Philadelphia, as well as a festive international food court.

Finally decided on that new tattoo? Need supplies for your next witches' sabbath? Head to **South Street.** Philadelphia's main entertainment strip is also one of its major shopping areas, with most shops open in the evenings. From Front Street to 9th Street you'll find more than 300 unusual stores—high-fashion clothing, New Age books and health food, avant-garde art galleries,—and 100 restaurants. You'll find a few of the national chains, but 95% of the stores are individually owned, selling things you won't find in the mall back home.

If you want local color, nothing compares with South Philadelphia's **Italian Market.** On both sides of 9th Street from Christian Street to Washington Street, and spilling out onto the surrounding blocks, hundreds of outdoor stalls and indoor stores sell such food items as spices, cheese, pasta, fruits, vegetables, freshly slaughtered poultry and beef; household items; clothing; shoes; and other goods. It's crowded and smelly, and the vendors can be less than hospitable—but the food is fresh and the prices are reasonable.

Philadelphia's landmark department store **John Wanamaker** (☎ 215/422–2000) is, sadly, up for sale. Philadelphians are wondering how much longer they'll be able to shop, enjoy the pipe organ concerts, the Christmas light shows, and tell their friends to "meet me at the eagle"— a traditional Philly rendezvous spot at the statue in the store's grand court (*see* Tour 3 *in* Chapter 2, Exploring Philadelphia).

Strawbridge and Clothier (☎ 215/629–6000), whose main store is at 8th Street and Market Street in the Gallery, is the other leading department store. Founded in 1868, it is still operated by the Clothier and Strawbridge families and is the only independent regional department store left in the country. Once a month, Strawbridge's has Clover Day, with special sale prices on items throughout the store.

What attraction could there be in the cultural wasteland of northeast Philadelphia that rivals the Liberty Bell and the zoo in popularity? **Franklin Mills Mall** (☎ 215/632–1500), with 1.7 million square feet, 220 stores, and 2 food courts, could be nicknamed the Disneyland of shopping. Discount outlet stores include Ann Taylor, Saks Fifth Avenue Clearinghouse, and Last Call from Neiman Marcus. The mall is nearly a mile in length, and the parking lot holds almost 9,000 cars. You will get lost.

Local stores have sales throughout the year. If you're looking for a particular item, check the daily newspapers. Most stores accept traveler's checks and Visa, MasterCard, and American Express. Diners Club, Carte Blanche, and Discover are less widely accepted. Policies on personal checks vary. As in many big cities, it's unwise to carry much cash.

Pennsylvania has a 6% sales tax, and the city adds another 1%. These do not apply to clothing, medicine, and food bought in stores.

Downtown shopping hours are generally 9:30 or 10 AM to 5 or 6 PM. Many stores close at 9 PM on Wednesday. Most downtown stores are closed on Sunday, but the Bourse and the Gallery are open 12–5.

Antiques

Many dealers cluster on Antiques Row—Pine Street between 9th and 12th streets.

W. Graham Arader (1308 Walnut St., ☎ 215/735–8811). This is the flagship store of a highly respected chain that stocks the world's largest selection of 16th- to 19th-century prints and maps, specializing in botanicals, birds, and the American West.

Architectural Antiques Exchange (715 N. 2nd St., ☎ 215/922–3669). Victorian embellishments from saloons and apothecary shops, stained and beveled glass, gargoyles, and advertising memorabilia and all manner of collectibles will entice many.

Calderwood Gallery (1427 Walnut St., ☎ 215/568–7475). Art Nouveau and Art Deco furniture, glass, bronzes, and rugs tempt discerning collectors.

M. Finkel and Daughter (936 Pine St., ☎ 215/627–7797). Late–18th- and early 19th-century American furniture, quilts, needlework, samplers, and folk art make this an important outpost for Americana buffs.

Freeman Fine Arts (1808 Chestnut St., ☎ 215/563–9275). This is not only the city's most prominent auction house but it's also America's oldest (founded in 1805). Examine furniture, china, prints, and paintings on Monday and Tuesday; bid for them on Wednesday. Freeman's auctioned one of the original flyers on which the Declaration of Independence was printed and posted throughout the city. It went for $400,000.

Gargoyles (512 S. 3rd St., ☎ 215/629–1700) has 11,000 square feet of antiques and reproduction decorative and architectural pieces—archways, mantels, entranceways, carousel horses, stained-glass windows, and ornate mirrors.

G. B. Schaffer Antiques (1014 Pine St., ☎ 215/923–2263). Eighteenth, 19th-, and early 20th-century American furnishings, stained glass, silver, porcelain, paintings, and prints.

Vintage Instruments (1529 Pine St., ☎ 215/545–1100). Antique strings and woodwinds. Specializes in violins and also carries American fretted instruments—banjos, guitars, and mandolins.

Art

For current shows in Philadelphia's numerous galleries, see listings in *Philadelphia* or the Weekend section of the Friday *Philadelphia Inquirer.*

Bauman Rare Books, **13**

Best of Philadelphia, **40**

Body Shop de le Parfumier, **28**

Book Trader, **32**

Bourse Building, **29**

Calderwood Gallery, **2**

Chef's Market, **41**

Destination Philadelphia, **27**

Food Hall at Strawbridge and Clothier, **21**

G.B. Schaffer Antiques, **17**

Gallery at Market East, **20**

Gargoyles, **39**

Gilbert Luber Gallery, **12**

Hand of Aries, **35**

Harry Sable, **24**

Hats In The Belfry, **30**

Hibberd's, **10**

I. Goldberg, **16**

J.E. Caldwell, **5**

Jack Kelmer, **23**

John Wanamaker, **4**

Kamikaze Kids, **36**

Kosmin's Camera Exchange, **15**

Locks Gallery, **25**

M. Finkel and Daughter, **18**

Market Place East, **22**

Mid-City Camera Exchange, **9**

Neo Deco, **34**

Robin's Bookstore, **6**

Robinson Luggage Company, **7**

Roth Camera Repairs, **14**

School Gallery of the Pennsylvania Academy of the Fine Arts, **3**

Snyderman Gallery, **38**

Third Street Jazz and Rock, **26**

Tower Records, **31**

University of the Arts' Rosenwald-Wolf Gallery, **8**

Vintage Instruments, **1**

W. Graham Arader, **11**

Wine and Spirits Shoppe, **20**

The Works, **37**

Zipperhead, **33**

Shopping (Sansom and Walnut Streets)

Ludlow St.

Ranstead St.

**Shops at
Liberty Place**

39

17

40 41 42

18 19

51 52

Ionic St.

Stock Exchange Pl.

43

44

Sansom St.

20 21 22 23 24

45

46

53 54

Moravian St.

55

25 26 27 28 29 30

47 48

56 57 58

31 32 33 34

35

59

36

49

50

60

17th St.

16th St.

Sydenham St.

15th St.

Chancellor St.

St. James St.

Locust St.

N

37

Bouvier St.

Latimer St.

Latimer St.

| 0 | 110 yards |
| 0 | 100 meters |

16

38

Rittenhouse Sq.

William H. Allen, **1**
Wine Reserve, **31**

South Street or scattered about downtown. Over the past few years, Old City has become the hottest gallery area. One evening a month, from October to June, on the "First Friday" you can wander 2nd and 3rd streets above Market Street going from gallery to gallery. It's like a refined block-party, with refreshments and performance artists.

I. Brewster (1628 Walnut St., ☎ 215/731–9200). Contemporary paintings and prints by Louis Icart, Erté, Andy Warhol, and Red Grooms.

David David Gallery (260 S. 18th St., ☎ 215/735–2922). American and European paintings, drawings, and watercolors from the 16th to the 20th centuries.

Helen Drutt (1721 Walnut St., ☎ 215/735–1625). Contemporary American and European artists, with a focus on ceramics and jewelry.

Janet Fleisher (211 S. 17th St., ☎ 215/545–7562). Twentieth–century self-taught American artists.

Gross-McCleaf Gallery (127 S. 16th St., ☎ 215/665–8138). Works by prominent and emerging artists, with emphasis on Philadelphia painters.

Locks Gallery (600 Washington Sq. South, ☎ 215/629–1000). Contemporary regional, national, and international painters, sculptors, and mixed-media artists.

Gilbert Luber Gallery (1220 Walnut St., ☎ 215/732–2996). Japanese and Chinese antique and contemporary prints and Thai and Balinese artifacts.

Muse Gallery (60 N. 2nd St., ☎ 215/627–5310). Established in 1978 by the Muse Foundation for the Visual Arts, Muse Gallery is a women's cooperative committed to increasing the visibility of women's artwork and presenting experimental work in a variety of media.

Newman Galleries (1625 Walnut St., ☎ 215/563–1779). A range of works, from 19th-century paintings to contemporary lithographs and sculpture. Strong on 20th-century painters from the Bucks County area.

School Gallery of the Pennsylvania Academy of the Fine Arts (1301 Cherry St., ☎ 215/972–7600). Rotating exhibits of works by faculty, alumni, and students.

University of the Arts' Rosenwald-Wolf Gallery (333 S. Broad St., ☎ 215/875–1116). Works by faculty and students, and local, national, and international artists.

Schwarz Gallery (1806 Chestnut St., ☎ 215/563–4887). Eighteenth-to 20th-century American and European paintings, concentrating on Philadelphia artists of the past.

Snyderman Gallery (303 Cherry St., ☎ 215/238–9576). One-of-a-kind handmade furniture pieces and glass objects.

The Works (319 South St., ☎ 215/922–7775). Contemporary, decorative, and applied American crafts in wood, fiber, ceramics, metals, and glass.

Books

AIA Bookstore (17th and Sansom Sts., ☎ 215/569–3188). Run by the Philadelphia chapter of the American Institute of Architects (AIA), this shop specializes in architectural theory, building construction, interior design, furnishings, blueprint posters, international magazines, and unusual gifts.

William H. Allen (2031 Walnut St., ☎ 215/563–3398). One of the city's best collections of used and scholarly books, specialties here are history, literature, and philosophy. Note the extensive collection of books on ancient Greece and Rome, in English and the original Greek or Latin.

Barnes and Noble (1901 Spraul Rd., Broomall, about 20 min outside Philadelphia, ☎ 610/353–3255). One of the largest and most popular mega-chains, Barnes and Noble bookstores provide a vast selection and elegant commercial interiors. Classical music in the background and strategically placed benches and chairs make browsing here particularly comfortable. The store that used to be on Chestnut Street in central Philly recently closed, but this superstore helps fill in the gap.

Bauman Rare Books (1215 Locust St., ☎ 215/546–6466). An antiquarian bookstore with volumes dating as far back as the 15th century, it's a treasure trove for collectors in the fields of law, science, literature, travel, and exploration. There is also a print and map collection.

Book Trader (501 South St., ☎ 215/925–0219). You'll find great browsing on the two floors of this eclectic used-book store; prices are on the high side. Open daily 10 AM–midnight.

Borders (1727 Walnut St., ☎ 215/568–7400). Some natives find this to be the friendliest bookstore in Philadelphia, and it's probably the biggest. You can sit on a couch, listen to live guitar music, and read for hours. The 110,000 titles and more than half-million books are spread over a three-level, 20,000-square-foot selling floor. Each of the 50 staffers had to pass a literature test to be hired. Bibliophiles get to know each other at the second-floor espresso bar. Saturday-morning children's programs are held at 11:30.

Encore (609 Chestnut St., ☎ 215/627–4557). A discount chain with a dozen locations in the area, Encore offers 30% off *New York Times* best-sellers and up to 80% off closeouts and remainders.

Joseph Fox (1724 Sansom St., ☎ 215/563–4184). A small bookstore specializing in art, architecture, and design.

Hibberd's (1306 Walnut St., ☎ 215/546–8811). Rare and used books, remainders, and a large selection of unusual art books are the sizeable draws for book aficionados.

How-to-Do-It Bookshop (1608 Sansom St., ☎ 215/563–1516). Want to build a computer, grow rutabagas, groom your poodle? If there's a book telling you how to do something, chances are this unique place (with over 40,000 titles) will have it.

Rittenhouse Bookstore (1706 Rittenhouse Sq., ☎ 215/545–6072). Known as the best medical bookstore in Philadelphia, this establishment may be able to get the book you want overnight if you can't find it in stock.

Robin's Bookstore (108 S. 13th St., ☎ 215/735–9600). Not the biggest bookstore in town, and maybe not the best, but definitely the sentimental favorite of devoteés of literature, poetry, and minority studies. Owner Larry Robin has been promoting literature and fighting literary censorship for more than 30 years. Robin's has an exceptional variety of hard-to-find intellectual titles. Book fans are drawn to its frequent poetry readings and book signings by local authors.

University of Pennsylvania Bookstore (3729 Locust Walk, ☎ 215/898–7595). With over 60,000 titles of both popular and scholarly volumes,

this bookstore is especially strong in linguistics, anthropology, psychology, and sociology. The Middle East section may be the only place in town to buy a book on Kurdish grammar.

Whodunit (1931 Chestnut St., ☎ 215/567–1478). The city's only store specializing in mysteries, spy stories, and adventure books. It also stocks out-of-print mysteries. Over 25,000 titles. Owner Art Bourgeau has published six mystery books and a nonfiction book on mystery writing.

Clothing

Women's Clothing
Asta De Blue (265 S. 20th St., ☎ 215/732–0550). A boutique in a brownstone off Rittenhouse Square, this is a hot place for upbeat, urban-contemporary clothing, jewelry, accessories and gifts. Key collections include Zelda, Ghost, and Annie Kwan. The owners say they have the largest collection of Arche footwear outside Manhattan.

Jaeger International Sportswear (1719 Walnut St., ☎ 215/751–9285). With its classic signature, Jaeger offers a European collection of distinctive clothing, from classics to the latest silhouettes and proportions.

Knit Wit (1721 Walnut St., ☎ 215/564–4760). High fashion clothes and accessories from sportswear to cocktail dresses are the focus here.

Mendelsohn (229 S. 18th St., ☎ 215/546–6333). Classic European and specialty clothing attract a devoted clientele.

Plage Tahiti (128 S. 17th St., ☎ 215/569–9139). This leading showcase for promising young high-fashion designers includes a wide selection of chic and charming swimwear.

Toby Lerner (117 S. 17th St., ☎ 215/568–5760). This spot offers high-fashion apparel with strong classic lines, plus a full line of shoes.

Men's Clothing
Allure (1509 Walnut St., ☎ 215/561–4242). Classic and stylish Italian clothing and furnishings draws a cosmopolitan crowd.

Boyd's (1818 Chestnut St., ☎ 215/564–9000). The largest, single-store men's clothier in the country. Its nine shops feature the traditional English look, avant-garde Italian imports, and dozens of other styles and designers. There are shops for extra tall, large, and short men; an excellent café for lunch; valet parking; and 60 tailors on the premises. Really! We counted them.

Brooks Brothers (1500 Chestnut St., ☎ 215/564–4100). The oldest men's clothing store in America (founded in New York in 1818). Synonymous with Ivy League business clothing: conservative suits, button-down shirts, and striped ties.

Structure (Shops at Liberty Place, 1625 Chestnut St., ☎ 215/851–0835) is hip and stylish, with relatively decent prices. They sell casual clothes, such as silk shirts and baggy pleated pants, in bold colors. Sales can yield real bargains.

Wayne Edwards (1521 Walnut St., ☎ 215/563–6801). Exclusive lines of classic contemporary designer clothing from Italy, Japan, France, and the United States.

Women's and Men's Clothing
Banana Republic (1716 Walnut St., ☎ 215/735–2247). This store is part of the national chain that helped make famous—and still sells—the photojournalist vest (with a plethora of pockets) and the Kenya

convertible pants (with the hidden zippers that convert them into shorts).

Burberrys Ltd. (1705 Walnut St., ☎ 215/557–7400). Named after Thomas Burberry, who designed the trench coat in the mid-1850s, this British-owned establishment features British raincoats, overcoats, sportcoats, and cashmere sweaters. High quality, high prices.

Destination Philadelphia (Bourse Bldg., 21 S. 5th St., ☎ 215/440–0233). A clothing store where every item bears some form of Philadelphia logo or design—from a soft pretzel to a line drawing of Billy Penn. Hats, jackets, sweatshirts, and more than 40 styles of T-shirts.

Hats In The Belfry (247 South St., ☎ 215/922–6770, and 125 S. 18th St., ☎ 215/567–0037). Designer hats, practical hats, formal hats, silly hats, Panamas, baseball caps, and more add the finishing touch to your outfit.

Neo Deco (414 South St., ☎ 215/928–0627). European-style contemporary clothing: sportswear, shoes, and jewelry.

Ultimate Sock (The Shops at Liberty Place, 1625 Chestnut St., ☎ 215/567–0801). Designer socks and hosiery by Hue, DKNY, Calvin Klein, and Hot Sox, plus hundreds of novelty socks—some even play music. Prices range from $4 to $20.

Urban Outfitters (1801 Walnut St., ☎ 215/569–3131). What started out just a few years ago as a storefront selling used jeans to students in West Philadelphia, is now a trend-setting chain found on campuses across the country. This Beaux Arts mansion now houses the flagship store, selling hip clothing, books, unusual toys, and apartment accessories.

Zipperhead (407 South St., ☎ 215/928–1123). As you enter this place, chances are you'll have to step around a teenager and his parents arguing whether or not to go in. For 15 years this has been the alternative clothing landmark for the spiked-hair-and-nose-ring set. Offerings here include motorcycle jackets, rock band T-shirts, and hard-to-find body jewelry for those-hard-to-pierce places.

Children's Clothing

Born Yesterday (1901 Walnut St., ☎ 215/568–6556). Unusual selection of clothing and toys for tots. Handmade goods, imported fashions, and styles you won't find elsewhere.

Children's Boutique (1717 Walnut St., ☎ 215/563–3881). A look between conservative and classic in infant to preteen clothes; complete wardrobes, specialty gifts, and handmade items.

Kamikaze Kids (527 S. 4th St., ☎ 215/574–9800). Handmade fashions by local designers for infants to preteens.

Food

Chef's Market (231 South St., ☎ 215/925–8360). Philly's ultimate gourmet supermarket prepares 60 to 70 different entrées every day, stocks several hundred kinds of cheeses, sells goods from its own bakery, and is a fish market and meat market. Packaged items include 150 varieties of imported jams, 40 olive oils, and 60 flavored vinegars.

Fante's (1006 S. 9th St., ☎ 215/922–5557). One of the oldest gourmet supply stores in the country, it has the largest selection of coffee makers and cooking equipment in the United States. It's located in the Italian Market. Family-owned since 1906, it is famous for oddball kitchen

gadgets such as truffle shavers, pineapple peelers, and croquembouche molds; it supplies restaurants and bakeries all over the country and overseas.

Food Hall at Strawbridge and Clothier (8th and Market Sts., ☎ 215/629–6000). You can eat in or take out breads, cheeses, salads, and ice cream. It features frequent cooking demonstrations with free samples—and check out its large candy department and charcuterie.

Godiva Chocolatier (Shops at Liberty Place, 1625 Chestnut St., ☎ 215/963–0810). At $3 for a single piece of hand-dipped fruit to $29 for a one-pound box, it doesn't get any sweeter than this.

Kitchen Kapers (213 S. 17th St., ☎ 215/546–8059). Fine cookware, French copper, cutlery, coffees, teas, and special foods.

Gifts and Novelties

Country Floors (1706 Locust St., ☎ 215/545–1040). Decorators love the ceramic and terra-cotta hand-painted tiles from the U.S. and all over Europe (mostly for floors and walls, but individual tiles can make great decorative art).

Dandelion (1718 Sansom St., ☎ 215/972–0999). Almost everything sold in this store is handmade: jewelry, ceramics, porcelains, and glass imported from Indonesia, India, and Africa. They also have Native American jewelry and handbuilt pots.

Best of Philadelphia (Bourse Bldg., 21 S. 5th St., ☎ 215/440–7016). Here's the fun place for cheap Philly schlock: over 100 different items, including earrings, flags, jigsaw puzzles, coloring books, Ben Franklin key chains, T-shirts, and, of course, Liberty Bells.

Hand of Aries (620 S. 4th St., ☎ 215/923–5264). Everything for the discriminating witch—books, candles, incense, tarot cards, ritual robes, capes, and long dresses (black only).

Holt's Tobacconist (1522 Walnut St., ☎ 215/732–8500). The city's oldest (1898) and largest purveyor of tobacco, cigars, and lighters, Holt's also has the city's largest selection of writing instruments.

Touches (225 S. 15th St., ☎ 215/546–1221). Upscale shoppers come to this attractive shop for its handmade shawls, handbags, belts, unusual jewelry, and children's gifts.

Urban Objects (1724 Sansom St., ☎ 215/557–9474). Eclectic collection of contemporary gifts, home accessories, and antiques (both authentic and reproductions), lamps, and pictures. Many objects are imported from Europe and Asia but are reasonably priced.

Warner Bros. Store (Liberty Place, 17th and Chestnut Sts., ☎ 215/981–0680). For those who love Bugs, Sylvester, Daffy, and Tweety on their mugs, T-shirts, key chains, puzzles, and golf club covers, this is the place. The store's gallery of animation art has 'toon lithographs for $150 and original cels for up to $1700.

Jewelry

J. E. Caldwell (Juniper and Chestnut Sts., ☎ 215/864–7800). A local landmark since 1839, the store is adorned with antique, handblown crystal chandeliers by Baccarat, making it as elegant as the jewels it sells. Along with traditional and modern jewelry, Caldwell's has one of the city's largest selections of giftware and stationery, and a bridal registry.

Bailey, Banks, and Biddle (16th and Chestnut Sts., ☎ 215/564–6200). Since 1832, it is known for diamond and gold jewelry, objets d'art, silver, crystal, and gift-wrap department.

Jack Kelmer (717 Chestnut St., ☎ 215/627–8350). Diamonds, gold jewelry, and gifts at below retail price.

Harry Sable (8th and Sansom Sts., ☎ 215/627–4014). In 1996 Harry ("king of the wedding bands") Sable marks his 50th year of selling engagement rings, diamond rings, gold jewelry, and watches.

Richard Kenneth (202 S. 17th St., ☎ 215/545–3355). Jewelry from the late-Georgian, Victorian, Art Nouveau, Art Deco, and '40s-retro periods are the highlights here. Kenneth also specializes in repairs and appraisals.

Luggage and Leather Goods

Deacon's Luggage (124 S. 16th St., ☎ 215/567–5584). Luggage, briefcases, and accessories at discount prices.

Robinson Luggage Company (Broad and Walnut Sts., ☎ 215/735–9859). Popular brands of luggage, leather, and travel accessories. The selection of briefcases and attaché cases is the largest in the Delaware Valley.

Perfumes

Crabtree and Evelyn (Bourse Bldg., 21 S. 5th St., ☎ 215/625–9256). Toiletries and soaps, many imported from Britain and France, as well as specialty foods.

The Body Shop de le Parfumier (Bourse Bldg., 21 S. 5th St., ☎ 215/922–7660). This "scent boutique" for men and women imports new fragrances, some not yet available elsewhere in the United States. Also carries cosmetics, perfume bottles, discontinued scents, and accessories.

Photography

Kosmin's Camera Exchange (927 Arch St., ☎ 215/627–8231). Film, motion picture equipment, slide projectors, screens, darkroom supplies, and a half-dozen brands of cameras.

Mid-City Camera Exchange (1316 Walnut St., ☎ 215/735–2522). Sales, service, rentals. This major "stockhouse" has a large line of darkroom equipment and all major camera brands in all formats. It also buys and trades used cameras.

Roth Camera Repairs (1015 Chestnut St., Jefferson Bldg. lobby, Room 102, ☎ 215/922–2498). If you have camera trouble, here's the place to have it fixed. Tourists should note that the store prides itself on extra-quick service.

Records and Music

Theodor Presser (1718 Chestnut St., ☎ 215/568–0964). The best selection of sheet music in Center City draws musicians from far and wide. The store specializes in classical, but also carries pop and will special order anything.

Third Street Jazz and Rock (20 N. 3rd St., ☎ 215/627–3366). Still some vinyl here (a few hard-to-find jazz and soul records) but now mostly

CDs, specializing in rock, New Wave, reggae, Caribbean, and African music. Salespeople are particularly knowledgeable.

Tower Records (610 South St., ☎ 215/574–9888). Open 9 AM to midnight 365 days a year, Tower stocks more than 250,000 CDs and tapes—the largest selection in the city. You can watch music videos on the 20 screens on three floors. Classical music lovers head over to the annex across the street.

Shoes

Beige (1715 Walnut St., ☎ 215/564–2395). Women's Italian leather shoes in sizes 4–12, priced toward the high end.

Bottino (121 S. 18th St., ☎ 215/854–0907). Men's shoes and accessories, all handmade and imported from Italy. Some very big feet get shod here including regular customers Michael Jordan and Sylvester Stallone.

Sherman Brothers Shoes (1520 Sansom St., ☎ 215/561–4550). An "off-price" retailer of men's shoes with name-brand merchandise, excellent service, and low prices. Extra-wide and extra-narrow widths, sizes to 15 and 16; 28 lines of shoes.

Strega (1521 Walnut St., ☎ 215/564–5932). A wide range of looks for men; exclusive footwear, the custom-made Edward Green line from England, and many top Italian designers.

Sporting Goods

Everyone's Racquet (132 S. 17th St., ☎ 215/665–1221). Everything related to racket sports: tennis, racquetball, badminton, squash. Next-day racket-stringing service.

Finish Line Sports (1915 Walnut St., ☎ 215/569–9957). Specialists in shoes and gear for triathlon sports: running, swimming, and cycling. Also aerobic and workout shoes and gear.

I. Goldberg (902 Chestnut St., ☎ 215/925–9393). An army-navy-and-everything store. Not stylish but practical, with emphasis on sporting apparel and camping gear. Crammed with government-surplus, military-style clothing, jeans and workclothes, unusual footware, and exclusive foreign imports. Huge stock of sizes. Rummaging here is a sport in itself.

Toys

Einstein Presents of Mind (1627 Walnut St., ☎ 215/665–3622). This place has everything from a large selection of nonfiction children's books to Gorbachev and KGB dolls to mechanical toys for executives—you name it—and they're all unique.

Fat Jack's Comicrypt (2006 Sansom St., ☎ 215/963–0788). For more than twenty years, Fat Jack (his real name is Mike) has been buying and selling old and new comics at catalogue prices. With over 500,000 available, this is the largest selection in the Philadelphia area.

Past, Present, Future (24 S. 18th St., ☎ 215/854–0444). Distinctive toys, handcrafted jewelry and ceramics, kaleidoscopes, and children's books.

What's Your Game (The Shops at Liberty Place, 1625 Chestnut St., ☎ 215/567–0772). Thousands of puzzles and games. French "Arjew" wooden puzzles; metal blacksmith "Tavern" puzzles.

Wine

Wine and Spirits Shoppe (819 Chestnut St., ☎ 215/560–6190). One of the best selections of fine wines and liquors in a city where liquor stores are state run. For a better selection you have to go to New Jersey.

Wine Reserve (205 S. 18th St., ☎ 215/560–4529). Selling fine wines and cognacs exclusively, this shop stocks wines you won't find in any other state store in Pennsylvania. You can pick up an extra bottle of Louis XIII Cognac for about $900.

Bargain Shopping

Cambridge Clothing Factory Outlet (1520 Sansom St., 2nd Floor, ☎ 215/568–8248). A manufacturers' outlet for men with 10 national brands starting at 40% off retail. Immediate alterations for out-of-town buyers.

Daffy's (1700 Chestnut St., ☎ 215/963–9996). Housed in an attractive Egyptian-deco–style building (formerly Bonwit Teller), Daffy's carries higher-end American and European designs for men, women, and children at 40–75% off list (sometimes even more with special markdowns).

Night Dressing (2100 Walnut St., ☎ 215/627–5244). Offers 50% off list prices on designer lingerie, 15% off hosiery.

Thos. David Factory Store (401 Race St., ☎ 215/922–4659). Upstairs they make it; downstairs they sell it—at almost wholesale prices. High-quality men's and women's business and sportswear.

4 Sports and the Outdoors

PHILADELPHIA SPORTS FANS have lots to cheer about. Their professional teams—the Eagles (football), Phillies (baseball), Flyers (ice hockey), and 76ers (basketball)—are all world-caliber and frequently make it to the playoffs. At the Spectrum or Veterans Stadium in the South Philadelphia sports complex, there is always a crowd: Philadelphians buy more tickets to pro sporting events than do residents of any other U.S. city.

Updated by
Rathe Miller

There are a myriad other sports attractions in the city, but two activities—and images—come immediately to mind. The first is one immortalized in a canvas by Thomas Eakins, Philadelphia's greatest painter, of a patrician oarsman rowing on the Schuylkill River in an elegant single scull. Today, the scene that Eakins depicted in the 19th-century is still enacted every week when scores of sculls are launched from Boathouse Row, a string of Victorian houses along Kelly Drive, now home to the city's many rowing clubs.

The second image, of course, is that of boxer Rocky Balboa, pungently captured by Sylvester Stallone in the *Rocky* movie series. Had Rocky been a real Philadelphia boxer, he would have fought at the Blue Horizon, the legendary fight club located at 1314 N. Broad Street (☎ 215/763–0500: The club has more than a thousand seats—but every one is close to the action.

Participant Sports and Fitness

Going out to the ball game has taken on new meaning in the "Decade of the Home Athlete," who is just as likely to be playing as observing. Philadelphia offers a wide variety of places for the player to test his skills.

Bicycling
A treat for cyclists is to ride along the east side of the Schuylkill River, cross Falls Bridge, and return on the west side of the river. This 8.2-mile loop takes about an hour of casually paced biking. Another great ride is Forbidden Drive in the Wissahickon (*see* Tour of Fairmount Park *in* Chapter 2, Exploring), a 5½-mile dirt and gravel bridle path along a stream. The **Bicycle Club of Philadelphia** (☎ 215/440–9983) organizes bike tours, from afternoon outings to week-long events. Bikes were available for rental at 1 Boathouse Row, presently undergoing renovation. Call Fairmount Park (☎ 215/685–0052) to find out the latest rental information.

Boating and Canoeing
Paddle or row through Fairmount Park along the scenic Schuylkill River, but yield the right of way to Olympic-caliber scullers speeding by. Rowboats and canoes had been available for rental at the **Public Canoe House** on Kelly Drive, now being renovated. Call Fairmount Park (☎ 215/685–0052) for the latest rental information.

Bowling
Bowling in Philadelphia seems to have lost some of its popularity. Alleys are no longer located downtown, but you can still bowl in other parts of the city. Two alleys worth trying are **Adams Lanes** (Adams Ave. and Foulkrod St., ☎ 215/533–1221, hours vary) and **Oregon Bowling Lanes** (24th St. and Oregon Ave., ☎ 215/389–2200, open daily 9 AM–11:30 PM).

Fishing

On the banks of Wissahickon Creek and Pennypack Creek, the catch varies but fishing is always good. Both creeks are stocked for the mid-April through December season. You'll need a license ($12.50–$25.50): You can get one at certain local sporting-goods stores and at K-Mart (424 Oregon Ave., ☎ 215/336–1778).

Golf

Philadelphia has six 18-hole courses that are open to the public. Cobbs Creek is the most challenging; Roosevelt is the easiest.

Cobbs Creek and Karakung. For those who love lots of golf action, these are two adjacent courses. Cobbs Creek plays in and around the creek itself, making for lovely vistas and challenging shots. It is the most difficult of the city courses. Karakung has hilly fairways and smaller greens. Both are par 71. *7200 Lansdowne Ave., ☎ 215/877–8707. Greens fees: $16–$22 weekdays, $19–$26 weekends and holidays.*

Franklin D. Roosevelt. A flat, relatively easy, par 69, which is particularly recommended for beginners. *20th St. and Pattison Ave., ☎ 215/462–8997. Greens fees: $18 weekdays, $21 weekends.*

J. F. Byrne. A short, but semi-challenging course, with small greens and water on six holes, rated par 67. *9500 Leon St., ☎ 215/632–8666. Greens fees: $16 weekdays, $20 weekends.*

Juniata. With lots of hills, trees, and the Frankford Creek running through it, Juniata is an impressive par 63. *L and Cayuga Sts., ☎ 215/743–4060. Greens fees: $16 weekdays, $19 weekends.*

Walnut Lane. Narrow, tree-lined fairways make this short (4500 yards) course a semi-challenging par 62. *Walnut La. and Henry Ave., ☎ 215/482–3370. Greens fees: $15 weekdays, $16 weekends.*

Outside Philadelphia, the privately owned **Valley Forge Golf Club** near Valley Forge National Historic Park is open to the public. Trees, doglegs, and small greens make this 6000 yard, par 71, a challenging 18-hole course. *401 N. Gulph Rd., King of Prussia, ☎ 610/337–1776. Green fees: $19 weekdays, $23 weekends.*

Health Clubs

Some of the downtown clubs allow nonmembers (with photo IDs) day guest privileges for around $10. Three good facilities are: **Gold's Gym** (834 Chestnut St., ☎ 215/592–9644); **12th Street Gym** (204 S. 12th St., ☎ 215/985–4092); and **Rittenhouse Square Fitness Club** (2002 Rittenhouse Sq., ☎ 215/985–4095).

Hiking

Hiking takes on an added exciting dimension when you opt for organized hikes with the following organizations:

Hosteling International/American Youth Hostels (☎ 215/925–6004). Arranges day hikes on weekends, and overnight hikes, mainly along the Horseshoe Trail, many starting from Valley Forge National Park.

Batona Hiking Club (☎ 215/659–3921). Hikers meet Sunday mornings at a central Philadelphia location (such as Broad and Arch Sts.) and carpool to hiking areas within a two-hour drive of the city, including the Appalachian Trail, the Delaware Water Gap, and the New Jersey Pine Barrens. Hikes range from 7 to 12 miles and tend to be more strenuous than those of the other clubs.

The Department of Recreation sponsors the **Wanderlust Hiking Club** (☎ 215/580–4847). Relatively easy hikes of 5 to 8 miles, many through

Fairmount Park and Pennypack Park, begin every Saturday afternoon at 1:30.

Horseback Riding

Of the numerous bridle paths coursing through Philadelphia, the most popular are the trails of the Wissahickon in the northwest, Pennypack Park in the northeast, and Cobbs Creek Park in the southwest. Riding academies that offer instruction and rentals include **Circle K Stables** (4220 Holmesburg Ave., ☎ 215/335–9975; $30/hr for lessons, $20/hr to rent) and **Ashford Farms** (River Rd., Miquon, ☎ 610/825–9838; trail ride fees are $25/hr, lessons $30–$40).

Ice Skating

You can skate outdoors—with the Delaware River and Benjamin Franklin Bridge as a backdrop—daily, from November to March, at the **Blue Cross RiverRink** (Penn's Landing between Market and Chestnut Sts., ☎ 215/636–1666). The **University of Pennsylvania Class of 1923 Ice Rink** (3130 Walnut St., ☎ 215/898–1923) is open to the public at various times through the school year.

Jogging and Running

Joggers can be seen traipsing up and down streets all over the city, but probably no area is favored more than Kelly and West River Drives, a scenic 8-mile route stretching from the Art Museum along one bank of the Schuylkill River, across Falls Bridge, and back down the other bank to the museum. Then, of course, there are the steps of the Art Museum itself, host to Rocky-like runners who raise their arms in salute to an early-morning jaunt.

Fairmount Park—especially along the river drives and Wissahickon Creek—is a natural for joggers and runners. Forbidden Drive along the Wissahickon offers more than 5 miles of soft-surface trail along a picturesque creek in a secluded valley. Only runners, walkers, bikers and horses—no motor vehicles allowed.

Similar to the trail along the Wissahickon, though not as nice, Pennypack Park in the northeast section of the city has an 8-mile, macadam trail along the Pennypack Creek. Those interested in the ultimate in running—through wide-open spaces on bike trails, horse trails, and grassy hills and dales—have to head outside of Philadelphia for Valley Forge National Park.

From dawn to dusk, the south walkway of the Benjamin Franklin Bridge provides a tough but rewarding 3.6-mile round-trip run, with a terrific view of the Delaware River waterfront.

Tennis

Fairmount Park has more than 100 free public courts, but many players must bring their own nets. Call the **Department of Recreation** (☎ 215/686–3600) for information.

Many indoor court facilities are in the Philadelphia area. The only one close to Center City, the **Robert P. Levy Tennis Pavilion,** has eight courts open weekdays 7 AM–11 PM, weekends 8 AM–10 PM (closed weekends July and Aug.) *3130 Walnut St.,* ☎ *215/898–4741. Yearly membership fee $70, plus $22–$26/hr.*

Spectator Sports

During the 1980s, Philadelphia became known as the "City of Champions," thanks to teams more accustomed to post-season play than not. Today, Philadelphians remains avid sports fans who support both pro-

fessional and collegiate teams. The major-league sports teams play their home games in the sports complex at Broad Street and Pattison Avenue—the Phillies and the Eagles at Veterans Stadium, the 76ers and the Flyers at the Spectrum. Some collegiate games are played there too; others are played on the campuses of the various colleges and universities.

Tickets to professional baseball, basketball, football, and hockey games are available at Veterans Stadium or the Spectrum, at Ticketron outlets, at ticket agencies, and by mail and phone from the respective teams.

Baseball
Philadelphia Phillies, Veterans Stadium, 3501 S. Broad St., Box 7575, 19101, ☎ 215/463–1000. Apr.–Oct.

Basketball
Philadelphia 76ers, The Spectrum, Broad St. and Pattison Ave., Box 25050, 19147, ☎ 215/339–7676. Nov.–Apr.

Collegiate, "Big Five" basketball features the teams from LaSalle, St. Joseph's, Temple, University of Pennsylvania, and Villanova. *Big Five Office, Hutchinson Gym, 220 S. 32nd St., 19104, ☎ 215/898–4747. Dec.–Mar.*

Bicycling
One of the world's top four bicycling events, the **CoreStates Pro Cycling Championship,** is held each June. The 156-mile race starts and finishes at Benjamin Franklin Parkway, with 10 loops including the infamous Manayunk "Wall." *☎ 215/636–1666.*

Football
Philadelphia Eagles, Veterans Stadium, 3501 S. Broad St., 19148, ☎ 215/463–5500. Sept.–Dec.

Hockey
Philadelphia Flyers, The Spectrum, Broad St. and Pattison Ave., 19148, ☎ 215/755–9700. Oct.–Apr.

Horse Racing
Thoroughbred racing takes place at **Philadelphia Park** (Street Rd., Bensalem 19020, ☎ 215/639–9000). Post time is usually at 12:30 PM daily except Wednesday and Thursday year-round. At **Garden State Park** (Rte. 70, Cherry Hill, NJ 08034, ☎ 609/488–8400) the post time is 7:30 PM Wednesday through Sunday. Thoroughbred racing runs January through June, harness racing September through December. For off-track betting, the **Turf Club Inner City** (1635 Market St., ☎ 215/246–1556) is open daily 11–11.

Rowing
The elegant boathouses, the regattas, the placid Schuylkill River, and a climate that allows an average of 360 rowing days a year all make Philadelphia the rowing capital of the world. From February to October, you can watch single and team races out on the river, usually from 5 AM to dusk. Dozens of major meets are held here every year including the largest rowing event in the country, the **Dad Vail Regatta,** held in May with up to 500 sculls from over 100 colleges (for spectators, free shuttle buses are provided from remote parking areas). Also in May, the **Stotesbury Cup Regatta** includes more than 2,500 students from 110 schools. More than a thousand individual and club member rowers compete in the 96-year-old **Independence Day Regatta,** held around July 4. For information on Dad Vail, ☎ 215/248–2600; all other events, ☎ 215/332–8531.

Track and Field

The **Penn Relays,** the world's largest and oldest amateur track meet, held the last week of April at the University of Pennsylvania's Franklin Field, features world-class performers in track and field. The **Philadelphia Distance Run,** the nation's top half-marathon, takes place in September. For more information on these events, call 215/685–0052. The **Philadelphia Marathon** (☎ 215/686–3645), runs through Center City and along the Schuylkill River and is held the Sunday before Thanksgiving. The **Broad Street Run** (☎ 215/686–3614), a 10-miler down Broad Street, is held in May.

Tennis

The **U.S. Pro Indoor Tennis Championships** take place at the Spectrum (☎ 215/336–3600), usually in February. More than 60 of the world's top pros compete.

5 Dining

NOT SO MANY YEARS AGO, a guide to fine dining in Philadelphia would have been one of the shortest—and saddest—books in the world. With very few exceptions, the local restaurant scene was a woeful collection of chop houses and pretentious "Continental" establishments that were expensive (at least for those days) and uniformly mediocre.

Updated by
Rathe Miller

Today Philadelphia is regarded as one of the hottest restaurant cities in the world. Seeds of change were evident in the mid-1970s. Small "boutique" restaurants began opening, particularly in the Society Hill section of town. A new core of demanding restaurant-goers and responsive restaurateurs became the nucleus of Philadelphia's widely-heralded "restaurant renaissance." Storefront restaurants began to offer food as highly personal as their decor: mismatched china and flatware, hand-me-down furniture, poster art, and jungles of hanging plants.

By 1990, Philadelphia had been almost completely transformed from a hash-and-mash gastronomic desert into a first-class restaurant city. These days, it's a town that lovingly supports America's finest dining establishment (according to some critics), Le Bec-Fin. It's enjoying the second generation of the restaurant renaissance but the "Early Attic" look has now been replaced with sleek settings—typified by the spectacular scene-arena of the Striped Bass, recently hailed by *Esquire* as "Restaurant of the Year."

FROM HAUTE CUISINE TO HOAGIES

For fine dining, you can choose from great steak houses, hotel gourmet dining, or French haute cuisine. The list of national cuisines reads like a roll call at the United Nations. Chinatown alone has over fifty restaurants and if you want Italian, South Philadelphia is an entire section of the city where the "red gravy" flows.

And then there is the "Philadelphia Cuisine" that doesn't get much attention from *Bon Appetit* or *Gourmet*: cheesesteaks, hoagies, soft pretzels with mustard, water ices—few Philadelphians aren't addicted to at least one of them. "We are the junk food capital of the world," says Mayor Ed Rendell. Visitors should not leave town before adequately sampling from the more than 100 varieties of Tastykakes (Butterscotch Krimpets are the number-one seller). Goldenberg's Peanut Chews, available at candy stands everywhere, can be habit forming.

Philly restaurants have always been reasonably priced (strikingly so by New York standards). While there are outposts of empty-the-wallet luxury dining, the fact remains that you can enjoy a meal at an excellent French restaurant such as Alouette for under $35. Only the fanciest restaurants require a jacket and tie for men (most places have a liberal dress policy: anything dressier than jeans and T-shirts is acceptable). Keep in mind that Philadelphia is a leading convention city (especially in the spring and fall), so it's always a good idea to make reservations for popular restaurants.

From the hundreds of restaurants in the city, we have selected a representative sampling to please every taste. They are grouped by type of cuisine and ranked by price category, and a handy neighborhood reference is provided along with the street address.

DISTRICT BY DISTRICT

Philadelphia's better restaurants are concentrated in the downtown area defined by the Schuylkill and Delaware Rivers, Vine Street to the

north, and Federal Street to the south. To help you find restaurants downtown, we've subdivided parts of that area into the following geographic areas: **Center City, Old City, Society Hill,** and **Chinatown.** Center City is bounded roughly by the Schuylkill River to the west, 6th Street to the east, Lombard Street to the south, and Race Street to the north. Old City is bounded by 6th Street, the Delaware River, and Race and Sansom streets. Society Hill is bounded by 6th Street, the Delaware River, Bainbridge Street, and Walnut Street. Chinatown lies between 9th and 11th and Vine and Arch streets.

We also include several restaurants in **West Philadelphia** (the part of the city west of the Schuylkill River), **South Philadelphia** (south of Bainbridge Street), and **Chestnut Hill** (in the northwest part of the city).

A good source for up-to-the-minute restaurant information is *Philadelphia*, a monthly magazine with extensive restaurant listings. The February issue features a major section on dining out, with listings for hundreds of local restaurants.

CATEGORY	COST*
$$$$	over $35
$$$	$25–$35
$$	$15–$25
$	under $15

** per person excluding drinks, service, and sales tax (7%)*

American-International

$$$$ **The Fountain Restaurant.** While dining here, you're charmed into feel-
★ ing glamorous and cosmopolitan. The grand window views overlooking Logan Circle's Swann Fountain are part of the trick, the confident service is another, but the best part is the food. Chef Jean-Marie Lacroix is constantly experimenting to create culinary excitement. Start with sharkfin galette with melted leeks and pressed caviar nage, then move on to such enticing entrées as American fois gras and duck confit on toasted brioche with shallot marmalade, or the sautéed venison medallions wrapped in homemade pasta and served with fried leeks and juniper-berry sauce. A special health menu offers foods low in cholesterol, calories, and sodium. The Fountain is nestled in the lavish but dignified lobby of the Four Seasons Hotel—a godsend for the frazzled traveler. ✕ *1 Logan Sq., Center City,* ☎ *215/963–1500. Reservations required. AE, D, DC, MC, V.*

$$$$ **Striped Bass Restaurant and Bar.** The biggest splash on Philadelphia's
★ dining scene in more than a decade, this all-seafood dining room offers a cutting-edge look and cuisine that has made it the city's most talked-about restaurant. Capitalizing on the existing grandeur of a former marble-pillar brokerage house, restaurateur/trendsetters Neil Stein and Joe Wolf have created a visually stunning room, with towering palms (accenting 28-foot ceilings), muslin-draped windows, terra-cotta tiles, and a spectacular 16-foot sculpture of a leaping striped bass made from hand-forged steel, hung over the full exhibition kitchen window. Chef Alison Barshak's food is art that comes out of the refrigerator and off the stove: red-curried grilled swordfish with lemongrass, coconut, and plantain chips; macadamia-crusted grouper with black beans and pineapple salsa; and, of course, herbed wild striped bass with roasted garlic mash. There is an extensive raw bar and the Chef's Table dinner—offered at a table strategically placed in the kitchen—offers a grand feast at very grand prices. Eat in the kitchen, however, and you'll miss the most exciting dining room in

Dining

Philadelphia. ✕ *1500 Walnut St, Center City,* ☎ *2 Reservations required. AE, MC, V.*

$$$ Café Nola. As they say in New Orleans, "Let the good times You can't help but have fun here at this outpost of "N'Awlins" cuisine. The dark, mirrored room with plants, tile floor and tin ceiling is alluring; try for a table on the raised section overlooking the action at the art deco–style mahogany bar. For 15 years, owners Judy DeVicaris and Bill Curry have been serving Big Easy cuisine to Philadelphians, and add plenty of their own touches such as a bouillabaisse with a splash of coconut milk or soft-shell crabs sautéed Creole style with avocado purée and corn sliced fresh from the cob. Those who love Nouvelle Orleans cuisine will opt for the Cajun popcorn—deep-fried rock shrimp or crawfish in a sherry remoulade sauce. For dessert, treat yourself to bananas Foster flambéed in brandy at your table. ✕ *328 South St., Society Hill,* ☎ *215/627–2590. Reservations advised. AE, D, DC, MC, V.*

$$$ The Chart House. People come here less for the food than the atmosphere: dramatic views of the Delaware River; a nautical theme combining ultramodern paintings, sculpture, and striking architecture; and a waterfall descending from the lobby to the lounge. The spacious dining area and lounge seat 250, yet afford a measure of intimacy lacking in many other large restaurants. For appetizers, try the oysters Rockefeller. All fish, including salmon, swordfish, and mahimahi, is flown in fresh daily and served grilled or baked. Mud pie, the house dessert, is coffee ice cream with a chocolate wafer crust topped with fudge, fresh whipped cream, and almonds. ✕ *555 S. Columbus Blvd., Society Hill,* ☎ *215/625–8383. Reservations accepted. AE, D, DC, MC, V.*

$$$ City Tavern. One step within these doors and 200 years of the city's history seems to disappear completely. You're transported back to 1773, when John Adams, George Washington, Thomas Jefferson, and the rest of the gang came here to hang out after putting in a hard day founding the country. More than a bit of legerdemain was needed to conjure up this bit of Olde Philadelphia: In 1975 chef-manager Walter Staib rebuilt this spot to the exact specifications and in the actual location of the original 1773 tavern. Today you can feast on foods and wines identical to those our forefathers ate in 1776—from West Indies pepper-pot soup to Martha Washington's turkey stew—served on china with authentic Colonial patterns and by waiters in period dress. For dessert, fresh fruit cobbler is served in a pewter dish. Wash it all down with a tankard of ale made according to Thomas Jefferson's recipe (available only here). There is live harpsichord music on Friday and Saturday nights. ✕ *138 S. 2nd St., Society Hill,* ☎ *215/413–1443. Reservations advised. AE, D, DC, MC, V.*

$$$ The Garden. A classic Philadelphia dining experience, this town-house-turned-restaurant has service inside and out: Dine outside on the canopied deck or at umbrella-covered tables in the garden. It's Mayor Ed Rendell's all-around favorite Philadelphia restaurant and gourmands find it fresher and more beautiful with every visit. Owner-chef Kathleen Mulhern's specialty-of-the-house is grilled Dover sole. Desserts are all homemade, including ice cream, sorbet, and the house favorite, white chocolate mousse. Two cruvinets (devices for keeping opened bottles of wine fresh) dispense glasses of selected red and white wines. ✕ *1617 Spruce St., Center City,* ☎ *215/546–4455. Reservations advised. AE, DC, MC, V. Closed Sun.; Sat. in July and Aug.*

$$$ The Marker. Located in the Adam's Mark hotel, the Marker has been growing more popular as its menu grows more adventurous. Popular

Dining

Frisancos Too
1501 E. Passyunk Ave. (near Dickinson)

5-10 p.m.

215 339-0199

Dinnie 11th & Christian Streets

entrées include jumbo lump crabcakes with smoked red-pepper butter, sautéed fillet of red snapper in a potato crust with avocado and green-onion relish, and pepper-seared tuna. Of the three dining room, many prefer the Library, which is a cozy room with a fireplace and built-in bookshelves. ✕ *City Line and Monument Rds., City Line area,* ☎ *215/581–5000. Reservations advised. AE, D, DC, MC, V.*

$$ Carolina's. Located a block from Rittenhouse Square, Carolina's opened in 1986 and has been a Center City hot spot ever since. The dining room's bentwood chairs seat 60 at vinyl-covered tables under a stamped tin ceiling. The extensive menu—sandwiches, pastas, salads, a dozen appetizers, and more than a dozen entrées—changes seasonally. Popular items are veal loaf with mashed potatoes and the Cobb salad (a deep-fried tortilla shell stuffed with chicken, avocado, blue cheese, black olives, tomato, and romaine). The pastry chef's specialties are Carolina's brownie sundae and Key lime pie. ✕ *261 S. 20th St., Center City,* ☎ *215/545–1000. Reservations advised. AE, DC, MC, V. No lunch Sat.*

$$ Downey's. The mahogany bar was salvaged from a Dublin bank; artwork and memorabilia cover the walls; and owner Jack Downey's antique radio collection is on display. Although the food is routine Irish fare, a lively crowd is always on hand. Irish stew and Irish whiskey cake are favorites. Downey's is popular with local athletes, especially baseball and hockey players. It has an oyster bar, outdoor sidewalk tables, and a second-floor, gaslit deck. Piano music nightly and the Sonny Troy Trio plays during Sunday brunch. ✕ *Front and South Sts., Society Hill,* ☎ *215/629–0525. Reservations advised. AE, D, DC, MC, V.*

$$ Friday, Saturday, Sunday. Located in what was in the '60s the Guilded Cage—Philadelphia's premier beatnik hangout—this small, neighborhood restaurant looks the way it did when it opened 20 years ago: fabrics are draped from the ceiling; mirrors and pinlights line the walls; classical and jazz music plays in the background. The blackboard menu has been replaced by a printed one, but the offerings still echo back to when this place *was* only open three days a week. A good appetizer is ravioli stuffed with wild mushrooms in a cream watercress sauce. Popular entrées include rack of lamb, Neapolitan pasta, and striped bass with artichoke heart stuffing. All desserts are made on the premises; vanilla cheesecake with a chocolate crust and fresh berry pureé topping tempts most people to linger. ✕ *261 S. 21st St., Center City,* ☎ *215/546–4232. Reservations advised. AE, D, DC, MC, V.*

$$ Lickety Split. A charter member of the '70s "restaurant renaissance," Lickety Split bills itself as "South Street's longest-running dinner party" and has hardly changed since it opened in 1972. It still has a plethora of plants, exposed brick walls, and pin lights; a waterfall flows in the upstairs lounge. Much of the original menu also remains—stir-fried vegetables, avocado stuffed with crabmeat, and rack of lamb with mustard-crumb coating. Newer offerings include the *fruitti de mare* (seafood stew) in a red sauce over pasta, and chicken Caesar salad in a deep-fried tortilla shell. The dessert tray changes weekly. ✕ *4th and South Sts., Society Hill,* ☎ *215/922–1173. Weekend reservations advised. AE, D, DC, MC, V.*

$$ Roller's. ★ A small, bustling, brightly lit place with floor-to-ceiling windows, Roller's is the best restaurant in Chestnut Hill, in the northwest corner of the city. Sit near the open kitchen and watch master chef (and owner) Paul Roller prepare duck with pear-port sauce; calves' liver with champagne vinegar and caramelized baby pearl onions; and, the chef's personal favorite, smoked pork chops with apple fritters. First-rate desserts include Linzer torte and lemon soufflé tart.

The wine list is varied. ✗ *Top of the Hill Plaza, Chestnut Hill,* ☎ *215/242–1771. Reservations advised. No credit cards. Closed Mon.; closed Sun. in July and Aug.*

$$ **Valley Green Inn.** Set in the heart of Fairmount Park, this national historic landmark is located in the middle of the Wissahickon Valley—a forested 5½-mile-long gorge, in the northwest section of the city. Built in 1850, the inn is filled with antique tools, glassware, kitchen utensils, and Wissahickon memorabilia. In season, you can eat out on the porch overlooking the ducks swimming in the creek. In winter, a fire blazes inside. People used to eat here *in spite of* the food, but since Suzanne Herst and Edward Doherty took over in 1994, the cuisine equals the setting. Rich appetizers include the wild mushrooms au gratin, and grilled polenta with blue cheese. Duck breast on porcini risotto and tuna poivre are two popular entrées. Call for directions. ✗ *Springfield Ave. and Forbidden Dr. between Chestnut Hill and Roxborough,* ☎ *215/247–1730. Reservations advised. D, MC, V.*

[handwritten: lunch M–Sat, 12–3, brunch on Sundays]

$$ **White Dog Cafe.** Canine memorabilia abound; the back of the menu explains why, telling the story of the 19th-century mystic Madame Blavatsky and how this restaurant got its name (a white dog once laid across Madame's ailing leg and cured it). Gingham and flea-market furniture give the White Dog a country-inn atmosphere. Owners Judy Wicks and Kevin Von Klaus have made the White Dog *the* restaurant in University City. Excellent regional cuisine uses the finest available local products, such as Bucks County broccoli served the day it is picked. Try the whole-grain breads and the oysters in thyme sauce with bacon. Also recommended is leg of lamb seasoned with a mixture of crushed black peppercorns, fennel, and mustard seeds. The small, lively bar serves 21 varieties of American boutique beer; the wine list is all-American. Tails, a "Victorian piano parlor," provides a plush setting for a quiet drink. ✗ *3420 Sansom St., West Philadelphia,* ☎ *215/386–9224. Reservations advised. AE, D, DC, MC, V.*

$ **The Restaurant School.** Here's the only place in Philadelphia where you can get haute cuisine and European service at a fraction of what you would normally expect to pay: a fixed price of $13.50 buys an appetizer and entrée. It is managed and staffed entirely by students attending the Restaurant School, an institution that has produced the chefs and owners of many Philadelphia restaurants. The menu occasionally offers Italian, Spanish, and German dishes, but is mainly traditional French cuisine. Set within a restored 1860 Victorian mansion in West Philadelphia (near the University of Pennsylvania), the dining area seats 120 in a glass-enclosed atrium enhanced with flowering plants and trees. ✗ *4207 Walnut St., West Philadelphia,* ☎ *215/222–4200. Reservations advised. AE, D, DC, MC, V. Closed Sun. and Mon.*

Diners and Philly Food

A joy for those who wish to strike a blow against fat-hating foodies, Philly's fast food is served up at city eateries that offset minimum decor with maximum flavor. Aficionados of all the Philly food mentioned below (with the exception of cheesesteaks) will be happy to know that gift packages can be shipped back home to Aunty Em by calling Philadelphia Favorites To Go (☎ 800/808–TOGO) or A Taste of Philadelphia (☎ 800/8–HOAGIE).

$ **The Famous Delicatessen.** The closest thing in Philadelphia to a classic New York deli, the Famous is renowned for its huge corned-beef and pastrami sandwiches—boxes of tin foil are handy to wrap up the half you won't be able to finish. Other favorites include carp, sable,

Nova Scotia salmon, herring, salami, and tongue. The bickering behind the counter is a show in itself; and if the waitress likes you, she may reward you with one of co-owner's Janie Auspitz's chocolate chip cookies. Beer is available. ✕ *4th and Bainbridge Sts., Society Hill,* ☎ *215/922–3274. AE MC, V.* ☺ *Mon.–Sat. 7 AM–6 PM, Sun. 7 AM–4 PM.*

$ **Lee's Hoagie House.** The hoagie is Philadelphia's official sandwich, and though "heros" and "zeppelins" are available in other cities, only the Philadelphia hoagie has that certain *je ne sais quoi.* The original store, founded in 1953 and named after owner Lee Seitchik, is still operating in the West Oak Lane section of the city; today, 23 other locations are now licensed to use Lee's name. Lee's offers a dozen different hoagies—tuna and turkey are gaining currency—but the classic is the Italian: pepper ham, genoa salami, cappicola, provolone, lettuce, tomato, onions, hot peppers, spices, and oil. You can request mayonnaise, but you'll be considered a wimp. ✕ *44 S. 17th St.,* ☎ *215/564–1264. No credit cards. Closed Sun.*

$ **Melrose Diner.** The classic Philadelphia diner, Melrose serves nothing elaborate but offers fresh, top-quality ingredients at diner prices. Entrées cost $5 to $9 ($11.50 for the sirloin). You can get breakfast 24 hours a day, including the house specialty, creamed chipped beef. Popular dishes include deviled crab cutlet made from backfin crabmeat, and 1620 shrimp (16–20 shrimps per pound), heavily breaded and fried. The on-premises bake shop has eight bakers. Favorite desserts are hot apple pie with vanilla sauce and butter-cream layer cake. Thirteen waitresses, most of whom are chewing gum and calling you "Hon," make new faces feel right at home. ✕ *1501 Snyder Ave., South Philadelphia,* ☎ *215/467–6644. No credit cards.* ☺ *24 hrs.*

$ **Pat's King of Steaks.** While a hoagie is a meal, a cheesesteak is an in-★ dulgence. Thin slices of steak, fried onions, and melted cheese (your choice of American, provolone, or Cheese Whiz) served on an 8-inch roll. You get it piping hot, dripping oil and juices onto the wax paper, the outdoor metal tables, and your clothes—until you acquire the proper eating stance. A side order of cheese fries, a fountain-made cherry coke, and a Tastykake for dessert, and you've had the ultimate Philadelphia culinary experience this side of Le Bec-Fin. Pat's, owned and run by the Olivieri family at this location for 65 years, claims to sell more cheesesteaks than anyone else, and they probably do. ✕ *1237 E. Passyunk Ave. (at the intersection of 9th and Wharton Sts.), South Philadelphia,* ☎ *215/468–1546. No credit cards.* ☺ *24 hrs.*

$ **Reading Terminal Market.** A Philadelphia treasure, the Reading Ter-★ minal Market is a potpourri of over 80 stalls, shops, lunch counters, and food emporiums within a one-square-block indoor farmers' market. You can choose from numerous cuisines—Chinese, Greek, Mexican, Japanese, Middle Eastern, Italian, soul food, vegetarian, and Pennsylvania Dutch. Food options include salad bar, seafood, deli, five bake shops, specialty hoagie shop, sushi bar, and Bassett's ice cream store. Lunch early to beat the rush. The Down Home Diner serves Brunswick stew made with rabbit. Fisher's is the place to try a Philadelphia soft pretzel—hot out of the oven and brushed with butter. ✕ *12th and Arch Sts., Center City,* ☎ *215/922–2317.* ☺ *Mon.–Sat. 8 AM–6 PM. Closed Sun.*

Chinese

$$$ **Susanna Foo.** Susanna's is the most expensive Chinese restaurant in ★ Philadelphia, and the best. Owners Susanna and E-Hsin Foo mounted a $1.5 million renovation in 1993, enlarging the room (a former steak

house), and adding a new kitchen. Chinese art and antiques create a space worthy of the kitchen's gourmet offerings. Best of all, they added an upstairs café to serve up their famous dim sum (the pheasant dumplings with shiitake mushroom sauce are fabulous). Downstairs, a favorite entrée is Eight Treasure Quails, made with Chinese sausage, lotus seeds, and sweet rice. The bar has a full wine list and imported beers. It's hard to resist the chocolate-covered fortune cookies, but Madame Foo always recommends the banana chocolate-mousse cake. ✕ *1512 Walnut St., Center City,* ☎ *215/545–2666. Reservations required. AE, DC, MC, V. Closed Sun.*

$ **Imperial Inn.** One of Philadelphia's larger and better-known Chinese restaurants, Imperial Inn is fancier than most other restaurants in Chinatown, with a dining room that cossets you with white linen, flowers, and chandeliers. The menu offers Cantonese, Szechuan, and Mandarin selections. The Imperial is known for its lunchtime dim sum—"finger-food" appetizers that you choose from a cart wheeled to your table. ✕ *142 N. 10th St., Chinatown,* ☎ *215/627–2299. AE, DC, MC, V.*

$ **Joe's Peking Duck House.** Joe Poon, the original owner-chef, is gone,
★ but this noisy little hole-in-the-wall is still the best Chinese restaurant in Chinatown. With its friendly atmosphere and plain environment, it's like many of the other 50 or so Chinese restaurants around 10th and Race streets, but the quality is better. Pat Lee, the new chef, continues Joe's tradition of excellent seafood, barbecued pork, and the house specialty, Peking duck. ✕ *925 Race St., Chinatown,* ☎ *215/922–3277. Reservations advised. No credit cards.*

French

$$$$ **La Truffe.** A Francophile's dream, La Truffe serves up classic and nou-
★ velle dishes in a felicitous French country-inn atmosphere. Specialties include such appetizers as *mille-feuille de pleurotte* (wild mushrooms in a puff pastry), traditional entrées like *carré d'agneau au thym* (rack of lamb with thyme sauce), and calorie-heavy desserts such as white chocolate mousse with fresh raspberry sauce. Many diners with a *goût de luxe* and a fat wallet opt for the truffle dishes in season (November to January). The prix-fixe dinner is $52.50. ✕ *10 S. Front St., Old City,* ☎ *215/925–5062. Reservations advised. Jacket and tie. AE, D, DC, MC, V. Closed Sun.*

$$$$ **Le Bec-Fin.** Only perfection can justify the prices this renowned land-
★ mark charges—about a $100 per person for dinner—and more often than not, Le Bec-Fin delivers. Here you'll find the finest in haute cuisine served in a setting Louis XVI would feel right at home in: dawn's-early-light-gold silk walls, crystal chandeliers, vases filled with cabbage roses, gilt-framed mirrors, and a bust of Marie-Antoinette peeking out of the corner. "The Fine Beak" (or more loosely "The Fine Palate") has won a zillion awards, with Craig Claiborne, of the *New York Times,* calling it "the finest French restaurant in the East." Owner-chef Georges Perrier is a perfectionist who spares nothing to inject excellence into every detail of his five-course prix-fixe dinner (which includes choice of appetizer, fish course, entrée, sorbet and cheese, and dessert cart). You'll be hard-pressed to say which dish is the most sensational. Leading contenders are the chopped snails sandwiched between two potato pancakes, the *filet d'agneau au curry de madras et son chutney de pommes* (lamb with curry and apple chutney), and the famous "pressed lobster" (with a $27 surcharge). For a grand finale, the *charrette de dessert*—a three-tiered cart with more than 30 sinful temptations—is rolled out, and you may succumb to as many pastries as you wish. If

you want a taste of the Beak without blowing the budget on dinner, lunch is a relatively modest $34, and Le Bar Lyonnais downstairs offers munchies with a French accent for about $10 a pop. ✕ *1523 Walnut St., Center City,* ☎ *215/567–1000. Reservations required. Jacket and tie. AE, D, DC, MC, V. Closed Sun.*

$$$ **Alouette.** Some people think Alouette is a French restaurant that serves Asian food; others think it's an Asian restaurant that specializes in French cuisine. East definitely meets West here, thanks to chef Fred Cherenfan, who trained under former owner/chef Kamol Phutlek. Main courses are often topped with tongue-tingling sauces—tamarind, lime and pineapple, Thai curry, and raspberry lemon. A favorite appetizer is snails in puff pastry with white-wine butter sauce. The elegant decor includes fresh flowers, candlelit tables, and a Victorian bar. The romantic, French flower-garden courtyard seats 20 people in summer. ✕ *4th and Bainbridge Sts., Society Hill,* ☎ *215/629–1126. Reservations advised weekdays, required weekends. AE, DC, MC, V. Closed Tues.*

$$$ **Ciboulette.** The food has always been exceptional at Ciboulette (French for chives), and now the setting equals the fare. In 1993 owner-chef Bruce Lim moved from his 35-seat minimalist space on Spruce Street to turn-of-the-century elegance in the former Bellevue Stratford Hotel. The restaurant now occupies the Pink and Gold rooms of what was once Philadelphia's most opulent hotel, with appointments—such as the original 1904 terrazzo mosaic floor (each tile 2½ inches deep)—that you will see in no other dining room in the city. For an appetizer, try the marinade of three-fish salad (sea bass, salmon, and tuna) with coriander. Chef Lim (who developed his talents at the excellent Fountain Restaurant in the Four Seasons Hotel) is proud of his rack of lamb, now done in mustard sauce. A new dessert cart offers over 20 desserts made daily on the premises. ✕ *200 S. Broad St., The Bellevue, 2nd Floor,* ☎ *215/790–1210. Reservations advised. AE, DC, MC, V.*

Italian

$$$$ **Monte Carlo Living Room.** Italian haute cuisine is served amid crystal chandeliers and imported furniture in two mirrored, candlelit dining rooms. Homemade pastas, pastries, and gelati are all recommended. Fish dishes are a specialty. Milk-fed veal stuffed with mozzarella and prosciutto, served with a mushroom sauce, is a popular entrée. The six-course "of the chef" dinner costs $65. Dancing in a private club upstairs is free to diners. ✕ *2nd and South Sts., Society Hill,* ☎ *215/925–2220. Reservations required. Jacket required. AE, DC, MC, V.*

$$$ **DiLullo Centro.** Occupying the former Locust Theater, this may be one of the most strikingly designed restaurants in Philadelphia. The two dining areas—one romantically dark, one brighter—have murals, etched glass, dark wood, and brass-and-glass partitions. Food is good to excellent, but some dishes are overpriced. Recommended pasta dishes are tortellini with bay scallops and a brandy tomato sauce, and the *tonnarelli* (mushroom pasta) with salmon. Best entrées include rack of lamb and the medallions of veal in a port-wine cream sauce. For dessert try the homemade gelati "flavor of the day." The excellent wine list has some hard-to-find Italian selections, including Arneis Montebertotto Bianco. ✕ *1407 Locust St., Center City,* ☎ *215/546–2000. Weekend reservations advised. AE, DC, MC, V. Closed Sun.*

$$$ **Osteria Romana.** You'll pay more than you're used to for Italian food,
★ but Osteria Romana is worth it. It's the finest Italian restaurant in Philadelphia. Its stucco walls are trimmed in dark wood and the white tile floors are styled after a Roman *ristorante*. The friendly staff makes

you feel at home. Pastas are ample enough for a relatively inexpensive entrée: Don't pass up the gnocchi. Top entrées include suckling pig; *fritto misto* (a mixture of squid, scallops, and shrimp in a delicate batter); and saltimbocca (veal, sage, and prosciutto in white wine with a dash of cream). Homemade gelato is the star dessert. The excellent wine list includes a Cervaro and a Montepulciano by Pepe. ✕ *935 Ellsworth St., South Philadelphia,* ☏ *215/271–9191. Reservations advised. AE, DC, MC, V. Closed Mon.*

$$$ Tiramisu. "The name is Italian for a 'pick-me-up,' " says chef-owner Alberto Delbello, explaining the name of his restaurant and the popular dessert in which he specializes. The intimate room is narrow, with a small bar at one end and a wood-burning fireplace at the other. Oil paintings from Italy line the exposed-brick walls. Delbello describes his fare as "nouvelle Jewish-Roman cuisine," with many items on the menu taken from *The Classic Cuisine of the Italian Jews,* by Edda Servi Machlin. You'll munch on matzoh with olive oil and garlic while you peruse the menu. For a fun appetizer try the baby artichokes with garlic. A memorable entrée is the veal scaloppine with mushrooms, rosemary, shallots, and, of course, garlic. The eponymous dessert is served in large portions and made with mascarpone, espresso coffee, chocolate shavings, ladyfinger cookies, a touch of liqueur and no garlic. ✕ *528 S. 5th St., Society Hill,* ☏ *215/925–3335. Reservations advised. AE, DC, MC, V.*

$$ Ristorante Primavera. Get here early: This popular Italian bistro seats only 36 and takes reservations only for parties of six or more. Cozy touches include soft track lighting, exposed brick walls, pink table linens, and wall-to-wall carpeting. *Insalata di frutti di mare* (seafood antipasto) with lemon juice, olive oil, and parsley is a huge but inexpensive seafood appetizer. If your appetite is smaller, go with the Caesar salad. Some entrées, such as the veal chop with shiitake mushrooms and white wine sauce, are good, but pastas and appetizers are the strong suits. Saltimbocca is delicious. For dessert, try the tiramisù, from the recipe book of the manager's grandmother. The wine list is small; service is friendly. ✕ *146 South St., Society Hill,* ☏ *215/925–7832. No credit cards.*

$$ ★ Victor Cafe. Looking for your waiter? He may be on the stairway singing a Verdi aria. At the Victor Cafe the waiters are opera singers and the kitchen plays second fiddle to the music. The northern Italian cuisine has improved now that the third generation of the Di Stefano family has taken charge, but people still come here more for the music and the atmosphere. Busts of composers adorn the shelves, and framed photos of opera singers line the walls. The family's record collection consists of 25,000 78 RPMs. ✕ *1303 Dickinson St., South Philadelphia,* ☏ *215/468–3040. Packed weeknights; weekends booked wks in advance. AE, DC , MC, V.*

$ Boccie Pizza. Two wood-burning ovens in a refurbished warehouse turn out both traditional and "nouvelle" pizzas. Design your own from 32 ingredients or choose one from the menu, such as the Moroccan (topped with lamb strips, scallions, and yogurt sauce), or the Indiana (barbecue sauce, Italian sausage cheddar and onion). Non-pizza entrées, pastas, sandwiches and a salad bar, are also available. ✕ *4040 Locust St., University City,* ☏ *215/243–2221. AE, D, DC, MC, V.*

$ Triangle Tavern. One of South Philadelphia's many neighborhood Italian bar-restaurants (only cheaper), the Triangle has lots of local color. Mussels are the specialty of the house; *calamari* (squid) with red sauce ("Italian gravy" to Philadelphia Italians) is also popular. Dusty's Trio has been providing live entertainment on Friday and Saturday nights

here for over 40 years. ✗ *10th and Reed Sts., South Philadelphia,* ☎ *215/467–8683. No credit cards.*

Japanese

$$ Tokio. Decor here is Japanese minimalist: A toy Godzilla guards the
★ four tables and sushi bar while Japanese rock plays in the background.
Sushi and sashimi, which are aesthetically presented at most Japanese
restaurants, are even more attractive here. Try one of the combination
dishes ranging in price from $9 to $23. A $10 dish includes octopus,
yellowtail, eel, and a ring of rice adorned with flying-fish eggs. If you
can't fathom raw fish, consider the sukiyaki or the yosenabe—they're
cooked at your table; you decide when they're done. Green tea ice cream
is the house dessert. Owner Madame Saito presides over both the
sushi bar and the elegant Champignon room, with a French and Thai
menu, next door. ✗ *124 Lombard St., Society Hill,* ☎ *215/922–7181.
AE, DC, MC, V.*

$$ Aoi. So much is happening here that dining may seem incidental. The
sleek black interior with its geometric neon shapes, floor-to-ceiling
video screen, and—at the mahogany bar—personal TV sets, has a mys-
terious ambience. The menu is mostly Japanese: sashimi, sushi, and
maki sushi. *Chirashi sushi* is an assortment of *surimi*, salmon roe,
giant clam, and squid garnished with vegetables atop vinegared rice.
"All-you-can-eat" sushi for $24.50 is offered Thursday through Sat-
urday. For dessert try the green tea ice cream. ✗ *1210 Walnut St.,
Center City,* ☎ *215/985–1838. Reservations advised on weekends.
AE, D, DC, MC, V.*

Mexican

$$ Tequila's. Chef Carlos Molina makes this the place to go for Mexican
★ food in Philadelphia. For appetizers, skip the *nachitos obligatorios* and
try one of the citric seviches (such as fish and shrimp stuffed in pineap-
ple). The best entrée is the *pescado frito,* a whole fish (usually red snap-
per or grouper) marinated in citrus, fried, and served with a garlic sauce.
Others to sample are *chiles rellenos*—poblano peppers stuffed with
ground beef mixed with fruit or cheese—and the defatted duck baked
in a ground squash-seed sauce. The colorful decor includes photos of
Pancho Villa and Emiliano Zapata and alcoves containing Mexican glass-
ware and ceramics. For dessert, many favor the *crepe ve Cajeta* with
goat's-milk syrup. Select from 10 different Mexican beers and 10
brands of tequila. ✗ *1511 Locust St., Center City,* ☎ *215/546–0181.
AE, DC, MC, V.*

Middle Eastern

$$ Marrakesh. Some find Marrakesh cramped and a little frayed around
★ the edges, but if you're up for it, it's a fun dining experience. People
who don't like eating with their hands—well, they'll survive. There
are no utensils here, and diners sit on low cushioned benches at
hammered-brass tables. After you wash your hands with warm water
and dry them on towels, you're served a $20 prix fixe seven-course
banquet: salads, *bastilla* (meat pie with chicken, almonds, and scram-
bled eggs), chicken and lamb with honey and almonds, couscous with
vegetables, fresh fruit, baklava, and sweet mint tea. ✗ *517 S. Leith-
gow St., Society Hill,* ☎ *215/925–5929. Reservations required. No
credit cards. No lunch.*

$$ The Middle East. More than just a restaurant, the Middle East is a show.
It has mirrors, Oriental rugs on the walls, and gilded portraits worthy

of a sultan's harem. Monday through Thursday you'll hear an eclectic selection of live music; Friday and Saturday, it's the famous Middle East belly dancers. (Join them if you feel adventurous.) The owners, the Tayoun family, have filled the menu with dishes from their ancestral Lebanon and other Middle Eastern countries. Lamb is the staple—on the shank, braised with tomatoes; in moussaka; on kebabs; and ground raw in *kibbie nayee* (raw lamb and wheat germ), the national dish of Lebanon. American food, including meatless Pritikin dishes, is also available. ✕ *126 Chestnut St., Old City,* ☎ *215/922–1003. Reservations advised. AE, D, DC, MC, V.*

$ **Chef Theodore.** Don't let the setting in a nondescript shopping strip dissuade you—Chef Theodore is the best Greek restaurant in Philadelphia. The bargain-priced *meze* combination platter includes *baba ganoush* (roast eggplant dip), *humus* (ground chick peas with sesame paste), *taramousalata* (salty caviar spread), *tzatziki* (whipped yogurt with cucumbers and lemon), marinated octopus, stuffed grape leaves, calamata olives, and feta cheese. Among a dozen nightly specials are braised lamb with *avgolimono* (lemon) and dill sauce, served with artichoke hearts. All entrées are served in portions that are a challenge to finish. You can end your meal with good Greek coffee and sweet but not overly rich desserts. ✕ *1100 S. Delaware Ave., South Philadelphia,* ☎ *215/271–6800. AE, MC, V. Closed Mon.*

Seafood

$$$$ **Old Original Bookbinder's.** Today, Philadelphia's most famous restaurant has become more of a landmark (the original opened in 1865) than an essential stop for the devoted diner. There's a photo of Elizabeth Taylor with owner John Taxin on the wall, three bars and seven dining rooms, and a touristy gift shop, complete with cans of Booky's most popular soups (including snapper with sherry). The place remains a favorite haunt of celebrities, politicians, and athletes, who come to enjoy the seafood, which is well prepared but not necessarily the best you'll ever eat. Booky's is often criticized for being overpriced (entrées range from $17 to $30) and you'll spring for the top end if you order one of the celebrated lobsters (which are selected from a tank and cooked to order—to the chagrin of more sensitive diners). All the same, Bookbinder's remains *the* landmark among Philly restaurants. ✕ *125 Walnut St., Society Hill,* ☎ *215/925–7027. Reservations advised. AE, D, DC, MC, V.*

$$$ **Bookbinder's Seafood House.** Son of Bookbinder's is actually owned by the original founding family (who sold the larger establishment to new owners in the 1940s). Here, you'll find the best mussels in red sauce in Philadelphia—one reason why this place remains extraordinarily popular. Less expensive than Old Original, the Seafood House has typical seafood restaurant decor like stuffed swordfish mounted on the walls and fishermen's nets dangling from the ceiling. The menu features lobster Coleman (lobster stuffed with chunks of crabmeat), crab imperial, fresh stone crabs, snapper soup, and baked crabs, and usually offers the freshest fare from Chesapeake Bay trawling. ✕ *215 S. 15th St., Center City,* ☎ *215/545–1137. Reservations advised. AE, D, DC, MC, V.*

$$ **Sansom Street Oyster House.** This Philadelphia favorite serves first-★ rate raw oysters plus clams, fish, shellfish, and grilled and blackened dishes. It's an unpretentious place with dark wood paneling and uncovered tables. The family collection of over 200 oyster plates covers the walls. The menu changes daily and includes nonseafood items like steak and chicken. House-specialty desserts are apple Brown Betty and bread pudding with whiskey sauce. ✕ *1516 Sansom St., Center City,*

☎ *215/567–7683. Reservations accepted only for 5 or more. AE, D, DC, MC, V. Closed Sun.*

Steaks

$$$$ **Morton's of Chicago.** With a tuxedoed maître d' and the atmosphere of a private club, Morton's is a steak house catering largely to money market men and women. It's hard to imagine how any of them do any useful work in the afternoon after finishing off the house specialty, a 24-ounce porterhouse. The balcony-level dining area overlooks the main dining room,which has an art deco bar and walls lined with bottles of wine. Choose your cut of meat or fish from raw items on a cart wheeled to your table; it will be cooked to your specifications. ✗ *1 Logan Sq. (on 19th St.), Center City,* ☎ *215/557–0724. Reservations advised. AE, DC, MC, V.*

$$$ **The Saloon.** Here's a steak house with Italian specialties. Everything it does is big: big pieces of meat, big drinks, big prices. Big money went into the antique turn-of-the-century decor—mahogany paneling, mirrors, and stained glass. For an appetizer, try radicchio salad with shiitake mushrooms, served warm. The antipasto Italiano is a sampler of all the appetizers. For an entrée, order the off-the-menu special risotto with abundant porcini mushrooms, or cannelloni filled with veal in one of the excellent tomato sauces. Desserts include fruit tarts, rum cake, and tiramisù. ✗ *750 S. 7th St., South Philadelphia,* ☎ *215/627–1811. Reservations advised. AE. Closed Sun.*

Thai

$ **Thai Garden East.** In 1988 Heng Leevongcharoen and his wife, Rudee,
★ opened Thai Garden in West Philadelphia. It quickly became the leading Thai restaurant in the city. In 1990 Chef Leevongcharoen moved to Center City, next door to the new Convention Center, and created Thai Garden East. The contemporary ambience is different, but the food that made both restaurants popular is as good, and as inexpensive, as ever. The *miena cum* appetizer—toasted peanuts, coconut chips, and lime piled on spinach leaves spiced with chopped chili and Thai plum sauce—is delectable. *Chu chee* (curried duck) and Thai-style barbecued chicken with sweet-and-sour sauce are among the excellent entrées. For dessert try Thai custard. ✗ *101 N. 11th St., Chinatown,* ☎ *215/629–9939. Reservations advised. AE, D, DC, MC, V.*

Vietnamese

$ **Van's Garden.** Van's is probably the least expensive Asian restaurant
★ in Philadelphia, yet it's first rate. Hodgepodge decor includes flocked red-and-black wallpaper, linoleum floors, and blond wood wainscoting. A superb appetizer is grilled meatballs wrapped in rice paper, with carrots, radishes, cucumbers, noodles, and a thick, brown bean sauce for dipping—a sort of Vietnamese hoagie. Among entrées, you can get 10 sweet-and-sour shrimp in a tempura-like batter. Barbecued shrimp on vermicelli at $7.95 is the most expensive item on the menu. Dinner here is a superb value. For a variation on a dessert theme, try rice pudding with taro and coconut juice. ✗ *121 N. 11th St., Chinatown,* ☎ *215/923–2439. BYOB. AE, D, DC, MC, V.*

Brunch

Sunday brunch is a Philadelphia tradition. Scores of local establishments open their doors on Sunday mornings for blissful breakfasts and brunches,

serving everything from the traditional bagels and lox at Famous Deli to the more unusual rock shrimp and grits baked in cream with pepper jack cheese and roasted peppers found at the White Dog Cafe.

Brunch connoisseurs will not want to miss Sunday morning at the **Four Seasons Hotel** (*see* Chapter 6, Lodging), where for from about $34 to $38, diners can feast on one of two sumptuous buffets amid crystal, linen, and massive floral arrangements. The hearty buffet at Swann Lounge Cafe features cooked-to-order omelets and waffles, as well as vegetable stir-fries, pasta, and three carving stations (beef, lamb, and veal). In the adjacent, more elegant, Fountain Restaurant, diners can choose from either the menu or the buffet, which specializes in fish, including a caviar dish. The menu features roasted Maine lobster with a Parisian of apples and avocados in a Sauterne sauce. A New Age jazz trio plays from 11 to 3. Children eat for half price. Reservations recommended.

Another classy (and expensive) brunch experience is at **Founders** on the 19th floor of the Hotel Atop the Bellevue (*see* Chapter 6, Lodging). Sky-high views; a stained-glass, 30-foot dome; soaring archways; and Victorian turn-of-the-century details add up to one of the most magnificent dining rooms in the city. The cost is $29.50 (half price for kids under 12).

The following restaurants offer Sunday brunch: Alouette, Café Nola, Carolina's, Chart House, Ciboulette, Downey's, Famous Deli, Lickety Split, The Marker, Roller's, Valley Green Inn, and White Dog Cafe. For descriptions, addresses, and phone numbers, *see* Dining, *above*.

6 Lodging

By Rathe Miller
and Michael
Schwager

Updated by
Rathe Miller

PHILADELPHIA HOTELS RUN THE GAMUT from world class to commonplace, from a five-star 1,200-room hotel with every luxury to an endearingly personal nine-room Colonial inn. While many are utilitarian hotels or national chains, many others are experiences in themselves. Aside from youth hostels and bed-and-breakfasts, the city has only a few moderately priced hotels; most are expensive.

Because the number of rooms—13,120—is small for a city with a population of nearly a million and a half, it occasionally can be difficult to find a place to stay. The Philadelphia Marriott, adjacent to the Pennsylvania Convention Center, opened in January 1995, giving the downtown area another 1,200 rooms. You're likely to encounter problems on the weekend of the Army-Navy football game (usually the weekend after Thanksgiving weekend) and when large conventions move into town. Advance reservations are usually advised. The city has no central reservation office.

Hotels are listed geographically, according to six neighborhoods. The **Benjamin Franklin Parkway/Museum Area** runs along the Benjamin Franklin Parkway from 16th Street to the Philadelphia Museum of Art. The **Historic District** on the east side of downtown centers on Independence Hall and extends to the Delaware River. The **Shopping/Theater District** encompasses a few blocks on either side of Broad Street, near Walnut Street. A half dozen hotels are clustered around the **Airport District,** near Philadelphia International Airport. Several are in **University City,** near the campus of the University of Pennsylvania in West Philadelphia; two are in the **City Line** area; and one is in **Chestnut Hill** in the northwest part of the city.

Accommodations are ranked according to the following price categories. Unless otherwise noted, all rooms have private bath. Note, as with all major city-center lodgings, many hotels offer special weekend packages and rates.

CATEGORY	COST*
$$$$	over $150
$$$	$100–$150
$$	$50–$100
$	under $50

All prices are for a standard double room; excluding 12% tax (7% sales tax plus 5% hotel tax).

Philadelphia has no off-season rates, but most hotels offer discount packages for weekends, when demand from business people and groups subsides. Besides substantially reduced rates, these packages often include an assortment of free features such as breakfast, parking, cocktails or champagne, and the use of exercise facilities.

When not included as a package feature, most downtown hotels charge an average of $15 a day for parking.

To reserve a room in any property in this chapter, you can contact **Fodor's new toll-free lodging reservations hot line** (☎ 1–800–FODORS–1 or 1–800–363–6771; 0800–89–1030 in Great Britain; 0014/800–12–8271 in Australia; 1800–55–9101 in Ireland).

The Benjamin Franklin Parkway/Museum Area

$$$$ **Four Seasons.** If you were a film director who wanted a location for
★ a romantic hotel-room view of Philadelphia, you would choose a room
 here, overlooking the fountains in Logan Circle and the Benjamin
 Franklin Parkway. Built in 1983, the eight-story U-shaped hotel has
 the most attractive public areas, best service, and finest hotel dining
 in the city—and block-long hallways that some guests don't like.
 Guest-room furniture is Federal style, dark and stately. All rooms look
 out on either Logan Circle or the interior courtyard, thanks to picture
 windows (and, in some rooms, private verandas). Then there are those
 Four Seasons touches: libraries in each room, a health menu available
 from room service and in the restaurant, alcoves in regular rooms, and
 one-inch-thick bathroom rugs. Philadelphia's most expensive hotel
 provides terry robes and a complimentary shoeshine—hang your shoes
 in the bag on your doorknob and they come back sleekly polished the
 next morning. The Fountain Restaurant, nestled in the lobby, is one
 of the best in town. Weather permitting, the Swann Courtyard Cafe is
 an excellent spot for a drink and a kiss. ⊞ *1 Logan Sq. (near major
 museums), 19103,* ☎ *215/963–1500 or 800/332–3442,* ℻ *215/963–
 1439. 371 rooms. 2 restaurants, outdoor café, room service, 6 no-smok-
 ing floors, indoor pool, exercise room, sauna, concierge. AE, D, DC,
 MC, V.*

$$$$ **Wyndham Franklin Plaza.** This was Philadelphia's biggest and busiest
 hotel until the Philadelphia Marriott opened in 1995, but the public
 has benefitted from the competition. All public areas and guest rooms
 have been updated and renovated, and while it is still primarily a con-
 vention hotel, it now caters to individual travelers with a variety of
 new, added amenities and services. The 70-foot atrium lobby encom-
 passes two restaurants, a bar, and numerous sitting areas. Room decor
 is modern, in gray and silver with chrome chairs, full-length mirrors,
 cable TV, voice mail, coffeemakers, and hair dryers. Seventy percent
 of the rooms are no-smoking. ⊞ *16th and Vine Sts., 19103,* ☎
 215/448–2000 or 800/822–4200, ℻ *215/448-2864. 758 rooms, in-
 cluding 38 suites. Room service, pool, exercise room, beauty salon, bar-
 bershop, health club privileges, concierge. Children under 18 stay free
 in parents' room. AE, D, DC, MC, V.*

$$ **Center City Hotel.** If you're willing to stay a bit away from downtown
 (and in less-than-average lodgings), you'll find a bargain here. The three-
 story, Y-shaped building was a Ramada Inn till 1994 and at press time
 was scheduled to become a Best Western. Rooms are done in mauve
 and taupe with oak-finish furniture and individual climate control. The
 best views face south toward the Benjamin Franklin Parkway, the
 Rodin Museum, and the downtown skyline. ⊞ *501 N. 22nd St.,
 19130,* ☎ *215/568–8300,* ℻ *215/557–9448. 183 rooms, including
 5 suites. Restaurant, outdoor café, room service, pool, parking. AE,
 D, DC, MC, V.*

The Historic District

$$$$ **Sheraton Society Hill.** Conveniently located for visits to the historic dis-
 trict, this redbrick, neo-Colonial building is two blocks from Penn's
 Landing, three blocks from Head House Square, and three blocks
 from Independence Hall. The hotel has a pleasant four-story atrium
 lobby framed by archways and balconies, filled with trees and plants,
 and lit by wrought-iron lanterns. Rooms are furnished traditionally but
 have modern conveniences such as a bar, remote-control TV, voice mail,
 modem ports in telephones, and coffeemakers. Fourth-floor rooms fac-

ing east toward the Delaware River have the best view. A pianist plays regularly in the atrium lobby. ⚑ *1 Dock St., 19106,* ☎ *215/238–6000 or 800/325–3535,* FAX *215/922–2709. 365 rooms, 17 suites. Restaurant, bar, room service, indoor pool, health club. AE, D, DC, MC, V.*

$$$ **Best Western Independence Park Inn.** From the rooms facing busy Chestnut Street you'll hear the clop-clop of carriage horses as well as the roar of city buses. The five-story building is a former dry-goods warehouse built in 1856; it opened in 1988 as a hotel. The high-ceiling guest rooms are modern with Colonial touches and come standard and deluxe (deluxe includes king-size bed and parlor). VCRs and videos are available for a small charge. Complimentary Continental breakfast is served in a courtyard dining room with a glass ceiling. ⚑ *235 Chestnut St., 19106,* ☎ *215/922–4443 or 800/624–2988,* FAX *215/922– 4487. 36 rooms. In-room modem lines, health club privileges. AE, D, DC, MC, V.*

$$$ **Holiday Inn Independence Mall.** "Independence Mall" in the name is no exaggeration: This is one of the most convenient hotels to the downtown historic area. To complement its location, all rooms are done in Colonial decor with Ethan Allen furniture, including poster beds and wing chairs. Children under 19 stay free in parents' rooms; children under 12 eat free. ⚑ *4th and Arch Sts., 19106,* ☎ *215/923–8660 or 800/THE–BELL,* FAX *215/923–4633. 364 rooms, 7 suites. Restaurant, bar, pool. AE, D, DC, MC, V.*

$$ **Comfort Inn at Penn's Landing.** The low price is the most noteworthy attraction here, with a complimentary deluxe breakfast as an additional lure. The 10-story hotel, opened in 1987, provides basic accommodations and service. Decor is contemporary, with oak furniture and a mauve color scheme. A bar enlivens the small, nondescript lobby. Tucked between the Benjamin Franklin Bridge, Delaware Avenue, and I–95, the location has more noise than charm—but if you're lucky enough to get a room on one of the upper floors facing the river, you'll enjoy a good view of the Benjamin Franklin Bridge beautifully lit up at night. A nice plus is the courtesy van service to points all over Center City; in a minute's time, foot power will bring you to the nearby Betsy Ross House. ⚑ *100 N. Christopher Columbus Blvd., 19106,* ☎ *215/627– 7900 or 800/228–5150,* FAX *215/238–0809. 185 rooms, including 3 suites. Lobby lounge, free parking. AE, D, DC, MC, V.*

Other accommodations in or around the Historic District include the Shippen Way Inn, Society Hill Hotel, Thomas Bond House, and the Bank Street Hostel (*see* Bed-and-Breakfasts *and* Youth Hostels, *below*).

The Shopping/Theater District

$$$$ **Doubletree Hotel Philadelphia.** You can sit in the four-story atrium lobby lounge and observe one of the busiest corners in Philly's shopping and theater district. Opened in 1983 as the Hershey, it was a Hilton until 1993. The rooms, renovated in 1994, are decorated in earth-tones and have modern furnishings. The hotel's sawtooth design gives each room a peaked bay window with a whopping 180-degree view. East-side rooms get a panoramic view of the city, the Delaware River, and New Jersey. ⚑ *Broad and Locust Sts., 19107,* ☎ *215/893–1600 or 800/822–TREE,* FAX *215/893–1663. 427 rooms, including 8 suites. Restaurant, lobby lounge, indoor pool, sauna, health club, racquetball. AE, D, DC, MC, V.*

$$$$ **Holiday Inn Select Center City.** This is an above-average Holiday Inn, centrally located between Benjamin Franklin Parkway, Rittenhouse Square, and City Hall. The 25-floor hotel opened in 1971 and completed a $10.5 million renovation in 1994. All rooms have a green-

Lodging

Adam's Mark, **3**

Airport Hilton, **29**

Bank Street Hostel, **23**

The Barclay, **11**

Best Western Independence Park Inn, **25**

Center City Hotel, **1**

Chamounix Mansion, **2**

Chestnut Hill Hotel, **5**

Clarion Suites, **20**

Comfort Inn at Penn's Landing, **22**

Days Inn, **31**

Doubletree Guest Suites at the Airport, **28**

Doubletree Hotel Philadelphia, **17**

Four Seasons, **8**

Holiday Inn Airport South, **32**

Holiday Inn Select Center City, **9**

Holiday Inn City Line, **4**

Holiday Inn Independence Mall, **21**

Holiday Inn Midtown, **18**

Hotel Atop the Bellevue, **16**

International House, **6**

Latham, **13**

Penn Tower, **7**

Philadelphia Marriott, **19**

The Rittenhouse, **10**

Ritz-Carlton, **14**

Sheraton Society Hill, **27**

Shippen Way Inn, **33**

Society Hill Hotel, **24**

Thomas Bond House, **26**

Travelodge Hotel Stadium, **30**

The Warwick, **12**

Wyndham Franklin Plaza, **15**

440 yards
400 meters

Willow St.

Callowhill St.

6th St.

Wood St.
30

Vine St.

Franklin Square

Benjamin Franklin Bridge

Front St.

30 76

20

Cherry St.

Race St.

Quarry St.

Elfreth's Alley

U.S. Mint

22

2nd St.

Arch St.

Arch St.

21

phia ion Center/ Terminal Market Filbert St.

Commerce St.

Market St.

Delaware River

Penn's Landing

Ranstead St.

Independence Hall

Chestnut St.

Bank St.

23

Letitia St.

24

25

Front St.

Independence Square

Ionic St.

Sansom St.

26

Sansom St.

10th St.

Walnut St.

27

Washington Square

Locust St.

5th St.

4th St.

3rd St.

Delaware Ave.

Spruce St.

2nd St.

95

9th St.

8th St.

7th St.

6th St.

Pine St.

Delancey St.

N

KEY

Lombard St.

- - - - Market-Frankford Subway
——— Broad St. Subway
- - - - Subway-Surface Subway
——— Airport Train

South St.

33

28 29 30 31 32

and-beige color scheme and contemporary decor. The "Select" properties offer extra amenities, including voice mail, iron and ironing boards, coffeemakers, cable TV, in-room modem lines, hairdryers, and *USA Today.* ☎ *1800 Market St., 19103,* ☎ *215/561–7500 or 800/HOLIDAY,* ℻ *215/561–4484. 445 rooms, including 2 suites. Restaurant, bar, 13 no-smoking floors, pool, exercise room. AE, D, DC, MC, V.*

$$$$ **Hotel Atop the Bellevue.** A Philadelphia institution for 92 years, the
★ elegant Bellevue hotel reopened in 1989, thanks to a three-year, $150 million renovation which transformed the hotel's lower floors into offices and retail space. The Barrymore Room, topped by a 30-foot stained-glass dome, and the seven-story Conservatory atrium are just two of the hotel's lavish public areas. Founders, with views of the city from its 19th-floor location, ranks among the most visually impressive dining rooms in town. From the champagne toast available at registration to the telephones in the bathrooms, a stay at the Bellevue is full of luxurious touches. Rooms are large and each has an entertainment center with color TV, stereo, and VCR; minibar; and in-room modem lines. Guests have free use of the Sporting Club, the best health club in town. There are also two floors of shops. ☎ *Broad and Walnut Sts., 19102,* ☎ *215/893–1776 or 800/221–0833,* ℻ *215/732–8518. 170 rooms. Restaurant, bar, lobby lounge, room service, shops, concierge. AE, D, DC, MC, V.*

$$$$ **Latham.** Once known as the finest business-traveler's hostelry in America, this is a small, elegant hotel with a European accent and an emphasis on personal service. Doormen clad in vests and riding boots welcome you to the lobby. A concierge is on duty daily from 10 to 8. All rooms have marble-topped bureaus and Louis XV-style writing desks, full-wall mirrors, hair dryers, and makeup mirrors; most have minibars. The weekend package includes a deluxe room, valet parking, and gourmet breakfast. ☎ *17th St. at Walnut St. (1 block from Rittenhouse Sq.), 19103,* ☎ *215/563–7474 or 800/528–4261,* ℻ *215/568–0110. 139 rooms. Restaurant, piano bar, health club privileges, business services. AE, D, DC, MC, V.*

$$$$ **Philadelphia Marriott.** If you like big, bustling hotels, this is your place. Opened in January 1995, this convention hotel—the biggest in Pennsylvania—cost $200 million, takes up an entire city block, and has corridors even the staff gets lost in. For an intrinsically impersonal place, it does go to a lot of effort to meet special needs (iron and ironing board in each room, 24-hour workout room, kids' menu from room service) and offers some of the lowest rates in its price category. The five-story lobby atrium features a water sculpture, piano music (live and taped), and greenery (real and fake). The 1,200 guest rooms are big, beige, and bland; half come with two queens, the rest with kings; all have full-length mirrors and extra counter space in the well-lit bathrooms. For no extra cost you can request one of the 250 "rooms that work," with adjustable work table, and extra lighting and outlets. The seventh-floor health club has the size and facilities of a good, small independent club. ☎ *1201 Market St., 19107,* ☎ *215/625–2900 or 800/699–1201,* ℻ *215/625–6000. 1200 rooms, including 54 suites. 2 restaurants, 2 lobby lounges, sports bar, room service, indoor pool, concierge, business services. AE, D, DC, MC, V.*

$$$$ **The Rittenhouse.** This luxury hotel takes full advantage of its Rittenhouse Square location: many of the rooms and both restaurants overlook the city's classiest park. The expansive white-marbled lobby leads to the Mary Cassatt Tearoom and Lounge and a cloistered garden. The 33-story building's sawtooth design gives the guest rooms their unusual shape, with nooks and alcoves. Each room is outfitted with an array of amenities: two TVs, three telephones, an entertainment center in an

armoire, a fully-stocked minibar, and a king-size bed. Ninth-floor rooms facing the square have the best views. ⚇ *210 West Rittenhouse Sq., 19103,* ☎ *215/546–9000 or 800/635–1042,* FAX *215/732–3364. 98 rooms, including 11 suites. 2 restaurants, bar, room service, 3 no-smoking floors, health club, concierge, business services, valet parking. AE, D, DC, MC, V.*

$$$$ **Ritz-Carlton.** Ritzy it is: a million dollars' worth of art on display, mantelpieces from Italy, silk walls in the bar, and for all those ladies who wear baubles from Bailey, Banks, and Biddle, a "security" elevator from the downstairs porte cochere to the main lobby. Opened in November 1990, the 15-story building is nestled between the twin blue towers of Liberty Place (and adjacent to the Shops at Liberty Place—more than 70 stores, boutiques, and restaurants). All rooms have an elegant, Colonial motif; most have king-size beds, although rooms with oversize twins are available. All the typical luxury amenities are here: entertainment center in armoire, honor bar, complimentary shoeshine, valet laundry service, bathroom telephone, terry robes, hair dryers, and bathroom scale. You'll also find a complimentary copy of *Philadelphia* magazine and souvenir Ritz-Carlton bookmark. ⚇ *17th and Chestnut Sts. (at Liberty Pl.), 19103,* ☎ *215/563–1600 or 800/241–3333,* FAX *215/567–2822. 290 guest rooms, including 15 suites. 2 restaurants, bar, lobby lounge, room service, health club, baby-sitting, concierge. AE, D, DC, MC, V.*

$$$ **The Barclay.** There's something special about staying at a hotel that
★ has hosted Katherine Hepburn, Eugene Ormandy, Katherine Cornell, and the Grateful Dead—just to mention some of the celebrities that have made this grande dame of a hotel their Philadelphia pied-à-terre. During its heyday, in the '30s and '40s, half of Broadway stayed here when plays would have their Philly run before opening in New York. Today, the stars may have departed but the stardust remains. The elegant, dark-paneled lobby leads to a registration area sparkling with a half dozen crystal chandeliers and matching wall fixtures. Guest rooms were renovated in 1994 and have hardwood floors and Oriental rugs. Many of the rooms have four-poster beds—most with canopies. Furniture has old-world charm throughout, and in most rooms TV sets are concealed in handsome armoires. And, of course, how nice that Rittenhouse Square is right outside the front door. ⚇ *Rittenhouse Sq. E., 19103,* ☎ *215/545–0300 or 800/421–6662,* FAX *215/545–2896. 105 rooms, including 18 suites. Restaurant, lobby lounge, concierge. AE, DC, D, MC, V.*

$$$ **Holiday Inn Midtown.** Rooms are more spacious than average here—perhaps because they're older (this Holiday Inn opened in 1964 and was renovated in 1992). All guest rooms have contemporary furnishings and a light, floral motif. Rooms facing south to Walnut Street have the best views. Drive in off Walnut Street for valet parking. The location is excellent: one block from the Broad Street Subway, near the theater and shopping district, and three blocks from the new Convention Center. No-smoking guest rooms are a special feature. ⚇ *1305 Walnut St., 19107,* ☎ *215/735–9300 or 800/HOLIDAY. 166 rooms. Pool. AE, D, DC, MC, V.*

$$$ **The Warwick.** Half of the rooms here are apartments, which makes for an interesting mix of guests in business suits and residents in shorts and sneakers all crossing the lobby (nicely brightened by mirrors and 18-foot Palladian windows) in a constant stream of activity. A $5 million renovation was completed in 1992, with spacious guest rooms refurbished in "English country style." Bathrooms are marble, with an ivy-green motif. A nice touch is the current issue of *Philadelphia* magazine in your room. ⚇ *1701 Locust St., 19103,* ☎ *215/735–6000*

or 800/523–4210, FAX *215/790–7766. 153 rooms, including 47 suites. Restaurant, bar, coffee shop, health club privileges. AE, DC, MC, V.*

The Airport District

A 20-minute drive or taxi ride away from most sightseeing and entertainment, these hotels are less expensive than those found downtown. While some of these hotels are within sight of industrial parks, they all enjoy a convenient location near the airport—a real plus for business travelers.

$$$ **Airport Hilton.** Enjoy a swim in the unique lobby pool of the Airport Hilton before jumping on a free shuttle bus for the ride to your airport terminal across the street. During the week, this is mostly a business travelers' hotel. Rooms have wood-and-wicker dressing tables and bureaus, and cable TV. 🏨 *4509 Island Ave., 19153,* ☎ *215/365–4150 or 800/445–8667,* FAX *215/365–3875. 330 rooms, including 2 suites. Restaurant, sports bar, pool, sauna, exercise room, free parking. Weekend rates. AE, D, DC, MC, V.*

$$$ **Doubletree Guest Suites at the Airport.** A glass-walled elevator whisks
★ you to your floor at this all-suite hotel, where rooms front balconies overlooking the light-flooded atrium lobby and restaurant. Suites are standard or deluxe; deluxe have larger living rooms and better views. Each accommodation has a king-size bed in the bedroom and a queen-size foldout in the living room, three telephones, two remote-control TV/clock-radios, honor bars, and coffeemakers, plus complimentary in-suite coffee packages and daily newspapers. The hotel has a wide range of weekend and theme packages. 🏨 *4101 Island Ave., 19153,* ☎ *215/365–6600 or 800/424–2900,* FAX *215/492–8471. 251 suites. Restaurant, lobby lounge, indoor pool, exercise room, free parking, airport shuttle. AE, D, DC, MC, V.*

$$$ **Holiday Inn Airport South.** A $3 million renovation in 1993 converted the lobby's "Floridian" theme to a more traditional look—with green marble, darker colors, and fireplaces. The slightly oversize rooms have pastel color schemes with light-color wood furniture. It's 3 miles west of the airport. 🏨 *45 Industrial Hwy. (Rte. 291), Essington 19029,* ☎ *610/521–2400 or 800/HOLIDAY,* FAX *610–521–1605. 306 rooms. Restaurant, pool, exercise room, airport shuttle. Weekend rates. AE, D, DC, MC, V.*

$$ **Travelodge Hotel Stadium.** This circular high-rise building was a Ramada Inn till 1993. Rooms have coffeemakers, refrigerators, and remote-control cable TV. Upper floors have a good view of the city. 🏨 *20th St. and Penrose Ave., 19145,* ☎ *215/755–6500 or 800/228–2828,* FAX *215/465–7517. 208 rooms. Restaurant, bar, airport shuttle. AE, D, DC, MC, V.*

$$ **Days Inn.** Even though this new hotel is surrounded by highways and is across the street from the airport, special construction makes it quiet. The sunny, pastel-green corridors of the five-story L-shaped building lead to pleasant and spacious rooms. 🏨 *4101 Island Ave., 19153,* ☎ *215/492–0400 or 800/325–2525,* FAX *215/365–6035. 177 rooms. Café, no-smoking rooms, airport shuttle. Children under 18 free and senior-citizen rates. AE, D, DC, MC, V.*

University City

Part of West Philadelphia, just across the Schuylkill River, this area is a five- to 10-minute drive from Center City. Slightly less expensive than downtown, the hotels are on the campus of the University of Penn-

sylvania, and near Drexel University and the Civic Center, the city's secondary convention facility.

$$$ **Penn Tower.** The University of Pennsylvania purchased and renovated this 21-floor former Hilton in 1987. It is located on the eastern edge of the campus, a good stone's throw from the Civic Center, University Museum, Franklin Field, 30th Street Station, Drexel University, and University Hospital. All rooms were renovated in 1993 with traditional mahogany furnishings, cable TV, and data ports for personal-computer usage. Rooms have excellent views east to Center City and west across campus. A big plus is free use of the university's own athletic facilities, including an Olympic-size pool. ☎ *34th St. and Civic Center Blvd., 19104,* ☎ *215/387–8333 or 800/356–PENN,* 📠 *215/386–8306. 175 rooms, including 7 suites. Restaurant, bar. AE, D, DC, MC, V.*

$ **International House.** This residence for students and professors from around the world is located on the University of Pennsylvania campus. Rooms are available year-round, but guests must have an affiliation with an educational institution. The high-rise building has an unusual, poured-concrete, tiered design and an oddly barren atrium. Both the public areas and the rooms themselves have a rough-hewn, spartan feel. Single rooms share bath and living room; double rooms have two single beds and private bath. No children permitted. ☎ *3701 Chestnut St., 19104,* ☎ *215/387–5125,* 📠 *215/895–6535. 379 rooms. Café, lobby lounge. MC, V.*

City Line

If you prefer to stay outside the bustle of downtown and enjoy free parking, you'll like the two hotels here. It's only a 10-minute ride on the Schuylkill Expressway to Center City under favorable conditions; however, visitors should take note that the expressway is frequently under construction and heavily congested.

$$$ **Adam's Mark.** This 23-story hotel is one of the tallest in Philadelphia. Request a room on the upper floors facing south toward Fairmount Park and the downtown skyline. There's nothing special about the rooms, which are on the small side. The big attraction here is the nighttime activity: Quincy's, a turn-of-the-century nightclub, plus two restaurants—one set in a re-created, paneled English library, the other in a French orangerie—a popular lounge, and a sports bar. Lines form early for the action at all these spots. ☎ *City Ave. and Monument Rd., 19131,* ☎ *215/581–5000 or 800/444–2326,* 📠 *215/581–5089. 515 rooms, including 56 suites. 2 restaurants, nightclub, sports bar, hair salon, indoor and outdoor pools, health club. AE, D, DC, MC, V.*

$$$ **Holiday Inn City Line.** This eight-story Holiday Inn is perfectly ordinary, but it's a good value in a choice location. You could stay here to save money and just walk across the parking lot to all the eateries and nightspots of the Adam's Mark hotel. A five-minute walk takes you to six other restaurants. In the lobby you can sink into an overstuffed easy chair and watch swimmers in the glass-enclosed pool. ☎ *4100 Presidential Blvd., 19131,* ☎ *215/477–0200 or 800/642–8982,* 📠 *215/473–5510. 343 rooms. Restaurant, indoor pool. AE, D, DC, MC, V.*

Chestnut Hill

Staying here, about a 25-minute drive from downtown, puts you among some of Philadelphia's finest homes and shops. This ritzy neighborhood has more than 120 shops—from Oriental-rug dealers to

bookstores, clothing boutiques, crafts and music stores, and cheese shops. Nearby is the Wissahickon Valley of Fairmount Park.

$$ **Chestnut Hill Hotel.** Here's a Colonial inn in the heart of Chestnut Hill. Built as a hotel in 1899, the four-story building was renovated in 1983. Ask to see the rooms first; they vary widely in size and ambience. Some have mahogany reproductions of 18th-century furniture, including four-poster beds. A packet of brochures in each room describes area shops and sights. Adjacent to the hotel is a farmer's market and shopping complex. ☎ *8229 Germantown Ave., 19118,* ☎ *215/242–5905 or 800/628–9744,* FAX *215/242–8778. 28 rooms, including 3 suites. 3 restaurants. AE, DC, MC, V.*

Bed-and-Breakfasts

For many visitors, it's the particularly gracious welcome. Others enjoy the personal touch of the owner. Still others like to wake up in a room filled with Victorian antiques or to enjoy the chance to leave behind today's hustle and bustle for a weekend. Whatever the reason, many travelers enjoy the distinctive personalities of bed-and-breakfast hostelries when on the road. These often less expensive alternatives to hotels are modeled after the European tradition of a room and meal in a private house or small hotel.

These bed-and-breakfasts offer considerable diversity in urban, suburban, and rural settings. Services and policies vary. Some B&Bs accept children and pets; others offer monthly rates and provide free transportation from airports and bus or train terminals. Breakfasts range from hearty to elegant.

$$$ **Society Hill Hotel.** This 1832 former longshoreman's house is one of the smallest hotels in the city—but it boasts an outdoor café, piano bar, and restaurant. Fresh flowers adorn all of its 12 guest rooms, which are furnished with antiques, brass beds, and lamps. The breakfast tray is brought to your room with fresh-squeezed juice and freshly baked muffins and croissants. Readers have written to say that the hotel is beginning to show its age and they hope that a renovation is in the works. ☎ *301 Chestnut St., 19106,* ☎ *215/925–1394,* FAX *215/925–3780. 12 rooms, including 6 suites. Restaurant, bar, café. AE, DC, MC, V.*

$$$ **Thomas Bond House.** Spend the night in the heart of Old City the way Philadelphians did 226 years ago. Built in 1769 by a prominent local physician, this four-story house recently underwent a faithful, meticulous restoration of everything from its molding and wall sconces to the millwork and flooring. All rooms have 18th-century features such as marble fireplaces and four-poster Thomasville beds. It doesn't get any more Colonial than this. ☎ *129 S. 2nd St., 19106,* ☎ *215/923–8523 or 800/845–BOND,* FAX *215/923–8504. 12 rooms, including 2 suites. AE, D, DC, MC, V.*

$$ **Shippen Way Inn.** Imagine the historic Betsy Ross House turned into
★ a bed-and-breakfast and you'll have an idea of what to expect at the Shippen Way Inn. In 1987, Raymond Ruhle and his family restored two adjacent, working-class, 18th-century houses to create this Colonial-style inn. Guest rooms vary in size and appeal, but most have original exposed wooden beams and wide plank floors, period wall stenciling, and original and reproduction antiques. The communal living room has a fireplace and TV. You can enjoy tea in the quiet of the walled-in garden out back, before walking a block to shops and nightlife along South Street. ☎ *416-18 Bainbridge St.,* ☎ *215/627–7266 or 800/245–4873,* FAX *215/271–2660. 9 rooms. AE, MC, V.*

B&B Reservation Services

$–$$$ Bed and Breakfast Connections–Philadelphia. Its selection of more than 100 host homes and inns includes a Colonial town house, a converted 1880s bank-style barn, and an 18th-century farmhouse on the Main Line. Prices range from $30 to $175. ⌧ *Box 21, Devon 19333,* ☎ *610/687–3565 or 800/448–3619. AE, MC, V.*

$–$$ Bed and Breakfast—The Manor. This service has various locations throughout Philadelphia and surrounding areas, including Amish country. Many hosts supply transportation for a nominal fee. Some accommodate the handicapped. Prices range from $45 to $85. ⌧ *Box 416, 830 Village Rd., Lampeter 17537,* ☎ *717/464–9564 or 800/461–7BED. MC, V.*

Youth Hostels

Youth hostels provide dormitory-style accommodations for less than you'd pay to park your car at a downtown hotel. They also offer a sense of adventure and a chance to share living, eating, and sleeping quarters with travelers from all over the world.

The American Youth Hostel Regional Office and Travel Center is at 624 South 3rd Street (☎ 215/925–6004).

$ Chamounix Mansion. Here's the cheapest place to stay in Philadelphia—$10 a night if you are an American Youth Hostel member, and $3 more if you are the guest of an AYH member. Located on a wooded bluff overlooking the Schuylkill River (and, unfortunately, the Schuylkill Expressway), it feels like it's out in the country. This restored 1802 Quaker country estate is loaded with character. The entrance hall is lined with flags; period rooms have antiques; walls display old maps, sketches, and paintings. Hard to find; call for directions. ⌧ *Chamounix Dr., 19131,* ☎ *215/878–3676 or 800/379–0017. 6 rooms for 48 people, shared baths and kitchen. MC, V. Closed Dec. 15–Jan. 15.*

$ Bank Street Hostel. Independently owned and managed by David Herskowitz, Bank Street opened in 1992 and, at $15 a night, is a downtown-Philly lodging bargain. It's located on the cusp of Olde City and Society Hill in a 140-year-old manufacturing building that's been combined with two neighboring buildings. Guests gather around the pool table and 48-inch TV. ⌧ *32 South Bank St., 19106,* ☎ *215/922–0222 or 800/392–4678. 3 rooms for 54 people. No credit cards.*

7 The Arts and Nightlife

THE ARTS

OF ALL THE PERFORMING ARTS, it is music for which Philadelphia is most renowned and the Philadelphia Orchestra of which its people are most proud. Considered one of the world's best symphony orchestras, it rose to fame under the batons of former conductors Leopold Stokowski and Eugene Ormandy, with Riccardo Muti—musical director of the La Scala Opera in Milan—recently ending a 12-year tenure at the helm. Maestro Muti must have felt quite at home in Philly since the orchestra performs at the Academy of Music, an acoustically superb concert hall built in 1857 and modeled after La Scala. Orchestra concerts during the September-to-May season are still among the city's premier social events. If you can get tickets, go. You'll see one of the city's finest groups in an opulent setting, with many Philadelphians dressed to match the occasion.

Updated by
Rathe Miller

The Opera Company of Philadelphia also performs at the Academy. They've gained national prominence several years ago with their performance of *La Bohème* on PBS's Great Performances—the most widely watched opera telecast in the history of public television. OCP annually welcomes the world's greatest tenor to its stage when Luciano Pavarotti attends the finals of the Luciano Pavarotti International Voice Competition.

There is no shortage of live entertainment, ranging from the Philly Pops to the Mellon Jazz Festival. There are also summer concerts of popular and classical music at the Robin Hood Dell East and at Fairmount Park's Mann Music Center. Many rock groups stop in Philadelphia on their national tours, playing at Spectrum, Tower Theater, or Veterans Stadium.

Of course, Philly holds a special place in pop music history. *American Bandstand,* hosted by Dick Clark, began as a local dance show. When it went national in 1957, it gave a boost to many hometown boys, including Fabian, Bobby Rydell, Frankie Avalon, and Chubbie Checker. The city's rock-and-roll tradition began in 1955 with Bill Haley and the Comets. In the 1970s, the Philadelphia Sound—a polished blend of disco, pop, and rhythm and blues—came alive through Kenny Gamble and Leon Huff; its lush sound has been kept alive by chart-toppers such as Hall and Oates and Patti LaBelle.

For current performances and listings, the best guides to Philly's performing arts are the "Guide to the Lively Arts" in the daily *Philadelphia Inquirer,* the "Weekend" section of the Friday *Inquirer,* the "Friday" section of the *Philadelphia Daily News,* and the Donnelley Directory Events Hotline (☎ 215/337–7777, ext. 2540). Two weekly papers, the *City Paper* and the *Philadelphia Weekly,* with extensive listings of concerts and clubs, are available free in newsboxes all over center city. Check also at the Visitors Center (16th St. and John F. Kennedy Blvd.). "UpStages" (☎ 215/893–1145) at Liberty Place (1650 Market St.) and at the Philadelphia Arts Bank (Broad and South Sts.) has discount tickets, often up to 50%, to productions and concerts around town.

Theater

Forrest Theater (1114 Walnut St., ☎ 215/923–1515) has major Broadway shows. Recent productions of *Cats, La Cage Aux Folles, Les Misérables,* and *Phantom of the Opera* have played here.

Annenberg Center (3680 Walnut St., ☎ 215/898–6791), a performing arts complex on the University of Pennsylvania campus, has four stages, from the 120-seat Studio to the 970-seat Zellerbach Theater. Something is going on almost all the time—including local and touring company productions of musical-comedy, drama, dance, and children's theater productions.

Merriam Theater (250 S. Broad St., ☎ 215/732–5446). Formerly the Shubert, and part of the University of the Arts, the Merriam presents Broadway tours and student productions of musicals and dramas.

Walnut Street Theater (9th and Walnut Sts., ☎ 215/574–3550). Founded in 1809, this is the oldest English-speaking theater in continuous use in the United States. The schedule includes musicals, comedy, and drama in a lovely auditorium where almost every seat is a good one.

Wilma Theater (2030 Sansom St., ☎ 215/963–0345), under artistic director Blanka Zizka, has gained favorable critical notices for its innovative work with American and European drama. In 1996 it will move to a new $20 million building at Broad and Spruce streets. Its season runs from September to June.

Philadelphia Theater Company (1714 Delancey St., at Plays and Players, ☎ 215/592–8333). Philadelphia and world premieres of works by contemporary American playwrights are performed here. The company also produces Stages, a program showcasing new plays by American playwrights.

Society Hill Playhouse (507 S. 8th St., ☎ 215/923–0210). The main stage features contemporary works; the Second Space Cabaret Theater has musical-comedies.

American Theater Arts for Youth (Seaport Museum, Penn's Landing, ☎ 215/563–3501) features musicals and live productions of the National Theater for Children.

Philadelphia Festival Theater for New Plays (3680 Walnut St., ☎ 215/898–3900) focuses on works by new playwrights. Its season runs from January through June. Award–winning playwright Bruce Graham is the interim artistic director.

Freedom Theater (1346 N. Broad St., ☎ 215/765–2793) is the oldest and most active African-American theater in Pennsylvania. Performances are held September through June.

Brick Playhouse (623 South St., ☎ 215/592–1183). Above the Montserrat Restaurant, in a space that seats 70, this two-year-old theater group develops and produces new works by local playwrights.

Concerts

Philadelphia Orchestra. The world-renowned ensemble performs at the Academy of Music (Broad and Locust Sts., ☎ 215/893–1900) from September to May. Riccardo Muti ended his 12-year tenure in 1992 and passed the baton to the new musical director, Wolfgang Sawallisch, who emphasizes the German repertoire. In June and July, a series of

noted soloists and guest conductors perform with the orchestra in an outdoor amphitheater, the Mann Music Center (West Fairmount Park, ☎ 215/878–7707). In addition to regular seating, you can bring a blanket and sit on the grassy slope under the stars as you listen to guest performers such as André Watts and Itzhak Perlman.

Concerto Soloists of Philadelphia (9th and Walnut Sts., ☎ 215/574–3550), directed by Marc Mostovoy, performs chamber music from September to June.

Philadelphia Chamber Music Society presents a classical music series of 27 concerts, including Music from Marlboro, at the Pennsylvania Convention Center (12th and Arch Sts., ☎ 215/569–4690) from October to May.

Robin Hood Dell East (Strawberry Mansion Dr., East Fairmount Park, ☎ 215/477–8810) is the site for rhythm-and-blues and soul music concerts on Monday and Wednesday evenings in July and August.

Philly Pops (☎ 215/735–7506), conducted by Peter Nero, performs at the Academy of Music from October to May and, occasionally, at other local events.

All-Star Forum (☎ 215/735–7506). Impresario Moe Septee and his 55-year-old organization bring visiting orchestras, recitals by stars such as Itzhak Perlman and Isaac Stern, ballets, and special musical events to the Academy of Music.

Mellon PSFS Jazz Festival (☎ 215/636–1666 or 610/667–3559) presents a series of 40 concerts and events (most with low ticket prices or free) in June at locations around town. The top names in jazz perform, including Pat Martino, Wynton Marsalis, and Chick Corea.

Philadelphia Folk Festival (Old Pool Farm, near Schwenksville, ☎ 215/242–0150) was first held in 1962 and is the oldest continuously running folk festival in the country, taking place each year during the last week in August. Performers have included Doc Watson, Taj Mahal, Joan Baez, and Judy Collins.

Opera

Opera Company of Philadelphia (510 Walnut St., ☎ 215/928–2100) has four productions a year at the Academy of Music between October and April featuring such stars as Luciano Pavarotti. All performances are in original languages with computerized English "supertitles" above the stage.

Savoy Company (☎ 215/735–7161), the oldest Gilbert and Sullivan company in the country, stages one G&S operetta each May or June at the Academy of Music and at Longwood Gardens.

Dance

The **Philadelphia Dance Alliance** (☎ 215/564–5270) is a good source of information on dance concerts, local companies, and touring companies visiting town.

Pennsylvania Ballet (☎ 215/551–7000), under artistic director Roy Kaiser, dances on the stages of the Academy of Music and the Merriam Theater, from October to June. The *Nutcracker* production at Christmastime is a perennial favorite.

Philadelphia Dance Company (Philadanco) (☎ 215/387–8200) performs modern dance in June at the ArtsBank (601 S. Broad St., ☎ 215/545–

0590) and September at Annenberg Center (3680 Walnut St., ☎ 215/898–6791).

Film

Philly's magnificent old movie palaces are all gone, as are the classic film repertory houses like Roxy Screening Room and TLA. Center City filmgoers thank their stars for the Ritz movie theaters and the new United Artist Riverview Plaza (1400 S. Delaware Ave., ☎ 215/755–2219), a clean, civilized multiplex. Avoid what's left of the first-run theaters on Chestnut Street west of Broad Street—they're frequented by rowdy urban youths.

Ritz Five (214 Walnut St., ☎ 215/925–7900) and **Ritz at the Bourse** (4th St. north of Chestnut St., ☎ 215/440–1181) are the finest movie theaters in town for avant-garde and foreign films. Both have comfortable seats, clean surroundings, a first-rate sound system, and courteous audiences and staff.

Philadelphia Festival of World Cinema (3701 Chestnut St., ☎ 215/895–6593) is a 12-day event in May filled with screenings, seminars, and events attended by critics, scholars, and filmmakers and cinema buffs.

NIGHTLIFE

Nightlife in Philadelphia is far better than it used to be (when they supposedly rolled up the sidewalks at 8 o'clock). Today you can listen to a chanteuse in a chic basement nightclub; dance till 3 AM in a smoky bistro; and watch street jugglers, mimes, and magicians on a Society Hill corner.

South Street between Front and 9th streets is still the hippest street in town. One-of-a-kind shops, bookstores, galleries, restaurants, and bars attract the young and the restless by the droves. In the past few years, **Main Street** in Manyunk, in the northwest section of the city, has become a smaller, tamer version of South Street. Dozens of new clubs have also opened up along the **Delaware River waterfront,** most of them near the Benjamin Franklin Bridge; a water taxi shuttles revelers between them.

Bars and clubs can change hands or go out of business faster than a soft pretzel goes stale. For current information check the entertainment pages of the *Philadelphia Inquirer,* the *Philadelphia Daily News,* and *Philadelphia* magazine. You can also call radio station WRTI's "Jazz Line," an extensive, up-to-the-minute listing of music in town, at 215/204–5277. For information about Penn's Landing events call 215/923–4992.

Bars, Lounges, and Cabarets

Dirty Frank's. Frank is long gone, but this place is still dirty, cheap, and a Philadelphia classic. An incongruous mixture of students, artists, journalists, and resident characters such as Jaitch DeLeon and F. Baggs Piglatano crowd around the horseshoe-shape bar and engage in friendly mayhem. *347 S. 13th St.,* ☎ *215/732–5010.* ☉ *Mon.–Sat. 11 AM–2 AM. No credit cards.*

Khyber Pass. It's small and loud, with lots of action. The music is all live, including alternative and rock, national and local talent. With over 100 brands, it has probably the best selection of beers in town. *56 S.*

2nd St., Olde City, ☏ *215/440–9683.* ⊗ *Mon.–Sat. noon–2 AM. No credit cards.*

Mia's. This upscale "meet market" bar and restaurant off the lobby of the Warwick Hotel is a popular after-work place for the business crowd. *17th and Locust Sts.,* ☏ *215/545–4655.* ⊗ *Daily 5 PM–2 AM. AE, D, DC, MC, V.*

Happy Rooster. Owner "Doc" Ulitsky provides the best selection of after-dinner drinks and liqueurs in the city. French, Russian, and Gypsy music plays in the background. *118 S. 16th St., Downtown,* ☏ *215/563–1481. Jacket required.* ⊗ *Mon.–Sat. 11:30 AM–2 AM. AE, DC, MC, V.*

Hepburn's. Philadelphia's only women's bar, but men are welcome (in fact, Wednesday night is "men's night"). Downstairs is a friendly lounge with a pinkish glow; upstairs is a disco, two pool tables and an outdoor deck. *254 S. 12th St.,* ☏ *215/545–8088.* ⊗ *Daily 4 PM–2 AM. No credit cards.*

Swann Lounge. Dance to piano music and a trio in an elegant hotel lounge. *Four Seasons Hotel, 18th St. and Benjamin Franklin Pkwy., Center City,* ☏ *215/963–1500.* ⊗ *Piano music weekdays 6–10 PM; Viennese buffet with trio and dancing, Fri. and Sat. 9 PM–1 AM. AE, D, DC, MC, V.*

Trocadero. This spacious rock 'n' roll club occupies a former burlesque house where W. C. Fields and Mae West performed. A lot of the old decor remains: mirrors, pillars, and balconies surround the dance floor. Most every band on the way up that's passing through Philly plays here for an under-30 crowd. On other nights, local DJs host dance parties. *1003 Arch St., Chinatown,* ☏ *215/923–7625.*

Woody's. This is Philadelphia's most popular gay bar. *202 S. 13th St.,* ☏ *215/545–1893.* ⊗ *Daily 11 AM–2 AM. No credit cards.*

Comedy Club

Comedy Cabaret atop the Middle East. Philly's one enduring comedy club presents national names and local talent. There's a dinner/show special at the Middle East restaurant downstairs. *126 Chestnut St., Olde City,* ☏ *215/625–JOKE.* ☛ *$10 cover, plus 2-drink minimum.*

Dancing and Discos

Katmandu. Large and usually crowded, this is an indoor/outdoor Caribbean restaurant and bar that features live music nightly—world, reggae, rock—and a "Wild Island" dance party on Saturday nights. *Columbus Blvd. south of Spring Garden St.,* ☏ *215/629–7400.* ⊗ *Daily 11:30 AM–2 AM. AE, DC, MC, V.*

Maui Entertainment Complex. If you're idea of heaven is ersatz tropical ambience, beach volleyball, and waitresses in cut-offs and bikini tops hawking beakers and individual shots of the drink-of-the-moment to a crowd in their 20s, this place is for you. Dancing happens indoors and out on the city's biggest dance floor to live bands (rock, alternative, progressive) and to radio DJ dance-party broadcasts. *Pier 53 North, 1143 Columbus Blvd.,* ☏ *215/423–8116.* ☛ *Covers range from $5–$7.* ⊗ *Thurs.–Sun. 8 PM–2 AM.*

Dave & Buster's. Call this a big "amusement park" for the somewhat grown-up. A short list of what's going on includes: two restaurants,

five bars, pool tables, pinball and video games, "just for fun" black-jack and poker, a virtual reality shooting game, and an outdoor deck overlooking the river. *325 N. Columbus Blvd.,* ☏ *215/413–1951.* ☼ *Mon.–Thurs. 11 AM–1 AM, Fri.–Sat. 11 AM–2 AM, Sun. 11 AM–8 PM.*

Monte Carlo Living Room. The DJ at this sophisticated watering hole plays Top-40 hits, European sounds, and South American music. An intimate room where all the furnishings, from the tapestries to the paintings, are European. The clientele are men in ties and women in dresses, between their 30s and 50s. *2nd and South Sts.,* ☏ *215/925–2220.* ☛ *$10 cover.* ☼ *Tues.–Sat. 5:30 PM–2 AM. Jacket required. AE, DC, MC, V.*

Pulsations. At the biggest, highest-tech disco in the area—20 miles from downtown Philly—a 28-foot starship glides over the dance floor and an alien robot emerges. Lots of neon, lots of lasers, and hydraulically lifted lights emerging from the dance floor. It has a 25,000-watt sound system and holds more than 2,000 people, most of them in their 20s and early 30s. *Rte. 1, Glen Mills,* ☏ *610/459–4140.* ☼ *Times vary nightly. AE, MC, V.*

Revival. Along with New Wave and contemporary music, this dance club in a 19th–century church has performance art, fashion shows, theme nights, and rock videos. It's also a showcase for new bands. *22 S. 3rd St., Old City,* ☏ *215/627–4825.* ☛ *$10 membership.* ☼ *Tues.–Sun. 9 PM–3 AM. AE.*

Jazz

Call the **Jazz Line** (☏ 215/204–5277) for an extensive listing of who's playing around town (plus a program guide for jazz radio WRTI 90.1 FM). You can also pick up a copy of the monthly *Jazz Philadelphia* (☏ 215/473–4273) at the Visitors Center (16th St. and John F. Kennedy Blvd.).

Liberties. This handsomely restored Victorian pub features live jazz Friday and Saturday. *705 N. 2nd St., Northern Liberties,* ☏ *215/238–0660.* ☼ *Daily 11 AM–2 AM. AE, MC, V.*

Ortlieb's Jazz Haus. Hear good jazz in a 100-year-old bar. The celebrated jazz organist Shirley Scott and her quartet occasionally perform. Tuesday night features a jam session for local musicians. *847 N. 3rd St., Northern Liberties,* ☏ *215/922–1035.* ☼ *Music 9:30 PM–1:30 AM. AE, DC, MC, V.*

Zanzibar Blue. A hip restaurant and bar adjoins the hottest jazz room in town. The best local talent plays six nights; nationally known names play on selected Sunday nights. There's a jazz brunch on Sundays from 11 AM to 2 PM, $15 per person. *305 S. 11th St.,* ☏ *215/829–0300.* ☼ *Jazz daily 8 PM–2 AM. AE, DC, MC, V.*

Miscellaneous

Painted Bride Art Center. By day it's a contemporary art gallery showing bold, challenging works. By night it's a "multidisciplinary, multicultural performance center," featuring performance art, prose and poetry readings, folk and new music, jazz, dance, and avant-garde theater. In 1996 this nonprofit educational institution celebrates its 27th season. *230 Vine St., Old City,* ☏ *215/925–9914.* ☼ *Gallery: Mon.–Sat. 10 AM–6 PM. Call for performance schedule. AE, MC, V.*

8 Bucks County

By Joyce
Eisenberg

Updated by
Rathe Miller

BUCKS COUNTY, about an hour's drive north of Philadelphia, could have remained 625 square miles of sleepy countryside full of old stone farmhouses, lush rolling hills, and quaint covered bridges if it hadn't been discovered in the '30s by New York's Beautiful Brainy People. Such luminaries as writers Dorothy Parker and S. J. Perelman and composer Oscar Hammerstein bought country homes here, a short drive from Manhattan. Pulitzer Prize- and Nobel Prize-winning author Pearl S. Buck chose to live in the area because it was "a region where the landscapes were varied, where farm and industry lived side by side, where the sea was near at hand, mountains not far away, and city and countryside were not enemies." Noted author James A. Michener, who won the 1947 Pulitzer Prize for his *Tales of the South Pacific,* was raised and worked in Doylestown. The region quickly gained a nickname: "The Genius Belt."

Over the years, Bucks County has become known for art colonies and antiques, summer theater, and country inns. And although parts of the county have fallen prey to urban sprawl and hyper-development, many areas of central and upper Bucks County remain as bucolic as ever. One of Bucks County's agrarian pursuits is a cottage vineyard industry. Four local wineries open their doors to visitors for tours and tastings.

A BIT OF HISTORY

Named after England's Buckinghamshire, Bucks County was opened by William Penn in 1681 under a land grant from Charles II. The county's most celebrated town, New Hope, was settled in the early 1700s as the industrial village of Coryell's Ferry. (One of the original gristmills is the home of the Bucks County Playhouse, which has been designated the State Theater of Pennsylvania.) The town was the Pennsylvania terminal for stagecoach traffic and Delaware River ferry traffic. Barges hauled coal along the 60-mile Delaware Canal until 1931.

Commerce built up New Hope but art helped sustain it. The art colony took root in the late 19th century and was revitalized first in the 1930s by New York theater folk and more recently with the formation of the New Hope–Lambertville Gallery Association, a cooperative network of gallery owners, artists, and the community. Today New York artists are again relocating to the region. In 1988, the James A. Michener Art Museum opened in the renovated Bucks County jail. It showcases 19th- and 20th-century American art. A $2 million-plus expansion, scheduled for 1996, will add a new wing honoring prominent Bucks County figures in the arts.

INNS AND OUTINGS

Bucks County is a daytripper's paradise, but since there's so much to see and enjoy, many visitors avail themselves of overnight stays at some of the prettiest inns in the Mid-Atlantic region. Among the leading destinations is New Hope, a hodgepodge of old stone houses, narrow streets and alleys, pretty courtyards, and charming restaurants. Summer weekends can be frantic here, with shoppers wandering through the tiny boutiques and galleries along Main Street. The Delaware Canal threads through town, and you can glide lazily along it in a mule-pulled barge.

Doylestown is the county seat. An important coach stop in the 18th century, the town is best known as the home of Henry Chapman Mercer, curator of American and Prehistoric Archaeology at the University of Pennsylvania Museum, master potter, self-taught architect, and

writer of gothic tales. When Dr. Mercer died in 1930 at the age of 74, along with a legacy of artistic creativity he left a magnificently bizarre castle named Fonthill, a museum displaying 50,000 implements and tools, and a pottery and tile works that still makes Mercer tiles.

The county is also a treasure trove for Colonial history buffs. Among the most interesting sites is Pennsbury Manor, a careful reconstruction of the brick Georgian-style mansion and estate William Penn built for himself in the late 1600s. On the banks of the Delaware, the 500-acre Washington Crossing Historic Park is situated where George Washington and his troops crossed the icy river on Christmas night 1776 to surprise the Hessian mercenaries at Trenton.

The Delaware River and the canal that follows its path offer opportunities for canoeing, kayaking, and fishing. Thousands float down the river each year in inner tubes or on rubber rafts. Joggers, hikers, bicyclists, cross-country skiers, and horse-back riders enjoy the 60-mile canal towpath.

The town of Lahaska is the center of antiques shopping in Bucks County. The bargain-price American treasures that made the area an antiques hunter's paradise are nowadays few and far between, but there is good prowling between New Hope and Doylestown all along U.S. 202 and in the 70 shops clustered in Peddler's Village, where you can find fine furniture, handcrafted chandeliers, handwoven wicker, and home-spun fabrics. One of three antique carousels in the county resides here as well. Another may be found at nearby Indian Walk, a mini-marketplace just south on Route 413 in Wrightstown.

For families, a premier attraction in Langhorne is Sesame Place, a theme park based on the public television series. There are shows starring Bert and Ernie, water play such as Big Bird's Rambling River raft ride, a computer gallery, and lots of colorful structures on which to climb and jump.

GETTING THE MOST FOR YOUR BUCKS

Although you can see all the major tourist attractions in a day-long whirlwind tour, plan to stay overnight in Bucks County. A number of houses and mills, some dating back to a half-century before the Revolution, are now quaint bed-and-breakfasts and excellent restaurants. A hearty meal, blissful sleep, and a day spent wandering along River Road (Route 32) are what make visits to Bucks County most enjoyable.

If you visit between mid-April and June, you can join in the county's annual celebration of the arts—Bucks Fever. This six-week festival features performances by local theater, dance, and music companies; exhibitions of sculpture, photography, crafts, and painting; walks and talks highlighting local history; and special events such as the Folkfest at the Mercer Museum, where more than 100 costumed craftsmen demonstrate their tinsmithing, blacksmithing, barrel-making, and wood-carving skills. In addition, there are militia drills, sheep shearing, a quilting bee, and wagon rides.

EXPLORING

Numbers in the margin correspond to points of interest on the Bucks County map.

Many Bucks County attractions are contained within the triangle formed by the towns of New Hope, Doylestown, and Newtown. Other

interesting sites are located along River Road (Route 32), from Pennsbury Manor north to charming river towns such as Erwinna. If you have just one day to visit Bucks County, begin at Fonthill in Doylestown, check out the antiques shops along U.S. 202, stroll through New Hope, and head north on River Road for dinner at one of the inns. For a longer stay, you can pick and choose among the attractions listed below. We begin in the southern part of the county, closest to Philadelphia, and work our way north.

❶ Situated on a gentle rise 150 yards from the Delaware River, **Pennsbury Manor** is the Georgian-style mansion and plantation William Penn built as his country estate. Living history demonstrations at the rebuilt manor house and work buildings on 40 of the estate's original 8,400 acres provide a glimpse of everyday life in 17th-century America. Among the antique furnishings in the house are some fine William and Mary and Jacobean pieces, among them some of William Penn's own furniture. Formal gardens, vineyards and orchards, an icehouse, a smokehouse, a bake and brew house, and collections of tools attest to the self-sufficient nature of Penn's early community. They also hint that, although history portrays Penn as a dour Quaker, as governor of the colony he enjoyed the good life by importing the finest provisions and keeping a vast retinue of servants and slaves. These extravagances led to his financial difficulties that resulted in a nine-month term in debtor's prison. The house can be seen only on the tour. *Tyburn Rd. E off U.S. 13, Morrisville 19067,* ☎ *215/946–0400.* ☛ *$5 adults, $4 senior citizens, $3 children 6–17.* ☉ *Tues.–Sat. 9–5, Sun. noon–5. Last tour at 3:30.*

❷ Six miles north is **Fallsington,** the pre-Revolutionary village where William Penn attended Quaker meetings. The village displays 300 years of American architecture, from a simple 17th-century log cabin to the Victorian excesses of the late 1800s. Three historic buildings, including the log cabin, have been restored and opened for guided tours. Ninety period homes surround the village, which is listed on the National Register of Historic Places. *Tyburn Rd. W off U.S. 13, Fallsington 19054,* ☎ *215/295–6567.* ☛ *$3.50 adults, $2.50 seniors, $1 children 6–18, reservations required. Many private homes are open to public on 2nd Sat. in Oct.*

❸ It was on the site of **Washington Crossing Historic Park,** on Christmas night in 1776, that General Washington and 2,400 of his men crossed the Delaware River, surprised the mercenary Hessian solders, and captured Trenton. A tall granite shaft surrounded by 13 cedar trees marks the point from which the soldiers embarked that snowy night. Attractions are divided between the Lower and the Upper Park, which are about 5 miles apart. In the Lower Park, the fieldstone **Memorial Building and Visitors Center** (Rte. 32, 7 mi south of New Hope) displays a reproduction of Emanuel Leutze's famous painting of the crossing (the original hangs in the Metropolitan Museum of Art in New York). Descendants of men who made that crossing sometimes come to gaze upon the painting and point out the resemblance between themselves and the soldiers in the boat. It's a vain and useless exercise: Leutze was in Düsseldorf, Germany, when he painted the figures and for his models, he used either young men from villages along the Rhine River or American artists living abroad. But past and present do merge—magically—during the annual Christmas Day reenactment of the crossing when local businessmen don Colonial uniforms and brave the elements in small boats (and it's a delightful experience to walk into nearby restaurants later in the day to discover troops, still in uniform, enjoy-

Bucks County

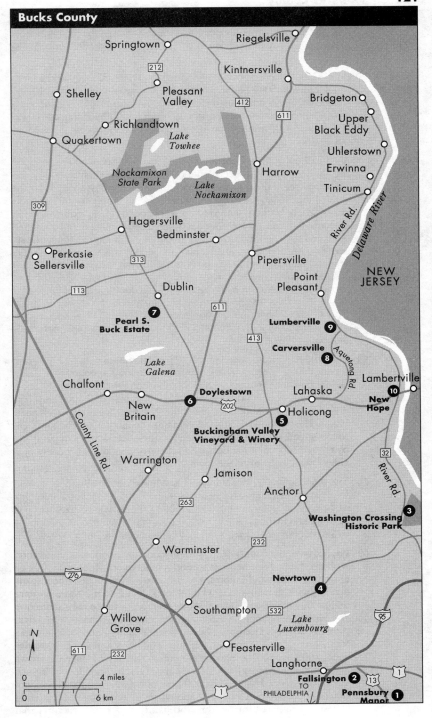

Springtown

Riegelsville

212

Kintnersville

Shelley

Pleasant Valley

412

Bridgeton

611

Richlandtown

Lake Towhee

Upper Black Eddy

Quakertown

Uhlerstown

Nockamixon State Park

Erwinna

Lake Nockamixon

Harrow

Tinicum

309

Hagersville

River Rd.

Delaware River

Bedminster

NEW JERSEY

Perkasie

313

Pipersville

Sellersville

Point Pleasant

113

Dublin

611

7

Pearl S. Buck Estate

413

Lumberville **9**

Carversville **8**

Lake Galena

Aquetong Rd.

Lambertville

Chalfont

Doylestown

Lahaska

10

County Line Rd.

New Britain

6

202

Holicong

New Hope

5

Buckingham Valley Vineyard & Winery

Warrington

Jamison

32

Anchor

River Rd.

263

3

Washington Crossing Historic Park

Warminster

232

276

Newtown **4**

Southampton

532

Lake Luxembourg

95

Willow Grove

611

232

Feasterville

Langhorne

1

N

Langhorne

13

0 4 miles

Fallsington **2**

0 6 km

1

TO PHILADELPHIA

Pennsbury Manor **1**

ing their holiday bird). The **McConkey Ferry Inn** where Washington and his staff had Christmas dinner while waiting to cross the river is nearby. Also open is **Taylor Mansion,** a completely restored 19th-century residence.

In the Upper Park, about 5 miles north on Route 32, stop at the landmark **Bowman's Hill Tower,** named after a surgeon who sailed with Captain Kidd. Washington used the hill as a lookout point. You can get a much better view of the countryside than he did by riding the elevator up the 110-foot-tall memorial tower. ☉ *Apr.–Nov., Tues.–Sun. 10–4:30.*

One-half mile north of the tower, the 80-acre **Wildflower Preserve** (☎ 215/862–2924) has been planted with hundreds of species of wildflowers, trees, shrubs, and ferns native to Pennsylvania. Take the guided tour (Mar.–Oct., $2 per person, $4 per family) or follow short trails clearly marked so as to bring you back to your starting point. At the same location, the **Platt Bird Collection** displays more than 100 stuffed birds and 600 eggs. Also in the Upper Park is the **Thompson-Neely House,** an 18th-century farmhouse furnished just as it was when the Colonial leaders planned the attack on Trenton in the kitchen. *Washington Crossing Historic Park, Rtes. 532 and 32,* ☎ *215/493–4076.* ☛ *Grounds free. 45-min walking tour of 5 historic park buildings, plus tower: $4 adults, $3 senior citizens, $2 children 6–17, available at Visitors Center, Thompson-Neely House, and Tower.* ☉ *Tours Tues.–Sat. 9:30, 11, 12:30, 2, 3:30; Sun. 12:30, 2, 3:30. Park: Tues.–Sat. 9–5, Sun. noon–5 year-round.*

❹ Until the real estate boom of the 1980s, **Newtown** was a busy village serving the commercial needs of the surrounding rural community. Today, it's the bustling center of sprawling suburban development. The town takes pride in its many 18th- and 19th-century homes and inns; the downtown historic district is on the National Register of Historic Places. The Newtown Historic Association building (Court St. and Center Ave., ☎ 215/968–4004) contains regional antiques and paintings by renowned local artist Edward Hicks. An association brochure provides a walking tour of the town.

❺ The **Buckingham Valley Vineyard & Winery** is a small family-owned winery that produces distinguished estate-bottled varietal wines. One of the state's first farm wineries, the vineyards and wine cellars are open to tours and tastings. *Rte. 413, 2 mi south of Rte. 202,* ☎ *215/794–7188.* ☛ *Free self-guided tour.* ☉ *Tues.–Sat. 11–6 Sun. noon–4.*

❻ **Doylestown,** the county seat, is a showcase of American architecture, with the stately Federal brick buildings of Lawyers' Row, and gracious Queen Anne, Second Empire, and Italianate-style homes. The historic district, with its nearly 1,200 buildings, is listed on the National Register of Historic Places. Three walking tours highlighting the architecture and history of Doylestown are mapped out in a brochure available at the **Central Bucks Chamber of Commerce** (Fidelity Bank Building, 115 W. Court St.) and at area B&Bs, inns, and bookstores. The most unusual buildings in Doylestown are those created by Henry Chapman Mercer. Bucks County has seen its share of eccentrics but, even in such august company, Henry Mercer stands out. Expert in prehistoric archaeology, homespun architect, and writer of gothic tales, Dr. Mercer is best remembered for the three brilliantly theatrical structures that are found on **Mercer Mile**, all constructed exclusively with reinforced concrete, a method perfected by Mercer in the early part of this century.

You almost expect to see a dragon puffing smoke outside **Fonthill,** Henry Chapman Mercer's storybook home. Mercer, a Harvard-educated millionaire, designed the house in 1910, modeling it after a 13th-century Rhenish castle. Outside, the stone mansion bristles with turrets, towers, and balconies. Inside, the multilevel structure is truly mazelike: Mercer built his castle from the inside out—without using blueprints!—and Gothic doorways, sudden stairways, dead-ends, and countless inglenooks follow one after the other, all creating a fairy-tale effect. Fonthill's wealth of books, prints, and Victorian engravings is enhanced by the setting: the ceilings and walls are embedded with tiles from Mercer's own kilns and ancient tiles from around the world. From room to room—every chamber has a different shape—each step of the way yields amazing discoveries and charming antiques. All in all, Mercer succeeded in creating one of the most unique abodes in America. *Swamp Rd. (Rte. 313) and E. Court St., Doylestown 18901,* ☎ *215/348–9461.* ☛ *$5 adults, $4.50 senior citizens, $1.50 children.* ◯ *Mon.–Sat. 10–5, Sun. noon–5. Hr-long guided tours. Reservations suggested.*

The **Moravian Pottery and Tile Works** are on the grounds of the Fonthill estate. Here "Mercer" tiles, the unique Arts and Crafts–style picture tiles—that adorn such structures as Graumann's Chinese Theater in Hollywood, the Pocantico Hills residence of John D. Rockefeller, and the Harvard Lampoon building—are still made. As author and Bucks County resident James Michener described them, "Using scenes from the Bible, mythology, and history, Henry Chapman Mercer produced wonderfully archaic tiles about 12 or 14 inches square in powerful earth colors that glowed with intensity and unforgettable imagery." Reproductions of Mercer's tiles can be bought in the Tile Works Shop. The factory, built in 1912, resembles a Spanish mission with an open-ended courtyard. *130 Swamp Rd., Doylestown 18901,* ☎ *215/345–6722.* ☛ *$2.50 adults, $2 senior citizens, $1 children 7–17.* ◯ *Daily 10–4:45. 45-min self-guided tours every ½ hr; last tour at 4. Closed major holidays.*

An archaeologist, Mercer worried that the rapid advance of progress would wipe out evidence of America's productivity before the Industrial Revolution. Consequently, from 1895 to 1915 he scoured the back roads of eastern Pennsylvania buying folk art, tools, and articles of everyday life that might otherwise have been destroyed. His collection, representing every craft, including more than 50,000 objects from before the age of steam, is displayed at the **Mercer Museum,** which he opened in 1916. This must be one of the most incredible attics in the world: You'll need a chin-wrap when you catch sight of the four-story central court, crammed with log-sleds, cheese presses, fire engines, boats, and bean hullers, most suspended by wires from the walls and ceiling. The Spruance Library on the third floor holds 20,000 volumes on Bucks County history. *84 S. Pine St., Doylestown 18901,* ☎ *215/345–0210.* ☛ *$5 adults, $4.50 senior citizens, $1.50 children and students.* ◯ *Mon. and Wed.–Sat. 10–5, Tues. 10–9, Sun. noon–5. Self-guided tours.*

Across the street is the new **James A. Michener Art Museum,** endowed by the bestselling novelist, a native of Doylestown. The arts museum occupies the buildings and grounds of the former Bucks County Jail, which dates from 1884. A 23-foot-high fieldstone wall surrounds seven exhibition galleries, an outdoor sculpture garden, and a Gothic-style warden's house. The collection and changing exhibits (photography, crafts, textiles, sculpture, and painting) focus on 19th- and 20th-century American art and Bucks County art. A $2.2 million ex-

pansion in 1993 renovated the two original galleries and added five new ones, including a re-creation of Michener's Doylestown study. The Mari Sabusawa Michener Wing, scheduled to open in 1996, will add a library, archives, and 12 exhibition rooms, each honoring a prominent Bucks County arts figure. *138 S. Pine St., Doylestown 18901,* ☎ *215/340–9800.* ☛ *$5 adults, $4.50 senior citizens, $1.50 students.* ⊙ *Tues.–Fri. 10–4:30, weekends 10–5.*

From Doylestown, you can detour to Green Hills Farm, Pearl S. Buck's country home (built in 1835) where she wrote nearly 100 novels, children's books, and works of nonfiction while raising seven adopted children and caring for many others. The house still bears the imprint of the girl who grew up in China and became the first American woman to win both the Nobel and Pulitzer prizes. She is best known for *The* ❼ *Good Earth.* The **Pearl S. Buck Estate** is filled with her collection of Asian and American antiques and personal belongings. The Pearl S. Buck Foundation, which supports Amerasian and other displaced children in Asia, operates out of offices on the property. *520 Dublin Rd., Perkasie, PA 18944,* ☎ *215/249–0100 or 800/220–2825.* ☛ *$5 adults, $4 senior citizens and students 6–17, $5 families (parents with children under 19).* ⊙ *Tours Tues.–Sat. 10:30, 1:30 and 2:30; Sun. 1:30 and 2:30. Closed Jan., Feb. and major holidays.*

The road from Doylestown to New Hope (Rte. 202) is studded with antiques shops, especially around Lahaska. (*See* Shopping, *below*).

Before you get to New Hope, take a scenic detour by making a left turn onto Aquetong Road and straight into one of the most beautiful byways of the state, the drive along the Delaware Canal Towpath. Wind through fields and woods dotted with old houses and barns to the tiny, ❽ old mill village of **Carversville.** Stop in at the **Carversville General Store** where locals gather for gossip and take-out coffee and pick up picnic supplies. Then continue past the ball field to Fleecydale or Old Carversville roads. (Ignore the "Road Closed" sign; it's been there for years.) Both of these back-country roads lead to River Road (Route ❾ 32) in **Lumberville,** where you can picnic along the canal or on Bull's Island, accessible by the footbridge across the Delaware River. Open since 1770, the **Lumberville Store** in Lumberville is the focus of village life, the place to mail letters, buy groceries, and rent a bicycle. Across the street stands the **Black Bass Hotel,** a famous Colonial-period inn (*see* Dining and Lodging, *below*) once the country retreat of President Grover Cleveland, which has a stunning river view from its indoor dining room and outdoor deck.

Past Lumberville are the towns of Point Pleasant (*see* Sports and the Outdoors, *below,* for information on renting a canoe or inner tube) and Erwinna. Between these two villages run some of the most Edenic stretches of the **Delaware Canal Towpath** (*see* Sports and the Outdoors, *below*). This is the section of Bucks Country that is reminds certain travelers of the Cotswolds of England: all charming bridge-keeper lodges, corkscrew bends in the road, and vistas so picturesque they seem to drip off the canvas (drivers, beware of the artists often painting at the easels by the side of the road). For the complete daytrip, make the drive up river to at least **Tinicum**—once home to Dorothy Parker and S.J. Perelman—which today attracts visitors for its Sand Castle Winery, Tinicum Outdoor Antiques Show (held in early June), and 126-acre Tinicum Park, one of the most active in the county park system.

The cosmopolitan village of **New Hope** is a mecca for artists, shoppers, and lovers of old homes—and hordes of day-trippers and back-

packers on summer weekends. Listed on the National Register of Historic Places, the town is easy to explore on foot; the most interesting sights and stores are clustered along four blocks of Main Street and on the cross streets—Mechanic, Ferry, and Bridge streets—which lead to the river. Unfortunately, other streets have succumbed to tourist blight. For true charm, and even better antiques, take Bridge Street over the bridge spanning the Delaware to the New Jersey village of Lambertville, which features a delightfully chic assemblage of shops, galleries, historic houses, and fine restaurants. For a good orientation to New Hope, take the Bucks County Carriages horse-drawn tour (*see* Guided Tours *in* Bucks County Essentials, *below*), which starts by the cannon alongside the Logan Inn.

The **Parry Mansion** is a stone house built in 1784 by wealthy lumbermill owner Benjamin Parry and occupied by five generations of his family. The furnishings reflect decorative changes from 1775 to the Victorian era—including candles, white-washed walls, oil lamps, and wallpaper. *S. Main and Ferry Sts.*, ☎ *215/862–5148.* ☛ *$3.* ☉ *May–Dec. Fri.–Sun. 1–5.*

TIME OUT Family-owned **Gerenser's Exotic Ice Cream** has been making ice cream—with 14% butterfat—since 1943. "Exotic" is no exaggeration: Polish plum brandy, African violet, and Indian loganberry are three of the more than 40 flavors. *22 S. Main St., New Hope,* ☎ *215/862–2050.*

Beginning in 1832, coal barges plied the Delaware Canal. Today, the mules pull barges filled with relaxing tourists. The **Mule Barge Ride** is a one-hour narrated excursion past Revolutionary-era cottages, gardens, and artists' workshops. A barge historian/folk singer is aboard. *New and S. Main Sts., New Hope,* ☎ *215/862–2842.* ☛ *$7.50 adults, $6.75 senior citizens, $5.50 students over 11, $4.50 children under 12.* ☉ *Apr. and Nov. 1–Nov. 15, Wed. and weekends at 11:30, 1, 2, 3, 4:30; May 1–Oct. 31, daily at 11:30, 1, 2, 3, 4:30, 6.*

The **New Hope & Ivyland Rail Road** makes a 9-mile, 50-minute scenic run from New Hope to Lahaska. The train crosses a trestle used in the rescue scenes in the old "Perils of Pauline" movies. The New Hope depot is an 1891 Victorian gem embellished with a witch's hat on the roof. Theme trains include wine-and-cheese trains, Halloween haunted trains, Santa trains at Christmas, and Sunday brunch trains. *W. Bridge and Stockton Sts.*, ☎ *215/862–2332.* ☛ *$7.95 adults, $6.95 senior citizens, $3.95 children 2–11.* ☉ *May–Oct., daily; Nov., Wed.–Mon.; Dec., Fri.–Sun.; Jan.–Apr., weekends and holidays; trains run hourly 11–4. Reservations required for theme trains.*

North of New Hope, the two-lane River Road (Route 32) winds scenically along the Delaware. It is a lovely drive with charming old inns, a winery, and ancient stone houses hidden around bends in the road. You'll pass through a series of tiny river towns along the way, many with a general store, inn, and restaurant. Stop for lunch at an inn or picnic along the river and take a walk or ride a bike along the towpath.

What to See and Do with Children

Mule Barge Ride (*see* Exploring, *above*).

New Hope & Ivyland Rail Road (*see* Exploring, *above*).

Sesame Place. Let the good times roll, crawl, climb, and jump at this recreation park designed for children—ages 3 to 15—who love "Sesame Street." Kids go wild playing on Cookie Mountain and their imagi-

nations can run free in Twiddlebug Land, the larger-than-life attraction themed around the tiny critters in the flower box outside Ernie and Bert's window. What kid could resist climbing a giant bag of marbles or discovering Ernie's Bed Bounce? There's even Sesame Island, a tropical-style water park. Tots splish-splash at the Rubber Duckie Pond, while adults love the Big Slipper or the Sesame Streak. Don't forget your bathing suit! The highlight for most is Sesame Neighborhood, a replica of the street on the popular public-TV show. *100 Sesame Rd. (off Oxford Valley Rd.), Langhorne,* ☎ *215/757–1100.* ☛ *$22.95, children under 3 free; parking $4.* ☉ *Mid-May–mid-Sept., daily; early May and mid-Sept.–mid-Oct. weekends. Peak season hrs (July–Aug.), 9–8; call for spring and fall hrs.*

Sportland America. Just up the road from Sesame Place in Langhorne, this huge indoor arcade offers batting cages, miniature golf, roller skating, a gladiator wall climb, and a velcro jumping wall. *9 Cabot Blvd. E, Langhorne,* ☎ *215/547–7766.* ☉ *Sun.–Thurs. 10–10, Fri. and Sat. 10–12:30 AM.*

Haunted Hayride. A spook-filled evening ride through 256 acres of sinister woods, complete with a visit to a haunted house. *Bucks County River Country, Upper Black Eddy,* ☎ *215/297–8406.* ☛ *$12–$15.* ☉ *Oct. Thurs.–Sun. at 6 PM.*

Off the Beaten Track

Eleven covered bridges are all that remain of the 36 originally built in Bucks County. Although the romantically inclined call them "kissing bridges" or "wishing bridges," the roofs were actually intended to protect the supporting beams from the ravages of the weather. The bridges are examples of the lattice-type construction of overlapping triangles, without arches or upright beams. They are delightful to stumble upon, but if you're serious about including them in your itinerary, contact the Bucks County Tourist Commission (☎ 215/345–4552 or 800/836–2825) to request their "Bucks County Covered Bridges Tour" brochure, which provides directions, driving distances, and a brief history of each bridge.

In 1966 President Lyndon B. Johnson greeted nearly 100,000 pilgrims who had come to Doylestown for the dedication of a new shrine—**The National Shrine of Our Lady of Czestochowa.** Since then, millions, including Pope John Paul II, many U.S. presidents, and Lech Walesa, have made a pilgrimage to this Polish spiritual center in Doylestown. The complex includes a modern church with huge panels of stained glass depicting the history of Christianity in Poland and the United States. The gift shop and bookstore sell religious gifts, many of them handcrafted and imported from Poland, and the cafeteria serves hot Polish and American food on Sunday. *Ferry Rd. off Rte. 313, Doylestown,* ☎ *215/345–0600.* ☉ *Daily 9–4:30; most principal holidays are celebrated Sun. at noon at the Polish mass.*

SHOPPING

Antiques

Bucks County has long been known for its antiques shops featuring everything from fine examples of early American craftsmanship to fun kitsch. There are formal and country furnishings plus American, European, and Asian antiques. Many shops (and another winery) are located along a 4-mile stretch of U.S. 202 between Lahaska and New

Hope and on intersecting country roads. Shops are generally open on weekends with weekday hours by appointment: It's best to call first.

The Pink House (W. Bridge St., New Hope, ☎ 215/862–5947): magnificent European 18th- and 19th-century furnishings and textiles. **Hobensack & Keller** (Bridge St., New Hope, ☎ 215/862–2406): antique and authentic reproduction garden ornaments, cast-iron furniture, fencing and Oriental rugs. **Olde Hope Antiques** (U.S. 202 and Reeder Rd., ☎ 215/862–5055): hooked rugs, Pennsylvania German textiles, hand-painted furniture, and folk art. **Katy Kane** (34 W. Ferry St., New Hope, ☎ 215/862–5873): antique, vintage, and designer clothing, accessories, and fine linens, by appointment. **Lahaska Antique Courte** (U.S. 202 opposite Peddler's Village, ☎ 215/794–7884 or 215/794–8695): 12 shops of American and European furniture and decorations.

The **Heritage Collectors' Gallery** (161 Peddler's Village, Lahaska, ☎ 215/794–0901) exhibits and sells historical artifacts and original documents owned or signed by everyone from Washington and Napoléon to Elvis and Freud. You might see a baseball inscribed by Babe Ruth, letters signed by Lincoln, or an autographed copy of Amelia Earhart's book. Prices for original items range from $200 to $30,000.

Across the river bridge from New Hope is Lamberville, NJ, which features more than 20 high-style antiques shops.

Art Galleries

Many New York artists have relocated to Bucks County and more than 30 galleries in New Hope and neighboring Lambertville (across the river in New Jersey) showcase paintings, prints, and sculpture. The **Golden Door Gallery** (52 S. Main St., New Hope, ☎ 215/862–5529) displays works by Bucks County painters, sculptors, and printmakers. The New Hope Information Center (*see* Bucks County Essentials, *below*) can tell you about other galleries.

Auctions

At **Brown Brothers** (Rte. 413 south of Rte. 263, Buckingham, ☎ 215/794–7630), three or four auctioneers simultaneously offer auctions in various categories—jewelry, silver, linens, tools, books, frames, furniture, and box lots. ☉ *Sept.–May, Sat. 8–3; June–Aug., Thurs. 4–9:30.*

Flea Markets

Rice's Sale and Country Market (Green Hill Rd. near Peddler's Village, Solebury, ☎ 215/297–5993) has been in operation for more than a century. It opens Tuesday at 6 AM, when the local antiques dealers check out the goods, and closes at 1:30 PM. There are bargains on canned goods, clothing, linens, shoes, back-issue magazines, and plants. Call for additional Saturday and holiday openings.

Gift Ideas

New Hope's streets are lined with shops selling crafts and handmade accessories, art, and contemporary wares. **Peddler's Village** (U.S. 202 and Rte. 263, Lahaska, ☎ 215/794–4000) began in the early '60s when Earl Jamison bought a 6-acre chicken farm, moved local 18th-century houses to the site, and opened a Carmel, California–inspired collection of 70 specialty shops and restaurants. Today, the 42-acre village peddles books, cookware, toys, leather goods, clothes, jewelry, dried wreaths, posters, candles, and a host of other decorative items. The

new Carrousel World features a carrousel museum, circus art, and an operating 1926 Grand Denzel merry-go-round. Crowd-drawing seasonal events include a Strawberry Festival in May, a Teddy Bear's Picnic in July, and a Scarecrow Festival in September. On the grounds is the Golden Plough Inn (☎ 215/794–4004), a 60-room country inn decorated with Early American country furnishings.

SPORTS AND THE OUTDOORS

Along the Delaware Canal Towpath

Many travelers compare the heart of Bucks County to the Cotswolds region of England and one of the best ways to experience the beauty of Bucks is take a stroll along the grassy towpath of the Delaware Canal, one of Pennsylvania's most picturesque byways. Dotted with fieldstone bridge-tender houses and clapboard toll-collector offices— now private studios and homes—and shaded by magnificent trees, the path is a bit of the old world that has seemingly never changed. Constructed in 1832 to allow access for coal barges, the canal and towpath are known today as the **Delaware Canal State Park** (Box 184, Upper Black Eddy, PA 18972, ☎ 610/982–5560). If you're interested in nature walks and guided tours, give the **Friends of the Delaware Canal** (☎ 215/862–2021) a call for their seasonal calendar of events.

Travelers on their own can enjoy the 60-mile towpath for biking, hiking, jogging, and, in the winter, cross-country skiing. In winter the canal freezes over to from a great ice-skating rink. A recommended six-mile route for hikers and bikers starts at Lumberville; from there cross the pedestrian bridge to Bull Island State Park; go south on the New Jersey side along the Delaware & Raritan Canal to Stockton. Cross the river again to Center Bridge, Pennsylvania, and head back up the towpath to Lumberville. Stop at the Stockton Grocery on Bridge Street in Stockton for picnic supplies.

Ballooning

Keystone State Balloon Tours organizes hot-air balloon flights over Bucks County followed by a champagne reception back on land. Flights are scheduled at dawn or in late afternoon, when the winds are best. *Van Sant Airport, just off Rte. 611, Headquarters and Cafferty Rds., Erwinna,* ☎ *610/294–8034.* ☛ *$125 per person.* ☉ *Year-round, daily, weather permitting. Reservations required.*

Biking

Kiddle Cyclery (Rtes. 413 and 202, Buckingham, ☎ 215/794–8958) rents 3- to 10-speed road bicycles. Closed some Sundays. **Lumberville Store Bicycle Rental Co.** (River Rd., 8 mi north of New Hope, ☎ 215/297–5388) rents mountain bikes with wide tires. They can direct you to scenic bike routes.

Camping

Many of the parks throughout the county have canoes for rent, trails for biking and hiking, and camping facilities. The largest and best-equipped is **Nockamixon State Park** (Rte. 563, Quakertown), which has a 1,450-acre lake, boating and boat rental, swimming pool, bike path and bike rental, hiking trails, ice skating and sledding in winter, trap shooting, and picnic areas. Other fine

parks include **Tohickon Valley Park** (Point Pleasant) and **Ralph Stover Park** (Pipersville), county and state parks respectively, joined along Tohickon Creek near Point Pleasant; and **Lake Towhee** east of Applebachsville. In the south, **Core Creek Park** (Langhorne) is a 1,200-acre facility with fishing and boating on Lake Luxembourg; and **Neshaminy State Park** is near Croydon. For those who wish to camp out near the Delaware Canal Towpath, check out **Tinicum Park.** Call the County Parks (☎ 215/757–0571) or State Parks (☎ 215/453–5000).

Canoeing/Tubing

Over 100,000 people a year—from toddlers to grandparents in their 80s—negotiate the Delaware River on inner tubes or canoes from **Point Pleasant Canoe & Tube** (☎ 215/297–8823). It also rents rafts and kayaks. The Point Pleasant site on River Road is open daily April through October. A bus transports people upriver to begin three- or four-hour tube or raft rides down to the base. No food, cans, or bottles are permitted on the tube rides. Wear sneakers you don't mind getting wet and lots of sunscreen. Life jackets are available at no charge. Reservations are required.

Fishing

Fishermen are drawn to the Delaware River and Lake Nockamixon for small-mouth bass, trout, catfish, and carp. The most popular event is the annual shad run (early April to early June), which has spawned a festival and street fair in Lambertville, NJ, the last weekend in April. The required fishing license can be purchased at any area sporting-goods shop; a five-day tourist license costs $20.50; a trout stamp costs an extra $5.50. For a license and tips on where to fish, try the **Nockamixon Sports Shop** (Rte. 313 and 5th St., Perkasie, ☎ 215/538–9553) or **Dave's Sporting Goods** (1127 N. Easton Rd., Rte. 611, north of Doylestown, ☎ 215/766–8000).

Horseback Riding

Haycock Riding Stables (Old Bethlehem Rd., Perkasie, ☎ 215/257–6271) escorts riders on one- and two-hour trips through Nockamixon State Park. **West End Farm** (River Rd. in Phillips Mill, north of New Hope, ☎ 215/862–5883) offers one-hour escorted trail rides along the Delaware Canal. Both operate by reservation.

DINING AND LODGING

Dining

Bucks County has no regional specialties to call its own. What makes dining here unique are the enchanting settings, ranging from French-style auberge to Colonial-era manor. Diners can enjoy a fine meal served with a dollop of history in restored mills, pre-Revolutionary taverns, stagecoach stops, and elegant Victorian mansions.

CATEGORY	COST*
$$$$	over $30
$$$	$20–$30
$$	$10–$20
$	under $10

per person for a 3-course meal, without wine, tax (6%), or service

Lodging

Although Bucks County has limited lodging options for families, it offers numerous choices to couples. Accommodations ranging from modest to elegant can be found in historic inns, small hotels, and bed-and-breakfasts. Most hostelries include breakfast with their room rates. Plan and reserve early—as much as three months ahead for summer and fall weekends. Unless otherwise stated, all accommodations listed below require a two-night minimum stay on weekends and a three-night minimum stay on holiday weekends. Many inns prohibit or restrict smoking. Unless otherwise indicated, all rooms have private bath and hotels are open year-round. Since many inns are historic homes furnished with fine antiques, they often bar young children.

CATEGORY	COST*
$$$$	over $105
$$$	$85–$104
$$	$60–$84
$	under $60

double occupancy, based on peak (summer) rates, not including sales and room tax (8%)

Carversville

Dining

$$$ **The Carversville Inn.** Its out-of-the-way location has made this circa-
★ 1813 inn one of the area's best kept secrets. Chef Will Mathias's regional American cuisine with a southern flair is now a favorite among locals. The menu changes seasonally, but you can always count on interesting and innovative sauces such as roast red-pepper horseradish on a grilled filet mignon or rosemary demi-glacé sauce on roast duck. On Friday evenings look for complimentary hors d'oeuvres at the bar. ✕ *Carversville and Aquetong Rds.,* ☎ *215/297–0900. AE, MC, V. Closed Mon.*

Doylestown

Dining

$$$$ **Cafe Arielle.** This French bistro serves delicious grilled seafood dishes
★ (including tuna steak), prime meats, and pistachio-encrusted rack of lamb in an open kitchen atmosphere amid country French furnishings and striking artwork. ✕ *100 S. Main St. in the Doylestown Agricultural Works,* ☎ *215/345–5930. Reservations advised. AE, DC, MC, V. Closed Mon. and Tues.*

$$$$ **Russell's 96 West.** The chef-proprietor Russell Palmer artistically presents classical French cuisine—with an accent on Southern France—in a restored 1846 town house. The seasonally changing menu may include rack of lamb, sautéed duck with soy and ginger, and Norwegian salmon with a reduction sauce of tomato, scallion, and bacon. Vegetables are bought from local organic farmers. Dinner and the lighter lunch are also served on the patio in warm weather. Russell will prepare a surprise six-course dinner for $55 per person. ✕ *96 W. State St.,* ☎ *215/345–8746. Reservations advised. AE, D, DC, MC, V. Closed Sun.*

Dining and Lodging

$$$–$$$$ **Sign of the Sorrel Horse.** Catering to weary (and hungry) travelers, this inn features one of the finest restaurants in the area. The 1714 gristmill houses two dining areas—the formal Escoffier Room and the ca-

sual New York/Paris Café. Chef Jon Atkin grows his own herbs and does wonders with fresh game dishes. His wife, Monique, oversees the dining rooms and his son, Christian, combs state stores for the best varietals (wines). For espresso and desserts, repair to the Waterwheel Lounge. If you plan to stay the night, you'll be put up in a 1714 gristmill that once supplied flour for Washington's army and lodged Lafayette, and is now charmingly decorated in the style of a French auberge. Guest rooms are filled with period antiques; one has a fireplace and one has a Jacuzzi. ⌗ *4424 Old Easton Rd.,* ☏ *215/230– 9999,* FAX *215/230–8053. 6 rooms with bath. 2 restaurants. Reservations advised. Jacket required for Escoffier Room. Children over 12 welcome. AE, DC, MC, V.*

Lodging

$$$$ **Pine Tree Farm.** A Colonial farmhouse dating from 1730 was redecorated with cheerful country antiques in light and airy rooms. The glass-enclosed garden room in the rear of the house overlooks 16 acres of pine trees, a pond, and the pool. Breakfast, served poolside in summer, features poached eggs Florentine and homemade apple muffins. Room 1 is a favorite. ⌗ *2155 Lower State Rd., 18901,* ☏ *215/348– 0632. 4 rooms. Pool. No smoking. No children. AE, MC, V.*

$$$$ **Highland Farms.** If this house could talk . . . or rather, sing. This Bucks
★ County estate was the home of lyricist Oscar Hammerstein from 1941 to 1961. Situated not far from the field where *Oklahoma* co-creator could enjoy what he originally called "corn as high as a cow's eye," this pretty 1840s federal-style country home often hosted the greats of Broadway and even Hollywood—Henry Fonda was once married to Mrs. Hammerstein's daughter. Today, the house welcomes travelers and is elegantly furnished with antiques and Hammerstein family memorabilia. A four-course country breakfast is served in the formal dining room or on the brick patio overlooking the 60-foot pool; at night, settle in with one of the films from the video library stocked with Rodgers and Hammerstein favorites. ⌗ *70 East Rd., 18901,* ☏ *215/340– 1354. 4 rooms, 2 with bath. Pool, tennis court. Children over 12 welcome. AE, MC, V.*

$$$ **Doylestown Inn.** In the middle of town at the crossroads of U.S. 611 and 202, this witch's-hat-topped Victorian hotel dates to 1902. Renovated in 1990, guest rooms feature richly stained furnishings and moldings while others are furnished with painted country-pine armoires and hand-stenciled walls. Mercer tiles are found in the lobby and there's one in each bathroom floor. A nice plus is live musical entertainment most nights in the restaurant and lounge. ⌗ *18 W. State St., Doylestown, 18901,* ☏ *215/345–6610,* FAX *215/345–4017. 21 rooms, 1 suite. AE, D, DC, MC, V.*

$$$–$$$$ **The Inn at Fordhook Farm.** The Burpee family (of seed catalogue fame) country estate is now a B&B loaded with family memorabilia and antiques. Built in 1760 and purchased in 1888 by W. Atlee Burpee, the house has high-ceilinged spacious bedrooms (one with a Mercer tile fireplace) brightened with floral prints, a large Federal-style living room, and a dining room with another tile fireplace. The full country breakfast featuring oatmeal buttermilk pancakes, cream cheese-filled French toast, and homegrown berries is served in the Burpee family dining room. The carriage house, with its dark wood paneling and vaulted cathedral ceiling, is a more modern alternative to the main house. ⌗ *105 New Britain Rd., 18901,* ☏ *215/345–1766,* FAX *215/345– 1791. 5 rooms, 3 with bath in main house, 2 with bath in carriage house. 60 acre-park, badminton, croquet. Children over 12 welcome. AE, MC, V.*

Erwinna

Dining and Lodging

$$$$ **Evermay on-the-Delaware.** The Barrymores used to play croquet on
★ the lovely sweep of lawn in front of this cream-colored clapboard
house, one of the prettiest Victorian mansions along the Delaware. Today,
Evermay is as popular for its restaurant as for its stylish hostelry. Ron
Strouse, who has cooked at La Varenne in Paris and with the late James
Beard in New York, serves an impressive prix-fixe six-course dinner.
His contemporary American menu changes constantly and offers a choice
of two entrées, such as grilled tuna with fresh tomato salsa or chicken
on linguine with basil and pine nuts, and includes champagne, hors
d'oeuvres, and a cheese course. Upstairs (try to book a room with a
river view) and in the nearby carriage house, guest rooms are filled with
antiques and fresh flowers. Breakfast of fresh fruit compote, croissants,
juice, and coffee is served in the glassed-in conservatory. Could any-
thing be nicer than taking pre-dinner sherry or afternoon tea in the stately
parlor warmed by its twin fireplaces? ⌆ *River and Headquarters Rds.,
13 mi north of New Hope,* ☎ *610/294–9100. 11 rooms in main
house, 4 in carriage house; 1-bedroom cottage. Restaurant (reserva-
tions required a month in advance; dinner Fri.–Sun. and holidays at
7:30). MC, V.*

$$$$ **Golden Pheasant Inn.** One of the prettiest places along the Delaware
★ Canal, this 1857 Bucks County landmark has been lovingly restored
into a rustic yet elegant French auberge by Michel and Barbara Faure,
a husband and wife team of chef and hostess. Romance reigns in the
solarium, where diners eat beneath potted plants—and the stars—in
a renovated greenhouse (overlooking the banks of the Delaware Canal,
gorgeously illuminated at night); Other diners prefer the fieldstone
room—all gleaming copper cooking vessels, pierced tin chandeliers,
and silk hydrangeas in Quimper pots. An ex-chef at Paris's Ritz Hotel,
Michel Faure deliciously melds the culinary traditions of the New and
Old Worlds: Medallions of boned duck with a marinade of apricot
brandy, salmon in a lobster-and-champagne sauce adorned with
Kennsett Square mushrooms, and lighter-than-air chocolate mousses
are three favored choices. Upstairs there are six guestrooms, all with
four-poster beds and river or canal views, and often booked months
in advance (note that some rooms front River Road, a heavily trafficked
thoroughfare). ⌆ *River Rd.,* ☎ *610/294–9595. Reservations advised.
6 rooms with bath. AE, MC, V.*

Lodging

$$$$ **Issac Stover House.** Talk-show host Sally Jesse Raphael's 1837 brick
★ mansion is a delightful B&B full of personality. Theme rooms include:
Shakespeare & Co., Cupid's Bower, Emerald City with Wizard of Oz
memorabilia, the Amore Room adorned with watercolor prints of
Italy, and more. The opulent Victorian sitting room features pink swag
curtains and makes it easy for guests to sink into romantic dreams at
night. Full breakfast is served on a sunny porch or in the breakfast room.
The inn is set on 13 acres of woods and meadows across River Road
from the Delaware River. ⌆ *845 River Road, 18920,* ☎ *610/294–8044.
7 rooms, 5 with bath. AE, MC, V.*

Holicong

Lodging

$$$$ **Barley Sheaf Farm.** If Bucks County was once known as the "Genius
★ Belt," this famous estate was probably its buckle. Home to cele-
brated playwright George S. Kaufman—author and collaborator

of such jewels as *Dinner at Eight, A Night at the Opera,* and *You Can't Take It With You*—the house was then called "Cherchez la Farm." During the theatrical heyday of Bucks County, from 1936 to 1953, these very rooms rang with the laughter of such visitors as John Steinbeck and the Marx Brothers. Today, when guests journey to the end of the long, maple-fringed drive, they'll find Barley Sheaf Farm, as the estate is now known. The inn's 30-acre parklike setting includes the 1740 fieldstone mansion, a duck pond, a swimming pool, and a meadow full of sheep. Guests retire to bedrooms that are a medley of floral prints, brass, and four-poster beds. A hearty breakfast is served on the glass-enclosed sunporch. Rooms in the adjacent cottage are smaller but share the same country antique decor. ☎ *Box 10, U.S. 202, 18928,* ☎ *215/794–5104,* ℻ *215/794–5332. 10 rooms. Pool, badminton, croquet, meeting rooms. Children over 8 welcome. AE, MC, V.*

$$–$$$$ **Ash Mill Farm.** This country B&B is a handsome 18th-century fieldstone manor house set on 10 acres. The parlor has high ceilings, ornate moldings, and deep-silled windows; rooms feature Irish and American antiques and thoughtful extras such as thick terry-cloth robes, hair dryers, and down comforters on canopy or four-poster beds. A full country breakfast is served to the strains of Mozart or Vivaldi. Afternoon tea and homebaked treats are offered by a cozy fire, in the garden, or on the sunny front porch with a view of resident sheep. ☎ *Box 202, Rte. 202, 18928,* ☎ *215/794–5373. 5 rooms, 2 suites. Golf privileges. Children over 14 welcome. No credit cards.*

Lahaska

Dining

$$$ **Jenny's.** American regional cuisine is served in a Victorian or a country French room. Lobster and crab sauté and filet Chesterfield (filet mignon with cheddar cheese, bacon, and horseradish sauce) are favorites. Live jazz and blues are featured Friday and Saturday nights and Dixieland music during brunch on Sunday. ✕ *U.S. 202, Peddler's Village,* ☎ *215/794–4020. Reservations advised. AE, D, DC, MC, V. No dinner Mon.*

$$ **The Spotted Hog.** This casual country bistro in the Golden Plough Inn serves American cuisine such as New York strip steak, grilled chicken with macadamia lime butter, Philadelphia cheesesteaks, interesting pizzas, and sundaes. The bar serves 35 American microbrewery beers. Live bands play folk, country, and pop on Thursday, Friday, and Saturday evenings and Sunday afternoons. ✕ *Peddler's Village, Rte. 202 and Street Rd.,* ☎ *215/794–4030. AE, D, DC, MC, V.*

Lodging

$$$–$$$$ **Golden Plough Inn.** Nestled within historic Peddler's Village, this inn
★ features 22 spacious guest rooms, many with four-poster beds, rich fabrics, and cozy window seats that beautifully evoke 19th-century Bucks County. All rooms are equipped with air-conditioning, remote control TV, a small refrigerator, and a complimentary bottle of champagne, and some have a fireplace or a Jacuzzi. Thirty-eight other guest rooms are scattered about the village, in an 18th-century farmhouse, a historic carriage house, and Merchant's Row. There is a complimentary Continental breakfast or a credit toward breakfast on the à la carte menu. ☎ *Peddler's Village, Rte. 202 and Street Rd., 18931,* ☎ *215/794–4004,* ℻ *215/794–4008. 60 rooms, including 22 suites. Restaurant. Children welcome. AE, D, DC, MC, V.*

Lumberville

Dining and Lodging

$$$$ Black Bass Hotel. In casting about for Bucks County favorites, natives invariably put this inn near the top of the list. Actually, it's been a favorite stopover along the Delaware River for more than 240 years. While it sits snug within a region that witnessed many incidents of American Revolution history, don't look for any GEORGE WASHINGTON SLEPT HERE plaques: the hotel and its clientele were loyalists to the British Crown, and, coincidentally, its current owner, Herb Ward, is as Anglophile as they come. He's even adorned the inn with a fabulous collection of British royal memorabilia. A wayside inn (and we do mean wayside, since the hotel's facade sits directly on Route 22), the Black Bass also features an excellent restaurant and a beautiful outdoor deck overlooking the river—just the place for a picture–perfect summer dinner. ⛺ *Rte. 32 (8 miles upriver from New Hope)*, ☎ *215/297–5770, FAX 215/297–0262. 9 rooms, 2 with bath. AE, DC, MC, V.*

New Hope

Dining

$$$$ La Bonne Auberge. Some critics consider this to be Bucks County's most
★ elite and expensive restaurant, thanks to the owners—chef Gerard Caronello, a native of Lyon, France, and his wife, Rozanne, of Great Britain. Consistently classic French cuisine is served in this pre-Revolutionary farmhouse. A small parlor features the original hearth and low beamed ceilings. The Terrace Room, used for dining, has a modern country-French ambience. Specialties include grilled salmon with a light lobster sauce served on the side and rack of lamb. A four-course table d'hôte menu, available Wednesday and Thursday evenings in addition to the regular menu, is a bargain. A bit hard to locate, the restaurant is within a residential development called Village 2; when you call for reservations, easy travel directions are always supplied. ✕ *Village 2 off Mechanic St.,* ☎ *215/862–2462. Reservations required. Jacket required. AE. Closed Mon. and Tues.*

$$$–$$$$ Odette's. In 1961, Parisian actress Odette Myrtil Logan converted a former canal lock house into a stylish restaurant. The atmosphere is French country bistro; the cuisine, Continental with a menu that changes seasonally. A "Lite-Bites" menu also is available during most serving hours. Belgian waffles and eggs Benedict are made table-side during Sunday buffet brunch. Some of the dining rooms command a view of the river. Entertainment consists of a piano bar, cabarets, and art shows. ✕ *S. River Rd., 4 mi south of New Hope,* ☎ *215/862–2432. Reservations advised; request a river view. AE, DC, MC, V.*

$$$ Hotel du Village. Diners partake of country French fare in a converted private school. Chef-owner Omar Arbani prepares tournedos Henri IV, fillet with béarnaise sauce; sweetbreads with mushrooms in madeira sauce; and fillet of sole in curried butter, topped off by extravagant desserts. Dinner is served in a Tudor-style room with working fireplaces or on the sunporch. ✕ *Phillips Mill and N. River Rds.,* ☎ *215/862–5164 or 215/862–9911. Reservations advised weekends. AE, DC. Closed Mon. and Tues. No lunch.*

$$$ Martine's. Reminiscent of a quaint English pub with a beamed ceiling, plaster over stone walls, and an oversize fireplace, Martine's is more popular with locals than with visitors. The eclectic menu features filet mignon au poivre, pasta, duckling, and seafood paella. Outdoor dining is on a small patio. ✕ *7 E. Ferry St.,* ☎ *215/862–2966. Reservations advised weekends. AE, MC, V.*

$$$ **Mother's.** One of New Hope's most popular dining spots, Mother's main claims to fame are its truly sinful desserts, chocolate mousse bombe and mocha Amazon. Homemade soups, pasta, and unusual pizzas stand out among the selections on the extensive menu. In summer, meals are also served in the garden. Expect to wait; it's always crowded here. ✕ *34 N. Main St.,* ☎ *215/862–9354. Reservations advised. AE, D, MC, V.*

$$ **Havana Bar and Restaurant.** The American regional and contemporary fare offered by the Havana is enhanced by its hickory-grilled specialties. Dishes featured are sesame onion rings, a Chinese vegetable sandwich, and spice-fried redfish. The bar serves exotic elixirs enlivened by jazz bands Thursday through Sunday nights and karaoke Monday nights. The view of Main Street is ideal for people-watching, especially from the outdoor patio. ✕ *105 S. Main St.* ☎ *215/862–9897. AE, D, DC, MC, V.*

Dining and Lodging

$$–$$$$ **The Logan Inn.** A 1988 face-lift of one of the oldest inns in continuous operation in North America has helped to restore its original Colonial charm. Established in 1727 as an extension of the Ferry Tavern, the Ferry Inn accommodated passengers who used the Delaware River ferry to Lambertville. George Washington is said to have stayed here at least five times—and one can only imagine what he would think of the hoards of daytrippers and backpackers that stroll right outside the inn, smack dab in the busiest part of town. Rooms are decorated with original and reproduction Colonial and Victorian furnishings and canopy beds. Some rooms have river views. Full or Continental breakfast on the tented patio is included. Ask Gwen the innkeeper about haunted room No. 6! As for the friendly restaurant, the Logan serves three menus: lunch (11:30–4), dinner (4:30–closing), and a popular all-day Café Menu with such favorites as nachos, buffalo wings, salads, burgers, and pizzas. ▥ *10 W. Ferry St., 18938,* ☎ *215/862–2300. 16 rooms with bath. Restaurant. Reservations advised. Children welcome. AE, D, DC, MC, V.*

Lodging

$$$$ **The Whitehall Inn.** Guest rooms at the 18th-century manor house of
★ what was once a gentleman's horse farm are furnished with period antiques, canopy beds, and patterned wallpaper. Guests get a bowl of fresh fruit and bottle of mineral water upon arrival and will find chocolate truffles and velour robes in their room. The spacious parlor has sofas and rocking chairs facing a blazing fireplace. The four-course candlelit gourmet breakfast is served at tables set with white linen, English china, and heirloom silver; in the afternoon, high tea is served. In the nearby stables, you'll find the owner's dressage horses. ▥ *1370 Pineville Rd., 18938,* ☎ *215/598–7945. 6 rooms, 4 with bath. Pool. No smoking. AE, D, DC, MC, V.*

$$–$$$$ **The Wedgwood Inn.** Three buildings comprise the Wedgwood Inn
★ B&B lodgings: a blue "painted lady" 1870 Victorian house with frilly woodwork, a gabled roof, wraparound porch, and a porte-cochere; a Federal-style 1840 stone manor house; and the Aaron Burr House, another 1870 Victorian building added to the inn's properties in 1990. Minutes from downtown, the collection of inns graces 2½ acres of landscaped grounds with gazebos and gardens. Wedgwood pottery, antiques, fireplaces, and wood-burning stoves add to its charm. Continental-plus breakfast and afternoon tea are served in the sunporch, gazebo, or guest room. ▥ *111 W. Bridge St., 18938,* ☎ *215/862–2570. 19 rooms with bath, including 4 suites and a carriage house. Pool and tennis privileges. No smoking. AE, MC, V.*

$$$ **Hotel du Village.** Flower-filled grounds surrounding the large, old stone boarding school create the feeling of an English manor house. The guest rooms are decorated with country furniture and a Continental breakfast is served in the parlor. ⊡ *Phillips Mill and N. River Rds.,* ☎ *215/862–5164 or 215/862–9911. 20 rooms with bath. Pool, 2 tennis courts. No children on weekends. AE, DC.*

$$–$$$ **Best Western New Hope Inn.** This comfortable motel is a few minutes from New Hope and 30 minutes from Sesame Place. On weekends, guests can enjoy entertainment in the lobby lounge. It is one of the few spots in Bucks County that welcomes children. ⊡ *6426 Lower York Rd. (Rte. 202), 18938,* ☎ *215/862–5221 or 800/467–3202,* ⅏ *215/862–5847. 159 rooms. Restaurant, lobby lounge, pool, tennis court. AE, D, DC, MC, V.*

$ **New Hope Motel in the Woods.** A clean, modern, one-story motel, with wood-paneled guest rooms, offers the lowest rates in the area and welcomes families. ⊡ *400 W. Bridge St., 18938,* ☎ *215/862–2800. 28 rooms. Pool. D, DC, MC, V.*

Newtown

Dining

$$$$ **Jean Pierre's.** Owner-chef Jean Pierre Tardy, formerly executive chef
★ at Philadelphia's distinguished Le Bec-Fin, prepares classic French cuisine in a quaint country French setting. Salmon stuffed with lobster and herb–encrusted rack of lamb with a rosemary lamb jus are two of the chef's favorites. ✕ *101 S. State St.,* ☎ *215/968–6201. Reservations required. AE, D, DC, MC, V. Closed Mon. No lunch weekends.*

Dining and Lodging

$$$–$$$$ **Temperance House.** This meticulously restored 1772 inn and hostelry also contains a restaurant that serves fine Continental cuisine. Homemade soup stocks and an in-house charcuterie ensure an appealing range of dishes featuring rack of lamb, roast Long Island smoked duck, and lean-generation pork; beef, fresh-catch, and chicken preparations change each day. Request hearthside seating in the room adorned with reproductions of artwork by Edward Hicks of *Peaceable Kingdom* fame. Listen to live jazz Friday and Saturday nights, and enjoy a Cajun brunch accompanied by Dixieland jazz on Sunday. Each room in the 1772 inn is decorated with a different style of furniture: the Benetz Suite has bent willow-and-twig furniture; the Edward Hicks Suite has rich period mahogany and walls stenciled in a pattern derived from a "Peaceable Kingdom" mosaic tile. Continental breakfast is served buffet style in the dining room. ⊡ *5–11 S. State St., 18940,* ☎ *215/860–0474. 13 rooms with bath and suites. Reservations advised. AE, DC, MC, V.*

Upper Black Eddy

Lodging

$$$$ **Bridgeton House on the Delaware.** Wide, screened porches and a terrace provide close-up views of the Delaware River and the bridge to Milford, New Jersey. Guest rooms are decorated with wall and ceiling folk murals by the self-described artist-in-residence. The informal sitting room has white wood walls, and a glass wall overlooking the river. A two-course gourmet country breakfast is served, as is afternoon tea and sherry. Request a river view: while other rooms face the road directly outside the front entrance, riverfront rooms feature French doors to private screened porches; in the penthouse, the marble fireplace and huge windows are delightful. ⊡ *Box 167, River Rd., 18972,* ☎

610/982–5856. 10 rooms, including 3 suites. Children under 8 welcome weekdays. AE, MC, V.

THE ARTS

Theater

The **Bristol Riverside Theatre** (120 Radcliffe St., Bristol, ☎ 215/788–7827), a professional regional theater, has five major shows a year along with a holiday production. Children's theater is offered on Saturday mornings throughout the season, classical music concerts on Sunday evenings, and concerts and revues during the summer.

The **Bucks County Playhouse** (S. Main St., New Hope, ☎ 215/862–2041). Housed in an historic mill, the Playhouse has been in continuous use as a theater since 1939, when it featured summer stock. The Playhouse stages Broadway musical revivals—most recently *Guys and Dolls, South Pacific,* and *A Chorus Line*—and is famous for its wonderful production of *Show Boat,* which was broadcast on PBS's "Great Performances."

The **New Hope Performing Arts Festival** (held at the Solebury School just outside New Hope, ☎ 215/862–9894 July and August, 215/862–9307 for off-season information or to be put on the mailing list) is dedicated to original and innovative works in theater, music, and performing arts. The summer festival, with scheduling varying from year to year, includes classical music and children's programming during the July and August season.

BUCKS COUNTY ESSENTIALS

Getting Around

By Car

Bucks County is a large area—40 miles long and up to 20 miles across—and is almost impossible to tour without a car. From Philadelphia, the most direct route is to follow I–95 north to Exit 31 (New Hope); turn left at the bottom of the exit ramp and follow to Route 532. Turn right onto 532 north, left onto Route 32 north and travel about 7 miles to New Hope, a total of about 40 miles from Philadelphia.

By Bus

Greyhound Lines (☎ 800/231–2222) has two buses a day to Doylestown from Philadelphia. The trip takes 75–90 minutes and costs $7 one way, $14 round-trip.

By Train

SEPTA (☎ 215/580–7800) provides frequent service from Philadelphia (Market Street East, Suburban, and 30th Street stations) to Doylestown on the R5 line. The trip takes up to 85 minutes.

Guided Tours

Nancy Neely (☎ 215/822–6692) will drive you around the county in your car. A Bucks County tour guide for over 20 years, she will take you off the main roads, show you the covered bridges, and amuse you with local color. Reservations required.

Marlene Miller of Executive Events Inc. (☎ 215/766–2211) offers customized group tours and tour groups for individual travelers in 28-pas-

senger minivans. Some tour themes include covered bridges, historic mansions, arts, wineries, antiques, and shopping.

Bucks County Carriages (☎ 215/862–3582) offers 20-minute horse-drawn carriage tours. Horses are "parked" at Logan Inn in New Hope, near the bakery in Peddler's Village, and at the Lambertville Station in Lambertville, N.J. Daytime and evening rides vary according to season and departure location. A ride to a catered picnic at a shaded spot by a brook, and customized tours—perhaps from your B&B to dinner and back—are available by reservation.

Coryell's Ferry Ride and Historic Narrative (☎ 215/862–2050) is a half-hour sightseeing ride on the Delaware River in a 65-foot, 49-passenger stern-wheeler.

Ghost Tours of New Hope (☎ 215/957–9988) offers a one-hour lantern-led walk which explores the haunting tales of the area. The tour was designed by psychic investigator Adi-Kent Thomas Jeffrey, author of *The Bermuda Triangle* and a former Bucks County resident.

Mule Barge Ride (*see* Exploring, *above*).

New Hope & Ivyland Rail Road (*see* Exploring, *above*).

Important Addresses and Numbers

Emergencies
Dial 911 in an emergency. The county's central emergency room is at **Doylestown Hospital** (595 W. State St., Doylestown, ☎ 215/345–2200).

Visitor Information
Bucks County Tourist Commission (Box 912, Doylestown 18901, ☎ 215/345–4552 or 800/836–2825). *On the Fonthill property.* ◯ *Weekdays 8:30–5:30, Sat. 10–4, May–Sept.*

Central Bucks Chamber of Commerce (Fidelity Bank Building, 115 W. Court St., Doylestown 18901, ☎ 215/348–3913). Free brochure with walking tours and other tourist information is available. ◯ *Weekdays 8:30–4:30.*

New Hope Information Center (1 W. Mechanic St., at Main St., New Hope 18938, ☎ 215/862–5880 for an automated menu of information, or 215/862–5030 for a travel counselor). It is a convenient place to stop or contact in advance for information about New Hope and its surrounding attractions. The center also offers a free lodging referral service. ◯ *Daily, usually 10–5, but hrs vary seasonally.*

9 Lancaster County

By Joyce
Eisenberg

Updated by
Rathe Miller

THE PLAIN AND FANCY LIVE SIDE BY SIDE in Lancaster County, some 65 miles west of Philadelphia. This is Pennsylvania Dutch Country, where horse-drawn buggies and horn-tooting cars jockey for position on picturesque country roads. Travelers to the region are amazed to find whole communities of the Plain People—as the Old Order Amish are called—who shun telephones, electricity, and the whole world of American gadgetry. Visitors feel they are magically stepping back one hundred years in time.

The tourists come to see the Old Order Amish, one of the most conservative of the Pennsylvania Dutch sects. Clinging to a centuries-old way of life, the Amish shun the amenities of modern civilization, using kerosene or gas lamps instead of electric lighting, horse-drawn buggies instead of automobiles. Ironically, in turning their backs on the modern world, they have attracted the world's attention.

WHEN TO VISIT
This bucolic region can be hectic, especially on summer weekends and in October, when the fall foliage attracts crowds. Its main arteries, U.S. 30 (also known as the Lincoln Highway and Lancaster Pike) and Route 340 (sometimes called the Old Philadelphia Pike), are lined with souvenir shops and outlet stores. The farmers markets and family-style restaurants are often crowded with busloads of tourists. But there is still much charm here in the general stores, one-room schoolhouses, country lanes, and picture-perfect farms, many of which welcome overnight guests. There are pretzel factories to tour, quilts to buy, and a host of attractions for railroad buffs. The trick is to visit the top attractions and then get off the beaten path. If possible, plan your trip for early spring, September, or Christmas season, when it is less crowded. Visitors should note that although many restaurants, shops, and farmers markets close Sunday for the Sabbath, commercial attractions remain open.

THE CULTURE OF THE PENNSYLVANIA DUTCH
Pennsylvania Dutch is a collective phrase for more than 35 Amish, Mennonite, and Brethren sects. Despite their name, they aren't Dutch at all. Rather, they are descendants of German and Swiss immigrants who came to the Lancaster area to escape religious persecution. "Dutch" is a corruption of "Deutsch," meaning German.

The Mennonite movement, named after its leader Menno Simons, began in Switzerland in the 16th century, the time of the Reformation. It was a radical religious group that advocated nonviolence, separation of church and state, adult baptism, and individual freedom in choosing a religion. In 1710, eight families led by Mennonite Bishop Hans Herr accepted William Penn's invitation to settle in Lancaster County.

In 1693, Swiss Mennonite Bishop Jacob Amman, whose stricter beliefs and interpretation of church tenets had attracted a following, broke off from the movement. His followers, the Amish, also settled in Lancaster. Today, there are 135,000 Amish people living in North America; Lancaster County has the second-largest Amish community in the nation, with 16,000 people. (Holmes County, Ohio, is first.) That the number of Amish has doubled in the last two decades suggests that theirs is still a viable alternative lifestyle.

The Amish religion and way of life stress separation from the world, caring for others of the faith, and self-sufficiency. What may appear as odd behavior results from religious convictions based on Biblical

interpretation. The Amish, who reject compulsory school attendance and military registration, do not accept social security benefits or purchase life or property insurance.

Old Order Amish send their children to one-room schoolhouses with eight grades to a room. They avoid larger public schools to prevent the exposure of their children to the influence of "outsiders." The Supreme Court has ruled that Amish children need not attend school beyond the eighth grade. Telephones, television, radio, and electric appliances are not permitted. Farmers work with teams of mules to plow, plant, and harvest their crops. Families ride in horse-drawn buggies. Men and women wear plain clothing which has remained unchanged for centuries.

Although some changes have been thrust upon them by the government, the Amish do change and update some rules themselves. Some have telephones in their barns or on the edge of their property for emergency use only; many will accept a ride in an automobile or take public transportation. They live a lively, rich life of discipline and caring. They seek to be at peace with themselves, their neighbors, their surroundings, and their God.

HISTORIC LANCASTER, HERSHEY, AND GETTYSBURG

Although the Amish are a prime attraction, they are not the only lure to Lancaster County. Lancaster (which the English named after Lancashire) is an intriguing city to explore. Very residential, with blocks of charming row houses, it served as the nation's capital for one day during the American Revolution when Congress fled Philadelphia after the Battle of Brandywine. It is also one of the nation's oldest inland cities, dating from 1710. Historic sites in the area include Wheatland, the home of James Buchanan, Pennsylvania's only contribution to the White House.

You can spend a full day following Oregon Pike (Rte. 272) northeast from the Landis Valley Museum, an exhibit devoted to rural life before 1900. Ephrata Cloister provides a look at a religious communal society of the 1700s. It was founded in 1728, when dissident brethren split from a group that had arrived in 1724. And Main Street in Lititz, founded in 1756, offers an architectural treat for strollers.

Western Lancaster County, which includes the towns of Marietta, Mount Joy, and Columbia, is a quieter part of the county where visitors can bicycle down winding lanes, sample local wines and authentic Mennonite cooking, and explore friendly, uncrowded villages. Its history is rooted in the Colonial period. The residents are of Scottish and German descent, and architecture varies from log cabins to Victorian homes. There are a number of good restaurants, inns, and farms that accept guests.

If you've brought your children as far as Lancaster, you may want to continue north to Hershey, the "Chocolate Town" founded in 1903 by Milton S. Hershey. Here the street lights are shaped like giant Hershey Kisses and the number one attraction is Hersheypark, an 87-acre theme park with kiddie rides and thrill rides, theaters, and live shows. Hershey's Chocolate World offers tours into the simulated world of chocolate production.

Finally, you may wish to journey to the battlefields and museums of Gettysburg, also within driving distance. Here—as in many other destinations in Lancaster County—you can journey back in time.

EXPLORING

Most visitors come to Pennsylvania Dutch Country to get a glimpse of the Amish and their lifestyle. Below are suggestions for one-day tours, plus itineraries for additional touring. Train lovers will appreciate the Strasburg attractions; history and architecture buffs will enjoy the sites in and around the city of Lancaster. There is information on a tour following Oregon Pike north from Lancaster and some suggestions for seeing the western part of Lancaster County. For an extended tour of south-central Pennsylvania, the sites and attractions of Gettysburg and Hershey are also included.

Discovering the Real Amish

Numbers in the margin correspond to points of interest on the Lancaster County map.

❶ **People's Place,** a "people-to-people interpretation center," provides an excellent introduction to the Amish, Mennonites, and Hutterites. A 30-minute multiscreen slide show titled "Who Are the Amish?" features close-ups of Amish life and perceptive narration. Geared toward children, **Amish World** is a hands-on exhibit on transportation, dress, schools, the effects of growing old, and mutual aid. Children can try on bonnets and play in the "feeling box." Don't miss the collection of wood sculptures by Aaron Zook. "Hazel's People," a feature film starring Geraldine Page and set in the Mennonite community, is shown Monday through Saturday from Memorial Day through Labor Day at 7:30 PM (separate admission fee). *Rte. 340, Intercourse, ☎ 717/768–7171. ☛ $3.50 adults, $1.75 children. ☺ Memorial Day–Labor Day, Mon.–Sat. 9:30–9:30, until 5 in winter.*

❷ Following Route 340 west to Bird-in-Hand will bring you to **Abe's Buggy Rides.** Abe chats about the Amish during a 2-mile spin down country roads in an Amish family carriage. No ☏. ☛ *$10 adults, $5 children 3–12. ☺ Mon.–Sat. 8 AM–dusk.*

TIME OUT For lunch (actually, they serve dinner all day) try one of the family-style Pennsylvania Dutch restaurants such as the **Amish Barn** on Rte. 340. At **Good 'N Plenty** (on Rte. 896) you'll share a table with about a dozen other customers and be treated to hearty regional fare, including traditional "sweets and sours." There's no menu; they just bring out the food (*see* Dining and Lodging, *below*). Although it doesn't serve family style, **Bird-in-Hand Family Restaurant** on Rte. 340 is an excellent place to sample local specialties such as apple dumplings and chicken pot pie.

Several furnished farmhouses offer a simulated, up-close look at how the Amish live. Note that these are commercial, not Amish-run, enterprises.

❸ **The Amish Farm and House** offers 40-minute tours through a 10-room circa 1805 house furnished in the Old Order Amish style. A map guides visitors to the farmstead's animals, waterwheel, and barns. *2395 Lincoln Hwy. E (U.S. 30), Lancaster, ☎ 717/394–6185. ☛ $5 adults, $4.50 senior citizens, $3 children 5–11. ☺ Daily 8:30–5, until 4 in winter, 6 in summer.*

❹ **The Amish Village** also offers guided tours through an authentically furnished Amish house. Afterward, visitors may wander about the grounds of the village, which includes a one-room schoolhouse, a blacksmith shop, and an operating smokehouse built for the Amish Village by Amish craftsmen. *Rte. 896 between U.S. 30 and Rte. 741, Strasburg, ☎ 717/687–*

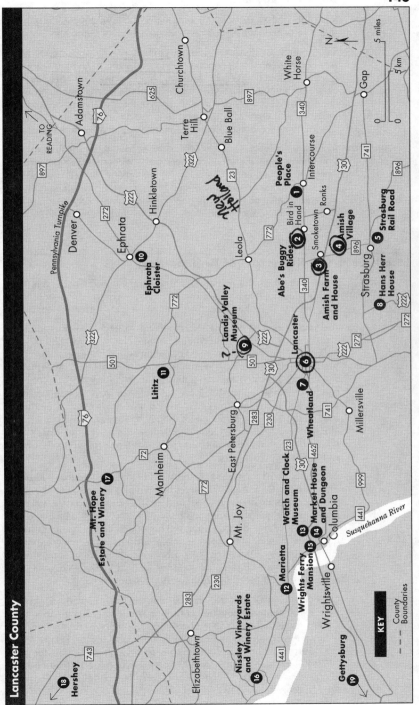

143

Lancaster County

8511. ☛ *$5.50 adults, $1.50 children 6–12.* ☉ *Daily 9–5 spring and fall, 9–6 in summer. House tours weekends 10–4 in winter.*

Save an hour or two to explore the country roads on your own. Many Amish farms (they're the ones with windmills and green blinds) are clustered in the area between Ephrata and New Holland. Drive the side roads between routes 23 and 340; visit the roadside stands and farms where hand-painted signs entice you with quilts or farm-fresh produce and eggs. Drive in and chat with the Amish—they always welcome polite inquiries. For take-home goodies and gifts, stop at a farmers market.

TIME OUT To sample the local ice cream, order one of the 18 farm-fresh flavors at **Lapp Valley Farm.** It also sells homemade root beer and has animals to entertain the children. *Mentzer Rd., between New Holland and Intercourse (from Intercourse, follow Rte. 340 1 mi east, turn left on New Holland Rd., left on Peters Rd., and right on Mentzer Rd.),* ☎ *717/354-7988.* ☉ *Mon.–Thurs. noon–dark, Fri. 8 AM–dark, Sat. 8 AM–7 PM or later.*

Strasburg: The Romance of Railroading

If you love trains, the area around Strasburg will look like heaven. Train aficionados could easily spend an entire day in the town. To get to Strasburg from U.S. 30, head south on Route 896 and turn left on Route 741.

❺ The Strasburg Rail Road is a scenic 9-mile round-trip excursion from Strasburg to Paradise on a rolling antique chartered in 1832 to carry milk, mail, and coal. Passengers can chug along in the open coach featured in *Hello Dolly.* Called America's oldest short line, the Strasburg run features wooden coaches pulled by an iron steam locomotive. You can lunch in the dining car or buy a box lunch in the restaurant at the station and alight at Groff's Grove along the line for a picnic lunch. *Rte. 741, Strasburg,* ☎ *717/687–7522.* ☛ *Round-trip: $7 adults, $4 children 3–11.* ☉ *Apr.–Oct. daily, Nov.–Mar. weekends; closed 1st 2 wks in Jan.* ☉ *Trains depart every 30–60 min depending on season; call for an exact schedule.*

Across the road from the Strasburg Rail Road, the **Railroad Museum of Pennsylvania** features 75 pieces of train history, including 13 colossal engines built between 1888 and 1930; 12 railroad cars including a Pullman sleeper that operated from 1855 to 1913; sleighs; and railroad memorabilia documenting the history of Pennsylvania railroading. More than 50 of the pieces are kept indoors in the newly expanded Hall of Rolling Stock. *Rte. 741, Strasburg,* ☎ *717/687–8628.* ☛ *$6 adults, $5 senior citizens, $4 children 6–17.* ☉ *Mon.–Sat. 9–5, Sun. noon–5. Closed Mon. from Nov.–Apr.*

On a smaller scale, antique and 20th-century model trains are on display at the **National Toy Train Museum,** the showplace for the Train Collectors Association. There are five operating layouts plus hundreds of locomotives and cars in display cases, nostalgia films, and many "push-me" buttons. *Paradise La., just north of Rte. 741, Strasburg,* ☎ *717/687–8976.* ☛ *$3 adults, $2.75 senior citizens, $1.50 children 5–12.* ☉ *May–Oct. and Christmas wk, daily 10–5; Apr. and Nov.–mid-Dec., weekends only; closed Jan.–Mar.*

Next door at the **Red Caboose Motel** N-5 cabooses have been converted into motel units and a casual restaurant. **Abe's Buggy Rides** depart from the motel for 20- to 30-minute horse-drawn-carriage rides along scenic back roads. *Rte. 896, 1½ mi south of U.S. 30, Strasburg,* ☎ *717/687–*

5000. ☛ *Rides: $10 adults, $5 children 3–12.* ⊙ *Departures June–Aug., Mon.–Sat.; Sept.–May, Sat. only.*

If you fancy fancy cars, **Gast Classic Motorcars Exhibit** has a changing display of more than 50 antique, classic, sports, and celebrity cars. *Rte. 896, Strasburg,* ☏ *717/687–9500.* ☛ *$6 adults, $3.50 children 7–12.* ⊙ *Memorial Day–Labor Day, daily 9–9; Labor Day–Memorial Day, Sun.–Thurs. 9–5, Fri. and Sat. 9–9.*

Choo Barn, Traintown, USA, is a family hobby that got out of hand. What started in 1945 as a single train chugging around the Groff family Christmas tree is now a 1,700-square-foot display of Lancaster County in miniature with 14 trains and 140 figures and vehicles in O-gauge. Every five minutes a house catches on fire and fire engines turn on their hoses to extinguish the blaze; flag bearers march in a Memorial Day parade; animals perform in a three-ring circus. Periodically, the overhead lights dim and it is nighttime; streetlights glow and locomotive headlights pierce the darkness. *Rte. 741, Strasburg,* ☏ *717/687–7911.* ☛ *$3 adults, $1.50 children 5–12.* ⊙ *Apr.–Dec., daily 10–5 (later in summer); closed Jan.–Mar.*

Lancaster: Heart of Pennsylvania Dutch Country

❻ If you have another day to spend in Pennsylvania Dutch Country, tour the city of **Lancaster** and surrounding attractions or follow Oregon Pike north along the route described below.

The Historic Lancaster Walking Tour, a 90-minute stroll through the heart of this charming old city, is conducted by costumed guides who impart lively anecdotes about local architecture and history. *Tours leave from the downtown visitor center at S. Queen and Vine Sts., near Penn Sq.,* ☏ *717/392–1776.* ☛ *$5 adults, $4 senior citizens, $2 students.* ⊙ *Tours Mon.–Sat. 10 and 1:30, Sun. 1:30, Apr.–Oct.; rest of yr by reservation only.*

Central Market began with open-air stalls in 1742. The current Romanesque building was constructed in 1889, and is one of the oldest covered markets in the country. This is where the locals shop for fresh fruit and vegetables, meats (try the Lebanon bologna), flowers, and baked goods such as sticky buns and shoofly pie. It's a good place to pick up food for a picnic. *Penn Sq.,* ☏ *717/291–4723.* ⊙ *Tues. and Fri. 6–4, Sat. 6–2.*

The **Demuth Foundation** includes the restored 18th-century home, studio, and garden of Charles Demuth, one of America's first modernist artists. The complex includes a museum shop and the oldest operating tobacco shop (1770) in the country. *114 E. King St.,* ☏ *717/299–9940.* ☛ *Free.* ⊙ *Tues.–Sat. 10–4, Sun. 1–4. Closed Jan.*

The Old City Hall, reborn as the **Heritage Center Museum,** shows the work of Lancaster County artisans and craftsmen—clocks, furniture, homemade toys, *fraktur* (ornate folk calligraphy), and Pennsylvania long rifles. Some exhibits are on display permanently, while others are rotated. *King and Queen Sts.,* ☏ *717/299–6440.* ☛ *Donation requested.* ⊙ *Tues.–Sat. 10–4.*

Rock Ford Plantation and Kauffman Museum show antiques and folk art. The antiques are in a 1794 Georgian-style house once owned by Edward Hand, George Washington's adjutant general; the Zoe and Henry Kauffman collection of pewter, brass, firearms, and furniture is displayed in the restored barn. *Lancaster County Park at 881 Rock*

Ford Rd., ☎ 717/392–7223. ☛ *$4.50 adults, $3.50 senior citizens, $2 children 6–12. Guided 45-min tours.* ☉ *Apr.–Oct., Tues.–Sat. 10–4, Sun. noon–4. Closed Nov.–Mar.*

❼ Wheatland was the home of the only president from Pennsylvania, James Buchanan. The restored 1828 Federal mansion displays the 15th president's furniture just as it was during his lifetime. A one-hour tour includes an entertaining profile of the only bachelor to occupy the White House. *1120 Marietta Ave. (Rte. 23), 1½ mi west of Lancaster,* ☎ *717/392–8721.* ☛ *$5.50 adults, $4.50 senior citizens, $3.50 students, $1.75 children 6–12.* ☉ *Apr.–Nov., daily 10–4. Victorian Christmas exhibit 1st 2 wks of Dec. Closed mid-Dec.–Mar.*

❽ Artist Andrew Wyeth's ancestors were members of the Herr family and the **Hans Herr House** is the subject of several Wyeth paintings. Today, the house is owned by the Lancaster Mennonite Historical Society, which aims to correct misconceptions about the Mennonite religion with exhibits about their way of life in its Visitors Center. The 45-minute tours cover the grounds and the 1719 sandstone house, a former Mennonite meeting place. The house, the oldest in Lancaster County, is considered the best example of medieval-style German architecture in North America. *1849 Hans Herr Dr., 5 mi south of Lancaster off U.S. 222,* ☎ *717/464–4438.* ☛ *$3.50 adults, $1 children 7–12.* ☉ *Mon.–Sat. 9–4, Apr.–Nov. Closed Dec.–Mar.*

❾ Follow Oregon Pike (Rte. 272) north from Lancaster to the **Landis Valley Museum,** an outdoor museum of Pennsylvania/German rural life and folk culture before 1900. Owned by brothers Henry and George Landis, the farm and village is now operated by the Pennsylvania Historical and Museum Commission. From May through October, you can visit over 15 historical buildings, from a farmstead to a country store, and see daily demonstrations of such skills as spinning and weaving, pottery making, and tinsmithing, the products of which are for sale in the Weathervane Shop. There are guided tours from November to April. *2451 Kissel Hill Rd. (just off Oregon Pike), Lancaster,* ☎ *717/569–0401.* ☛ *$7 adults, $6 senior citizens, $5 children 6–17.* ☉ *Tues.–Sat. 9–5, Sun. noon–5. Closed Nov.–Apr.*

❿ In the 1730s, a radical religious communal society took root in the town of Ephrata. A living example of William Penn's Holy Experiment, the monastic Protestants of the **Ephrata Cloister** lived an ascetic life of work, study, and prayer. They ate one meal a day of grain, fruit, and vegetables, and encouraged celibacy (the last sister died in 1813). The society was best known for a cappella singing, fraktur, its medieval German architecture, and its publishing center. Robed guides lead 45-minute tours of three restored buildings; then visitors can tour the stable, print shop, and craft shop by themselves. *Rtes. 272 and 322, Ephrata,* ☎ *717/733–6600.* ☛ *$5 adults, $4 senior citizens, $3 children 6–17.* ☉ *Mon.–Sat. 9–5, Sun. noon–5.*

⓫ The town of **Lititz,** west of Ephrata, was founded by Moravians who settled in Pennsylvania to do missionary work among the Indians. It's a lovely town with a tree-shaded main street lined with 18th-century cottages and shops selling antiques, crafts, clothing, and gifts. Around the main square are the Moravian communal residences, a church dating from 1787, and a hospital that treated the wounded during the Revolutionary War. Pick up a Historical Foundation walking tour brochure at the General Sutter Inn (*see* Dining and Lodging, *below*).

TIME OUT **The General Sutter Inn** (Main St. and Rte. 501, ☎ 717/626–2115) was named after the man who founded Sacramento in 1839, 10 years before the discovery of gold on his California property started the gold rush. A Victoriana lover's delight, this inn has a pretty coffee shop and a more formal restaurant. In summer, you can linger on the brick patio.

At the nation's oldest pretzel bakery, the **Julius Sturgis Pretzel House,** you can see pretzels twisted by hand and baked in brick ovens the same way Julius Sturgis did it in 1861. At the end of the 20-minute guided tour, visitors can try their hand at the almost extinct art of pretzel twisting. *219 E. Main St., Lititz,* ☎ *717/626–4354.* ☞ *$1.50.* ☉ *Mon.–Sat. 9–4:30.*

The first thing you'll notice in Lititz is the smell of chocolate. It emanates from the **Wilbur Chocolate Company's Candy Americana Museum and Factory Candy Outlet** (48 N. Broad St., Lititz, ☎ 717/626–1131), which features a candymaking demonstration (with free samples), a small museum of candy-related memorabilia, and a retail store. ☉ *Mon.–Sat. 10–5.*

Western Lancaster County: Peaceful Backwaters and Fine Wineries

Some visitors avoid the crowds and commercialism of eastern Lancaster County by staying in the sleepy towns along the Susquehanna River—Columbia, Marietta, Maytown, Bainbridge, Mount Joy, and Elizabethtown.

⑫ With architecture ranging from log cabins to more recent Federal and Victorian homes, 48% of the town of **Marietta** is listed on the National Historic Register. The restored river town, now seeing life as an artists' community, is perfect for strolling along, admiring the well-preserved facades and peeking into the art galleries and antiques shops.

TIME OUT Between Marietta and Columbia, pull off Route 441 at **Chickies Rock County Park.** Follow the trail from the parking area to Chickies Rock, an outcropping high above the water, for a commanding view of the Susquehanna River as it snakes through the valley.

⑬ **The Watch and Clock Museum of the National Association of Watch and Clock Collectors** displays a large and varied collection of timepieces, specialized tools, and related items from the primitive to the modern. There's a 19th-century Tiffany globe clock, a German Black Forest organ clock with 94 pipes, and the showstopper, the Engle Clock—an 1877 timepiece intended to resemble the famous astronomical cathedral clock of Strasbourg, France. It took clockmaker Stephen D. Engle 20 years to complete and has 48 moving figures. *514 Poplar St., Columbia,* ☎ *717/684–8261.* ☞ *$3 adults, $2.50 senior citizens, $1 children 6–17.* ☉ *Tues.–Sat. 9–4; May–Sept. Sun. 12–4.*

⑭ The **Market House and Dungeon,** built in 1869, is one of the oldest continuously operating farmers markets in the state. You can buy handcrafted jewelry, baked goods, meat, fruits, and vegetables from local farms. The basement of the market used to be a dungeon; you can still see the ground-level windows through which prisoners were shoved down a chute into the darkness. *308 Locust St. (off of Rte. 441), Columbia,* ☎ *717/684–2468.* ☉ *Farmers market: Fri. 7–4, Sat. 7–noon. Dungeon by appointment only; contact the Susquehanna Heritage Visitors Center, 3rd and Linden Sts., Columbia 17512,* ☎ *717/684–5249.*

⑮ **Wrights Ferry Mansion** is the former residence of English Quaker Susanna Wright, a silkworm breeder whose family helped open Colonial Pennsylvania west of the Susquehanna. The 1738 stone house showcases period furniture in the Philadelphia William & Mary and Queen Anne styles and a great collection of English needlework, ceramics, and glass, all pre-dating 1750. *38 S. 2nd St., Columbia,* ☎ *717/684–4325.* ☛ *$5 adults, $2.50 students 6–18.* ☉ *May–Oct., Tues., Wed., Fri., Sat. 10–3.*

Two wineries operate in the western part of the county. At the 52-acre
⑯ **Nissley Vineyards and Winery Estate,** you can review the grape-growing and wine-making process on a self-guided wine tasting tour. *140 Vintage Dr., northwest of Columbia near Bainbridge, 1½ mi off Rte. 441,* ☎ *717/426–3514.* ☛ *Free.* ☉ *Mon.–Sat. 10–5, Sun. 1–4.*

⑰ At the **Mt. Hope Estate and Winery,** it's an elegant 1800s mansion, not vineyards, that's the focus of the tour. The mansion is a 19th-century delight, complete with turrets, hand-painted 18-foot ceilings, Egyptian marble fireplaces, gold-leaf wallpaper, and crystal gas chandeliers. Tours are led by costumed guides and followed by a formal wine tasting of Mt. Hope Wines. There are lovely estate gardens for strolls. *North of Manheim on Rte. 72, ½ mi from Exit 20 of the Pennsylvania Turnpike,* ☎ *717/665–7021 ext. 125.* ☛ *$5 adults, $2 those under 21.* ☉ *Tours May and June weekends, July–Sept. daily; by reservation only.*

The **Pennsylvania Renaissance Faire** (☎ 717/665–7021) runs weekends from August to mid-October on the grounds of the Mt. Hope Estate and Winery. The winery is transformed into a 16th-century English village with human chess matches, jousting and fencing tournaments, street performances, craft demonstrations, jesters, and Shakespearean plays. ☛ *$15.95 adults, $7 children 5–11.* ☉ *Aug.–Labor Day, Sat.–Mon. 11:30–7; Sept.–mid-Oct., weekends 10:30–6.*

Hershey: The "Chocolate Town"

⑱ **Hershey** celebrates chocolate without guilt, from streetlights shaped like foil-wrapped kisses to avenues named Chocolate and Cocoa. Situated about 30 miles northwest of Lancaster, its attractions offer activities for kids of all ages (call 800/HERSHEY for brochures).

At **Hersheypark** they take the saying, "You are what you eat," seriously. Where else can you find walking Hershey Bars and dancing Reese's Peanut Butter Cups? Only here, living on 100 acres that include 50 rides, games of chance, and five theaters. The park originated in 1907 as a playground for Hershey chocolate-factory employees. Among its historic attractions are the Comet, a 1946-vintage wooden roller coaster, and a carousel built in 1919 with 66 hand-carved wooden horses. *Rte. 743 and U.S. 422, Hershey, 17033,* ☎ *717/534–3090.* ☛ *$24.95 adults, $15.95 senior citizens and children 3–8; includes ZooAmerica (see below).* ☉ *Memorial Day–Labor Day, daily 10:30–10 (some earlier closings); May and Sept., weekends only.*

Within the grounds of Hersheypark is **ZooAmerica,** an 11-acre wildlife park. On display are more than 250 animals from throughout North America in re-creations of their natural habitats. ☎ 717/534–3860. ☛ *$4.75 adults, $4.25 senior citizens, $3.50 children 3–12 (or Hersheypark admission).* ☉ *Mid-June–Aug., daily 10–8; Sept.–May, daily 10–5.*

An automated ride through **Hershey's Chocolate World** has taken the place of touring the actual factory, which stopped welcoming visitors

when the crowds became too large. Chocolate pilgrims may learn how Hershey products are made, taste-test their favorite Hershey confection, and buy gifts. Chocolate World also serves as the town's official visitors center. ☎ *717/534–4900.* ☛ *Free.* ☾ *Mon.–Sat. 9–5; in summer, daily 9–8.*

The **Hershey Museum** preserves the story of Milton Snavely Hershey, who founded the town bearing his name and just about everything in it. The main exhibit, "Built on Chocolate," displays Hershey artifacts and memorabilia. Chocolate bar wrappers and cocoa tins show their evolution through the years, while black and white photos of the town from the '30s, '40s, and '50s are hung side by side with color photos of the same sites today. ☎ *717/534–3439.* ☛ *$4.25 adults, $3.75 senior citizens, $2 children 3–15.* ☾ *Memorial Day–Labor Day, daily 10–6; Labor Day–Memorial Day, daily 10–5.*

Hershey Gardens began with a single 3½-acre plot of 8,000 rose bushes and has grown to include 10 themed gardens on 23 landscaped acres. The gardens come to life in spring as thousands of bulbs burst into bloom. Flowering displays last until fall, when late roses open their petals. *Hotel Rd. near the Hotel Hershey,* ☎ *717/534–3439.* ☛ *$4.25 adults, $3.75 senior citizens, $2 children 3–15.* ☾ *Apr.–Oct., daily 9–5.*

Chocolatetown Square is a one-acre park downtown where free concerts are held. *Look for the wooden gazebo just off the intersection of Cocoa and E. Chocolate Aves. For information on upcoming events,* ☎ *717/534–3411.*

The **Hotel Hershey** (*see* Lodging, *below*) dates back to 1933, when Milton Hershey embarked upon his own personal jobs program to lift his town out of the depression, as does the downtown **Hershey Theater,** located in the rear of the Community Building. Before each showing, the theater ceiling is transformed into the nighttime sky as images of clouds drift across star-filled heavens. Other depression-era projects Milton Hershey launched are the 9,000-seat **Hersheypark Arena** and 25,000-seat **Hersheypark Stadium,** both on the theme park grounds.

Gettysburg: A Living Battlefield

If you continue west from Lancaster on U.S. 30 to Adams County, about 55 miles distant, you will arrive at the site where Confederate dreams of independence died. From July 1 to 3, 1863, 51,000 Americans were killed, wounded, or counted as missing in battle. **Gettysburg** honors these casualties with more than 1,000 markers and monuments, 20 museums, and a 5,000-acre national park.

The **Gettysburg Travel Council** (35 Carlisle St., ☎ 717/334–6274, ℻ 717/334–1166) offers free brochures and maps of attractions surrounding the battlefield. The **Gettysburg National Military Park Visitors Center** (97 Taneytown Rd., ☎ 717/334–1124) offers a free map with an 18-mile driving tour through the battlefield. Private, licensed guides may also be hired at the center. Narrated tours aboard open-air, double-decker buses depart every 15 to 45 minutes from the **Gettysburg Tour Center** (778 Baltimore St., ☎ 717/334–6296).

To best understand the battle, begin at the military park visitors center, where an **Electric Map** uses colored lights to illustrate deployments and clashes during the three days of fighting. Sit on the south side for the best view. ☛ *$2 adults, $1.50 senior citizens, children under 16 free.* ☾ *Showings every 45 min 8:15–4:15, till 5:15 in summer.*

The **Cyclorama Center** contains a 19th-century, in-the-round painting that puts viewers in the center of Pickett's Charge, the South's ill-fated frontal assault during the last day of the battle. ☛ *$2 adults, $1.50 senior citizens.* ◔ *Showings daily, every 30 min, 9–4:30.*

To stand near the site where the Gettysburg Address was delivered, cross the street to the **National Cemetery.** ☛ *Free.* ◔ *Daily, dawn–dusk.*

Facing the battlefield entrance, the **National Civil War Wax Museum** exhibits 200 life-size figures in 30 scenes, a reenactment of the Battle of Gettysburg, and an animated Abraham Lincoln delivering his Gettysburg Address. *297 Steinwehr Ave.,* ☎ *717/334–6245.* ☛ *$4.50 adults, $2.50 children 13–17, $1.75 children 6–12.* ◔ *Daily 9–7. Jan. and Feb., weekends only 9–5.*

The **Hall of Presidents** re-creates in wax the nation's chief executives from Washington to Clinton, as well as their wives (with reproductions of their inaugural gowns). *789 Baltimore St.,* ☎ *717/334–5717.* ☛ *$5.25 adults, $3.25 children 6–11.* ◔ *Summer, daily 9–9; spring and fall, daily 9–5; closed Dec.–Feb.*

Soldier's National Museum depicts the 10 major battles of the Civil War in miniature dioramas plus a life-size encampment scene from the night of July 2, 1863. *777 Baltimore St.,* ☎ *717/334–4890.* ☛ *$5.25 adults, $3.25 children 6–11.* ◔ *Summer, daily 9–9; spring and fall, daily 9–5; closed Dec.–Feb.*

The **Lincoln Train Museum** brings to life Lincoln's journey from Washington to Gettysburg in 1863. A 12-minute ride simulates the sights, sounds, and most of all the feel of traveling on a period railcar. *Business Rte. 15,* ☎ *717/334–5678.* ☛ *$5.25 adults, $3.25 children 6–12.* ◔ *Summer, daily 9–10; spring and fall, daily 9–5; closed Dec.–Feb.*

Along U.S. 30, which runs through the center of town, the **Lincoln Room Museum** houses the bedroom where the president finished writing his famous address. **General Lee's headquarters** may also be found along this road, west of town. *Lincoln Room: 12 Lincoln Sq.,* ☎ *717/334–8188.* ☛ *$3.25 adults, $3 senior citizens, $1.75 children 9–18.* ◔ *Summer, daily 9–7:30; reduced hrs off-season. Lee's headquarters: Rte. 30 W (near the Quality Inn),* ☎ *717/334–3141.* ☛ *$1.50 adults, children under 12 free.* ◔ *Mar.–Nov., daily 9–9.*

A general and president from a later time, Dwight D. Eisenhower, was also associated with Gettysburg. Ike's retirement farm adjoining the battlefield is administered by the park service as the **Eisenhower National Historic Site.** ☎ *717/334–1124.* ☛ *$3.75 adults, $1.75 children 13–16, $1.15 children 6–12.* ◔ *Apr.–Oct., daily 9–5; Nov.–Mar., Wed.–Sun. 9–5; closed mid-Jan.–mid.-Feb.*

What to See and Do with Children

Abe's (*see* Discovering the Real Amish *in* Exploring, *above*) or **Ed's Buggy Rides** (Rte. 896 near Herr Rd., Strasburg, ☎ 717/687–0360).

Dutch Wonderland. With 44 acres of games and rides, the amusement park is ideally suited for families with younger children. Most rides are tame. The rides are supplemented by diving shows, an animated bear show, and concerts. *U.S. 30, east of Lancaster,* ☎ *717/291–1888.* ☛ *$11 for 5 rides; $16 for unlimited rides; children under 3 free.* ◔ *Memorial Day–Labor Day, daily 10–7 or later; Easter–Memorial Day and Labor Day–Oct. 31, weekends only.*

Indian Echo Caverns is one of the largest caves in the northeastern United States. A 45-minute guided walking tour explores the underground wonderland. Bring a sweater; no strollers are allowed. *Off U.S. 322, Hummelstown,* ☎ *717/566–8131.* ☛ *$7 adults, $3.50 children 4–11.* ☉ *Summer, daily 9–6; rest of yr 10–4.*

National Wax Museum. Wax figures represent important people in Lancaster County history. Visitors view scenes from daily life and watch a simulated barn raising. *2249 Lincoln Hwy. E, Lancaster,* ☎ *717/393–3679.* ☛ *$4.75 adults, $4.25 senior citizens, $3 children 5–11.* ☉ *Daily 9–6 or later, until 9 in summer.*

People's Place (*see* Discovering the Real Amish *in* Exploring, *above*).

Strasburg Rail Road (*see* Strasburg *in* Exploring, *above*).

National Toy Train Museum (*see* Strasburg *in* Exploring, *above*).

Off the Beaten Track

The **Green Dragon Farmers Market and Auction** is an old traditional agricultural market with a country carnival atmosphere. Each week livestock and agricultural commodities are auctioned in the morning. Local Amish and Mennonite farmers tend many of the 450 indoor and outdoor stalls selling meats, fruits, vegetables, fresh-baked pies, and dry goods. One of the state's largest farmer's markets (occupying 30 acres), it also has a flea market and an evening auction of small animals. Try the sticky buns at Rissler's Bakery and the sausage sandwiches at Newswanger's. *955 N. State St., just off Rte. 272, Ephrata,* ☎ *717/738–1117.* ☉ *Fri. 9 AM–10 PM.*

SHOPPING

Crafts

Although craftspeople in the Lancaster County area produce fine handiwork, folk art, quilts, and needlework, much of the best work is sold to galleries nationwide and never shows up in local shops. Among the few places to see fine local crafts are the **Weathervane Shop** at the Landis Valley Museum (2451 Kissel Hill Rd., Lancaster, ☎ 717/569–9312). Craftsmen sell the wares they make in on-site demonstrations—tin, pottery, leather, braided rugs, weaving, and chair-caning.

The Tin Bin (20 Valley Rd. off Rte. 501, Neffsville, ☎ 717/569–6210) features handmade tinware and pottery, and reproductions of 18th-century lighting devices. **The Artworks at Doneckers** (100 N. State St., Ephrata, ☎ 717/738–9503) houses studios where you can watch painters, sculptors, and potters at work. There are also art, fine crafts, and antiques galleries. **Pandora's** (Rte. 340 just east of U.S. 30, Lancaster, ☎ 717/299–5305, call ahead) sells antique quilts and textiles made in Lancaster County. At **Witmer's Quilt Shop** (1070 W. Main St., New Holland, ☎ 717/656–9526), you'll find both new and antique quilts. Though pricey, old quilts have proven to be good investments.

The Mennonite Central Committee operates **Selfhelp Crafts of the World Gifts and Tea Room** (Rte. 272 north, just north of the Cloister in Ephrata, ☎ 717/721–8400). A job-creation program designed to aid developing countries, the store has more than 3,000 items—including jewelry, Indian brass, onyx, needlework, baskets, toys,

handwoven Pakistani rugs, and odd musical instruments—from Bangladesh, Botswana, Brazil, and about 30 other countries. Sales in January and July offer some terrific bargains. Each week for lunch the Nav Jiwan (Hindi for "new life") Tea Room features the cuisine of a different country.

Kitchen Kettle Village (Rte. 340, 10 miles east of Lancaster, in Intercourse, ☎ 717/768–8261 or 800/732–3538) consists of 32 shops showcasing local crafts, including decoy carving; furniture making; leather tooling; relish, jam, and jelly making; and tin punching. The Kling House Restaurant (*see* Dining, *below*) is open for breakfast and lunch. Closed Sunday.

Outlets

It appears that Lancaster is trying to compete with Reading as the Factory Outlet Capital of the Universe. U.S. 30 is lined with outlets: Some are factory stores, which offer first-quality goods at large discounts; others call themselves outlets but don't have real bargains. It's a good idea to find out the retail prices of whatever you want before you leave home. With 120 stores and counting, from Lenox to London Fog and the huge Reading China & Glass, **Rockvale Square Factory Outlet Village** (U.S. 30 and Rte. 896, ☎ 717/293–9595) is the largest outlet center in Lancaster. The latest addition to outlet row is **MillStream Factory Shops** (Rte. 30 west of Rockvale, near Dutch Wonderland, ☎ 717/392–7202), a collection of 52 designer outlets including Ann Taylor and Brooks Brothers.

Antiques

On Sundays, antiques hunters frequent the huge antiques malls located on Route 272 between Adamstown and Denver, 1 mile west of Pennsylvania Turnpike Exit 21. As many as 5,000 dealers may turn up on summer festival Sundays. **Renninger's Antique and Collector's Market** (☎ 717/336–2177), **Barr's Auctions** (☎ 717/336–2861), and **Stoudt's Black Angus** (☎ 717/484–4385) all feature indoor and outdoor booths. Dealers display old books and prints, Victorian blouses, corner cupboards, pewter and local stoneware, and lots of furniture. Barr's is open on Saturday, also. Several antiques cooperatives (Log Cabin Antique Center, Weaver's, Southpoint) also line the stretch.

Americana

Genuine Civil War artifacts and stirring canvases depicting the battle are the spoils of a visit to Gettysburg. The town's artist-in-residence, **Dale Gallon,** may be found at **Old Gettysburg Village** in the center of the tourist district (777 Baltimore St., ☎ 717/334–8666). For a shopping experience that is more like visiting a museum, **The Horse Soldier** (☎ 717/334–0347), another village shop, sells authentic Civil War mementos ranging from swords to photographs. For Civil War histories stop by **Farnsworth Military Impressions** (401 Baltimore St., ☎ 717/334–8838).

Farmers Markets

Farmers markets offer the most unusual shopping experiences in the area. The **Central Market** in Lancaster (*see* Lancaster *in* Exploring, *above*) and **Green Dragon Farmers Market and Auction** in Ephrata (*see* Off the Beaten Track, *above*) are the best; if you can't shop there, try **Bird-in-Hand Farmer's Market** (Rte. 340, Bird-in-Hand, ☎ 717/393–9674),

a conveniently located market with produce stands, baked goods, gift shops, and outlets. Market open Wednesday through Saturday; Friday and Saturday only in winter. **Meadowbrook Farmer's Market** (Rte. 23, Leola, ☎ 717/656–2226) is popular for its edible goodies as well as its flea-market items, crafts, collectibles, country store, and 50%-off Lone Star Outlet store. Open Friday and Saturday year-round, more days in summer. The county's newest farmers market may be found at the **Artworks at Doneckers** (*see* Crafts, *above*).

SPORTS AND THE OUTDOORS

Ballooning

Great Adventure Balloon Club offers a bird's-eye view of Pennsylvania Dutch Country. As part of the crew, you help inflate the balloon, maneuver the controls, and land the craft in a farmer's field. You spend an hour airborne, about three hours total. A chase van drives you back to the starting point. *Lancaster,* ☎ *717–397–3623.* ☛ *$135 per person.* ☉ *Daily year-round, weather permitting. 1-day advance reservation required.*

Bicycling

The Pennsylvania Department of Transportation (☎ 717/787–7350) is working on a state bicycling resource directory covering touring, mountain biking, racing, and bike clubs. Planned publication 1996.

Camping

The Pennsylvania Dutch Visitors Bureau has a complete list of area campgrounds. Some of the best include:

Mill Bridge Village and Campresort, which is attached to a restored 18th-century village. *½ mi south of U.S. 30 on S. Ronks Rd.,* ☎ *717/687–8181 or 800/645–2744. Snack shop, summer entertainment, free buggy rides, stream fishing.*

Muddy Run Park offers lovely campgrounds in the southern end of the county set among 700 acres of woodland and rolling fields that surround a 100-acre lake. Environmental programs include nature walks, bird-watching (including evening "owl prowls"), and fly–fishing workshops. *172 Bethesda Church Rd. W, Holtwood,* ☎ *717/284–4325. Snack bar, general store, playground, boating, fishing.*

Spring Gulch Resort Campground is a glorious farmland and forest setting with 400 sites (pleasantly shaded) and rental cottages. A full schedule of weekend activities includes country dances and chicken barbecues. *Rte. 897 between Rtes. 340 and 322, New Holland,* ☎ *717/354–3100 or 800/255–5744. Lake, two heated pools, spa, miniature golf, tennis and volleyball courts, fishing, game room, square dances, exercise classes.*

In Gettysburg, **Artillery Ridge Campground** provides a place to pitch a tent or park an RV one mile south of the military park visitors center. *610 Taneytown Rd.,* ☎ *717/334–1288. Swimming, fishing, horse and bicycle rentals.*

Golf

The **Lancaster Host Resort and Conference Center** (U.S. 30, Lancaster, ☎ 717/299–5500) has 27 holes for regulation golf; carts are not re-

quired. *Greens fees: $28 for 18 holes, $11.50 per person for cart. Rental clubs available.*

The **Country Club of Hershey** (☎ 800/900–4653) maintains two private 18-hole courses that are available to guests of the Hotel Hershey (greens fees around $60); plus, the **South Course** (☎ 717/534–3450), a short, but demanding 18 holes that is open to the public (greens fees $22–$43). **Spring Creek Golf** (☎ 717/533–2847), a nine-hole course, was originally built by Milton Hershey for youngsters to hone their stroke (greens fees $9 for nine holes). The **Hotel Hershey** (☎ 717/533–2171) offers nine holes on the hotel grounds (greens fees $10 for nine holes).

Hiking and Walking

The National Park Service provides free walking-tour maps of the **Gettysburg National Military Park,** available at the Visitors Center (97 Taneytown Rd., ☎ 717/334–1124). Short one-mile loops include the sites of some of the battle's most pivotal engagements. Longer 9- and 3.5-mile trails also are marked. In western Lancaster County, **Chickies Rock County Park,** off Rte. 441, between Marietta and Columbia, offers stunning views of the Susquehanna River.

DINING AND LODGING

Dining

Like the German cuisine that influenced it, Pennsylvania Dutch cooking is hearty and uses ingredients from local farms. To sample regional fare, eat at one of the several bustling restaurants in the area where diners sit with perhaps a dozen other people and the food is passed around in bowls family style. Meals are plentiful and basic—fried chicken, ham, roast beef, dried corn, buttered noodles, mashed potatoes, chowchow, bread, pepper cabbage—and that's only a partial listing. Entrées are accompanied by traditional "sweets and sours," vegetable dishes made with a vinegar-and-sugar dressing. This is the way the Amish, who hate to throw things out, preserve leftover vegetables.

Don't forget to indulge your sweet tooth with shoofly pie, snitz pie, all kinds of pies, even for breakfast. Bake shops in this area are proud to point out that this is the region that invented the hole in the donut (by cutting out the center of *fastnacht* cakes)—even the English word *dunk* comes from Pennsylvania Dutch *dunke*.

Lancaster County has numerous smorgasbords and reasonably priced family restaurants along with a number of Continental and French restaurants in contemporary settings and quaint historic inns. Unless otherwise noted, liquor is served.

CATEGORY	COST*
$$$$	over $30
$$$	$20–$30
$$	$10–$20
$	under $10

per person for a 3-course meal, excluding wine, 6% tax, and service

Lodging

Lancaster County lodgings are much like the people themselves—plain or fancy. You can rough it in one of the many campgrounds in the area,

meet a family by staying in their B&B or on their farm, or indulge yourself at a full-frills resort. A good selection of moderately priced motels cater to families. The Pennsylvania Dutch Visitors Bureau has a listing of all area B&Bs and farms that welcome guests. Rates are highest in summer; at most hotels off-season rates are greatly reduced. Unless otherwise indicated, all rooms have private bath and hotels are open year-round.

CATEGORY	COST*
$$$$	over $100
$$$	$80–$100
$$	$60–$79
$	under $60

double occupancy, based on peak (summer) rates, excluding 6% tax

Adamstown

Dining

$$$ Stoudt's Black Angus. Prime rib cut from certified Angus beef is the specialty of this popular Victorian-style restaurant, adjacent to the Black Angus antiques mall. Also notable are its raw oyster bar and German dishes such as Wiener (veal) and Schwabian (pork) schnitzel. Stoudt's beer, brewed right next door, is on tap. On weekends from July through October, a Bavarian Beer Fest featuring German bands, a pig roast, and ethnic food takes over Brewery Hall. ✕ *Rte. 272,* ☎ *717/484–4385. Reservations advised Fri.–Sun. Brewery tours Sat. at 3, Sun. at 1. AE, DC, MC, V. Lunch Sun. only.*

Bird-in-Hand

Dining

$$ Amish Barn Restaurant. Pennsylvania Dutch cuisine is served family style, which means generous helpings of meat and produce, breads, and home-baked pies. Apple dumplings are a specialty. You can choose from an à la carte menu or order a family-style meal. No liquor is served. ✕ *Rte. 340 between Bird-in-Hand and Intercourse,* ☎ *717/768–8886. Reservations advised summer weekends. AE, D, MC, V. ☉ Apr.–Dec. daily; winter Fri.–Sun. only.*

$ Bird-in-Hand Family Restaurant. This family-owned, diner-style restau-
★ rant enjoys a good reputation for hearty Pennsylvania Dutch home cooking. The menu is à la carte. There is a lunch buffet weekdays. No liquor is served. ✕ *2760 Old Philadelphia Pike,* ☎ *717/768–8266. MC, V. Closed Sun.*

Lodging

$$–$$$ Village Inn of Bird-in-Hand. The Victorian flavor of this three-story country inn, built in 1852, is tempered by the modern comforts of down-filled bedding, cable TV, and phones. Continental breakfast, an evening snack, and a two-hour tour of the area are complimentary. ⊡ *Box 253, 2695 Old Philadelphia Pike (Rte. 340), 17505,* ☎ *717/293–8369. 11 rooms, including 2 deluxe suites with Jacuzzis. Pool and tennis privileges at nearby Bird-in-Hand Family Inn. AE, D, MC, V.*

$$ Bird-in-Hand Family Inn. Plain, clean, comfortable rooms in a family-owned motel praised for its friendly staff. ⊡ *Box 402, 2740 Old Philadelphia Pike, 17505,* ☎ *717/768–8271 or 800/537–2535. 100 rooms. Restaurant, tennis courts, playground, indoor and outdoor pools. AE, D, DC, MC, V.*

Churchtown

Lodging

$–$$$$
★

Churchtown Inn. This restored 1735 fieldstone mansion, overlooking an Amish farm, has two beautiful Victorian parlors, a collection of handmade quilts and antique music boxes, and cozy, elegant bedrooms with pencil-post canopied, brass, and high-back Victorian beds. The day dawns in the glass-enclosed garden room with a five-course breakfast including goodies such as Grand Marnier French toast, oatmeal and granola pancakes, and homemade coffee cake and ends in the parlor with an evening beverage hour, during which one of the innkeepers, a former music director, plays the piano and sings. Guests are invited to a nearby Amish home for dinner. Special-event weekends are held from mid-November through May, featuring road rallies, murder mysteries, barbecues, a formal Victorian costume ball, and professional concerts. ☒ *On Rte. 23 between Morgantown and New Holland, 5 mi from Pennsylvania Turnpike exit 22., 2100 Main St., Churchtown, 17555,* ☎ *717/445–7794. 8 rooms, 6 with bath; carriage house. Children over 12 welcome. 2-night minimum weekends, 3-night minimum holiday weekends. MC, V.*

Denver

Dining

$

Zinn's Country Diner. Local specialties are served here daily from 6 AM to 11 PM. On the property are a gift shop, two miniature golf courses, batting cages, basketball courts, and an arcade. Complete children's dinners $2.99–$3.99. Antiques malls are nearby. No liquor is served. ✕ *Rte. 272 north at Pennsylvania Turnpike exit 21,* ☎ *717/336–2210. D, MC, V.*

Lodging

$$–$$$$

Black Horse Lodge and Suites. The lodge has contemporary rooms with balcony or patio overlooking spacious grounds, which include fitness stations, a picnic pavilion, and a barbecue area. It is convenient to antiques malls and offers a free Continental breakfast. ☒ *Rte. 272, 1 mi north of Pennsylvania Turnpike exit 21. Box 343, 17517,* ☎ *717/267–7563,* 𝗙𝗔𝗫 *717/336–1110. 74 rooms. Restaurant, pool, basketball, playground. AE, D, DC, MC, V.*

East Petersburg

Dining

$$$
★

Haydn Zug's offers American-Continental dining in an 1850s house with tasteful Williamsburg furnishings. Its specialties include lamb tenderloins, veal Vienna, crab cakes, and fresh fish. James Beard wrote about their cheesy chowder; *Bon Appetit* profiled the establishment. A tavern menu is also available. ✕ *Rte. 72 and State St., Lancaster,* ☎ *717/569–5746. Reservations advised. AE, MC, V.*

Ephrata

Dining

$$$

The Restaurant at Doneckers. Classic and country French cuisine is served downstairs amid Colonial antiques and upstairs overlooking a country garden. The kitchen is known for its chateaubriand for two, sautéed whole Dover sole, daily chef's veal special, and salmon. The service is fine; the wine cellar is extensive. From 2:30 to 4 light fare is served. ✕ *333 N. State St.,* ☎ *717/738–9501. Reservations advised. AE, D, DC, MC, V. Closed Wed.*

Lodging

$$–$$$$ **Smithton Inn.** The B&B is in a historic former stagecoach inn with
★ seven lovingly furnished guest rooms and one four-room suite.
The rooms have antiques and reproductions, fireplaces, and canopy
beds; the third floor suite has a skylight, cathedral ceiling, and
Franklin stove fireplace. Nice touches abound: oversize goose-down
pillows, nightshirts, magazines, and fresh flowers. Outside are a lily
pond, a fountain, English lawn furniture, and a lovely garden. Full
breakfast is included. ⊞ *900 W. Main St., 17522,* ☎ *717/733–6094.
8 rooms, 1 suite. Well-behaved children and pets welcome by pre-
arrangement. 2-night minimum Sat. and holidays. No smoking. AE,
MC, V.*

$$–$$$ **The Inns at Doneckers.** Four properties dating from the 1770s to
1920s have been tastefully furnished with French country antiques
and decorated by hand-stenciling. Rooms are light and airy, and
the price includes Continental breakfast. ⊞ *318–324 N. State
St., 17522,* ☎ *717/738–9502. 40 rooms, including 13 suites. AE,
D, DC, MC, V.*

Gettysburg

Dining

$$$ **Farnsworth House Inn.** Housed in a building that still shows bullet holes
from the battle, the restaurant at this B&B serves up Civil War–era dishes
such as game pie, peanut soup, and spoon bread. The outdoor garden,
with sculptures, fountains, and a waterfall, provides a tranquil setting
in which to ponder the events of 1863. ✕ *401 Baltimore St,* ☎
717/334–8838. AE, D, MC, V.

Lodging

$$$–$$$$ **Best Western Gettysburg Hotel 1797.** The hotel is a pre–Civil War
structure in the heart of the historic downtown district, but the in-
terior was completely rebuilt in 1991. Some suites have fireplaces and
whirlpool tubs. Ask about the cannonball from the Battle of Gettysburg
still embedded in the brick wall across the street. ⊞ *1 Lincoln Sq.,
17325,* ☎ *717/337–2000,* ℻ *717/337–2077. 83 rooms. AE, D,
DC, MC, V.*

Hershey

Dining

$–$$ **Pippin's.** Pub-style food in an early American setting is a good value
at this family-oriented restaurant, located in Tudor Square just outside
Hersheypark. Its convenient location is also a short walk away from
Chocolate World, Hershey Museum, and the arena and stadium. ✕
100 W. Hershey Park Dr., ☎ *717/534–3821. AE, D, MC V. Closed
Jan.–Mar.*

Lodging

$$$$ **Hershey Lodge & Convention Center.** This bustling, expansive, mod-
ern resort caters to families and has two casual restaurants where kids
can be kids, plus a somewhat more formal room for adult dining. ⊞
W. Chocolate Ave. and University Dr., 17033, ☎ *717/533–3311 or
800/533–3131. 457 rooms. 3 restaurants, nightclub, cinema, indoor
and outdoor pools, 2 tennis courts, exercise center, miniature golf, play-
ground. AE, D, DC, MC, V.*

$$$$ **Hotel Hershey.** The grande dame of Hershey, this gracious Spanish-
style hotel is a quiet and sophisticated resort with lots of options for
recreation, starting with the golf course that lushly surrounds the hotel.
Opened in 1933 as part of Milton S. Hershey's building program to

lift his town out of the Great Depression, the Hershey was nicely refurbished in time for the hotel's 60th anniversary. Ask for one of the recently renovated rooms—they're spruced up but they've still got an evocative Old World feel. The hotel is next to Hersheypark, which automatically makes it popular with families. Dining options include The Fountain Cafe, the formal Circular Dining Room, and the casual Clubhouse Café. AP, MAP, and EP available. ⌖ *Hotel Rd. Box 400, 17033,* ☎ *717/533–2171 or 800/533–3131. 241 rooms. 3 restaurants, indoor-outdoor pool, 3 tennis courts, bowling, golf. AE, D, DC, MC, V.*

Intercourse

Dining

$$ Stoltzfus Farm Restaurant. Homemade Pennsylvania Dutch foods are served family style in a small country farmhouse, with most ingredients home grown on the farm. Most dishes are so tasty (especially the ham loaf with vinegar and brown sugar), you'll want the recipes—and the owners will happily supply you with them. ✕ *Rte. 772 E, ½ mi east of Rte. 340,* ☎ *717/768–8156.* ⊙ *May–Oct., Mon.–Sat.; Apr. and Nov., Fri. and Sat. only; closed Dec.–Mar. MC, V.*

$ Kling House. The Kling family home has been converted into a charming, casual restaurant featuring American cuisine at breakfast and lunch. Cranberry chicken, London broil, and snitz and knepp (dried apple and potato dumpling) entrées come with complimentary appetizer of red-pepper jam and cream cheese with crackers. The soups are homemade, and the desserts are luscious. A children's menu is available. ✕ *Kitchen Kettle Village, Rtes. 340 and 772,* ☎ *717/768–8261. Reservations advised. D, MC, V. Closed Sun. Dinner served Thurs.–Sat.*

Lancaster

Dining

$$$–$$$$ The Log Cabin. Steak, lamb chops, and seafood are prepared on a
★ charcoal grill in this 1928 expanded log cabin which was a speakeasy during Prohibition. The atmosphere is elegant and the setting is embellished with an impressive art collection. ✕ *11 Lehoy Forest Dr. (off Rte. 272, 5 mi north of Lancaster),* ☎ *717/626–1181. Reservations advised. AE, MC, V.*

$$$ Market Fare. The cuisine is American, and steaks, seafood, and veal are served in a cozy dining room with upholstered armchairs and 19th-century paintings, drawings, and photographs. Homemade soups and breads highlight the diverse menu. A children's menu and a light menu are also available. The café upstairs offers light breakfast, quick lunch, and carryout. ✕ *Market and Grant Sts. (across from Central Market),* ☎ *717/299–7090. Reservations advised. AE, D, DC, MC, V.*

$$–$$$ Olde Greenfield Inn. Continental cuisine and a fine wine cellar form part of the attraction in this gracious circa-1780 restored farmhouse. House specialties include roast duckling with raspberry sauce, Cajun beef with shrimp, and jumbo lump crab cakes. Lighter entrées, like seafood crepes, are also available. A piano player is in the lounge on weekends. Guests can dine on the patio. ✕ *595 Greenfield Rd.,* ☎ *717/393–0668. Reservations advised. AE, D, DC, MC, V. Closed Sun. evening.*

$$ Center City Grill. This casual but elegant bar and restaurant has a convenient downtown location for those exploring the city center. The varied "global menu" goes from Thai chicken in peanut-and-ginger sauce to gourmet pizzas to quiche Lorraine. Dancing most nights to a DJ,

and live jazz on Sunday evenings. A children's menu is available. ✕ *10 S. Prince St.,* ☎ *717/299–3456. AE, D, DC, MC, V.*

$$ **The Pressroom.** The menus look like newspapers and headline banners hang over the bar in this upscale bistro with an amusing *USA Today* ambience. Set in an old warehouse with an open kitchen and exposed baking hearth, the menu runs towards sandwiches (named after newspaper cartoon characters), salads, pizza, and pasta dishes. During summer months, there is seating in the park outside. ✕ *16–18 W. King St.,* ☎ *717/295–1316. AE, MC, V.*

$ **Lancaster Dispensing Co.** Fajitas, salads, sandwiches, and nachos are served until midnight in this stylish Victorian pub. The selection of imported beers is extensive. On the weekend, you can enjoy live music. ✕ *33–35 N. Market St.,* ☎ *717/299–4602. AE, MC, V.*

Lodging

$$$$ **Best Western Eden Resort Inn.** Spacious contemporary rooms (request
★ a room at poolside) and attractive grounds contribute to a pleasant stay here. The inn has a stunning tropical indoor pool and whirlpool under a retractable roof. The award-winning chef in Arthur's is noted for seafood and pasta; the Sunday buffet brunch in the skylit Eden Courtyard is excellent. Fun food is presented in Garfield's. Encore provides live entertainment. ⌂ *222 Eden Rd. (U.S. 30 and Rte. 272), 17601,* ☎ *717/569–6444 or 800/528–1234,* ℻ *717/569–4208. 275 rooms, 40 residential-style Club Suites. 2 cinemas, indoor and outdoor pools, tennis court. AE, D, DC, MC, V.*

$$$–$$$$ **King's Cottage.** This elegant Spanish mansion, which is on the National Register of Historic Places, has been transformed into a B&B furnished with antiques and 18th-century English reproductions, and has an outdoor goldfish pond. Full breakfast and afternoon tea are included. The cottage suite has a fireplace, Jacuzzi, and king-size canopy bed. ⌂ *1049 E. King St., 17602,* ☎ *717/397–1017 or 800/747–8717, 10 rooms. Children over 12 welcome. 2-night minimum weekends. D, MC, V.*

$$$–$$$$ **Lancaster Hilton Garden Inn.** An new, elegant hotel popular with corporate travelers offers oversize rooms, many with cathedral ceilings and large desks. The "BounceBack Weekend" package with breakfast is a bargain. ⌂ *Intersection of Rtes. 72 and 283, 17601,* ☎ *717/560–0880 or 800/HILTONS. 155 rooms. Restaurant, indoor pool, exercise room. AE, D, DC, MC, V.*

$$–$$$$ **Lancaster Host Resort and Conference Center.** This sprawling family resort sports a striking marble lobby and comfortable, contemporary rooms with cherrywood furnishings. The golf course and grounds are beautifully landscaped. A camp program for children ages 1–12 takes place daily during the summer and on weekends throughout the year. A variety of packages are available. ⌂ *2300 Lincoln Hwy. E (Rte. 30), 17602,* ☎ *717/299–5500 or 800/233–0121. 330 rooms. 2 restaurants, piano bar, indoor-outdoor pool, 27 holes of golf, miniature golf, 4 indoor and 8 outdoor tennis courts. AE, DC, MC, V.*

$$$ **Willow Valley Family Resort and Conference Center.** This mom-and-pop operation has blossomed into a large and stylish family resort. The striking skylit atrium lobby is surrounded by attractive rooms. There are moderately priced rooms, but the ones overlooking the atrium are the most attractive and most expensive. Since it is Mennonite owned, there is no liquor permitted on the premises. Several packages offer seasonal discounts. ⌂ *2416 Willow St. Pike, 17602,* ☎ *717/464–2711 or 800/444–1714,* ℻ *717/464–4784. 353 rooms. 2 restaurants, outdoor pool, 2 indoor pools, 9-hole golf course, 2 tennis courts. AE, D, DC, MC, V.*

$–$$$ **Your Place Country Inn.** This small new hotel close to the outlets and attractions has country furnishings handmade by Amish and local craftsmen. Continental breakfast is included. ⌑ *2133 Lincoln Hwy. E, 17602, ☎ 717/393–3413. 79 rooms. Restaurant, pool. AE, D, MC, V.*

Lititz

Lodging

$$–$$$$ **General Sutter Inn.** The oldest (1764) continuously run inn in the state
★ is a Victoriana lover's dream reminiscent of "Grandma's house." Its decor ranges from Pennsylvania folk art to Louis XIV sofas and marble-topped tables. The inn is at the crossroads of town, within easy walking distance of the Wilbur Chocolate Factory, Julius Sturgis Pretzel House, and the many 18th-century buildings of the historic district. The dimly lit tavern is a good place to mingle with local folks. Children are welcome. ⌑ *Corner of Rtes. 501 and 772, 17543, ☎ 717/626–2115, ℻ 717/626–0992. 12 rooms, including 2 family suites. Restaurant, bar, coffee shop. AE, D, MC, V.*

$$–$$$$ **Swiss Woods.** Innkeepers Werner and Debrah Mosimann designed this Swiss-style chalet while they were still living in Werner's native Switzerland. They planted it on 30 acres in Lititz, creating a comfortable, friendly, European-style bed-and-breakfast with light pine wood furnishings, a contemporary country decor, and goose-down comforters. The chalet is surrounded by extensive flower gardens and is nestled on the edge of the woods overlooking Speedwell Forge Lake. ⌑ *500 Blantz Rd., 17543, ☎ 717/627–3358 or 800/594–8018, ℻ 717/627–3483. 6 rooms, 1 suite. Hiking, boating, fishing. No smoking. Children welcome. 2-night minimum weekends Easter–Jan. 1, 3-night minimum holiday weekends. D, MC, V.*

Marietta

Dining and Lodging

$$–$$$ **Railroad House.** In a historic hotel on the east bank of the Susquehanna River, this restaurant has a split personality. Upstairs, classic American cuisine reigns, with steaks, seafood, veal, poultry, and pastas flavored with herbs from the on-premises garden; downstairs, a light tavern menu offers gourmet pizza, wings, sandwiches, soups, and salads. In warm weather, you can dine out on the patio in the garden. On Saturday nights, the Victorian era is re-created with strolling minstrels. The adjoining bed-and-breakfast was originally built in 1820 to service canal and river traffic. It now welcomes guests to Victorian-style rooms refurbished with antiques and Oriental rugs. Full breakfast is served. ⌑ *W. Front and S. Perry Sts., ☎ 717/426–4141. Reservations advised. 12 rooms, 8 with bath. Children welcome. MC, V.*

Mount Joy

Dining

$$–$$$$ **Groff's Farm.** Abe and Betty Groff's 1756 farmhouse restaurant has
★ received national attention for its hearty Mennonite fare. Candlelight, fresh flowers, and original Groff Farm country fabrics and wall coverings contribute to the homey ambience. House specialties include chicken Stoltzfus, farm relishes, and cracker pudding. Dinner begins with chocolate cake. Lunch is à la carte, dinner à la carte or family style served at your own table. ✕ *650 Pinkerton Rd., ☎ 717/653–2048, ℻ 717/653–1115. Reservations required for dinner, advised for lunch.*

Dinner seatings Tues.–Fri. between 5 and 7:30, Sat. at 5 and 8. AE, D, DC, MC, V. Closed Sun. and Mon.

$–$$$$ **Bube's Brewery.** The only intact, pre-Prohibition brewery in the United States contains three unique restaurants. **The Bottling Works** in the original bottling plant of the brewery serves steaks, light dinners, salads, burgers, and subs. **Alois's** offers prix-fixe six-course international dinners (reservations required; closed Mon.) in a Victorian hotel attached to the brewery. **The Catacombs** serves traditional steak and seafood dishes in the brewery's aging cellars 43 feet below street level. A feast master, with his wenches, presides over a medieval-style dinner on Sunday nights. Wine and ale flow, musicians entertain, and diners participate in the festivities. Reservations are required, at $30 per person. In addition, Bube's Brewery features an outdoor beer garden open in summer. ✕ *102 N. Market St.,* ☎ *717/653–2056. AE, D, MC, V.*

Dining and Lodging

$$–$$$$ **Cameron Estate Inn.** A sprawling Federal redbrick mansion, once the
★ summer home of Simon Cameron, Abraham Lincoln's first secretary of war, the Cameron Estate Inn welcomes guests to both its hostelry and fine restaurant. Some guests just enjoy the candlelit, Federal-style dining room and its menu, which specializes in American cuisine presented with French flair. After veal Cameron (medallions sautéed with wine and capers served over pasta) or broiled Norwegian salmon with pineapple and sweet pepper relish, other travelers repair to the guestrooms upstairs. The rooms beckon with Oriental rugs, antique and reproduction furniture, and canopy beds; seven have working fireplaces. The lovely porch overlooks the inn's 15 wooded acres. Continental breakfast is included. ⌂ *Donegal Springs Rd., 17552,* ☎ *717/653–1773,* FAX *717/653–9432. 18 rooms, 16 with bath. Restaurant (reservations required), access to tennis courts and pool nearby. No children under 12. AE, D, DC, MC, V.*

Ronks

Dining

$$ **Miller's Smorgasbord.** Miller's presents a lavish spread with a good
★ selection of Pennsylvania Dutch foods. Breakfast is sensational here with omelets, pancakes, and eggs cooked to order, fresh fruits, pastries, bacon, sausage, potatoes, and much more. It's one of the few area restaurants open Sunday. ✕ *2811 Lincoln Hwy. E (U.S. 30),* ☎ *717/687–6621 or 800/669–3568. Reservations for dinner only. Breakfast Dec.–May, weekends. AE, D, MC, V.*

Lodging

$$$ **Hershey Farm.** This continually expanding motel overlooks a picture-perfect pond and a farm. The handy restaurant features family-style and smorgasbord meals. Ask for one of the large rooms in the new building. ⌂ *240 Hartman Bridge Rd., Ronks 17572,* ☎ *717/687–8635 or 800/827–8635,* FAX *687–8638. 59 rooms, 28 no-smoking. Restaurant, pool. AE, D, MC, V.*

Smoketown

Dining

$$ **Good 'N Plenty.** Don't bother to ask for a menu here: they just bring out heaps of Pennsylvania Dutch cuisine. More than 650 can be served at this bustling, family-style restaurant, nicely set within a remodeled Amish farmhouse. ✕ *Rte. 896, ½ mi north of U.S. 30,* ☎ *717/394–7111. MC, V. Closed Sun. and Jan.*

Lodging

$$ Mill Stream Motor Lodge. Long a popular choice, and renovated a few years back, this motel overlooks a picturesque stream. Request a room in the rear to get the prettiest view. Breakfast is available in the restaurant but no alcohol is served. ⊡ *Rte. 896, 17576,* ☎ *717/299–0931,* FAX *717/295–9326. 52 rooms, 3 suites. Restaurant; exercise and pool privileges at Willow Valley, a sister property. 2-night minimum weekends. AE, D, MC, V.*

$–$$ Smoketown Motor Lodge. In the carriage house behind this redbrick
★ Federal-style motel lies one of the Pennsylvania Dutch Country's best-kept secrets. Three ground floor rooms are finished in rough-hewn pine paneling and exposed ceiling beams, and have queen-size beds and plush carpeting. The Carriage Room, largest of the three, features a huge bathroom with sunken tub and separate shower and dressing areas. Rooms in the main motel building are a good value as well. ⊡ *109 E. Brook Rd. (Rte. 896), 17576,* ☎ *717/397–6944. 17 rooms. MC, V.*

Strasburg

Dining

$$$ Iron Horse Inn. This charming, rustic, candlelit restaurant is housed in the original 1780s Hotel Strasburg. Best bets are the catch-of-the-day, the homemade breads, and, for dessert, the great, warm apple pie. There's live entertainment on weekends and an extensive wine list. ✗ *135 E. Main St. (Rte. 741),* ☎ *717/687–6362. Reservations advised. AE, D, DC, MC, V. Closed Mon. Dec.–May.*

$$ Washington House Restaurant. This restaurant at the Historic Strasburg Inn offers fine candlelight dining in two Colonial-style dining rooms. The American menu features steaks, jumbo lump crab cakes, and wild game. The lunch buffet is bountiful. ✗ *Rte. 896 (Historic Dr.),* ☎ *717/687–7691 or 800/872–0201. AE, D, DC, MC, V.*

Lodging

$$$–$$$$ Timberline Lodges. Beautiful lodges nestled on a hillside put you close enough to Strasburg to hear the train whistles but far away enough to hear the birds. The lodges, which sleep from two to eight people, have stone fireplaces, balconies, TV, and furnished kitchens. There are also five motel units ($). ⊡ *44 Summit Hill Dr., 17579,* ☎ *717/687–7472. 11 lodges, 5 motel units. Restaurant, bar, pool, playground. 2-night minimum weekends. AE, D, MC, V.*

$$$ Strasburg Village Inn. This historic circa-1788 house has rooms ele-
★ gantly appointed in the Williamsburg style. Most have canopy or four-poster beds; two have Jacuzzis. A sitting/reading room is on the second floor; an old-fashioned porch overlooks Main Street. Full breakfast in the adjacent ice cream parlor is included, except on Sunday, when it's Continental only. ⊡ *1 W. Main St., 17579,* ☎ *717/687–0900 or 800/541–1055. 11 rooms. AE, D, MC, V.*

$$–$$$ Fulton Steamboat Inn. At Lancaster's busiest intersection, across
★ from rows of outlet stores, sits a small lake, man-made waterfalls, piped-in sounds of a river, and a hotel that looks just like a steamboat. Named after Lancaster native Robert Fulton, who built the first successful passenger steamer in 1807, the hotel will delight all land-locked boaties. Inside, the decor is nicely coordinated, right down to the costumed staff that looks at home in the Victorian-style lobby. The inn has three levels: The uppermost deck features whirlpool baths and private outdoor decks, the middle level has staterooms with two queen-size beds, and the bottom level has cabins with nautical nuances and rigged with bunk beds, making it a good choice for fam-

ilies with children. Rooms have turn-of-the-century–style furnishings, microwaves, remote control TV, and mini-refrigerators. Package plans include meals and admission to area attractions. ⚐ *Rtes. 30 and 896, Box 333, 17579,* ☎ *717/299–9999 or 800/922–2229 outside PA,* ⅎⱯⱾ *717/299–9992. 95 rooms. Restaurant, indoor pool, exercise room, game room. 2-night minimum weekends, 3-night minimum holidays. AE, MC, V.*

$$$ **Historic Strasburg Inn.** The newly renovated, Colonial-style inn is set on 58 peaceful acres overlooking farmland. The rooms come with double beds only. Continental plus breakfast is included. ⚐ *Rte. 896 (Historic Dr.), 17579,* ☎ *717/687–7691 or 800/872–0201. 103 rooms. Pets allowed. 2 restaurants, pool, exercise room, volleyball. AE, D, DC, MC, V.*

$ **Red Caboose Motel.** This motel consists of 37 railroad cabooses that have been converted into a string of rooms: heavenly accommodations, needless to say, for railroad buffs, who will delight in the N5-style cabooses, some dating back to 1910, and perched on railroad tracks. Half a caboose sleeps two; a family gets a whole car (one double bed, four bunks). Even the furnishings are fun—TV sets are built into pot-bellied stoves. ⚐ *303 Paradise La. (off Rte. 741), 17579,* ☎ *717/687–6646. 40 units, including 7 efficiency suites. Restaurant, playground. AE, D, MC, V.*

Wrightsville

Dining

$$$$ **Accomac Inn.** Outside, a magnificent Susquehanna River setting
★ soothes and rewards the weary traveler; inside, Queen Anne furnishings—reminiscent of Williamsburg—warm the eye. This inn beckons the beholder to savor the bounty of both a landscape and a fine kitchen. The menu is basically American cuisine with French accents. Tableside cooking is featured with dishes such as duck flambéed in Curaçao, bananas Foster, and crepes Suzette. Specialties include fresh rack of New Zealand lamb, veal, venison, and seafood. The remarkable wine list boasts 250 selections. ✗ *Across Susquehanna River from Marietta (take Rte. 30 west to Wrightsville exit, turn right and follow signs),* ☎ *717/252–1521. Reservations advised. AE, MC, V.*

Farm Vacations

A number of farm families open their homes to visitors and allow them to observe, and even participate in, day-to-day farm life. Your hosts may teach you how to milk a cow and feed chickens. They serve you breakfast with their family, and invite you to church services. Make reservations weeks in advance: Most farms are heavily booked during the summer tourist season.

$ **Jonde Lane Farm.** Breakfast with the family is served every day but Sunday at this working dairy and poultry farm. There are four guest rooms including one family room, which can sleep up to seven people; two shared baths. Ponies, chickens, and cats are conspicuous. Guests can fish on the property. ⚐ *1103 Auction Rd., Manheim 17545,* ☎ *717/665–4231.* ☉ *Easter–Thanksgiving. No credit cards.*

$ **Olde Fogie Farm.** Milk the goats and bottle-feed the calves on this organic farm. The old frame home has an Amish cookstove, a petting farm, a creek, a pond, and a new stable for pony rides. ⚐ *106 Stackstown Rd., Marietta 17547,* ☎ *717/426–3992. 1*

room with bath, 1 shares bath with family, 2 efficiency apartments. No credit cards.

$ **Rocky Acre Farm.** Sleep in a 200-year-old stone farmhouse, which was once a stop on the Underground Railroad. This is a dairy farm with calves to feed, cows to milk, and dogs, kittens, roosters, and sheep—in the meadow, of course—to enjoy. Guests can go fishing and boating in the creek. A full hot breakfast is served daily. ⌧ *1020 Pinkerton Rd., Mt. Joy 17552,* ☎ *717/653–4449. 5 rooms with bath, 2 efficiency units with shared bath. No credit cards.*

$ **Verdant View Farm.** Don and Virginia Ranck's 1896 farmhouse sits on about 122 acres devoted to dairy and crop farming. Guests use five rooms on the second floor, one with a private bath. Hearty breakfasts are served in the family dining room every day but Sunday. ⌧ *429 Strasburg Rd., Paradise 17562,* ☎ *717/687–7353. No credit cards.*

THE ARTS

Theater

Dutch Apple Dinner Theater (510 Centerville Rd. at U.S. 30, Lancaster, ☎ 717/898–1900). A candlelight buffet plus Broadway musicals and comedies are the draws in this 400-seat theater. Recent seasons have included *Camelot, Nunsense,* and *Fiddler on the Roof.* Matinees and dinner shows. Call for reservations.

The **Fulton Opera House** (12 N. Prince St., Lancaster, ☎ 717/397–7425). This restored 19th-century theater is America's oldest theater in continuous use, and a National Landmark. Recently, a major $9.5 million renovation was completed. The theater is now home to the Fulton Theater Company, the Actors Company of Pennsylvania, the Lancaster Symphony Orchestra, and the Lancaster Opera.

Sight & Sound Entertainment Centre (Rte. 896, Strasburg, ☎ 717/687–7800) is a 1,372-seat, state-of-the-art theater—the largest Christian entertainment complex in the nation—presenting concerts and Bible-based theatrical productions with lavish costumes, special effects, and live animals.

LANCASTER COUNTY ESSENTIALS

Getting Around

By Car

From Philadelphia, take the Schuylkill Expressway (I–76) west to the Pennsylvania Turnpike. Lancaster County attractions are accessible from Exits 20, 21, and 22. For a more scenic route, follow U.S. 30 (Lancaster Pike) west from Philadelphia. It's about 65 miles; allow 90 minutes.

By Bus

Greyhound Lines (☎ 800/231–2222) has three runs daily between Philadelphia and the R&S Bus Terminal (22 West Clay St.) in Lancaster. The ride takes two hours, 20 minutes. Fares are $15 one way, $30 round-trip.

By Train

Amtrak (☎ 215/824–1600 or 800/USA–RAIL) has regular service from Philadelphia's 30th Street Station to the Lancaster Amtrak Sta-

tion, 53 McGovern Avenue. Trips take 80 minutes. Fares are $9 one way, $18 round-trip.

Guided Tours

Amish Country Tours (Rte. 340 between Bird-in-Hand and Intercourse, ☎ 717/768–8400 or 800/441–3505) has a variety of large bus or mini-van tours. Most popular is the four-hour Amish farmlands trip. Featured are stops at an Amish farmhouse, a wine tasting, and shopping for crafts. On Tuesday, tours to Hershey are available.

Brunswick Tours (National Wax Museum, U.S. 30 E, Lancaster, ☎ 717/397–7541) provides private guides who will tour with you in your car.

The Mennonite Information Center (2209 Millstream Rd., Lancaster, ☎ 717/299–0954) has local Mennonite guides who will join you in your car. These knowledgeable guides will lead you to country roads, produce stands, and Amish craft shops, and also acquaint you with their religion.

Rutts Tours (3564 Old Philadelphia Pike, Intercourse, ☎ 717/768–8238) has guides who will join you in your car.

For an aerial tour, try **Glick Aviation** at Smoketown Airport (311 Airport Dr. off Rte. 340, Smoketown, ☎ 717/394–6476). Eighteen-minute flights in a four-seater plane (pilot plus three) provide a splendid view of rolling farmlands.

You can rent or purchase a cassette tape for the self-guided **Auto Tape Tour of Pennsylvania Dutch Country.** Minimum driving time is 90 minutes. *Available at Dutch Wonderland and the National Wax Museum (2249 U.S. 30 E, Lancaster , ☎ 717/291–1888).*

Tapetours sells a self-guided auto tour for $12. It begins at the Pennsylvania Dutch Convention & Visitors Bureau on Greenfield Road; the 28 stops take three to four hours. *Available from Brunswick Tours* (see above).

Important Addresses and Numbers

Emergencies

Dial **911** for police, fire, or ambulance. There are three emergency rooms in the city of Lancaster: **Community Hospital of Lancaster** (1100 E. Orange St., ☎ 717/397–3711), **Lancaster General Hospital** (555 N. Duke St., ☎ 717/299–5511), and **St. Joseph's Hospital** (250 College Ave., ☎ 717/291–8211). For non-emergency referrals, call the Lancaster City & County Medical Society, ☎ 717/393–9588.

PHARMACY
Weis Pharmacy (1603 Lincoln Hwy. E, Lancaster, ☎ 717/394–9826). ☉ *Weekdays 9–9, Sat. 9–6.*

Strasburg Pharmacy (326 Hartman Bridge Rd., Rte. 896, 2 mi south of Rte. 30, Strasburg, ☎ 717/687–6058). ☉ *Weekdays 9–9, Sat. 9–5.*

Visitor Information

The Pennsylvania Dutch Convention & Visitors Bureau (Greenfield Rd. exit of U.S. 30 E, Dept. 2201, 501 Greenfield Rd., Lancaster 17601, ☎ 717/299–8901 or 800/735–2629) has many brochures and maps, direct phone connections to local hotels, and a 14-minute multi-image slide presentation, "There Is a Season," a visual journey through pic-

turesque Pennsylvania Dutch Country that serves as a good introduction to the area. ⊙ *Daily 9–5, later in summer.* ☛ *Slide presentation: $2 adults, $1 children 6–12.*

The Mennonite Information Center (2209 Millstream Rd., Lancaster 17602–1494, ☎ 717/299–0954) serves mainly to "interpret the faith and practice of the Mennonite Church to all who inquire." It has information on local inns and Mennonite guest homes as well as a 20-minute video about the Amish and Mennonite people. Next door is the "only actual-size model" of the Hebrew Tabernacle, complete with an Ark of the Covenant. ⊙ *Mon.–Sat. 8–5.* ☛ *Hebrew Tabernacle: $4 adults, $2 children 7–12.*

Intercourse Tourist Information Center (3614 Old Philadelphia Pike, Intercourse 17534, ☎ 717/768–3882) provides travel advice on one of the Dutch Country's most popular towns. ⊙ *Mar.–Dec., Mon.–Sat. 10–5.*

10 Excursions

THE BRANDYWINE VALLEY

By Joyce
Eisenberg

Updated by
Rathe Miller

CHANCES ARE THAT TRAVELERS journeying to the Brandywine Valley will feel a strong sense of déjà vu. Every hundred yards, there seems to be a scene so hauntingly familiar that first-time visitors feel they've visited this area before, a vista so picturesque it virtually drips off the canvas. When Andrew Wyeth immortalized the unique landscape of the Brandywine Valley—creating some of the most beloved works in 20th-century American art—he caused many travelers to flock to this valley and fall in love with its peaceful byways. Using colors quintessentially Brandywine—the earthen brown of its hills, gray slate of its stone farmhouses, and dark green of its spruce trees—the famous American realist artist captured the unique personality of the valley: decidedly private, unostentatiously beautiful. Wyeth struck pay dirt by painting its vistas, and, today, visitors continue to do so, for when they travel to the Brandywine Valley, many feel they have discovered a tucked-away treasure.

KINGDOM OF THE DU PONTS

The Brandywine Valley actually incorporates parts of three counties in two states: Chester and Delaware counties in Pennsylvania, and New Castle County in Delaware. Winding through this scenic region (about 25 miles south of Philadelphia), the Brandywine River flows lazily from West Chester, Pennsylvania, to Wilmington, Delaware. Although in spots it's more a creek than a river, it has nourished many of the valley's economic and artistic endeavors. While paintings of the Wyeth family distilled the region's mystery, it was the regal du Pont family that provided more than a dollop of magnificence, recontouring the land with grand gardens, mansions, and mills. Their kingdom was founded by the family patriarch, Pierre-Samuel du Pont, who had escaped with his family from post-Revolutionary France and settled in northern Delaware. The Du Pont company was founded in 1802 by his son Éleuthère Irénée (E. I.), who made the family fortune first in gunpowder and iron, and later in chemicals and textiles.

E. I. and five generations of du Ponts lived in Eleutherian Mills, the stately family home on the grounds of a black-powder mill that has been transformed into the Hagley Museum. The home, from which Mrs. Henry du Pont was driven after accidental blasts at the powder works, was closed in 1921. Louise du Pont Crowninshield, a great-granddaughter of E. I., restored the house fully before opening it to the public. Louise's brothers were busy, too. Henry Francis was filling his country estate, Winterthur, with furniture by Duncan Phyfe, silver by Paul Revere, decorative objects, and entire interior woodwork fittings salvaged from homes built between 1640 and 1840. More than 200 rooms were added to display his outstanding collection of American decorative arts.

Pierre devoted his life to horticulture. He bought a 1,000-acre 19th-century arboretum and created Longwood Gardens, where he entertained his many friends and relatives. Today, 350 acres of the meticulously landscaped gardens are open to the public. Displays range from a tropical rain forest to a desert; acres of heated conservatories, where flowers are in bloom year-round, create eternal summer. Pierre also built the grand Hotel du Pont in downtown Wilmington adjacent to company headquarters. No expense was spared; more than 18 French and

Italian craftsmen labored for two years carving, gilding, and painting. Alfred I. du Pont's country estate, Nemours, was named after the family's ancestral home in north-central France. It encompasses 300 acres of French gardens and a mansion in the Louis XVI style.

WYETH COUNTRY

For many travelers, the Brandywine Valley will always be Wyeth country first and foremost, for here is where three generations of artists found landscapes worthy of their talents. Although Andrew Wyeth is the most famous local artist, the area's artistic tradition began long before, when artist-illustrator Howard Pyle started a school in the valley. He had more than 100 students, including Andrew's father, N. C. Wyeth; Frank Schoonover; Jessie Willcox Smith; and Harvey Dunn. It was that tradition which inspired Andrew and his son Jamie.

In 1967, local residents formed the Brandywine Conservancy to prevent industrialization of the area and pollution of the river. In 1971, they opened the Brandywine River Museum in a preserved 19th-century gristmill. It celebrates the Brandywine School of artists in a setting much in tune with their world.

The valley is also the site of one of the more dramatic turns in the American Revolution, the Battle of Brandywine, and an offbeat museum, which celebrates the mushroom. The region is dotted with antiques shops, fine restaurants, cozy country inns, and reliable bed-and-breakfasts. Because there is a lack of agencies that offer guided tours, your best bet is to rent a car and explore on your own with the help of a map from one of the tourist information agencies listed at the end of this chapter.

Exploring

Numbers in the margin correspond to points of interest on the Brandywine Valley map.

If you start early enough, you can tour the valley's top three attractions—the Brandywine River Museum, Longwood Gardens, and Winterthur—in one day. If you have more time to spend in the valley, you can stop in to see the additional sites in Pennsylvania and then move on to Delaware.

❶ **Franklin Mint Museum,** a private mint that creates heirloom-quality collectibles, displays uniquely designed coins, precision die-cast model cars, porcelain dolls, objets d'art from the House of Igor Carl Fabergé, and sculpture in crystal, pewter, and bronze. *U.S. 1, Franklin Center, PA 19091,* ☎ *610/459–6168.* ☛ *Free.* ☼ *Mon.–Sat. 9:30–4:30, Sun. 1–4:30.*

❷ **Brandywine Battlefield State Park,** in Chadds Ford, is a popular stop for history buffs. Nearby is the site of the Battle of Brandywine, where British General William Howe and his troops defeated George Washington on September 11, 1777. The Continental Army then fled to Lancaster, leaving Philadelphia vulnerable to British troops. The Visitors Center has audiovisual materials and displays about the battle. On the site are two restored farmhouses that once sheltered Washington and Lafayette. *U.S. 1, Chadds Ford, PA 19317,* ☎ *610/459–3342.* ☛ *Park free; house tours $3.50 adults, $2.50 senior citizens, $1.50 children 6–17.* ☼ *Tues.–Sat. 9–5, Sun. noon–5.*

❸ In a converted Civil War–era gristmill, the **Brandywine River Museum** showcases the art of Chadds Ford native Andrew Wyeth, a major American realist painter, and of his family: his father, N. C. Wyeth,

Brandywine Valley

illustrator of many children's classics; his sisters Henriette and Carolyn; and his son Jamie. The collection also emphasizes still life, landscape painting, and American illustration. Glass-walled lobbies display the river and countryside which inspired the Brandywine School. The museum uses a system of filters, baffles, and blinds to direct natural light. Outside the museum, visit a garden with regional wildflowers and follow a nature trail along the river. *U.S. 1 and Rte. 100, Chadds Ford, PA 19317, ☎ 610/388–7601. ☞ $5 adults, $2.50 senior citizens and students, children under 6 free. ☉ Daily 9:30–4:30. Closed Dec. 25.*

④ Longwood Gardens has established an international reputation for its colorful gardens featuring flowers and blossoming shrubs. In 1906, Pierre Samuel du Pont bought a simple Quaker farm, famous for its trees, and turned it into the ultimate estate garden. Fabulous seasonal attractions include magnolias and azaleas in spring, roses and water lilies in summer, fall foliage and chrysanthemums, and winter camellias, orchids, and palms. Bad weather is no problem as 3½ acres of exotic foliage, cacti, ferns, and bonsai are housed in heated conservatories. The new Heritage exhibit traces the last 300 years of evolution of the Longwood area. There are illuminated fountain displays on Tuesday, Thursday, and Saturday evenings in summer. *U.S. 1, Kennett Square, PA 19348, ☎ 610/388–1000. ☞ $10 adults ($6 Tues.), $6 youths 16– 20, $2 children 6–15. ☉ Daily 9–5, plus some evenings in summer and Thanksgiving–Christmas.*

⑤ Phillips Mushroom Place is a small museum devoted exclusively to a fungus—the mushroom. Mushrooms are Pennsylvania's number one cash crop and most are grown in Kennett Square. The history, lore, and growing process of mushrooms is explained with dioramas, ex-

hibits, and an 18-minute film. The gift shop sells a mushroom giftpack suitable for mailing. *U.S. 1, ½ mi south of Longwood Gardens, Kennett Square, PA 19348,* ☎ *610/388–6082.* ☛ *$1.25 adults, 75¢ senior citizens, 50¢ children 7–12.* ☉ *Daily 10–6.*

6 Henry Francis du Pont housed his 89,000 objects of American decorative art in a nine-story mansion called **Winterthur.** The 1640–1860 furniture, silver, paintings, and textiles are displayed in period room settings. Surrounding the museum are 1,000 acres of landscaped lawns, gardens, and virgin forest. "Winterthur's Yuletide Tour" (Nov. 15–Dec. 31) showcases the holiday traditions of early America. The Galleries, opened in 1992, houses permanent displays and changing exhibits of decorative arts and crafts. *Rte. 52, Winterthur, DE 19735, 5 mi south of U.S. 1,* ☎ *302/888–4600. Variety of tours (all include garden tram); no children under 12 on reserved tours.* ☛ *$8–$21, with discounts for senior citizens and children.* ☉ *Mon.–Sat. 9–5, Sun. 12–5.*

7 **Hagley on the Brandywine** offers a glimpse of the du Ponts at work. A restored, mid-19th-century mill community on 240 landscaped acres, Hagley is the site of the first Du Pont black-powder mills. The museum's exhibits, including a restored workers' community, depict the dangerous work of the early explosives industry. The tour includes stops at Eleutherian Mills, an 1803 Georgian-style home which was furnished by five generations of du Ponts, and a French Renaissance–style garden. Allow about two hours for your visit. The coffee shop is open for lunch except in winter. *Rte. 141 between Rte. 100 and U.S. 202, Wilmington, DE 19807,* ☎ *302/658–2400.* ☛ *$9.75 adults, $7.50 senior citizens and students, $3.50 children 6–14, $26.50 family.* ☉ *Mar. 15–Dec., daily 9:30–4:30; Jan.–Mar. 14, weekends 9:30–4:30; winter tours, weekdays at 1:30.*

8 **Nemours Mansion and Gardens,** a 300-acre country estate built for Alfred I. du Pont in 1910, is a modified Louis XVI château showcasing European and American furnishings, rare rugs, tapestries, and art. The gardens, reminiscent of those at Versailles, are landscaped with fountains, pools, and statuary. The estate can only be seen on the guided two-hour tours. *Rockland Rd., between Rte. 141 and U.S. 202, Wilmington, DE 19899,* ☎ *302/651–6912. Visitors must be over 16.* ☛ *$10.* ☉ *May– Nov.; tours Tues.–Sat. at 9, 11, 1, and 3; Sun. at 11, 1, and 3. Reservations advised.*

9 **Delaware Art Museum.** The museum features the paintings of Howard Pyle, a Wilmington native and "father of American illustration," and his students—N. C. Wyeth, Frank Schoonover, and Maxfield Parrish. It also houses the largest American collection of 19th-century English pre-Raphaelite paintings and decorative arts and a children's participatory gallery. *2301 Kentmere Pkwy., Wilmington, DE 19806,* ☎ *302/571–9590.* ☛ *$5 adults, $3 seniors citizens, $2.50 children.* ☉ *Tues.–Sat. 10–5, Sun. noon–5.*

10 In contrast to the opulent French-inspired du Pont homes is **Rockwood,** a quietly elegant English-style country house and a fine example of rural Gothic architecture. Built in 1851 by Joseph Shipley, a Quaker merchant, the house is now a museum filled with 17th- to 20th-century American, European, and Asian decorative arts and furnishings. There is a guided tour of the mansion. *610 Shipley Rd., Wilmington, DE 19809,* ☎ *302/761–4340.* ☛ *$5 adults, $4 senior citizens, $1 children 5–16.* ☉ *Tues.–Sun. 11–3. Closed Sun. Jan. and Feb.*

Dining and Lodging

Dining

It seems that almost every restaurant in the Brandywine Valley serves what is called Continental-American cuisine, yet most also feature local specialties—fresh seafood from the Chesapeake Bay and dishes made with Kennett Square mushrooms.

CATEGORY	COST*
$$$$	over $40
$$$	$25–$40
$$	$15–$25
$	under $15

per person for a 3-course meal, excluding wine, tip, and 6% tax

Lodging

Many Brandywine Valley accommodations call themselves bed-and-breakfasts because they provide beds and serve breakfast, but they are far from the typical B&B—which is usually a room in a private home—and are more accurately characterized as inns or small hotels.

Unless otherwise indicated, all rooms have private bath and the hotel is open year-round.

CATEGORY	COST*
$$$$	over $100
$$$	$80–$100
$$	$65–$80
$	under $65

double occupancy, excluding 6% tax

Chadds Ford

DINING

$$$ Chadds Ford Inn. Within walking distance of the Brandywine River Museum, this inn is a popular choice for visitors to the valley. Once a lively former rest stop on the Wilmington-Philadelphia-Lancaster commerce route, the inn now welcomes guests to a Colonial-period dining room, complete with candlelight, stone hearts, and Wyeth prints. Continental-American dishes such as roasted salmon with fresh ginger and sun dried tomatoes purée, and pecanwood-smoked free-range chicken with roasted corn and andouille are served up in generous portions. ✗ *Rte. 100 and U.S. 1,* ☎ *610/388–7361. Reservations advised. AE, DC, MC, V. Sun. brunch.*

LODGING

$$$$ Brandywine River Hotel. This small, modern, two-story hotel is across the highway from the Brandywine River Museum. Tasteful Queen Anne furnishings, classic English chintz, and florals create a homey feeling. Ten suites have fireplaces and Jacuzzis. Complimentary Continental breakfast and afternoon tea are served in a lovely dining room. ▨ *Rte. 100 and U.S. 1, Chadds Ford, PA 19317,* ☎ *610/388–1200. 40 rooms. AE, D, DC, MC, V.*

Glen Mills

LODGING

$$$$ Sweetwater Farm. A handsome 18th-century fieldstone farmhouse
★ has been lovingly restored into a homey inn serving hearty breakfasts. A shaded porch lined with rockers overlooks the 50-acre horse farm; no other houses are in sight. Rooms have fresh flowers, fragrant potpourri, and reproductions of period furnishings, including some canopy beds. Rooms in the newer section (circa 1815) of the house are larger.

☎ *50 Sweetwater Rd., Glen Mills, PA 19342,* ☎ *610/459–4711. 6 rooms, 5 cottages. Pool, horseback riding. 2-night minimum weekends. AE, MC, V.*

Kennett Square

DINING AND LODGING

$$$–$$$$ **Longwood Inn.** This small, family-owned motel offers affordable accommodations with simple, traditional furnishings, and offers travelers the convenience of a fine restaurant. Live Maine lobsters, Chesapeake seafood dishes, and mushroom specialties are served in a relaxed Williamsburg-style setting. Homemade desserts with an Amish flavor include apple turnovers and rice pudding. ☎ *815 E. Baltimore Pike (U.S. 1), ½ mi south of Longwood Gardens,* ☎ *610/444–3515. 27 rooms. Restaurant (reservations advised for dinner), lounge. AE, D, DC, MC, V.*

LODGING

$$$ **Meadow Spring Farm.** Anne Hicks's farmhouse is a gallery for her family's antiques, dolls, teddy bears, and Santas. Rooms have Amish quilts and televisions. A full country breakfast is served daily on the glassed-in porch. Children are welcome here, and they will particularly enjoy the farm animals. ☎ *201 E. Street Rd., Kennett Square, PA 19348,* ☎ *610/444–3903. 6 rooms, 4 with bath. Pool, hot tub, fishing. No credit cards.*

Mendenhall

DINING

$$$$ **Mendenhall Inn.** Continental and American cuisine is served in this 1790s Quaker mill building with its old beams still intact. Crab imperial, prime rib, and game are featured. For lunch, request a table with a courtyard view; at Saturday dinner, ask for the Mill Room upstairs. ✕ *Rte. 52, 1 mi south of U.S. 1,* ☎ *610/388–1181. Reservations advised for lunch, required for dinner. Jacket and tie (except in tavern). AE, D, DC, MC, V.*

LODGING

$$$$ **Fairville Inn.** Halfway between Winterthur and Longwood Gardens,
★ Ole and Patti Retlev's inn offers bright, airy rooms furnished with Queen Anne and Hepplewhite reproductions. There's a main house, built in 1826; a remodeled barn; and a carriage house. Request a room in the back of the property, away from traffic. The main house has a striking living room with a large fireplace. The Fairville serves complimentary light breakfast and afternoon tea. Note that this inn is not suitable for children under 10. ☎ *Rte. 52 (Kennett Pike), Box 219, Mendenhall, PA 19357,* ☎ *610/388–5900,* FAX *610/388–5902. 13 rooms, 2 suites. AE, D, MC, V.*

Thornton

DINING

$$$ **Pace One.** This is a friendly, casual spot, set within a 250-year-old barn with poplar beams and stone walls. Country specialties are the forte, such as pork chops stuffed with cornbread and sausage and marinated, broiled fish. Chocolate fondue and fudge cake head the list of tempting desserts. ✕ *Glen Mills and Thornton Rds.,* ☎ *610/459–3702. Reservations advised. AE, DC, MC, V. No lunch Sat.*

West Chester

DINING

$$$$ **Dilworthtown Inn.** Fresh seafood from the Chesapeake, local quail, and
★ smoked pheasant are among the entrées served at this inn. Vegetables

and herbs are grown in the garden across the road. The wine cellar is stocked with over 14,000 bottles. ✕ *Old Wilmington Pike and Brinton's Bridge Rd.,* ☎ *610/399–1390. Reservations advised. Jacket required. AE, D, DC, MC, V. No lunch.*

Wilmington
DINING

$$$$ **Green Room.** For years Philadelphians have trekked to Wilmington to
★ celebrate special occasions in the famous Hotel du Pont restaurant. Classic French cuisine is served in Edwardian splendor under a gold-encrusted ceiling with massive Spanish chandeliers and high French windows. Harp music accompanies formal dinners. ✕ *Hotel du Pont, 11th and Market Sts.,* ☎ *302/594–3100. Reservations advised. Jackets required. AE, D, DC, MC, V.*

LODGING

$$$$ **Hotel du Pont.** The hotel is an elegant 12-story building with an old-world feel built in 1913 by Pierre-Samuel du Pont. The lobby has a spectacular old-world ceiling, polished marble walls, and carved paneling. Rooms feature antique reproductions and original art; request a newly renovated room. ▣ *11th and Market Sts., Wilmington, DE 19801,* ☎ *302/594–3100 or 800/441–9019,* FAX *302/594–3108. 216 rooms. 3 restaurants lobby lounge, theater next door. AE, D, DC, MC, V.*

Brandywine Valley Essentials

Getting Around
BY CAR

Take U.S. 1 south from Philadelphia; Brandywine Valley is about 25 miles from Philadelphia and many attractions are on U.S. 1. To reach Wilmington, pick up U.S. 202 south just past Concordville, or take I–95 south from Philadelphia.

BY BUS

From Philadelphia, **Greyhound Lines** (☎ 800/231–2222) has about 10 daily departures to the Wilmington terminal at 101 North French Street. The trip takes one hour.

BY TRAIN

Amtrak (☎ 215/824–1600 or 800/872–7245) has frequent service from Philadelphia's 30th Street Station to the Wilmington Station at Martin Luther King Jr. Boulevard and French Street on the edge of downtown. It's a 25-minute ride.

Guided Tours

Colonial Pathways (Box 879, Chadds Ford, PA 19317, ☎ 610/388–2654) guides escort you—in your car—for full-day excursions. You can plan the itinerary, or have them do it for you. Call for reservations.

Important Addresses and Numbers
VISITOR INFORMATION

The Brandywine Valley Tourist Information Center (U.S. 1 north of Kennett Sq., ☎ 610/388–2900 or 800/228–9933) in the Longwood Progressive Meeting House at the entrance to Longwood Gardens has information on attractions, lodging, and restaurants. Open daily, May–Sept. 10–6; Oct.–Apr. 10–5. The center is run by the **Chester County Tourist Bureau,** which has its main office at the Government Services Center, 601 Westtown Rd., West Chester, PA 19382, ☎ 610/344–6365.

For good road maps and visitors' guides, contact the **Delaware County Convention and Visitors Bureau** (200 E. State St., Suite 100, Media,

PA 19063, ☎ 610/565–3679 or 610/565–3666 for tape of events) and the **Greater Wilmington Convention and Visitors Bureau** (1300 Market St., Suite 504, Wilmington, DE 19801, ☎ 302/652–4088).

VALLEY FORGE

Valley Forge National Historical Park preserves the area where George Washington's Continental Army endured the bitter winter of 1777–78. It is an area rich in history, offering an awesome beauty that seems to whisper of the past. It wouldn't be incongruous for the area's inns and lodges to sport signs boasting: "Washington Slept Here." He did have to sleep somewhere. But it is doubtful that Washington enjoyed any peaceful nights as he struggled with the morale problems that beset his troops.

The army had just lost the battles of Brandywine, White Horse, and Germantown. While the British occupied Philadelphia, Washington's soldiers were forced to endure horrid conditions—blizzards, inadequate food and clothing, damp quarters, and disease. Many men deserted and, although no battle was fought at Valley Forge, 2,000 American soldiers died.

But the troops won one victory that winter—a war of the will. The forces slowly regained strength and confidence under the leadership of Prussian drillmaster Friedrich von Steuben. In June 1778, Washington led his troops away from Valley Forge in search of the British. Fortified, the Continental Army was able to carry on the fight for five years more.

For the day-tripper interested in early-American history, a visit to the monuments, markers, huts, and headquarters in Valley Forge National Historical Park, 20 miles from Center City, Philadelphia, is illuminating. If the weather is fine, consider renting a bicycle or packing a lunch and picnicking at one of three park sites. Other nearby attractions include Mill Grove, the home of naturalist John James Audubon; the studio and residence of craftsman Wharton Esherick; and The Court and Plaza, one of the nation's largest shopping complexes.

If you stay overnight in Valley Forge, check the schedule for the **Valley Forge Music Fair** (Route 202, Devon 19133, ☎ 610/644–5000). This theater-in-the-round presents top names in entertainment, with recent performances by Diana Ross, the Pointer Sisters, and Tom Jones. The **People's Light and Theater Company** (39 Conestoga Rd., Malvern 19355, ☎ 610/644–3500), a pioneer of the regional theater movement, offers classics and modern productions throughout the year.

Exploring

Numbers in the margin correspond to points of interest on the Valley Forge map.

❶ **Valley Forge National Historical Park,** administered by the National Park Service, is the site of the 1777–78 winter encampment of General George Washington and the Continental Army. Stop first at the Visitor Center for an 18-minute orientation film, exhibits, and a map for a 10-mile, self-guided auto tour of the park attractions. Stops include reconstructed huts of the Muhlenberg Brigade, and the National Memorial Arch, which pays tribute to the soldiers who suffered through the infamous winter. Other sites include the bronze equestrian statue

on the encampment of General Anthony Wayne and his Pennsylvania troops; Artillery Park, where the soldiers stored their cannons; and the Isaac Potts House, which served as Washington's headquarters. From June through September, you can purchase an auto-tour cassette tape for $8 or rent a tape and player for $10.

The park contains 7 miles of paved trails for jogging or bicycling, and hiking trails. Visitors can picnic at any of three designated areas. A leisurely visit to the park will take no more than half a day. *Rtes. 23 and 363, Box 953, Valley Forge, PA 19481, ☎ 610/783–1077.* ☛ *Washington's headquarters: $2 adults 17–61.* ☉ *Daily 9–5. Closed Dec. 25.*

❷ The **Valley Forge Historical Society Museum** tells the Valley Forge story with military equipment and Colonial artifacts plus a large collection of items that belonged to Martha and George Washington. The nearby Chapel Cabin Shop sells homemade goodies such as Martha's 16-Bean Soup and blue-barb jam. *Alongside the Washington Memorial Chapel on Rte. 23,* ☎ *610/783–0535.* ☛ *$1.50 adults, 50¢ children 2–12.* ☉ *Mon.–Sat. 9:30–4:30, Sun. 1–4:30. Closed Thanksgiving, Dec. 25, Jan. 1, and Easter.*

❸ **Mill Grove** was the first American home of Haitian-born artist and naturalist John James Audubon. Built in 1762, the house is now a museum displaying Audubon's major works, including reproductions, original prints, his paintings of birds and wildlife, and the double-elephant folio of his *Birds of America.* The attic has been restored to a studio and taxidermy room. The Audubon Wildlife Sanctuary has 170 acres with a marked hiking trail along Perkiomen Creek. *Audubon and Pawlings Rds., Box 7125, Audubon, PA 19407,* ☎ *610/666–5593.*

☛ *Free.* ⊙ *Museum: Tues.–Sat. 10–4, Sun. 1–4. Grounds: Tues.–Sun. 7 AM–dusk. Closed Thanksgiving, Dec. 25, and Jan. 1.*

On the Horseshoe Trail, two miles west of Valley Forge park, is the
④ **Wharton Esherick Museum,** the former home and studio of the "Dean of American Crafts." Best known for his sculptural furniture, Esherick shaped a new aesthetic in decorative arts by bridging art with furniture. The museum houses 200 samples of his work—paintings, woodcuts, furniture, and wood sculptures. The studio, in which everything from the light switches to the spiral staircase is hand-carved, is one of his monumental achievements. *Box 595, Paoli, PA 19301,* ☎ *610/644–5822.* ☛ *$5 adults, $3 children under 12.* ⊙ *Sat. 10–5, Sun. 1–5 for hourly guided tours. Reservations required. Group tours weekdays. Closed Jan. and Feb.*

⑤ For lunch or an afternoon of browsing, head for **The Court and Plaza** at King of Prussia, one of the nation's largest shopping complexes. These two adjacent malls contain more than a dozen restaurants, 300 shops and boutiques, and a half dozen major department stores, including Bloomingdale's and a stunning new branch of Philadelphia's own Strawbridge and Clothier. *Rte. 202 and N. Gulph Rd.,* ☎ *610/265–5727.* ⊙ *Mon.–Sat. 10–9:30, Sun. 11–5.*

Dining and Lodging

For price categories, see *Dining and Lodging in The Brandywine Valley, above.*

King of Prussia

DINING

$$$ **Bocconcini.** Updated American and northern Italian specialties (tortellini
★ alla panna with prosciutto, mushrooms, and cream) are served amid majestic marble columns and hanging vines interlaced on cherrywood ceiling beams. Italian desserts include tiramisù, cannoli, and ricotta cheesecake. ✗ *Plaza Hotel at Valley Forge, N. Gulph Rd. and 1st Ave.,* ☎ *610/265–1500. Reservations advised. AE, D, DC, MC, V.*

$$$ **Kennedy Supplee Restaurant.** French and northern Italian cuisine is served in the seven dining rooms of a circa 1852 Italian Renaissance mansion overlooking Valley Forge National Historical Park. ✗ *1100 W. Valley Forge Rd.,* ☎ *610/337–3777. Reservations advised. AE, MC, V. No lunch weekends.*

$$$ **Lily Langtry's Victorian Theater and Restaurant.** This lavishly appointed Victorian-era restaurant/cabaret serves American and Continental dishes, but the campy Las Vegas-style entertainment—corny comedians, showgirls, and some fine singers and dancers—is the real draw here. ✗ *Sheraton Valley Forge Hotel, N. Gulph Rd. and 1st Ave.,* ☎ *610/337–5459. Reservations advised. AE, D, DC, MC, V.*

LODGING

$$$ **Sheraton Plaza Hotel.** The Sheraton Plaza Hotel and the Sheraton Valley Forge (*see below*) flank the Valley Forge Convention Center and share several restaurants and nightclubs. Contemporary rooms here are minisuites with Jacuzzis for two and numerous telephones and TV sets. There are excellent breakfast and champagne-dinner-theater package. ⊞ *N. Gulph Rd. and 1st Ave., 19406,* ☎ *610/265–1500 or 800/325–36535,* ⅏ *610/962–3892. 160 rooms. Restaurant, pool, exercise room, theater, comedy club. AE, D, DC, MC, V.*

$$$$ **Sheraton Valley Forge Hotel.** A bustling high rise catering to groups
★ and couples escaping to Jacuzzi-equipped fantasy theme suites—a prehistoric cave, a wild-and-woolly jungle, the outer-space-like "Outer

Limits." There are excellent breakfasts and a champagne-dinner-theater package. ⚐ *N. Gulph Rd. and 1st Ave., 19406,* ☎ *610/337–2000 or 800/325–3535,* ␧ *610/768–3222. 326 rooms, including 72 fantasy suites. 2 restaurants, dinner theater, pool, health club. AE, D, DC, MC, V.*

$$$ **Comfort Inn at Valley Forge.** Spacious, modern rooms with king-size beds, three phones, VCR, stocked refrigerators, and remote control TV make this new five-story hotel a good buy. A complimentary deluxe Continental breakfast is offered. ⚐ *550 W. DeKalb Pike (Rte. 202N), 19406,* ☎ *610/962–0700 or 800/222–0222,* ␧ *610/962–0218. 121 rooms. Fitness center. AE, D, DC, MC, V.*

Valley Forge Essentials

Getting Around

BY CAR

Take the Schuylkill Expressway (I–76) west from Philadelphia to Exit 25 (Goddard Blvd.). Take Route 363 to North Gulph Road and follow signs to Valley Forge National Historical Park. Exit 25 also provides easy access to The Court and Plaza shopping complex.

BY BUS

On weekdays, the **SEPTA** (☎ 215/580–7800) Bus 125 leaves from 16th Street and John F. Kennedy Boulevard (departing hourly starting at 5:30 AM) for King of Prussia Plaza, and continues on to Valley Forge National Historical Park. On Saturday, transfer at the plaza to the "Royersford" Bus 99, which goes through the park. Bus 99 departs hourly. On Sunday Bus 99 does not run; Bus 125 goes as far as the Sheraton Valley Forge Hotel, less than a 1-mile walk from the park, but along busy roads.

Guided Tours

The Valley Forge National Historical Park Bus Tour (☎ 610/783–1077) is a narrated minibus tour that originates from the park Visitor Center (Rte. 23 and N. Gulph Rd.). Passengers can alight, visit sites, and reboard. Tours are scheduled from June through September; times vary. Tours cost $5.50 for adults, $4.50 children 5–16, children under 5 free.

Important Addresses and Numbers

VISITOR INFORMATION

Valley Forge Convention and Visitors Bureau (600 W. Germantown Pk., Suite 130, Plymouth Meeting, PA 19462, ☎ 610/834–1550 or 800/441–3549). Call or write for information packet.

Valley Forge Country Funline (☎ 610/834–8844) offers information about special events and exhibits 24 hours a day.

READING

After enjoying the richness of Valley Forge's past, you may want to head onto the Pennsylvania Turnpike and continue north to Reading (*Red*-ing), a city of 81,000 residents, but one which swells considerably thanks to hordes of shop-till-you-droppers. They arrive by car, bus, and train, attracted to the city's claim to fame as the "Outlet Capital of the World." Once, the city had another claim to fame: founded by William Penn's sons Thomas and Richard, it was celebrated in the 19th-century as the terminus of the Reading Railroad. Today, most visitors hop right off the bus and head for the outlets. Not for nothing does the city continues to draw thousands of bargain hunters enticed

with those alluring promises of savings up to 75% off retail: there are outlets for clothing, pretzels, candy, luggage, jewelry, shoes, pet food—even tropical fish!

This method of merchandising began when local factories and mills started selling overruns and seconds to employees. Eventually, small stores sprang up inside the factories. About 10 million visitors a year, many coming in bus excursions from all over the East Coast, now visit some 300 outlets located within a 4-mile radius. A large number of outlets are grouped together in former factory complexes.

In recent years, outlets with narrow wooden stairs and sawdust on the floors have given way to upscale shopping. Most outlets now are indistinguishable from normal retail stores, complete with carpeting, fitting rooms, sales clerks, and classical music playing in the background. Designer labels, including Ralph Lauren, Oleg Cassini, Calvin Klein, Karl Lagerfeld, Mark Cross, Coach, and Yves St. Laurent, are discounted.

It's easy to get caught up in the buying frenzy as you browse through racks marked $10 and under, but not all the buys are bargains. If an item is marked "irregular," look it over carefully. It may be fine or it might have holes in the sleeves. There is no sales tax on clothing in Pennsylvania.

Reading is an easy 75-minute drive from Philadelphia and the major outlets can be scanned in a day. Most outlet complexes have cafeterias or food courts. If you want another day to shop or sightsee, you have numerous overnight options since the success of the outlet stores has lead to a hotel and restaurant renaissance.

Sitting prettily atop Mt. Penn on Skyline Drive is the Pagoda, a seven-story building of Japanese design, which provides an expansive view of the city. Skyline Drive is a meandering road with miles of unspoiled vistas. The Daniel Boone Homestead, a renovation of the frontiersman's home, and the Mary Merritt Doll Museum, make good diversions after a shopping spree.

Exploring

Numbers in the margin correspond to points of interest on the Reading Environs and Reading maps.

❶ If you can't wait to load up your shopping bag, stop at the **Manufacturers Outlet Mall** when you exit the Pennsylvania Turnpike in Morgantown (Exit 22). "MOM" looks like any modern suburban enclosed shopping mall and has 50 stores on one level including Van Heusen, Pennsylvania Furniture House, Arrow, and London Fog. Attached to the mall is a 200-room Holiday Inn (☎ 610/286–3000) and indoor recreation center with pool. The food court serves lunch and dinner. *Exit 22, Pennsylvania Turnpike, Rtes. 23 and 10, ☎ 610/286–2000. ☉ Mon.–Sat. 10–9, Sun. noon–5.*

❷ The **VF Outlet Village** offers some of the best buys and the largest variety of goods in the city. Situated in what was once the world's largest hosiery mill, the complex originally sold surplus hosiery, sleepwear, and lingerie. Today it consists of nine major buildings on more than 900,000 square feet, with more than 90 outlets. The VF Factory Outlet store offers a vast selection of Lee jeans, women's sleepwear, and lingerie from Vanity Fair and Lollipop, Healthtex, and Jantzen and Jansport activewear at half price. Designers Place, with a three-story glass atrium, shopping amenities, and about 15 upscale outlets including Anne Klein, Perry Ellis, Carole Little, and Tommy Hilfiger. *Park Rd. and Hill*

Reading Environs

Ave., Wyomissing, ☎ *610/378–0408 or 800/772–8336. Food court. Shuttle buses take shoppers to and from the parking lot.* ☉ *Weekdays 9–9, Sat. 9–6, Sun. 10–5.*

❸ The **Reading Outlet Center** occupies a former silk-stocking mill in the heart of the city and now houses more than 70 shops on four floors plus stores in nearby buildings. An elevator and new signs now make getting around the store easier. Items for sale range from coffee and cosmetics to sporting goods and wine. There's a Polo/Ralph Lauren outlet, Fashion Flair's Izod Lacoste clothes, Timberland, Burberry's, and Corning. Russ–Villager–Crazyhorse occupies a new site nearby at 832 Oley Street. *801 N. 9th St.,* ☎ *610/373–5495. Restaurant.* ☉ *Mon.–Sat. 9:30–8, Sun. 11–5.*

❹ **Outlets on Hiesters Lane** is a grouping of three outlet buildings along one city block at the northern end of downtown Reading. Except for a linen outlet and the dinnerware at the Mikasa Factory Store, most stores sell coats, clothes, and shoes. There's Burlington Coat Factory Warehouse, Luxury Linen, Baby Depot, and Kids Depot. *Corner of Hiesters La. and Kutztown Rd.,* ☎ *610/921–8130.* ☉ *Most stores Mon.–Sat. 9:30–5:30, Sun. noon–5.*

❺ **Reading Station** bills itself as the "upscale outlet experience." This $23 million outlet complex is modeled after a turn-of-the-century Pennsylvania railroad village on the site of the former Reading Company railroad. The five buildings surrounding the courtyard display railroad memorabilia and house restaurants and about 30 factory outlet stores, including WestPoint Steven's Bed, Bath & Linens, Calvin Klein, and He–Ro Group featuring Oleg Cassini. *951 N. 6th St.,* ☎ *610/478–7000.* ☉ *Mon.–Thurs. and Sat. 9:30–7, Fri. 9:30–9, Sun. 11–5.*

Reading

Blue Marsh Lake, a 6300–acre park with an 1150–acre lake, is run by the U.S. Army Corps of Engineers as a recreational park with hiking, picnicking, and swimming. *Leesport, PA, 5 miles northwest of Reading on Route 183,* ☎ *610/376–6337.* ☉ *Daily 8 AM to dusk.*

❻ The Pagoda, a seven-story Japanese castle attached to the top of Mt. Penn by 10 tons of bolts, offers a panoramic view of the Reading area. Built in 1908 as a mountaintop resort, it underwent a $2 million renovation in 1993 and is now the home of the Berks Arts Council. Art gallery on second floor with changing exhibits. *Skyline Dr.,* ☎ *610/655–6374.*

❼ Crystal Cave's 45-minute guided walking tours wind through illuminated stalactites and stalagmites in distinctive formations like the "ice cream cone," "totem pole," and innumerable others. *From Reading, take U.S. 222 north 15 mi to Kutztown exit, follow signs;* ☎ *610/683–6765.* ☛ *$7.50 adults, $4.50 children 4–11.* ☉ *Daily 9–5, extended summer hrs. Closed Dec.–Feb.*

❽ The **Daniel Boone Homestead,** 10 miles east of Reading, is where the great frontiersman lived until the age of 16. The rebuilt homestead has been furnished to typify rural life in this part of the state. Offered are a half-hour house tour and unguided tours of the blacksmith shop, sawmill, and a log cabin built in 1737. *Daniel Boone Rd. off U.S. 422,* ☎ *610/582–4900.* ☛ *$4 adults, $3 senior citizens, $2 children 6–17.* ☉ *Tues.–Sat. 9–5, Sun. noon–5. Closed Mon. except Memorial Day, Labor Day, and July 4.*

❾ It's a small world at the **Mary Merritt Doll Museum** where you'll find rare dolls—rag dolls, French bisque dolls, mechanical dolls, and more—crafted between 1725 and 1900. Also on display are toys, exquisitely

fashioned miniature period rooms, and elaborate dollhouses. **Merritt's Museum of Childhood** has an eclectic collection of 18th-century Pennsylvania Dutch fraktur (hand-painted birth and marriage certificates), tin and iron toys, Colonial lighting devices, and early baby carriages. *Both on Rte. 422 in Douglassville, 1 mi east of Boone Homestead,* ☎ *610/385–3809.* ☛ *$3 adults, $2.50 senior citizens, $1.50 children 5–12.* ☉ *Mon.–Sat. 10–5, Sun. 1–5. Closed major holidays.*

⓾ **Hawk Mountain Sanctuary,** a 2,330-acre refuge 28 miles north of Reading, is visited by more than 20,000 migrating raptors—hawks, bald eagles, ospreys, and falcons—each fall. In other seasons, you can spot songbirds, grouse, and white-tailed deer and other mammals; hike along the sometimes rocky trails; and picnic at a lookout offering a bird's-eye view of the spectacular scenery. Bring binoculars and proper footgear. No pets allowed. *Hawk Mountain Road, 8 miles west of Kempton,* ☎ *610/756–6961.* ☛ *$4 adults, $3 senior citizens, $2 children 6–12.* ☉ *Visitor Center Dec.–Aug., daily 9–5; Sept.–Nov., daily 8–5. Closed Thanksgiving, Dec. 25, and Jan. 1.*

Dining

For price categories, see Dining and Lodging in The Brandywine Valley, above.

$$$$ **Joe's.** Now accorded shrine status by mushroom lovers everywhere, Joe's is the celebrated family restaurant of the Czarneckis. Thanks to the success of Jack Czarnecki's *Joe's Book of Mushroom Cookery* and *A Cook's Book of Mushrooms*—the definitive mushroom cookbooks—and the national attention they received, new legions of mushroom fans have been popping up faster than cepes after a rainstorm. These aficionados all head here to enjoy unusual dishes enriched by the exotic accents of wild and domestic mushrooms (morels, slippery jacks, woodblewits, and boletes, among others), most of which are handpicked by the family. The menu's highlights include wild game dishes, such as bear and antelope, but the "don't miss" item remains the extraordinary wild mushroom soup. ✕ *7th and Laurel Sts.,* ☎ *610/373–6794. Reservations advised on weekends. AE, D, DC, MC, V. Closed Sun. and Mon. No lunch.*

$$$ **Dans.** Located across from Reading's City Park, Dans (two guys named Dan run the place) is one of the region's best bets for contemporary American cuisine. Each menu selection seems more tantalizing than the next: baked brie in a cashew crust with blueberry marmalade, orange-glazed Achiote pork loin, cavatappi pasta with sausage and sage. Remember to spare room for the Strawberries Chantilly—berries served with whipped cream on flaky pastry floating in a puddle of light but intensely flavorful caramel sauce. At lunchtime, moderately priced salads and sandwiches entice. Thanks to the tranquil decor, a great glass of wine, and attentive service (how carefully they pace those reservations), dining at Dans is always a relaxed affair—welcome relief for shoppers after a hectic day. ✕ *1049 Penn St., at 11th St.,* ☎ *610/373–2075. Reservations advised. AE, D, MC, V. Closed Mon.*

$$ **The Peanut Bar.** Free peanuts (throw the shells on the floor), video games, and good burgers and fries make this 1930s-style tavern and restaurant a fun outing. Besides such fun foods as Buffalo chicken wings and cheese balls, the chef serves up some gourmet meals, including Maryland crab cakes and Tandoori chicken. Beers from local breweries are featured. ✕ *332 Penn St.,* ☎ *610/376–8500 or 800/515–8500. Reservations advised. AE, D, MC, V. Closed Sun.*

$ Arner's. This chain of family restaurants has four locations, all with the look and feel of spruced-up diners. The menu features American favorites with a Pennsylvania Dutch influence, such as pork chops, chicken pot pie, meatloaf, apple dumplings, and homemade pastries and pies. The bountiful salad bar and daily specials make this a hard-to-beat bargain. ✗ *9th and Exeter Sts., Reading,* ☎ *610/929–9795; Howard Blvd., Mt. Penn,* ☎ *610/779–6555; 1714 Bern Rd., Berkshire Mall,* ☎ *610/372–6101; 4643 Pottsville Pk., Tuckerton,* ☎ *610/926–9002. AE, D, MC, V.*

Lodging

$$$$ Sheraton Berkshire Inn. Recent renovations, including the addition of a striking art deco lobby and marble-tile floors, have made this an exceptionally attractive property. It's worth the extra $20 a night to upgrade from a standard room to an extra-large executive room in the tower. ⊞ *U.S. 422 W, on Papermill Rd., Wyomissing 19610,* ☎ *610/376–3811 or 800/325–3535,* 🆉 *610/375–7562. 256 rooms, 4 bi-level suites. 2 restaurants, nightclub, indoor pool, fitness center. AE, D, DC, MC, V.*

$$$ Inn at Reading. Housed in a well-kept, elegant complex, the inn's large rooms feature remote-control cable TV and traditional cherrywood furnishings, including some four-poster beds. Request a room close to the lobby. The Publick House restaurant serves excellent meals. ⊞ *1040 Park Rd. and Warren St., Wyomissing 19610,* ☎ *610/372–7811 or 800/383–9713,* 🆉 *610/372–4545. 250 rooms. Restaurant, nightclub, pool, playground. AE, DC, MC, V.*

$ Hampton Inn. This small hotel has stylish contemporary rooms, a new fitness center, and business facilities. The spacious King Special, just $5 more than a double, has a separate sitting area, king-size bed, and remote-control cable TV. Complimentary deluxe Continental breakfast is served. ⊞ *1800 Papermill Rd., Wyomissing 19610,* ☎ *610/374–8100 or 800/426–7866,* 🆉 *610/374–2076. 125 rooms. AE, D, DC, MC, V.*

Reading Essentials

Getting Around
BY CAR
Take the Schuylkill Expressway (I–76) west from Philadelphia to the Pennsylvania Turnpike. Go west to Exit 22, take I–176 north to U.S. 422 and then west into downtown Reading.

BY BUS
Greyhound Lines (☎ 800–231–2222) has frequent runs to the Intercity Bus Terminal, Third and Court streets, in Reading. Most buses make the trip in 90 minutes, although some locals take more than three hours. Check the schedule carefully.

Important Addresses and Numbers
VISITOR INFORMATION
Reading & Berks County Visitors Bureau (Factory Village Complex, Park Rd. and Hill Ave., Box 6677, Wyomissing, PA 19610, ☎ 610/375–4085 or 800/443–6610) provides outlet maps and guides. ⊘ *Jan.–June, weekdays 9–5, Sat. 10–2; July–Dec., weekdays 9–7, Sat. 10–3, Sun. 10–2.*

11 Portraits

THE SEARCH FOR INTELLIGENT LIFE

WELL, NOT EXACTLY a newcomer. I've been living here four years now, long enough to regard the scaffolding on City Hall tower as a permanent part of the architecture, long enough not to expect drivers to yield the right of way at pedestrian crossings, long enough to accept the litter, if not the dog ca-ca, as a natural part of the environment.

But even though I've been here a while, living in Center City, I'm still poking around trying to see whether Philadelphia is culturally more like London, or Calcutta, or Sauk Centre, Minnesota. Coming to a conclusion isn't easy because no one knows for sure what "culture" is or how you might experience it or why it's a good thing to have. Some people think you can get it at a specific outlet, like Lincoln Center in New York or The Kennedy Center in Washington. Others—Matthew Arnold, for example—think it's not a commodity at all, but a state of mind, not easily come by and acquired by a prolonged immersion in "the classics," whatever they may be. A Nazi storm trooper in a popular German play of the 1930s thought he could detect it easily and was prepared to protect his loved ones from its pernicious influences. "Whenever I hear the word 'culture,'" he said, "I release the safety catch on my pistol." Today the word can cause plenty of confusion, as the *Inquirer* unwittingly reveals each Sunday by titling one of its sections "Entertainment and the Cultural Arts." This awards equal time to symphony and opera and dance and country music and prole movies, thus suggesting that the "Cultural Arts" include anything not edible or portable or obviously utilitarian that readers can be enticed to spend money on.

And the *Inquirer* may be right. For T. S. Eliot, culture included much more than art, music, and beautiful letters. It embraced, he said, "all the characteristics and interests of the people." For the British that included, he maintained, the dart board and (ugh) "boiled cabbage cut into sections."

If that's what culture means, I'd have to look into cheesesteaks and soft pretzels with mustard, Frank Rizzo's impressive bod and the pitiable performances of the Iggles. But for me culture still means what it meant before anthropologists began using the term to include everything. For me it still designates things that don't make money, that engage your mind and imagination, that address your aesthetic sense and gratify your curiosity and connect you with the past. Culture invites you to think about time and history. It means things that government is disinclined or embarrassed to subsidize. It means those things that institutions are always begging for funds to house and maintain and exhibit. It is comparable to those things a philistine school board, considering the annual budget, would stigmatize as "frills."

Before moving to Philadelphia I lived in Princeton for many years, and there "my city" was New York, an easy cultural commuting distance away. I'd visited Philadelphia a few times, once for an opera, once for a road-show play, once for some soccer at Veterans Stadium, once for a not-so-hot seafood dinner. But because I knew very little about Philadelphia and its cultural operations, I consulted the estimable *Places Rated Almanac* (1981 edition). This rated American urban areas on the basis of their presumed cultural attractiveness according to various criteria, not all of which were plausible. From the *Almanac* I learned that Philadelphia ranked seventh among metropolitan areas for its number of actors. But the problem is that Philadelphia's are now mostly waiters. ("Hi. My name is Gary. We have a number of specials tonight I'd like to tell you about.") I learned also that Philadelphia's public library system ranked seventh in the United States, beaten not just by New York and Chicago and Boston (no surprise there) but astonishingly enough, by Cleveland and—shock!—Cincinnati. Another of the *Almanac*'s measures of cultural adequacy was the number of authors in residence. New York had a reputed 4,382, Philadelphia only 449, just

above Detroit (395). There weren't many dancers here, but a lot of painters and sculptors and a vast number of musicians and composers, giving Philadelphia a ranking for music fourth in the nation, just behind New York, Los Angeles, and Chicago. Considering all its criteria of cultural desirability together, the *Almanac* concluded that Philadelphia ranked seventh in the country, a ranking earned in very large part, I'd say, by the efforts of Stokowski, Ormandy, and Muti. Above Philadelphia: New York, Washington, Chicago, Boston, Los Angeles, and San Francisco. Below it: Denver, Minneapolis, Dallas, Buffalo, Baltimore, Houston, and Atlanta, not to mention Fort Smith, AR; Greeley, CO; and Laredo, TX. At the bottom of the list of 277 places ranked is poor Lafayette, LA, apparently a locus of bowling alleys, fast-food dispensaries, porn theaters, and dirt auto-racing tracks.

Now, if you need a shot of civic pride, look into the second edition of the *Almanac,* dated 1985. Philadelphia is now ranked sixth in the country as a metropolitan area rich in the arts and—hold your hats—first in the country (out of 328 metropolitan areas) in higher education. Eat your heart out, Boston: You're only 14th.

But as I confronted such statistics and tried to make sense of them, I remembered something more about Philadelphia, and it was mighty encouraging. Long ago, when I was returning to the States after living a year in London and encumbered with a whole lot of household stuff to bring back, friends advised encountering U.S. Customs in Philadelphia rather than New York. "People are nicer there," they said, and they were right. No one at the Philadelphia airport displayed open envy or contempt because of my good fortune in spending a year abroad. No one was rude for the fun of it. The sensitive questioning of the customs officer allowed me to bring in all my stuff without any trouble at all. This was a memorable experience of Philadelphia niceness, and since then I've had many more.

But there's a problem with niceness. It exacts cultural costs. I hadn't lived here very long before I sensed a deadly critical vacuum in Philadelphia. The most awful things—books, plays, restaurants, buildings, public utterances—passed without complaint or satire or abuse. I got the impression that Philadelphians really cared as little about a strenuously earned excellence as about spotless streets, a safe, well-run mass transit system, and an uncorrupt judiciary.

BECAUSE NO ONE SEEMS to care enough, literary culture in Philadelphia has suffered a notable erosion. The major book publishers have decamped, and with them the agents and most of the editors and writers. The book trade has been largely taken over by chains, mass-market bookstores where no one has heard of Flaubert or Veblen, let alone Montaigne or Sir Thomas Browne. And books are not authoritatively reviewed here. In one Sunday book review section of the *Inquirer* recently, there were 10 full reviews. All were by either *Inquirer* staff people, some apparently recruited from the mail room, or freelance writers. There were no national authorities whatsoever reviewing books, and this left the unhappy impression that the amateur and the parochial were good enough for Philadelphia. Not that the *Inquirer* hasn't some good, sharp critics, such as Carlin Romano on books, William B. Collins on theater, Elaine Tait on restaurants, and pre-eminently Thomas Hine on architecture and urban imagery. But the general critical tone in Philadelphia is soft and nice, rather like the local pretzel, and that's no way to encourage a culture for grown-ups.

If literary culture here seems in decline, theater is, of course, in a worse state. The curse here is the lack of a permanent, stable repertory company with knowledge and taste. By this lack Philadelphia betrays its cultural inferiority not just to New York, but to San Francisco and Washington, not to mention New Haven and Cambridge, MA. One of my bitter disappointments in moving here was discovering that whatever it does, the immensely expensive Annenberg complex at the University of Pennsylvania does not consider it a duty to stage plays in the historical repertory, which means not only that I can't profit from repeated attendance at *Antony and Cleopatra, Major Barbara, Six Characters in Search of an Author* and *Krapp's Last Tape,* but that, worse, the

local students can't. I think they're being cheated.

Having said that, I must recognize that there's wonderful stuff here, even if it takes some nosing around to find it. That's because Philadelphia culture is decentralized. You don't find it all in one place, or even in one district. If this were New York, the building of the Pennsylvania Academy of Fine Arts on Broad Street would probably have been torn down years ago and its contents consolidated with those of the Philadelphia Museum of Art. The same with the Rodin Museum. And Philadelphia's culture is unique for another reason. It's rather shy. New York has the pompous Morgan Library, looking like a rich man's palace designed to awe beholders. Philadelphia has the Rosenbach Museum and Library, established in a town house on a quiet domestic street. It seems the same here with the least important cultural things. It took me some time to notice, passing almost daily, that Firstrust Savings Bank on Rittenhouse Square provides a lending library for its clients. But there's little indication in front that you can borrow books there as well as money. That suggests Philadelphia's cultural style at its best: Don't shout, just quietly and modestly deliver something good. And wait for the culture clients to find it.

ADECENTRALIZED CULTURE like Philadelphia's has large and subtle advantages. Other cities' "cultural centers" give the impression that culture can be assembled all in one place. That makes it seem a luxury isolated from real life and thus fit to be ignored. But when it's spread all around, you can't help meeting some of it all the time, passing and perhaps dropping in to the Balch Institute or the Atwater Kent or the Afro-American or American Jewish museums, or the Historical Society of Pennsylvania or The University Museum, or noticing the delightful group of "Dutch Renaissance" buildings on Walnut Street between 19th and 20th streets. And the more you walk around, the more you're likely to notice that there's an oboe repair shop on Pine Street.

The Gideon Bibles placed in hotel rooms offer specific "how-to" advice for alleviating common spiritual and psychological maladies. For example, "If you are weary and discouraged, read Matthew 11:28-30," or "When your friends seem to go back on you, read I Corinthians 13." In the same way, here are some nuggets of cultural therapy for Philadelphians, all possible because of a happily decentralized culture.

- When you feel that residence in or around Philadelphia is beginning to blunt your sense of humor, as well as of beauty, go to the art museum and contemplate Oldenburg's hypertrophied cherry wood multiple plug, hung up near the ceiling. You will smile.

- While at the museum, if you feel the need of a sexual lift combined with artistic refreshment, seek out Duchamps's *Etant Donnés*. More or less X-rated, it has to be kept from the children and thus is not easy to find. But it's eminently worth the search and inquiries.

- When you are persuaded that these days "young people are no good," devoted only to drink and drugs and dumb movies, go hear a recital by the devoted kids at the Curtis Institute. And when you've convinced yourself that the federal government and its agencies are distinguished by no artistic instincts whatsoever, go hear the Curtis students in a free noontime recital at, of all places, the Federal Reserve Bank on 6th Street, presented in its own civilized, comfortable, small auditorium.

- When you feel that, despite your costly education, your ability to entertain two conflicting ideas simultaneously is feebler than it should be, go to the corner of 15th and Market streets and study— really study—the *Clothespin*. Or is it lovers embracing? Is it a clothespin becoming lovers or lovers becoming a clothespin? Or both at once?

- When you feel that Philadelphia radio offers little but proletarian call-in shows, turn to WFLN (95.7 FM) for 24 hours of intelligent music, with lots of Baroque from midnight to morning.

- When you're overcome with the depressing conviction that Philadelphia is

hopelessly provincial, ruinously out of touch with Europe and Asia and the world's significant history, join the Alliance Française and speak French, and after that drop into the Rosenbach to contemplate the manuscript of Joyce's *Ulysses*. Then look into The University Museum. If you were sent by *The Last Emperor*, try exercising your imagination on the crystal ball, which once delighted the Dowager Empress.

- If your experience of contemporary politics, and especially tax policy, has persuaded you that the rich and famous of all places are necessarily selfish swine and always have been, spend an hour in "The Titanic and Her Era" exhibit at the Maritime Museum at Penn's Landing. There you can reacquaint yourself with the fact that boundlessly rich men within living memory sacrificed themselves when the chips were down and the odds very bad, so that their wives and children could live.

It's a mind-expanding experience to wonder if you would do the same, and if not, why not.

- When wearied and bored by the sight of the new business architecture all over town, which gives the impression that plate glass and aluminum are interesting, stroll across the Schuylkill and regale yourself with the facade of the original Drexel Institute Main Building (Chestnut at 32nd). Enjoy the sexy muse or angel or whatever at the top; they don't make them like that anymore. Contemporary women have breasts that good, but no wings.

— Paul Fussell

Long a Philly fan, Paul Fussell is one of the city's most noted wits and raconteurs.

PORTRAIT OF AN AMISH FAMILY

YOU'LL SPOT JACOB Stoltzfus working his fields with a team of horses as you drive the back roads of Lancaster County. You will certainly encounter his somber black buggy on one of the traffic-choked highways. You might exchange a few words with his wife, Becky, in her plain dark dress and white cap, if you happen to stop by their farmhouse to buy fresh eggs or inspect the homemade quilts she has for sale. If you're on the right road at the right time, you might see their younger children playing in the yard of a one-room schoolhouse. And on certain Sundays, you may pass the farmhouse where the Stoltzfus family and other Amish people gather to worship.

Stoltzfus is the most common of a dozen Amish family names; Jacob and Becky and their children are fictitious but typical of the more than 16,000 Amish (pronounced *Ah*-mish) in this area. Their roots and religious traditions reach back to 16th-century Europe. Every detail of their lives, from their clothing to the way they operate their farms, is an expression of their faith in God and their separateness from "the world"; every detail is dictated by the *Ordnung,* the rules of their church.

Becky Stoltzfus, like Amish women of any age, wears a one-piece dress in a dark color (bright colors and printed patterns are forbidden). The sleeves are long and straight, her full skirt hemmed modestly halfway between knees and ankles. The high, collarless neck is fastened shut in front with straight pins; buttons and safety pins are forbidden although the Ordnung of some church districts allows hooks and eyes. Over her shoulder she wears a shawl the same color as her dress, pinned in front and back to the waistband of an apron also in the same color. Since apron strings tied in a bow are considered frivolous and therefore forbidden, her apron is also pinned. She wears black stockings rolled below the knee and black low-heeled oxfords. At home in warm weather, Becky and her family go barefoot.

Soon after her daughters were born, Becky made sure they wore the white organdy prayer cap. When Katie turned 12, she changed to a black cap for the Sunday preaching; after she marries she will wear the white cap all the time. The head coverings may look identical to outsiders but subtle differences tell the Amish a great deal about one another. The width of the front part, the length of the ties, the style of the seams, the way the pleats are ironed all indicate where the woman lives and how conservative or liberal her church district is.

Becky has never cut or curled her hair, nor has she let it hang loose. She pins it in a plain knot at the back of her neck. She parts little Hannah's hair in the middle, plaits it, and fastens the two little braids in the back. When Becky is away from home she wears a black bonnet with a deep scoop brim over her prayer cap.

The clothes Jacob wears are also carefully dictated by the Ordnung of his church district. For Sunday preaching he wears a *Mutze,* a long, black frock coat with split tails and hook-and-eye closings but no collar or lapels. His vest is also fastened with hooks and eyes. Jacob's broadfall or "barn-door" trousers have no fly, just a wide front flap that buttons along the sides; they have no creases and no belt— homemade suspenders hold them up. There are buttons on his shirt, the number specified by the Ordnung. Colored shirts are permitted, but stripes and prints are out. Neckties are forbidden.

When he's not dressed up, Jacob hangs up his Mutze and puts on a *Wamus,* a black sack coat with either a high round neck or V-neck and neither lapels nor outside pockets. Sometimes the Wamus has hooks and eyes, but more liberal church districts allow buttons. Buttoned sweaters are sometimes permitted, and there are also buttons on the long greatcoats some older men wear in cold weather.

In winter Jacob and his sons wear broad-brimmed black felt hats; in summer they switch to straw. Ben and Ezra, Jacob's

younger boys, have been wearing hats with three-inch brims since they were little. Sam, the oldest son, wears a hat with a crease around the top of the crown, a sign (along with his sprouting beard) that he is newly married. The hat is a status symbol among the Amish. The grandfather's hat is higher in the crown than the father's and its brim is four inches wide. At the top of the hierarchy, the bishop who preaches at the Sunday service is recognizable by his hat's high rounded crown and its brim, the broadest in the district.

The width of an Amish man's hat brim also signifies his degree of conservatism: The broader the brim, the more conservative the wearer. Young rebels like Jacob's middle son Joe sometimes trim their hat brims to just a little less than the prescribed width.

Jacob's long beard is as much the mark of an Amish man as a broad-brimmed hat. He shaves only his upper lip, since mustaches are against the rules. He cuts his hair straight around, well below the ears. Ben and Ezra have theirs parted in the middle, with bangs across the forehead. Cutting it short—up to the earlobe, as Joe did—is another form of rebellion.

THE STYLE OF THE AMISH BUGGY is as carefully prescribed as the style of his hat. The Stoltzfus family owns a black carriage with a gray top and big wooden wheels. The battery-powered side lamps, reflectors, and bright orange triangles have been added as required by Pennsylvania state law. The iron-tire wheels are precisely set, toed in slightly, farther apart at the top than at the bottom. A gear assembly at the pivot of the front axle adds stability. The brakes are operated by hand, an iron block pressed hard against the rear tire. This kind of brake is prescribed by the Ordnung; different groups permit different kinds of brakes. The Ordnung tells the buggy owner whether or not he may have roll-up side curtains or sliding glass doors, and if he is allowed a dashboard, a whipsocket, and other variations. The Stoltzfus family also owns a farm wagon and young Joseph was given his own horse and open one-seater when he turned 16.

The waiting list is long for handmade buggies. Carriage-making used to be a non-Amish occupation, but the growing Amish population, the toll of wrecked carriages, and the need for approved work in addition to farming have brought some Amish into the trade. The carriage maker is in a more liberal church district that allows power tools.

Incidentally, the Amish can—and do—ride in cars owned by non-Amish people and travel on trains, buses, and even airplanes and taxis. But they are not allowed to *own* a car. Teenage Amish boys sometimes manage to buy a car and hide it out of sight of their families. They are not subject to the rules of the Ordnung until they have been baptized, an event that takes place in their late teens or early 20s after they've had time to sow some wild oats.

No electric wires lead from the power lines along the road into the neat, well-kept buildings of the Stoltzfus farm, a difference that distinguishes Amish farms from their non-Amish neighbors'. The farms are small, no more than 50 or 60 acres, which is all that can be handled by a farmer limited to horse power. Tractors, like electricity, are taboo among most of the Amish.

The Stoltzfuses' house is spacious and uncluttered. There is no wall-to-wall carpeting to vacuum; rather, plain, unpatterned linoleum covers the floor. There are no curtains to wash or draperies to clean; although some church districts allow plain curtains on the lower half of the windows, this district permits only dark-green roller shades. There are no slipcovers to launder or upholstery to shampoo, because upholstered furniture is not allowed.

Becky has a large kitchen where the family eats around a big wooden table. Afterward Becky and Katie and Hannah clean up the kitchen, wash the dishes, and put away leftover food in the gasoline-operated refrigerator. A one-cylinder engine in the cellar chugs noisily, powering the water pump, but many Amish families still rely on windmills or water power. A creek that runs through a farm also supplies water. Although labor-saving devices are generally forbidden, Becky does have a washing machine that runs by gasoline.

Her stove burns kerosene; she would prefer bottled gas, but that is forbidden by the Ordnung of her district. She uses a treadle sewing machine and sews by the bright and steady light of a gasoline lamp.

About once a year, it is the Stoltzfuses' turn to host the every-other-Sunday preaching service. As many as 175 people may attend: There are 90 members in the district, and double that number counting unbaptized children. The removable partitions built into the downstairs walls are folded back and furniture moved aside. The district's backless oak benches are brought in and set up in rows. For that one Sunday morning the entire district fills the big house for the long service, staying on for a hearty lunch that Becky has been preparing for days.

Jacob and Becky Stoltzfus are fluent in English, but the language they speak among themselves is Pennsylvania Dutch, a German dialect related to the dialects spoken in the part of Germany from which their Amish ancestors came. It is primarily a spoken language and spelling varies with the writer. "Dutch" actually means *Deutsch*, or German, and some scholars call the dialect "Pennsylvania German." Many Pennsylvanians of German descent speak the dialect, but among the Amish it is the "mother tongue," the first language an Amish child learns to speak and another mark of separation from the world.

When Hannah, Becky's youngest child, starts school, she will learn to speak and read and write in the language of "the world." Jacob and Becky want their children to know English, because their survival depends on good business relationships with English-speaking people. Sometimes when the Amish converse in English, they resort to dialect translated literally into English. The results are the quaint expressions that amuse tourists and inspire souvenir manufacturers to decorate switchplates and cocktail napkins with "typical Amish" expressions like "Outen the light" and "Throw Papa down the stairs his hat."

About the same time Hannah Stoltzfus starts to learn English, she will also be taught High German, the language of religion. The family Bible is written in High German, and she and her brothers and sisters must learn to read it. By the time they are baptized in their late teens, they will be able to understand most of the Sunday sermon and to join in the prayers and hymns. Most Amish can't carry on a conversation in High German and have no need to do so unless they are ordained church officials who must preach sermons and pray. But everyone needs to be able to read and to listen.

THE OUTSIDER MAY NOT NOTICE the inconspicuous building on a back road where Ben and Ezra and Annie Stoltzfus attend school, along with eight grades of children in one room taught by a young Amish woman with only an eighth-grade education. Amish children are not sent to public school, and Amish schools continue only as far as the eighth grade. That's time enough to learn the basics of reading, writing, and arithmetic! The *real* education for their lives takes place at home, on the farm.

At age five, Hannah Stoltzfus would be old enough for kindergarten—if the Amish had one. But they believe children should be at home with their parents until they are six. Annie loves school and wishes she could continue, while her brothers can hardly wait until their 14th birthdays, the end of school for them. Schools are built to serve children within a 2-mile radius so that no one has far to walk. Some children go to old, one-room schoolhouses once owned by the public school district. When districts consolidated, the Amish bought the obsolete schools and remodeled them—not modernizing them, but ripping out the electric wiring. Since none was available near the Stoltzfus farm, the Amish fathers in that area built a plain cinder-block structure with big windows to take advantage of natural light.

Stepping into an Amish schoolhouse is like entering a time machine and emerging 70 or more years in the past. At 8:30 the teacher pulls the rope to ring the old-fashioned bell on the roof. Ben and Ezra and Annie come early, after they've finished their farm chores, so they have a chance to play before school begins. When the bell rings, the children line up and file through the big front door into the cloakroom. They hang their hats and jackets on

pegs, line up their lunch boxes, and go quietly to their carefully refinished old-fashioned desks.

The school day begins with the roll call. During peak periods of farm work, the Amish close down the schools for a few days; they stop earlier in the spring than the public schools. They make up for the time by taking only a short Christmas break and celebrating none of the national holidays. Except in the case of illness, everyone stays home to work or goes to school to learn.

Next, the teacher reads to the pupils from the German Bible, then everyone recites the Lord's Prayer in German. Except for the lessons in reading German Scriptures and prayers, the teacher speaks exclusively English in the classroom.

Beside the teacher's desk is a "recitation bench." There are more than 30 students in the eight grades, and each class of three or four or five comes forward by turns to recite its lessons. There is no competition to come up with the answer first, and they all respond in a singsong chorus.

Because it is essential to the work of a farmer, arithmetic is considered very important. Picking readers (books) for the pupils was not easy. The parents want the subject matter to be farm children, not city life; they want the stories to teach a moral lesson; fairy tales, myths, and fantasies are taboo. The Amish think most modern readers are too worldly, showing families with clothes, cars, and too many material possessions. Outsiders would consider the books they use hopelessly outdated.

During the 15-minute morning recess, Ezra and Ben and the other boys resume their baseball game. One of the rules of the Amish schoolyard is that children are never allowed to stand around by themselves; everyone must be included in the group. Annie and the older girls play blindman's bluff; the younger ones, joined by their teacher, race around in a game of tag.

During recess and lunchtime, the yard rings with conversation in English, Pennsylvania Dutch, and mixtures of the two. Parents disagree about which language should be used in the schoolyard. More pragmatic parents want their children to become as fluent as possible in English. The

more traditional argue that using English when it's not necessary helps to drive a wedge between the Amish child and the Amish community.

The Amish want their children to learn to work together as a group, not to compete as individuals. Preserving tradition is a goal; reasoning abstractly is not. Asking too many questions is not acceptable. Discipline is strict; the only voices heard in the schoolroom are those of the teacher and the pupils who are reciting. The Amish expect pupils to master the material unquestioningly: Memorization replaces reasoning in a culture dominated by oral tradition. Rapid learning is not considered an advantage; thoroughness is valued more. Teachers believe that intellectual talents are a gift from God and that children should be encouraged to use the gift by helping others in the school.

BEFORE THE DAY IS OVER, there is time for singing. Singing is a vital part of the Amish tradition, important in their religious life and in their social life as well. There are no harmonized-part songs for the Amish; unaccompanied unison singing is the universal rule. The Amish have their own style of singing, in which the leader (*Vorsanger*) sings the first word and everybody else joins in for the rest of the line.

When it's time to go home, students put away their books, sweep out the room, line up the desks neatly, wash the old-fashioned slate blackboards, and clap the erasers until they are clean. In cold weather they carry in the wood for the stove and take turns cleaning out the ashes and banking tomorrow's fire.

For years public school authorities were in conflict with the Amish. Truancy laws were enforced and Amish fathers were often arrested and jailed for refusing to send older children to school. But in 1972 the United States Supreme Court ruled that the Amish are exempt from state compulsory education laws that require a child to attend beyond the eighth grade; they found that such laws violate Constitutional rights to freedom of religion.

Today, the Amish accept the idea of sending their children to school for eight years to learn what they need to survive in the

20th-century rural economy. But what an Amish child really needs to know in order to survive in the Amish culture he learns from his parents and from other adults in the community. Most of the practical knowledge of farmers and housewives is acquired not in books but in a family apprenticeship.

The marriage of Jacob and Becky Stoltzfus is a very practical affair. The Amish are quite realistic about their expectations. They do not marry for "love" or "romance" but out of mutual respect and the need for a partner in the kind of life they expect to live. The farmer needs a wife and they both need children. Marriage is essential to the Amish community; divorce is unknown; separation is rare. Marriage is the climax of the rite of passage that begins with baptism, the signal of the arrival of adulthood and sober responsibility. It signifies that young people have really joined the community.

From the time they reach the age of *Rum Schpringe* ("running around"—about 16 for boys, a bit younger for girls) and for the next half-dozen years until each marries, Joe Stoltzfus and his sister Katie do much of their socializing at Sunday night singings usually held at the farm where the preaching service took place in the morning. Singings are functions of the church district, which helps keep dating and eventually marriage within the group. In Lancaster County, young people from several church districts with similar interpretations of the Ordnung may get together for a joint singing. Although the main activity is singing hymns, these occasions are more social than religious.

At the more conservative singings, boys sit on one side of a long table in the barn and girls sit on the other, and between joking and teasing they take turns in the role of Vorsanger. The hymns they sing are the "fast tunes" (some of them familiar Protestant hymns) rather than the "slow tunes" or chants sung at the preaching service. At around 10 o'clock the singing ends and the girls serve snacks. The couples, now paired off—Joe is with Leah Zook, as usual, and Katie has somehow ended up with Reuben Beiler—start home.

Although outsiders believe that the social life of an Amish teenager begins with a singing and ends with a buggy ride home at a respectably early hour, Amish dating is actually much livelier. Among the more liberal groups, the old-fashioned singings can turn quickly into rowdy, foot-stomping hoedowns. A few bring out harmonicas, guitars, and other forbidden instruments; older boys haul in cases of beer. Few outsiders attend these events.

On the "off Sunday" when there is no preaching service, Joe and Leah and other young unmarried people go courting—but always in secret. Before they marry, they are never seen together in public as a couple except as they leave a singing or a barn dance.

Bundling, the practice of courting in bed fully clothed, is usually attributed to the Amish. Actually it is an English word with no equivalent in Amish dialect, and the custom dates back to New England where it had more to do with keeping warm in a cold house than with sex. No one is quite sure whether the Amish do or don't, but the consensus is that the girl's parents, rather than the Ordnung, have the final say. Leah's father and Jacob Stoltzfus have both said "no."

THERE IS A SAYING that if a boy can persuade his girl to take off her prayer cap, she'll have sex with him. Evidently that doesn't happen often because the rate of premarital pregnancies among the Amish is quite low. Premarital sex is forbidden, birth control is taboo, and sex education is nonexistent. The Amish child growing up on a farm isn't ignorant of the reproductive process, but human "facts of life" usually remain somewhat mysterious until the age of marriage.

When Jacob's son Sam married Sarah Beiler, their wedding was held after the harvest in November. December is the second most popular month for weddings, and there are traditionally only two possible days in the week for the ceremony: Tuesday and Thursday. Sarah chose Thursday. There was no honeymoon, but every weekend throughout the winter the couple went to visit relatives. Now they're living on the Stoltzfus farm.

The average age at marriage of Amish couples has been rising because of the problems of accumulating enough money

to establish a household and to acquire land. Many Amish parents retire while they are still relatively young, especially if they have a son who needs a farm. Sam and Sarah have moved into the "grandfather's house," a section of Jacob's farmhouse built to accommodate a second generation. In a few years, when Sam assumes full responsibility for the farm and has children, he and Sarah will move into the larger part of the house and Jacob and Becky will move into the grandfather's house.

Recently Sam told his parents that a new little "woodchopper" or "dishwasher" is expected, the first grandchild of Jacob and Becky. A new generation of the Stoltzfus family and for the Amish community is on the way.

The roots that nourish Amish beliefs and bring vitality to Amish tradition reach back hundreds of years. Theirs is a complex story of persecution from without and division within. Remembrance of the past is a part of the present for the Amish every day of their lives, not something reserved for Sunday worship and special ceremonies.

TO UNDERSTAND THE AMISH as something more than a quaint anachronism, turn back the calendar to 16th-century Europe. The poor, by far the majority, were exploited by the rich and powerful few. The Roman Catholic Church wielded tremendous influence and many blamed the church for society's ills. When Martin Luther launched the Protestant Reformation in 1517, he had many opponents in addition to the Roman Catholic Church. One was Ulrich Zwingli, a radical Swiss Protestant, who in turn opposed Conrad Grebel. Grebel's followers wanted to establish free congregations of believers baptized as adults who made a confession of faith and committed themselves freely to a Christian life. Backing Zwingli, the Great Council of Zurich announced that babies must be baptized within eight days after their birth or the parents would be exiled.

This marked the beginning of Anabaptism, which means "rebaptized." Regarded as radically left wing, the Anabaptist movement posed a threat to both Roman Catholic and Protestant establishments. Anabaptist leaders were imprisoned, beaten, tortured, and killed until, by the end of the 16th century, nearly all the Anabaptists of Switzerland and Germany had been put to death.

But the movement spread through Central and Western Europe. Menno Simons, a former Roman Catholic priest, became one of those persecuted for Anabaptist preaching. His followers were called Mennonites (In Switzerland they were known as the Swiss Brethren). And although they were hounded by Catholics and other Protestants, dissension began to grow among the Mennonites themselves. A principal source of disagreement was the interpretation of the *Meidung,* the practice of shunning church members who had broken a rule. Shunning was based on St. Paul's advice to the Corinthians to avoid keeping company and eating with sinners. The Mennonites interpreted this to mean the member was to be subjected to Meidung only at communion. But Jacob Amman, a young Mennonite bishop, insisted that the Meidung meant that the rule-breaker must be shunned totally; even his wife and family must refuse to have anything whatever to do with him until he repented and had been forgiven.

The controversy grew and in 1697 the stubborn and fiery Jacob Amman broke away from the Mennonites. His followers, known as the Amish, were as stubborn and inflexible as Amman himself and they became known for their unwillingness to change. Although differences in details of clothing were not a primary issue, they did become symbolic of the split. The Amish became known as the *Haftlers* (Hook-and-eyers) while the more worldly Mennonites were called the *Knopflers* (Buttoners).

Meanwhile, King Charles II of England granted a large province in the American colonies to William Penn. A devout Quaker, Penn believed he could offer refuge, freedom, and equality to the persecuted. Penn arrived in 1682, and the following year Francis Daniel Pastorius of the Frankfort Land Company brought the first group of Mennonites to Pennsylvania. They established themselves in Germantown, northwest of Philadelphia. The first Amish immigrants left Switzerland

and the Palatinate of Germany in 1727, settling near Hamburg north of Reading. When Indian raids threatened that community, the Amish moved toward the southwest.

By the start of the Revolutionary War, about half of the 225,000 Pennsylvania colonists were German, but only a small minority were Amish and Mennonite. Although the Germans were excellent farmers, Benjamin Franklin dismissed them as "stupid boors." The English scorned them and tried to Anglicize them. But the Amish and Mennonites were determined to hold on to their religion, which was a way of life that included their language and their plain dress.

The Amish of Pennsylvania were all of one conservative mind until 1850, when a schism divided the Amish into two main factions. The more progressive group built meeting houses, which earned them the label "Church Amish," to distinguish them from the stricter "House Amish," who continued to worship in their homes. Since then, innumerable splits have been caused by various interpretations of the Meidung (as happened in the days of Jacob Amman) or by different details of the Ordnung—by Haftlers who want to live more like Knopflers but still remain Amish.

Every society changes to some extent and in every society there are a few people who cannot adjust. The Amish are no exception. Many leave; there is generally a shortage of young men in the Amish community because most of the dissidents who leave are male. But some exert pressure for changes in the Ordnung that result in splits. Today there are 7 Amish, 21 Mennonite, and 9 Brethren groups in the Lancaster area.

The ultimate control exerted by the Amish to keep the members in strict adherence to the Ordnung is the Meidung. No one will speak to the person, eat with him, conduct business with him, or have anything whatever to do with him while he is under the ban. It can last for a lifetime, unless the sinner mends his ways, begs for forgiveness, and is readmitted to fellowship by a unanimous vote of the congregation.

Visitors are sometimes surprised to learn that "Pennsylvania Dutch" and "Amish" are not synonymous. Many of the early settlers of Pennsylvania came from Germany at Penn's invitation; many were farmers, most were Protestant, and they spoke the same dialect. Despite these similarities, the Amish refer to all non-Amish as "English." These English are the Pennsylvania Dutch who permit hex signs on their farms (the Amish do not) and whose ancestors decorated useful items such as furniture and dishes with colorful peasant-style designs. The work of Amish craftsmen is competent but plain.

The Amish are generally friendly and hospitable people. Tape recorders and cameras are not welcome, but a visitor sincerely interested in the Amish people who does not act like an interrogator can quietly learn something about their unique way of life.

— *Carolyn Meyer*

MORE PORTRAITS

Fiction

"Writing fiction set in Philadelphia is tough," says *Philadelphia Inquirer* columnist Steve Lopez. "There is nothing you can make up that is any more unbelievable or preposterous than what actually happens here." Nonetheless, Lopez succeeded with *Third and Indiana,* a hardedged story set in Philadelphia's "badlands." *God's Pocket,* by Pete Dexter; *South Street,* by David Bradley; and *Payback* by Philip Harper, also capture the grittier side to the City of Brotherly Love.

History and Background

Philadelphia, a 300-Year History, edited by Russell F. Weigley, is the best overall text. *1787: The Day to Day Story of the Constitutional Convention* and Catherine Drinker Bowen's *Miracle at Philadelphia* tell the story of the Constitution.

For biographies of seven Philadelphians, read *Philadelphia: Patricians and Philistines, 1900 to 1950,* by John Lukacs. *Puritan Boston and Quaker Philadelphia* by E. Digby Baltzell, compares the two cities and the differing characters of their people.

Other selections are *Christopher Morley's Philadelphia* edited by Ken Kalfus; and *Philadelphia—A Dream for the Keeping,* by John Guinther.

Sightseeing and Touring

Walking Tours of Historic Philadelphia, by John Francis Marion, though a bit dated, has wonderful walks detailed by the late, well-known Philadelphiaphile. The Foundation for Architecture's *Philadelphia Architecture: A Guide to the City* contains maps, photos, biographies of noted Philadelphia architects, and descriptions of almost 400 sites. *Cultural Connections, Museums and Libraries of Philadelphia and the Delaware Valley,* by Morris J. Vogel, has photos and text on sites throughout the region.

Guides to Philadelphia's spectacular collection of outdoor art include: *Sculpture of a City,* by the Fairmount Park Art Association, with text and photos; *Philadelphia's Outdoor Art: A Walking Tour,* by Roslyn F. Brenner, describing more than 50 works of art along Benjamin Franklin Parkway; and *Public Art in Philadelphia,* by Penny Balkin Bach, the most comprehensive work on the subject. Garden lovers will want to study *Gardens of Philadelphia and the Delaware Valley,* by William M. Klein, Jr., which has beautiful photographs.

Other selections are *Country Walks Near Philadelphia,* by Alan Fisher; *Philadelphia One-Day Trip Book,* by Jane Ochevhausen Smith; *Philadelphia and its Countryside,* by Ruth Hoover Seitz; and *The Mid-Atlantic's Best Bed & Breakfasts* by Fodor's Travel Publications.

INDEX

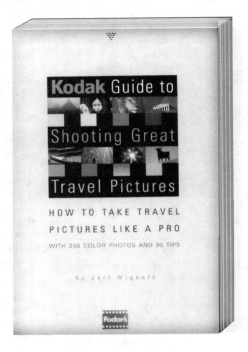

Fodor's Travel Publications

Available at bookstores everywhere, or call 1–800–533–6478, 24 hours a day.

Gold Guides
U.S.

Alaska	Florida	New Orleans	Santa Fe, Taos, Albuquerque
Arizona	Hawaii	New York City	Seattle & Vancouver
Boston	Las Vegas, Reno, Tahoe	Pacific North Coast	The South
California	Los Angeles	Philadelphia & the Pennsylvania Dutch Country	U.S. & British Virgin Islands
Cape Cod, Martha's Vineyard, Nantucket	Maine, Vermont, New Hampshire	The Rockies	USA
The Carolinas & the Georgia Coast	Maui	San Diego	Virginia & Maryland
Chicago	Miami & the Keys	San Francisco	Waikiki
Colorado	New England		Washington, D.C.

Foreign

Australia & New Zealand	Egypt	London	Provence & the Riviera
Austria	Europe	Madrid & Barcelona	Scandinavia
The Bahamas	Florence, Tuscany & Umbria	Mexico	Scotland
Bermuda	France	Montréal & Québec City	Singapore
Budapest	Germany	Moscow, St. Petersburg, Kiev	South America
Canada	Great Britain	The Netherlands, Belgium & Luxembourg	South Pacific
Cancún, Cozumel, Yucatán Peninsula	Greece		Southeast Asia
Caribbean	Hong Kong		Spain
China	India	New Zealand	Sweden
Costa Rica, Belize, Guatemala	Ireland	Norway	Switzerland
Cuba	Israel	Nova Scotia, New Brunswick, Prince Edward Island	Thailand
The Czech Republic & Slovakia	Italy		Tokyo
	Japan	Paris	Toronto
Eastern Europe	Kenya & Tanzania	Portugal	Turkey
	Korea		Vienna & the Danube

Fodor's Special-Interest Guides

Branson	Fodor's London Companion	Kodak Guide to Shooting Great Travel Pictures	Walt Disney World for Adults
Caribbean Ports of Call	France by Train	Shadow Traffic's New York Shortcuts and Traffic Tips	Where Should We Take the Kids? California
The Complete Guide to America's National Parks	Halliday's New England Food Explorer	Sunday in New York	Where Should We Take the Kids? Northeast
Condé Nast Traveler Caribbean Resort and Cruise Ship Finder	Healthy Escapes	Sunday in San Francisco	
	Italy by Train		
Cruises and Ports of Call		Walt Disney World, Universal Studios and Orlando	

Special Series

Affordables
Caribbean
Europe
Florida
France
Germany
Great Britain
Italy
London
Paris

Fodor's Bed & Breakfasts and Country Inns
America's Best B&Bs
California's Best B&Bs
Canada's Great Country Inns
Cottages, B&Bs and Country Inns of England and Wales
The Mid-Atlantic's Best B&Bs
New England's Best B&Bs
The Pacific Northwest's Best B&Bs
The South's Best B&Bs
The Southwest's Best B&Bs
The Upper Great Lakes' Best B&Bs

The Berkeley Guides
California
Central America
Eastern Europe
Europe
France
Germany & Austria
Great Britain & Ireland
Italy
London
Mexico

Pacific Northwest & Alaska
Paris
San Francisco

Compass American Guides
Arizona
Chicago
Colorado
Hawaii
Hollywood
Las Vegas
Maine
Manhattan
Montana
New Mexico
New Orleans
Oregon
San Francisco
Santa Fe
South Carolina
South Dakota
Southwest
Texas
Utah
Virginia
Washington
Wine Country
Wisconsin
Wyoming

Fodor's Español
California
Caribe Occidental
Caribe Oriental
Gran Bretaña
Londres
Mexico
Nueva York
Paris

Fodor's Exploring Guides
Australia
Boston & New England
Britain
California
Caribbean
China
Egypt
Florence & Tuscany
Florida
France
Germany
Ireland
Israel
Italy
Japan
London
Mexico
Moscow & St. Petersburg
New York City
Paris
Prague
Provence
Rome
San Francisco
Scotland
Singapore & Malaysia
Spain
Thailand
Turkey
Venice

Fodor's Flashmaps
Boston
New York
San Francisco
Washington, D.C.

Fodor's Pocket Guides
Acapulco
Atlanta
Barbados

Jamaica
London
New York City
Paris
Prague
Puerto Rico
Rome
San Francisco
Washington, D.C.

Rivages Guides
Bed and Breakfasts of Character and Charm in France
Hotels and Country Inns of Character and Charm in France
Hotels and Country Inns of Character and Charm in Italy

Short Escapes
Country Getaways in Britain
Country Getaways in France
Country Getaways Near New York City

Fodor's Sports
Golf Digest's Best Places to Play
Skiing USA
USA Today The Complete Four Sport Stadium Guide

Fodor's Vacation Planners
Great American Learning Vacations
Great American Sports & Adventure Vacations
Great American Vacations
National Parks and Seashores of the East
National Parks of the West

Teach Yourself VISUALLY™
Windows® 10 Anniversary Update

Paul McFedries

Visual
A Wiley Brand

Teach Yourself VISUALLY™ Windows® 10 Anniversary Update

Published by
John Wiley & Sons, Inc.
10475 Crosspoint Boulevard
Indianapolis, IN 46256

www.wiley.com

Published simultaneously in Canada

Library of Congress Control Number: 2016947156

ISBN: 978-1-119-31118-8 (pbk); ISBN: 978-1-119-31119-5 (ebk);
ISBN: 978-1-119-31108-9 (ebk)

Manufactured in the United States of America

10 9 8 7 6 5 4 3 2 1

Trademark Acknowledgments

Contact Us

For general information on our other products and services, please contact our Customer Care Department within the U.S. at 877-762-2974, outside the U.S. at 317-572-3993 or fax 317-572-4002.

For technical support please visit www.wiley.com/go/techsupport.

Credits

Executive Editor
Jody Lefevere

Project Editor
Sarah Hellert

Technical Editor (previous edition)
Vince Averello

Copy Editor
Scott Tullis

Production Editor
Athiyappan Lalith Kumar

Manager, Content Development & Assembly
Mary Beth Wakefield

Vice President, Professional Technology Strategy
Barry Pruett

About the Author

Paul McFedries is a full-time technical writer. Paul has been authoring computer books since 1991, and he has more than 90 books to his credit. Paul's books have sold more than four million copies worldwide. These books include the Wiley titles *Teach Yourself VISUALLY macOS Sierra*, *Teach Yourself VISUALLY Excel 2016*, *The Facebook Guide for People Over 50*, and *iPhone 6 Portable Genius*. Paul is also the proprietor of Word Spy (www.wordspy.com), a website that tracks new words and phrases as they enter the language, and Word Spy Press (https://wordspy.com/index.php?page=press), books for people who love words. Paul invites you to drop by his personal website at www.mcfedries.com or follow him on Twitter @paulmcf or @wordspy.

Author's Acknowledgments

It goes without saying that writers focus on text, and I certainly enjoyed focusing on the text that you'll read in this book. However, this book is more than just the usual collection of words and phrases. A quick thumb-through the pages will show you that this book is also chock full of images, from sharp screenshots to fun and informative illustrations. Those colorful images sure make for a beautiful book, and that beauty comes from a lot of hard work by Wiley's immensely talented group of designers and layout artists. I thank them for creating another gem. Of course, what you read in this book must also be accurate, logically presented, and free of errors. Ensuring all of this was an excellent group of editors that included project editor Sarah Hellert, copy editor Scott Tullis, and technical editor (previous edition) Vince Averello. Thanks to all of you for your exceptional competence and hard work. Thanks, as well, to Wiley executive editor Jody Lefevere for asking me to write this book.

How to Use This Book

Who This Book Is For

This book is for the reader who has never used this particular technology or software application. It is also for readers who want to expand their knowledge.

The Conventions in This Book

❶ Steps

This book uses a step-by-step format to guide you easily through each task. Numbered steps are actions you must do; bulleted steps clarify a point, step, or optional feature; and indented steps give you the result.

❷ Notes

Notes give additional information — special conditions that may occur during an operation, a situation that you want to avoid, or a cross reference to a related area of the book.

❸ Icons and Buttons

Icons and buttons show you exactly what you need to click to perform a step.

❹ Tips

Tips offer additional information, including warnings and shortcuts.

❺ Bold

Bold type shows command names, options, and text or numbers you must type.

❻ Italics

Italic type introduces and defines a new term.

Table of Contents

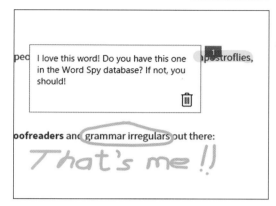

Table of Contents

Chapter 5 Getting Social with Windows

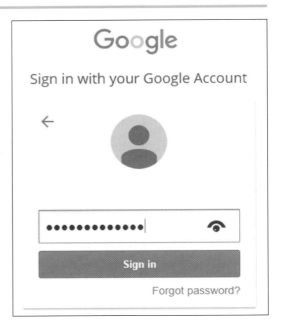

Chapter 6　Performing Day-to-Day Tasks with Apps

Table of Contents

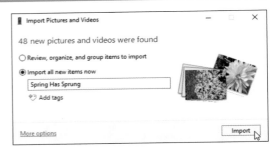

Florence Trip

Monday, May 30, 2016 8:58 AM

····

Things To Do
- [] Rent apartment
- [] Renew passport
- [] Purchase Euros
- [] Rent car
- [] Purchase camera battery

How do you want to open this file?

Keep using this app

Photos
Photos are easily enhanced, organized for you, and ready to edit and share.

Other options

Paint

Windows Photo Viewer

Look for an app in the Store

More apps ↓

☐ Always use this app to open .jpg files

OK

Table of Contents

Chapter 13 Implementing Security

Chapter 14 Maintaining Windows

Getting Started with Windows

To do something useful with your computer and with Windows 10, you need to explore the screen, connect to your network, and learn how to work with apps.

Explore the PC Screen

Before getting to the specifics of working with Windows 10, take a few seconds to familiarize yourself with the basic elements of the screen. These include the desktop, the Start button, and the taskbar. In most cases, you only see the Start button and the taskbar when you move the mouse pointer to the bottom of the screen.

This section covers the screen you see on a PC. If you are using a Touch PC or a tablet, see the next section, "Explore the Tablet Screen."

A Desktop Icon

An icon on the desktop represents a program or Windows feature. A program you install often adds its own icon on the desktop.

B Mouse Pointer

When you move your mouse, this pointer moves along with it.

C Desktop

This is the Windows "work area," meaning that it is where you work with your programs and documents.

D Start Button

You use this button to start programs and launch many of Windows' features.

E Search Box

You use this box to search for items on your PC or on the Internet.

F Taskbar Icons

You use these icons to launch some Windows features with just a mouse click.

G Taskbar

The programs you have open appear in the taskbar. You use this area to switch between programs if you have more than one running at a time.

H Notification Area

This area displays small icons that notify you about things that are happening on your computer. For example, you see notifications if your printer runs out of paper or if an update to Windows is available over the Internet.

I Time and Date

This is the current time and date on your computer. To see the full date, position the mouse pointer (⌖) over the time. To change the date or time, click the time.

I f you are using a touch-based PC or a tablet device, Windows 10 will automatically reconfigure the screen into *tablet mode*, which is designed to make it easier for you to navigate and launch items using touches and other gestures. However, you might find that using this new interface is not easier at first. To get more out of this interface and to learn how to operate your Touch PC or tablet, you need to familiarize yourself with Windows 10's tablet mode.

Explore the Tablet Screen

A Tablet mode displays the Start screen, which consists of *tiles* for several common apps.

B In an app, you can click **Back** (◀) to return to either the previous app screen or to the Start screen.

C To return directly to the Start screen, you can click **Start** (⊞).

1 To see more commands, click **Menu** (≡).

Windows displays a menu of commands.

2 To hide the commands, click **Menu** (≡) again.

D To toggle tablet mode on and off, you can click **Action Center** (▢) and then click **Tablet Mode**.

Put Windows to Sleep

You can make your computer more energy efficient by putting Windows into sleep mode when you are not using the computer. *Sleep mode* means that your computer is in a temporary low-power mode. This saves electricity when your computer is plugged in, and it saves battery power when your computer is unplugged.

In sleep mode, Windows keeps your apps open. This is handy because it means that when you return from sleep mode, after you sign in to Windows again, you can immediately get back to what you were doing.

Put Windows to Sleep

1 Click **Start** (⊞).

The Start menu appears.

2 Click **Power** (⏻).

3 Click **Sleep**.

Windows activates sleep mode.

Note: To return from sleep mode, press your computer's Power button.

Restart or Shut Down Windows

Y ou can restart Windows, which means that it shuts down and starts up again immediately. This is useful if your computer is running slowly or acting funny. Sometimes a restart solves the problem.

Alternatively, when you complete your work, you could shut down Windows. However, do not just shut off your computer's power because doing so can cause problems: If you have documents with unsaved changes, you may lose those changes; you also could damage one or more Windows system files, which could make your system unstable. Therefore, you should always follow the proper steps when shutting down your PC.

Restart or Shut Down Windows

1 Shut down all your running programs.

Note: Be sure to save your work as you close your programs.

2 Click **Start** (⊞).

The Start menu appears.

3 Click **Power** (⏻).

4 Click a command:

Ⓐ You can click **Restart** to shut down and then start your computer.

Ⓑ You can click **Shut Down** to turn off your computer.

7

Connect to Your Wireless Network

If you have a wireless access point and your computer has built-in wireless networking capabilities, you can connect to the wireless access point to access your network. If your wireless access point is connected to the Internet, then connecting to the wireless network gives your computer Internet access, as well.

Most wireless networks are protected with a security key, which is a kind of password. You need to know the key before attempting to connect. However, after you have connected to the network once, Windows remembers the password and connects again automatically whenever the network comes within range.

Connect to Your Wireless Network

① Click **Network** (📶).

Ⓐ Windows displays a list of wireless networks in your area.

② Click your network.

③ To have Windows connect to your network automatically in the future, click **Connect automatically** (☐ changes to ☑).

④ Click **Connect**.

If the network is protected by a security key, Windows prompts you to enter it.

5 Type the security key.

B If you want to be certain that you typed the security key correctly, you can temporarily click and hold **Display Password Characters** (👁).

6 Click **Next**.

Windows asks if it can locate the other computers and devices on your network.

7 Click **Yes**.

Windows connects to the network.

C The network icon changes from Disconnected (📶) to Connected (📶) to indicate that you now have a wireless network connection.

TIP

How do I disconnect from my wireless network?
To disconnect from the network, follow these steps:

1 Click **Network** (📶).

2 Click your network.

3 Click **Disconnect**. Windows disconnects from the wireless network.

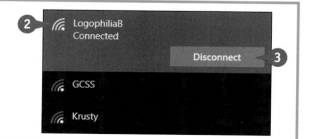

Switch to a Microsoft Account

You can get much more out of Windows by using a Microsoft account. When you connect a Microsoft account to your Windows user account, many previously inaccessible Windows features become immediately available. For example, you can use the Mail app to access your email and the OneDrive app to store documents online. You can also download apps from the Windows Store, access your photos and documents anywhere online, and even sync your settings with other PCs for which you use the same account.

Switch to a Microsoft Account

Start a Microsoft Account

1 Click **Start** (⊞).

2 Click **Settings** (⚙).

Windows opens the Settings app.

3 Click **Accounts**.

The Accounts window appears.

4 Click **Sign in with a Microsoft account instead**.

The Make It Yours window appears.

Configure an Existing Microsoft Account

A To create a new Microsoft account, you can click **Create one** and then skip to the next subsection, "Configure a New Microsoft Account."

1 Type your email address.

2 Type your password.

3 Click **Sign in**.

4 To finish configuring your existing account, skip to the subsection "Complete the Account."

TIP

Can I use a new Microsoft email address?
Yes, you can. Windows does not require that you use an Outlook.com email address from Microsoft, but you can use such an address if you do not want to use an existing address. In the Let's Create Your Account window, click the **Get a new email address** link and then type the username you want to use with Outlook.com. Your new address will be *username*@outlook.com.

continued ▶

How you proceed after you type your email address depends on whether you are creating a new Microsoft account or using an existing account. Using a Microsoft account with Windows can help if you forget your account password and cannot log in.

You can provide Microsoft with your mobile phone number, so if you ever forget your password, Microsoft will send you a text message to help you reset your password. You can also give Microsoft an alternative email address, or you can provide the answer to a secret question.

Switch to a Microsoft Account (continued)

The Let's Create Your Account window appears.

Configure a New Microsoft Account

1. Type your name.

2. Type the email address you want to use and select either **outlook.com** or **hotmail.com** from the list.

3. Type your password.

4. Click ⌄ and then click your country.

5. Click each ⌄ to select your date of birth.

6. Click **Next**.

Complete the Account

1. Click **Next**.

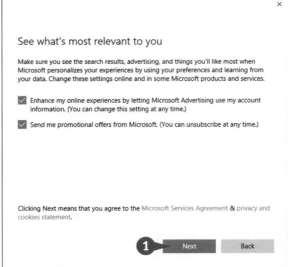

Windows asks you to verify your current account password.

2 Type your password.

3 Click **Next**.

Windows asks if you want to use a PIN with your account.

4 Click **Skip this step**.

Note: See the section "Set Up a Fingerprint Sign-In" in Chapter 13 to learn how to add a PIN to your account.

Windows connects the Microsoft account to your user account.

The next time you start Windows, you can use your Microsoft account email address and password to sign in.

TIP

If I no longer want to use a Microsoft account with Windows, can I remove it?

Yes, but you will no longer see any personal data on the Start screen, you will not be able to access your files online, and your settings will no longer sync between PCs. To remove the Microsoft account, click **Start** (⊞), click your user name in the upper-left corner, and then click **Change account settings**. In the Accounts window, click **Sign in with a local account instead**.

Manage my Microsoft account

Sign in with a local account instead

Install an App

If Windows does not come with an app that you need, you can obtain the app and then install it on your computer. How you start the installation process depends on whether you obtained the app from the Windows Store that comes with Windows or you downloaded the app from the Internet. If you purchased the app from a retail store and received a physical copy of the software, you install the app using the CD or DVD disc that comes in the package.

Install an App

Install from the Windows Store

1 Click **Start** (⊞).

2 Click **Store**.

Ⓐ You can also click **Store** (🗗) in the taskbar.

Note: You need a Microsoft account to install from the Windows Store, as described in the previous section, "Switch to a Microsoft Account."

The Windows Store appears.

3 Use these tabs or the Search box to locate the app you want to install.

4 Click the app from the results that appear.

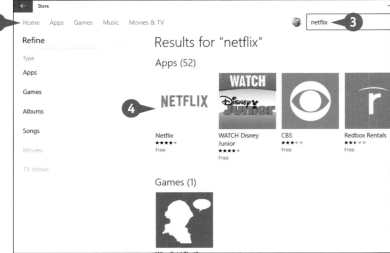

5 Click **Free**.

If the app is not free, click the price button instead, type your Microsoft account password, and then click **OK**.

Windows installs the app.

Install a File Downloaded from the Internet

1 Click **File Explorer** (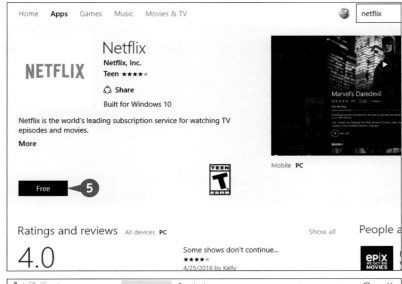).

2 Open your **Downloads** folder.

Note: If you saved the downloaded file in a folder other than Downloads, use File Explorer to find the downloaded file. To view a file with File Explorer, see Chapter 10.

The Downloads folder appears.

3 Double-click the file.

The software's installation app begins.

Note: For compressed files, extract the files and then double-click the setup file. See Chapter 10 for more information.

4 Follow the installation instructions the app provides.

TIPS

How do I install software from a CD or DVD?
Insert the disc and, when the AutoPlay dialog box appears, click **Run** *file*, where *file* is the name of the installation app (usually SETUP.EXE). Then follow the installation instructions the app provides (these installation steps vary from app to app).

How do I find my software's product key or serial number?
Look for a sticker attached to the back or inside of the CD case. Also look on the registration card, on the CD, or on the back of the box. If you downloaded the app, the number should appear on the download screen and on the email receipt you receive.

Start an App

To perform tasks of any kind in Windows, you can use one of the apps installed on your computer. The application you use depends on the task you want to perform. For example, if you want to surf the World Wide Web, you use a web browser application, such as the Microsoft Edge app that comes with Windows.

Before you can use an application, however, you must first tell Windows which application you want to run. You can start an app either from the Start menu or from the All Apps list.

Start an App

Using the Start Menu

1 Click **Start** (⊞).

A Your most frequently used apps appear here.

B Common Windows features appear here.

C The right side of the Start menu displays tiles for commonly used apps.

D The rest of your installed apps appear here.

2 Click the app you want to start.

The app runs.

E To close an app, you can click **Close** (✕) or press **Alt** + **F4**.

Note: If you are using a tablet PC, close an app by swiping down from the top edge of the screen and then dragging the app window all the way to the bottom of the screen.

Using the All Apps List

1 Click **Start** (⊞).

2 If you do not see the app you want, scroll down through the All Apps list.

3 Click the icon for the program you want to launch.

F To quickly navigate your apps alphabetically, you can click any letter and then click the letter that contains the app you want to start.

G If your program icon is in a submenu, you can click the submenu and then click the program icon.

Windows launches the app.

Is there an easier way to locate an app?
Yes, you can perform a search to locate it. Click inside the taskbar's Search box and then begin typing the name of the app. As you type, Windows displays a list of apps and other items that match the characters. When you see the app you want, click it to run the program.

What are tiles?
A tile is a method for displaying a shortcut that launches an app. Many tiles are *live*, which means that a tile's text changes to display the app's most recent information, such as the latest news or your most recently received email messages. See the section "Pin an App to the Start Menu" in Chapter 2 to learn how to add your own Start menu tiles.

Switch Between Running Apps

I f you plan on running multiple applications at the same time, you need to know how to easily switch from one application to another. In Windows, after you start one application, you do not need to close that application before you open another one. Windows supports a feature called *multitasking*, which means running two or more applications simultaneously. For example, you might keep your word processing application, your web browser, and your email application open all day. You can switch from one program to another using either the taskbar or the keyboard.

Switch Between Running Apps

Switch Apps Using the Taskbar

1 Position the mouse pointer (⍅) over the taskbar button of the program you want to switch to.

A Windows displays a thumbnail version of the app window.

2 Click the app's taskbar button.

Note: A program does not have to be minimized to the taskbar for you to use the program's taskbar button.

B Windows brings the program's window to the foreground.

Note: You can also switch to another window by clicking the window, even if it is in the background.

18

Switch Apps Using Task View

1 In the taskbar, click **Task View** (▯).

C Windows displays thumbnails for each running program.

2 Click the thumbnail of the program you want to switch to.

Windows switches to the program.

Is there an easy way to arrange windows so they do not overlap?
Yes, you can *snap* windows into place. To snap a window to the left half of the screen, drag the top of the window until the mouse pointer (⇖) hits the left edge of the screen, and then release. Similarly, drag a window to the right edge to snap it to the right. To snap a window to a quarter of the screen, drag the window to any corner.

How can I switch between apps using the keyboard?
Press and hold **Alt** and then press **Tab** to see thumbnail versions of the open windows. Press **Tab** until the window you want to work in is selected and then release **Alt**.

Update an App

You can ensure that you are using the latest version of an app by using the Windows Store to install an available update. After a software company releases an app, its programmers continue to work on it. They add new features, improve existing features, fix problems, and close security holes.

After fully testing these improvements and fixes, they place the new version of the app in the Windows Store, which alerts you that an update is available. You can then install the new version.

Update an App

1 Click **Start** (▦).

2 Click **Store**.

A You can also click **Store** (▤) in the taskbar.

The Windows Store app appears.

B This number tells you how many updates are available.

3 Click **Updates** (↓).

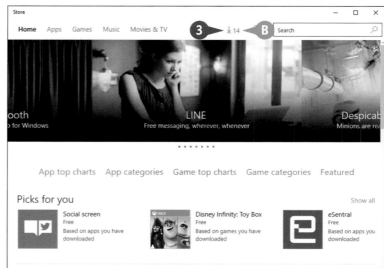

The Windows Store displays a list of the available updates.

④ To ensure that you are seeing all the available updates, click **Check for updates**.

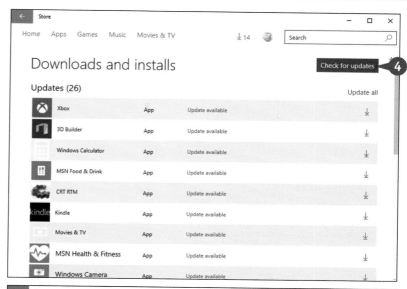

ⓒ If you prefer to update all the apps at the same time, you can click **Update all** and skip step **5**.

⑤ Click **Update** (↓).

Windows installs the app updates.

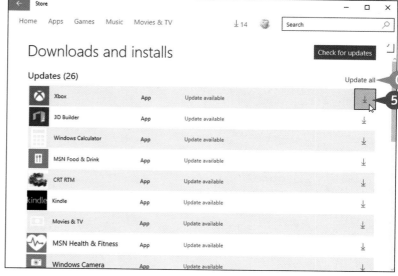

Can I automate the updates?
Yes. Instead of updating your apps manually, configure Windows to update the apps automatically. In the Store app, click your user icon, click **Settings**, and then click the **Update apps automatically** switch to **On**.

How do I update Windows?
By default, Windows is configured to automatically check for updated system files each day. If updates are available, Windows downloads and installs them. If you know of an important update, you can check for it manually if you would rather not wait for the automatic check. Click **Start** (⊞) and then click **Settings** (⚙) to open the Settings app. Click **Update & security** and then click **Check for updates**.

Uninstall an App

If you have an app that you no longer use, you can free up some hard drive space and reduce clutter on the Start screen by uninstalling that app. When you install an app, the program stores its files on your computer's hard drive, and although most programs are quite small, many require hundreds of megabytes of hard drive space. Uninstalling an app you do not need frees up the hard drive space it uses and removes its tile (or tiles) from the Start screen (if it has any there) and the Apps screen.

Uninstall an App

Uninstall via the Start Menu

1. Click **Start** (▦).

2. Use the Start menu or the All Apps list to locate the app you want to uninstall.

3. Right-click the app.

4. Click **Uninstall**.

Windows asks you to confirm.

5. Click **Uninstall**.

Windows removes the app.

Uninstall via Programs and Features

1 Type **uninstall**.

2 Click **Change or remove a program**.

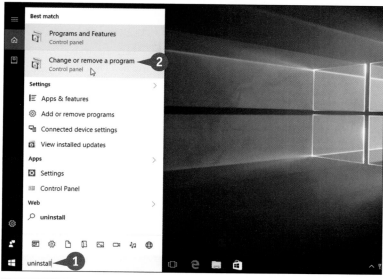

The Programs and Features window appears.

3 Click the app you want to uninstall.

4 Click **Uninstall** (or **Uninstall/ Change**).

The app's uninstall procedure begins.

5 Follow the instructions on the screen, which vary from app to app.

TIPS

How can I uninstall the app that is taking up the most space?

Click **Start** (⊞) and then click **Settings** (⚙) to open the Settings app. Click **System** and then click **Apps & features** to see a list of apps sorted by size. To remove an app, click it, click **Uninstall**, and then click **Uninstall** when Windows asks you to confirm.

What is the difference between an Automatic and a Custom uninstall?

The Automatic uninstall requires no input from you. It is the easiest, safest choice and therefore the one you should choose. The Custom uninstall gives you more control, but it is more complex and suitable only for experienced users.

Customizing Windows

Windows comes with a number of features that enable you to personalize your computer. Not only can you change the appearance of Windows to suit your taste, but you can also change the way Windows works to make it easier to use and more efficient.

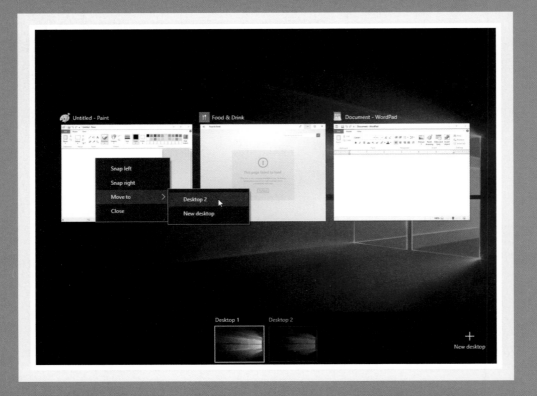

Pin an App to the Start Menu

You can customize the Start menu to gain quick access to the programs that you use most often. If you have an app that does not appear on the Start menu, you usually open the app by clicking the Start menu's All Apps command and then negotiating the menus and submenus that appear. For the apps you use most often, you can avoid this extra work by *pinning* their icons permanently to the right side of the main Start menu. After you have pinned an app, you can launch it by displaying the Start menu and clicking the app.

Pin an App to the Start Menu

1 Click **Start** (⊞).

2 Locate the app that you want to pin to the Start menu.

3 Right-click the app.

The app shortcut menu appears.

④ Click **Pin to Start**.

Ⓐ A tile for the pinned app appears on the right side of the Start menu.

Note: To remove an app tile from the Start menu, click **Start** (⊞), right-click the tile, and then click **Unpin from Start**.

Note: If you have a large screen, you can show more tiles on the Start menu. Click **Start** (⊞), click **Settings** (⚙), click **Personalization**, click **Start**, and then click the **Show more tiles** switch to **On**.

TIPS

Can I move an app tile within the Start menu?

Yes, you can move any app tile to a different position within the Start menu. To move a tile, click **Start** (⊞), press and hold the mouse button as you drag the tile to its new position, and then release the mouse button.

Can I change the size of a Start menu tile?

Yes. In all cases, you can select either a Small or Medium square. With some apps, you can also choose either a Wide rectangle or a Large square. To change the size, click **Start** (⊞), right-click the app's tile, click **Resize**, and then click the size you want.

Open the Settings App

You can configure and customize many aspects of your Windows system using the Settings app. Settings is the Windows app that you use for customizing and tweaking your PC. Many of the sections that follow in this chapter, including changing the Lock screen backgrounds and adding an app to the Lock screen, are performed using the Settings app. Settings also offers a wealth of other options that you can use to customize your PC.

Open the Settings App

Open the Settings App

① Click **Start** (⊞).

② Click **Settings** (⚙).

The Settings app appears.

Note: You can also open the Settings app by pressing ⊞+🄸.

Navigate the Settings App

1 Click a category.

The Settings app displays the category.

2 Click a tab.

3 Use the controls on the right side of the app window to modify the tab's settings.

Windows puts the new settings into effect.

A You can click **Back** (←) if you need to return to the previous screen.

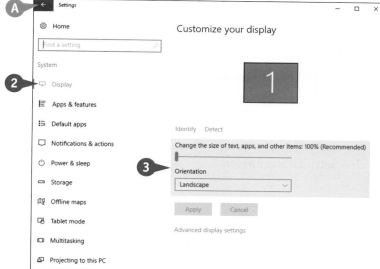

TIP

If I know which tab of the Settings app I want to use, is there a quick way to display it?
Yes, you can use the taskbar's Search box, which enables you to quickly search for the setting that you want to work with. Click inside the Search box and then begin typing the name of the tab or setting you want.

For example, if you want to go directly to the Accounts tab, type **accounts** and then click **Add, edit, or remove other people** in the search results. Note that Settings items appear in the search results with the Settings icon (⚙).

Change the Lock Screen Background

You can make your Lock screen more interesting by changing the image that appears as its background. Locking your computer is a useful safety feature because it prevents unauthorized users from accessing your files and your network. If you find yourself looking at the Lock screen frequently, you might prefer to see something other than the default image. Windows comes with several system pictures that you can use, or you can use one of your own pictures.

Change the Lock Screen Background

1 Open the Settings app.

Note: See the previous section, "Open the Settings App."

2 Click **Personalization**.

The Personalization settings appear.

3 Click **Lock screen**.

4 Click the **Background** ∨ and then click **Picture**.

Note: If you want to use a series of Microsoft Bing photos as the Lock screen background, click **Windows Spotlight**, instead.

5 To use a default image, click the thumbnail of the picture that you want to use.

6 To use one of your own pictures, click **Browse**.

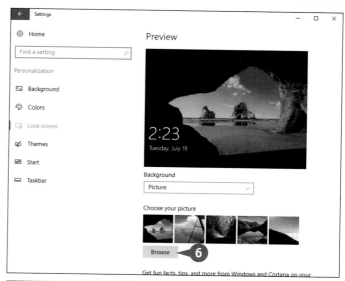

7 Click the picture that you want to use.

8 Click **Choose picture**.

The image appears the next time that you lock your computer.

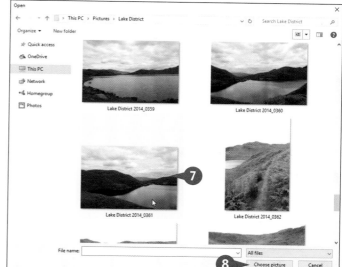

How do I lock my computer?

Click **Start** (⊞), click your user icon on the left side of the menu, and then click **Lock**. You can also press ⊞+L. You can configure Windows to automatically lock the computer after it has been idle for a specified amount of time. In the Search box, type **lock**. Click **Lock the computer when I leave it alone for a period of time**. Click **On resume, display logon screen** (☐ changes to ☑). Use the Wait text box to set the number of minutes of idle time after which Windows locks your PC. Click **OK**.

Add an App to the Lock Screen

When you lock your PC, Windows displays status icons for some apps. For example, the status icon for the Mail app shows the number of unread messages. The Lock screen also shows any new notifications that appear for the Calendar app, such as an upcoming appointment. If you lock your computer frequently, you can make the Lock screen even more useful by adding icons for other apps, including ones that support notifications.

Add an App to the Lock Screen

1 Open the Settings app.

Note: See the section "Open the Settings App" earlier in this chapter.

2 Click **Personalization**.

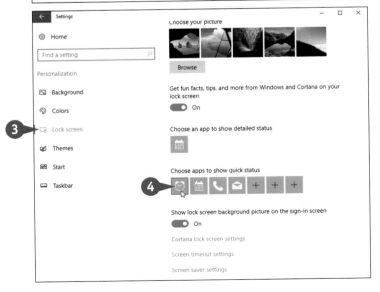

The Personalization settings appear.

3 Click **Lock screen**.

4 To set a quick status icon for an app, click a button.

The Choose an App window appears.

5 Click the app for which you want to add a quick status icon to the Lock screen.

6 Repeat steps **4** and **5** to set the other quick status icons.

A If you do not want an app associated with the icon, you can click **None**.

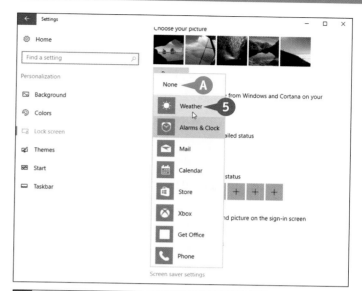

7 To choose which app displays its detailed status, click here and then click the app.

Note: If you do not want a detailed status, click **None**.

Windows puts the new settings into effect, and the apps appear on the Lock screen the next time that you use it.

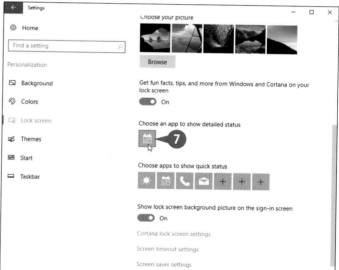

TIP

What is the difference between a quick status and detailed status?

A *quick status* means that the Lock screen shows only a small icon for an app, and that icon displays the number of recent or unread items, such as the number of unread email messages in the Mail app. A *detailed status* means that the Lock screen shows more information from the app. For example, if you have an upcoming event in the Calendar app, the Lock screen shows the details of that event, including the event title, location, and time.

Synchronize Settings Between PCs

If, besides your Windows desktop computer, you also have a Windows notebook, a Windows tablet, and a Windows smartphone, using the same Microsoft account on each platform means that you can synchronize data among them. You can sync customizations, such as backgrounds and themes; system settings, such as languages and regional settings; Microsoft Edge data, such as favorites and history; and app settings and more. This gives you a consistent interface across your devices and consistent data so that you can be more productive.

Synchronize Settings Between PCs

1 Open the Settings app.

Note: See the section "Open the Settings App" earlier in this chapter.

2 Click **Accounts**.

The Accounts settings appear.

3 Click **Sync your settings**.

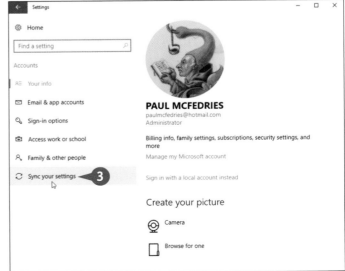

The Sync settings appear.

④ Click the **Sync settings** switch to **On**.

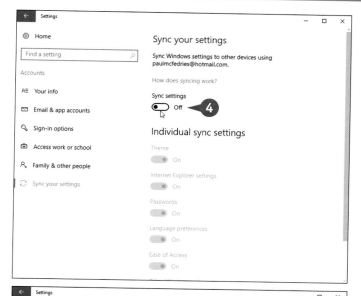

⑤ Under Individual Sync Settings, click the switch to **Off** beside each type of setting that you do not want to include in the sync.

The next time Windows syncs, it does not include the settings that you turned off.

TIP

Why is the Passwords switch disabled in my version of Sync Your Settings?
This occurs when you have yet to verify your identity on your PC. Verifying your identity means having a confirmation code sent to the mobile phone number associated with your Microsoft account. To verify your identity, use the taskbar's Search box to type **actions** and then click **View recommended actions to keep Windows running smoothly**. In the Security and Maintenance window that appears, you should see the message "Verify your identity on this PC." Click **Verify** to the right of that message, and then follow the instructions that appear for having the confirmation code sent to your mobile phone.

Access an App's Features

Depending on the app, you might see a few tabs across the top of the window, as well as a Search box in the upper-right corner of the window. However, almost all the apps that come with Windows include a strip running down the left side of the window. This is the app menu, and it gives you access to a number of features, including commands, settings, and views. This menu shows only icons at first, but you can open the menu to display the names of each feature. You can then click the feature that you want to use.

Access an App's Features

Display the Menu

1 Open the app that you want to work with.

2 Click **Menu** (≡).

Ⓐ The app menu expands to show the feature names.

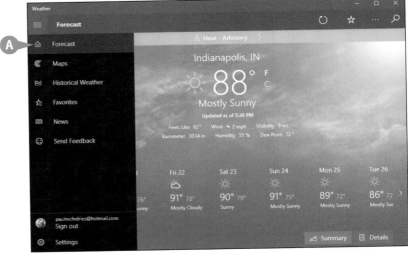

Hide the Menu

Note: If you click a menu feature, the app automatically hides the menu. You need to manually hide the menu if you decide not to select a feature.

1 Click **Menu** (≡).

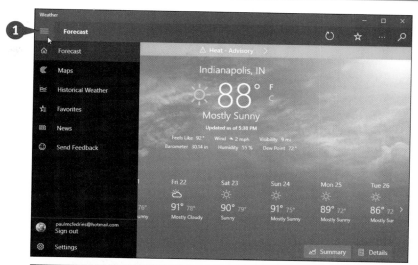

B The app hides the menu.

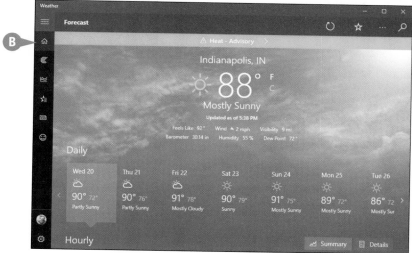

Do all apps use the Menu icon?
No. The so-called *Modern* apps that ship with Windows — including Mail, Calendar, People, Maps, News, and Weather — use the Menu icon (≡), as do some third-party apps. However, the so-called *Desktop* apps — including File Explorer, Paint, and WordPad — do not use this feature.

Are there more app features that I can access?
Yes, you can also display the Settings pane, which displays app-specific settings. The layout of the Settings pane varies between apps, but it usually includes commands for setting app preferences and options. To display an app's Settings pane, click **Menu** (≡) and then click **Settings** (⚙).

Pin an App to the Taskbar

Pinning an app to the Start menu, as described earlier in this chapter, is helpful because it puts the app just two clicks away. If you have an app that you use frequently, you might prefer to have that app just a single click away. You can achieve this by pinning the app to the taskbar. You can pin an app to the taskbar either from the Start menu or from the taskbar itself.

Pin an App to the Taskbar

Using the Start Menu

1 Click **Start** (⊞).

2 If you do not see the app you want to pin, scroll down through the All Apps list.

3 Locate the app that you want to pin to the taskbar.

4 Right-click the app.

5 Click **More**.

6 Click **Pin to taskbar**.

A An icon for the app now appears in the taskbar.

Using the Taskbar

1 Launch the app that you want to pin to the taskbar.

2 Right-click the running app's taskbar icon.

3 Click **Pin to taskbar**.

4 Click **Close** (✖).

B An icon for the app remains on the taskbar.

TIPS

Can I change the order of the taskbar icons?
Yes. Click and drag a taskbar icon to the left or right and then drop it in the new position. Note that this technique applies not only to the icons pinned to the taskbar, but also to the icons for any running programs.

How do I remove an app icon from the taskbar?
If you decide that you no longer require an app to be pinned to the taskbar, you should remove it to reduce taskbar clutter and provide more room for other app icons. To remove a pinned app icon, right-click the icon and then click **Unpin this program from taskbar**.

Adjust the Volume

While an audio or video file is playing, you can adjust the volume up or down to get its audio just right. If you are listening to media by yourself, you can adjust the volume to suit the music and your mood. However, if there are other people nearby, you will probably want to use the volume control to keep the playback volume low to avoid disturbing them. If you need to silence the media temporarily, you can mute the playback.

Adjust the Volume

1 In the taskbar, click **Volume** (◀�))).

The Volume window appears.

2 Click and drag the slider to set the volume level that you want.

Ⓐ You can also click **Mute** (◀�))) to mute the volume (◀)) changes to ◀✕).

Windows sets the system volume to the new level.

Set the Time Zone

To ensure that your system clock is accurate, you should set the time zone to correspond to your location. When Windows configures your computer, it performs a number of chores, including setting the current system time and time zone. However, for the time zone, Windows defaults to Pacific Time in North America. If this is not the time zone used where you live, you must select the correct one to ensure that you have the accurate system time.

Set the Time Zone

1 Open the Settings app.

Note: See the section "Open the Settings App" earlier in this chapter.

2 Click **Time & language**.

3 Click the **Time zone** ✓ and then click your time zone.

Windows adjusts the time to the new time zone.

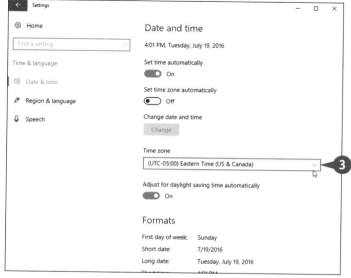

Configure Windows to Work with Multiple Monitors

You can improve your productivity and efficiency by using a second monitor. To work with an extra monitor, your PC must have a second video output port, such as VGA, DVI, or HDMI. If you do not have such a port, check with the manufacturer to see if an adapter is available that enables your PC to connect with an extra monitor.

After you have connected your PC and the external monitor, you then need to configure Windows to extend the Start screen to both the main screen and the second monitor.

Configure Windows to Work with Multiple Monitors

1 Connect the second monitor to your PC.

2 Open the Settings app.

Note: See the section "Open the Settings App" earlier in this chapter.

3 Click **System**.

The System settings appear.

4 Click **Display**.

5 Click the **Multiple displays** ⌄.

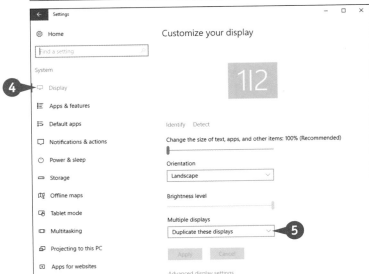

42

6 Click **Extend these displays**.

7 Click the monitor that you want to set as the main display.

8 Click **Make this my main display** (☐ changes to ☑).

9 Click **Apply**.

Windows connects to the second monitor and uses the selected monitor as your main display.

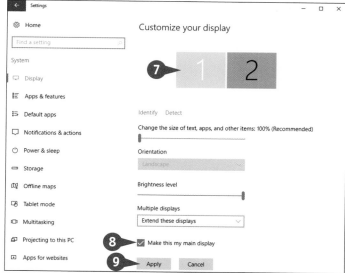

TIPS

Why does my mouse pointer stop at the right edge of the left screen?

This means that you need to exchange the icons of the left and right monitors. To do that, click and drag the left monitor icon to the right of the other monitor icon (or vice versa).

How do I configure Windows to stop using the external monitor?

Follow steps **2** to **4** in this section to open the Multiple Displays list and then click **Show only on 1**. You can also usually revert to using just the original PC screen by disconnecting the monitor from your computer.

Customize the Taskbar's Notification Area

You can customize how Windows displays the taskbar's notification area icons to ensure a particular icon is always visible or to turn off an icon's notifications.

The notification area shows only a few icons by default: Network, Volume, and Notifications, and notebook PCs also show the Power icon. You might want to customize the default arrangement. For example, many notification icons offer quick access to their programs' features when you right-click them. If there is an icon that you right-click frequently, you might want to configure the notification area to show the icon on the taskbar.

Customize the Taskbar's Notification Area

① In the taskbar's Search box, type **notification**.

② Click **Taskbar notification area**.

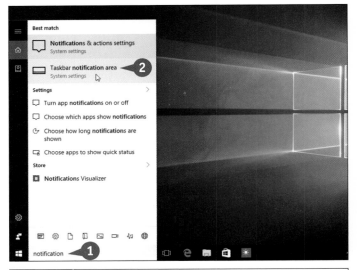

The Settings app displays the Notifications & Actions window.

③ Click **Select which icons appear on the taskbar**.

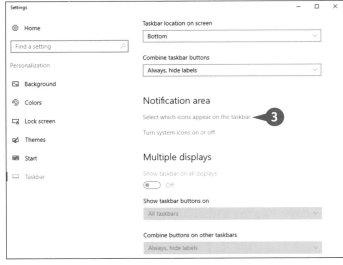

The Select Which Icons Appear on the Taskbar window appears.

④ Click the switch to **On** for each icon you want to display in the notification area.

⑤ Click **Back** (←) to return to the Notifications & Actions window.

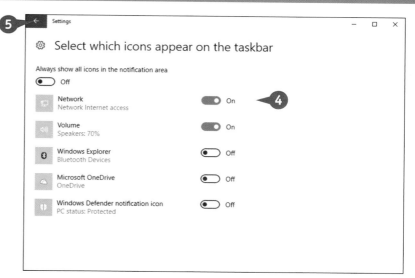

⑥ Click **Turn system icons on or off** (not shown).

⑦ Click the switch to **Off** for each system icon you want to prevent from appearing in the notification area.

Windows puts the new settings into effect.

Ⓐ You can click **Show hidden icons** (⌃) to see your hidden icons.

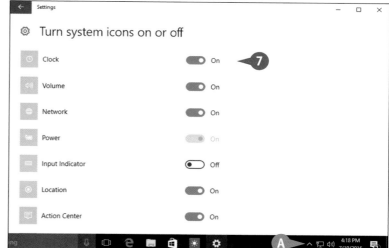

TIPS

Is there a faster way to show every icon on the taskbar?

Yes. Follow steps **1** to **3** to open the Select Which Icons Appear on the Taskbar window. Click the **Always show all icons in the notification area** switch to **On**.

Can I configure the taskbar to always appear on the screen?

Yes. The default taskbar state is hidden, and you display it by moving the mouse pointer (⌖) to the bottom of the screen. This gives you more desktop room, but if you would prefer not to perform this extra step to display the taskbar, right-click the taskbar, click **Properties**, and then click **Auto-hide the taskbar** (☑ changes to ☐). Click **OK**.

Set Up Multiple Desktops

You can make your PC screen easier to manage and less cluttered by organizing your running programs into two or more desktops. Each desktop includes only the windows of the programs that you have assigned to that desktop. For example, you might have a work desktop that includes only a word processor, a spreadsheet, and Microsoft Edge for research; a social desktop that includes only Mail, People, and Calendar; and a media desktop that includes only Music, Photos, and Videos. You can quickly switch from one desktop to another.

Set Up Multiple Desktops

Add a New Desktop

1 In the taskbar, click **Task view** (▣).

2 Click **New desktop**.

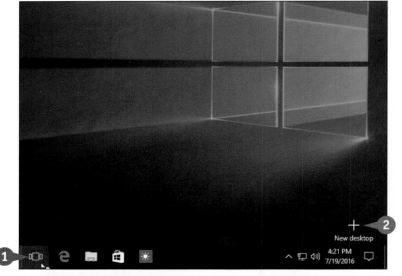

A Windows creates a new desktop.

B Your original desktop is shown as Desktop 1.

Switch to Another Desktop

1 In the taskbar, click **Task view** (▣) (not shown).

C You can position the mouse pointer (▷) over the other desktop to see the programs running within that desktop.

2 Click the desktop you want to use.

Windows switches to that desktop and displays its running programs.

Note: Any new programs you launch will now appear only in the selected desktop.

Move a Program to a Different Desktop

1 In the taskbar, click **Task view** (▣) (not shown).

2 Right-click the program you want to move.

3 Click **Move to**.

4 Click the desktop to which you want the program moved.

D You can also click **New desktop** to move the program to a new desktop.

Windows moves the program to the selected desktop.

TIPS

What shortcut methods can I use?
Press ⊞+Tab to open Task view. To switch between desktops, open Task view, press Tab to select a desktop thumbnail, use ← and → to highlight the desktop you want, and then press Enter. You can also press ⊞+Ctrl+D to create a new desktop and ⊞+Ctrl+D to close the current desktop.

How do I close a desktop?
Click **Task view** (▣) to display the desktop thumbnails. Position the mouse pointer (▷) over the desktop you want to close and then click **Close** (✕). If the desktop contained running programs, they are assigned to your original desktop.

Surfing the Web

This chapter shows you how to use Microsoft Edge (which replaces Internet Explorer in Windows 10) to navigate from site to site. You learn how to enter web page addresses, work with tabs, save your favorite sites, search for information, and more.

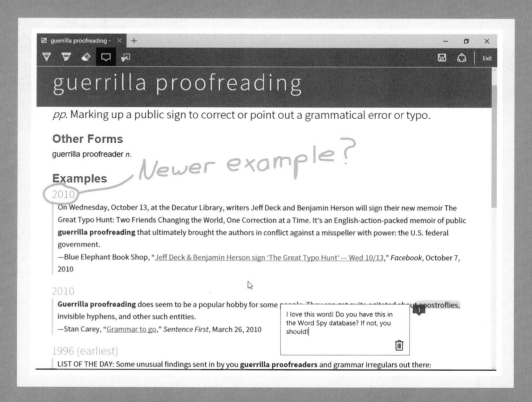

Open a Web Page

Although you usually navigate web pages by clicking links, if you know the address of a specific page, you can type it into the web browser to display it. Every web page is uniquely identified by an address composed of four basic parts: the transfer method (usually http, which stands for *Hypertext Transfer Protocol*), the website domain name, the directory where the web page is located on the server, and the web page filename. The website domain name suffix most often used is .com (commercial), but other common suffixes include .gov (government), .org (nonprofit organization), .edu (education), and country domains such as .ca (Canada).

Open a Web Page

Enter a Web Page Address

1 Click **Microsoft Edge** (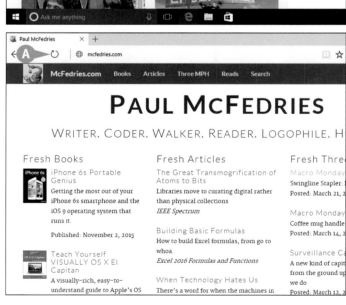).

2 Click in the address bar.

3 Type the address of the web page.

4 Click **Go** (→).

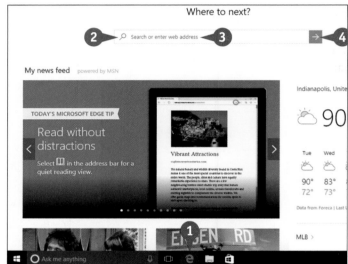

The web page appears.

A If you find that Microsoft Edge cannot display the page, this is usually a temporary glitch, so click **Refresh** (↻) to try loading the page again.

Select a Link

1 Position the mouse pointer (λ) over a link (λ changes to \Pointinghand).

Note: A link can be text or an image.

2 Click the link.

B The Status area shows the link address.

Note: The address shown in the status bar when you point at a link may be different than the one shown when the page is downloading. This happens when the website "redirects" the link, which happens often.

The linked web page appears.

C The web page title and address change after the linked page is loaded.

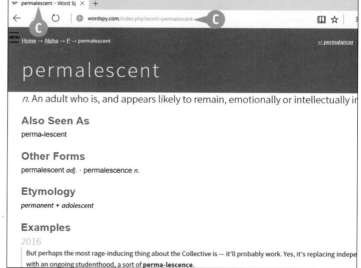

TIP

Are there any shortcuts that I can use to enter web page addresses?
Yes. Here are some useful keyboard techniques:

- After you finish typing the address, press `Enter` instead of clicking **Go** (\rightarrow).
- Most web addresses begin with *http://*. You can leave off these characters when you type your address.
- If the address uses the form http://www.*something*.com, type just the *something* part and then press `Ctrl`+`Enter`. Microsoft Edge automatically adds *http://www.* at the beginning and *.com* at the end.

Open a Web Page in a Tab

As you surf the web, you may come upon a page that you want to keep available while you visit other sites. That page may contain important information that you need to reference, or it might be a page that you want to read later on.

Instead of leaving the page and trying to find it again later, Microsoft Edge lets you keep the page open in a special section of the browser screen called a *tab*. You can use a second tab to visit your other sites and then resume viewing the first site by clicking its tab.

Open a Web Page in a Tab

Open a Web Page in a Tab

1 Right-click the link you want to open.

2 Click **Open in new tab**.

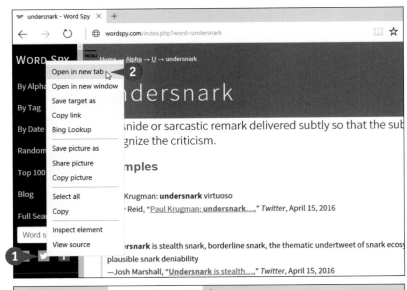

A A new tab appears with the page title.

3 Click the tab to display the page.

B You can also create a new tab by clicking **New Tab** (+).

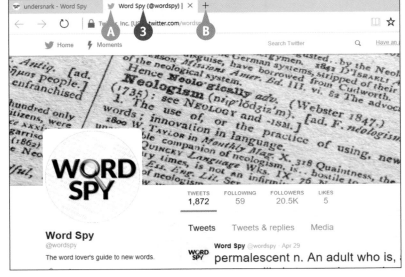

Navigate Tabs

1 Click **Scroll tab list backward**
(<) or **Scroll tab list forward**
(>) to display the tab you want.

Note: You see the tab scroll buttons only if Microsoft Edge does not have enough room to display all the tabs.

C You can hover the mouse pointer (\mathbb{k}) over a tab to see a thumbnail version of the page loaded in the tab.

2 Click the tab.

The web page loaded in the tab appears.

Close a Tab

1 Position the mouse pointer (\mathbb{k}) over the tab you want to close.

2 Click **Close Tab** (\times).

Are there any shortcuts I can use to open web pages in tabs?
Here are some useful keyboard techniques:

- Press and hold **Ctrl** and click a link to open the page in a tab.
- Press and hold **Ctrl** + **Shift** and click a link to open the page in a tab and display the tab.
- Type an address and then press **Alt** + **Enter** to open the page in a new tab.

- Press **Ctrl** + **Tab** or **Ctrl** + **Shift** + **Tab** to cycle through the tabs.
- Press **Ctrl** + **W** to close the current tab.
- Press **Ctrl** + **Alt** + **F4** to close every tab but the current one.

Navigate Web Pages

After you have visited several pages, you can return to a page that you visited earlier. Instead of retyping the address or looking for the link, Microsoft Edge gives you some easier methods.

When you navigate from page to page, you create a kind of "path" through the web. Microsoft Edge keeps track of this path by maintaining a list of the pages that you have visited. You can use that list to go back to a page. After you have gone back, you can also use that same list to go forward through the pages again.

Navigate Web Pages

Go Back

1 To go back one page, click **Back** (←).

The page appears.

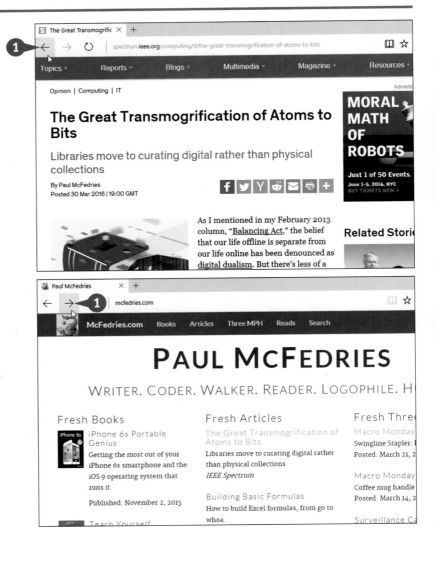

Go Forward

1 To go forward one page, click **Forward** (→).

Note: If you are at the last page viewed up to that point, Forward (→) is not active.

The page appears.

Find Text on a Page

When you are reading a page on the web, it is not unusual to be looking for specific information. In those situations, rather than read through the entire page to find the information you are looking for, you can search the web page text for the data. The Find on Page feature in Microsoft Edge lets you to do that by enabling you to search through the current page text for a specific word or phrase.

Find Text on a Page

1 Click **More** (⋯).

2 Click **Find on page**.

You can also press ⌃**Ctrl**+**F**.

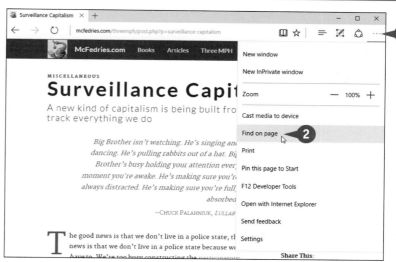

The Find on Page bar appears.

3 Type the word or phrase that you want to locate.

Ⓐ Microsoft Edge highlights the matching text on the page.

Ⓑ You can click **Next** (**>**) to cycle forward through the matches.

Ⓒ You can click **Previous** (**<**) to cycle backward through the matches.

4 When you are done, click **Close** (✕).

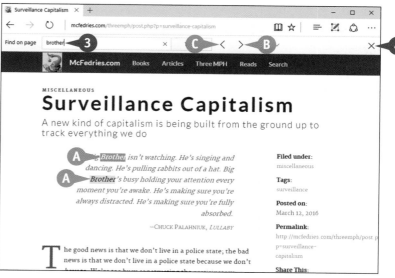

Navigate with the History List

Back and Forward (← and →) enable you to navigate pages only in the current browser session. To redisplay sites that you have visited in the past few days or weeks, you need to use the History list, which is a collection of the websites and pages you have visited over the past month.

If you visit sensitive places such as an Internet banking site or your corporate site, you can increase security by clearing the History list so that other people cannot see where you have been.

Navigate with the History List

1 Click **Hub** (≡).

2 Click **History** (🕐).

A The History list appears.

3 Click the day or week that you visited the site.

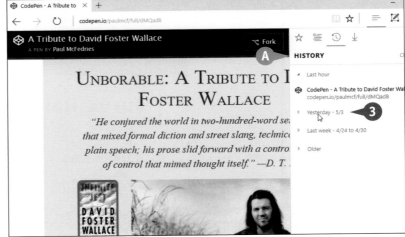

A list of pages you visited during that day or week appears.

④ Click the page you want to display.

The page appears.

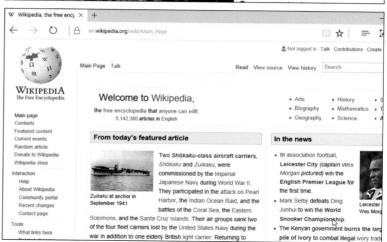

How do I clear my History list?
Follow steps **1** and **2** to display the History list and then click **Clear all history** to open the Clear Browsing Data pane. Click **Browsing history** (☐ changes to ☑). Click the other check boxes (☑ changes to ☐). Click **Clear**.

How do I clear individual pages from my History list?
Follow steps **1** and **2** to display the History list. Position the mouse pointer (��) over the page you want to clear and then click **Remove** (✕). If you want clear the history for an entire day, position the mouse pointer (��) over the day and then click **Remove** (✕).

Change Your Startup Page

Your startup page is the screen, web page, or collection of tabs that appears when you first start Microsoft Edge. The default startup page is the New Tab page, which displays a list of common sites and some suggested content. However, you can configure Microsoft Edge to open a specific web page or a collection of tabs as the startup page.

Change Your Startup Page

1 Click **More** (⋯).

2 Click **Settings**.

The Settings pane appears.

3 Click **A specific page or pages** (○ changes to ◉).

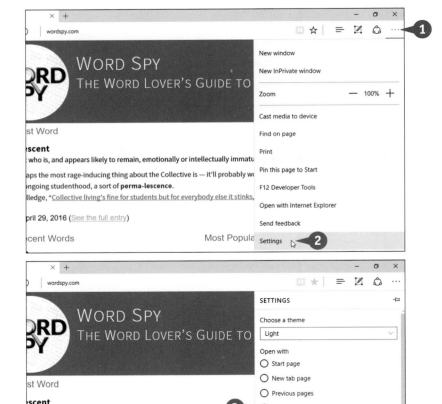

4 Click ⌄ and then click **Custom**.

5 Type the web page address.

6 Click **Add** (＋).

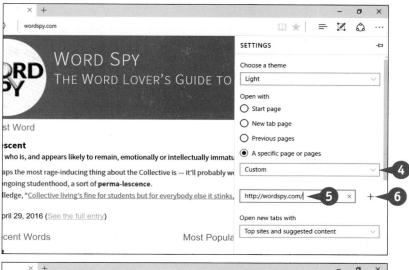

Ⓐ Microsoft Edge adds the web page to the list.

7 Repeat steps **5** and **6** to add more web pages, as needed.

Microsoft Edge displays these pages the next time you start the app.

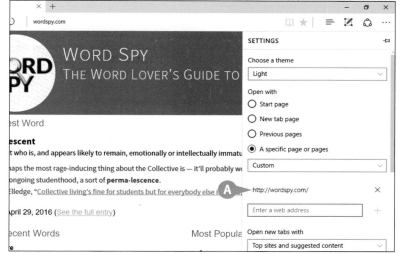

Can I get Microsoft Edge to load a tab without displaying a startup page?
Yes. Follow steps **1** and **2** to open the Settings pane. Click the **Open new tabs with** ⌄ and then click **A blank page**.

How can I get Microsoft Edge to open with the pages I was using when I last closed it?
Follow steps **1** and **2** to open the Settings pane. In the Open With section, click **Previous pages** (○ changes to ⦿). The next time you start Microsoft Edge, it will redisplay the pages you had open in tabs the last time.

Save Favorite Web Pages

If you have web pages that you visit frequently, you can save yourself time by saving those pages as favorites within Microsoft Edge. This enables you to display the pages with just a couple of clicks.

You save favorite pages in Microsoft Edge by adding them to a special section of the app called the Favorites list. Instead of typing an address or searching for one of these pages, you can display the web page by clicking it in the Favorites list.

Save Favorite Web Pages

Save a Favorite Web Page

1 Display the web page you want to save as a favorite.

2 Click **Add to favorites** (☆).

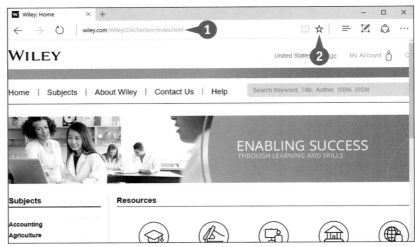

The Add to Favorites dialog box appears.

Note: You can also display the Add to Favorites dialog box by pressing <kbd>Ctrl</kbd>+<kbd>D</kbd>.

3 Click the **Favorites** tab.

4 Edit the page name, as necessary.

5 Click **Add**.

Microsoft Edge saves the web page as a favorite.

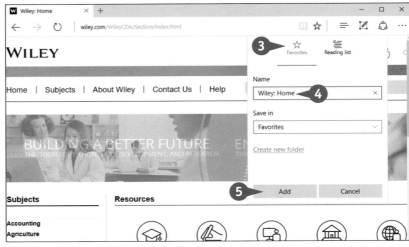

Display a Favorite Web Page

1 Click **Hub** (≡).

2 Click **Favorites** (☆).

The Favorites list appears.

3 Click the web page you want to display.

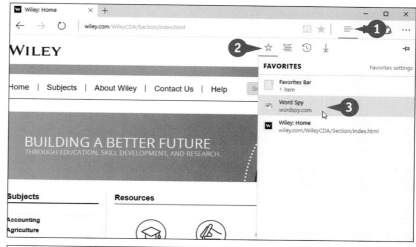

The web page appears.

A If you use your Favorites list a lot, you can make it easier to display the pages by keeping the Hub visible. Click **Hub** (≡) and then click **Pin this pane** (⊷). Microsoft Edge pins the Hub to the right side of the window.

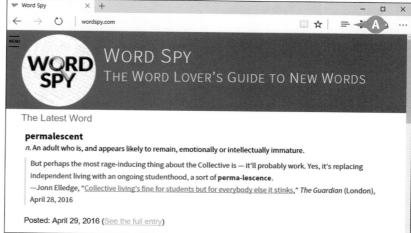

Is there an easy way to organize my favorites?
Yes, you can create Hub folders for storing related favorites. For example, you could create a folder for work, another for each of your hobbies, and so on. Follow steps **1** to **3** in the subsection "Save a Favorite Web Page" and then click **Create new folder**. Type a name for the folder and then click **Add** to save the favorite in that folder.

Can I save a page to read later when I am not online?
Yes, you can save the page to your Reading List. Follow steps **1** and **2** in the subsection "Save a Favorite Web Page" and then click **Reading List**. Edit the page name and then click **Add**. To read the page, follow steps **1** and **2** in the subsection "Display a Favorite Web Page" and then click **Reading List** (≣).

Take Advantage of the Favorites Bar

Y ou can use Microsoft Edge's Favorites bar to provide easy one-click access to those websites that you visit most often.

One of Microsoft Edge's most useful features is the Favorites bar, which appears below the address box. The Favorites bar is fully customizable, which means you can populate the Favorites bar with new buttons associated with the sites you visit most often. This section shows you how to display and populate the Favorites bar and takes you through a few Favorites bar customizations.

Take Advantage of the Favorites Bar

Display the Favorites Bar

1 Click **Hub** (≡).

2 Click **Favorites settings**.

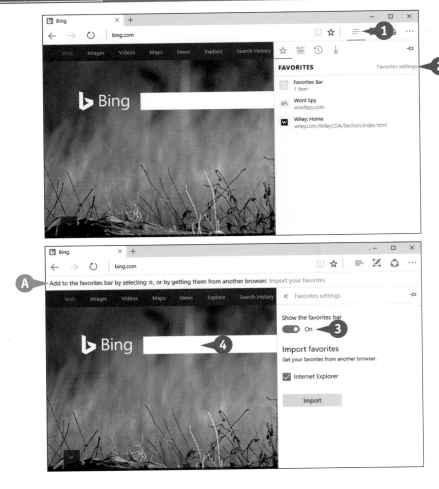

The Favorites Settings pane appears.

3 Click the **Show the favorites bar** switch to **On**.

Ⓐ Microsoft Edge displays the Favorites bar.

4 Click outside the Favorites Settings pane to close it.

Add a Web Page to the Favorites Bar

1 Navigate to the page that contains the link you want to add to the Favorites bar.

2 Click **Add to favorites** (☆).

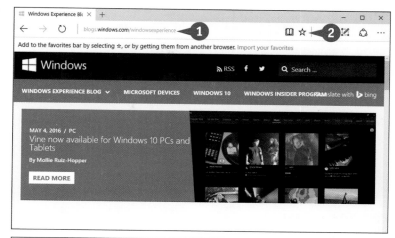

The Add to Favorites dialog box appears.

3 Edit the page name, as necessary.

4 Click the **Create in** ⌄ and then click **Favorites Bar**.

5 Click **Add**.

B Microsoft Edge adds the web page to the Favorites bar.

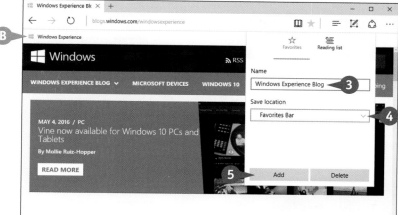

TIPS

Can I move or delete Favorites bar buttons?

Yes. To move a button, click and drag the button left or right and then drop it in the new position. To delete a button, right-click it and then click **Remove**.

How do I change the name of a button?

By default, Microsoft Edge uses the page title as the name of the Favorites bar button. If you do not like the default name, or if you would prefer something shorter or more descriptive, click **Hub** (≡), click **Favorites** (☆), and then click **Favorites Bar**. Right-click the button you want to edit, click **Rename**, type the new name, and then press **Enter**.

Create Web Notes

The Web Notes feature enables you to mark up a web page by annotating and highlighting page elements, adding your own text notes, and clipping part of the page.

When you read a paper document, you might often mark up the page with proofreading symbols, highlight passages, and add your own notes in the margins. Microsoft Edge offers Web Notes, which give you the same capabilities when you are reading a web page. These annotations are stored in Microsoft Edge, where you can view them or copy them to other apps.

Create Web Notes

Display the Web Note Tools

1 Navigate to the page you want to annotate.

2 Click **Make a Web Note** (✏️).

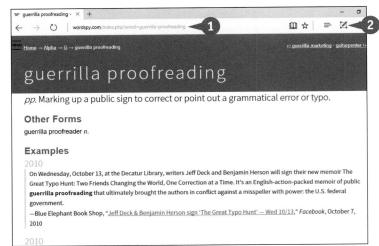

Ⓐ Microsoft Edge displays the Web Note tools.

Annotate a Web Page

1 Click the annotation tool you want to use:

Ⓑ You can click **Pen** (✏️) to draw lines or handwrite text.

Ⓒ You can click **Highlighter** (🖊️) to highlight page elements.

2 Click and drag on the page to create the annotation.

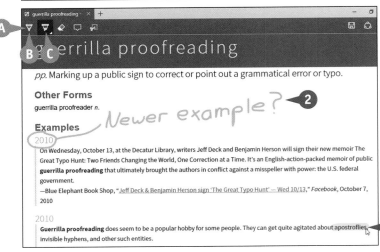

Add a Typed Note

1 Click **Add a typed note** (🖳).

2 Click the web page where you want the note to appear.

3 Type your note.

4 Click outside the text box.

Ⓓ You can click the typed note number to redisplay the text.

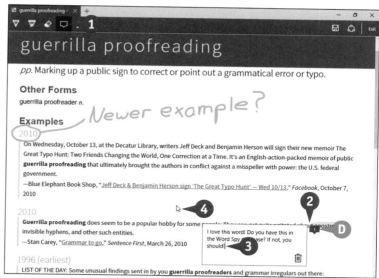

Save Your Web Notes

1 Click **Save Web Note** (🖫).

2 Click a location.

3 Fill in the note options, as needed. For example, if you are using OneNote (see Chapter 9), click ﹀ to select a section.

4 Click **Save**. If you are saving the note to Favorites, click **Add**, instead.

Microsoft Edge saves your web note to the Quick Notes section of the OneNote app.

5 Click **Exit**.

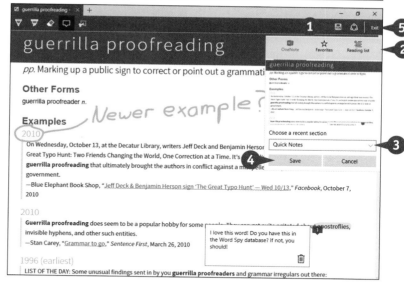

TIPS

How do I display a saved Web Note?
Microsoft Edge stores your saved Web Notes as favorites, so to display a saved Web Note, click **Hub** (≡), click **Favorites** (☆), and then click the saved note.

What is a web page clip?
A *clip* is a rectangular section of the web page that you can copy and then paste to another program, such as OneNote or Paint. To copy a clip, display the Web Note tools and then click **Clip** (🖾). Click and drag a rectangle over the area you want to save. When you release, Edge automatically copies the area.

Search for Sites

If you need information on a specific topic, Microsoft Edge has a built-in feature that enables you to quickly search the web for sites that have the information you require. The web has a number of sites called *search engines* that enable you to find what you are looking for. By default, Microsoft Edge uses the Bing search site. You use the Microsoft Edge address bar to enter a word or phrase that is representative of the information you seek. Microsoft Edge passes the word or phrase to Bing, which then looks for pages that match your text.

Search for Sites

1 Click inside the address bar.

Microsoft Edge selects the current address.

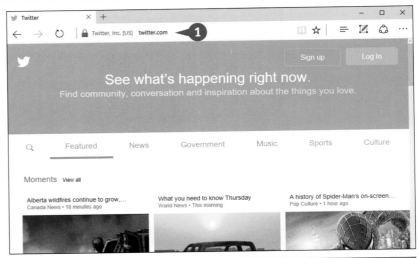

2 Type a word, phrase, or question that represents the information you want to find.

3 Press Enter.

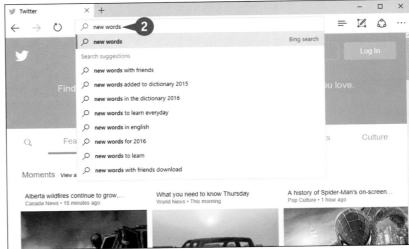

Ⓐ A list of pages that match your search text appears.

❹ Click a web page.

The page appears.

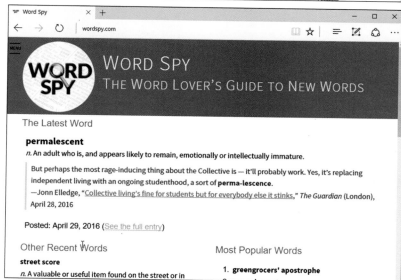

How can I get better search results?

Simple, one-word searches often return tens of thousands of *hits,* or matching sites. To improve your searching, type multiple search terms that define what you are looking for. To search for an exact phrase, enclose the words in quotation marks. If you want to find a page that includes one term or another, separate the two terms with the word OR (in capitals). If you want the results to exclude pages that contain a particular term, precede that term with a minus sign (–).

Download a File

Many websites make files available for you to use on your computer, so you need to know how to save them to your PC, a process known as *downloading*. After you have downloaded a file, you can open it on your computer as long as you have an app that can work with the type of file you downloaded. For example, if the file is an Excel workbook, you need either Excel or a compatible program. You can either open the downloaded file right away, or open it later by displaying your downloaded files.

Download a File

Download and Open a File

1 Navigate to the page that contains the link to the file.

2 Click the link to the file.

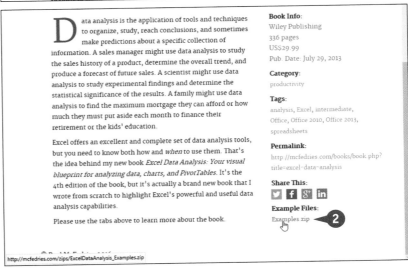

Microsoft Edge downloads the file to your PC and displays the Information bar.

3 Click **Open**.

A If you do not want to work with the file right away, you can click **Close** (**✕**), instead.

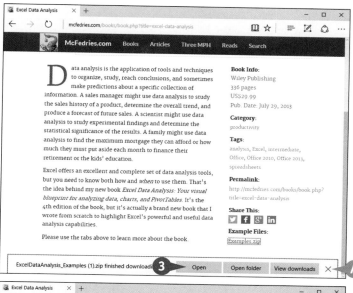

View Your Downloaded Files

1 Click **Hub** (≡).

2 Click **Downloads** (↓).

Note: If you have just downloaded a file, you can also click **View downloads** in the Information bar.

B Microsoft Edge displays the Downloads list.

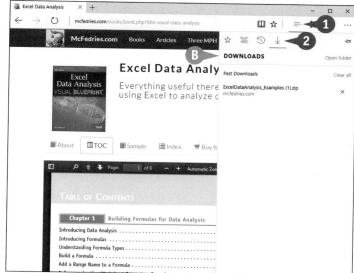

TIP

Is it safe to download files from the web?

Yes, as long as you only download files from sites you trust. If you ever notice that Microsoft Edge is attempting to download a file without your permission, cancel the download immediately because it is likely that the file contains a virus or other malware.

If you do not completely trust a file that you have downloaded, use an antivirus program, such as Microsoft Security Essentials (http://windows.microsoft.com/en-us/windows/security-essentials-download), Avast! Antivirus (www.avast.com), or AVG Internet Security (http://free.avg.com) to scan the file before you open it.

Sending and Receiving Email

You can use the Mail app to work with your email account. You can use Mail to send email messages and file attachments. You can also use Mail to receive and read incoming messages.

Configure an Email Account

Before you can send an email message, you must add your email account to the Mail application. This also enables you to use Mail to retrieve the messages that others have sent to your account.

You use Mail to set up web-based email accounts with services such as Hotmail and Gmail. Note, however, that if you are already signing in to Windows using a Microsoft account, then Windows automatically adds that account to the Mail app — so you need to follow the steps in this section only if you want to add another account to Mail.

Configure an Email Account

1 On the Start menu, click **Mail** (not shown).

Mail opens.

Note: If you are starting Mail for the first time and the app prompts you to add an account, skip to step **4**.

2 Click **Settings** (⚙).

The Settings pane appears.

3 Click **Manage Accounts**.

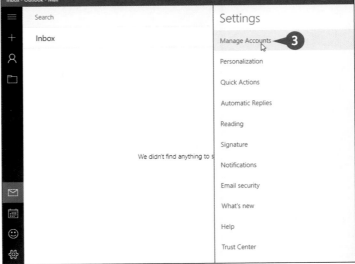

The Accounts pane appears.

4 Click **Add account**.

The Choose an Account menu appears.

5 Click the type of account that you want to add.

Mail asks for your account email address and password.

6 Type your email address.

7 Type your email password.

8 Click **Sign in**.

Mail adds your email account to the Accounts pane.

TIP

How do I add my Exchange account to Mail?
You will need to obtain from your Exchange administrator or provider the account's server address, domain name, and username — and you will need to know your account's email address and password, of course. In many cases, you can follow steps **1** to **4**. Click **Exchange** and follow steps **6** to **8**. If Mail cannot find your settings, enter your Exchange domain name and click **Sign in**. If Mail still cannot locate your account, click **Advanced**, enter the server address, and then click **Sign in**.

Send an Email Message

If you know the email address of a person or organization, you can send an email message to that address. Each address uniquely identifies the location of an Internet mailbox. An address takes the form *username@domain*, where *username* is the name of the person's account, and *domain* is the Internet name of the company that provides the person's email account.

When you send an email message, it travels through your email provider's outgoing mail server. This server routes the message to the recipient's incoming mail server, which then stores the message in the recipient's mailbox.

Send an Email Message

① In Mail, click **New mail** (▦).

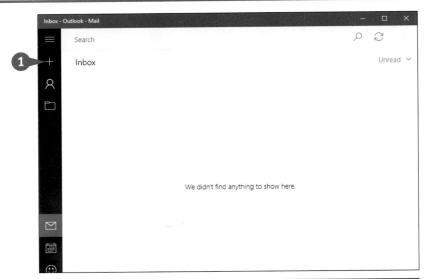

A message window appears.

② Type the email address of the recipient.

Ⓐ To send a copy of the message to another person, you can click **Cc & Bcc**, and then type that person's email address in the Cc field.

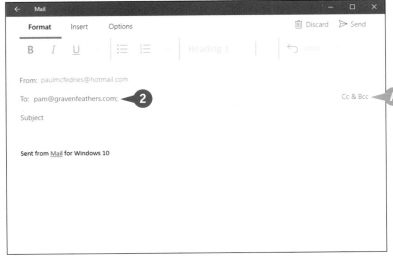

3 Type a subject for the message.

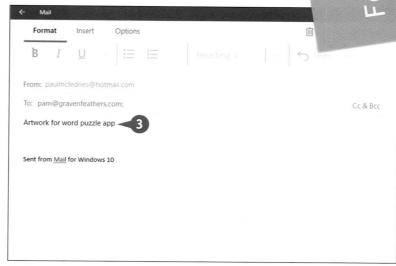

4 Type the message.

Note: See the next section, "Format the Message Text," to learn how to apply formatting to your message.

5 Click **Send**.

Mail sends your message.

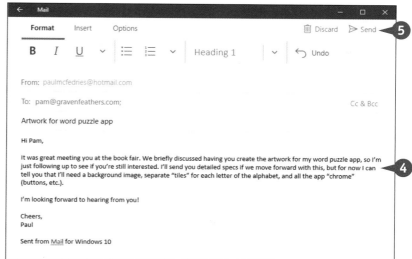

TIPS

Can I send my message to several people?
Yes. Besides adding a single address to each of the To and Cc lines, you can also add multiple email addresses to both To and Cc. After each address is complete, press Enter to begin a new line and then type the next address.

Can I send a copy to someone but not let the other recipients see that person's address?
Yes, this is known as a *blind carbon copy* (Bcc, sometimes also called a *blind courtesy copy*). To include a blind carbon copy with your message, click **Cc & Bcc** to add the Bcc field and then use that field to type the person's address.

mat the Message Text

You can add visual interest and make your message easier to read by formatting your message text. A plain email message is quick to compose, but it is often worth the extra time to add formatting to your text. For example, you can add bold or italic formatting to highlight a word or phrase. Mail supports a wide range of formatting options, including font colors, highlights, emoticons, bulleted lists, and numbered lists. All these formatting options have their place, but be careful not to overdo it, or you may make your message *harder* to read.

Format the Message Text

Format the Message Font

1 Select the text that you want to format.

2 Click the font formatting that you want to apply, such as **Bold** (**B**), **Italic** (***I***), or **Underline** (**U**).

A For more font options, you can click ✓.

Mail applies the font formatting to the text.

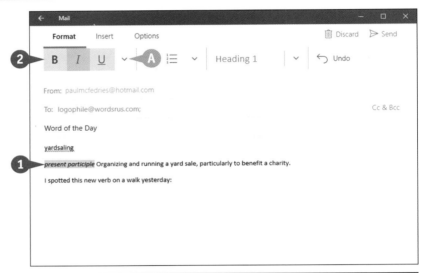

Format a Message Paragraph

1 Select the paragraph that you want to format.

2 Click the **Paragraph Formatting** ✓.

3 Click the paragraph formatting that you want to apply, such as Indents or Alignment.

B You can click **Bullets** (:≡) to convert the paragraphs to bullet points.

C You can click **Numbering** (:≡) to convert the paragraphs to a numbered list.

Mail applies the paragraph formatting to the text.

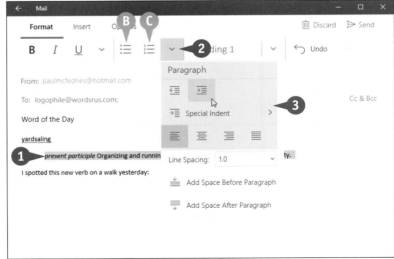

Apply a Style

① Select the text that you want to format.

② Click the **Styles** ∨.

③ Click a style.

Mail applies the style to the text.

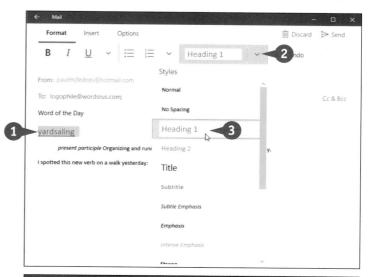

Insert a Picture

① Position the cursor where you want the picture to appear.

② Click the **Insert** tab.

③ Click **Pictures**.

The Open dialog box appears.

④ Select the location of the picture.

⑤ Click the picture.

⑥ Click **Insert**.

Mail adds the picture to the email message.

Can I make adjustments to a picture that I have inserted in my email message?

Yes. Click the picture and then click the **Picture** tab. Click **Rotate** to rotate the image, or **Crop** to crop unwanted portions of the image. You can use the sizing handles that appear around the image to adjust its size. If you are not happy with the new image dimensions, click the image, click the **Picture** tab, and then click **Reset Size**.

How do I set the message priority?

Setting the priority level of your message helps the recipient know how to handle your message. Click the **Options** tab and then click **High importance** (!) or **Low importance** (↓).

Add a File Attachment

If you have a document that you want to send to another person, you can attach the document to an email message. A typical email message is fine for short notes, but you may have something more complex to communicate, such as budget numbers or a slide show, or some form of media that you want to share, such as an image or a song. Because these more complex types of data usually come in a separate file — such as a spreadsheet, presentation file, or video file — it makes sense to send that file to your recipient as an attachment.

Add a File Attachment

1 Click the **Insert** tab.

2 Click **Files**.

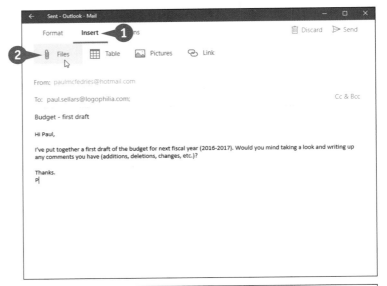

The Open dialog box appears.

3 Select the folder that contains the file you want to attach.

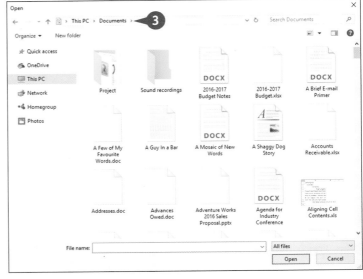

④ Click the file that you want to attach.

⑤ Click **Open**.

Ⓐ Mail attaches the file to the message.

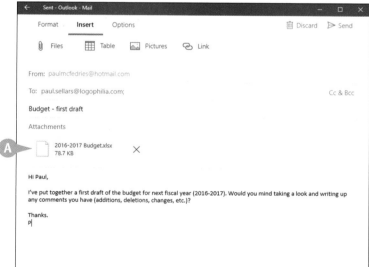

Is there a limit to the number of files that I can attach to a message?
There is no practical limit to the number of files that you can attach to a message. However, you should be careful with the total *size* of the files that you send. If you or the recipient has a slow Internet connection, sending or receiving the message can take an extremely long time. Also, many Internet service providers (ISPs) place a limit on the size of a message's attachments, which is usually between 2 MB and 10 MB. In general, use email to send only a few small files at a time.

Save a Draft of a Message

If you cannot complete or send your message right away, you can save it as a draft and open it again later. As you work on an email message, you might find that you need to give it more thought or that you have to do more research. Rather than discard your work, you can close the message and Mail will save it for you automatically. Mail stores the saved message in your account's Drafts folder. When you are ready to resume editing the message, you can open it from the Drafts folder.

Save a Draft of a Message

Save the Draft

1 Compose the message up to the point where you want Mail to save it.

2 Click **Back** (←).

Mail closes the message and saves the message to your Drafts folder.

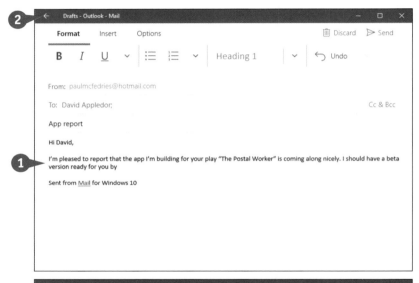

Open the Draft

1 Click **All Folders** (▣).

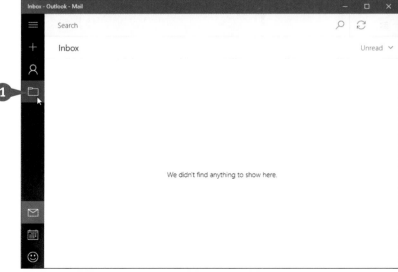

Mail displays your account folders.

2 Click **Drafts**.

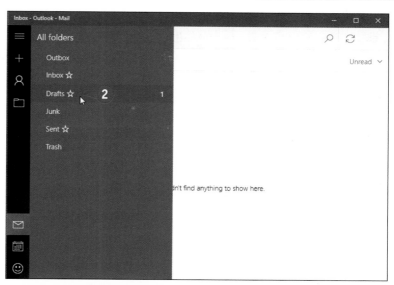

3 Click the draft that you want to open.

Mail opens the message for editing.

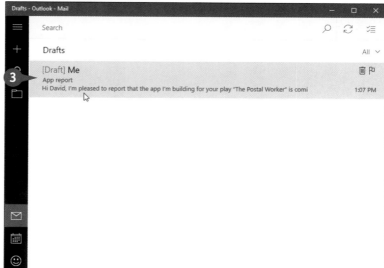

TIP

What are the other account folders used for?

Sent	Holds copies of outgoing messages that you have sent	Junk	Holds incoming messages that Mail has deemed to be unsolicited commercial emails, also known as *junk mail* or *spam*
Outbox	Holds outgoing messages that are in the process of being sent	Trash	Holds messages that you have deleted from other folders

Receive and Read Email Messages

When another person sends you an email message, that message ends up in your email account's mailbox on the incoming mail server maintained by your ISP or email provider. However, that company does not automatically pass along that message to you. Instead, you must use Mail to connect to your mailbox on the incoming mail server and then retrieve any messages waiting for you. By default, Mail automatically retrieves new messages as they arrive, but you can also check for new messages at any time.

Receive and Read Email Messages

Receive Email Messages

1 Click **Refresh** (↻).

Mail checks for new messages.

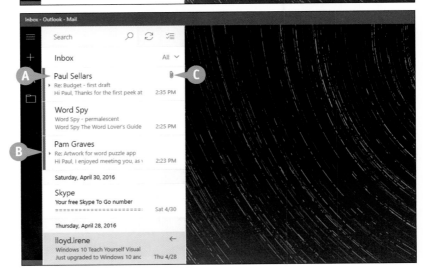

Ⓐ If you have new messages, they appear in your Inbox folder.

Ⓑ This bar appears beside messages that you have not yet read.

Ⓒ The 🔗 symbol means that the message has an attachment.

Read a Message

1 Click the message.

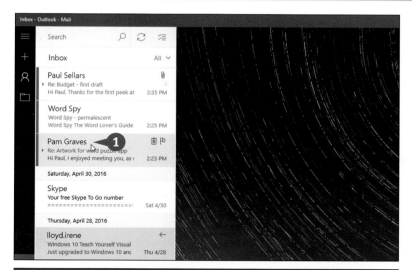

The message text appears in the preview pane.

2 Read the message text.

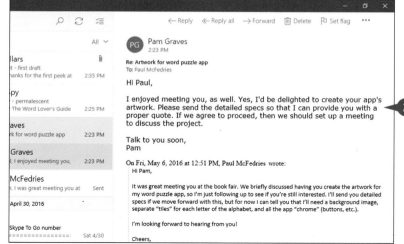

Why do new messages sometimes appear in my Inbox when I have not clicked Sync?
For certain types of accounts, Mail supports a feature called *push* that can send new messages to your Inbox automatically. In this case, when the mail server receives a new message, it immediately sends the message to your Inbox without your having to run the Sync command. Note that this feature works if you are using a Hotmail, Live.com, or Outlook.com email account, as well as a Gmail account.

Reply to a Message

When a message you receive requires some kind of response — whether it is answering a question, supplying information, or providing comments — you can reply to that message. Most replies go only to the person who sent the original message. However, you can also send the reply to all the people who were included in the original message's To and Cc lines. Mail includes the text of the original message in the reply, but you might want to edit the original message text to include only enough of the original message to put your reply into context.

Reply to a Message

1 Click the message to which you want to reply.

2 Click **Reply**.

A If you prefer to respond to all the message recipients, you can click **Reply all** instead.

Note: See the first Tip for more information.

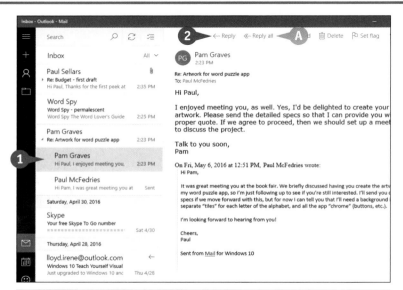

A message window appears.

B Mail automatically inserts the sender of the original message as the recipient.

C Mail also inserts the subject line, preceded by "RE:".

D Mail includes the original message's addresses (To and From), date, subject, and text at the bottom of the reply.

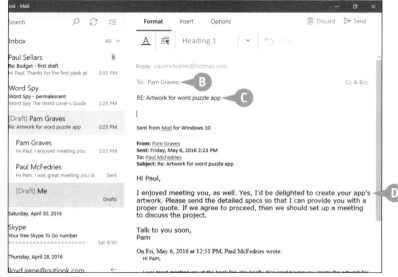

③ Edit the original message to include only the text relevant to your reply.

④ Click the area above the original message text.

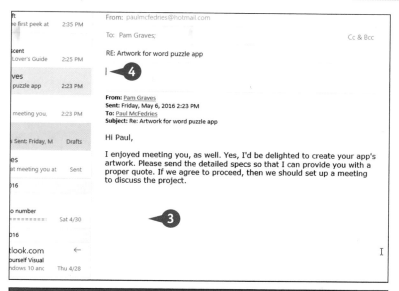

⑤ Type your reply.

⑥ Click **Send**.

Mail sends your reply.

Note: Mail stores a copy of your reply in the Sent folder.

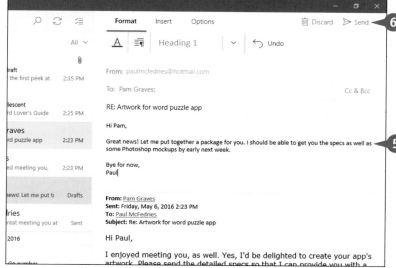

What is the difference between Reply and Reply All?

You can click **Reply** to respond only to the person who sent the message, or click **Reply all** to respond to the sender as well as any other addresses that the sender included in the original message's To and Cc fields.

Should I edit the original message text in my reply?

If the original message is short, you usually do not need to edit the text. However, if the original message is long, and your response deals only with part of that message, you will save the recipient time by deleting everything except the relevant portion of the text.

Forward a Message

If a message has information that is relevant to or concerns another person, you can forward a copy of the message to that person. You can also include your own comments in the forward.

In the body of the forward, Mail includes the original message's addresses, date, and subject line. Below this information, Mail also includes the text of the original message. In most cases, you will leave the entire message intact so that your recipient can see it. However, if only part of the message is relevant to the recipient, you should edit the original message accordingly.

Forward a Message

1 Click the message that you want to forward.

2 Click **Forward**.

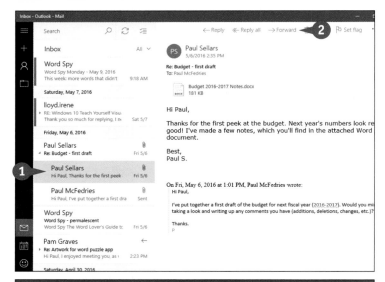

A message window appears.

Ⓐ Mail inserts the subject line, preceded by "FW:".

Ⓑ The original message's addresses (To and From), date, subject, attachments, and text are included.

3 Select or type the email address of the person to whom you are forwarding the message.

Ⓒ To send a copy of the message to another person, you can click **Cc & Bcc**, and then enter that person's email address in the Cc field.

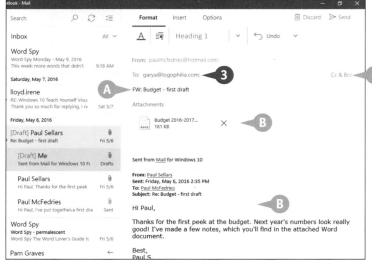

4 If necessary, edit the original message to include only the text relevant to your forward.

5 Click the area above the original message text.

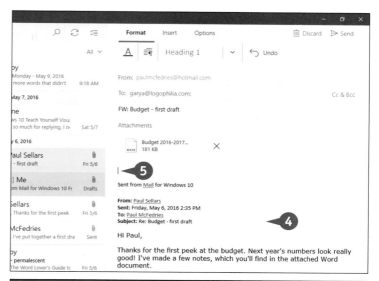

6 Type your comments.

7 Click **Send**.

Mail sends your forward.

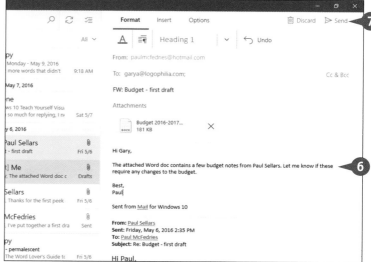

How do I view the text of a forward or reply after I have sent it?

When you send a forward or a reply (or an original message), Mail stores a copy of the message in the Sent folder. To view the message, click **All Folders** (▦) to display the All Folders list and then click **Sent**.

When I forward a message, is it possible to not include an attachment that came with the message?

Yes. After you click the message and then click **Forward**, the message attachment appears by default as part of the forwarded message. This is usually what you want, but you can remove the attachment by clicking **Remove** (✕).

Open and Save an Attachment

When a message comes in and displays the attachment symbol (a paper clip), it means that the sender has included a file as an attachment to the message. If you just want to take a quick look at the file, you can open the attachment directly from Mail. Alternatively, if you want to keep a copy of the file on your computer, you can save the attachment to your hard drive.

Be careful when dealing with attached files. Computer viruses are often transmitted by email attachments.

Open and Save an Attachment

Open an Attachment

① Click the message that has the attachment, as indicated by a paper clip (📎).

Ⓐ A list of the message attachments appears.

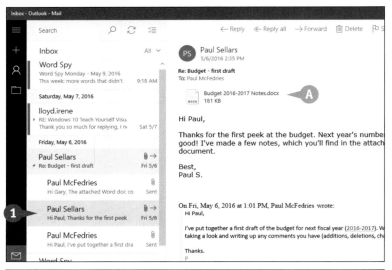

② Click the attachment that you want to open.

The file opens in the appropriate program.

Note: Instead of opening the file, you may see a message that says, "Windows can't open this type of file." This means that you need to install the appropriate program for the type of file. If you are not sure, ask the person who sent you the file what program you need.

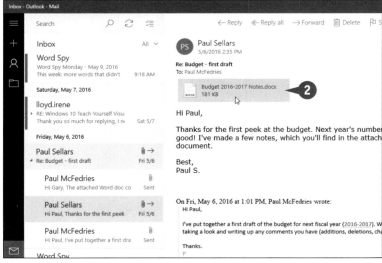

Save an Attachment

1 Click the message that has the attachment, as indicated by a paper clip (📎).

B A list of the message attachments appears.

2 Right-click the attachment that you want to save.

3 Click **Save**.

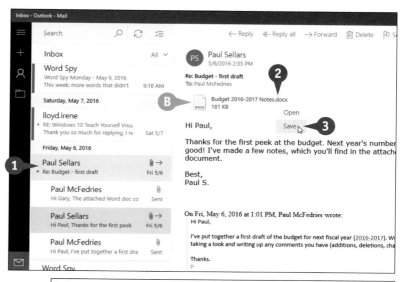

The Save As dialog box appears.

4 Click the folder where you want to store the file.

5 Edit the filename, if needed.

6 Click **Save**.

Mail saves the attachment to your PC's hard drive.

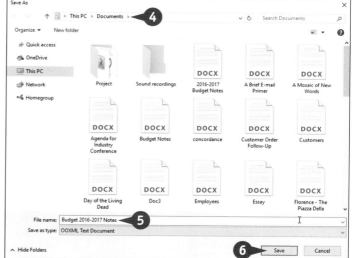

TIP

Why must I be careful when working with email attachments?

Email attachments are the most common way that nefarious users attempt to infect PCs with viruses and other malware. When you open such an attachment, the virus infects your computer and then, without your knowledge, uses your email program and your address book to send messages with more copies of itself attached. The nastier versions also mess with your computer by deleting data or corrupting files. Never open an attachment that comes from someone you do not know. If someone you know sends you an attachment unexpectedly, write that person back and confirm that he or she really did send the file.

Delete a Message

After you have used Mail for a while, you may find that you have a lot of messages in your Inbox folder. The more messages you have, the harder it becomes to find a message that you want and the more time-consuming it gets to navigate the messages. To keep the Inbox uncluttered and easier to navigate, you should delete any messages that you have already read and do not need to keep.

Note that when you delete a message, Mail actually sends it to the Trash folder. If you delete a message accidentally, you can retrieve it from the Trash folder.

Delete a Message

Delete a Message from the Inbox

1 Click the message that you want to delete.

2 Click **Delete**.

Note: If you have a tablet PC, you can also delete a message by swiping to the left across the message.

Mail removes the message from the Inbox and moves it to the Trash folder.

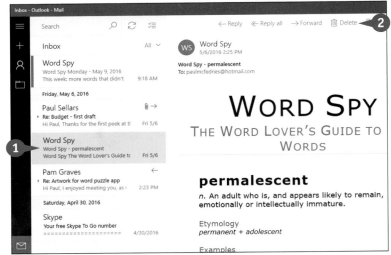

Restore a Deleted Message

1 Click **All Folders** (▣).

Mail displays the folders list.

2 Click **Trash**.

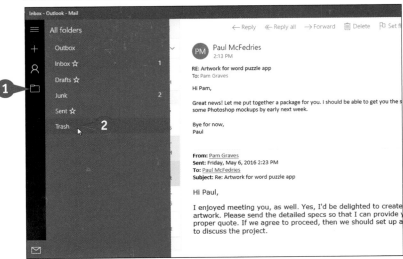

Mail opens the Trash folder.

3 Right-click the message that you want to restore.

4 Click **Move**.

Mail displays a list of folders.

5 Click **Inbox**.

Mail restores the message to the Inbox folder.

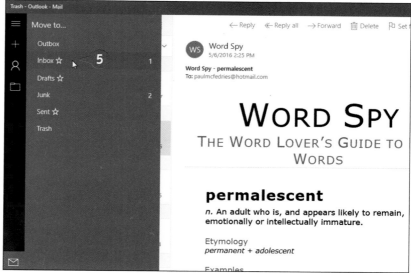

TIP

Can I remove a message permanently?

Yes, as long as you are sure you will never need to work with the message again, you can delete it permanently from your account. However, this operation is not reversible, so you really need to be certain that you no longer need the message.

Follow steps **1** and **2** in the subsection "Restore a Deleted Message" to open the Trash folder, right-click the message you want to remove, and then click **Delete**. Mail removes the message permanently from your account.

Create a Folder for Saving Messages

After you have used Mail for a while, you may find that you have a lot of messages in your Inbox folder. To keep the Inbox uncluttered, you can create new folders and then move messages from the Inbox to the new folders.

To help keep your messages organized, you should use each folder you create to save related messages. For example, you could create separate folders for people you correspond with regularly, projects you are working on, different work departments, and so on. By saving each message to the appropriate folder, you make it easier to find your messages in the future.

Create a Folder for Saving Messages

Create a Folder

1 Use a web browser to navigate to http://mail.live.com and sign in to your account.

2 Click **New folder**.

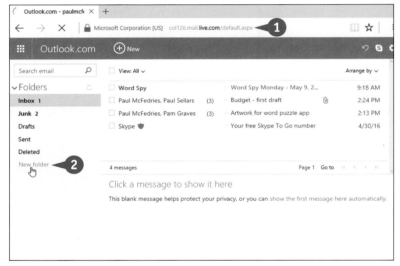

You are prompted to enter the folder name.

3 Type the name of the new folder.

4 Press `Enter` or click outside the text box.

The new folder is created.

Note: It might take a few minutes before the new folder appears in the Mail app.

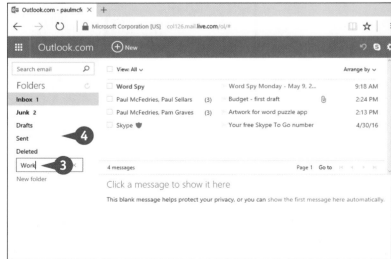

Move a Message to Another Folder

1 In Mail, right-click the message you want to move.

2 Click **Move**.

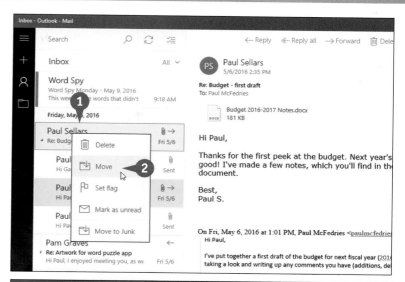

Mail displays the list of folders.

3 Click the folder you want to use as the destination.

Mail moves the message.

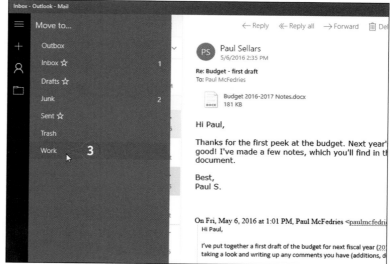

How do I rename a folder?

Use a web browser to sign in to your account. In the Folders list, right-click the folder you want to rename and then click **Rename**. In the text box, type the new name and then either press Enter or click outside the text box. You can rename only folders that you have created.

How do I delete a folder?

Use a web browser to sign in to your account. In the Folders list, right-click the folder you want to remove and then click **Delete**. You can delete only folders that you have created. When you delete a folder, you also delete any messages stored in that folder.

Configure Mail Options

The Mail app comes with a few options that you can configure to make the program suit the way you prefer to work. Several of these options are related to how you use swipe gestures in the Mail app, if you are running Windows on a touch PC or tablet. You can also configure the Mail app background image and whether the app displays notifications. Finally, you can also customize the signature text that appears in the body of the messages you create as well as in the replies and forwards you send.

Configure Mail Options

1 Click **Settings** (⚙).

The Settings pane appears.

2 To change the Mail app background image, click **Personalization**.

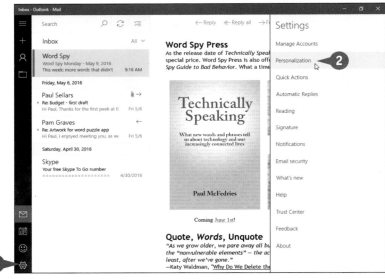

Mail displays the Personalization pane.

3 Click **Browse**.

The Open dialog box appears.

4 Click the image.

5 Click **Open**.

Ⓐ Alternatively, you can click one of the predefined images.

6 Click **Back** (❮) to return to the Settings pane.

7 Click **Reading** (not shown).

The Reading pane appears.

8 If you click the **Auto-open next item** switch to **On**, Mail automatically opens the next message after you use a swipe gesture to delete a message.

9 In the Mark Item as Read section, click an option to specify when Mail marks a message as having been read (○ changes to ◉).

10 Click **Back** (‹) to return to the Settings pane.

11 Click **Quick Actions** (not shown).

The Quick Actions pane appears.

12 If you do not want to use gestures on a tablet, click the **Swipe actions** switch to **Off**.

13 Click the **Swipe right / hover** ⌄ and click the action that Mail performs when you swipe right on a message.

14 Click the **Swipe left / hover** ⌄ and click the action that Mail performs when you swipe left on a message.

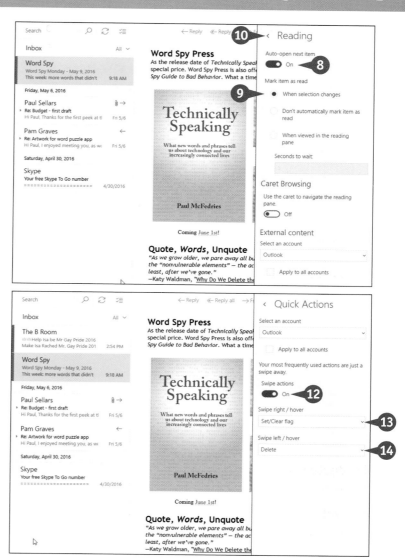

What is a flag?

A *flag* is an indicator that you can add to a message by clicking the message and then clicking **Flag**. Mail adds a flag icon (⚑) to the message, which serves as a visual reminder. This is useful if you need a prompt to follow up with a message or to perform some other action based on that message.

How can I add a signature?

A *signature* is a snippet of text that appears at the bottom of any message that you send, including original messages, replies, and forwards. To add a signature, click **Settings** (⚙), click **Signature**, click the **Use an email signature** switch to **On**, and then edit the signature.

Getting Social with Windows

You can use Windows to manage your social schedule. You can use the People app to store contact information, connect to social networks, and keep track of friends. You can use the Calendar app to schedule meetings, appointments, and other events.

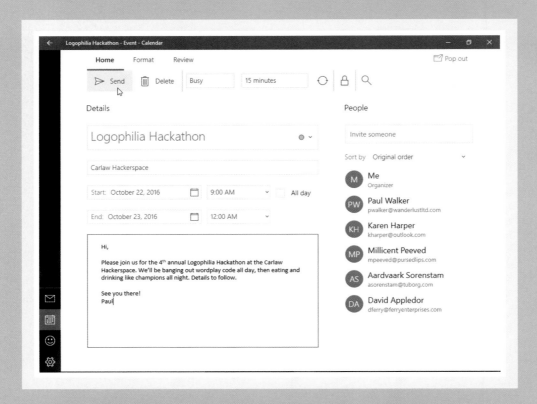

Create a Contact

You can easily store information about your friends, family, and colleagues, as well as send messages to them, by using the People app to create a contact for each person. Each contact can store a wide variety of information, such as a person's first and last names, company name, email address, phone number, and street address.

If you already have contacts on a social network such as Facebook or LinkedIn, you do not need to enter those contacts manually. Instead, you can connect your social network account to your Microsoft account, as described in the next few sections.

Create a Contact

1 Click **Start** (⊞).

2 Click **People**.

The People app loads.

3 Click **Add contact** (+).

The New Contact screen appears.

4 Type the contact's name.

5 Click the **Phone** ⌄ and then click the type of phone number that you want to enter.

6 Type the contact's phone number.

Ⓐ You can click **Add** (+) to add another phone number.

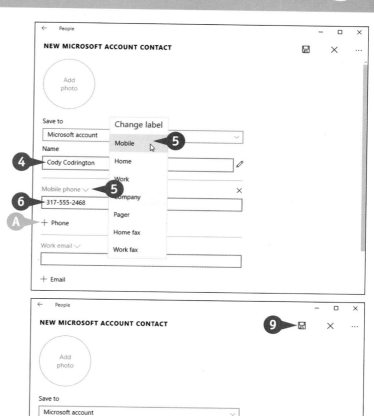

7 Click the **Email** ⌄ and then click the type of email address that you want to enter.

8 Type the contact's email address.

Ⓑ You can click the **Email** + to add another email address.

9 Click **Save** (💾).

The People app creates the new contact.

Is there an easy way to send an email to a contact?
Yes. Normally, you would use the Mail app, as described in Chapter 4. If you are already working in the People app, however, it is easier to click the person's entry in the Contacts list to open the contact and then click the email address you want to use.

How do I record a contact's physical address?
With the new contact open for editing, click the **Address** + and then click the label you want for the address. In the text boxes that appear, type the contact's Street address, City, State/province, Zip/postal code, and Country/region.

Add Your Google Account

You can add your Google account to Windows to access your Google contacts (as well as your Google calendar and email) from your Windows computer. To do so, you must provide Windows with your Google account login data.

After you have added your Google account, you can use the People app to view your Google contacts. You can use the Calendar app to view your Google events and appointments, and you can use the Mail app to view your Gmail messages.

Add Your Google Account

1 In the People app, click **More** (⋯).

2 Click **Settings**.

The Settings screen appears.

3 Click **Add an account**.

4 Click **Google**.

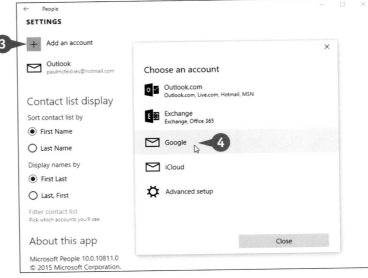

The People app prompts you for your Google login data.

5 Type your Google email address.

6 Click **Next**.

7 Type your Google password.

8 Click **Sign in**.

The People app shows you what it will do with your Google data.

9 Click **Allow**.

Windows connects your Google account to your Microsoft account.

10 Click **Done** (not shown).

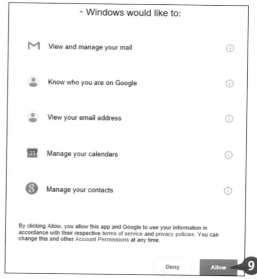

TIP

Can I control what type of Google content appears in Windows?
Yes, you can configure the type of content to sync between Google and Windows and how often that content syncs. In the People app, click **More** (⋯), click **Settings**, click **Gmail**, and then click **Change mailbox sync settings**. People displays the Gmail Sync Settings dialog box. Click the **Sync contacts and calendars** ⌄ and then click how often you want Windows to sync your Google data. In the Sync Options group, use the **Email**, **Calendar**, and **Contacts** switches to toggle each type of content on or off.

Add Your iCloud Account

You can add your iCloud account to Windows to access your iCloud contacts (as well as your iCloud calendar and email) from your Windows computer. To do so, you must provide Windows with your iCloud account login data.

After you have added your iCloud account, you can use the People app to view your iCloud contacts. You can use the Calendar app to view your iCloud events and appointments, and you can use the Mail app to view your iCloud messages.

Add Your iCloud Account

1 In the People app, click **More** (⋯).

2 Click **Settings**.

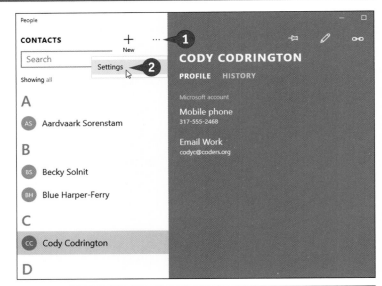

The Settings screen appears.

3 Click **Add an account**.

4 Click **iCloud**.

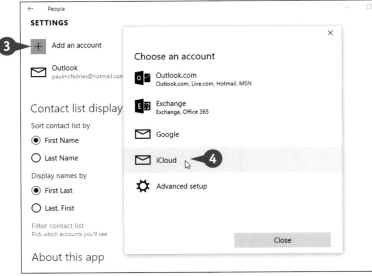

The People app prompts you for your iCloud login data.

5 Type your iCloud email address.

6 Type your iCloud password.

7 Click **Sign in**.

Windows connects your iCloud account to your Microsoft account.

8 Click **Done**.

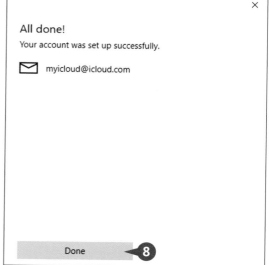

TIP

Can I control what type of iCloud content appears in Windows?

Yes, you can configure the type of content to sync between iCloud and Windows and how often that content syncs. In the People app, click **More** (···), click **Settings**, click **iCloud**, and then click **Change mailbox sync settings**. People displays the iCloud Sync Settings dialog box. Click the **Sync contacts and calendars** ⌄ and then click how often you want Windows to sync your iCloud data. In the Sync Options group, use the **Email**, **Calendar**, and **Contacts** switches to toggle each type of content on or off.

View a Contact

After you have added contacts and connected your other accounts to Windows, you can use the People app to view your contacts. The information that you see when you view a contact depends on how the contact was added to Windows. If you added the contact yourself, you see the information that you entered. If the contact was added by connecting another account to Windows, you see the data provided by that account. If you have many contacts, you can also use the People app's Search feature to locate the contact you want to view.

View a Contact

View a Contact

1 In the People app, scroll the Contacts list up or down to locate the contact you want to view.

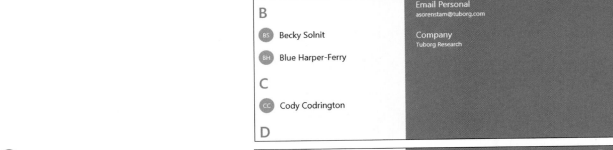

2 Click the contact.

A The People app displays the contact's data.

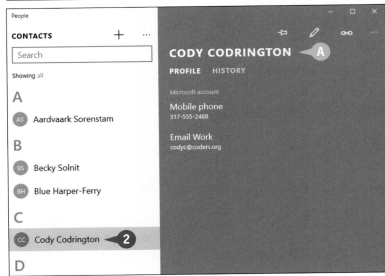

Search for a Contact

1. Click in the People app's Search box.

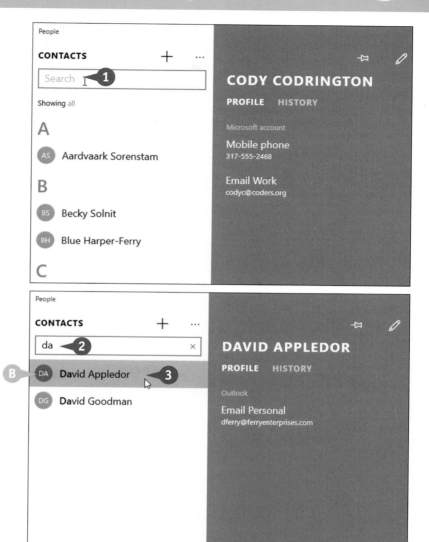

2. Begin typing the name of the contact you want to view.

B. People displays a list of contacts with names that match your typing.

3. When you see the contact you want to view, click the name in the search results.

 The People app saves the updated data.

Is there an easier way to navigate the Contacts list?
Yes. Click any of the letters that the People app uses to divide the Contacts list alphabetically. This converts the Contacts list to a grid of letters and you then click the letter you want to view.

How do I delete a contact?
If you no longer need a contact, you should delete it from the People app to reduce clutter in the Contacts list. First, use either of the techniques outlined in this section to locate the contact you want to remove. Right-click the contact and then click **Delete**. When the People app asks you to confirm, click **Delete**.

Edit a Contact

If you need to make changes to the information already in a contact, or if you need to add new information to a contact, you can edit the contact from within the People app. While editing a contact, you can modify the existing information, add new information to the contact, or delete existing information.

Edit a Contact

1 In the People app, click the contact you want to edit.

2 Click **Edit** (✐).

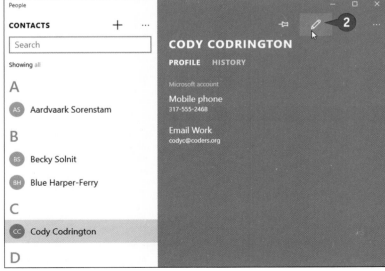

People makes the contact's fields available for editing.

③ Edit the existing fields as required.

④ To add a field, click the ✚ beside the field type you want to use and then type the data.

⑤ To remove a field, position the mouse pointer (⌖) over the field and then click **Remove** (✕).

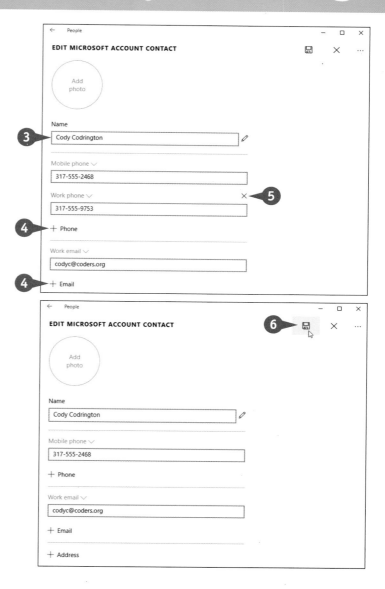

⑥ When you complete your edits, click **Save** (🖫).

People saves the edited contact.

TIP

Can I add other more detailed name data for a contact?
Yes, the People app offers multiple name fields: First Name, Last Name, Middle Name, Nickname, Title, Suffix, Phonetic First Name, and Phonetic Last Name. To specify any of this data, follow steps **1** and **2** to open the contact for editing, and then click **Edit** (✎) beside the Name field. In the Edit Name dialog box that appears, fill in the name fields as needed and then click **Done**.

Assign a Photo to a Contact

You can add visual interest to the People app and make it more useful by assigning photos to your contacts. By default, the People app shows a standard image for each contact. For your Microsoft account, that image is a generic headshot, but other accounts have different images. For example, Google's images consist of just the contact's initials. Assigning photos not only improves the look of the People app, but it also helps you remember your contacts, particularly if they are business colleagues or similar acquaintances that you do not see very often.

Assign a Photo to a Contact

1 In the People app, click the contact you want to work with.

2 Click **Edit** ().

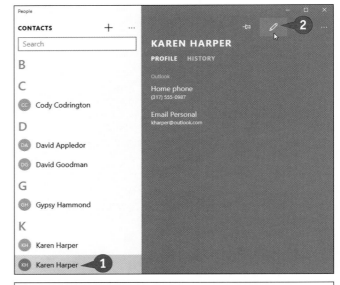

People opens the contact for editing.

3 Click **Add photo**.

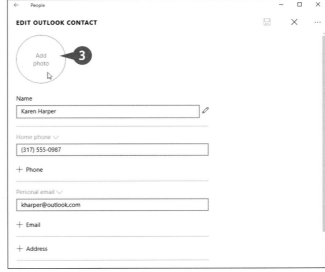

A version of the Photos app displays your photos.

4 Click the photo you want to add.

People prompts you to choose the area of the photo that you want to use for the contact.

5 Click and drag the photo to set the area you want to use within the circle.

6 Click and drag any of the four handles to set the size of the circle.

7 Click **Apply** (☑).

People adds the photo to the contact.

8 Click **Save** (💾).

People saves the edited contact.

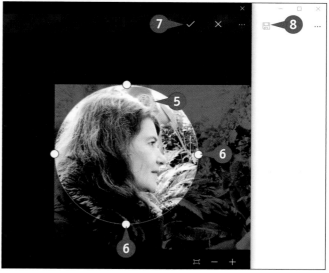

How do I change a contact's photo?

Follow steps **1** and **2** to open the contact for editing, and then click the existing photo to open the Photos app and see your photos. Click the new photo you want to use and then follow steps **5** to **8** to set the photo position and size and save your changes.

How do I remove a contact's photo?

If you no longer want to use a photo for a contact, you can delete it. Follow steps **1** and **2** to open the contact for editing. Right-click the existing photo and then click **Delete photo**. People removes the photo from the contact. Click **Save** (💾) to preserve your changes.

Add Extra Fields to a Contact

The People app offers several other fields that you can add to a contact to store more data about that person or company. The default editing screen shows only a few field types: Name, Phone, Email, and Address. However, People also supports many other field types that enable you to store data such as the contact's website address, company name, job title, and office location. You can also save personal data such as the name of the contact's significant other and the contact's birthday and anniversary. Finally, you can also add a Notes field to hold any other required data.

Add Extra Fields to a Contact

1 In the People app, click the contact you want to edit.

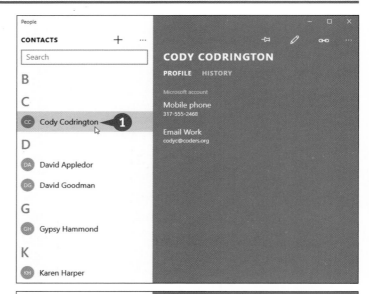

2 Click **Edit** ().

People makes the contact's fields available for editing.

3 Click the **Other** +.

4 Click the type of field you want to add.

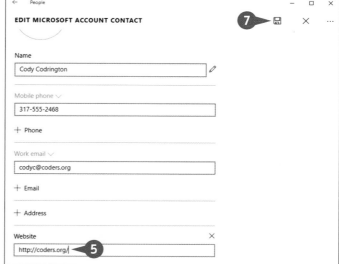

5 Fill in the data for the new field.

6 Repeat steps **3** to **5** to add extra fields as needed.

7 When you complete your edits, click **Save** (💾).

People saves the edited contact.

Is there a way to add a contact's website without having to memorize a long address?
Yes, you can copy the address from the Microsoft Edge web browser. In the taskbar, click **Microsoft Edge** (🔵) and then navigate to the contact's website. In the address bar, right-click the address, click **Select All**, and then either press Ctrl + C or right-click the selected address and then click **Copy**. Switch to the People app, follow steps **1** to **4** to add the Website field, click inside the field, and then either press Ctrl + V or right-click the field and then click **Paste**.

Filter the Contacts List

Y ou can make a long Contacts list easier to navigate and manage by filtering it to hide certain contacts. For example, if you mostly use People to locate contacts for phone calling or text messaging, you can filter the Contacts list to hide all those contacts who do not have a phone number. Similarly, if you have multiple accounts added to the People app, you might find that this creates many duplicate entries. You can fix this problem by filtering the Contacts list to hide all contacts from a particular account.

Filter the Contacts List

Hide Contacts Without Phone Numbers

1 In the People app, scroll to the top of the Contacts list.

2 Click **all**.

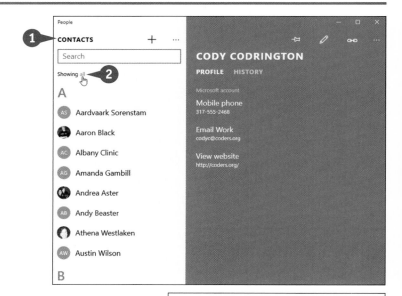

The Filter Contacts dialog box appears.

3 Click the **Hide contacts without phone numbers** switch to **On**.

4 Click **Done**.

People only shows those contacts who have at least one phone number.

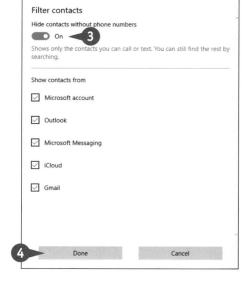

Hide Contacts by Account

1 In the People app, scroll to the top of the Contacts list.

2 Click **all**.

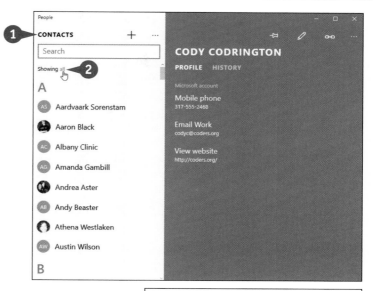

The Filter Contacts dialog box appears.

3 Click the account you want to hide (☑ changes to ☐).

4 Click **Done**.

People hides the contacts from the account you deselected in step **3**.

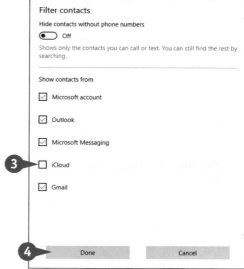

TIP

How do I remove an account from the People app?

If you find that you do not use the contacts from a particular account, or if a particular account contains all or mostly duplicate contacts of another account, you might prefer to remove that account entirely instead of just hiding it. Note, however, that removing an account also removes that account's email from the Mail app and its calendars from the Calendar app.

If you still prefer to remove the account, click **More** (⋯) and then click **Settings**. Click the account you want to remove and then click **Delete account**. When People asks you to confirm, click **Delete**.

Link Multiple Profiles for a Contact

Y ou can make your Contacts list more manageable and more useful by linking two or more contacts that are profiles of the same person. When you add multiple accounts to the People app, you might end up with the same contact listed two or more times. If those profiles contain different data — for example, one might contain personal information, whereas the other contains work information — it is a hassle to try to remember which is which. A better alternative is to link those profiles, which tells People to display all the contact's data in a single profile.

Link Multiple Profiles for a Contact

1 In the People app, click one of the profiles that you want to link.

2 Click **Link** (⚭).

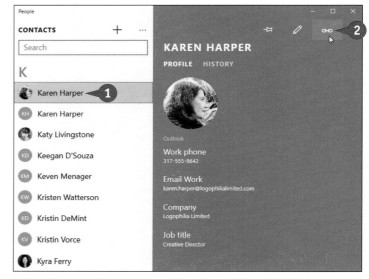

The Links for *Contact* screen appears (where *Contact* is the name of the contact you clicked in step **1**).

3 Click **Choose a contact to link**.

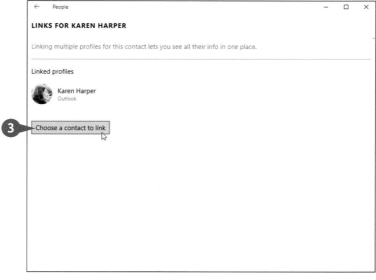

The Choose a Contact dialog box appears.

④ Click the contact you want to link.

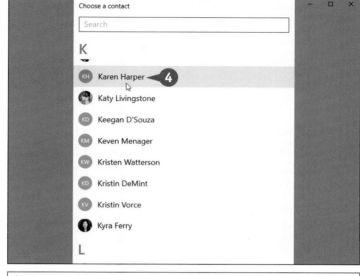

People links the contacts and returns you to the Links for *Contact* screen.

Ⓐ The linked contacts appear here.

⑤ Click **Back** (←) to return to the Contacts list.

The contact's Link icon (⊶) now displays the number of linked profiles.

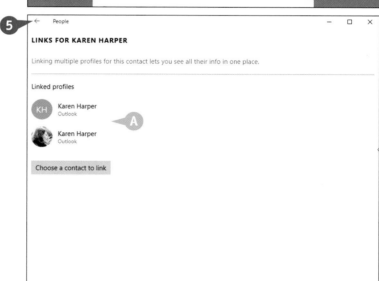

Can I remove a linked profile from a contact?

Yes. In some cases, you might find that you prefer to keep two separate profiles for a particular contact. For example, if you have separate business and personal profiles for a contact and both those profiles contain a great deal of information, you might find that the combined profile is too confusing or cluttered.

To unlink a profile from a contact, click the contact and then click **Link** (⊶). In the Links for *Contact* screen, click the linked profile that you want to remove. When People asks you to confirm, click **Unlink**.

View Your Calendar

Windows comes with a Calendar app to enable you to manage your schedule. To create an event such as an appointment or meeting, or an all-day event such as a conference or trip, you select the date when the event occurs.

Calendar lets you change the calendar view to suit your needs. For example, you can show just a single day's worth of events if you want to concentrate on that day's activities. Similarly, you can view a week's or a month's worth of events if you want to get a larger sense of what your overall schedule looks like.

View Your Calendar

View Events by Month

1 In the Start menu, click **Calendar** (not shown).

Note: When you first start Calendar, if Windows asks if the app can use your location, click **No**.

2 Click **Month**.

Your calendar for the month appears.

3 Click ∧ and ∨ to navigate the months.

Note: On a touchscreen PC, you navigate the months by swiping up and down on the screen.

View Events by Week

1 Click **Week**.

Ⓐ To see just Monday through Friday, you can click **Work week** instead.

Your events for the week appear.

2 Click ‹ and › to navigate the weeks.

Note: On a touchscreen PC, you navigate the weeks by swiping left and right on the screen.

View Events by Day

1 Click **Day**.

The events for a single day appear.

2 Click **<** and **>** to navigate the days.

Note: On a touchscreen PC, you navigate the days by swiping left and right on the screen.

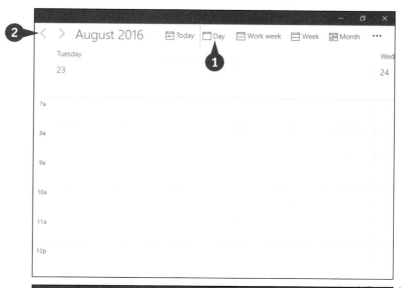

View Today's Events

1 Click **Today**.

Calendar navigates the current view to include today's date.

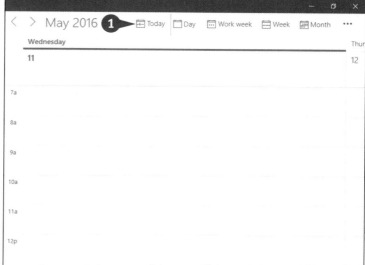

TIP

Are there any techniques that I can use to navigate the calendar?
Yes, you can use the mini calendar that appears on the left side of the Calendar window. If you do not see the mini calendar, click **Menu** (☰) in the upper-left corner of the Calendar window. Position the mouse pointer (⇩) over the mini calendar and then click ⌃ and ⌄ to navigate the months. (On a touchscreen PC, you navigate the months by swiping up and down on the mini calendar.) Then click the day you want to view.

Add an Event to Your Calendar

You can help organize your life by using the Calendar app to record your upcoming events — such as appointments, meetings, phone calls, and dates — on the date and time that they are scheduled to occur.

If the event has a set time and duration — for example, a meeting or a lunch date — you add the event directly to the calendar as a regular appointment. If the event has no set time — for example, a birthday, anniversary, or multiple-day event such as a sales meeting or vacation — you can create an all-day event.

Add an Event to Your Calendar

1 In the Calendar app, navigate to the date when the event occurs.

2 Click the time when the event starts.

Note: If you are currently in Month view, click the day the event occurs.

3 Type a name for the event.

4 Type the event location.

5 Click **More details**.

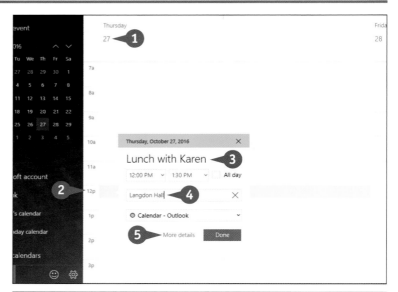

Calendar displays the event details screen.

6 If the start date and/or time is incorrect, use the Start controls to select the correct start time.

7 If the end date and/or time is incorrect, use the End controls to select the correct end time.

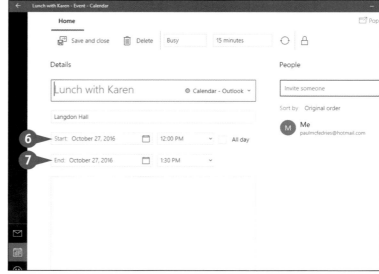

8 Use the large text area to type notes related to the event.

9 Click **Save and close**.

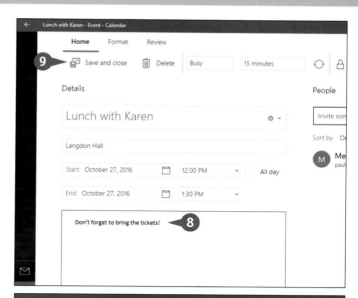

A Calendar adds the event to your schedule.

To make changes to the event, you can click it.

Create a Recurring Event

If you have an activity or event that recurs at a regular interval, you can create an event and configure it to automatically repeat in the Calendar app. This saves you from having to repeatedly add the future events manually because Calendar adds them for you automatically.

You can repeat an event daily, weekly, monthly, or yearly. If your activity recurs every day only during the workweek, such as a staff meeting, you can also set up the event to repeat every weekday.

Create a Recurring Event

1 Follow the steps in the previous section, "Add an Event to Your Calendar," to create an event.

2 Click **Repeat** (◯).

3 Click ✓ and then click the repeat interval that you want to use.

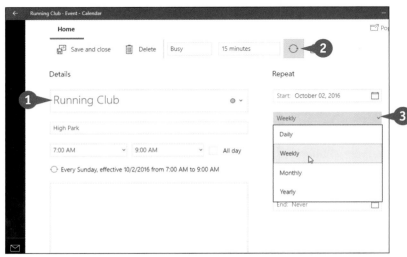

A You might also be able to further refine your choice, such as choosing the specific day of the week for the Weekly interval.

4 If needed, use the End calendar control to select the last recurrence.

5 Click **Save and close**.

Calendar adds the future events using the interval that you specified.

Note: To edit a recurring event, right-click it and then click either **Edit occurrence** to edit just that occurrence or **Edit series** to edit every occurrence.

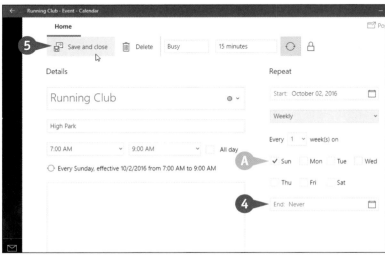

Add an Event Reminder

You can help make sure that you never miss a meeting, appointment, or other event by setting up the Calendar app to remind you before the event occurs. A *reminder* is a notification message that Windows displays at a specified time before the event occurs. By default, Calendar adds a 15-minute reminder to each event, but you can change that to a more suitable interval.

Add an Event Reminder

1 Follow the steps in the section "Add an Event to Your Calendar," earlier in this chapter, to create an event.

2 Click the **Reminder ⌄**.

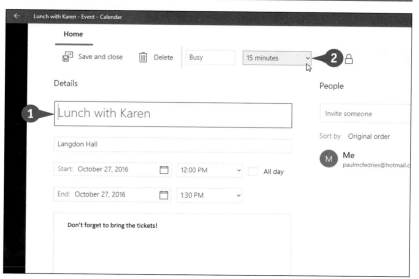

3 Click the length of time before the event that you want the reminder to appear.

4 Click **Save and close**.

Calendar saves the event and later reminds you of it beforehand, according to the time that you select.

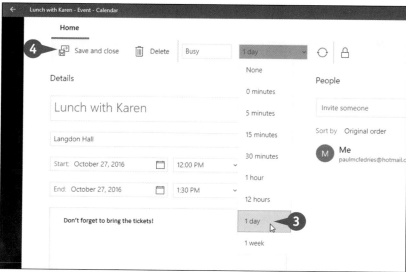

Send or Respond to an Event Invitation

The Calendar app has a feature that enables you to include people from your Contacts list in your event by sending them invitations to attend. If you receive an event invitation, you can respond to it to let the person organizing the event know whether you will be attending.

The advantage of this approach is that when other people respond to the invitation, Calendar automatically updates the event. When you receive an event invitation, the email message contains buttons that enable you to respond quickly.

Send or Respond to an Event Invitation

Send an Event Invitation

1. Follow the steps in the section "Add an Event to Your Calendar," earlier in this chapter, to create an event.

2. In the People list, specify a person that you want to invite:

 If the person is in your Contacts list, type the person's name.

 If the person is not in your Contacts, type the person's email address.

3. Press Enter.

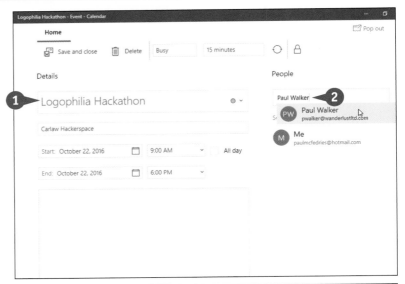

4. Repeat steps **2** and **3** for each person you want to invite.

5. Type a note that will appear with the invitation.

6. Click **Send**.

 Calendar saves the event and sends the invitation.

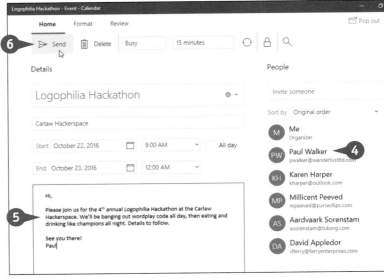

Handle an Event Invitation

1 Click **Mail** (✉).

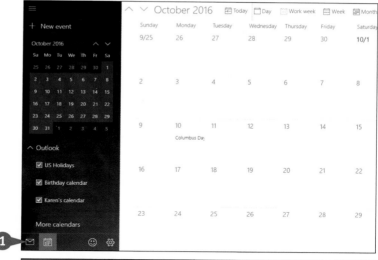

Windows switches you to the Mail app.

2 Click the invitation.

3 Click the button that represents your reply:

A You can click **Accept** if you can attend the event.

B You can click **Tentative** if you are currently not sure whether you can attend.

C You can click **Decline** if you cannot attend the event.

4 If you clicked either Tentative or Decline, choose whether you want to edit your response, send the response right away, or not send a response.

5 Click **Calendar** (📅) to return to the Calendar app.

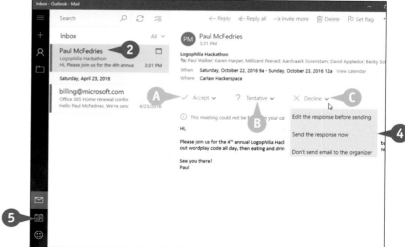

TIPS

If I click Tentative, how do I later either accept or decline the invitation?

When you click **Tentative**, Windows temporarily adds the event to the Calendar at the date and time specified in the invitation. To respond definitively, open the event details and then click either **Accept** (✓) or **Decline** (✗).

If I am not sure whether to accept an invitation, can I check my calendar?

Yes. The invitation message includes a link to your calendar that automatically displays the date on which the event occurs. Click the message and then click **View calendar**. Windows opens the Calendar app and displays the event date so that you can check your schedule.

Customize Your Calendar

Calendar is a useful tool right out of the box, but it comes with a decent collection of customization settings that you can use to make the app even better. For example, you can specify a first day of the week other than Sunday. You can also specify which days are in your workweek and which hours are in your workday. You can also display week numbers and change the Calendar colors.

Customize Your Calendar

1 Click **Settings** (⚙).

2 Click **Calendar Settings**.

The Calendar Settings pane appears.

3 Click the **First Day of Week** ⌄ and then click the day you prefer to use as the first of the week.

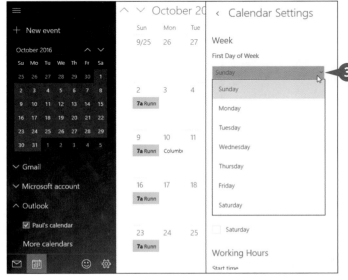

4 Use the **Days in Work Week** check boxes to define your workweek.

5 Click the **Start time** ∨ and then click the **End time** ∨ to define the beginning and end of your workday.

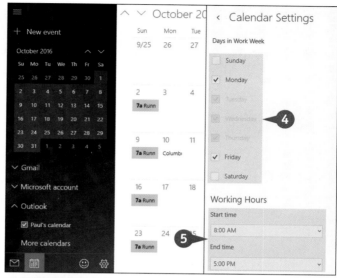

6 If you want to display week numbers in the calendar, click the **Week Numbers** ∨ and then click an option (see the Tip for an explanation).

7 In the Calendar Colors section, click the color option you prefer (○ changes to ◉).

8 Click outside the Calendar Settings pane to close the pane.

Calendar puts the new settings into effect.

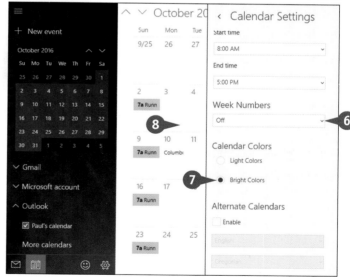

<div style="border:1px solid">

TIP

What is the difference between the two Week Numbers options?

Besides the default option of None, the Week Numbers list offers two numbering options:

First Day Of Year — If you select this option, Calendar designates week 1 as the week that contains January 1, even if that week contains one or more days from the previous year.

First Full Week — If you select this option, Calendar designates week 1 as the first full week that occurs in the year, even if the previous week contains one or more days from the current year.

</div>

Performing Day-to-Day Tasks with Apps

You can use the Windows apps to perform many useful tasks, including searching for apps, settings, and files; getting directions; looking up a weather forecast; tracking a stock; and getting the latest sports news.

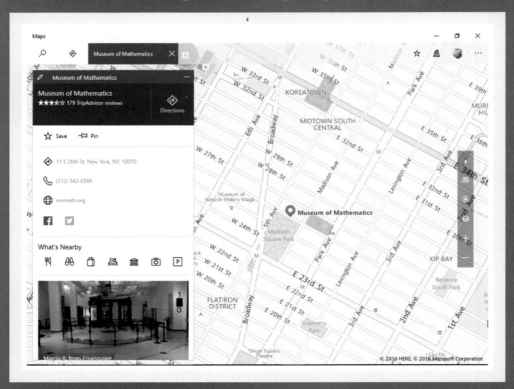

Search Your PC

After you have used your PC for a while and have created many documents, you might have trouble locating a specific file. You can save a great deal of time by having Windows search for your document.

You can use the Search feature to look for apps, system settings, and documents on your PC, as well as websites on the Internet. If you are working with File Explorer, you can also perform document searches using the Search box in a folder window.

Search Your PC

Search from the Taskbar

1 Click inside the Search box and type your search text.

A Windows displays the top apps, settings, and documents with names that include your search text.

B Windows displays other search results here, organized by category (such as Folders).

C If you see the app, setting, or document that you want, you can click it.

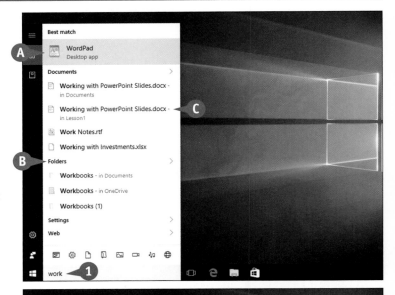

2 To see results from a specific category, click a heading, such as Documents.

D You can also use these icons to click a category, such as **Settings** (⚙️).

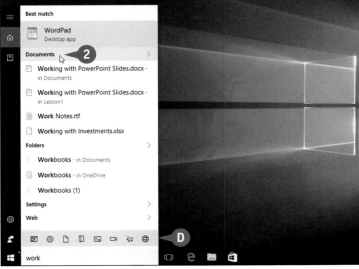

Windows displays the category items that match your search text.

③ Click the item you want.

Windows opens the app, setting, document, or website.

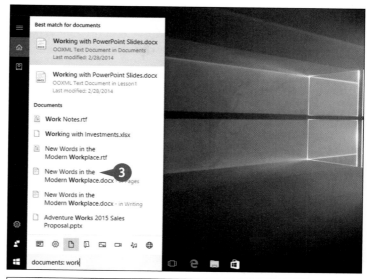

Search from a Folder Window

① Click **File Explorer** (▢).

② Open the folder you want to search.

③ Type your search text in the Search box.

Ⓔ As you type, Windows displays the folders and documents in the current folder with names, contents, or keywords that match your search text.

④ If you see the folder or document that you want, double-click it.

The folder or document opens.

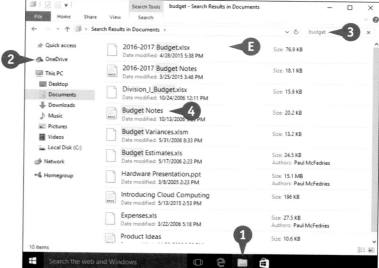

TIPS

Can I restrict my folder searches to a particular file type?

Yes, you can tell File Explorer to search only one of more than 20 different file types, including documents, music, and pictures. In File Explorer, click inside the Search box and then click the **Search** tab in the ribbon. Click the **Kind** ▼ and then click the type of file you want to find.

Is there any way to tell Windows that I specifically want to search for settings?

Not directly, but the Settings app does have a search feature. Click **Start** (⊞), click **Settings** (⚙), and then use the Find a Setting search box to type a word or phrase for the setting you want.

Configure the Cortana Voice Assistant

If you have a microphone attached to your PC, you can use it to search for information on your computer and on the web by using voice commands. To set up this feature, you need to configure Cortana, the Windows 10 voice assistant. Cortana knows what is on your PC and what is available on the web. Although you can still type searches as described in the previous section, "Search Your PC," once Cortana is configured you can run searches and other tasks using verbal commands that you speak into your microphone.

Configure the Cortana Voice Assistant

1 Click inside the Search box.

2 Click **Cortana can do much more**.

Windows lets you know that Cortana will collect information about you.

3 Click **Sure**.

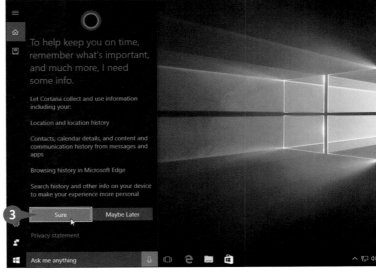

If you are not signed in with a Microsoft account, Cortana asks you to sign in.

④ Click **Sign in**.

The Choose an Account dialog box appears.

⑤ Click **Microsoft account** and then follow the prompts to set up your account.

Note: See Chapter 1 to learn how to switch to a Microsoft account.

You can now use Cortana to search your PC.

TIPS

How do I use Cortana?
Display the taskbar and then click **Talk** (🎤) inside the Search box. You then see the prompt "Ask me anything" in the Search box. You can then either speak your search text or specify an action, such as calling a contact, creating a calendar entry, setting an alarm or reminder, or taking a note.

How do I adjust Cortana's settings?
Click inside the Search box, click **Notebook** (📒), and then click **Settings** (⚙). Use the Settings pane to adjust the settings as needed. If you no longer want to use Cortana, click the **Cortana** switch to **Off**.

Get More Out of Cortana

The Cortana voice assistant gets more powerful with each new update of Windows 10, but to take advantage of that power you need to provide Cortana with information about yourself. This information can include your favorite sports teams, the type of food you like, or the academic field you study.

You can also use Cortana to streamline aspects of your life. For example, you can use Cortana to set up reminders to appear at specific times, when you arrive at or leave specific places, or when you interact with a specific person (for example, by sending email to or receiving from that person).

Get More Out of Cortana

Tell Cortana Your Preferences

1. Click inside the Search box to open Cortana.

2. Click **Notebook** (🗒).

3. Click a section.

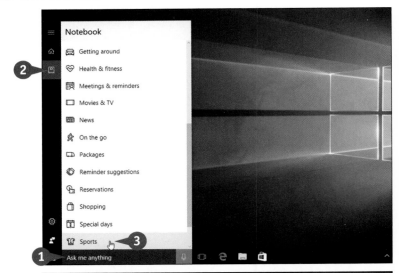

Cortana displays the options for that section.

4. Use the switches to toggle section features on and off.

5. Click an **Add** link to provide Cortana with specific information.

6. Click **Save**.

Cortana saves your data and uses it to provide you with better information and search results.

Set a Reminder

1 Click inside the Search box to open Cortana.

2 Click **Notebook** (⬛).

3 Click **Reminders** (not shown).

4 Click **Add** (➕).

Cortana prompts you to set up the new reminder.

5 Type the reminder text.

6 Select the type of reminder:

You can click **Person** to be reminded when you interact with the contact you specify.

You can click **Place** to be reminded when you arrive or leave the location you specify.

You can click **Time** to be reminded at the time you specify.

7 Click **Save**.

Cortana sets up and activates the reminder.

TIPS

Is there an easier way to invoke Cortana than always clicking Talk (🎤)?
Yes, you can configure Windows 10 so that you can invoke Cortana by saying "Hey Cortana" into your microphone. To set this up, click inside the taskbar's Search box and then click **Settings** (⚙). Click the **Hey Cortana** switch to **On**.

How do I clear the personal information that Cortana has saved about me?
Click inside the taskbar's Search box and then click **Settings** (⚙). Click **Change what Cortana knows about me in the cloud** to open the Personal Information window. Use the links provided to clear your personal information.

Configure Skype Video

You can use the Skype Video app to place phone calls to friends and family using your Internet connection. Note that, unlike regular phone calls, Skype Video lets you place *video calls*, which means you hear *and* see the other person. If either you or the person you call does not have a video camera, then Skype Video also enables you to place voice calls over the Internet.

Although you can sign up for a Skype account separately, this is not necessary because Windows 10 will assign you a Skype account automatically using your Microsoft account.

Configure Skype Video

1 Click **Start** (⊞).

2 Click **Skype**.

The Sign In screen appears.

3 Type your Skype or Microsoft account address.

4 Click **Next**.

Skype prompts you to enter your account password.

5 Type your password.

6 Click **Sign in**.

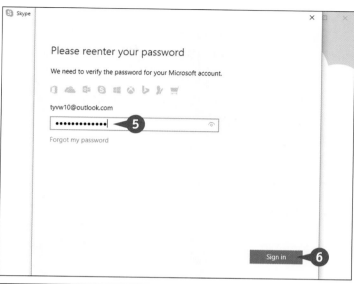

Skype completes the configuration and displays its main window.

TIPS

How do I change items such as my mobile phone number and current status?
Open Skype, click **Menu** (≡), and then click your user name. Skype displays your account info where you can edit your status and phone number.

Can I add multiple phone numbers to my Skype account?
Yes. Open Skype, click **Menu** (≡), and then click **Settings** to display the Skype Settings screen. Click **My phone numbers**. Microsoft Edge launches and displays your online Skype profile. Click **Add a phone number**, type the phone number you want to include, and then click **Add**.

Call Someone Using Skype Video

Once you have Skype Video set up on your PC, as described in the previous section, "Configure Skype Video," you are ready to make and accept some video calls. When you make a call, note that the other person has to accept the call before the conversation can begin. Similarly, when someone calls your PC, you can either accept or decline the incoming call. This means you do not have to answer a call if you are too busy or otherwise occupied.

Call Someone Using Skype Video

Initiate a Call

1. Click **Create a new conversation** (+).

2. Click **More** (···).

3. Click **Add people**.

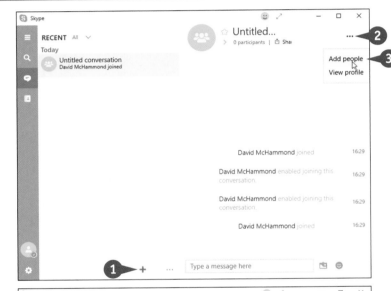

The Add Participants pane appears.

4. Type the name of the person you want to call.

5. When the person's name appears in the list, click the check box beside the name (○ changes to ⦿).

6. Click **Add**.

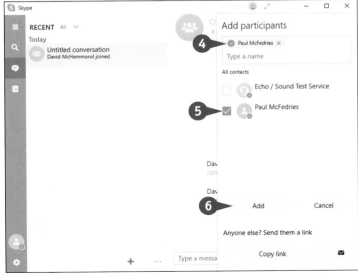

7 Choose the type of call you want to make:

A You can click **Call** (📞) to make a voice call.

B You can click **Video call** (📹) to make a video call.

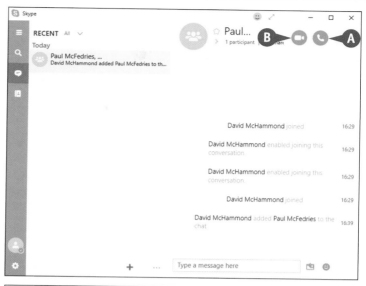

Accept a Call

1 Click **Video** (📹).

C If you want to use voice only, you can click **Audio** (🎤), instead.

D To decline the call, you can click **Ignore** (📞).

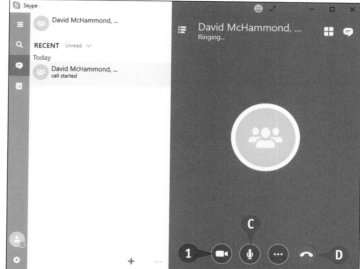

TIP

How do I add a Skype contact who is not in my address book?

Send that person a contact request. Follow steps **1** to **3** to display the Add Participants pane and then click **Copy Link** to place a copy of the conversation address in memory. Open Mail or some other communications app, start a new message, press Ctrl + V to paste the conversation address, and then send the message. When the other person clicks the link to join the conversation, he or she will be added to your contacts.

Display a Location on a Map

You can use the Maps app to display a location on a map. *Maps* is an app that displays digital maps that you can use to view just about any location by searching for an address or place name.

When you first start the Maps app, Windows asks if it can turn on location services, which are background features that help determine your current location and offer this information to apps such as Maps. For the best results with Maps, you should allow Windows to turn on location services.

Display a Location on a Map

1 Click **Start** (⊞).

2 Click **Maps**.

The first time that you start Maps, the app asks if it can use your location.

3 Click **Yes**.

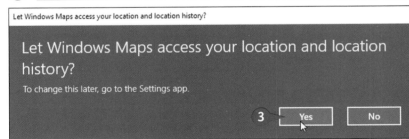

④ Type the address or the name of the location.

⑤ Click the location in the search results.

Ⓐ To see a list of matching locations, you can click **Search** (🔍) and then click the location you want.

Ⓑ Maps displays the location on the map.

Ⓒ Maps displays information about the location.

Ⓓ In the Navigation toolbar, you can click **Zoom in** (🔳) and **Zoom out** (🔳) to see more or less map detail.

Ⓔ You can click **Show my location** (🔘) to see your current location.

Ⓕ You can click **Close** (❌) to hide the location information.

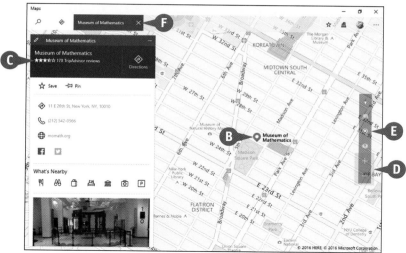

TIPS

How does Maps know my location?
First, it looks for known *Wi-Fi hotspots*, which are commercial establishments that offer wireless Internet access. Second, if you are connected to the Internet, Maps uses the location information embedded in your unique Internet Protocol (IP) address. Third, if your PC has a Global Positioning System (GPS) receiver, Maps uses this GPS data to pinpoint your location to within a few feet.

Can I turn off location services?
Yes. Click **Start** (🔳) and then click **Settings** (⚙). In the Settings app, click **Privacy**, click **Location**, and then click the **Location** switch to **Off**.

Get Directions to a Location

Besides displaying locations, Maps also recognizes the roads and highways found in most cities, states, and countries. This means that you can use the Maps app to get specific directions for traveling from one location to another.

You specify a starting point and destination for a trip, and Maps then provides you with directions for getting from one point to the other. Maps highlights the trip route on a digital map and also gives you specific details for negotiating each leg of the trip.

Get Directions to a Location

1 Click **Directions** (⬦).

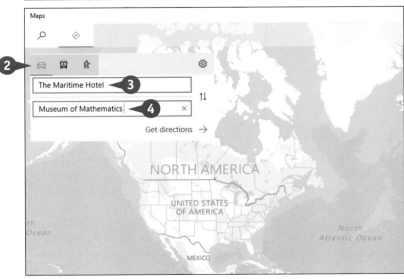

2 Click the travel method:
Driving (🚗), **Transit** (🚌), or
Walking (🚶).

Note: Maps assumes that you want
to start at your current location. If
that is true, skip step **3**.

3 Type the name or address of
the location where your journey
will begin.

4 Type the name or address of
your destination and then
press **Enter**.

A Maps displays an overview of the route.

B This area tells the distance and approximate traveling time by the chosen travel method.

C This area displays the various legs of the journey.

5 Click the first leg of the trip.

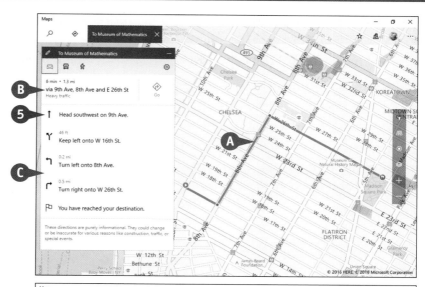

Maps zooms in to show you just that leg of the trip.

6 As you complete each leg of the trip, click the next leg for further instructions.

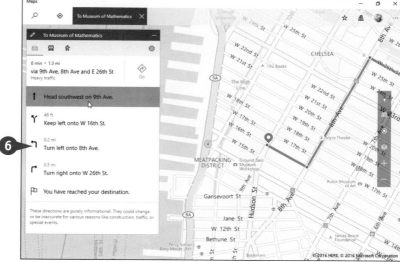

TIP

Can I get traffic information as I follow the directions provided by Maps?
Yes. In the Navigation toolbar, click **Map views** (⬚) and then click **Traffic** to see the current traffic conditions:

- Green means traffic is moving normally on that route.
- Yellow means traffic is slower than normal.
- Orange tells you that traffic is slow.
- Red means traffic is heavy.

Check Your Weather Forecast

You can use the Weather app to view your city's current conditions and five-day forecast. The Weather app takes advantage of the MSN Weather service provided by Microsoft, which uses several online weather resources to obtain up-to-the-minute conditions and forecasts.

The Weather app can check the forecast for a default location that your specify, or for your current location, which uses Windows location services to determine your location and display the forecast. If you would prefer to see the forecast for some other location, see the next section, "Check Another City's Weather Forecast."

Check Your Weather Forecast

Create a Default Location Forecast

1 Click **Start** (⊞).

2 Click **Weather**.

The Weather app appears. The first time you start the program, it asks you to specify a default temperature unit and location.

3 Click **Fahrenheit** or **Celsius** (○ changes to ◉).

④ Begin typing the name of the default location you want to use.

⑤ When you see the location in the list, click it.

Weather displays the location's current conditions and forecast.

Check Your Current Location Forecast

① Click **Settings** (⚙).

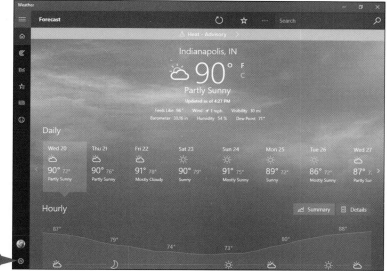

② Click **Always detect my location** (○ changes to ◉).

Weather asks for permission to use your location.

③ Click **Yes**.

Weather determines your current location.

④ Click **Back** (←).

Weather displays your current location's conditions and forecast.

TIPS

Why does the Weather app say, "Your location cannot be found"?
You have turned off location services. Click **Start** (⊞), click **Settings** (⚙), click **Privacy**, click **Location**, and then click the **Location** switch to **On**. Click the **MSN Weather** switch to **On**.

How can I see my city's forecast when I start the Weather app?
If your city is the only one added to Weather, then you see your forecast when you start the app. Otherwise, make your city the app's default location. To do this, open the Weather app, click **Settings** (⚙), click **Default Location** (○ changes to ◉), and then type the name of your city in the text box.

Check Another City's Weather Forecast

You can use the Weather app to view another city's current conditions and five-day forecast. The Bing Weather service uses online resources to obtain up-to-the-minute information on the current conditions and weather forecasts for hundreds of locations around the world. If you are going to be traveling to another city or if you are simply curious about the weather conditions elsewhere, you can use Maps to look up the weather forecast for most cities around the world.

Check Another City's Weather Forecast

1 In the Weather app, click **Menu** (☰).

The menu appears.

2 Click **Favorites**.

The Places screen appears.

3 Click **Add** (⊞).

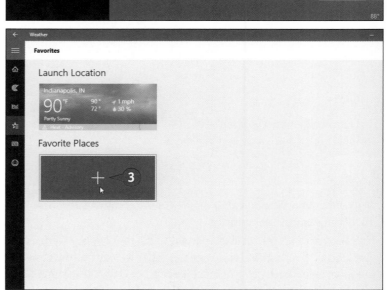

4 Type the name of the city whose weather you want to view.

A As you type, Weather displays place names that match.

5 When you see the location that you want, click it.

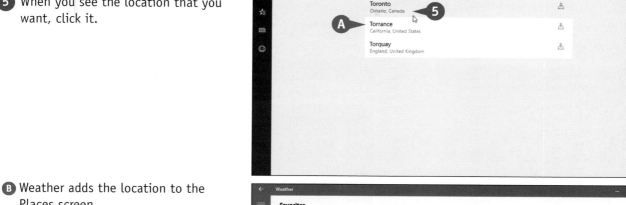

B Weather adds the location to the Places screen.

6 Click the location.

Weather displays the city's current conditions and forecast.

TIPS

How do I switch between Fahrenheit and Celsius?
In the Weather app, click **Menu** (≡) and then click **Settings** (⚙) to open the Weather app's Settings pane with the General tab displayed. Then click either **Fahrenheit** or **Celsius** (○ changes to ●).

How do I remove a city?
To remove a location from the Places screen, follow steps **1** and **2** to display the Places screen, right-click the city that you want to remove, and then click **Remove from Favorites** (✕).

Perform Calculations

You can use the Calculator app to make calculations and to convert numbers from one unit to another. The app comes with a Standard calculator that you can use for basic calculations such as addition, subtraction, multiplication, and division. For more advanced calculation, use either the Scientific or the Programmer calculator.

Calculator also comes with a number of converters that you can use to change one value to a different unit. For example, you can use the Length converter to change centimeters to inches, or the Weight and Mass converter to change kilograms to pounds.

Perform Calculations

Start the Calculator

1 Click **Start** (⊞).

2 Click **Calculator**.

The Calculator app appears.

Select a Calculator or Converter

1 Click **Menu** (≡).

2 Click the calculator or converter you want to use.

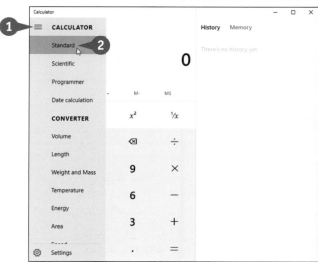

Perform a Calculation

1 Click the numeric buttons to enter a number.

2 Click an operator.

3 Repeat steps **1** and **2** as needed.

4 Click **Equals** (=).

Calculator displays the result.

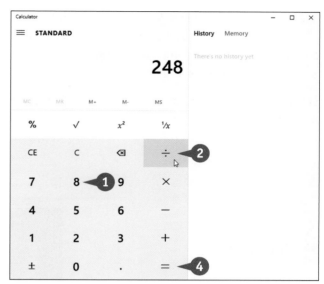

Perform a Conversion

1 Click the top ⌄ and then click the unit you want to convert from.

2 Click the bottom ⌄ and then click the unit you want to convert to.

3 Click the numeric buttons to enter the value you want to convert.

A Calculator displays the converted value.

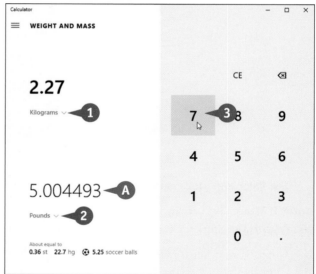

What is the Calculator app's Memory feature and how do I use it?

The Memory feature lets you perform a calculation, save the result, and then use that result as part of another calculation. To save a result to memory, perform the calculation and then click the **M+** button. To retrieve the result from memory, click the **MR** button.

Is there a way to rerun an earlier calculation?

Yes. Calculator saves your last few calculations in the History tab. To rerun a calculation, click **History** and then click the calculation. Note that you might need to scroll down the History list to see the calculation you want.

Get the Latest News

You can use the News app to read the latest news stories and to locate stories that are important to you. The News app aggregates news stories from a wide variety of web sources, including the Associated Press, Reuters, the *New York Times*, and CNN.

The News app's main page — called *Headlines* — displays stories in various categories, including Technology, Business, Politics, and Sports. If you are interested in other topics, you can customize News to show stories related to those topics.

Get the Latest News

1 Click **Start** (⊞).

2 Click **News**.

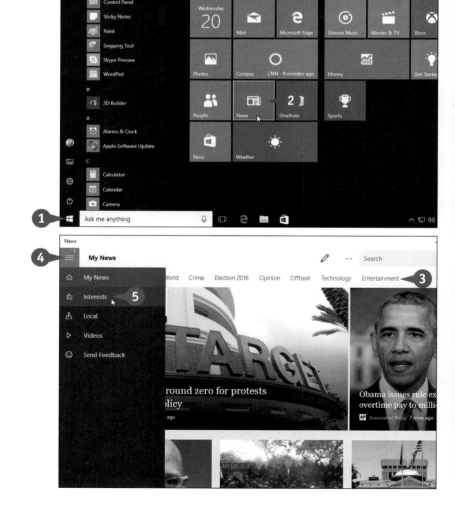

The News app appears.

Note: If News asks you to personalize the app by choosing interests, click **Skip**.

3 Click a category.

You can also scroll up and down to see the main stories in each category.

4 Click **Menu** (≡).

5 Click **Interests**.

The Interests page appears.

6 To add a new interest, use the Search box to type the name of the topic that you want to add.

A News displays topics that match.

7 Click the topic that you want to add.

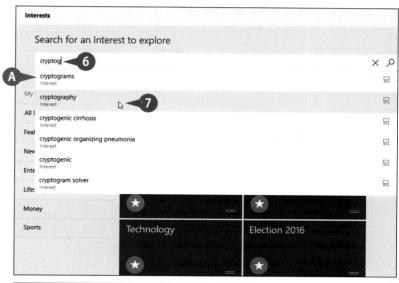

B News adds the topic to the bottom of the Interests page.

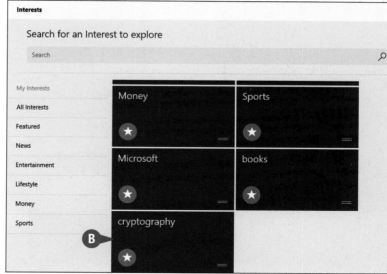

Can I see news that focuses on a particular country?

Yes. To see news from a particular country, click **Menu** (≡) and then click **Settings** (⚙) to open the News app's Settings pane with the General tab displayed. Use the **Choose edition** list to select the country whose news you want to view.

Can I see news that focuses on my current location?

Yes. To see news related to your location, click **Menu** (≡) and then click **Local**. When the app asks if it can use your location, click **Yes**. News displays stories and sources that are associated with your PC's current location.

Track a Stock

You can use the Money app to read the latest financial news stories, see the latest financial data, and create a list of stocks to track. The Finance app combines a wide variety of financial information in a single place.

The Money app's main screen — called *Home* — displays financial news; Dow statistics, NASDAQ information, and other index values; major stock activity; bond prices; interest rates; and more. You can also use the Money app to create a list — called a *watchlist* — of the stocks that you want to track.

Track a Stock

1 Click **Start** (⊞).

2 Click **Money**.

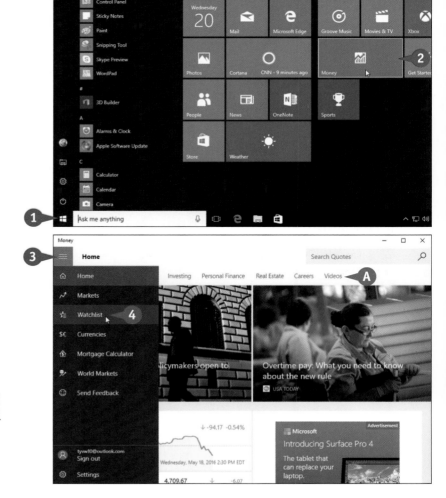

Note: If Money asks you to choose an edition, click the country and language you want to use and then click **Continue**.

The Money app appears.

Ⓐ To read the latest financial information, you can click a category.

You can also scroll up, left, and down to see the latest financial news and data.

3 Click **Menu** (☰).

4 Click **Watchlist**.

The Watchlist screen appears.

5 Click **Add** (✚).

Ⓑ If you have not yet added a stock to your watchlist, you can also click **Add** (✚) here.

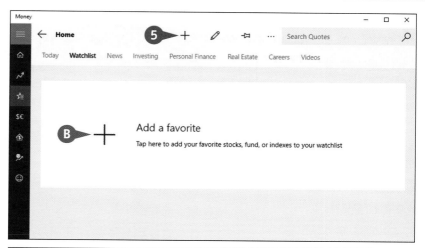

The Add to Watchlist screen appears.

6 Type the stock symbol or name of the stock that you want to add.

Ⓒ As you type, Money displays stocks that match.

7 When you see the stock that you want, click it.

Money adds the stock to the Watchlist screen.

Note: Your watchlist also appears on the MSN Finance screen.

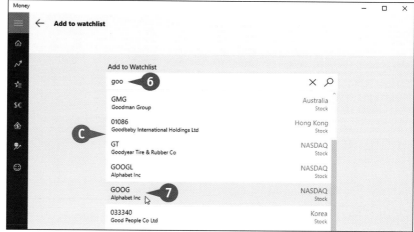

TIPS

How do I remove a stock from my watchlist?

Follow steps **1** to **4** to display the Watchlist screen, click **Edit** (✐), and then click **Remove** (✕) beside each stock you no longer want on the watchlist.

Is there a way to keep my watchlist on-screen so that I can monitor it?

Yes, you can snap Money to the edge of the screen. In Money, display the Watchlist screen. Now press ⊞+← to snap the window to the left side of the screen. If you prefer to snap the Money window to the right side, press and hold ⊞ and tap → until the window is in the position you want.

Follow Your Favorite Teams

You can use the Sports app to catch up on all your sports news. The Sports app combines a wide variety of sports news and information in a single place.

The Sports app's main screen — called *MSN Sports* — displays the top story of the day, other sports news, the day's schedule of upcoming games, and the latest scores from those games. You can also use the Sports app to create a list — called *My Favorites* — of the teams that you want to follow.

Follow Your Favorite Teams

1 Click **Start** (⊞).

2 Click **Sports**.

Note: If Sports asks you to choose an edition, click the country and language you want to use and then click **Continue**.

The Sports app appears.

A To read the latest sports information, you can click a category.

You can also scroll up, left, and down to see the latest sports news, schedules, and scores.

3 Click **Menu** (≡).

The menu appears.

4 Click **My Favorites**.

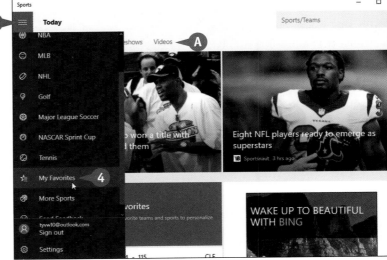

The My Favorites screen appears.

5 Click **Add** (➕).

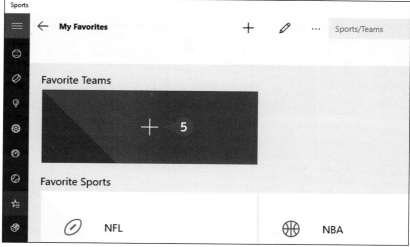

The Add to Favorites screen appears.

6 Type the name of the team that you want to add.

B As you type, Sports displays teams that match.

7 When you see the team that you want, click it.

Sports adds the team to the My Favorites page.

8 Repeat steps **5** to **7** for every team that you want to follow.

You can now see news, schedules, and stats by clicking a team in the My Favorites list.

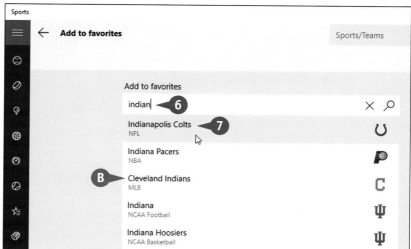

TIPS

How do I remove a team from the My Favorites list?
Follow steps **1** to **4** to display the My Favorites section. Click **Edit** (✎) and then click **Remove** (✕) beside each team you no longer want to follow.

Can I see more information about a particular sport?
Yes, the Sports app offers information on several sports leagues, including the National Football League, the National Basketball Association, Major League Baseball, and the National Hockey League. For each league, you see the latest news stories, a schedule of upcoming games, recent results, current standings, player statistics, and more. To select a league, click **Menu** (☰) and then click a league in the menu.

Record a Voice Message

I f you want to remember an idea or an inspiration, you could jot it down with pen and paper or use the Notepad program as described later in this chapter (see the section "Write a Note"). An alternative is to record a voice message using the Voice Recorder app. This is particularly handy if you are already using a microphone to send commands to the Cortana voice assistant. Voice Recorder also includes a feature that enables you to share your recordings with other people via email or instant messaging. To use Voice Recorder, you must have a microphone connected to your PC.

Record a Voice Message

1 Click **Start** (⊞).

2 Click **Voice Recorder**.

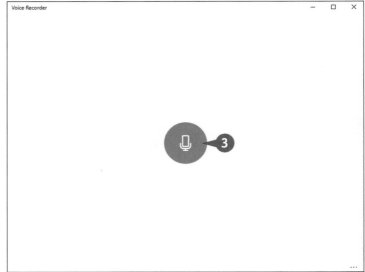

The Voice Recorder app appears.

3 Click **Record** (🎤).

Voice Recorder begins the recording.

4 Speak your message into your PC's microphone.

Ⓐ You can click **Pause** (Ⅱ) to temporarily stop the recording.

5 When the recording is complete, click **Stop recording** (☐).

Ⓑ Voice Recorder adds the recording.

6 Click **Rename** (✎).

7 Type a name for the recording.

8 Click **Rename**.

Voice Recorder saves the recording under the new name.

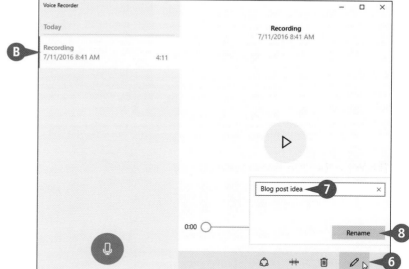

TIPS

How do I edit audio from the beginning or the end of the recording?

Click the recording you want to edit, then click **Trim** (⊬) to display the trim controls. On the left, click and drag the **Start** trim marker (●) to the right to cut audio from the beginning; on the right, click and drag the **End** trim marker (●) to the left to cut audio from the end. Click **Apply** (✓).

How do I share a recording?

Click the recording, click **Share** (△), then click the app you want to use, such as Mail. Fill in the rest of the details, such as the recipient address, then send the recording.

Create a Sway

You can use the Sway app to create online presentations that tell a story, outline an idea, present a product, display a newsletter, and more. A Sway is much like a presentation that you create with a program such as PowerPoint. In the same way that a PowerPoint file consists of one or slides arranged into a presentation, a *Sway* consists of one or more *cards* arranged in a *storyline*. Each card can contain a heading, text, an image or video, or even embedded tweets, maps, or charts.

Create a Sway

1 Click **Start** (⊞).

2 Click **Sway**.

The Sway app appears.

3 Click **Create New**.

A new Sway appears.

4 Type a title for the Sway.

A If you want to change the card background image, you can click **Background**.

5 Click **Insert Content** (✦).

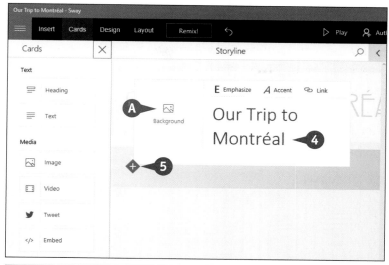

Sway displays boxes for each type of card you can insert.

6 Click the type of card you want to insert into your Sway.

B You can also click a content type in the Cards pane.

7 Fill in the card, depending on its type, such as text for a Text card, or a photo for an Image card.

8 Repeat steps **5** to **7** to complete your Sway.

9 To view your Sway, click **Play** (▷).

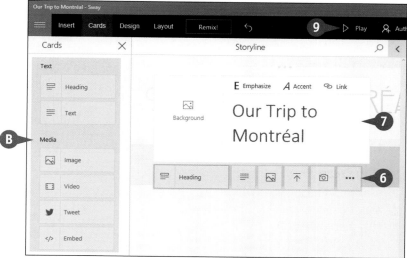

TIPS

Can I change the overall look of my Sway?
Yes. Sway comes with a number of pre-made designs that format your sway with colors, fonts, and textures. To apply a design, click the **Design** tab, then click one of the designs.

Can I import a PowerPoint presentation?
Yes, as well as Word documents and PDF files. Click **Menu** (≡) and then click **My Sways** to return to the main Sway window. Click **Import** to display the Open dialog box, click the file you want to import, and then click **Open**.

Set an Alarm

You can use the Alarms & Clock app to set an alarm to play at a specific time. You can set up the alarm to play once, or you can have it repeat on specified days. You can also choose the sound that Windows plays when the alarm goes off. Note that your PC must be turned on and awake for the alarm feature to work.

You can also use the Alarms & Clock app to set up a timer that counts down from a specified number of hours, minutes, and seconds, and to run a stopwatch for timing an event.

Set an Alarm

1 Click **Start** (⊞).

2 Click **Alarms & Clock**.

The Alarms & Clock app appears.

A Alarms & Clock comes with a default alarm already added. To modify this alarm, you can click it and then follow steps **4** to **9**.

B You can click **On/Off** to toggle the alarm on or off.

3 Click **New** (➕).

④ Set the time of the alarm.

⑤ Type a name for the alarm.

⑥ Click **Repeats** and then click the check box beside each day you want the alarm to ring (☐ changes to ☑).

⑦ Click **Sound** and then click a sound to play.

⑧ Click **Snooze time** and then click the interval the app uses when you select Snooze.

⑨ Click **Save** (🖫).

Ⓒ Alarms & Clock adds and activates the alarm.

Ⓓ To delete an alarm, you can click **Manage** (☰), and then click **Delete** (✕) beside the alarm.

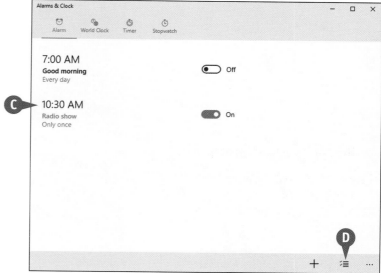

TIPS

How do I set a timer?
At the top of the Alarms & Clock app, click **Timer** and then click the displayed time to open the Edit Timer window. Edit the timer name and then use the Duration boxes to set the number of hours, minutes, and seconds for the timer. Click **Save** (🖫). When you are ready to start the timer, click **Play** (▷).

How do I use the stopwatch?
At the top of the Alarms & Clock app, click **Stopwatch**. Click **Play** (▷) to start the watch. To get a lap or split time, click **Laps/Splits** (🏳).

Write a Note

You can use the Notepad app to create simple text documents for things such as to-do lists and meeting notes. Word processing programs such as WordPad, as well as powerful note-taking apps such as the OneNote app covered in Chapter 9, are useful for creating complex and lengthy documents, but they feel like overkill when all you want to do is jot down a few simple notes. For these more basic text tasks, the Notepad app that comes with Windows is perfect because it offers a simple interface that is easy to learn and use.

Write a Note

Start Notepad

1. Click **Start** (⊞).

 The Start menu appears.

2. Click **Windows Accessories**.

3. Click **Notepad**.

 Notepad opens.

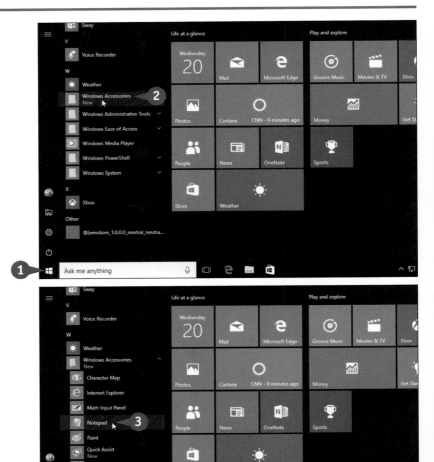

Write and Save a Note

1 Type your note text.

2 Click **File**.

3 Click **Save**.

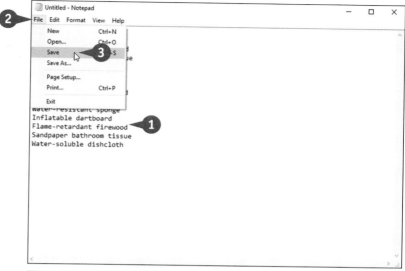

The Save As dialog box appears.

4 Type a name for the file.

5 Click **Save**.

Notepad saves the file.

TIPS

Can I create a temporary note?
Yes. If you just want to jot down a phone number, you can create the Windows equivalent of a sticky note by following steps **1** to **3** in the subsection "Start Notepad" and then clicking **Sticky Notes**.

What is the difference between Notepad and WordPad?
Notepad is called a *text editor* and you use it only to enter and edit text. WordPad is called a *word processing program* and you use it not only to enter and edit text, but also to format that text with fonts, sizes, and colors; apply bulleted and numbered lists; insert images; and more.

Working with Images

Whether you load your images from a digital camera or a scanner, download them from the Internet, or draw them yourself, Windows comes with a number of useful tools for working with those images. In this chapter, you learn how to import images from a camera, view your images, fix photo problems, and delete images.

Import Images from a Digital Camera

You can import photos from a digital camera and save them on your PC. If your camera stores the photos on a memory card, you can also use a memory card reader attached to your PC to upload the digital photos from the removable drive that Windows sets up when you insert the card.

To perform the import directly from your digital camera, you need a cable to connect your camera to your PC. Most digital cameras come with a USB cable. After you have the digital photos on your system, you can view or print the images.

Import Images from a Digital Camera

1 Plug in your camera or memory storage card reader.

Note: If you see a notification, click the notification and then skip to step **5**.

2 Click **File Explorer** (■).

3 Click **This PC**.

File Explorer displays a list of the devices attached to your PC.

4 Right-click your digital camera.

5 Click **Import pictures and videos**.

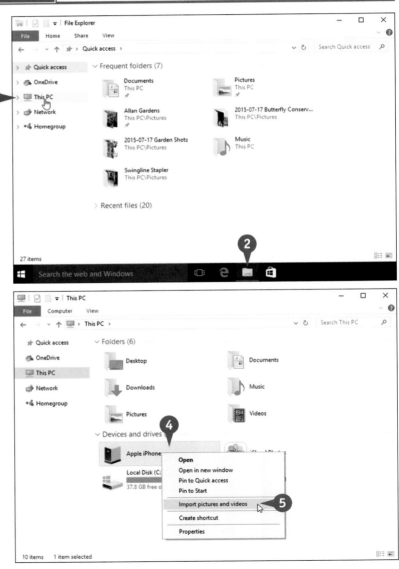

The Import Pictures and Videos dialog box appears.

6 Click **Import all new items now** (☐ changes to ✔).

7 Type a name to use for the import.

8 Click **Import**.

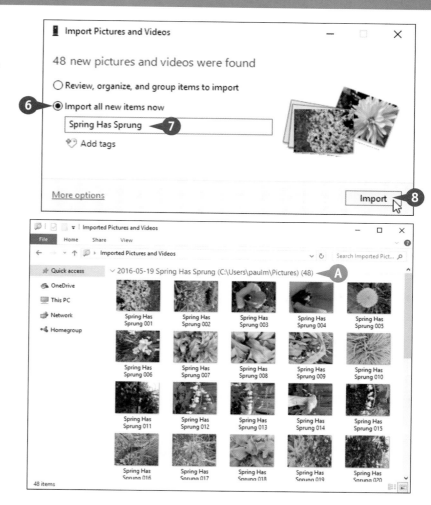

Windows imports the photos.

When the import is complete, File Explorer displays your imported photos.

Ⓐ The Photos app stores the imported photos in your Pictures library in a folder named after today's date.

How can I import just some of the photos on my camera?
If you want to import only a subset of your photos, follow steps **1** to **5** to open the Import Pictures and Videos dialog box. Click **Review, organize, and groups items to import** (☐ changes to ✔) and then click **Next**. You now see the camera photos grouped by date. Click **Select all** (⦿ changes to ◯) to deselect all the groups. Click the check box (☐ changes to ✔) and type a name for each group you want to import, and then click **Import**.

Scan an Image

You can create a digital copy of a photo or other image by using a document scanner, or the scanner component of an all-in-one printer. The scanner copies the image to your computer, where you can then store it as a file on your hard drive.

You can use a scanned image in many ways. For example, you can scan a photo to email to friends or publish on a web page. You can also scan a logo or other image to use in a document.

Scan an Image

1 Turn on your scanner or all-in-one printer and position a photo or other image on the scanner bed.

2 Click **Start** (⊞).

3 Click **Scan**.

The Scan window appears.

4 Use the File Type list to select the file type you want to use for the scanned image file.

5 Click **Show more**.

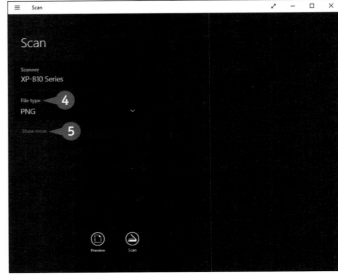

The Scan window displays extra settings.

6 Use the Color Mode list to select a mode that matches your image: Color, Grayscale, or Black and White.

7 Use the Resolution list to specify the scan resolution.

Note: The higher the resolution, the sharper the image, but the larger the resulting file.

8 Click **Preview**.

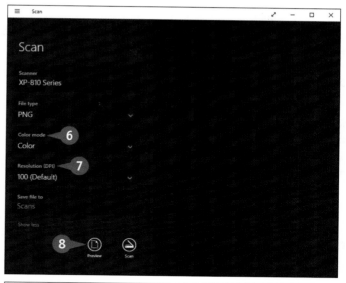

A A preview of the scan appears here.

9 Click and drag the round handles at the corners of the rectangle to set the scan area.

10 Click **Scan**.

Windows scans the image.

Navigate the Pictures Library

Before you can work with your images, you need to view them on your PC. You do that by using the Photos app to open the Pictures library, which is a special folder designed specifically for storing images.

To get more out of the Pictures library, you need to know not only how to open it, but also the basic techniques for opening any albums that you have stored in the library.

Navigate the Pictures Library

1 Click **File Explorer** (▭).

The File Explorer program window appears.

2 Click **Pictures**.

The Pictures library appears.

Ⓐ Items with folder icons are subfolders.

Ⓑ Items without folder icons are individual images.

③ Double-click a subfolder.

File Explorer displays the subfolder's images.

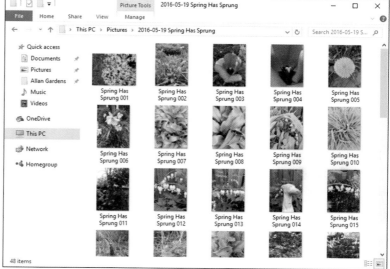

TIP

Do I have to use File Explorer to navigate the Pictures library?
No. Although File Explorer is often the easiest and fastest way to navigate the Pictures library, it is not the only way. An alternative method is to use the Photos app, which you launch by clicking **Start** (⊞) and then clicking **Photos**. You can then use the icons on the left to view the pictures by collection (▥) or by album (▣). See the next section, "View Your Images," for more information.

View Your Images

If you want to look at several images, Windows gives you two methods to navigate backward and forward through the images in the Pictures library. First, you can use File Explorer to open an individual image for viewing in the Photos app, and then navigate through the other images in the same folder. Second, you can use the Photos app directly to view your images by collection or by album.

View Your Images

View Individual Images

1 In File Explorer, open the folder that contains the images you want to view.

Note: See the previous section, "Navigate the Pictures Library," for details.

2 Double-click the first image that you want to view.

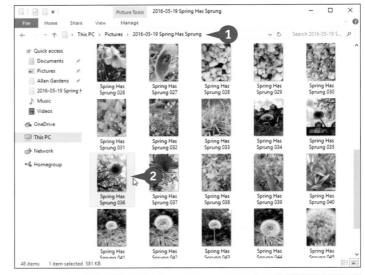

The image appears in the Photos app.

3 Click the right-pointing arrow (**>**) to scroll right.

The Photos app displays the next screen of images from the album.

4 Repeat step **3** to continue viewing the album images.

A You can return to the previous screen of images by scrolling left.

You can also press ➡ to see the next image and ⬅ to see the previous image.

View Images by Collection or Album

1 Click **Start** (⊞).

2 Click **Photos**.

The Photos app appears.

3 Click **Collection** (▦).

B Alternatively, you can click **Albums** (▦) to view your pictures by album.

4 Scroll up and down to view your images by collection or album.

Start a Slid...

Instead of vi...
in a slid...
each ph...
Alt...

TIP

Can I view an individual picture in a collection or album?
Yes. Scroll to the image you want to view and then click it. You can then navigate the images as described in the subsection "View Individual Images." To return to the collection or album, click the screen to display the controls, and then click the name of the collection or album that appears in the upper-left corner of the screen.

To Get Pictures go to tiles - File Explorer - This PC - Pictures

e Show

ewing your photos one at a time, you can easily view multiple photos by running them
show. You can run the slide show from within the Photos app. The slide show displays
oto for a few seconds and then automatically moves on to the next photo.

rnatively, you can view a slide show of images using the Photos tile on the Start menu. This slide
show uses recent images from your Pictures library.

Start a Slide Show

In the Photos App

1 In the Photos app, display
the collection or album that
contains the photos you want
to display in your slide show.

2 Click the first image you want
to display in the slide show.

Photos opens the image.

3 If you do not see the
application bar, click the screen.

The Photos application bar
appears.

4 Click **Slide show** (▣).

The Photos app begins the slide
show.

On the Photos Tile

1 In the Photos app, click **Settings** (⚙).

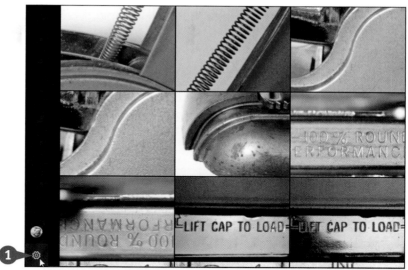

The Settings window appears.

2 In the Choose What to Show on the Photos Tile list, select **Recent photos**.

The next time that you display the Start screen, the Photos tile displays a slide show of recent images from your Pictures library.

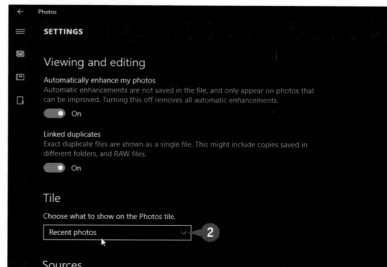

TIP

Can I change the speed at which the slide show displays the images?
No, not with the Photos app. However, you can adjust the speed if you start the slide show from File Explorer. Click **File Explorer** (▢) on the taskbar, open the **Pictures** library, and then click the folder that you want to view. In the ribbon, click the **Manage** tab and then click **Slide show** to start the show. To control the speed, right-click the screen to display the shortcut menu, and then click the speed that you want: **Slow**, **Medium**, or **Fast**.

Repair an Image

You can use Photos to improve the look of digital photos and other images. When you open an image in Photos, the application bar offers a number of tools for repairing various image attributes.

The easiest way to repair an image is to use the Auto Fix tool, which automatically adjusts an image's brightness, contrast, color temperature, tint, and saturation. You can also correct any of these elements manually, as well as remove red eye and hide photo flaws.

Repair an Image

Repair an Image Automatically

1. In Photos, display the image you want to repair.

2. If you do not see the application bar, click the screen.

 Photos displays the application bar.

3. Click **Auto fix** (🖋).

 Photos repairs the image automatically.

Repair an Image Manually

① In Photos, display the image you want to repair.

② If you do not see the application bar, click the screen.

Photos displays the application bar.

③ Click **Edit** (✐).

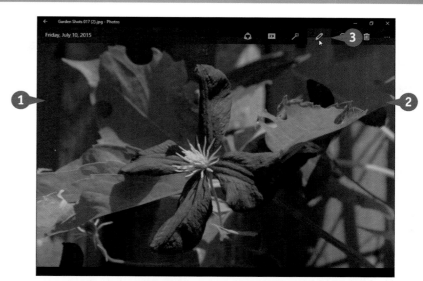

Photos displays the image editing tools.

④ Use the tools to repair the image as needed.

⑤ Click **Save** (🖫).

Photos saves your changes.

Ⓐ If you prefer to leave the original as is, you can click **Save a Copy** (🖫) instead.

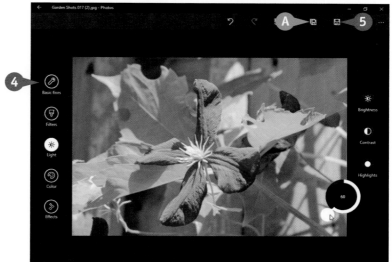

TIPS

How do I remove red eye from a photo?
When you take a picture with a flash, the light may reflect off the subjects' retinas, resulting in red eye. To fix this, follow steps **1** to **3** in the subsection "Repair an Image Manually," click **Basic fixes**, click **Red eye**, and then click each red eye.

Can I remove a small flaw in a photo?
Yes. Photos offers a Retouch tool that enables you to perform a *spot fix*, which replaces an element from the photo with colors from the surrounding area. To perform a spot fix, follow steps **1** to **3** in the subsection "Repair an Image Manually," click **Basic fixes**, click **Retouch**, and then click the flaw.

Add a Photo Effect

You can use Photos to enhance the look of an image by applying one or more of the effects offered by the Photos app.

The Vignette effect darkens the edges and corners of the photo, which adds a natural frame around the image and draws attention to the rest of the photo. The Selective Focus effect enables you to select a custom circular or elliptical area of the photo that remains in focus while the area outside the selection gets blurred. This enables you to really attract the viewer's eye to a particular part of the photo.

Add a Photo Effect

Display the Effects

1 In Photos, display the image you want to repair.

2 If you do not see the application bar, click the screen.

The application bar appears.

3 Click **Edit** (✏️).

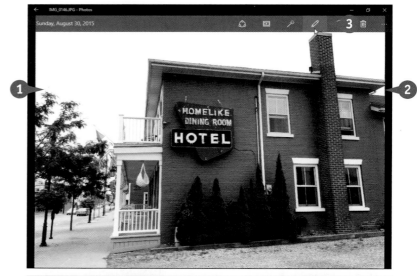

Photos displays the image editing tools.

4 Click **Effects**.

5 Click the effect you want to apply:

A You can click **Vignette** to apply the Vignette effect. In this case, proceed with the subsection "Apply a Vignette Effect."

B You can click **Selective focus** to apply the Selective Focus effect. In this case, proceed with the subsection "Apply a Selective Focus Effect."

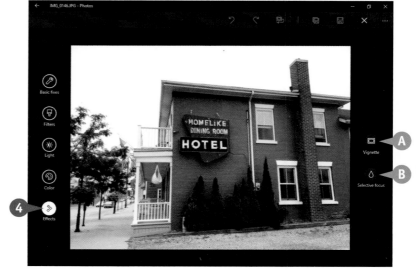

Apply a Vignette Effect

1 Click and drag the vignette indicator clockwise until the vignette is at the level you want.

Note: If you apply too much vignette, drag the indicator counterclockwise to reduce the effect.

Apply a Selective Focus Effect

1 Position the mouse pointer (⌖) inside the selective focus area (⌖ changes to ✥).

2 Drag the selective focus area to the portion of the photo that you want to remain in focus.

3 Click **Apply** (✔).

4 Click **Save** (🖫) (not shown).

Photos saves your changes.

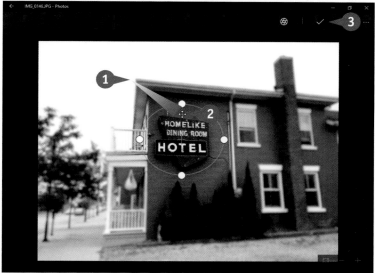

TIPS

How do I change the shape of the selective focus area?

By default, the selective focus area is a circle. This works best for most photos, but if you have a non-circular area, you can adjust the shape of the selective focus area by dragging any of the four white circles that appear on the border of the selective focus area.

Can I control the amount of blur in the Selective Focus effect?

Yes. Photos offers several blur strengths that you can apply. Follow steps **1** to **3** in the subsection "Apply a Selective Focus Effect" to display the Selective Focus tool. Click **Strength** (⚙) and then click the blur level you prefer: Maximum, Strong, Medium (the default), Weak, or Minimum.

Crop an Image

If you have an image containing elements that you do not want or need to see, you can often cut out those elements. This is called *cropping*, and you can do this with Photos. When you crop a photo, you specify a rectangular area of the photo that you want to keep. Photos discards everything outside the rectangle.

Cropping is a useful skill to have because it can help give focus to the true subject of a photo. Cropping is also useful for removing extraneous elements that appear on or near the edges of a photo.

Crop an Image

1 In Photos, display the image you want to crop.

2 If you do not see the application bar, click the screen.

The application bar appears.

3 Click **Edit** (✏️).

Photos displays the image editing tools.

4 Click **Basic fixes**.

5 Click **Crop**.

Photos displays a cropping rectangle on the photo.

6 Click and drag the photo or any corner of the rectangle to define the area you want to keep.

Note: Remember that Photos keeps the area inside the rectangle.

7 Click **Apply** (☑).

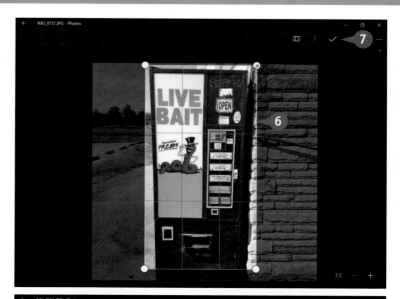

Photos applies the cropping.

8 Click **Save** (🖫).

Photos saves your changes.

Ⓐ If you prefer to leave the original as is, you can click **Save a copy** (🖫) instead.

TIP

Is there a quick way to crop a photo to a certain size?
Yes. Photos enables you to choose a specific ratio, such as 4 x 6 or 5 x 7. Repeat steps **1** to **5** to display the cropping rectangle over the image. Click **Aspect ratio** (▭). Click the ratio you want to use, such as 4 x 6 or 5 x 7. Repeat steps **7** and **8** to apply and save the cropping.

Rotate an Image

You can rotate and straighten an image using Photos. Depending on how you hold your camera when you take a shot, the resulting photo might show the subject sideways or upside down. To fix this problem, you can use Photos to rotate the photo so that the subject appears right-side up. You can rotate a photo either clockwise or counterclockwise.

Rotate an Image

1. Open the image you want to rotate.

2. If you do not see the application bar, click the screen.

 The application bar appears.

3. Click **Rotate** (icon) until the image is the way you want it.

Photos saves your changes.

Delete an Image

The images that you create may not always turn out perfectly. A photo may be blurry, or an edited image may not turn out the way that you want it to.

When you are viewing an album or watching a slide show, having a bad image can make the experience less pleasant. You can prevent that from happening by deleting an image you no longer want to work with or view. You can delete a single image or multiple images with a single command.

Delete an Image

1 Open the image you want to delete.

2 If you do not see the application bar, click the screen.

The application bar appears.

3 Click **Delete** (🗑).

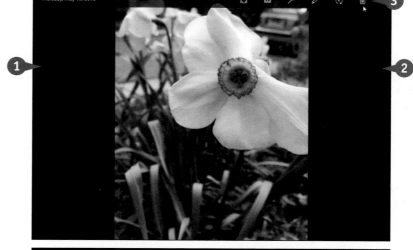

Photos asks you to confirm the deletion.

4 Click **Delete**.

Photos deletes the selected image or images.

Print an Image

You can print an image from the Pictures library, or from any subfolder in the Pictures library. When you activate the Print command, the Print Pictures dialog box appears. You can use this dialog box to choose a printer and a layout, and to send the image to the printer.

You can print a single image or multiple images. If you work with multiple images, you can print them individually or print two or more images per sheet.

Print an Image

1. Open the image you want to print.

2. If you do not see the application bar, click the screen.

 The application bar appears.

3. Click **More** (⦁⦁⦁).

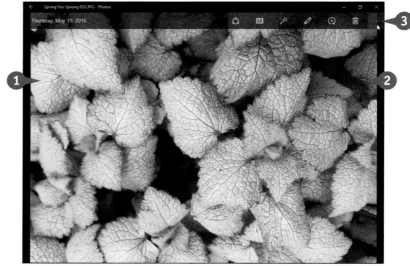

Photos displays more commands.

4. Click **Print**.

The Print pane appears.

Ⓐ Photos displays a preview of the printout.

5 Click ⌄ and click the printer you want to use.

6 Select the number of copies you want.

7 Click ⌄ and select the orientation of the photo.

Ⓑ If you want to set extra options such as the page layout or printout quality you prefer, you can click **More settings**.

8 Click **Print**.

Photos sends your image to the printer.

Which orientation should I use?
The orientation determines how Photos lays out the image on the page. If your image has a greater height than width, choose Portrait; if your image has a greater width than height, choose Landscape.

What type of paper should I use for my photo printouts?
You can purchase a variety of photo-quality paper types for printing your digital photographs. Photo-quality paper, though more expensive than multipurpose paper, is designed to create a more permanent image and improve the resolution and color of the printed image. Photo-quality paper comes in glossy and matte finishes. Be sure to select a photo-quality paper that your printer manufacturer recommends.

Take a Picture with Your PC Camera

I f your PC comes with a built-in camera or if you have an external camera attached to your PC, you can use the camera to take a picture of yourself, someone else, your surroundings — anything you want — using the Camera app.

The Camera app also gives you the option of recording a video. The Camera app stores each photo or video in a new album called *Camera Roll*, which appears in your Pictures library.

Take a Picture with Your PC Camera

1 Click **Start** (⊞).

2 Click **Camera**.

The first time that you start the Camera app, it asks for permission to use your location.

3 Click **Yes**.

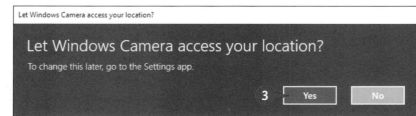

The Camera app loads.

A A live feed from the camera appears.

B If you want to adjust settings before taking the photo, you can click **More** (⋯) and then click **Settings**.

4 When you are ready to take the photo, click **Photo** (📷).

C If you want to record a video instead, you can click **Video** (📹).

The Camera app takes the photo or starts the recording.

5 If you are recording a video, click **Video** (📹) again when you are finished.

The Camera app saves your photo or video.

01:09

I accidentally clicked No when I first started the Camera app. How can I change this?
Click **Start** (⊞) and then click **Settings** (⚙). Click **Privacy** and then click the **Location** tab. Click the **Windows Camera** switch to **On**.

My video recordings take up lots of space. Can I fix this?
Yes, you can switch to a lower resolution, a lower frame rate, or both. Click **More** (⋯), click **Settings**, and then open the **Video recording** list in the Videos section. The default resolution is 640 x 480, but you can select a smaller resolution such as 320 x 240. For some cameras, you can also reduce the default frame rate of 30 frames per second (fps), to 15 fps or 12 fps to save space.

Working with Multimedia

If you are into movies, TV shows, or music, you will appreciate the Windows apps that help you play, organize, edit, and generally get the most out of your multimedia. This chapter gives you the details on all the Windows media apps.

Import Videos from a Digital Camera

You can import videos from a digital camera and save them on your computer. If your camera stores the videos on a memory card, you can also use a memory card reader attached to your PC to upload the digital videos from the removable drive that Windows sets up when you insert the card.

To perform the import directly from your digital camera, you need a cable to connect your camera to your PC. Most digital cameras come with a USB cable. After you have the digital videos on your system, you can view them.

Import Videos from a Digital Camera

1 Plug in your camera or memory storage card reader.

Note: If you see a notification, click the notification and then skip to step **5**.

2 Click **File Explorer** (📁).

3 Click **This PC**.

File Explorer displays a list of the devices attached to your PC.

4 Right-click your digital camera.

5 Click **Import pictures and videos**.

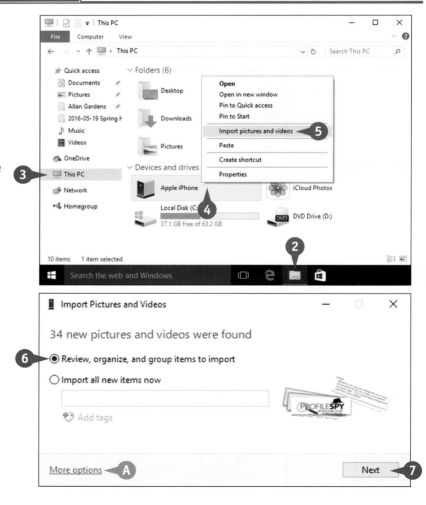

The Import Pictures and Videos dialog box appears.

6 Click **Review, organize, and group items to import** (○ changes to ⦿).

A To make sure your videos are imported into the Videos library, you can click **More options** and follow the instructions in the first Tip.

7 Click **Next**.

Windows displays the photos and videos that are on your camera.

Ⓑ Videos are indicated with a filmstrip graphic.

⑧ Click each video that you want to import (☐ changes to ✔).

Ⓒ If a group contains both photos and videos, you can click the group's **View all** link, and then click just the videos (☐ changes to ✔).

⑨ Type a name for each video import.

⑩ Click **Import**.

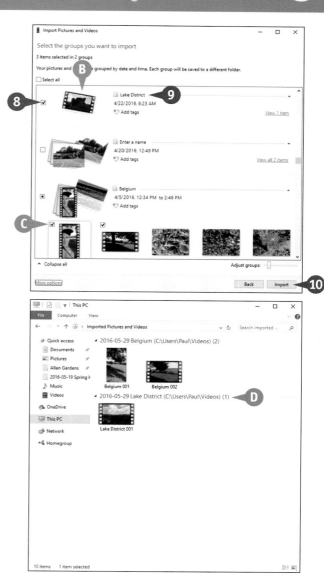

Windows imports the videos.

When the import is complete, File Explorer displays your imported videos.

Ⓓ Windows stores the imported videos in a folder named after today's date.

TIPS

How do I ensure my videos are imported into the Videos library?

Follow steps **1** to **5** to open the Import Pictures and Videos dialog box and then click **More options**. Click the **Import videos to** ⌄ and then click **Videos**. Click **OK**.

How can I get my imported videos to appear in the Movies & TV app?

In the Search box, type **movies** and then click the **Movies & TV** app. Click **Settings** (⚙), click **Choose where we look for videos**, and click **Add** (➕). Click the folder that Windows created when you imported your videos, click **Add this folder to Videos**, and then click **Done**.

Navigate the Videos Library

Before you can work with your videos, you need to locate them on your PC. You do that by using the Movies & TV app to open the Videos library, which is a special folder designed specifically for storing digital videos, movies, and TV shows.

To get more out of the Videos library, you need to know the basic techniques for opening any videos that you have stored in it. If you are looking for commercial movies or TV shows, you can also use the Movies & TV app to buy or rent a movie or to buy a TV show episode.

Navigate the Videos Library

1 Click **Start** (⊞).

2 Click **Movies & TV**.

Windows opens the Movies & TV app.

3 Click **Menu** (≡).

4 Click **Videos**.

The Movies & TV app displays the videos stored on your PC.

5 If the Video library contains one or more folders, click a folder.

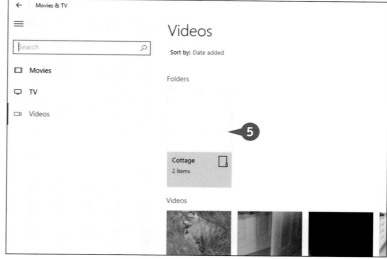

Ⓐ The Movies & TV app displays the digital videos in the selected folder.

Ⓑ You can click **Back** (←) to return to the previous section of the Movies & TV app.

TIPS

How can I get my Camera app videos to appear in the Movies & TV app?

Open the Movies & TV app, click **Settings** (⚙), click **Choose where we look for videos**, click **Add** (➕), select the **Pictures** folder, click **Camera Roll**, click **Add this folder to Videos**, and then click **Done**.

How do I get movies and TV shows?

Click **Start** (⊞), click **Store** to open the Store app, and then click **Movies & TV**. Click a movie or TV section heading (such as New Movies or Featured TV Shows); locate the movie, TV show season, or TV show episode; and then click either **Buy** or **Rent**.

Watch a Video

After you know how to use the Movies & TV app to navigate your Videos library, as shown in the previous section, "Navigate the Videos Library," you can use the app to select and play a video that you have on your PC. The Movies & TV app plays the video full screen on your PC, so you get the best viewing experience. When you have the video playing, you can pause and restart the playback, and you can use a special tool called the *scrubber* to quickly fast-forward or rewind the video to the spot that you want.

Watch a Video

Start a Video

1 In the Movies & TV app, locate the video you want to play.

2 Click the video.

The Movies & TV app begins playing the video.

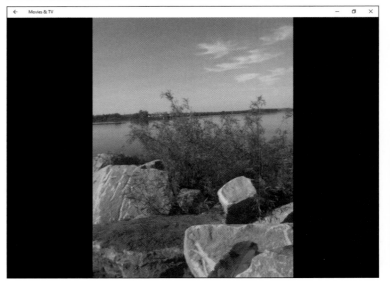

Control the Video Playback

1 Click the screen.

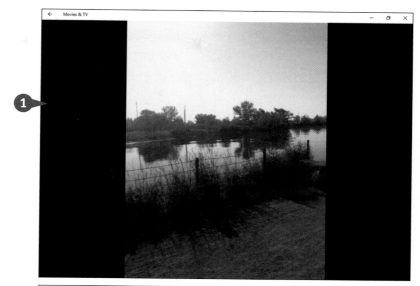

The Movies & TV app displays the playback controls.

A You can click **Pause** (❚❚) to stop and restart the playback.

B You can click and drag the scrubber to rewind or fast-forward the video.

C You can click the timeline to jump to that position in the video.

TIPS

How do I play a movie or TV show that I purchased or rented from the Windows Store?

After your purchase or rental has been downloaded to your PC, it appears in the Movies & TV app. Click **Start** (▦) and then click **Movies & TV** to open the Movies & TV app. Click **Menu** (≡) and then click either **Movies** or **TV**.

How do I play a DVD?

Unfortunately, Windows 10 does not come with an app for playing DVDs, so you will need to obtain a third-party app. A good choice is VLC, by VideoLAN. In the Store app, search for the app named "VLC for Windows Store."

Play a Music CD

You can play music CDs in Windows Media Player. When you first insert an audio disc in your PC's optical drive (that is, a drive capable of reading CDs and DVDs), Windows asks what action you want to perform with audio CDs, and you can tell it to play them using Windows Media Player.

The CD appears in the Now Playing window, and if you have an Internet connection, you see the name of each track as well as other track data. You can control some playback options using the Now Playing window, but you can also switch to the Media Player library for more options.

Play a Music CD

Play a CD

1 Insert a music CD into your computer's optical drive.

A Windows displays an audio CD notification.

2 Click the notification.

Windows displays a list of actions you can take when you insert an audio CD.

3 Click **Play audio CD**.

Note: If you see the Welcome to Windows Media Player dialog box, click **Recommended settings** (○ changes to ◉) and then click **Finish**.

The Windows Media Player Now Playing
window appears and begins playing the
audio CD.

Skip a Track

④ Click **Next** (▶▶|) to skip to the next track.

⑤ Click **Previous** (|◀◀) to skip to the
previous track.

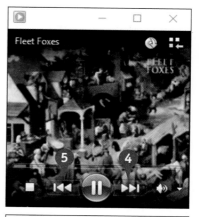

Pause and Resume Play

⑥ Click **Pause** (⏸).

Windows Media Player pauses playback.

⑦ Click **Play** (▶).

Windows Media Player resumes playback
where you left off.

TIPS

Can I change the CD's audio levels?
Yes, Windows Media Player has a graphic equalizer component
you can work with. To display it, right-click the **Now Playing**
window, click **Enhancements**, and then click **Graphic equalizer**.
To choose a predefined set of levels, click **Default** and then click
a preset value such as Rock or Classical. Alternatively, you can
use the sliders to set your own audio levels.

**Can I display something other than
album art during playback?**
Yes. Right-click the **Now Playing**
window and then click **Visualizations**
to see a list of visualization categories.
Click a category and then click the
visualization you want to view.

continued ▶

You can use the playback buttons at the bottom of the Windows Media Player library to control how a CD plays. For example, you can easily switch from one song to another on the CD. You can also use the Repeat feature to tell Windows Media Player to start the CD over from the beginning after it has finished playing the CD. Windows Media Player also offers the Shuffle feature, which plays the CD's tracks in random order. If you want to learn how to import music from the CD to Windows Media Player, see the next section, "Copy Tracks from a Music CD."

Play a Music CD (continued)

Stop Play

8 Click **Stop** (■).

Windows Media Player stops playback.

If you click **Play** (▶) after clicking **Stop** (■), the current song starts over again.

9 Click **Switch to Library** (⊞) to open the Windows Media Player library window.

The Windows Media Player library window opens.

Play Another Song

10 In the details pane, double-click the song you want to play.

Windows Media Player begins playing the song.

Ⓐ This area displays the current song title, the album title, and the song composer (if one is listed).

Repeat the CD

11 Click **Turn Repeat On** (↻).

Windows Media Player restarts the CD after the last track finishes playing.

Note: To turn on Repeat from the Now Playing window, press Ctrl + T.

Play Songs Randomly

12 Click **Turn Shuffle On** (⤨).

Windows Media Player shuffles the order of play.

Note: To turn on Shuffle from the Now Playing window, press Ctrl + H.

TIPS

Why does my details pane not list the song titles?
Windows Media Player tries to gather information about the album from the Internet. If it cannot ascertain song titles, it displays track numbers instead. To add your own titles, right-click each song title you want to change, click **Edit**, type your text, and press Enter.

Can I keep the Now Playing window in view at all times?
Yes. You can configure the Now Playing window so that it stays on top of any other window that you have open on your desktop. Right-click the Now Playing window and then click **Always show Now Playing on top**.

197

Copy Tracks from a Music CD

You can add tracks from a music CD to the library in Windows Media Player. This enables you to listen to an album without having to put the CD into your optical drive each time. The process of adding tracks from a CD is called *copying*, or *ripping*, in Windows.

You can either rip an entire CD directly from the Now Playing window, or rip selected tracks using the library. You can also use the tracks to create your own playlists and to create your own custom CDs.

Copy Tracks from a Music CD

Rip an Entire CD Using the Now Playing Window

1. Insert a CD into your computer's optical drive.

 The Now Playing window appears.

2. Click **Rip CD** (🔘).

 Windows Media Player begins ripping the entire CD.

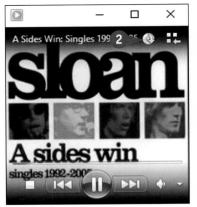

Rip Selected Tracks Using the Library

1. Insert a CD into your computer's optical drive.

 If the Now Playing window appears, click **Switch to Library** (▦).

 Ⓐ Windows Media Player displays a list of the CD's tracks.

2. Click the CD tracks that you do not want to copy (☑ changes to ☐).

3. Click **Rip CD**.

Windows Media Player begins copying the track or tracks.

B The Rip Status column displays the copy progress.

C After each file is copied, the Rip Status column displays a Ripped to Library message.

D The copy is complete when all the tracks you selected display the Ripped to Library status.

TIPS

How do I remove a track from the library?

In the library, click **Music**, click **Album**, and then double-click the album that you ripped to display a list of the tracks. Right-click the track that you want to remove and then click **Delete**.

Can I adjust the quality of the copies?

Yes, by changing the *bit rate*, which is a measure of how much of the CD's original data is copied to your computer. This is measured in kilobits per second (Kbps); the higher the value, the higher the quality, but the more hard drive space each track takes up. Click **Rip Settings**, click **Audio Quality**, and then click the value you want.

199

Navigate the Music Library

Before you can work with your songs and albums, you need to locate them on your PC. You do that by using the Groove Music app to open the Windows Music library, which is a special folder designed specifically for storing digital music.

To get more out of the Music library, you need to know the basic techniques for opening any albums that you have stored in it. You can also use the Groove Music app to purchase commercial albums or songs.

Navigate the Music Library

1 Click **Start** (⊞).

2 Click **Groove Music**.

Windows opens the Groove Music app.

3 Click **Menu** (≡).

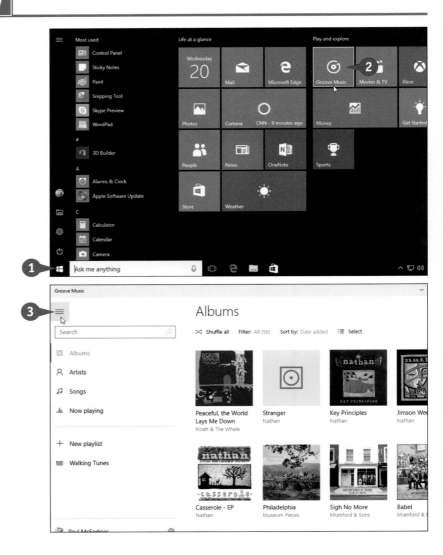

The Music library appears.

4 Click a music category.

A The music in that category appears.

5 Click a category item.

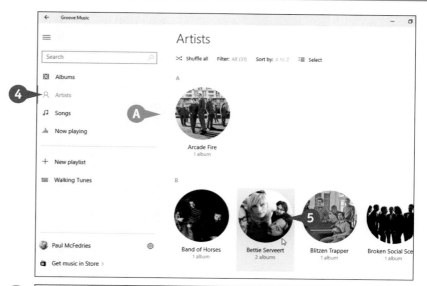

B If the category item contains multiple subitems, Groove Music displays those subitems.

C You can click **Back** (←) to return to the previous section of the Groove Music app.

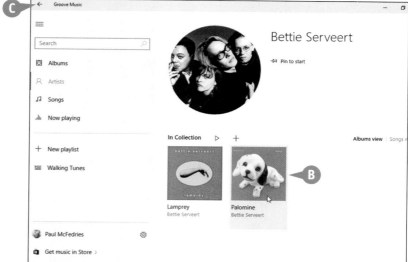

TIPS

What if a song that I want to play does not appear in the Music library?

If your song is outside the Music library, the Groove Music app does not see it. Click **Settings** (⚙), click **Choose where we look for music**, and click **Add** (➕). Locate and click the folder that contains your music, and then click **Add this folder to Music**.

How do I buy an album?

Click **Start** (⊞), click **Store** to open the Store app, and then click **Music**. Either use the Search box to look for the artist or album title, or click a section heading, and locate the album. Click the album and then click the price button.

Play Music

If you want to listen to music while using your PC, and your PC has either built-in or connected speakers, you can use the Groove Music app to play tunes from your Music library. You can listen to all the songs on an album, all the songs from a particular artist, or individual songs.

The Groove Music app offers several features for controlling the music playback. You can also play albums, artists, and songs in random order and play albums and artists repeatedly.

Play Music

Start Groove Music

1 Use the Groove Music app to display your music.

Note: See the previous section, "Navigate the Music Library," for details.

2 Click the item that contains the music you want to play.

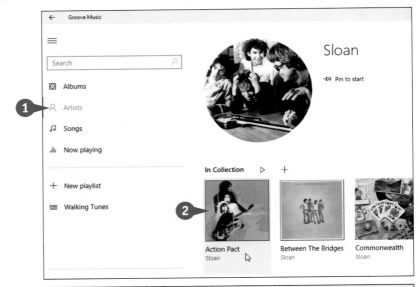

The Groove Music app opens the item and displays a list of songs.

3 Click **Play** (▷).

A You can also click a song and then click **Play** (▷).

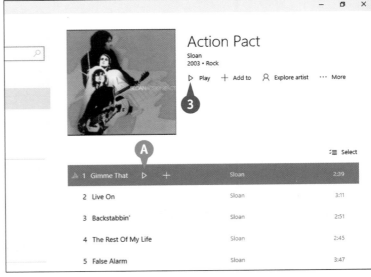

Control the Music Playback

B When you play music, the Groove Music app displays the playback controls.

C You can click **Pause** (▮▮) to stop and restart the playback.

D You can click and drag the scrubber to rewind or fast-forward the current song.

E To control the volume, you can click **Volume** (◀》) and then click and drag the slider.

F You can click **Next** (▷▮) to jump to the next song.

G You can click **Previous** (▮◁) to return to the beginning of the current song; click **Previous** (▮◁) again to jump to the previous song.

Create a Playlist

A *playlist* is a collection of songs that represents a subset of your total music collection. A playlist can include audio tracks you ripped from a music CD, songs downloaded from the Internet, or music purchased through the Xbox Music Store.

You can use the Groove Music app to create customized playlists that include only the songs you want to hear. For example, you might want to create a playlist of upbeat or festive songs to play during a party or celebration. Similarly, you might want to create a playlist of your current favorite songs to play during a workout.

Create a Playlist

1 Click **Menu** (≡).

2 Click **New playlist**.

Groove Music prompts you to name the new playlist.

3 Type a name for the new playlist.

4 Click **Save**.

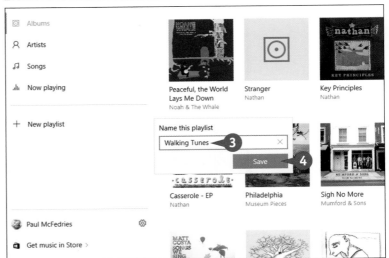

5 Click a song that you want to add to the playlist.

6 Click **Add to**.

7 Click the name of your playlist.

Groove Music adds the song to the playlist.

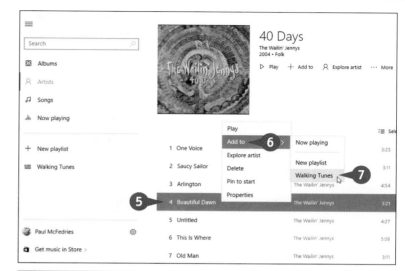

8 Click **Menu** (≡).

9 Click the playlist.

A Groove Music displays a list of the songs you added.

10 Click **Play** (▷) to listen to the playlist.

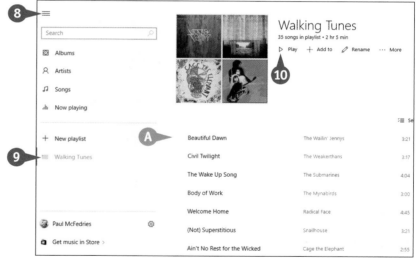

TIPS

How do I make changes to an existing playlist?
Click the playlist to open it. To change the playlist name, click **Edit** (▦), type the new playlist name, and then click **Save**. To change the song order, click and drag songs up and down, or right-click a song and then click either **Move up** or **Move down**. To delete a song from the playlist, right-click the song and then click **Remove from playlist**.

How do I delete a playlist?
Click the playlist to open it, click **More** (···), and then click **Delete**. When Groove Music asks you to confirm, click **Delete**.

Switch Between PC Speakers and Headphones

I f you have connected a pair of headphones to your PC, you can use those headphones to listen to music or to hear the sound from videos, TV shows, and movies. If you want to listen through your PC's built-in sound system instead, you must disable the headphones by disconnecting them. To avoid that hassle, you can leave your headphones connected and use Control Panel's Sound feature to switch between sound output devices.

Switch Between PC Speakers and Headphones

1 In the Search box, type **control**.

2 Click **Control Panel**.

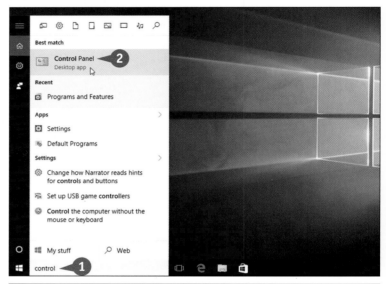

The Control Panel appears.

3 Click **Hardware and Sound**.

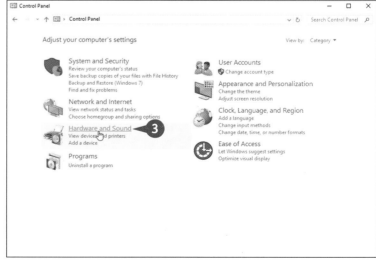

The Hardware and Sound window appears.

④ Click **Manage audio devices**.

The Sound dialog box appears with the Playback tab selected.

⑤ Click the audio device you want to use for the sound playback.

⑥ Click **Set Default**.

⑦ Click **OK**.

Windows now uses the device you set as the default for sound playback.

TIPS

I am hard of hearing in one ear. How do I turn up the headphone sound for that ear?
Follow steps 1 to 4, click your headphones, click **Properties**, click the **Levels** tab, and then click **Balance**. In the Balance dialog box, drag the slider marked either L (left) or R (right) to the level you prefer and then click **OK**.

How can I prevent wide fluctuations in volume between the different media that I play?
Activate the Loudness Equalization feature, which makes all your PC's sounds equally loud. Follow steps 1 to 4, click your headphones, click **Properties**, click the **Enhancements** tab, click **Loudness Equalization** (☐ changes to ☑), and then click **OK**.

Editing Documents

To be productive with Windows, you need to know how to work with documents. In this chapter, you learn how to create, save, open, and work with documents and OneNote notebooks.

Create and Save a Document

When you are ready to create something using Windows, in most cases you begin by launching a program and then using that program to create a new document to hold your work. Many Windows programs (such as WordPad and Paint) create a new document for you automatically when you begin the program. However, you can also use these programs to create another new document after you have started the program.

After you create a document and make any changes to it, you must save the document to preserve your work.

Create and Save a Document

Create a New Document

① Click **File**.

② Click **New**.

The program creates the new document.

Note: In most programs, you can also press **Ctrl**+**N** to create a new document.

Save a Document

① Click **File**.

② Click **Save**.

Note: In most programs, you can also press **Ctrl**+**S** or click **Save** (⊟).

Note: If you saved the document previously, your changes are now preserved. You do not need to follow the rest of the steps in this section.

If this is a new document that you have never saved before, the Save As dialog box appears.

3 Click **Documents**.

Note: In most programs, the Documents library is selected automatically when you save a document.

A Windows opens the Documents library.

4 Click in the File Name text box and type the name you want to use for the document.

Note: The name you type can be up to 255 characters long, but it cannot include the following characters: < > , ? : " \ *.

5 Click **Save**.

The app saves your document in the folder you specified.

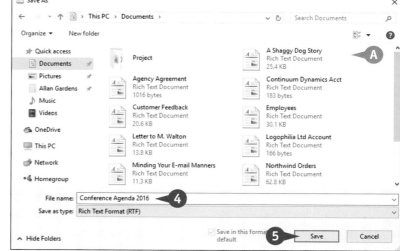

TIPS

Why do I need to save a document?
As you work on a document, Windows stores the changes in your computer's memory. However, Windows erases your PC's memory whenever you shut down or restart the computer. Without saving, you would lose all the changes you have made to your document. Saving the document preserves your changes on your computer's hard drive.

Do I have to save all my files to the Documents library?
No. You can create a subfolder within Documents. In the Save As dialog box, click **New folder**, type the name of the folder, press Enter, double-click the new folder, and then follow steps **4** and **5**.

Open a Document

To work with a document that you have saved in the past, you typically need to open the document in the program that you used to create it. When you save a document, you save its contents to your PC's hard drive, and those contents are stored in a separate file. When you open the document using the same application that you used to save it, Windows loads the file's contents into memory and displays the document in the application. You can then view or edit the document as needed.

Open a Document

1 Start the program you want to work with.

2 Click **File**.

A If you see the document you want in a list of the most recently used documents on the File menu, you can click the name to open it. You can then skip the rest of the steps in this section.

3 Click **Open**.

Note: In most programs, you can also press <kbd>Ctrl</kbd>+<kbd>O</kbd> or click **Open** (📂).

The Open dialog box appears.

4 Click **Documents**.

Note: In most programs, the Documents library is selected automatically when you open a document.

B If you want to open the document from some other folder, you can click here, click your username, and then double-click the folder.

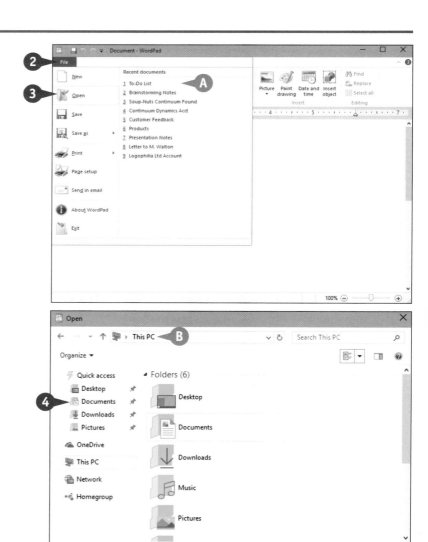

C Windows opens the Documents library.

5 Click the document name.

6 Click **Open**.

D The document appears in the program window.

TIPS

Is there a more direct way to open a document?
Yes, there is. You do not always need to open the program first. Instead, use File Explorer to open the folder that contains the document and then double-click the document. Windows automatically launches the program and opens the document.

Is there a quick way to locate a document?
Yes, Windows offers a documents search feature, which is handy if your Documents library contains many files. Use the taskbar's Search box to type some or all of the document's filename, click **Search my stuff**, and then click the Documents tab.

Change the Text Font

You can add visual appeal to a document by changing the font formatting. The font formatting includes attributes such as the typeface, style, size, or special effects.

A *typeface* — also called a *font* — is a distinctive character design that you can apply to the selected text in a document. The *type style* refers to formatting applied to text, such as **bold** or *italics*. The *type size* refers to the height of each character, which is measured in *points*; 72 points equal one inch. *Special effects* are styles that change the appearance of the text, such as <u>underline</u> and ~~strikethrough~~.

Change the Text Font

1 Select the text you want to format.

2 Display the font options.

Ⓐ In WordPad, you display the font options by clicking the **Home** tab.

Note: In many other programs, you display the font options by clicking Format in the menu bar and then clicking the Font command.

3. In the Font list, click ▼ and then click the typeface you want.

4. In the Size list, click ▼ and then click the type size you want.

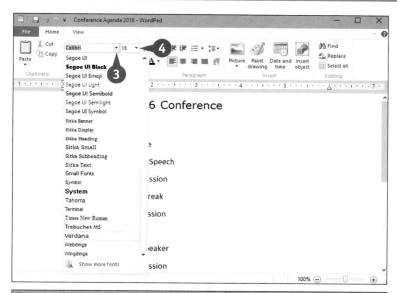

5. For bold text, click **Bold** (**B**).

6. For italics, click **Italic** (*I*).

7. For underlining, click **Underline** (**U**).

8. For color, click the **Font color** ▼ and then click a color.

B. The program applies the font formatting to the selected text.

Note: Here are some shortcuts that work in most programs: For bold, press Ctrl + B; for italics, press Ctrl + I; for underline, press Ctrl + U.

TIP

How can I make the best use of fonts in my documents?

- Use one or two typefaces to avoid the "ransom note" look.

- Avoid overly decorative typefaces because they are often difficult to read.

- Use bold only for document titles, subtitles, and headings.

- Use italics only to emphasize words and phrases, or for the titles of books and magazines.

- Use larger type sizes only for document titles, subtitles, and, possibly, headings.

- In general, dark text on a light background is the easiest to read.

Find Text

In large documents, when you need to find specific text, you can save a lot of time by using the program's Find feature. In short documents that contain only a few dozen or even a few hundred words, finding a specific word or phrase is usually not difficult. However, many documents contain hundreds or even thousands of words, so finding a word or phrase becomes much more difficult and time consuming.

You can work around this problem by using the Find feature, which searches the entire document in the blink of an eye. Most programs that work with text — including the Windows WordPad and Notepad programs — have the Find feature.

Find Text

1 Click **Find**.

A In WordPad, you display the Editing options by clicking the **Home** tab.

Note: In many programs, you run the Find command by clicking **Edit** in the menu bar and then clicking the **Find** command, or by pressing `Ctrl` + `F`.

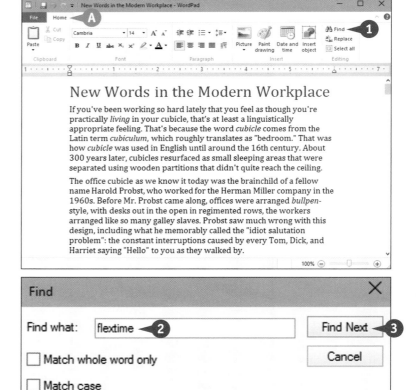

The Find dialog box appears.

2 Click in the Find What text box and type the text you want to find.

3 Click **Find Next**.

B The program selects the next instance of the search text.

Note: If the search text does not exist in the document, the program displays a dialog box to let you know.

4 If the selected instance is not the one you want, click **Find Next** until the program finds the correct instance.

5 Click **Close** (✕) to close the Find dialog box.

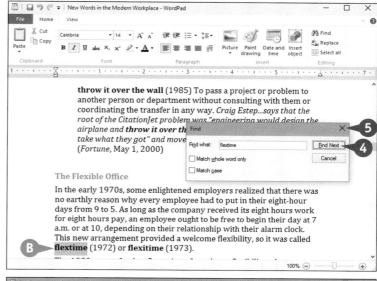

C The program leaves the found text selected.

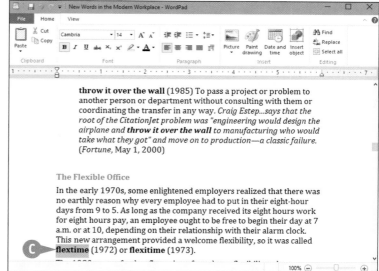

A search for a word such as *the* also matches larger words such as *theme* and *bother*. How can I avoid this?

In the Find dialog box, click **Match whole word only** (☐ changes to ☑). This tells the program to match the search text only if it is a word on its own.

A search for a name such as *Bill* also matches the non-name *bill*. How do I fix this?

In the Find dialog box, click **Match case** (☐ changes to ☑). This tells the program to match the search text only if it has the same mix of uppercase and lowercase letters that you specify in the Find What text box.

Replace Text

You can make it easier to replace multiple instances of one word with another by taking advantage of the program's Replace feature. Do you need to replace a word or part of a word with some other text? If you have several instances to replace, you can save time and do a more accurate job if you let the program's Replace feature replace the word for you. Most programs that work with text — including the Windows WordPad and Notepad programs — have the Replace feature.

Replace Text

1 Click **Replace**.

A In WordPad, you display the Editing options by clicking the **Home** tab.

Note: In many programs, you run the Replace command by clicking **Edit** in the menu bar and then clicking the **Replace** command, or by pressing Ctrl + H.

The Replace dialog box appears.

2 Click in the Find What text box, and type the text you want to find.

3 Click in the Replace With text box, and type the text you want to use as the replacement.

4 Click **Find Next**.

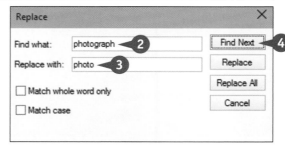

B The program selects the next instance of the search text.

Note: If the search text does not exist in the document, the program displays a dialog box to let you know.

5 If the selected instance is not the one you want, click **Find Next** until the program finds the correct instance.

6 Click **Replace**.

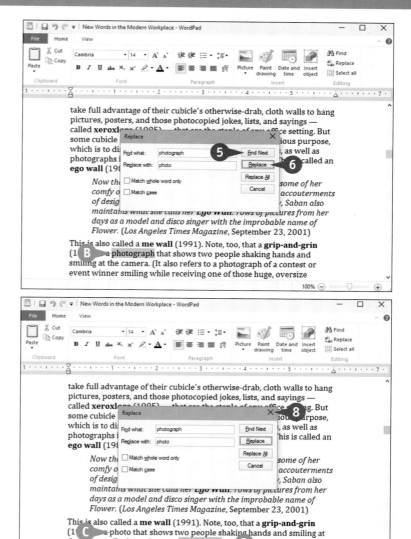

C The program replaces the selected text with the replacement text.

D The program selects the next instance of the search text.

7 Repeat steps **5** and **6** until you have replaced all the instances you want to replace.

8 Click **Close** (**X**) to close the Replace dialog box.

TIP

Is there a faster way to replace every instance of the search text with the replacement text?
Yes. In the Replace dialog box, click **Replace All**. This tells the program to replace every instance of the search text with the replacement text. However, you should exercise some caution with this feature because it may make some replacements that you did not intend. Click **Find Next** a few times to make sure the matches are correct. Also, consider clicking **Match whole word only** and **Match case** (changes to ✔), as described in the previous section, "Find Text."

Insert Special Symbols

You can make your documents more readable and more useful by inserting special symbols that are not available via your keyboard. The keyboard is home to a large number of letters, numbers, and symbols. However, the keyboard is missing some useful characters. For example, it is missing the foreign characters in words such as café and Köln. Similarly, your writing might require mathematical symbols such as ÷ and ½, financial symbols such as ¢ and ¥, or commercial symbols such as © and ®. These and many more symbols are available in Windows via the Character Map program.

Insert Special Symbols

1 Click **Start** (⊞).

2 Click **Windows Accessories**.

3 Click **Character Map**.

The Character Map window appears.

4 Click the symbol you want.

5 Click **Select**.

Ⓐ Character Map adds the symbol to the Characters to Copy text box.

6 Click **Copy**.

7 Click **Close** (✕) to shut down Character Map after you choose all the characters you want.

220

8 In your document, position the cursor where you want to insert the symbol.

B In WordPad, you display the Clipboard options by clicking the **Home** tab.

9 Click **Paste**.

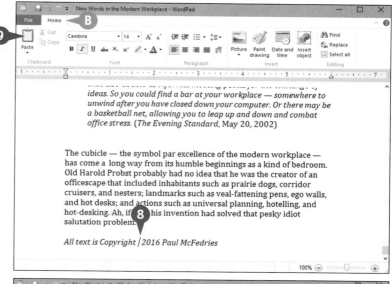

C The program inserts the symbol.

TIPS

When I click a symbol, Character Map sometimes displays a "keystroke" in the status bar. What does this mean?

This tells you that you can insert the symbol directly into your document by pressing the keystroke shown. For example, you can insert the copyright symbol (©) by pressing Alt + 0 1 6 9. When you type the numbers, be sure to use your keyboard's numeric keypad.

Are there even more symbols available?

Yes, dozens of extra symbols are available in the Character Map program's Webdings and Wingdings typefaces. To see these symbols, click the Font list ▼ and then click either **Webdings** or **Wingdings**.

Make a Copy of a Document

Whe you need to create a document that is nearly identical to an existing document, instead of creating the new document from scratch, you can save time by making a copy of the existing document and then modifying the copy as needed. For example, you might have a résumé cover letter that you want to modify for a different job application. Similarly, this year's conference agenda is likely to be similar to last year's. Instead of creating these new documents from scratch, it is much faster to copy the original document and then edit the copy as needed.

Make a Copy of a Document

1 Start the program you want to work with and open the original document.

2 Click **File**.

3 Click **Save as**.

The Save As dialog box appears.

4 Click **Documents**.

Note: In most programs, the Documents library is selected automatically when you run the Save As command.

(A) Windows opens the Documents library.

(5) Click in the File Name text box and type the name you want to use for the copy.

Note: The name you type can be up to 255 characters long, but it cannot include the following characters: < > , ? : " \ *.

(6) Click **Save**.

The program closes the original document and opens the copy you just created.

(B) The filename you typed appears in the program's title bar.

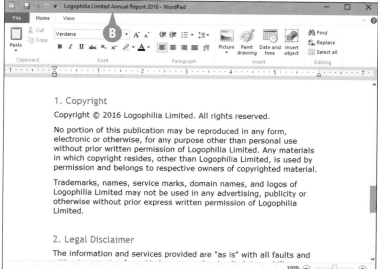

Create a OneNote Notebook

You can use the OneNote app to record and save miscellaneous bits of information, including text, lists, drawings, images, web pages, and tables of data. All of this is stored in a special file called a *notebook*. Within each notebook you can organize your data within *sections*, where each section is devoted to a particular subject. Each section is then divided into one or more *pages*, and you use these pages to enter your data.

Note that your Windows user account must be connected to a Microsoft account to use OneNote.

Create a OneNote Notebook

1 Click **Start** (⊞).

2 Click **OneNote**.

3 The first time you start OneNote, the app takes you through a few introductory screens (not shown). On each screen, click **Next** (>) to continue.

4 Click **Start using OneNote**.

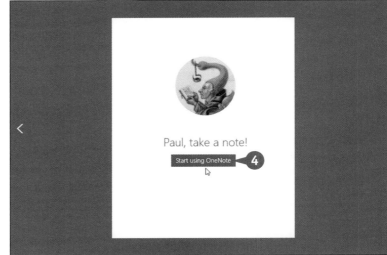

The OneNote app appears.

5 Click the screen.

6 Type a name for the notebook.

7 Press Enter.

OneNote creates a new notebook and populates it with a single section and page.

Ⓐ You can click **Menu** (≡) to hide the OneNote sidebar.

Ⓑ To name the section, you can right-click it, click **Rename Section**, and then type the name.

Ⓒ You can click here to add a title for the page.

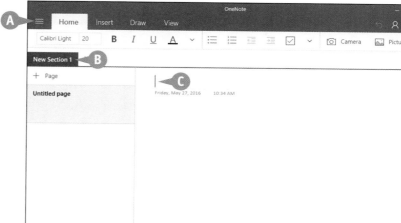

TIPS

Can I create more than one notebook?
Yes, you can add more notebooks if you have data to keep separate. Click **Menu** (≡), click **Add** (➕) to the right of the Notebooks heading, type a name for the new notebook, and then press Enter.

Can I delete a notebook?
Yes, but you cannot delete a notebook using the OneNote app. Instead, you must use the online version of OneNote. Log in to http://onedrive.live.com. Click **Documents**, position the mouse pointer (⌖) over the OneNote notebook, and then click the file's check box (☐ changes to ☑). Click **Manage** and then click **Delete**.

Add Pages and Sections to a Notebook

You can keep your notes organized and easy to find by taking advantage of OneNote's pages and sections. Each OneNote notebook consists of one or more sections, which you use to break down the notebook's overall topic or theme into smaller, more manageable subjects.

You can further break down each section into one or more pages, which are the OneNote items within which you add text, images, lists, and other data. You can add as many sections and pages as you need to keep your notes organized.

Add Pages and Sections to a Notebook

Add a Page

1 Click the section in which you want to add the page.

2 Click **Add** (+).

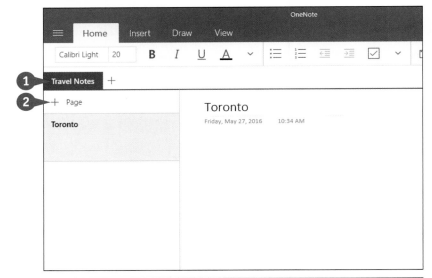

OneNote adds a page to the section.

3 Type a title for the page and press **Enter**.

OneNote sets the page title.

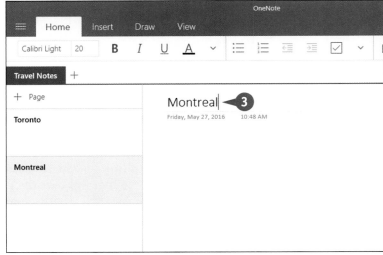

Add a Section

1 Click **Add** (**+**).

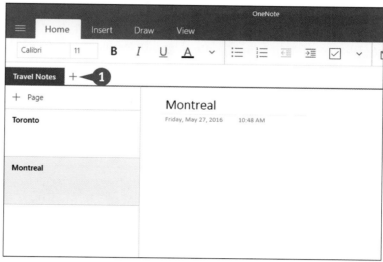

OneNote adds a section to the notebook.

2 Type the section name and press **Enter**.

OneNote sets the section title.

A OneNote adds a blank page to the new section.

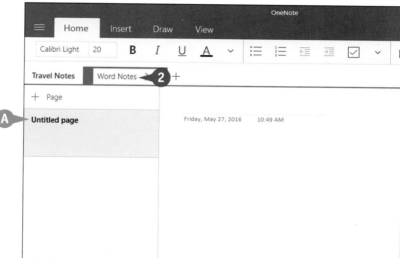

TIPS

How do I rename a section or change a section's color scheme?

To change the section name, right-click the section tab, click **Rename Section**, type the new name, and then press **Enter**. To change the section's color scheme, right-click the section tab, click **Section Color**, and then click the color you want to use.

How do I delete a page or section?

To delete a page, right-click the page in the Pages list, click **Delete Page**, and then click **Delete Page** to confirm. To delete a section, right-click the section tab, click **Delete Section**, and then click **Delete Section** to confirm.

Add Text Notes

Once you have your sections and pages, your next step is to fill your pages with content. OneNote makes it easy to insert everything from simple text notes to pictures to entire files. All OneNote content appears inside a *container*, which is essentially a box that surrounds the content. After you have some content inside a container, you can move the container around on the page, edit or format the container content, and more.

Most page content consists of text notes, and OneNote makes it very simple to add text to a page.

Add Text Notes

Add a Text Note

1 Click the section you want to use.

2 Click the page you want to use.

3 Click inside the page at the position where you want the text to appear.

A OneNote adds an insertion point cursor.

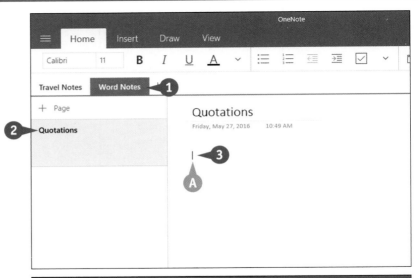

4 Type your text.

B OneNote adds a container around your text.

5 When your text note is complete, click outside the container.

OneNote adds the text note to the page.

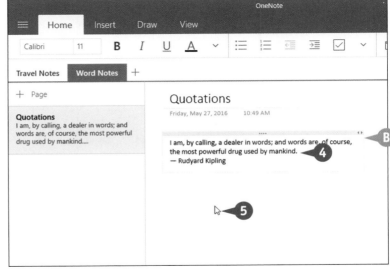

Size a Text Note Container

1 Position the mouse pointer (◌) over the right edge of the container (◌ changes to ⟷).

2 Click and drag the mouse pointer (⟷) right for a larger container, or left for a smaller container, and then release the mouse.

OneNote resizes the container and adjusts the text to fit the new size.

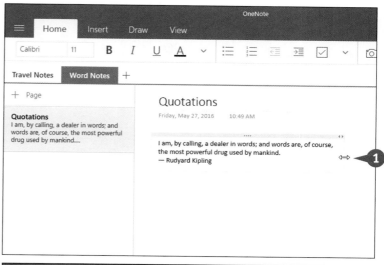

Move a Text Note Container

1 Position the mouse pointer (◌) over the middle of the top edge of the container (◌ changes to ✥).

2 Click and drag the mouse pointer (✥) to the position you want and then release the mouse.

OneNote moves the container to the new position.

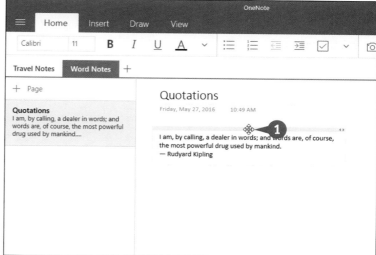

TIP

How do I format note text?

Select the note text you want to format and then click the **Home** tab to display the text note formatting options. You can click **Bold** (**B**), **Italic** (*I*), or **Underline** (U) to apply those font styles to the text. You can also click the Font formatting ❯ to apply the subscript, superscript, or strikethrough effect.

Add an Image to a Notebook Page

Although you will populate your OneNote notebooks mostly with text notes, you can also insert other types of content, including images. You can either insert an image file from your PC's hard drive or, if your computer has a camera attached, take a photo and insert it directly into the page. As with text notes, OneNote adds an image to the page within a container that you can move and size as needed.

Add an Image to a Notebook Page

1 Click the section you want to use.

2 Click the page you want to use.

3 Click inside the page at the position where you want the image to appear.

4 Click the **Insert** tab.

5 Click **Picture**.

Ⓐ If you want to add a photo using your PC's camera, you can click **Camera**, instead.

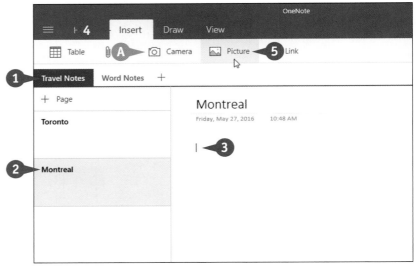

The Open dialog box appears.

6 Click the image.

7 Click **Open**.

OneNote opens the image for editing.

⑧ Edit the image as needed.

Ⓑ For example, you can click **Crop** (◻) to crop the image before inserting it.

⑨ Click **Insert all**.

OneNote inserts the image into the page.

Ⓒ To rotate or flip the image, you can right-click it, click **Picture**. To rotate 90 degrees, click either **Rotate Right** or **Rotate Left**; to flip, click with **Flip Horizontal** or **Flip Vertical**.

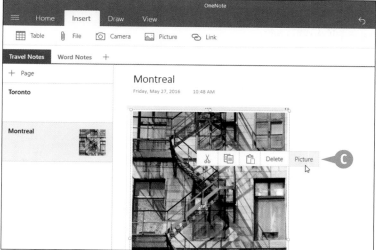

TIPS

How do I add a title or caption to the image?
Adding a title or caption is a good idea, especially if other people will be viewing your notebook. To add a title to the image, press Enter and then type the title above the image. To add a caption, double-click inside the space just below the image (but still in the image placeholder) and then type your caption.

Can I insert other types of files?
Yes, you can insert PDF files, text files, Microsoft Office documents, and more. To insert a file, follow steps 1 to 4, click **File**, click **Insert as Attachment**, select the file, and then click **Open**.

Work with Notebook Lists

Many OneNote notes consist of lists of items. If you have a list that does not require a particular sequence, you can add the items to a page as a bulleted list. If you have a list that does require a sequence, then you can add the items to the page as a numbered list instead.

One of the most common OneNote list types is the to-do list, which is a collection of tasks, each with a leading check box. When you complete a task, you activate its check box.

Work with Notebook Lists

Create a Bulleted or Numbered List

1. Click the section you want to use.

2. Click the page you want to use.

3. Click inside the page at the position where you want the list to appear.

4. Click the **Home** tab.

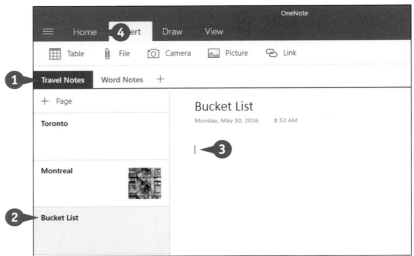

5. Click the type of list you want to add:

 A. You can click **Bulleted List** (:☰) to create a list with bullets.

 B. You can click **Numbering** (:☰) to create a list with numbers.

 OneNote adds the list to a container.

6. Click inside the container and type your list items, pressing **Enter** after each item.

7. When you are done, click outside the container.

 OneNote adds the list to the page.

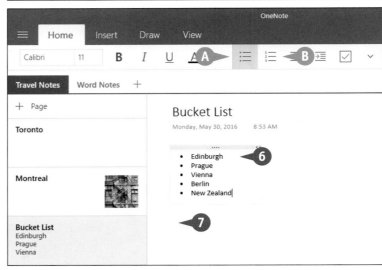

Create a To-Do List

1 Click the section you want to use.

2 Click the page you want to use.

3 Add the to-do list.

4 Select all the items in the list.

5 Click **Tag as To Do** (☑).

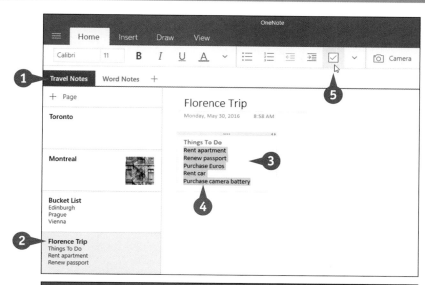

Ⓒ OneNote adds a check box to the left of each item.

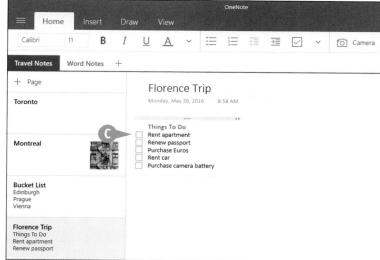

233

Print a Document

When you need a hard copy of your document, either for your files or to distribute to someone else, you can get a hard copy by sending the document to your printer. Most applications that deal with documents also come with a Print command. When you run this command, the Print dialog box appears. The Print dialog box enables you to choose the printer you want to use as well as to specify how many copies you want to print. Many Print dialog boxes also display a preview of your document before you print it.

Print a Document

① Turn on your printer.

② Open the document you want to print.

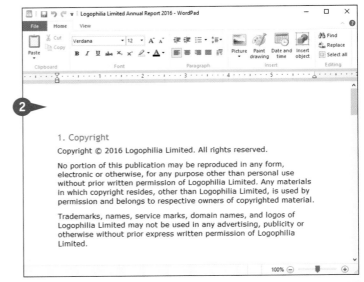

③ Click **File**.

④ Click **Print**.

Note: In many programs, you can select the **Print** command by pressing Ctrl + P or by clicking **Print** (🖨).

The Print dialog box appears.

Note: The layout of the Print dialog box varies from program to program. The WordPad version shown here is a typical example.

5 If you have more than one printer, click the printer you want to use.

6 Click the **Number of copies** to specify the number of copies to print.

7 Click **Print**.

A Windows prints the document. The print icon appears in the taskbar's notification area while the document prints.

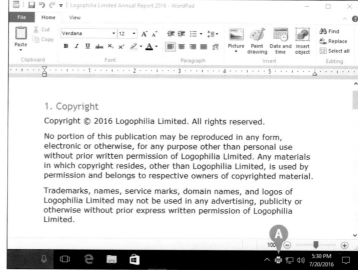

How do I print only part of a document?

Most programs support the following methods:

- Print selected text: Select the text and then, in the Print dialog box, click **Selection** (○ changes to ◉).
- Print a specific page: Place the cursor on the page and then, in the Print dialog box, click **Current Page** (○ changes to ◉).
- Print a range of pages: In the Print dialog box, click **Pages** (○ changes to ◉), type the first page number, a dash (–), and the last page number (for example, 1–5).

Working with Files

This chapter shows you how to work with the files on your computer. These easy and efficient methods show you how to view, select, copy, move, rename, and delete files, as well as how to restore accidentally deleted files, how to extract files from a compressed folder, and more.

Select a File

Before you can use File Explorer to do any work with one or more files, you first have to select the files so that Windows knows which ones you want to work with. For example, before you can move files to a new location, you must first select the files you want to move. You can select just a single file, two or more files, or a group of files, or all the files in a folder. Although you learn specifically about selecting files in this section, the technique for selecting folders is exactly the same.

Select a File

Select a Single File

1. Click **File Explorer** (📁).

2. Open the folder containing the file.

3. Click the file.

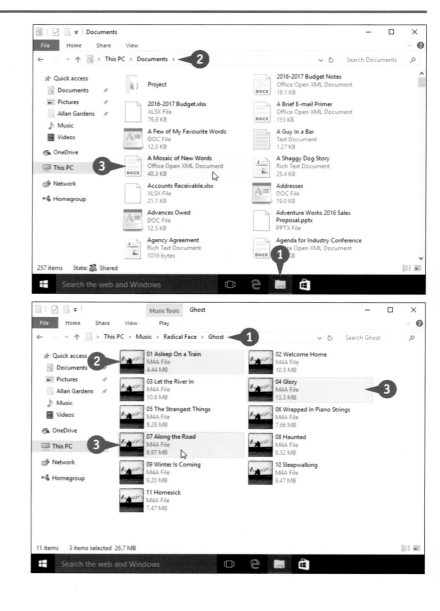

Select Multiple Files

1. Open the folder containing the files.

2. Click the first file you want to select.

3. Press and hold Ctrl and click each of the other files you want to select.

Select a Group of Files

1. Open the folder containing the files.

2. Position the mouse pointer (⇗) slightly above and slightly to the left of the first file in the group.

3. Click and drag the mouse pointer (⇗) down and to the right until all the files in the group are selected.

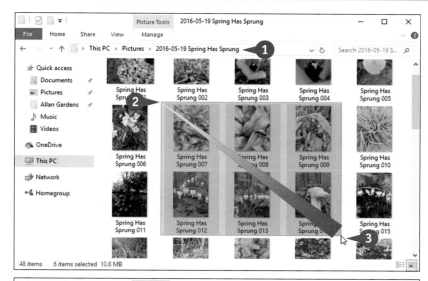

Select All Files

1. Open the folder containing the files.

2. Click the **Home** tab.

3. Click **Select all**.

Note: A quick way to select all the files in a folder is to press `Ctrl`+`A`.

Ⓐ File Explorer selects all the files in the folder.

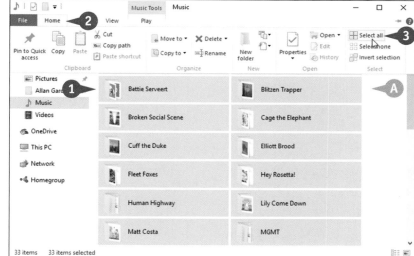

TIP

How do I deselect a file?

Depending on the situation, there are a few ways to deselect files:

- To deselect a single file from a multiple-file selection, press and hold `Ctrl` and click the file you want to deselect.

- To deselect all files, either click the **Home** tab and then click **Select none**, or click an empty area within the folder.

- To reverse the selection — deselect the selected files and select the deselected files — click the **Home** tab and then click **Invert selection**.

Change the File View

You can configure how Windows displays the files in a folder by changing the file view. This enables you to see larger or smaller icons or the details of each file.

You can choose a view such as Small Icons to see more files in the folder window. A view such as Large Icons or Extra Large Icons enables you to view images as thumbnail versions of each picture. If you want to see more information about the files, choose either the Tiles view or Details view.

Change the File View

1 In File Explorer, open the folder containing the files you want to view.

2 Click the **View** tab.

3 In the Layout section, click **More** (⇟).

Windows displays the Layout gallery.

4 Click the view you want.

Ⓐ File Explorer changes the file view (this example shows Tiles view).

Preview a File

Windows enables you to view the contents of some files without opening them. This makes it easier to select the file you want to work with because it means you do not have to run an application to see the file's contents. Previewing the file is faster and uses fewer system resources. Windows previews only certain types of files, such as text documents, rich text documents, web pages, images, and videos.

Preview a File

1 In File Explorer, open the folder containing the file you want to preview.

2 Click the **View** tab.

3 Click **Preview pane**.

A The Preview pane appears.

4 Click a file.

B The file's contents appear in the Preview pane.

C You can click and drag the left border of the Preview pane to change its size.

Note: When you are finished with the Preview pane, you can click **Preview pane** on the View tab to close it.

Copy a File

You can use Windows to make an exact copy of a file. This is useful if you want to back up an important file by making an extra copy on a flash drive, memory card, or other removable disc. Similarly, you might require a copy of a file if you want to send the copy on a disc to another person. This section shows you how to copy a single file, but the steps also work if you select multiple files. You can also use these steps to copy a folder.

Copy a File

1. In File Explorer, open the folder containing the file you want to copy.

2. Select the file.

3. Click the **Home** tab.

4. Click **Copy**.

 Windows places a copy of the file in a special memory location called the Clipboard.

5. Open the location you want to use to store the copy.

6. Click the **Home** tab.

7. Click **Paste**.

 Ⓐ Windows inserts a copy of the file in the location.

Move a File

When you need to store a file in a new location, the easiest way is to move the file from its current folder to another folder on your computer. When you save a file for the first time, you specify a folder on your PC's hard drive. This original location is not permanent; you can move the file to another location on the hard drive. This section shows you how to move a single file, but the steps also work if you select multiple files or move a folder.

Move a File

1 In File Explorer, open the folder containing the file you want to move.

2 Select the file.

3 Click the **Home** tab.

4 Click **Cut**.

Windows places the file in the Clipboard.

5 Open the folder to which you want to move the file.

6 Click the **Home** tab.

7 Click **Paste**.

Ⓐ Windows moves the file to the new location.

Rename a File

You can change the name of a file, which is useful if the current name of the file does not accurately describe the file's contents. By giving your document a descriptive name, you make it easier to find the file later.

Make sure that you rename only those documents that you have created or that someone else has given to you. Do not rename any of the Windows system files or any files associated with your programs, or your computer may behave erratically, or even crash.

Rename a File

1 In File Explorer, open the folder that contains the file you want to rename.

2 Click the file.

3 Click the **Home** tab.

Note: In addition to renaming files, you can also rename any folders that you have created.

4 Click **Rename** (or press F2).

A text box appears around the filename.

5 Type the new name you want to use for the file.

Note: If you decide that you do not want to rename the file after all, press Esc to cancel the operation.

Note: The name you type can be up to 255 characters long, but it cannot include the following characters: < > , ? : " \ *.

6 Press Enter or click an empty section of the folder.

The new name appears under the file's icon.

Create a New File

You can quickly create a new file directly within a file folder. This method is faster, and often more convenient, than running a program's New command. In Windows, you can create several different file types, such as a Bitmap Image (a drawing), Rich Text Document (a WordPad file), Text Document (a Notepad file), and Compressed (Zipped) Folder (which combines multiple files in a single file, as described in the section "Extract Files from a Compressed Folder," later in this chapter). You can also create a new folder.

Create a New File

1 In File Explorer, open the folder in which you want to create the file.

2 Click the **Home** tab.

3 Click **New item**.

4 Click the type of file you want to create.

A If you click **Folder**, Windows creates a new subfolder.

Note: The New Item menu on your system may contain more items than you see here because some programs install their own file types.

B An icon for the new file appears in the folder.

5 Type the name you want to use for the new file.

6 Press Enter.

Delete a File

When you have a file that you no longer need, instead of leaving the file to clutter your hard drive, you can delete it. Make sure that you delete only those documents that you have created or that someone else has given to you. Do not delete any of the Windows system files or any files associated with your programs, or your computer may behave erratically or crash.

Delete a File

1 In File Explorer, open the folder that contains the file you want to delete.

2 Click the file you want to delete.

Note: If you need to remove more than one file, select all the files you want to delete.

Note: See the section "Select a File," earlier in this chapter, to select multiple files.

3 Click the **Home** tab.

4 Click the top half of **Delete**.

Note: Another way to select the Delete command is to press Delete.

A Windows removes the file from the folder.

Note: Another way to delete a file is to click and drag it to the desktop Recycle Bin icon.

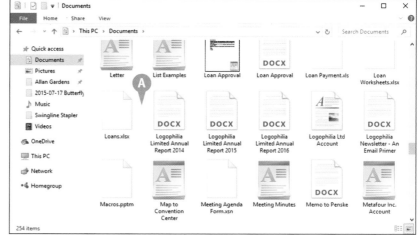

Restore a Deleted File

If you delete a file in error, Windows enables you to restore the file by placing it back in the folder from which you deleted it. You can restore a deleted file because Windows stores each deleted file in a special folder called the Recycle Bin, where the file stays for a few days or a few weeks, depending on how often you empty the bin or how full the folder becomes.

Restore a Deleted File

1 Double-click the desktop **Recycle Bin** icon.

Note: If you have a touch PC, open File Explorer, click the first **>** in the address bar, and then click **Recycle Bin**.

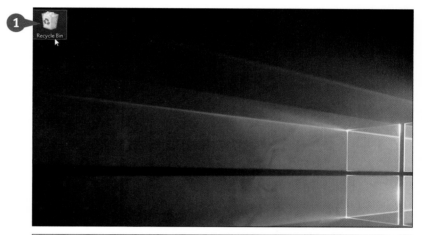

The Recycle Bin folder appears.

2 Click the file you want to restore.

3 Click the **Manage** tab.

4 Click **Restore the selected items.**

The file disappears from the Recycle Bin and reappears in its original folder.

Add a File to Your OneDrive

If you are using Windows under a Microsoft account, then as part of that account you get a free online storage area called *OneDrive*. You can use the special OneDrive folder on your PC to move or copy any of your files to your OneDrive. This is useful if you are going to be away from your computer but still require access to a file. Because the OneDrive is accessible anywhere you have web access, you can view and work with your file without using your computer.

Add a File to Your OneDrive

Move a File to Your OneDrive

1 In File Explorer, open the folder that contains the file you want to move.

2 Click and drag the file to the **OneDrive** folder.

A As you drag, if you hover the file over **OneDrive**, File Explorer expands OneDrive to let you see your other OneDrive folders.

3 Drop the file on the OneDrive folder you want to use.

B File Explorer moves the file to the OneDrive folder.

Copy a File to Your OneDrive

1. In File Explorer, open the folder that contains the file you want to copy.

2. Press and hold Ctrl and then click and drag the file to the **OneDrive** folder.

C. If needed, you can hover the file over **OneDrive** to see your other OneDrive folders.

3. Drop the file on the OneDrive folder you want to use.

D. File Explorer copies the file to the OneDrive folder.

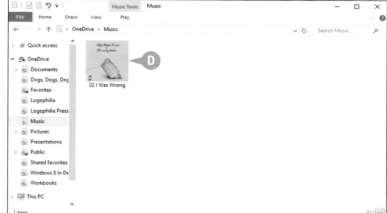

How do I access my OneDrive online?

You need to open Microsoft Edge and navigate to the OneDrive site, http://onedrive.live.com. After you are logged in to your OneDrive, you can use it to create new folders, rename files, delete files, and more.

Can I create new documents using OneDrive?

Yes. As part of your OneDrive, Microsoft gives you access to the Office Web Apps, which are scaled-down, online versions of the Microsoft Office applications. To create a document using one of these programs, navigate to your online OneDrive, click **New**, and then click **Word document**, **Excel workbook**, **PowerPoint presentation**, **OneNote notebook**, **Excel survey**, or **Plain text document**.

Extract Files from a Compressed Folder

If someone sends you a file via email, or if you download a file from the Internet, the file often arrives in a *compressed* form, which means the file actually contains one or more files that have been compressed to save space. To use the files on your computer, you need to extract them from the compressed file.

Because a compressed file can contain one or more files, it acts like a kind of folder. Therefore, Windows calls such files *compressed folders*, *zipped folders*, or *Zip archives*. You can view these files or extract them from the folder.

Extract Files from a Compressed Folder

View Compressed Folder Files

1. In File Explorer, open the folder containing the compressed folder.

Ⓐ The compressed folder appears as a folder icon with a zipper.

2. Double-click the compressed folder.

Ⓑ File Explorer displays the contents of the compressed folder.

Note: File Explorer is only displaying the contents of a compressed folder; it has not extracted the files. To extract the files, follow the steps in the next subsection.

Extract Compressed Folder Files

1 In File Explorer, open the folder containing the compressed folder.

2 Click the compressed folder.

3 Click the **Extract** tab.

4 Click **Extract all**.

The Select a Destination and Extract Files dialog box of the Extract Wizard appears.

5 Type the location of the folder into which you want to extract the files.

C You can also click **Browse** and choose the folder.

6 If you want to open the folder into which you extracted the files, click **Show extracted files when complete** (☐ changes to ☑).

7 Click **Extract**.

Windows extracts the files.

TIP

How can I create a compressed folder?
Follow these steps:

1 Select the files and folders you want to store in the compressed folder.

2 Right-click any selected item.

3 Click **Send to**.

4 Click **Compressed (zipped) folder**.

The compressed folder appears.

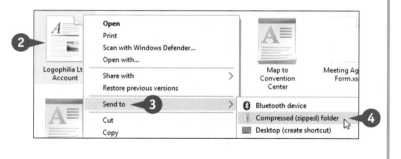

Specify a Different Program When Opening a File

You can open a file in a different program from the one normally associated with the file. This enables you to use the other program's features to work on the file.

You may have situations where you prefer to open a particular file with a different program. For example, double-clicking a picture file opens it in the Photos app. However, you may prefer to open the picture file in Paint or some other image-editing program so that you can make changes to the picture. This section shows you how to open any document in another program.

Specify a Different Program When Opening a File

1 In File Explorer, open the folder that contains the file you want to open.

2 Click the file.

3 Click the **Home** tab.

4 Click the **Open** ▼.

Ⓐ If the program you want to use appears here, you can click the program and skip the remaining steps.

5 Click **Choose another app**.

Windows asks how you want to open this file type.

6 Click **More apps**.

Ⓑ Windows displays a full list of programs you can use to open the file.

7 Click the program you want to use to open the file.

Ⓒ If the program you want to use does not appear in the list, you can click **Look for another app on this PC**, and use the Open With dialog box to specify the program.

8 Click **OK**.

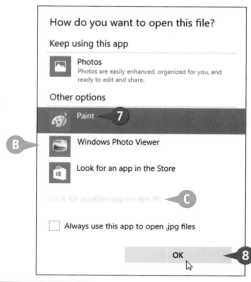

Windows opens the file in the program you chose.

How can I open every file of the same type in the new program?

If you want to open every file of the same type — such as Text Document files or Rich Text Format files — in the same program, follow steps **1** to **6** and then click **Always use this app to open .*ext* files** (☐ changes to ☑), where *.ext* is the file extension of the file type you are working with.

Can I set the default program for multiple file types?

Yes. In the taskbar's Search box, type **set default**, click **Default Programs**, and then click **Set your default programs**. Click the program you want to use, click **Choose defaults for this program**, click each file type you want to open with the program (☐ changes to ☑), and then click **Save**.

Sharing Your Computer

If you share your computer with other people, you can create separate user accounts so that each person works only with his own documents, programs, and Windows settings. This chapter shows you how to create and change user accounts, how to log on and off different accounts, how to share documents between accounts, and how to connect and work with a homegroup.

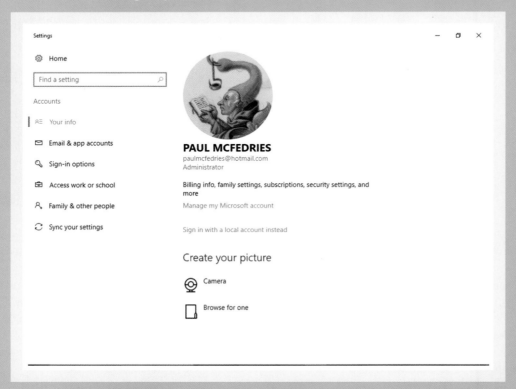

Display User Accounts

To work with user accounts, you need to display the Windows Accounts settings. A *user account* is a collection of Windows folders and settings associated with one person. In this chapter, you learn how to create new user accounts, change a user account's picture, change a user account's password, and delete a user account. To perform any of these tasks, you must first display the Accounts screen of the Settings app.

Display User Accounts

1 Click **Start** (⊞).

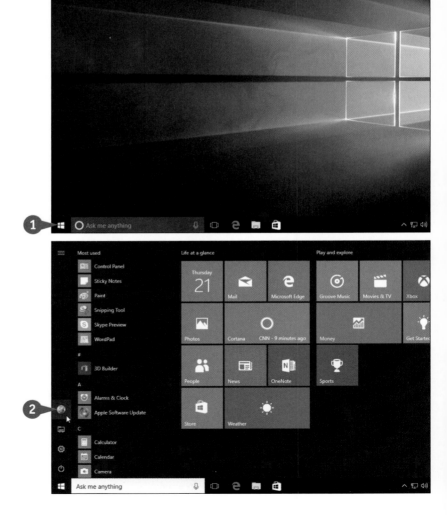

The Start menu appears.

2 Click your user account.

3 Click **Change account settings**.

The Accounts screen appears.

A Information about your account appears here. Later, after you have switched to another account, information for the current account appears in this spot.

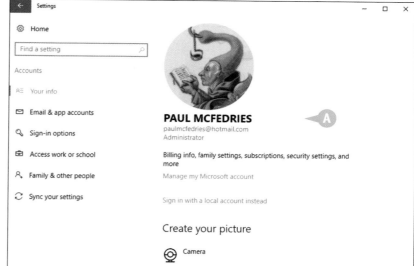

How do user accounts help me share my computer with other people?

Without other people having their own user accounts, anyone who uses your computer can view and even change your documents, Windows settings, email accounts and messages, Microsoft Edge favorites, and more.

With user accounts for each person, users get their own folders (Documents, Pictures, Music, and so on), personalized Windows settings, email accounts, and favorites. In short, users get their own versions of Windows to personalize without interfering with anyone else's. Also, user accounts enable you to safely share documents and folders with people who use your computer and with people on your network.

Create a User Account

If you want to share your computer with another person, you need to create a user account for that individual. This enables the person to log on to Windows and use the system. The new user account is completely separate from your own account. This means that the other person can change settings, create documents, and perform other Windows tasks without interfering with your settings or data.

You can create a local user account or a Microsoft account. For maximum privacy, you should safeguard each account with a password.

Create a User Account

1 Display the Accounts screen of the Settings app.

Note: See the previous section, "Display User Accounts," to learn how to display the Accounts screen.

2 Click **Family & other people**.

3 Click **Add someone else to this PC**.

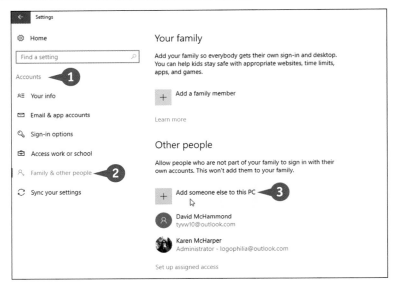

The How Will This Person Sign In screen appears.

4 For a local account, click **I don't have this person's sign-in information**.

Note: If you want to create a Microsoft account instead, see Chapter 1 for more information.

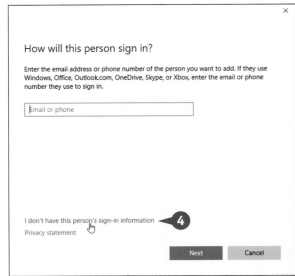

5 Click **Add a user without a Microsoft account**.

The Create an Account for this PC screen appears.

6 Type the name you want to use for the new account.

7 Type the password.

Note: The password characters appear as dots for security reasons.

8 Type the password again.

9 Type a hint that will help you or the user remember the password.

10 Click **Next**.

Windows creates the account and adds it to the Other Users section.

How do I create a secure password?

It is a good idea to use secure passwords that a nefarious user cannot guess. First, do not use an obvious password such as the user's account name or the word "password." Second, make sure the password is at least eight characters long. Finally, use at least one character from at least three of the following four sets: lowercase letters, uppercase letters, numbers, and symbols.

Switch Between Accounts

After you have created more than one account on your computer, you can switch between accounts. This is useful when one person is already working in Windows and another person needs to use the computer.

When you switch to a second account, Windows leaves the original user's programs and windows running. This means that after the second person is finished, the original user can sign on again and continue working as before.

Switch Between Accounts

1 Click **Start** (⊞).

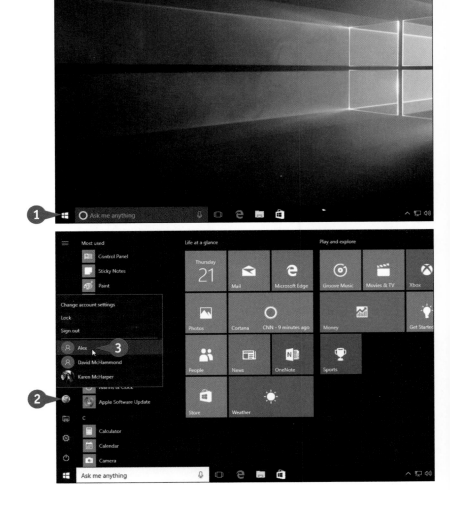

The Start menu appears.

2 Click your user account.

3 Click the user account you want to switch to.

Windows prompts you for the user account password.

④ Type the password.

⑤ Click **Submit** (➡).

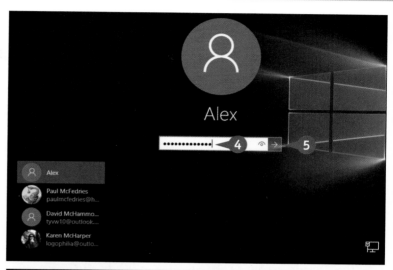

ⓐ The user's picture now appears in the Start menu, and the user's name appears when you hover the mouse pointer () over the account picture.

Note: The first time you switch to a new account, Windows takes a few moments to configure the account.

TIP

What happens if I forget my password?

When you set up your password as described in the previous section, "Create a User Account," Windows asks you to supply a hint to help you remember the password. If you cannot remember your password, follow these steps: In the sign-on screen, leave the password text box blank. Click **Submit** (➡). Windows tells you the password is incorrect. Click **OK** to return to the sign-on screen. Windows displays the password hint.

Change Your User Account Picture

You can add visual interest to your user account as well as make it easier to tell one user account from another by adding a picture to the account. When you create a user account, Windows assigns it a default picture, which appears in the user's Start screen tile, the Accounts screen of the Settings app, and the sign-on screen. Unfortunately, this default picture is a generic silhouette of a person's head and upper torso, so it is not very interesting or useful. If you have a more suitable picture that you would prefer to use, you can change your picture.

Change Your User Account Picture

1 Click **Start** (⊞).

The Start menu appears.

2 Click the user account.

3 Click **Change account settings**.

The Settings app appears with the Your Info tab displayed.

4 Click **Browse for one**.

The Open dialog box appears.

5 Click the picture you want to use.

6 Click **Choose picture**.

Ⓐ The Your Info tab appears and displays the new picture.

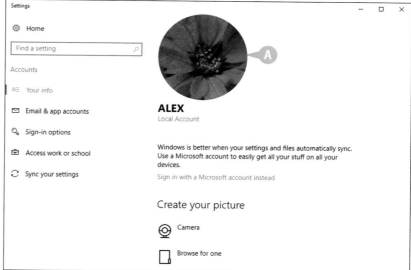

How do I use a webcam photo as my user account picture?
Repeat steps **1** to **3** and then click **Camera** to open the Camera app. Position yourself within the screen and then click the screen to take the picture. The Camera app displays the photo and adds a rectangle that defines the area of the photo it will use for your account picture. Click and drag the rectangle to the position you want. Click and drag the rectangle corners to set the size and shape of the rectangle. Click **OK**.

Change a User's Password

If you set up a user account with no password, or if you find it difficult to remember your password, you can change the password. Assigning a password to each user account is good practice because otherwise someone who sits down at the PC can sign in using an unprotected account.

It is also good practice to assign a strong password to each account, so that a malicious user cannot guess the password and gain access to the system. Whether you want to assign a password or create a password that is stronger or easier to remember, you can use Windows to change an existing password.

Change a User's Password

1 If you want to change another user's password, sign in as that user.

2 Display the Accounts screen of the Settings app.

Note: See the section "Display User Accounts," earlier in this chapter, to learn how to display the Accounts screen.

3 Click **Sign-in options**.

4 Under Password, click **Change**.

Note: If the account has no password, click **Add** in the Password section.

Windows prompts you to verify your current password.

Note: If the account has no current password, skip to step **7**.

5 Type your current account password.

6 Click **Next**.

Windows prompts you for the new password.

7 Type the new password.

8 Type the new password again.

A If you are not sure whether you typed a password correctly, you can click and hold **Display Password Characters** (👁) to temporarily display the password.

9 Type a hint.

10 Click **Next**.

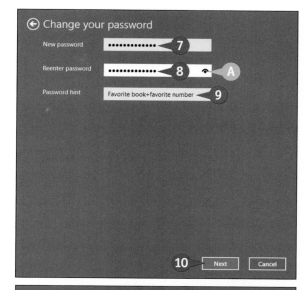

11 Click **Finish**.

Windows updates the user account password.

Are there any other precautions I can take to protect my password?
Yes, besides creating a strong password, you can safeguard your password by following these guidelines:

• Do not tell anyone your password.

• Do not write down your password.

• Make your password easier to remember by using a mnemonic device. For example, you could use the first letters as well as any numbers that appear in the name of a favorite book or movie.

Delete an Account

If you create a user account temporarily, or if you have a user account that is no longer needed or no longer used, you can delete that account. This reduces the number of users that appear in the Users tab of the Settings app, as well as the Windows sign-on screen, which can make these screens a bit easier to navigate. Deleting a user account also means that Windows reclaims the hard drive space that the account uses, which gives you more room to store files in your other accounts.

Delete an Account

1 Sign out of the user account you want to delete.

Note: To sign out of an account, click **Start** (⊞), click the user account on the Start menu, and then click **Sign out**.

2 Display the Accounts screen of the Settings app.

Note: See the section "Display User Accounts," earlier in this chapter, to learn how to display the Accounts screen.

3 Click **Family & other users**.

The Family & Other Users screen appears.

4 Click the user account you want to delete.

5 Click **Remove**.

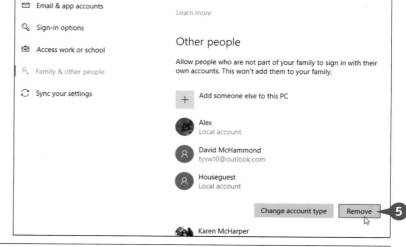

The Delete Account and Data dialog box appears.

6 Click **Delete account and data**.

Windows deletes the account.

TIP

Why can I not delete my original Windows account?
Windows configures the original user account as the administrator account on the computer, which means it is the only account allowed to perform tasks such as creating and deleting user accounts. Windows does not allow you to delete this account because it requires that there always be at least one administrator account on the computer. When you are logged in with another account, you cannot access the Other Accounts screen, so you cannot use it to delete your original Windows account.

Create a Homegroup

You can share documents and media easily with other Windows computers by creating a homegroup on your network. A homegroup simplifies network sharing by making it easy to share documents with other computers and users who are also connected to that homegroup.

You use one Windows computer to create the homegroup, and then you use the homegroup password to join your other Windows computers. For more information, see the next section, "Join a Homegroup."

Create a Homegroup

1 In the taskbar's Search box, type **homegroup**.

2 Click **HomeGroup**.

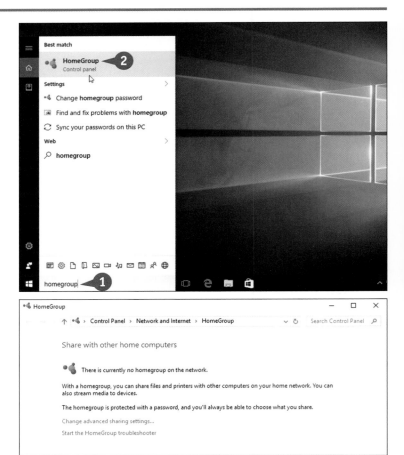

The HomeGroup window appears.

3 Click **Create a homegroup**.

Windows displays an overview of what you can do with a homegroup.

4 Click **Next** (not shown).

The Create a Homegroup dialog box appears.

5 Select **Shared** for each item you want to share with the homegroup, such as pictures or documents.

6 Click **Next**.

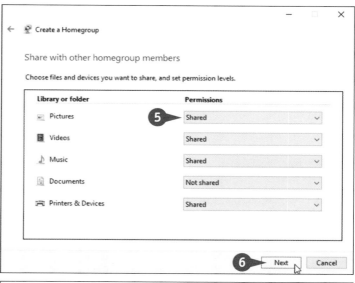

Windows displays the homegroup password.

7 Make a mental note of the homegroup password.

8 Click **Finish**.

You can now join your other computers to the homegroup, as described in the next section. Note that a computer must be running Windows 7 or later to join a homegroup.

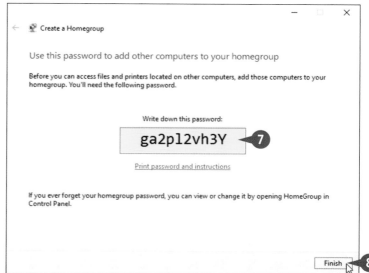

TIPS

I have lost my homegroup password. How do I view it again?

The easiest method is to repeat steps **1** and **2** to display the HomeGroup window and then click **View or print the homegroup password**. The window that appears displays the homegroup password.

How can I change the homegroup password?

Follow steps **1** and **2** to display the HomeGroup window. Click the **Change the password** link and then click **Change the password** to generate a new homegroup password. If one or more computers have already joined the homegroup, you need to provide them with the new password.

Join a Homegroup

If your network has a homegroup, you can join your Windows computer to that homegroup. This enables you to access shared resources on other homegroup computers, and to share your own resources with the homegroup.

This section assumes you or someone else on your home network has already set up a homegroup as described in the previous section, "Create a Homegroup," and that you have the homegroup password.

Join a Homegroup

1 In the taskbar's Search box, type **homegroup**.

2 Click **HomeGroup**.

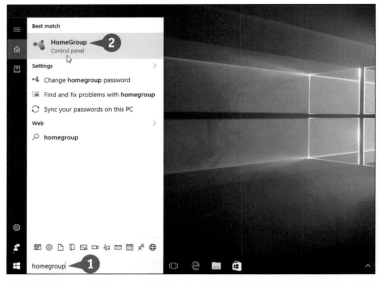

The HomeGroup window appears.

3 Click **Join now**.

Windows displays an overview of what you can do with a homegroup.

4 Click **Next** (not shown).

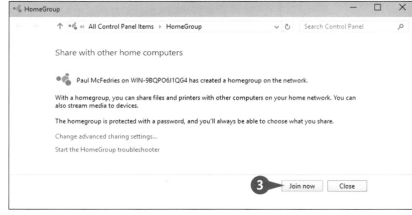

The Share with Other Homegroup Members dialog box appears.

5 Select **Shared** for each item you want to share with the homegroup, such as pictures or documents.

6 Click **Next**.

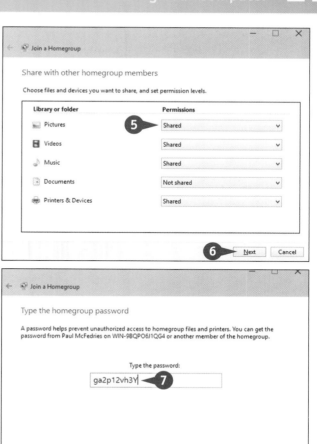

Windows prompts you for the homegroup password.

7 Type the homegroup password.

8 Click **Next**.

Windows joins the homegroup.

9 Click **Finish**.

You can now access other homegroup computers and share your files with the homegroup.

When I try to join a homegroup, Windows tells me my password is not correct. What am I doing wrong?

First, double-check that you have been given the correct homegroup password and that you are typing that password correctly. Second, understand that homegroup passwords are case-sensitive, so you must type the uppercase and lowercase letters exactly as they appear in the original homegroup settings. Make sure your keyboard does not have Caps Lock turned on.

Can I leave a homegroup if I no longer need it?

Yes. Follow steps **1** and **2** to display the HomeGroup window. Click **Leave the homegroup.** When Windows asks you to confirm, click **Leave the homegroup**.

Share a Document or Folder

You can share documents and folders of your choice with your homegroup, if your network has one. You can also share a document or folder with other users set up on your computer.

Sharing a document or folder enables you to work on a file with other people without having to send them a copy of the file. You can set up each document or folder with View or View and Edit permissions. View permission means that users cannot make changes to the document or folder; View and Edit permission means that users can view and make changes to the document or folder.

Share a Document or Folder

Share with the Homegroup

1. Click **File Explorer** (▢).

2. Open the folder containing the item you want to share.

3. Click the document or folder you want to share.

4. Click the **Share** tab.

5. Click **Homegroup (view)**.

Ⓐ To allow homegroup users to make changes to the item, you can click **Homegroup (view and edit)** instead.

Share with a Specific User

1. Open the folder containing the item you want to share.

2. Click the document or folder you want to share.

3. Click the **Share** tab.

4. Click **Specific people**.

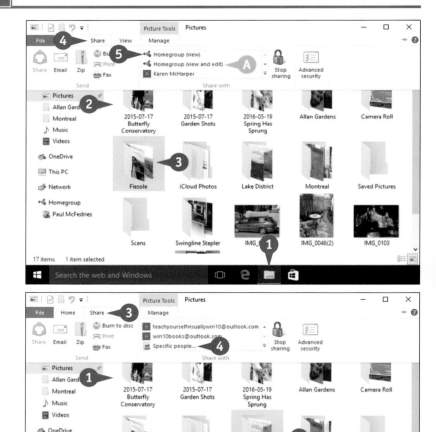

The File Sharing dialog box appears.

5 Click ⌄ and then click the name of the user.

6 Click **Add**.

7 Click ▼ and then click the permission level.

Note: Read permission is the same as View, and Read/Write is the same as View and Edit.

8 Click **Share**.

Windows shares the document or folder.

Ⓑ When you open the folder, you see State: Shared in the status bar.

TIPS

How do the other users access the shared document or folder?

Send them the address in the final File Sharing dialog box. You have two choices: Click **e-mail** to send the address via email, or click **copy** to copy the address to memory. You can then open a program such as WordPad, click **Edit**, and then click **Paste** to paste the address.

Can I see all the documents and folders that I am sharing with other users?

Yes, you can do this in two ways. In the final File Sharing dialog box, click **Show me all the network shares on this computer**. Alternatively, in any folder window, click **Network** and then double-click your computer.

View Network Resources

To see what other network users have shared in your homegroup, you can use the Homegroup folder to view the other computers and see their shared resources. To get access to the shared homegroup resources, you must know the homegroup's password and have joined the homegroup, as described earlier in the section "Join a Homegroup." If your network does not have a homegroup, you can use the Network folder instead. A network resource can be a folder, hard drive, CD or DVD drive, flash drive, printer, scanner, or other shared device.

View Network Resources

View Homegroup Resources

1 Click **File Explorer** (🗔).

2 Click the **Homegroup** folder.

Ⓐ Windows displays icons for each user who is sharing data in the homegroup.

3 Double-click the user who is sharing the resource you want to access.

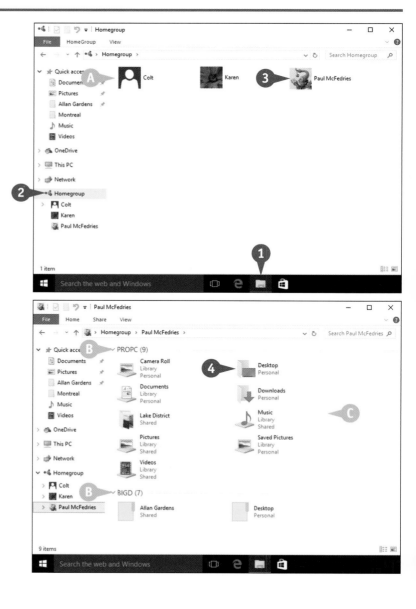

Windows displays the resources the user is sharing.

Ⓑ If the user has an account on multiple PCs, you see a section for each PC.

Ⓒ The resources that the user is sharing on the computer appear here.

4 Double-click an icon to access the resource.

View Network Resources

1. In File Explorer, click the **Network** folder.

Ⓓ Windows displays icons for each computer that is sharing resources.

2. Double-click the computer that is sharing the resource you want to access.

Ⓔ The resources the computer is sharing appear here.

3. Double-click an icon to access the resource.

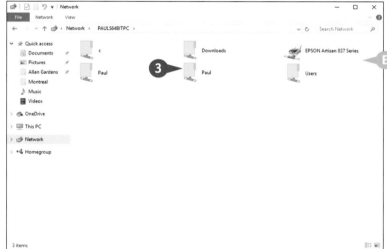

TIPS

How can I fix network problems?

If you are having homegroup trouble, launch File Explorer, click the **Homegroup** folder, click the **Homegroup** tab, and then click **Start troubleshooter**. If you are having network trouble, right-click the network icon in the taskbar's notification area and then click **Troubleshoot problems**. In both cases, follow whatever repair techniques Windows suggests.

How do I change my computer's network name?

In the taskbar's Search box, type **name** and then click **View your PC name**. Windows opens the PC screen of the Settings app. Click **Rename PC**, use the Rename Your PC text box to type the new name, click **Next**, and then click **Restart now**.

Getting More from a Tablet PC

Windows comes with many features designed to help you get the most out of your tablet PC. In this chapter, you learn how to use gestures, type with and configure the touch keyboard, add a second monitor, and more.

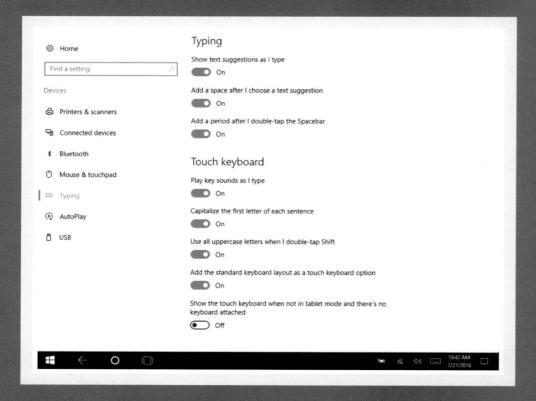

Understanding Gestures

You can get the most out of your Windows tablet by learning the various gestures that you can use to initiate actions, manipulate data, and control the elements on your screen. Traditional computers use the mouse and keyboard to input data and make things happen. A tablet lacks these input devices; instead, you must rely on your fingers because tablets are built to respond to touches on the glass screen surface. Some tablets also come with a small penlike device called a *stylus,* which you can use instead of your finger for some actions.

Tap

Use your finger to touch the screen and then immediately release it. You use this gesture to initiate an action.

Double-Tap

Tap and release the screen twice, one tap right after the other. You also use this gesture to initiate an action, although mostly with older desktop programs.

Tap and Hold

Press your finger on the screen for a second or two. This gesture usually displays a menu of options related to whatever screen object you are pressing.

Slide

Place your finger on the screen, move your finger, and then release. You use this gesture either to move an object from one place to another or to scroll the screen in the same direction as your finger.

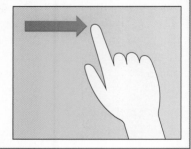

Swipe

Quickly and briefly run your finger along the screen. Windows has specific swipe gestures that display screen elements. For example, you swipe up from the bottom of the screen to display the taskbar.

Pinch

Place two fingers apart on the screen and bring them closer together. This gesture zooms out on whatever is displayed on the screen, such as a photo.

Spread

Place two fingers close together on the screen and move them farther apart. This gesture zooms in on whatever is displayed on the screen, such as a photo.

Turn

Place two fingers on the screen and turn them clockwise or counterclockwise. This gesture rotates whatever is displayed on the screen, such as a photo.

Using Gestures to Control Windows

To use your tablet efficiently and accurately, you need to know how to use gestures to control Windows. Using a tablet is a different experience than using a regular computer, but Windows was built with the tablet in mind, so it is intuitive and easy to learn.

If you have never used a tablet PC before, the main difference is that you use your fingers (or stylus) to run applications, select items, and manipulate screen objects. This might seem awkward at first, but it will come to seem quite natural if you practice the techniques shown here as much as you can.

Using Gestures to Control Windows

Initiate an Action

1 Position your finger or the stylus over the object that you want to work with.

2 Tap the screen.

Depending on the object, Windows either selects the object or performs some operation in response to the tap, such as displaying more of the Start menu.

Swipe the Screen

1 Quickly move your finger or the stylus across the screen in a swipe motion:

A You can swipe left from the right edge of the tablet to display the Notifications pane.

B You can swipe right from the left edge of the tablet to display Task View for switching between running applications.

C You can swipe (or slide) up or down to navigate an app's screens.

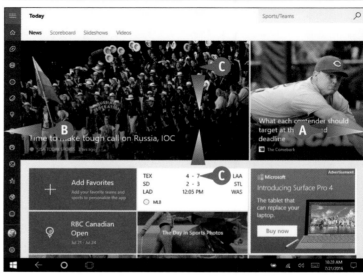

Shut Down an App

1 Place your finger or stylus at the top edge of the app screen.

2 Slide down until the app window turns into a thumbnail, and then slide the thumbnail down to the bottom of the screen.

Windows shuts down the app.

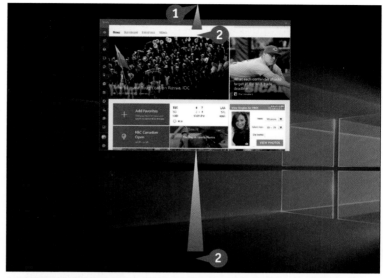

Move an Item

1 Position your finger or the stylus over the item that you want to move.

2 Tap and hold the item and immediately begin moving your finger or the stylus.

D The object moves along with your finger or the stylus.

3 When the object is repositioned where you want it, lift your finger or the stylus off the screen to complete the move.

TIP

How do I use gestures to select files and folders in File Explorer?
You can use the following techniques:

- To select a single file or folder, tap it.

- To select multiple, adjacent files or folders, tap and hold the screen above and to the left of the first item, and then slide your finger or stylus down and to the right until you have selected the items you want.

- If you have a physical keyboard, you can select multiple, nonadjacent files or folders by tapping the first one, pressing and holding **Shift**, and then tapping the other items you want to select.

Input Text with the Touch Keyboard

If you are using a tablet, or a PC in tablet mode, you do not have a physical keyboard available. To input text, Windows offers the *touch keyboard*, which is a virtual keyboard that appears on the screen. You input text using this keyboard by tapping the keys. Windows offers several touch keyboard types, and some characters are difficult to find, so you need to know how to use the touch keyboard to get the most out of Windows.

Input Text with the Touch Keyboard

Select a Keyboard

1 In an app, tap the text box area in which you want to insert text.

A Windows displays the touch keyboard.

2 Tap **Keyboard** (⌨).

Windows displays the keyboard options.

B You can tap ⌨ for the default keyboard.

C You can tap ⊞ for the split keyboard.

D You can tap ✐ for the writing pad.

Input Text

1 Tap the keys for the characters that you want to input.

Windows inserts the text.

E To enter an uppercase letter, you can tap **Shift** (⬆) and then tap the letter.

F To delete the previous character, you can tap **Backspace** (⌫).

2 To enter numbers and other symbols, tap **&123**.

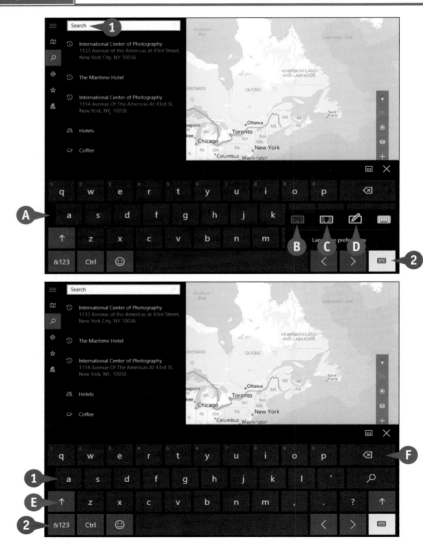

Windows displays the numbers
and symbols.

3 Tap **More** (⊙) to see more
symbols.

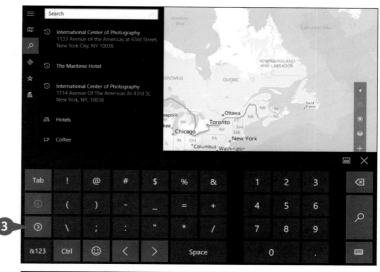

4 To see more symbols, tap and
hold a key.

G Windows displays the extra
symbols.

5 Slide your finger to the symbol
that you want and then release.

H You can tap **Back** (⊙) to return
to the previous symbols.

I You can tap **&123** to return to
the letters.

6 When you are done, tap
Close (✖) to hide the keyboard.

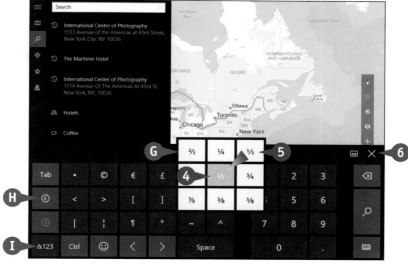

TIP

How do I write text with the stylus?
Follow steps **1** and **2** in the subsection
"Select a Keyboard" and then tap **Writing
Pad** (✍). Use the stylus to handwrite the
text in the writing pad (**A**). As you
write, Windows converts your writing to
text and adds it to the text box. To insert
a space, tap **Space** (▭) (**B**).

Configure the Touch Keyboard

The touch keyboard offers a number of features that make it easier to use. For example, the touch keyboard automatically adds a period and space when you double-tap the spacebar, and it automatically capitalizes the first letter of each sentence.

However, the touch keyboard also has some features that you might not like — such as the noise it makes each time you tap a key. You can use the Settings app to turn on the touch keyboard features that you like and turn off the features that you do not like.

Configure the Touch Keyboard

① Tap **Settings** (⚙).

The Settings app appears.

② Tap **Devices**.

The Devices screen appears.

3 Tap **Typing**.

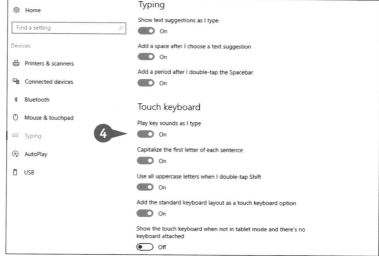

4 Under Touch Keyboard, tap each option **On** or **Off**, according to your preferences.

Windows applies your new settings to the touch keyboard.

TIP

What is the standard keyboard layout?

If you tap the **Add the standard keyboard layout as a touch keyboard option** switch to **On** in step **6**, the next time that you use the keyboard, tap ⌨ and then tap ⌨. This presents a normal keyboard.

Configure Your Tablet to Work with a Second Monitor

You can improve your productivity and efficiency by using a second monitor. To work with an external monitor, your tablet must have a video output port, such as VGA, DVI, or HDMI. If you do not have such a port, check with the manufacturer to see if an adapter is available that enables your tablet to connect with an external monitor.

After you have connected your tablet and the external monitor, you then need to configure Windows to extend the Start screen to both the tablet screen and the external monitor.

Configure Your Tablet to Work with a Second Monitor

1 Connect the second monitor to your tablet.

2 Tap **Settings** (⚙).

The Settings app appears.

3 Tap **System**.

The System screen appears.

4 Tap **Display**.

5 Tap the **Multiple displays** ✓ and then tap **Extend these displays**.

6 Tap the monitor that you want to set as the main display.

7 Tap **Make this my main display** (☐ changes to ✓).

8 Tap **Apply**.

Windows connects to the second monitor, uses it to extend the desktop, and uses the monitor that you selected as your main display.

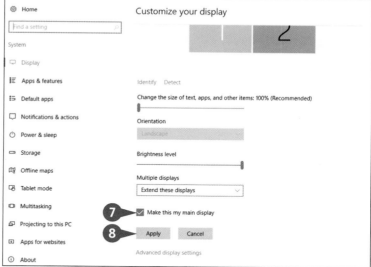

TIP

Why does my cursor stop at the right edge of the left screen?
Ideally, you should be able to move your cursor continuously from the left monitor to the right monitor. If you find that the cursor stops at the right edge of your left monitor, it means that you need to exchange the icons of the left and right monitors. To do that, follow steps **1** to **6**, and then tap and drag the left monitor icon to the right of the other monitor icon (or vice versa).

Adjust Screen Brightness

You can extend the battery life of your tablet by turning down the screen brightness. Your tablet screen uses a lot of power, so turning down the brightness also reduces battery drain.

On the other hand, if you have trouble seeing the data on your tablet screen, you can often fix the problem by *increasing* the screen brightness. This is not a problem when your tablet is running on AC power. However, you should not use full screen brightness for very long when your tablet is running on its battery because a bright screen uses a lot of power.

Adjust Screen Brightness

1 Tap **Power** (🖳).

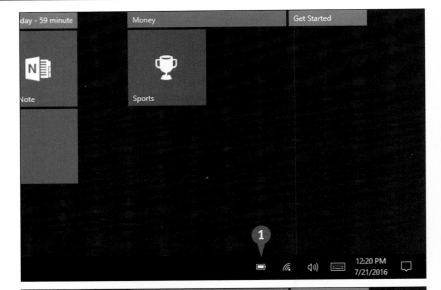

The Power options appear.

2 Tap the brightness setting to cycle through one of four screen brightness values: 25%, 50%, 75%, and 100%.

Windows puts the new brightness setting into effect.

Monitor Battery Life

You can use the Power icon in the Desktop taskbar's notification area to monitor your tablet's remaining battery power. When the battery is at maximum charge, the icon shows as all white. As the battery charge falls, the amount of white in the icon also falls. You can also position your stylus cursor over the icon or tap the icon to see a tool tip that shows you the current battery level.

Monitor Battery Life

1 Tap **Power** (🔲).

Ⓐ The current battery level appears here.

Implementing Security

Threats to your computing-related security and privacy often come from the Internet and from someone simply using your computer while you are not around. To protect yourself and your family, you need to understand these threats and know what you can do to thwart them.

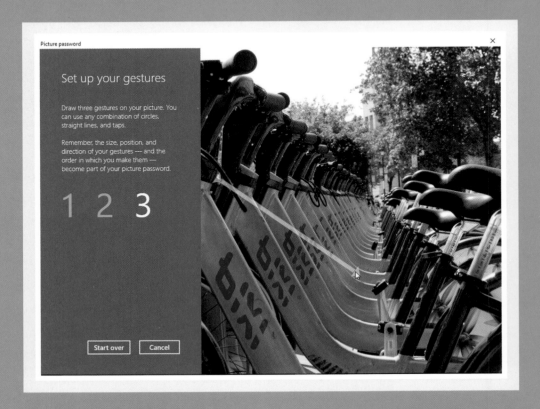

Understanding Windows Security

Before you get to the details of securing your computer, it helps to take a step back and look at the security and privacy tools that Windows makes available.

These tools include your Windows user account password, User Account Control, locking your PC, Windows Firewall, Windows Defender, and the private browsing feature in Microsoft Edge. Taken all together, these features represent a *defense-in-depth* security strategy that uses multiple layers to keep you and your data safe and private.

User Account Password

Windows security begins with assigning a password to each user account on the computer. This prevents unauthorized users from accessing the system, and it enables you to lock your computer. For more information, see the section "Lock Your Computer," later in this chapter.

User Account Control

User Account Control asks you to confirm certain actions that could conceivably harm your system. When you are using your main Windows user account, which is your computer's administrative account, you click **Yes** to continue; for all other accounts, you must enter the administrative account's username and password to continue.

Locking Your PC

Protecting your PC with a password prevents unauthorized access, but what happens when you leave your desk? If you remain logged on, a person who sits down at your computer can view and work with your files. Instead of shutting down your computer when you leave your desk, you can lock your system. Anyone who tries to use your computer must first enter your password.

Windows Firewall

When your computer is connected to the Internet, it is possible for another person to access your computer and infect it with a virus or cause other damage; as a result, Windows comes with its Windows Firewall feature turned on. This prevents intruders from accessing your computer while you are online.

Help protect your PC with Windows Firewall

Windows Firewall can help prevent hackers or malicious software from gaining access to your PC through the Internet or a network.

Private networks Connected

Networks at home or work where you know and trust the people and devices on the network

Windows Firewall state: On

Windows Defender

Spyware is a software program that installs itself on your computer without your knowledge or consent. This type of program surreptitiously gathers data from your computer, steals your

Malware Detected
Windows Defender is taking action to clean detected malware

passwords, displays advertisements, and hijacks your web browser. To prevent spyware from installing on your computer, Windows includes the Windows Defender program.

InPrivate Web Browsing

The Microsoft Edge Explorer web browser normally collects data as you navigate from site to site. Most of this data is used to improve your browsing experience, but it can also be used to track your online activities. If you plan on

Browsing InPrivate

🔍 Search or enter web address →

When you use InPrivate tabs, your browsing data (like cookies, history, or temporary files) isn't saved on your PC after you're done. Microsoft Edge deletes temporary data from your PC after all of your InPrivate tabs are closed.

visiting private or sensitive sites, you can turn on InPrivate browsing, which tells Microsoft Edge not to collect any data during your browsing session. For more information, see the section "Browse the Web Privately," later in this chapter.

Reset Your PC

Your computer contains a lot of information about you, including your personal files, your Microsoft Edge favorites, your email messages, and your Windows settings. If you plan on selling or donating your computer, you can use the Reset Your PC feature to securely remove your data while installing a fresh copy of Windows.

Reset this PC

If your PC isn't running well, resetting it might help. This lets you choose to keep your files or remove them, and then reinstalls Windows.

Get started

Check for Security Problems

In Windows, the Security and Maintenance window displays messages about the current state of your computer. In particular, it warns you if your computer has any current security problems. For example, Security and Maintenance tells you if your computer does not have virus protection installed or if the Windows Defender spyware database is out of date. Security and Maintenance will also warn you if your computer is not set up to download updates automatically and if important security features such as User Account Control are turned off.

Check for Security Problems

1 In the taskbar's Search box, type **security**.

2 Click **Security and Maintenance**.

The Security and Maintenance window appears.

3 Review the messages in the Security section.

4 Click a message button to resolve the security issue, such as clicking **Turn on now** if Windows Defender is turned off.

5 Click **Security**.

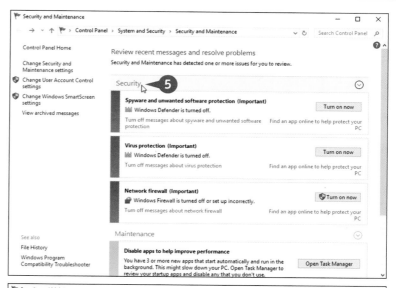

6 Scroll down the Security and Maintenance window.

A Security and Maintenance displays a summary of all your system's security settings.

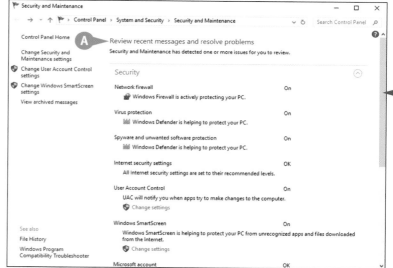

TIPS

Can I control which messages I see in Security and Maintenance?
Yes. Follow steps **1** and **2** to open the Security and Maintenance window, and then click **Change Security and Maintenance settings**. Click any security or maintenance message you no longer want to see (☑ changes to ☐). Click **OK**.

Do I always have to open the Security and Maintenance window to resolve security issues?
No. In many cases, you can resolve the issue directly without opening Security and Maintenance. In the taskbar's notification area, click **Action Center** (▣) and examine the window that appears. If you see a security issue, it should also display a link that you can click to resolve the issue.

Create a Picture Password

You can make it easier to sign in to your Windows computer by creating a picture password. This is particularly true for a tablet PC. If you find that it is taking you a long time to sign in to Windows using your tablet's touch keyboard, you can switch to a picture password instead. In this case, your "password" is a series of three gestures — any combination of a click, a straight line, or a circle — that you apply to a photo. Windows displays the photo at startup, and you repeat your gestures, in order, to sign in.

Create a Picture Password

1. In the taskbar's Search box, type **password**.

2. Click **Sign-in options**.

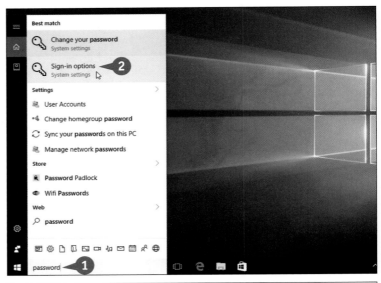

The Settings app appears and displays the Sign-in Options screen.

3. Under Picture Password, click **Add**.

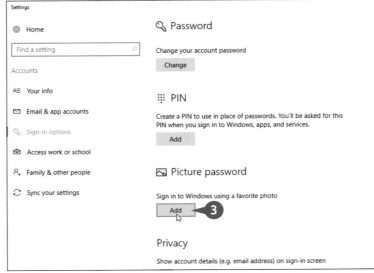

Windows prompts you for your account password.

④ Type your password.

⑤ Click **OK**.

The Welcome to Picture Password screen appears.

⑥ Click **Choose picture**.

TIPS

Is a picture password safe to use?
Yes. The biggest drawback is that it is possible for a malicious user to view and possibly even record your gestures using a camera. Unlike a regular text password for which the characters appear as dots to prevent someone from seeing them, gestures have no such protection.

Does the picture password replace my text password?
No. Your picture password is applied to your user account along with your existing text-based password. As you see in the next Tips section, it is not difficult to bypass the picture password and sign in using the text password, so you should still protect your PC with a strong text password.

continued ▶

Create a Picture Password (continued)

In the same way that you should not choose a regular account password that is extremely obvious, such as the word *password* or your username, you should take care to avoid creating an obvious picture password. For example, if you are using a photo showing three faces, an obvious picture password would be a click on each face.

A good picture password not only uses all three available gestures, but also uses them in nonobvious ways. To ensure that you have memorized your picture password, you should sign out of your account a few times and then sign back on using the picture password.

Create a Picture Password (continued)

The Pictures screen appears.

7 Click the picture that you want to use.

8 Click **Open**.

The How's This Look screen appears.

9 Drag the picture so that the image is positioned where you want.

10 Click **Use this picture**.

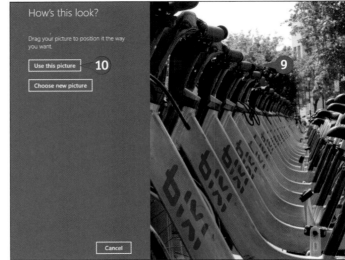

The Set Up Your Gestures screen appears.

⑪ Use your finger or a stylus to draw three gestures.

⑫ Repeat the gestures to confirm.

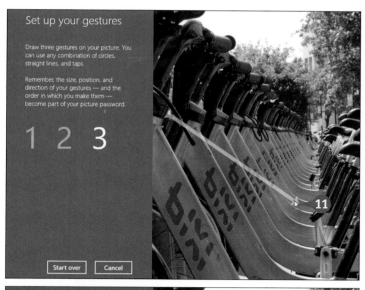

⑬ Click **Finish**.

The next time that you sign in to Windows, you will be prompted to enter your picture password gestures.

 TIPS

What happens if I forget my gestures?
At the sign-on screen, click **Sign-in options** and then click **Microsoft account** to sign in with your regular password. To get a reminder of your picture password gestures, follow steps **1** and **2** in this section, click **Change**, type your user account password, and click **OK**. In the Change Your Picture Password screen, click **Replay**. Click the picture to see each gesture.

Can I change my picture password?
Yes. Open the Change Your Picture Password screen as described in the preceding Tip, choose a new picture, if necessary, and then run through your gestures.

Set Up a Fingerprint Sign-In

You can ensure that only you can access your PC and you can avoid the insecurity of using passwords and gestures in public, by using your fingerprint to sign in to Windows.

If your PC comes with a built-in fingerprint reader, or you have an external reader attached to your PC, you can use the Windows Hello feature to teach Windows your fingerprint and use it to sign in. Because your fingerprint is unique, this ensures that only you can access your PC. Also, if you are in a public place, you do not have to enter a password or use sign-in gestures that could be observed by a nearby snoop.

Set Up a Fingerprint Sign-In

1 In the taskbar's Search box, type **fingerprint**.

2 Click **Set up fingerprint sign-in**.

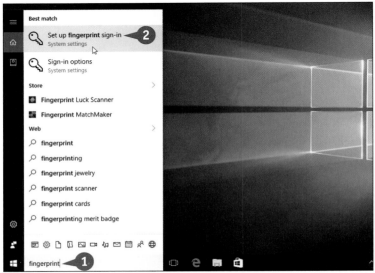

The Settings app appears and displays the Sign-in Options screen.

3 Under Fingerprint, click **Set up**.

Note: If the Set Up button is disabled, you must assign a PIN to your Microsoft account. In the Sign-in Options screen, click **Add** under the PIN heading and follow the prompts to assign a PIN to your account.

The Windows Hello Setup dialog box appears.

4 Click **Get started**.

Windows prompts you for your account PIN.

5 Type your PIN.

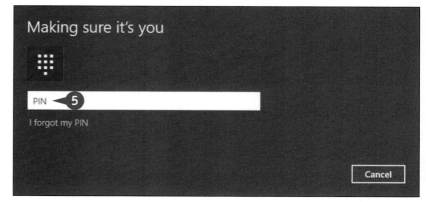

Making sure it's you

PIN 5

I forgot my PIN

Cancel

Windows Hello prompts you to scan your fingerprint.

6 Swipe your finger across your PC's fingerprint reader.

7 Repeat the swipe until the scan is complete.

8 Click **Close**.

The next time that you start your PC, you will be prompted to swipe your finger across the fingerprint reader to sign in.

Windows Hello Setup ×

X

Scan your finger on the fingerprint reader.

We'll need to scan your fingerprint a few times to set up Windows Hello.

Close **8**

TIPS

What do I do if Windows does not recognize my fingerprint swipe when I try to sign in?
At the sign-on screen, click **Sign-in options** and then click **Microsoft account** to sign in with your regular password.

How do I stop using my fingerprint for signing in to Windows?
To remove your fingerprint from the sign-in options, follow steps **1** and **2** in this section to display the Settings app's Sign-in Options window. Under the Fingerprint section, click **Remove**.

Lock Your Computer

You can enhance your computer's security by locking the device when you leave it unattended. Protecting your account with a password prevents someone from logging on to your account, but what happens when you leave your computer unattended? If you remain logged on to the system, any person who picks up your computer can use it to view and change files.

To prevent this, you can lock your computer. After your computer is locked, anyone who tries to use your computer will first have to enter your password.

Lock Your Computer

Lock Your Computer

1. Click **Start** (⊞).

2. Click your user account.

3. Click **Lock**.

Windows locks your computer and displays the Lock screen.

Unlock Your Computer

1 On the Lock screen, press **Enter** to display the sign-in screen.

2 Click inside the Password text box.

3 Type your password.

4 Click **Submit** ().

Windows unlocks your computer and restores your desktop.

TIP

How can I quickly access the Lock command?

If you need to leave your desk in a hurry, Windows offers a couple of quick methods for locking your computer. Probably the quickest way to lock your computer is to press +. Alternatively, press **Ctrl**+**Alt**+**Delete** and then click **Lock**.

Configure Your PC to Lock Automatically

You can configure Windows to automatically lock your computer after it has been idle for a specified time.

The previous section describes how to lock your computer to prevent unauthorized access when you leave your PC. However, the hard part is *remembering* to do it. If you are late for a meeting or other appointment, locking your machine is probably the last thing on your mind as you dash out the door. To ensure that some snoop cannot access your PC if you forget to lock it, you can configure Windows to lock automatically after a period of inactivity.

Configure Your PC to Lock Automatically

1 In the taskbar's Search box, type **screen saver**.

2 Click **Change screen saver**.

The Screen Saver Settings dialog box appears.

3 Click **On resume, display logon screen** (☐ changes to ☑).

④ Use the **Wait** ⬍ to set the number of minutes of idle that must pass before Windows locks your computer.

⑤ Click **OK**.

Windows now automatically locks your PC when it has been idle for the number of minutes you specified in step 4.

Does my computer lock when it goes into sleep mode?
Yes, Windows is also configured by default to display the logon screen when your computer wakes up from sleep mode. To make sure this setting is activated, click **Start** (⊞) and then click **Settings** (⚙) to launch the Settings app. Click **Accounts** to open the Accounts window and then click the **Sign-in options** tab. Click the **Require sign-in** ⌄ and then click **When PC wakes up from sleep.**

Browse the Web Privately

If you visit sensitive or private websites, you can tell Microsoft Edge not to save any browsing history for those sites. If you regularly visit private websites or websites that contain sensitive or secret data, you can ensure that no one else sees any data for such sites by deleting your browsing history, as described in the Tip section. However, if you visit such sites only occasionally, deleting your entire browsing history is overkill. A better solution is to turn on the InPrivate browsing feature in Microsoft Edge before you visit private sites. This tells Microsoft Edge to temporarily stop saving any browsing history.

Browse the Web Privately

1 Click **Start** (▦).

2 Click **Microsoft Edge**.

Ⓐ Alternatively, you can click **Microsoft Edge** (e) if you see it in the taskbar.

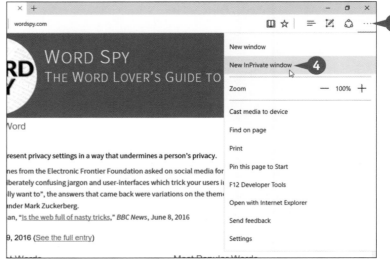

3 Click **More** (···).

4 Click **New InPrivate window**.

You can also activate InPrivate by pressing Ctrl + Shift + P.

A new Microsoft Edge window appears.

B The InPrivate indicator appears in the upper-left corner of the window.

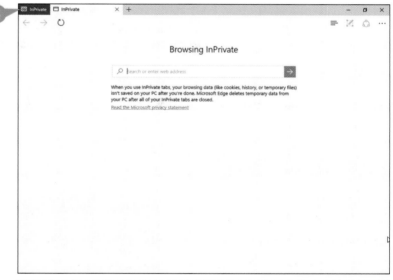

5 Surf to and interact with websites as you normally would, such as the banking site shown here.

6 When you are done, click **Close** (✕).

Microsoft Edge closes the InPrivate window and turns off InPrivate browsing.

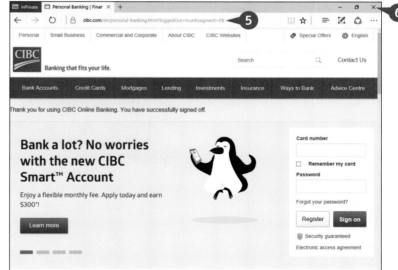

TIP

What is browsing history?
Microsoft Edge maintains a list of the sites that you visit, as well as text and passwords that you have typed into forms, the names of files that you have downloaded, and *cookies*, which are small text files that store information such as site preferences and site logon data. Saving this history is dangerous because other people who use your computer can just as easily visit or view information about those sites. You eliminate this risk by visiting such sites using an InPrivate browsing session. To delete your browsing history, click **More** (⋯), click **Settings**, click **Choose what to clear**, click **Browsing history** (☐ changes to ✔), and then click **Clear**.

Control Your Private Information

By default, Windows enables apps to access many aspects of your system, such as the camera, microphone, and internal antennas such as Wi-Fi and Bluetooth. Windows also enables apps to access personal information such as your location, account information, contacts, and calendar. This access improves your app experience in most cases, but you might be uncomfortable sharing so much with apps, particularly third-party apps. In that case, you can turn off access to your system resources and to your private information, either globally or just for specific apps.

Control Your Private Information

1 Click **Start** (⊞).

2 Click **Settings** (⚙).

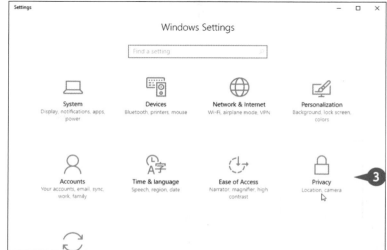

The Settings app appears.

3 Click **Privacy**.

The Privacy screen appears.

4 Click **Location**.

5 Click the **Location** switch to **Off** to prevent apps from using your location.

6 To remove all location information from your PC, click **Clear**.

Windows removes all your location information.

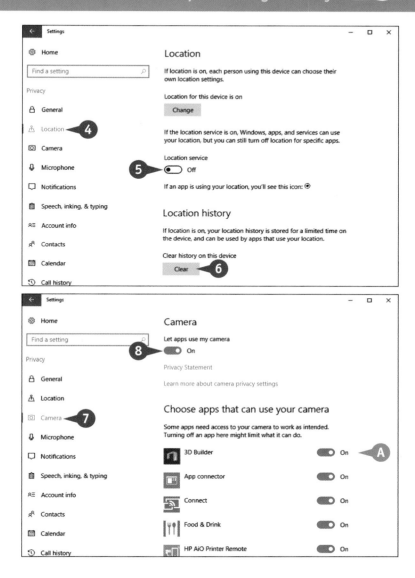

7 For each resource that you no longer want to allow apps to access, click the resource tab.

8 Click the switch that controls global access to **Off**.

Ⓐ Alternatively, you can use the app-specific switches to turn off access for individual apps.

The next time you display the Start menu, you will not see any personal information in the tiles.

TIPS

How do I prevent Windows from showing apps and documents that I have used recently?
Click **Start** (⊞), click **Settings** (⚙), click **Personalization**, and then click **Start**. To prevent Windows from showing the apps you use most often, click the **Show most used apps** switch to **Off**. To hide recently used documents, click the **Show recently opened items in Jump Lists on Start or the taskbar** switch to **Off**.

How do I stop an app's notifications?
If an app's notifications contain private information, you can turn them off. Click **Start** (⊞), click **Settings** (⚙), click **System**, and then click **Notifications & actions**. Beside the app for which you want notifications disabled, click the switch to **Off**.

Reset Your Computer to Preserve Privacy

As you use your computer, you accumulate a large amount of personal data: documents, installed apps, Microsoft Edge favorites, email messages, photos, and much more. If you are selling your computer or giving it away, you probably do not want the recipient to have access to all that personal data. To prevent this, you can reset the computer, which deletes all your personal data and reinstalls a fresh copy of Windows.

Reset Your Computer to Preserve Privacy

Note: This section assumes that you have copied your personal files to a backup destination, such as an external hard drive.

1 In the taskbar's Search box, type **reset**.

2 Click **Reset this PC**.

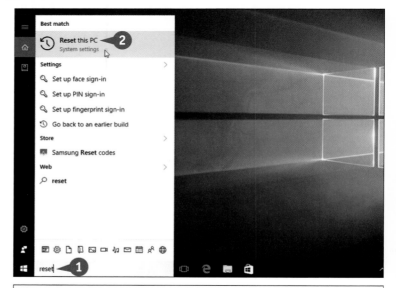

The Settings app opens the Update & Security window with the Recovery tab displayed.

3 Under Reset this PC, click **Get started**.

Windows asks how you want to remove your personal files.

④ Click the removal option that you want.

Note: For more information about the removal options, see the Tip.

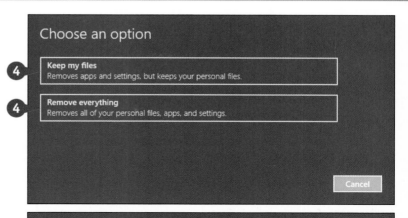

Windows displays a list of apps that will be removed during the reset process.

⑤ Click **Next**.

The Ready to Reset This PC screen appears.

⑥ Click **Reset**.

Windows resets your computer.

TIP

What is the difference between removing my files and fully cleaning the drive?
The Keep My Files option deletes your apps and your Windows settings, but it leaves your files on your PC, so this is not the option you want if you are giving away or selling your PC. Instead, you want the Remove Everything option, which not only removes your apps and your custom Windows settings, but it also removes all your personal files.

Maintaining Windows

To keep your system running smoothly, maintain top performance, and reduce the risk of computer problems, you need to perform some routine maintenance chores. This chapter shows you how to delete unnecessary files, check for hard drive and other device errors, back up your files, and more.

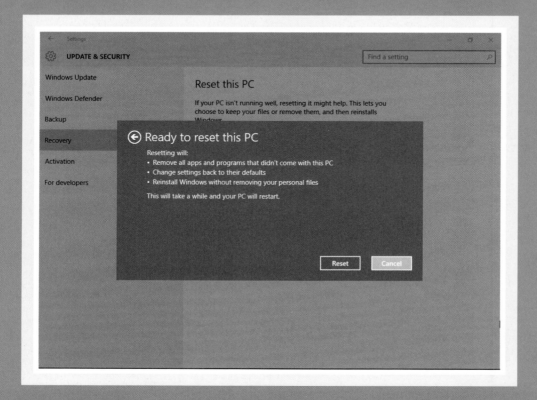

Check Hard Drive Free Space

To ensure that your PC's hard drive does not become full, you should periodically check how much free space it has left. This is important because if you run out of room on your hard drive, you cannot install more programs or create more documents, and your PC's performance will suffer.

Of particular concern is the hard drive on which Windows is installed, usually drive C. If this hard drive's free space becomes low — say, less than about 20 or 25GB — Windows runs slowly. With normal computer use, you should check your hard drive free space about once a month.

Check Hard Drive Free Space

Note: You can also check the free space on a CD, DVD, memory card, or flash drive. Before you continue, insert the disc, card, or drive.

1. Click **File Explorer**.

 File Explorer appears.

2. Click **This PC**.

 The This PC folder appears.

3. Click the **View** tab.

4. Click **Tiles**.

A Information about each drive appears along with the drive icon.

B This value tells you the amount of free space on the drive.

C This value tells you the total amount of space on the drive.

D This bar gives you a visual indication of how much disk space the drive is using.

E Windows is installed on the drive with the Windows logo (⊞).

F The used portion of the bar appears blue when a drive still has sufficient disk space.

G The used portion of the bar turns red when a drive's disk space becomes low.

5 Click **Close** (✕) to close the This PC window.

TIP

What can I do if my hard drive space is becoming low?

You can do three things:

- **Delete Personal Files**. If you have personal files — particularly media files such as images, music, and videos — that you no longer need, delete them.
- **Remove Programs**. If you have programs that you no longer use, uninstall them (see Chapter 1).
- **Run Disk Cleanup**. Use the Disk Cleanup program to delete files that Windows no longer uses. See the next section, "Delete Unnecessary Files."

Delete Unnecessary Files

To free up hard drive space on your computer and keep Windows running efficiently, you can use the Disk Cleanup program to delete files that your system no longer needs. Although today's hard drives are quite large, it is still possible to run low on disk space, particularly because today's applications and media files are larger than ever.

Run Disk Cleanup any time that your hard drive free space becomes too low. If hard drive space is not a problem, run Disk Cleanup every two or three months.

Delete Unnecessary Files

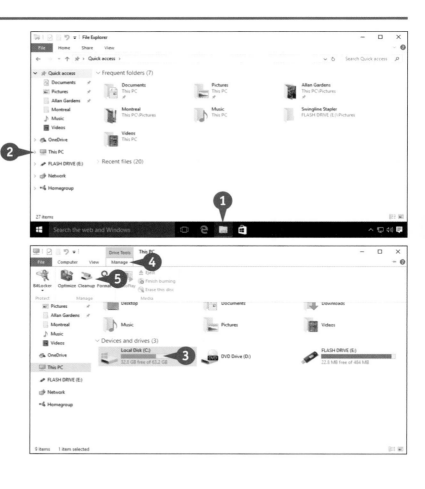

1 Click **File Explorer**.

File Explorer appears.

2 Click **This PC**.

The This PC folder appears.

3 Click the hard drive you want to clean.

4 Click the **Manage** tab.

5 Click **Cleanup**.

After a few moments, the Disk Cleanup dialog box appears.

🅐 This area displays the total amount of drive space you can free up.

🅑 This area displays the amount of drive space the activated options will free up.

⑥ Click the check box (☐ changes to ☑) for each file type that you want to delete.

🅒 This area displays a description of the highlighted file type.

⑦ Click **OK**.

Disk Cleanup asks you to confirm that you want to delete the file types.

⑧ Click **Delete Files**.

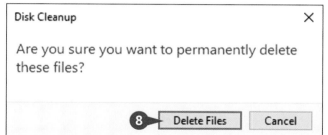

What types of files does Disk Cleanup delete?

Here are the main file types that it deletes:

- **Downloaded Program Files**. These are small web page programs downloaded onto your hard drive.
- **Temporary Internet Files**. These are web page copies stored on your hard drive for faster viewing.
- **Delivery Optimization Files**. These are files used by Windows' Delivery Optimization service.
- **Recycle Bin**. These are files that you have deleted since you last emptied your Recycle Bin.
- **Temporary Files**. These are files used by programs to store temporary data.
- **Thumbnails**. These are miniature versions of images and other content used in folder windows.

Refresh Your Computer

If you find that your computer is running slowly or that frequent program glitches are hurting your productivity, you can often solve these problems by resetting your PC's system files. The Reset this PC feature reinstalls a fresh copy of Windows. It also saves the documents, images, and other files in your user account, some of your settings, and any Windows apps that you have installed. However, Reset this PC does *not* save any other PC settings (which are reverted to their defaults) or any desktop programs that you installed.

Refresh Your Computer

1 In the taskbar's Search box, type **reset**.

2 Click **Reset this PC**.

The Settings app runs and selects the Recovery tab.

3 Under Reset this PC, click **Get started**.

Reset this PC asks you to choose a reset option.

4 Click **Keep my files**.

Reset this PC displays a list of software you will need to reinstall.

5 Click **Next**.

6 Click **Reset**.

Reset this PC reboots the computer and refreshes the system files.

TIP

How do I refresh my computer if I cannot start Windows?

1 Insert your installation disc or recovery drive and then restart your computer.

2 Boot to the disk or drive.

3 In the Windows Setup dialog box, click **Next**.

4 Click **Repair your computer**.

5 Click **Troubleshoot**.

6 Click **Reset this PC**.

7 Click **Keep my files**.

8 Click your user account, type your account password, and then click **Continue**.

9 Click **Reset**.

Create a Recovery Drive

You can make it easier to troubleshoot and recover from computer problems by creating a USB recovery drive. If a problem prevents you from booting your computer, then you must boot using some other drive. If you have your Windows installation media, you can boot using that drive. If you do not have the installation media, you can still recover if you have created a recovery drive. This is a USB flash drive that contains the Windows recovery environment, which enables you to refresh or reset your PC, recover a system image, and more.

Create a Recovery Drive

1 Insert the USB flash drive you want to use.

2 In the taskbar's Search box, type **recovery drive**.

3 Click **Create a recovery drive**.

The User Account Control dialog box appears.

4 Click **Yes**.

Note: If you are using a standard account, enter your PC's administrator credentials to continue.

The Recovery Drive Wizard appears.

5 Click **Next**.

The Recovery Drive Wizard prompts you to choose the USB flash drive.

6 Click the drive if it is not selected already.

7 Click **Next**.

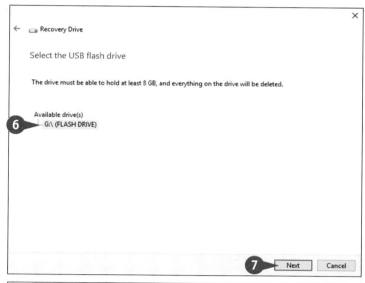

The Recovery Drive Wizard warns you that all the data on the drive will be deleted.

8 Click **Create**.

The wizard formats the drive and copies the recovery tools and data.

9 Click **Finish** (not shown).

TIPS

Can I use any USB flash drive as a recovery drive?
No. The drive must have a capacity of at least 16GB. Windows erases all data on the drive, so make sure the flash drive does not contain any files you want to keep.

How can I make sure the recovery drive works properly?
You should test the drive by booting your PC to the drive. Insert the recovery drive and then restart your PC. How you boot to the drive depends on your system. Some PCs display a menu of boot devices; select the USB drive from that menu. In other cases, a message tells you to press a key.

Keep a History of Your Files

There may be times when backing up a file just by making a copy is not good enough. For example, if you make frequent changes to a file, you might want to copy not only the current version, but also the versions from an hour ago, a day ago, a week ago, and so on. In Windows, these previous versions of a file are called its *file history*, and you can save this data for all your documents by activating a feature called File History.

Keep a History of Your Files

Set the File History Drive

1 Connect an external drive to your PC.

Note: The drive should have enough capacity to hold your files, so an external hard drive is probably best.

Note: If you see a notification, click it, click **Configure this drive for backup**, and then skip steps 3 and 4.

2 In the taskbar's Search box, type **file history**.

3 Click **File Backup settings**.

The Settings app runs and displays the Backup tab.

4 Click **Add a drive**.

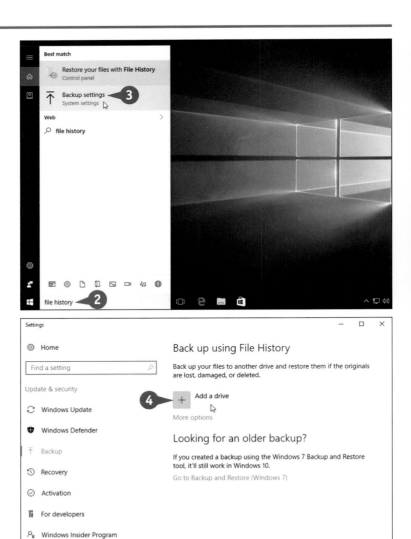

The Select a Drive window appears.

5 Click the drive you want to use.

Activate File History

1 Click the **Automatically back up my files** switch to **On**.

Note: Windows activates File History automatically, so in most cases you can skip this step.

Windows activates File History and begins saving copies of your files to the external drive.

TIP

Is it okay to disconnect the external hard drive temporarily?

Yes. However, if you need to remove the external drive temporarily (for example, if you need to use the port for another device), you should turn off File History before disconnecting the external drive. Follow steps **2** and **3** to open the Backup tab and then click the **Automatically back up my files** switch to **Off**. When you are ready to resume saving your files, follow steps **1** to **3** to reconnect the drive and open the Backup tab, and then click the switch to **On**.

Restore a File from Your History

If you improperly edit, accidentally delete, or corrupt a file through a system crash, in many cases you can restore a previous version of the file. Why would you want to revert to a previous version of a file? One reason is that you might improperly edit the file by deleting or changing important data. In some cases, you may be able to restore that data by going back to a previous version of the file. Another reason is that the file might become corrupted if the program or Windows crashes. You can get a working version of the file back by restoring a previous version.

Restore a File from Your History

1 In the taskbar's Search box, type **restore files**.

2 Click **Restore your files with File History**.

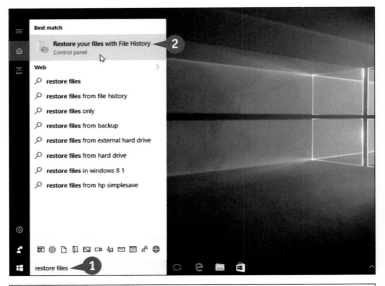

The Home - File History window appears.

3 Double-click the library or folder that contains the file you want to restore.

4 Open the folder that contains the file.

5 Click **Previous Version** (◄) until you open the version of the folder you want to use.

6 Click the file you want to restore.

7 Click **Restore to Original Location** (⟳).

If the original folder has a file with the same name, File History asks what you want to do.

8 Select an option:

Ⓐ You can click **Replace the file in the destination** to overwrite the existing file with the previous version.

Ⓑ You can click **Skip this file** to do nothing.

Ⓒ You can click **Compare info for both files** to decide which file you prefer to keep.

Windows restores the previous version.

TIPS

Can I restore a folder?
Yes, because Windows also keeps track of previous versions of folders, which is useful if an entire folder becomes corrupted. Follow steps **1** to **5**, click the folder you want to restore, and then click **Restore to Original Location** (⟳).

What should I do if I am not sure about replacing an existing file with a previous version?
Click **Compare info for both files** in the Replace or Skip Files dialog box. In the File Conflict dialog box, click the check box beside both versions (☐ changes to ☑) and then click **Continue**. This leaves the existing file as is and restores the previous version with (2) appended to the name.

Check Your Hard Drive for Errors

To keep your system running smoothly, you should periodically check your hard drive for errors and fix any errors that come up. Because hard drive errors can cause files to become corrupted, which may prevent you from running a program or opening a document, you can use the Check Disk program to look for and fix hard drive errors.

Check Your Hard Drive for Errors

1 Click **File Explorer**.

File Explorer appears.

2 Click **This PC**.

3 Click the hard drive that you want to check.

4 Click the **Computer** tab.

5 Click **Properties**.

The hard drive's Properties dialog box appears.

6 Click the **Tools** tab.

7 Click **Check**.

A If Windows tells you that the drive has no errors, you can click **Cancel** and skip the rest of these steps.

8 Otherwise, click **Scan drive**.

Windows checks the hard drive.

9 When the check is complete, click **Close**.

Note: If Check Disk finds any errors, follow the instructions the program provides.

TIPS

What is a "bad sector"?
A *sector* is a small storage location on your hard drive. When Windows saves a file on the drive, it divides the file into pieces and stores each piece in a separate sector. A bad sector is one that, through physical damage or some other cause, can no longer be used to reliably store data.

How often should I check for hard drive errors?
You should perform the basic hard drive check about once a week. Perform the more thorough bad sector check once a month. Note that the bad sector check can take several hours, depending on the size of the drive, so perform this check only when you will not need your computer for a while.

Check Your Devices for Errors

To help ensure that your system is operating smoothly and efficiently, you should periodically check for errors associated with the devices attached to your computer. Device errors usually mean either that you cannot work with a device entirely, or that the device behaves erratically or unexpectedly. You can use the Windows Devices and Printers feature to check your installed devices for errors. You can also use Devices and Printers to troubleshoot your problem devices, and in most cases, Windows will be able to fix the problem automatically.

Check Your Devices for Errors

Check for Devices with Errors

1 In the taskbar's Search box, type **devices**.

2 Click **Devices and Printers**.

The Devices and Printers window appears.

3 Examine the device icons for errors.

A Windows indicates devices with errors using this icon: (⚠).

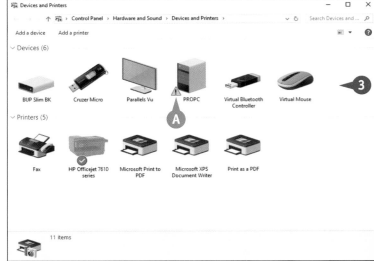

Begin Device Troubleshooting

1 Click a device that has an error.

2 Click **Troubleshoot**.

The Devices and Printers troubleshooting wizard appears and displays the first fix.

3 Click **Apply this fix**.

Devices and Printers applies the fix. If this does not solve the problem, Devices and Printers displays the next fix.

B If you are certain this fix is not the solution, you can click **Skip this fix** instead.

4 Repeat step **3** until the problem is resolved.

TIPS

What is a device driver?
It is a small program that Windows uses to communicate with a device. Many hardware problems are the result of either not having a device driver installed, or having an incorrect driver installed. Most devices come with discs that have the correct device driver, so you should insert that disc when troubleshooting. You can also obtain the latest device driver from the manufacturer's website.

What if Devices and Printers cannot solve the problem?
In this case, you need to either return the device to the manufacturer for repair or replacement, or take it to a local computer shop for fixing.

Index